KT-478-561

Lost for Words

Lost for Words

The Hidden History of the Oxford English Dictionary

Lynda Mugglestone

Yale University Press
New Haven and London

Copyright © 2005 by Lynda Mugglestone

All rights reserved. This book may not be reproduced in whole or in part, in any form (beyond that copying permitted by Sections 107 and 108 of the U.S. Copyright Law and except by reviewers for the public press), without written permission from the publishers.

For information about this and other Yale University Press publications, please contact:
U.S. Office: *sales.press@yale.edu* yalebooks.com
Europe Office: *sales@yaleup.co.uk* www.yalebooks.co.uk

Set in Sabon MT by J&L Composition, Filey, North Yorkshire
Printed in Great Britain by St Edmundsbury Press Ltd

Library of Congress Cataloging-in-Publication Data

Mugglestone, Lynda.
Lost for words: the hidden history of the Oxford English dictionary/
Lynda Mugglestone. — 1st ed.
p. cm.
Includes bibliographical references (p.) and index.
ISBN 0–300–10699–8 (alk. paper)
1. Oxford English dictionary. 2. Encyclopedias and dictionaries—History and criticism. 3. English language—Lexicography.
4. English language—Etymology. I. Title.

PE1617.094M84 2005
423—dc22 2004029344

A catalogue record for this book is available from the British Library

10 9 8 7 6 5 4 3 2 1

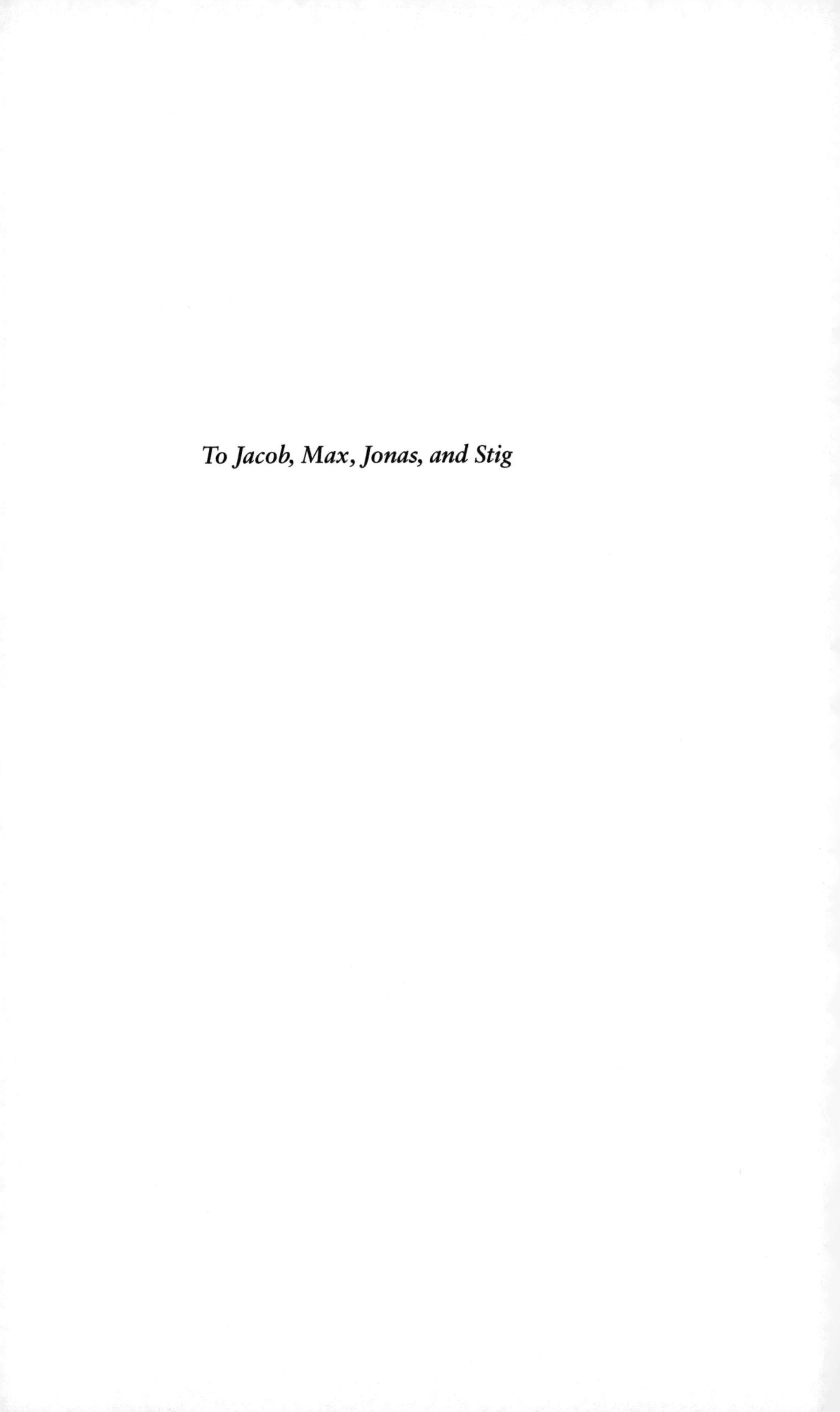

To Jacob, Max, Jonas, and Stig

Contents

List of Illustrations ix
Preface xi
Acknowledgements xxiii
Abbreviations xxv

Chapter 1 The Ideal Dictionary 1

Chapter 2 Palimpsests 37

Chapter 3 Lost Words 70

Chapter 4 Science and the Principles of Selection 110

Chapter 5 'I am not the editor of the English language' 143

Chapter 6 Ended but not Complete 179

Chapter 7 Into the Future 209

Notes 222
References 252
Index 267

Illustrations

Figure 1	Annotations and deletions by W. W. Skeat on the proofs of the first fascicle of the dictionary.	xii–xiii
Figure 2	The four editors of the *OED*.	2
Figure 3	Murray's annotated copy of the Preface to Part I.	72
Figure 4	The compass of the language.	75
Figure 5	Jowett's suggested revisions on the title page of the dictionary.	156
Figure 6	Annotated and illustrated letter from J. A. H. Murray to Mr Darlington.	180–81
Figure 7	James Murray and his assistants.	186
Figure 8	James Murray in his Scriptorium.	213

Preface

This book, like many others, began with a chance discovery. In this instance it was of a set of stray proof sheets from the very first fascicle of the first edition of the *Oxford English Dictionary*. Dating from late October 1883 (some four months before this section of the dictionary appeared in published form), the proofs aptly recorded the words from *abandon* to *Anglo-Saxon*. The provisional version of the dictionary which they provided was, however, notably different from the finished text. The latter was regularly to be praised for its immaculate typography and impeccable presentation. As R. McLintock declared in 1889, its status was exemplary in this respect: 'every typographical device possible for attaining the maximum of clearness and the maximum of consideration has been employed'.[1] The assembled entries of the proofs were instead marked by a mass of scrawled annotations and suggested deletions, presenting a textual layer that contrasts sharply with the clarity that McLintock would later commend (see fig.1). Words such as *angerful*, *angering*, *angeled*, and *angelence* were firmly crossed through. 'Omit these words, the sense of which is obvious' states a forthright instruction in the margin. 'Useless', avers a further handwritten comment by the side of *anencepheloid* ('Partially, or tending to be, anencephalous'). *Anginous* drew a similar response. If the *OED* had originally been conceived as an 'inventory' of English (in an image that resonates with its intended neutrality),[2] then the subjectivity of these responses was disturbing, not least since they suggested that the inventory could and should be partial and selective. Entries such as *abirritant* ('Any soothing agent which causes diminution of irritation'), together with derivative forms such as *abirritation* and *abirritative*, were likewise recommended for omission. 'Rubbish! Mere tradesman's make-up', exclaims a trenchant remark alongside *anerithmoscope* ('a magic lantern for displaying pictorial . . . advertisements, changing them automatically by means of electricity'). A double question mark appears next to *abashless* ('Unabashed, shameless;

the reverse of *bashful*'), explicitly querying its right to appear in the dictionary. Even the presence of an illustrative citation from Robert Browning did not, it seemed, guarantee a place.[3]

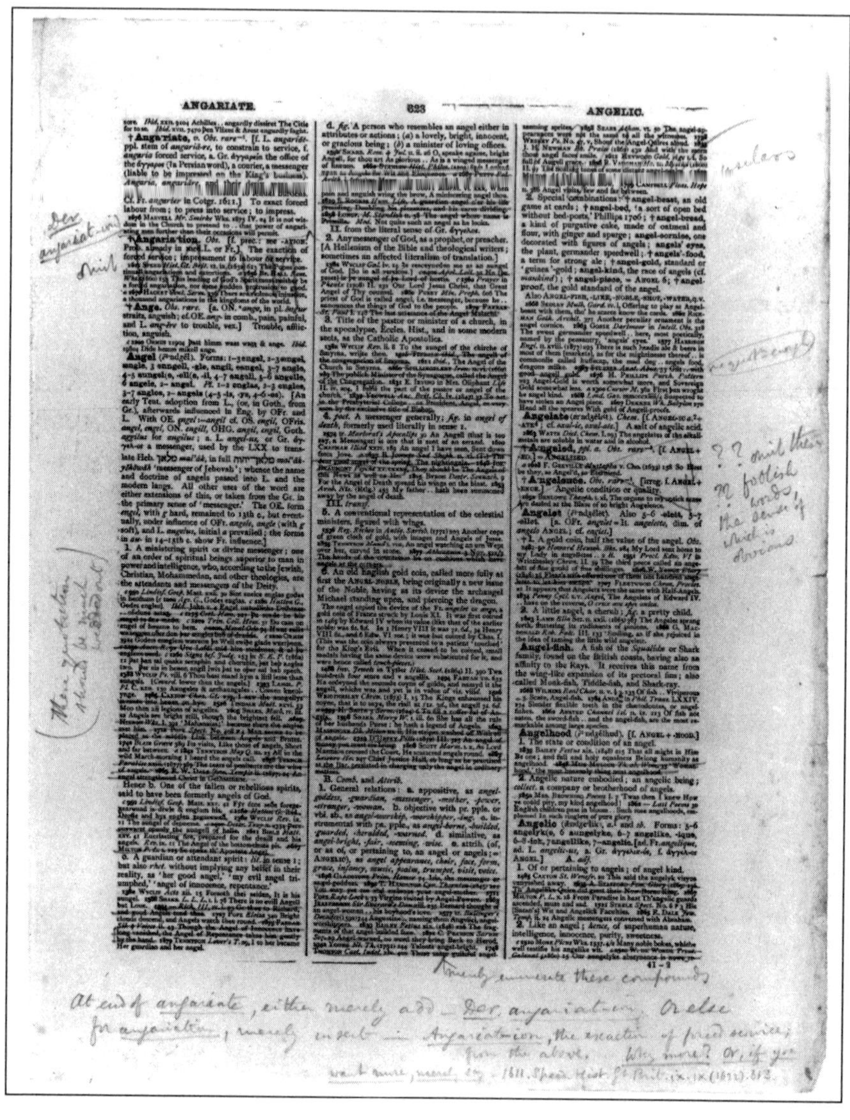
ANGARIATE 323 ANGELIC

At end of angariate, either merely add — Der. angariation. Or else for angariation, merely insert — Angariation, the exaction of forced service, from the above. Why more? Or, if you want more, merely cite — 1611 Speed Hist. Gt Brit. ix. ix (1632). 812.

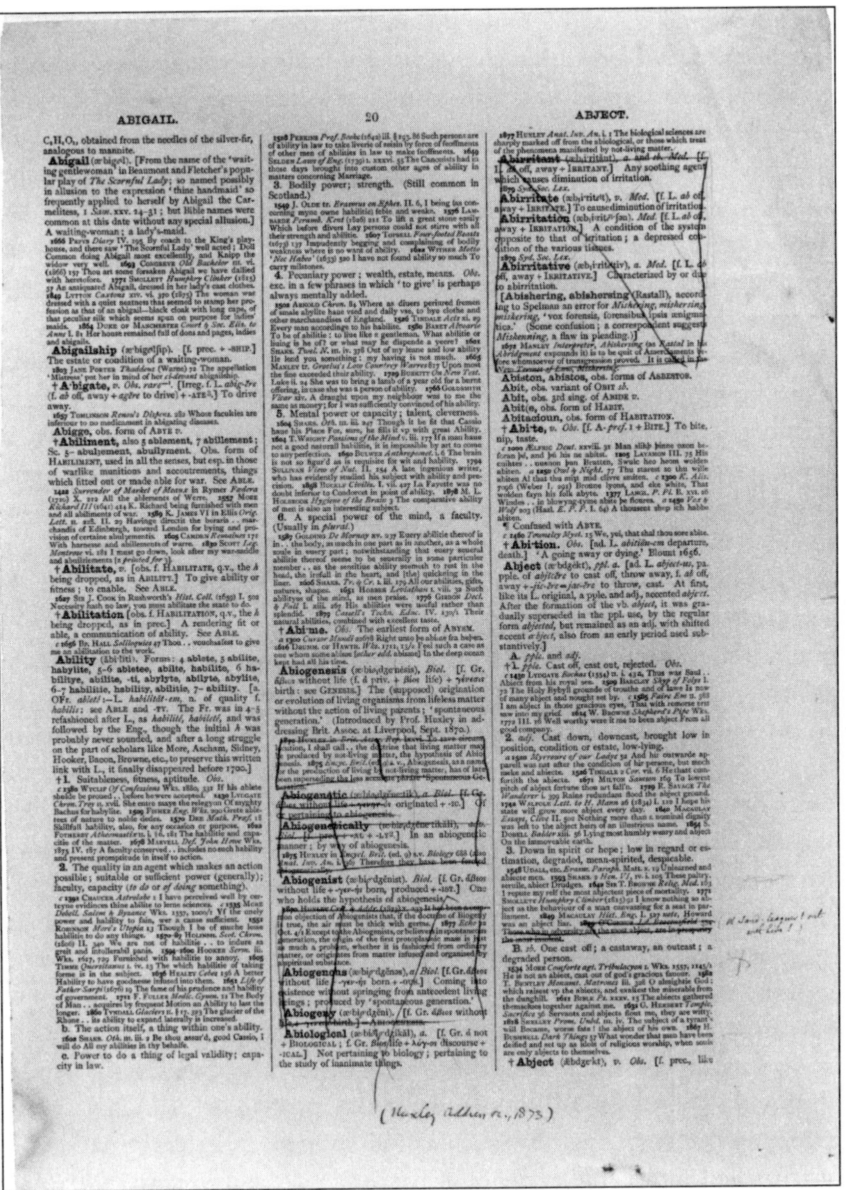

ABIGAIL. 20 ABJECT.

Figure 1 Annotations and deletions by W. W. Skeat on the proofs of the first fascicle of the dictionary.

The reading of proofs for the *OED* was clearly not confined to the correction of incidental error (though this was naturally important too).[4] Instead, as these proofs seemed to reveal, it could also examine the very principles on which the dictionary was to be based, the kinds of entries – and data – which it should include. 'This and the three following are mainly newspaper words', as a further handwritten comment records alongside *anglophobe*, *anglophobia*, *anglophobic*, *anglophobist*. The same hand – that of the American scholar Fitzedward Hall, erstwhile Professor of Sanskrit at King's College, London and one of the most diligent critical readers for the dictionary[5] – crossed through their entries, contesting their status as legitimate forms. 'Newspaper words' evidently did not operate as a term of commendation. Hall's comments were not, however, appended as a form of gratuitous censure. Instead they confirmed his role as one of those men (and women) who 'systematically and continuously, have read the proofs, to improve the work as a whole by criticism, or to enrich it by additions', as James Murray (editor of the *OED* from 1878 to 1915) noted in 1888 in his Preface to the dictionary's first volume.[6] Criticism was part of Hall's intended remit, just as it was for Walter Skeat, the Cambridge medievalist, or James Johnston, a Scottish minister (and one-time assistant on the dictionary), or Henry Hucks Gibbs (Lord Aldenham), a director of the Bank of England from 1853 to 1901 and an assiduous member of the Philological Society. A range of others added their own voluntary contributions in similar ways. The popular writer on history, Edith Thompson (whose *History of England* was in print for some thirty years), together with her sister Peronnet, annotated the drafts of the dictionary until its very end. The retired physician William Sykes sent detailed missives from Gosport, just as other readers did from all over the country, as well as from abroad. The *OED* was always a collective enterprise. 'We do but follow the example of the Grimms, when we call upon Englishmen to come forward and write their own Dictionary for themselves', the *Proposal* for the dictionary proclaimed in August 1859.[7] Ordinary readers – Englishwomen as well as men – sent in the quotations which supplied the vital evidence of past and present usage. Editors, voluntary sub-editors, and the critical readers in their different ways crafted these into the entries that make up the finished text. Long before the reviews which greeted the publication of the individual fascicles, each and every entry had been the subject of a critical process which operated virtually without limits.

While the discovery of potential faults and inconsistencies was of course critical in itself, especially because of the authoritative reputation which the *OED* aimed to achieve, the annotations, emendations and suggestions which feature prominently on almost every sheet of proofs (whether those located in the Murray Papers or the more extensive runs which remain in the archives of Oxford University Press) often move beyond the identification of occasional errors or stylistic infelicities. 'I *cannot* agree', 'I have *never* heard it so pronounced' are among the forthright comments of the critical readers, as they dispute the versions of the dictionary which had been presented for their inspection. Murray's later definition of *criticism* (which appeared in 1893 in the fascicle *Consignant–Crouching*) at times seemed all too apposite to his experiences in editing the dictionary. 'The action of criticizing, or passing judgement upon the qualities or merits of anything', he wrote, adding '*esp.* the passing of unfavourable judgement; fault-finding, censure'. These preliminary versions of the dictionary often emerge as a site of conflict and dissent, offering contrasting views of usage which were not always easily reconciled. While Fitzedward Hall condemned *abashless* in his characteristic black ink, Murray could nevertheless proffer his own opposing view on precisely the same page. 'Capital word, well-formed, vigorous', he retorts in the margin of the proof which Hall had duly returned, affirming his decision to retain the word.

The proofs can in this respect often generate a particularly immediate form of reception and response. Here editorial uncertainties can be acknowledged and specific help sought. 'The sense is far from clear', Murray wrote to Skeat, for example, in the midst of drafting *inmew* ('to mew or coop up'). 'Can you offer any suggestions?' Skeat duly obliged. Henry Bradley, appointed as second editor of the dictionary in 1888, similarly confessed temporary defeat to Sir Frederick Pollock, alongside the proof entry for *freelance* ('A term used by writers denoting . . . military adventurers, often of knightly rank'). Bradley's earliest citation was from Charlotte Yonge in 1855, yet he felt sure that the word must be earlier. Pollock who, like so many others, regularly gave up his spare time to dictionary matters, recommended writing to Yonge herself. A cousin of Henry Hucks Gibbs as well as a sub-editor for the dictionary, Charlotte Yonge would, he felt, be sure to help. A new citation from Sir Walter Scott duly emerged, locating usage of *freelance* over a quarter of a century earlier than had been possible in the initial version of the proofs. Suggestions of this kind, isolating possible sources and alternative readings – or different entries altogether – can densely occupy adjacent margins in the surviving proof sheets. Moreover, as Murray's comments on *abashless* suggest, it was by no means merely outside readers for the dictionary who participated in these patterns of conspicuous reassessment. 'Absolute folly, a waste of space', 'absolutely superfluous', 'too trivial and obvious', Murray would point out alongside many of the sense-distinctions and citations included in Bradley's first version of *go*. A refrain of 'not wanted' appears again and again as his co-editor's careful work was cast aside. As here, Murray's role as editor-in-chief of the *OED* would often prove him to be the most critical reader of all.

Lying in the basements of Oxford University Press, and in Murray's own papers at the Bodleian Library in Oxford, innumerable proof sheets, together with an abundance of letters and other archival resources, record the often forgotten details by which the dictionary first came into being. The proofs in particular – uncatalogued, in an order by no means alphabetical, and hitherto almost entirely unexamined – provide an unparalleled scholarly resource, offering a hidden history of a work which often was to be commended as 'the most complete and the most authoritative lexicon of our time'.[8] They cover in fact much of the alphabetic span of the *OED*, creating a series of temporary points of stasis in which words, senses, definitions, and citations can all differ, and in which consensus between the different editors could be difficult and at times, as we shall see, even impossible. If popular opinion tends to invest the word of the lexicographer with some of the same power as the Word of God – so much so that the dictionary and the Bible are often perceived as twin (and equally incontestable) sources of authority, one secular and the other divine – then these conflicts over the history and interpretation of words offer a striking corrective to this view. What now appears to the user of the dictionary as a clear-cut account of the 'biography' of each word, revealing the immanent truths of history, is, in the proofs, instead set down in ways which attest a range of possibilities which had to be resolved before the text could assume its final form. As Murray later recorded, one sense of *proof* is that of 'testing or making trial of anything, . . . [a] test, trial, experiment; examination, probation; assay'. The proofs in this sense participate in a wider and collective experiment, determining the forms the dictionary might have taken, the words it might have included, the senses it might have recorded, and the citations from popular as well as canonical sources which it might have given – against those which did indeed make their way into the finished text.

In the scholarly graffiti which the proofs bear, it becomes especially clear that marginalia can prove far from marginal in the value they assume for the further understanding of the history of the *OED*. 'Annotations – glosses in the margin . . . are consistently undervalued in studies of the history of authorship and publishing', the critic Evelyn Tribble has asserted.[9] As she affirms, writings of this kind habitually present an unofficial and often unguarded set of judgements which stand alongside the main body of a text. The marginalia of the *OED* must assume a special status in this respect. While critical annotations on style and content litter, for example, a copy of *John Ruskin. The Early Years* in the English Faculty Library at Oxford,[10] the comments which pervade the proofs of the *OED* are significantly different. In the first place, the latter are deliberately invited, thereby possessing a form of authority which is forever unattained by the pointed jibes which appear in individual copies of printed texts. As proofs sent out to specified individuals – co-editors, critical readers, outside experts, and specialists – these preliminary versions of the dictionary literally invited defacement, stressing their own ephemerality, their provisionality, their potential for change. Moreover, unlike the anonymous remarks which deface the Ruskin biography, the comments on the *OED* are usually attributable, either because they are signed with the writer's initials, or because the proof sheets in question still have the address of the recipient on the reverse (a common practice when sending out the sheets for comment to external readers for the dictionary) or because the handwriting can be matched with the range of other archival letters either in the Murray Papers in the Bodleian or in the archives of Oxford University Press. Walter Skeat's comments on the proofs of the first fascicle are, for instance, unsigned. Nevertheless his remarks can be precisely collated with two letters within the Murray Papers. In the first Skeat amplifies the suggestions he had made on the proof. *Anerithmoscope* was merely 'coined . . . to puff an ephemeral toy' and should be omitted, he advised; 'omit ridiculous compounds, the sense of which is perfectly obvious', he further specified for words such as *angelicalness*, *angelically*. 'Omit *anglicify*, *anglicity*, *anglicization*, *anglicized* – all useless', another comment instructs.[11] In the second letter, having evidently been taken to task over his ill-advised responses, Skeat proffers a profuse apology to Murray himself. 'I am sure I am infinitely sorry if I seem to make silly suggestions . . . as to my *disputing* every word, I should as soon think of flying', he wrote.[12] He had merely thought the dictionary was in need of condensation and so, he added, 'I naturally "went for" what seemed to me to be the least vital parts'. Murray in this instance would insist upon his own editorial judgement, retaining all of Skeat's contested words in the relevant portion of the dictionary.

Rather than the impulsive – and often highly personal – reactions which mark the non-specialist annotation, the comments on the proofs of the *OED* can be seen to exist as part of a far wider pattern of organized response. Still more significantly, the information and opinions they present were often integrated into the final forms of the text, providing the source of substantive changes and specific rewriting. Definitions, senses, labels, pronunciation – or indeed the practice of inclusion altogether – might shift as a result of the critical annotations which the readers collectively returned to the dictionary. Critical reading and critical revision could often prove to be precisely the same thing, providing a common pattern in the making of the dictionary by which proof and response were collated and subsequently combined, offering new interpretations of where the facts of language might be said to lie. The same – or perhaps indeed still greater – value attaches to the revisions and remarks which derive from the individual editors. As Helen Jackson has pointed out, 'authorial reflections and revision are marginalia of a special kind'. If in general, as Jackson avers, these remain merely 'refinements to the text . . . of limited interest as a rule, to anyone but the producer',[13] the proofs of the *OED* once more present a somewhat different case. Individual editors can and do add their own marginal annotations to what becomes, in effect, a multi-layered text which offers an explicit context for lexicographical debate and difference. This in itself provides internal – and often unique – evidence of the complex decisions which attended the dictionary from its very first pages. The value of these is incontestable, not least in supplementing the gaps in the history of the dictionary's making.

The lack of detailed knowledge about the day-to-day processes by which the dictionary came into being has formed something of a cliché in lexicographical criticism. 'It is indeed remarkable how little is known about the working methods of O.E.D. readers and editors', Jürgen Schäfer stated in 1980.[14] 'A record of editorial decisions by its editors and other workers unfortunately does not exist', Roderick McConchie echoed seventeen years later.[15] The same premisses recur in the opening paragraph of Darrell Raymond's *Dispatches from the Front*. 'The OED is largely silent about its own history, both in anecdotal material and in what can be inferred from the entries', he writes; 'consistency, accuracy, and completeness make the OED a unique reference work, but by their very nature these virtues conceal the people and events involved in the Dictionary's development'.[16] Yet the proofs can tell a different story, breaking the silence of which Raymond writes and revealing editorial decisions and dilemmas at first hand.

Murray's expression of the difficulties involved 'in deciding whether a word on or near the frontier line in any direction shall or shall not be included' receive vivid illustration in the deletions which mark the extant proofs.[17] The same is true for editorial decisions on a range of other senses or citations. While the published pages of the *OED* can be seen to stand as the final stage in the narrative of its making, it is in the proofs and revises, especially when combined with the abundant personal letters and other archival documents which still survive, that a more complex history is revealed. Rather than possessing Jackson's 'limited interest', the proofs instead liberally reveal the controversies and conflicts, the quibbles over labels, citations, canonicity, and legitimacy as they took place. It was, after all, not just in the first fascicle that suggestions for omissions were made. Instead, as Chapters 3 and 4 explore, this was a pervasive pattern throughout the making of the dictionary, changing the record of the language as finally offered to our view.

The examination of archival sources of this kind provides a collective history for the making of the *OED* which, in a variety of ways, can serve to change a number of the conventional images with which the dictionary is often surrounded. The deliberate omission of words, the culling of citations, the controversies about science ('very recent and very vile', as Skeat wrote on the proofs alongside suggested entries for *lipacidaemia* and *lipaciduria*), the frustrations which attended the making of a dictionary originally intended to encompass the language – but for which space remained tight, often leading to pragmatic restraint where lexicographical liberality would have been the chosen ideal – are all features that recurrently emerge. Behind the printed page lies another, at times very different, version in which compromises were reluctantly made and in which imperatives other than including the entirety of English often assumed prominence. Editing the *OED* was a heroic endeavour of a kind unforeseen when Murray first began. 'I chose the Dictionary; but it was, I felt, a great sacrifice', he later wrote. Yet the reality was even harder than he had envisaged. If he had 'dreamed of 10 years hard work', it had instead 'proved a lifetime'. And, as he added, 'half of my time was not enough: the Dictionary demanded it all.'[18] Murray did not exaggerate. As the following chapters will show, the history of the first edition of the *OED* was one of unprecedented difficulty – and unparalleled dedication.

The first chapter of this book covers the detailed history of this first edition, examining the origins of an attempt to craft what was widely seen as an 'ideal' dictionary – as well as the problems which, in wider terms, affected its intended realization. As always, translating abstract ideas into physical reality would present unforeseen complexities. The pragmatics of publication regularly impinged on the original aspirations for the *OED*, while editorial conflicts and inadequacies of data brought still further difficulties. Henry Bradley's definition of *editor* ('One who prepares the literary work of another person, or number of persons for publication, by selecting, revising, and arranging the material') assumes a neutrality which conspicuously occludes the strain which making the *OED* so often caused. Chapter 2 looks in detail at the image of the proofs and the interactions of readers, editors, and critics as these came to influence the form of countless entries in the finished text. While *proof-reading* was, ironically, not included in the dictionary's first edition, the import of the changes made at this stage of the text, especially in imposing the canonical at the expense of that regarded as less so, cannot be ignored. Chapter 3 examines the lost words of the *OED* as witnessed by the proofs, collating different preliminary versions of the dictionary to examine the patterns of loss and attrition, particularly in light of the economic pressures which affected the dictionary through much of the 1890s. Space was a critical issue with a critical outcome for a wide range of words. Chapter 4 examines the language of science and the dictionary, not least since the attitudes of many critics – and indeed of the Delegates of Oxford University Press[19] – was often that such words should not be included at all. Scientific 'jargon' in the nineteenth century, in spite of – and at times, precisely because of – the salience of Darwinism remained a problematic issue. While contemporary scientists stressed the significance of the advances being made ('I firmly believe in the advent of an English epoch in science and art which will lick the Augustan . . . into fits', as the wide-ranging biologist Thomas Huxley averred),[20] the legitimacy of the language in which such discoveries were phrased remained a matter of debate.

Chapter 5 deals with other problems which surround the popular image of the dictionary. While the *OED* had, from the very beginning, striven to assimilate a new and descriptive science of language – stressing the claims of objectivity and empiricism in the needful recording of the reality of language in use – popular sensibilities instead often inclined to the prescriptive, to the search for an authorized norm. It was the latter which many expected the dictionary to provide. The fact that such a view could be held even by members of the Philological Society – and by those who wrote and commented on the dictionary – made such conflicts especially difficult. Murray's prose was a target for prescriptive censure as he strove to craft the 'General Explanations' of the dictionary;[21] the labelling and phrasing of countless other aspects of the *OED* would, as we shall see, reveal the persistent problems which lay behind the attempt to impose neutrality as a cardinal lexicographic aim. Race, class, gender, as well as the prevalent images of correctness, all at times fractured the ideal of the impartial inventory of words. Chapter 6 focuses on the ending of the first edition, placing the dictionary in the twentieth century when the burgeoning usage of, for example, the First World War meant that the dictionary was noticeably incomplete even as it approached its formal conclusion. Serial publication – and the fact that the first fascicle of the dictionary *A–Ant* had been published, with no possibility of change or alteration, in 1884 while the final fascicle *Wise–Wyzen* would not appear until 1928 – clearly exacerbated these problems.[22]

As Murray and his co-editors were all too aware, time and language are in continuous flux. While they could not have foreseen the development of an on-line *OED* – the subject of the concluding chapter – they would undoubtedly have appreciated the scope it offered for a further stage in realizing the world of words in which they had spent much of their own lives. Evolution in lexicographical terms had provided the keynote of Murray's Romanes Lecture in 1900, given in the Sheldonian Theatre in Oxford on 22 June. The English dictionary, like language itself, was 'a growth that has slowly developed itself adown the ages', as he informed his assembled audience.[23] Stasis in both was ultimately impossible. An earlier statement, made in the *Academy* in 1881, encapsulates Murray's true – and enduring – sense of the *OED*. 'We are doing for England and the English tongue a work which will be built upon, extended, and completed', he said.[24] If the precise details of its physical form were subject to change, rendering a supplement to the first edition necessary a mere five years after its completion, and necessitating four further supplementary volumes in 1972–86, as well as *OED2* in 1989, the three volumes of *Additions* which appeared in 1993–97 (and the ongoing revisions which will make up *OED Online*),[25] the essence of the dictionary would, as Murray stressed, ultimately remain the same. The dictionary 'will itself never grow old', he affirmed. In its changing record of the language, encompassing past as well as present, it would outlive individual editions and editors alike.

Acknowledgements

Acknowledgements are due primarily to the Secretary to the Delegates of Oxford University Press for the generous permission to use materials in the *Oxford English Dictionary* archives and to reproduce the photographs on pp. 2, 186, and 213, and to the staff of Room 132 in the Bodleian Library, Oxford, for their unfailing courtesy and help with reference to the archived Murray Papers. I would also like to thank the Bodleian Library for permission to reproduce a number of illustrations from the latter. My thanks are also due to Professor Eric Stanley for a range of valuable critical comments on lexicographical history (and on earlier drafts of this book) and to April Warman who has acted as research assistant on the bibliography. My thanks also go to John Simpson, Penny Silva, and Peter Gilliver at the *Oxford English Dictionary* for their many useful comments on the art and craft of dictionary-making.

Abbreviations

CWW	K. M. E. Murray, *Caught in the Web of Words. James A. H. Murray and the* Oxford English Dictionary (New Haven and London: Yale University Press, 1977)
DNB	*Dictionary of National Biography*
EETS	Early English Text Society
MP	Murray Papers, Bodleian Library, Oxford
OED1	J. A. H. Murray, H. Bradley, W. A. Craigie, and C. T. Onions (eds), *A New English Dictionary on Historical Principles* (Oxford: Clarendon Press, 1884–1928)
OED2	J. A. Simpson and E. S. C. Weiner (eds), *The Oxford English Dictionary First Edited by James A. H. Murray, Henry Bradley, W. A. Craigie, and C. T. Onions combined with A Supplement to the Oxford English Dictionary edited by R. W. Burchfield and Reset with Corrections, Revisions, and Additional Vocabulary*, 20 vols (Oxford: Clarendon Press, 1989); CD-Rom (Oxford: Clarendon Press, 1992)
OEDS	R. W. Burchfield (ed.), *A Supplement to the Oxford English Dictionary*, 4 vols (Oxford: Clarendon Press, 1972–86)
OED Online	J. Simpson (ed.), *Oxford English Dictionary* (3rd edn), *OED Online* (Oxford: Clarendon Press, 2000–) <http://dictionary. oed.com>
OUP	Oxford University Press

CHAPTER 1

The Ideal Dictionary

'I wanted to see an ideal Dictionary & to show what I meant by one', James Murray wrote to the politician James Bryce in 1903,[1] reflecting in detail upon his editorship of the work which we now know as the *OED*. The original title of the dictionary – and that which appeared on the individual fascicles throughout the first edition – gives a clearer picture of the lexicographical departures in which Murray and his co-editors were then engaged. *A New English Dictionary on Historical Principles*, its title pages announced, stressing alike the originality and the historicism which formed a salient part of the ideals to which Murray referred.[2] The further statement on each title page that the dictionary was 'founded mainly on the materials collected by the Philological Society' and that it was assisted by 'many scholars and men of science' highlighted other aspects of a work which was deliberately new in more than name alone. Science and wide-ranging scholarship, alongside a commitment to objective accuracy of information (in place of the *ipse dixit* pronouncements which had so often marked the dictionaries of the past), all played their part in the reformed agendas of this new lexicographical endeavour. 'It is now common knowledge among scholars that no discussion as to the origin or meaning of a word can be fully based until one has considered what the Oxford Dictionary says', a review of 1902 declared. Informally, as this moreover confirms, the dictionary was already the 'Oxford' dictionary, its name increasingly synonymous with the authoritative investigation of the past and present of the national tongue.

By 1903 Murray's editorship of the dictionary, under both formal and informal titles, was already in its twenty-sixth year. This in itself signalled the complexity of ideals – and their realization – as they impinged upon the making of the *OED*. The original contract with Oxford University Press had been signed in 1879, stipulating an allotted time span of ten years, and an allotted space of four volumes. Murray had been confirmed as its single editor. Yet by 1889 publication of the dictionary was merely midway through C and in the second of what would turn out to be ten volumes (and 125 separate parts). This was in many ways less than ideal, particularly when seen from the standpoint of the Delegates of Oxford University Press. Appointed from the senior academic staff of the university, the Delegates were actively involved in the work of the Press; their approval was necessary before any book was accepted for publication. Delays such as those which surrounded the dictionary were, for them, a cause of serious concern. Murray had by that point been joined by a second editor, Henry Bradley, an erstwhile corresponding clerk from Sheffield and, like Murray himself, an autodidact with an enviable zest for knowledge.[3] By the dictionary's end, two further editors – William Craigie and Charles Onions – would have made their appearance, each with a separate editorial team (see fig. 2). The final part of the dictionary appeared in 1928, forty-nine years after the optimistic projections of the contract which Murray had initially signed.

Figure 2 The four editors of the *OED*. Clockwise from top left: James Murray, Henry Bradley, Charles Onions, and William Craigie.

Ideals are, by definition, often elusive. 'Ideals . . . can only be approached, but never reached', as Murray states in a 1796 quotation from F. Nitsch which he included in the dictionary's entry for *ideal*. 'The notion of an *ideal*, of something which for whatever reason, *ought to be*, as distinguished from *what is*', he further added from John Grote's *Examination of the Utilitarian Philosophy* of 1870. For the *OED*, these images remained all too pertinent. What was the nature of an 'ideal' dictionary? What could, in reality, be achieved? To what extent, for example, could a dictionary encompass the language, especially if it intended – as the *OED* did – to engage with both past and present of the native tongue?[4] What compromises might have to be enforced – or resisted? These and other questions would recur throughout the long gestation of the first edition. Murray's definitions of *ideal* reflected the dilemmas he faced. On one hand an ideal remained on the level of abstraction: 'A conception of something, or a thing conceived, in its highest perfection, or as an object to be realized or aimed at; a perfect type; a standard of perfection or excellence'. On the other, it was something that endeavour might indeed secure: 'An actual thing or person regarded as realizing such a conception, and so as being perfect in its kind; a standard proposed for imitation'. The act of editing the *OED* found him, and his co-editors, regularly trapped in discourses of this kind. The Delegates of OUP would at times urge a stance less concerned with perfectibility. 'It would be in vain if . . . the pursuit of an unattainable standard in particular minutiae were to end in the non completion of the Dictionary', warned Philip Lyttelton Gell who acted as Secretary to the Delegates (or, in modern terms, the Press's chief executive) between 1884 and 1898.[5] Nevertheless, for those engaged in the making of the dictionary the desire to transcend previous lexicographic achievement proved a mainstay of their work. Words, senses, etymologies, citations, as well as the art of definition – and the sheer range of entries which the dictionary included – regularly saw the *OED* striving to surpass both predecessors and contemporaries.

The essential mutability of lexicographic ideals is of course all too clear. The agendas which informed Robert Cawdrey's *Table Alphabeticall* in 1604 (the first monolingual English dictionary) were, for instance, by no means shared by his counterparts in later centuries. His intent to elucidate 'hard vsuall, English wordes' for the benefit of 'ladies, gentlewomen, or other vnskilfull persons' was entirely in keeping with the lexical expansion of the Renaissance which had rendered many new importations – including *ideal* itself – opaque for many speakers of the language. '*Ideall*, proper', Cawdrey glossed.[6] His dictionary remains an act of translation, intentionally facilitating the wider use of 'hard words' which had newly been deemed English. Linguistic ideals in the eighteenth century relied on a somewhat different construction. 'My idea of an English dictionary', as Samuel Johnson declared in 1747, is that 'by which the pronunciation of our language may be fixed, and its attainment facilitated; by which its purity may be preserved, its use ascertained, and its duration lengthened'.[7] Eight years later his *Dictionary of the English Language* reflected corresponding images of selection and control. *Extraordinary* was condemned as 'a colloquial barbarism used for ease of pronunciation'; *nowadays*, in spite of being used by Shakespeare, was 'barbarous'.[8] By the nineteenth century, such ideals had changed again. 'A century does much to change law and language . . ., more to change the scope and method of our knowledge concerning them', as the *Saturday Review* averred in 1884, reviewing the first part of the *OED* to reach publication.[9] Even if we habitually refer to 'the dictionary', with all the embedded associations of monolithic and unitary truth which this phrase suggests, it is clear that dictionaries – and their constituent parts – prove all too susceptible to the constraints of time and change.

What was regarded as the unideal state of English lexicography in the mid-nineteenth century underpinned the origins of the *OED*. Long before Murray's involvement, Richard Chenevix Trench had delivered two lectures on 'Some Deficiencies in our English Dictionaries' to the London Philological Society.[10] Trench's work on language already included his well-received *Study of Words* (1851) which had originally been given as a course of lectures at the Diocesan Training School in Winchester, as well as his *English Past and Present* of 1855. His audience in 1857 at the Philological Society included men such as the social activist and lawyer Frederick Furnivall (one of the founders of the Working Men's College in London) and the philologist and barrister Hensleigh Wedgwood (brother of Emma Darwin), as well as the classicist Henry Malden and the wide-ranging scholar of language, Richard Morris. Wedgwood later produced his own three-volume *Dictionary of English Etymology* (1859–65); Morris edited twelve works for the Early English Text Society (providing a mass of detail on the language of the texts thereby edited), as well as publishing important works on early English and the history of English grammar. The energetic Furnivall was to be associated with the *OED* until his death in 1910, publishing over fifty works on language and early literature.[11] Trench had joined the Philological Society only in 1857, the year in which he gave his lectures, but it had been founded some fifteen years earlier. Furnivall had been a member since 1847.

The Society strove to promote a new linguistic scholarship in which philology was no longer, as it had been for Johnson, a 'barren' and 'dusty desart' in need of enlivening by the addition of 'verdure and flowers'.[12] For its members philology was fertile terrain, the site of new discoveries and new understanding. Johnson's own associate, the orientalist William Jones, had left England in 1783 and moved to India where he became the first English scholar to master Sanskrit. His deduction that Sanskrit, Greek, and Latin must all share a common source set the foundation for a new understanding of the linguistic laws of change and development. Comparative philologists such as Jacob Grimm, Franz Bopp, and Rasmus Rask followed, demonstrating hitherto hidden relationships of form and meaning in their own research. English scholars such as John Kemble (who had worked with Grimm in Germany) and Benjamin Thorpe (who had been studying with Rask in Copenhagen) made their own contributions.[13] In London the Philological Society, originally based at University College, duly stressed its commitment to 'the investigation of the Structure, the Affinities, and the History of Languages; and the Philological Illustration of the Classical Writers of Greece and Rome'. Papers on the 'Philological Ethnography of South America' (given by Sir R. H. Schombuck in 1846) and on the 'Personal Pronouns and Numerals of the Mallicolo and Erromanga Languages' (delivered by the Reverend C. J. Abraham in 1852) demonstrated the adherence of its members to the new forms of knowledge emanating from the Continent. If linguistic scholarship was thereby transformed, the implications for lexicography were also clear. Already in 1819 Franz Passow had stressed the canonical principle that 'every word should be made to tell its own story'. It was this which informed the methodology of his edition of J. G. Schneider's *Kritisches griechisch–deutsches Handwörterbuch*. No longer were lexicographers to frame or distort evidence by the assertion of their own edicts. Patterns of significant change were instead revealed by dictionary entries which operate as miniature biographies, documenting the life-history of individual words by means of empirically substantiated facts. In a similar implementation of these new insights of philology, the scholars of German (and collectors of fairy tales) Jacob and Wilhelm Grimm had been at work since 1840 on the *Deutsches Wörterbuch*, the first part of which was published in 1852 (and which was completed long after their deaths). In France the lexicographer and philosopher Émile Littré was likewise midway through crafting his *Dictionnaire de la langue française*, deliberately incorporating a strongly historical base alongside evidence of contemporary French usage.[14]

In contrast, as Trench and others realized, lexicography in England could seem strikingly anachronistic. Countless reprints and abridgements of Johnson's *Dictionary* continued to appear throughout the nineteenth century. If these gained some additional features (pronunciation, largely excluded by Johnson, became a common feature following the work of Thomas Sheridan and John Walker),[15] they were still remote from the achievements which could be observed elsewhere in Europe. Passow's insights had been implemented by H. Liddell and R. Scott in 1843, but only in the context of their *Greek–English Lexicon Based on the German Work of Francis Passow*. The *Lexicon* did not address the native language in its own right. Other English dictionary-makers such as Charles Richardson had of course stressed the departures from Johnson's work which time had rendered necessary. 'No man can possibly succeed in compiling a truly valuable Dictionary of the English Language, unless he entirely desert the steps of Johnson', Richardson had categorically affirmed.[16] His own *New Dictionary* of 1836, however, merely revealed other fallibilities in its adherence to the etymological principles of Horne Tooke.[17]

Trench's lectures of 1857 homed in on the weaknesses he saw before him as he surveyed existing lexicographical work in English. 'The vocabulary of our Dictionaries is seriously deficient', he stated. Johnson was censured for his inconsistent treatment of obsolete words, not least because of the element of partiality which self-evidently intervened in their representation. With disdain, Trench quoted Johnson's statement that 'obsolete words are admitted when they are found in authours not obsolete, or when they have any force or beauty, that may deserve revival'. 'I will not pause . . . to enquire what a lexicographer has to do with whether a word deserves revival or not', Trench countered, going on to criticize the fact that 'Johnson does not even observe his own rule of comprehension, imperfect and inadequate as that is.' Other axioms of philological enquiry had likewise been ignored. 'It is in every case desirable that the *first* authority for a word's use in the language . . . should be adduced', Trench stressed.[18] Yet here too Johnson had been seriously amiss: 'I doubt whether Johnson even so much as set this before him as an object desirable to be obtained'. Surveying the word-books of the past, Trench comprehensively catalogued their imperfect registering of archaic words, their inconsistencies in representation, their unsystematic grasp of lexical history, as well as their problems in elucidating meaning and synonymy.

In their place, Trench was to proffer a vision of a new and ideal lexicography which, in effect, established the founding principles of the *OED*. The partialities of earlier dictionaries were firmly discarded. In their place is a new stress on the dictionary as an inventory, and the dictionary-maker as a historian. Both redefinitions preclude the subjective engagement with data which had marked previous work. As Trench insisted, notions that a dictionary was a normative guide to correctness were entirely mistaken. The metaphor of the inventory instead emphasized the need to itemize the contents of the lexicon. It did not require evaluation, the interpellation of personal opinion. Such considerations were irrelevant. As a result, even if the maker of dictionaries 'may think of this article which he inserts in his catalogue, that it had better be consigned to the lumber-room with all speed, or of the other, that it had only met its deserts when it was so consigned long ago; . . . his task is to make his inventory complete'. Indeed, Trench stressed, if the lexicographer 'begins to pick and choose, to leave this and to take that, he will at once go astray'.[19] Against the kind of lexicographical dictatorship exhibited in Johnson's stated dislike of words such as *nowadays* or *shabby* ('A low word that has crept into conversation and low writing; but ought not to be admitted into the language') were placed desiderata of an entirely new kind – the dictionary-maker would no longer attempt 'to sort the wheat from the chaff' but would instead simply bring all within the linguistic harvest of the dictionary. Johnson's willingness to include certain tranches of vocabulary at the expense of others was accordingly dismissed. 'Nor are all words which are not found in the vocabulary, to be lamented as omissions', Johnson had reassured his readers, commenting on the deliberate absence of the 'casual and mutable' diction which he saw as characterizing the 'laborious and mercantile part of the people'.[20] Trench found little reassurance in such precepts. The thrust of his lectures embraced the ideal of inclusivity, emphasizing the need for 'impartial hospitality' in the attempt to encompass the whole of the English language.

History – the image of the biography of each and every word – provided further validation of the new directions which Trench sought to impose. '*Historian*: A writer of facts and events', Johnson had written in his own *Dictionary*. It was this commitment to verifiable truth rather than individual caprice which Trench repeatedly commended. A dictionary for Trench was a 'historical monument, the history of a nation contemplated from one point of view'.[21] Even if his own susceptibilities occasionally emerge within his rhetoric of objectivity,[22] his lectures stand as a radical restatement of the future of English lexicography. What was needed, he declared, was not a 'patch upon old garments, but a new garment throughout'.[23] The original plan for a supplement to existing dictionaries, mooted by the Philological Society earlier that year (and formalized in the committee established in June 1857 for the collection of hitherto unregistered words), was clearly inadequate. By January 1858 it was evident that the inspirational agenda which Trench proposed could only be satisfied by the attempt to create a new English dictionary in entirety. The formal *Proposal for the Publication of a New English Dictionary by the Philological Society* which appeared in the following year comprehensively affirmed a number of resolutions based on Trench's work. 'The first requirement of every lexicon is, that it should contain *every word occurring in the literature of the language it professes to illustrate*', it stated. The principle of lexicographic neutrality was likewise adopted as a canonical precept: 'We entirely repudiate the theory, which converts the lexicographer into an arbiter of style'.[24] Even if the language of scientific works is treated with some caution, being excluded in part from that evidence which a dictionary should rightly scrutinize in its making,[25] the general pattern of departure was clear. Just as Johnson in the eighteenth century had hoped that his own dictionary might be a work by which 'we may no longer yield the palm of philology without a contest to the nations of the continent', then so too might this new dictionary of the Philological Society redress, at least in part, the all too evident deficits in nineteenth-century linguistic scholarship and the documentation of the English word-hoard.

Abstractions and Actualities

The preparatory translation of Trench's ideals into physical reality began well. By the end of 1857, Trench had secured seventy-six volunteers who were already engaged in the reading of 121 books in the endeavour to bring an accurate record of English usage into being. Even at this stage it was clear that the proposed work would be a wide-ranging activity, involving many people. Over a hundred 'collectors' were involved by the time the *Proposal* of 1859 appeared. This actively asked for still more contributors who would be willing to give up their time to look for 'remarkable words' and to examine the 'principal 18th or 19th century writers' or to read 'any work' in earlier periods.[26] Practice and precedent went hand in hand, and the proposal explicitly invokes the example of the Grimms in Germany in using volunteers to collect the material for their own dictionary. Herbert Coleridge, grandson of Samuel Taylor Coleridge and author of the eminently scholarly *Glossarial Index to the Printed English Literature of the Thirteenth Century* (1859), assumed the editorship of the new dictionary in 1860. Confident of what might be achieved within a relatively short space of time, he ordered the construction of a set of fifty-four pigeonholes in which the emerging facts about word history and usage could be assembled. Contributors in both England and America duly sent in slips on each of which they had written a precisely dated quotation from a given work. This established the methodology which, with some slight modifications, would remain in use throughout the first edition as well as afterwards. It was the accumulation of these handwritten slips which provided the critical evidence by which the evolution of words and senses would be documented. Up to 100,000 could be gathered together for due classification in Coleridge's economical system of filing. 'When he had filled [the pigeon-holes], it would be time to begin to make the Dictionary', he told Frederick Furnivall who was at that point playing an enthusiastic role on the literary and historical committee for the great work.

Coleridge, despite already realizing some of the problems which the use of volunteer readers might entail, made optimistic projections for the publication of the dictionary. 'In about two years we shall be able to give our first number to the world', he announced in 1860, adding that 'were it not for the dilatoriness of many contributors' it would be possible to 'name an even earlier period'.[27] The facts of Coleridge's own life history nevertheless intervened after merely a single specimen page (*Affect–Affection*) had been printed. As Furnivall wrote in 1861, the projected dictionary had received a 'severe blow' from the early death of its first editor. Consumption had claimed Coleridge's life earlier that year and Furnivall deliberately presents a picture of heroic sacrifice and the utmost scholarly dedication in his tribute to his colleague. After all, Furnivall stressed, it was in the service of the dictionary that Coleridge had 'caught the cold which resulted in his death. All through his illness he worked for it whenever leisure and strength allowed; and his last attempt at work – two days before he died – was to arrange some of its papers'.[28] It was to be Furnivall himself who took charge of the dictionary until well into the next decade, assuming responsibility for the reading programme and for the further organization of voluntary sub-editors who would give the raw material some semblance of order.

It is commonplace to disparage Furnivall's connection with the dictionary at this time. Certainly no further part of it went to press in spite of the prognostications Coleridge had made before his untimely death. Instead Furnivall's redoubtable zeal and energy went into the establishment of authoritative sources on which a future dictionary might depend, as well as into the extension of the reading programme for such sources. Lists of books annotated in Furnivall's hand record the industry of these years. George Perkins Marsh, who lectured on English in Columbia University, applied himself to W. Nye's *Art of Gunnery* of 1670. Miss Nesbitt searched through the 1793 *Selections from the Harleian Miscellany* while Mrs Campbell, another volunteer, worked at a 1793 copy of Thomas Best's *Art of Angling*. Meanwhile Miss F. Scott was reading Lord Chesterfield's *Letters*, and Miss J. Scott (perhaps her sister?) tackled Bentham's *Rationale of Reward*. For the new philology the accuracy of the historical record was vital. To obviate mistakes, readers were 'asked to cut passages out of the printed texts wherever possible, as copying is often hard to read'.[29] Yet, as Furnivall and his army of volunteer readers often found, the linguistic record of earlier eras of the language was fallible, depending on texts which had been imperfectly edited, and on readings which were in many cases unsubstantiated. Given Trench's stress on the signal importance of knowing the precise point at which a word first came into use, such imperfections of data potentially compromised the wider achievements that the dictionary might make. It was for these reasons that Furnivall established (among others) the Early English Text Society in 1864, the Ballad Society and the Chaucer Society in 1868, the New Shakspere [sic] Society in 1873, and the Wyclif Society in 1886. 'Mr. Furnivall has in this work inaugurated a new era in philology', the phonetician Alexander Ellis declared to the Philological Society.[30] Meanwhile Furnivall continued to lecture on English at the London Working Men's College and, during formal working hours, he pursued a career as a solicitor. His socialist beliefs moreover continued to establish a firm foundation for the linguistic democracy which the dictionary was intended to enact. As Furnivall emphasized in his circulars to the readers for the dictionary, the work in the making was by no means merely to be a 'National Portrait Gallery' of the great and the good. Instead it was to be a realm in which 'all the members, of the race of English words' would find equal representation.[31]

If energy and enthusiasm were dominant facets of Furnivall's personality, his talents for administrative organization were, as we shall see, perhaps less pronounced. The tally of over one and three-quarter tons of material generated by the reading programme at this time (and duly delivered to James Murray after he began his own editorship of the dictionary project) stands as eloquent testimony to the exertions that Furnivall's approach could produce. Yet work for the dictionary lost momentum over these years as readers and sub-editors wearied of a scheme which seemed to have no hope of speedy publication. An early agreement with Trübner & Co. foundered as the scale of the dictionary became apparent. Even Furnivall's plan to produce a concise dictionary using some of the materials came to nothing. While some sub-editors – such as the exemplary Henry Hucks Gibbs – maintained a connection with the dictionary which would last well into the next century, many ultimately lapsed in their endeavours. By 1869 only a few readers were continuing to send in new material. Furnivall himself maintained his habits of excerpting his reading – and especially his morning newspaper – for the benefit of the dictionary,[32] but within ten years of Coleridge's death it seemed as if what was already referred to as 'the Big Dictionary' was doomed to be a chimera. Even Furnivall was compelled to admit that activities had declined to such an extent by 1872 that a 'fresh report' was unnecessary 'since progress in the Dictionary work has been so slight'.[33] As Alexander Ellis sadly noted in his Presidential Address to the Philological Society two years later, the dictionary 'remains, and may for some time remain, merely one of the things we have tried to do'.[34]

Yet only a few years later all had changed. Further abortive negotiations for publishing the dictionary with Macmillan were replaced by encouraging discussions with Oxford University Press. The phonetician Henry Sweet, then President of the Philological Society, wrote to the Delegates of the Press in 1877 with a persuasive account of what the plans for the dictionary had so far been able to achieve. He made not so much a request for them to consider publication as a deliberately phrased offer – a 'share in what promises to be . . . very safe & remunerative'.[35] The Press, he suggested, could thereby partake in the revolution in English lexicography which the dictionary so clearly represented. 'Our proposed dictionary has . . . the field almost entirely to itself, and its fullness of material gives it many years' start of any possible rival', Sweet persuasively informed them. The materials gathered during Furnivall's years in charge were presented as attractive bait and Sweet eloquently discoursed on what had already been accomplished, suggesting a project which seemed on the point of realization, a risk-free venture which would benefit Press and Philological Society alike. The 'mass of material' was very great, Sweet assured the Delegates. Moreover during nineteen years of work over half of the alphabet had been sub-edited so that all relevant words were already in 'a shape fit for publication'. Even the other half of the alphabet consisted of 'sorted slips'.[36] And, he stressed, the citations were the 'essential groundwork'. 'Whatever may be the character of the editing, these will always retain their value', Sweet conclusively maintained; 'their collection, it may safely be said, constitutes half of the whole undertaking'.

The 'character of the editing' mentioned by Sweet was also encouraging. The proposed editor of the new work was James Murray himself, a man of a very different temperament to the maverick Furnivall ('there is no saying what he may do in one of his mad fits', Murray would later comment).[37] A schoolmaster at Mill Hill School in London, Murray originally came from Denholm near Hawick in Scotland. His own life could stand as one of the testimonies of Victorian self-help related by Samuel Smiles.[38] Murray was the son of a tailor, and his childhood and adolescence had been marked by his intellectual vigour, his quest for knowledge. He taught himself Latin at twelve and French (as well as Greek) a few years later. As he afterwards recalled, he had 'a sort of mania for languages, learning every new language that I had a chance of'.[39] Archaeology, entomology, biology, and natural science were all favourite pursuits. He had risen to become assistant master as Hawick Grammar School by the age of seventeen. Two years later he became master of the Hawick 'Subscription Academy'. Coming to London in 1864 for the sake of his first wife's health and taking a position as a clerk at the Chartered Bank of India, he had gradually been able to gain the scholarly contacts he needed and, from 1870, to resume his teaching career at Mill Hill, an independent school founded in 1807. Having joined the Philological Society in 1868, Murray had moreover begun to make a name for himself in linguistic scholarship, publishing his *Dialect of the Southern Counties of Scotland* in 1873. This book secured his reputation. 'By its insistence on the true principles of philological inquiry, which at that time were familiar in this country only to a few . . ., it had an appreciable effect on the progress of linguistic science in general', Henry Bradley later recorded.[40] Murray's 1878 article on 'The English Language' for the *Encyclopaedia Britannica* further confirmed him 'as one of the most accomplished scholars in English philology', as Bradley also vouchsafed. With his reserve and scholarly decorum, his dedication and commitment to philology, as well as his competence in the new territories of linguistic science, Murray seemed – both personally and professionally – the ideal candidate to assume the editorship of the proposed dictionary.

The Delegates of OUP were attentive, not least since the eminent comparative philologist Friedrich Max Müller (a Delegate since 1870) was clearly in favour of the proposal. Max Müller, as the *Dictionary of National Biography* records, was in the nineteenth century 'the standard authority on philology in the estimation of the English public'. His lectures on the science of language at the Royal Institution in 1861 and 1863 had been a triumphant success, prompting widespread discussion on the subject of language and the fruits of philological enquiry. In 1864 he had even been asked to give a private lecture to Queen Victoria during which, as Max Müller recalled, 'she listened very attentively, and did not knit at all'.[41] By 1872, as Müller's biographer has stressed, 'largely through Müller's own writings and speeches, the claims and value of the science of Comparative Philology had been established and its far-reaching importance recognized'.[42] As the other Delegates realized, Max Müller was indeed in a position to validate – or otherwise – Sweet's claims for the dictionary. 'The great advance of Philology of late years has completely changed the conditions of a good dictionary', Sweet had argued; 'what is now required is fullness of citations and historical method, . . . treated according to the latest results of linguistic science'. Max Müller concurred. The proposed dictionary was, he wrote, 'an undertaking of such magnitude, in which one might almost say the national honour of England is engaged'. Indeed 'no effort should be spared to make the work as perfect as possible'. As he realized, here at last was England's chance to assume a comparable philological status with France and Germany.[43] Max Müller's report was vital for the dictionary's acceptance by the Press. Though he began a private correspondence with Murray as he sought to clarify the finer details of the project,[44] the positive tone of his recommendations to the Delegates served in effect to ensure the future publication of the Dictionary. As he stressed to Murray, it already had the makings of 'a really scholarlike and classical work'. Murray's later entry for *classical* would confirm the salience of Max Müller's praise: 'Of the first rank or authority; constituting a standard or model; especially in literature'.

The formal contract between the Philological Society and Oxford University Press was signed on 1 March 1879. Its details, however, had already been systematically discussed in a series of private letters. Four months earlier, Murray had agreed with Bartholomew Price (Sedleian Professor of Natural Philosophy and, more critically in this context, Secretary to the Delegates until 1884) that 'the time estimated for the preparation of the Dictionary (with due assistance) is 10 years'. And as Murray had solemnly vowed in the same letter, 'I agree to complete the work within that time, as far as it shall be found to be possible'.[45] According to the plan thereby set out, the first three years were to be devoted to the further collection of data and to the full arrangement of the material which was already in hand. After that point publication would begin. Nevertheless, a careful reading of Murray's letters from this period reveals the presence of a number of qualifying phrases. As he had stated, the dictionary would be completed 'as far as it shall be found to be possible'. Similarly a time span of ten years would suffice provided that Murray received 'due assistance'. Against the time limits specified by the contract, such phrases allowed a certain latitude of interpretation, an element of flexibility should it be needed. As Murray carefully explained to Price, at the conclusion of the three years of preliminary organization, 'copy might *begin* to be *regularly* and *continuously* sent in to the Press'. Or conversely, as events would indeed prove, it might not.

This is not to suggest that Murray was being deliberately duplicitous at this stage. While he would make his own modifications and developments to the planned dictionary, he was in essence inheriting rather than initiating a project. The difference was important. Though other members of the Philological Society had stressed the incalculable worth of what had been achieved ('*the collection of material is simply invaluable*', Walter Skeat had informed him in 1876),[46] Murray was aware that he was also inheriting what was literally an unknown quantity (as well as quality) of material. Even the enthusiastic Skeat had been forced to admit that some of it might be in a 'sad jumble'. A note of caution was realistic. Contrary to the pressures which Price attempted to exert, Murray therefore declared that he 'was not prepared to bind [himself] to have the portions A–E ready for press' by 1882. He nevertheless remained relatively optimistic about what might be achieved with only a few years' work. 'I should rather expect to have A–E well advanced', he assured Price.[47]

Murray's first task as editor was of course to assume possession of the accumulated materials which had been vaunted by Sweet in his letter of 1877. Like his predecessor, Murray organized a system of pigeonholes, though these far exceeded the modest scale which had been adopted by Herbert Coleridge. Over a thousand lined the walls of Murray's Scriptorium, a corrugated iron shed built in February 1879 in the garden of his house at Mill Hill where Murray still retained most of his duties as a teacher. Here, with one assistant, Sidney Herrtage, and the help of two women 'of fair education' from the nearby village (as well as his brother-in-law Herbert Ruthven who was to be in charge of the clerical work), Murray began the task of sorting two decades' worth of intermittent industry on the dictionary. What he termed 'primitive chaos' awaited him, a situation which Murray felt compelled to admit to the Philological Society at its Anniversary Meeting on 16 May 1879.[48] While 'one or two of the letters were in excellent order', gaps and absences were often conspicuous in the mass of slips which Furnivall had delivered. Alongside fundamental problems of illegibility and the imperfect recording of data, it had already been discovered that whole sections of the original material were missing. That for Q had, as Murray reminded Furnivall in May, apparently been taken for sub-editing by the Reverend J. Sheppard in 1862. It had, however, never been heard of since. '*Is it lost*?' Murray demanded; 'will you enquire about [it]?'[49] H too was missing. After originally declaring it to be in America, Furnivall recalled that the relevant alphabetic section was in fact in Florence. He promised that it would reach Murray by June. He managed to find X in one of the darker recesses of his dictionary cupboard and promised to send that along too.[50] P was particularly elusive, especially its opening sections. The trail had gone cold in 1868, when the original sub-editor had died in Ireland.[51] Rather than editing a dictionary which was supposed to transform English lexicography, Murray found himself engaged in various acts of detection and often futile quests. A Mr Jackson in Plymouth was, for instance, initially reputed to have the dictionary material for P though, when contacted, he admitted responsibility only for *Pea* onwards, and the first third of E. Murray's irate letters to Furnivall, berating him for the 'mass of utter confusion' which he had found in the existing materials, were, as this indicates, all too justified. The fact that, as the discussions with OUP had specified, Murray himself had agreed to 'engage, pay for, and be responsible for all Editorial assistance' made the implications still more severe.[52] As Murray informed one of his correspondents over a year later, much of the material still remained unsorted. The dictionary was behind schedule before even a single word had been set in type.

The original material for the *OED* would remain a disappointment, both personally and professionally. Murray confessed many years later to Fitzedward Hall that there were 'numberless puzzles about the early history of the Philological Society's materials' which he had 'long despaired of unravelling'. If their quantity had been impressive (Murray estimated there to be around 2.5 million slips in 1880), their quality proved to be less so. With a few exceptions, including those supplied by Hall, 'the original materials are bad enough, and are rarely to be trusted'.[53] Fewer than one-sixth of these would be used in the dictionary as it came to be published, belying the claims of its title page and the stated value of the 'materials collected by the Philological Society'. Instead, as Murray confirmed, it was the new *Appeal to the English-Speaking and English-Reading Public to Read Books and Make Extracts for the Philological Society's New Dictionary* which he instigated in May 1879 that was the real source of the vast majority of the dictionary's evidence.

Rather than the 'incubus of rubbish & error', as Murray came to characterize the dictionary materials he had inherited, the new *Appeal* would ultimately act as a form of renaissance for the dictionary. Together with his own editorship, and the newly formalized arrangements with OUP, it placed the dictionary on a new and public footing. The *Appeal*, along with the lists of books for which it hoped to attract volunteer readers for the dictionary, was widely circulated. Two thousand copies were sent to university professors and college lecturers, to headmasters and personal friends, as well as to the members of the Philological Society. Moreover, rather than being confined to the pages of arcane periodicals or scholarly journals, the *Appeal* was commented on in the popular press, and was mentioned in a wide range of publications in Britain and abroad.[54] 'This is work in which anyone can join', the *Academy* urged in its own report; 'even the most indolent novel-reader will find it little trouble to put a pencil-mark against any word or phrase that strikes him, and he can afterwards copy out the context at his leisure'.[55] Murray's more measured prose in the *Appeal* itself – 'In order that [the progress of the Dictionary] may be certain, and that it may have that complete and representative character which has been its aim from the beginning, . . . the Committee wants help from its readers in Great Britain, America, and the British Colonies, to finish the volunteer work so enthusiastically commenced twenty years ago'[56] – hence came to stand alongside a range of far more impassioned pleas for assistance. 'Gentle reader', Harold Harley admonished in the *Sweep Papers*, 'do not imagine that *you* have no concern in this great work':

> Whence came those hundreds and thousands of slips which you beheld? Where does the Philological Society look for the million more that will be required? They call upon you, and upon all who speak and read our mother-tongue, to help them . . . But if you cannot yourself take part in this great national work, you can at least persuade some friend to do so, or you can help by lending early copies of seventeenth or eighteenth century books.[57]

Dire consequences were foretold for the 'wilful reader' who might 'obstinately refuse to add a single stone to this noble structure'. As Harley warned, such people would be convicted of disregarding 'the honour of helping to raise a lasting monument of our language'.

Soon Murray's *Appeal* was having the effects he desired. Demand was such that a second edition – and an extended lists of texts – was necessary within a month; a third appeared in January 1880. By mid-May of 1879

Murray was able to tell the Philological Society that 165 readers had already pledged their services. By September, as a report in the *Athenaeum* confirmed, this had increased to almost 400, with over 81,600 slips having been delivered to Murray's Scriptorium.[58] One year later, these figures had increased to 754 readers, with a total of 1,568 books either having been read and excerpted or in the process of being read. This had already produced 361,670 slips. Many readers were strikingly prodigious in their activities on behalf of the dictionary. Within the first year of the appeal Thomas Austin, working in Oxford, had provided 11,000 slips (and over 150,000 more by 1888); a Miss Foxall in Edgbaston in Birmingham sent 4,500 by 1880; the children's writer Jennett Humphreys dispatched 9,200 (mainly attesting eighteenth-century usage) over the same time. American readers, as Murray also recorded, had responded with particular enthusiasm. 'I do not hesitate to say that I find in Americans an ideal love for the English language as a glorious heritage', he stressed to the Philological Society.[59] Works which appeared on the original list of books, such as George Puttenham's *Arte of English Poesie* (1589) and Sir Philip Sidney's *Arcadia*, were willingly undertaken, as was the reading of Bunyan and Dekker and, for the later periods, Blake and Godwin, Tom Paine and Matthew Arnold. While the anonymous *Art of Fair Building* or the plays and poems of Congreve remained unassigned by June 1879, these too had been taken up by the time of the revised list which accompanied the third edition of the *Appeal* in January of the following year.

The public proved astonishingly receptive to the ideals which Murray set before them. Explicit appeals to their patriotism in terms of 'a new Dictionary worthy of the English language' spurred on their endeavours. As Murray admitted, if the compilation of the lengthy 'Lists of Books for Which Readers are Wanted' had undeniably been 'a long and arduous work',[60] then the response the lists continued to receive made the labour worth while. The Murray Papers in the Bodleian Library contain the letters of countless individuals who wrote directly to Murray, pledging their services, their desire to contribute to the work of the dictionary. 'I noticed a statement in the Guardian a few days ago, suggesting that any persons desirous of undertaking "amateur dictionary-making" – I think that, or something like it, was the phrase – should write', noted Berkeley Wesley, for example, in April 1879; 'I have given some little attention to philology, and take an interest in the study', he added.[61] William White wrote one day later, having read Murray's 'appeal for help from any of the old boys' in the *Mill Hill Magazine*: 'Only say what you want done and how I am to do it'.[62]

Professor H. Helwich was assiduously reading Caxton by January 1880, finding 'plenty of new words'. C. Y. Potts sent 200 slips recording unregistered usages in the *Times* and the *Athenaeum* in August 1881; Murray received 1,300 slips from Richardson's *Pamela* in March 1883, enclosed in a letter from Gibbs.[63] These numbers were by no means unusual. On average Murray received around 1,000 slips a day during 1882 alone, all of which had to be sorted in the Scriptorium alongside the original materials.

The day-to-day dedication of these volunteers is striking. 'I have made time to send quotations by taking a few minutes from dinner time or tea time', one correspondent, John Randall, wrote to Murray in 1884; 'sometimes, I have given an hour or two on Saturday afternoon, sometimes I have sat up until twelve on Saturday evening, and sometimes I have got up earlier than usual on Monday mornings, that, before going to work, I might copy those sentences in which I had noticed strange words'.[64] Randall's work exemplifies the many acts of individual industry by which the dictionary was to come into being. In this respect at least, progress was transparently being made. The *Appeal* had stressed the intention of the dictionary 'to contain *all* English words, ordinary and extraordinary' and readers responded in kind.[65] Yet the increase in new material paradoxically served to heighten Murray's awareness of the deficits in what had already been collected. If by 1881 the number of readers had risen to well over 800 while 656,900 citations had been delivered to the Scriptorium, then it was simultaneously all too clear that these achievements did not necessarily bring the dictionary any nearer to its promised publication. Instead Murray found himself struggling to complete a preliminary section of the dictionary's first fascicle that in reality would not even cover the first letter of the alphabet. Against the confident proclamations of the 1879 *Appeal* ('It is intended that a first part of 400 pages containing the letter A shall be ready in 1882'), ideal and actuality forcibly began to diverge.

By this stage Murray was able to calculate with far more precision the real demands of the dictionary. His private correspondence with Henry Hucks Gibbs reveals the dilemmas in which he found himself. After all, the fact was now patent – at least within the Scriptorium – that 'the work *cannot* be done in anything approaching to the time which we first named'.[66] Even twelve years would, as Murray realized, be inadequate. Instead 'the very shortest period which the work will . . . take' was, in total, sixteen or seventeen years. And even this relied on the notably unrealistic premiss that Murray could somehow cover thirty-three words a day. Drafting the single entry for *approve* had, however, taken almost a whole day. 'The terrible word *Black* & its derivatives', as Murray was at that point perhaps fortunately unaware, would later take over three months.[67] When other elements of writing the dictionary were factored in – such as the reading and correction of the proofs and revises – it became evident that even seventeen years was a serious underestimate of the time which would be needed to complete the dictionary. Work on the proofs, as we shall see in the next chapter, was to be one of the most onerous activities in the making of the *OED*, occupying a minimum of three to six hours a day and often leaving little time for what Murray termed the 'real work' of lexicography.

Murray was rightly anxious. 'The thing worries me, and interferes with my mental peace, more perhaps than you can realize', he wrote to Gibbs. Against his better instincts, he felt forced to conceal the true situation from the Delegates. His underlying fear was of the moment at which they realized the real duration of the dictionary. Then, he despairingly conjectured, 'the majority (who care nothing specially for English, & do not realize *a priori* the grandeur of the work) might put up their backs & say, We won't stand this, we will rather stop it'. In the wider interests of the dictionary, and its completion, he felt it best to conceal the facts 'till we get the work fairly launched', at which point its value might be realized and the Delegates might in turn be satisfied with what they had taken on. It was a complex game to play and one which was unsuited in many ways to Murray's scrupulous sense of honour.[68] Like the Delegates, he had signed the contract in good faith. Like them, he found himself betrayed by its stated terms. What all had set out to do was simply impossible.

The Dictionary and the Delegates

By 1882, and already committed to changing the form of the dictionary to six volumes rather than the four originally agreed,[69] some of the Delegates were having their own reservations about the progress of the dictionary. Rather than sitting back and waiting for its production, they developed the habit – much to Murray's annoyance – of actively attempting to engage in its making.[70] More to the point, they also had their own set of lexicographic ideals which did not always accord with those of the Philological Society. Well versed in Johnsonian models of the dictionary in which the evidence of writers such as Milton and Shakespeare had been deemed to set the standard for 'good' usage, many Delegates were disconcerted by a dictionary which seemed to validate the non-canonical, and the ephemera of modern newspapers and magazines, as equally legitimate sources of evidence. Trench's credo of the inventory was at times lost on them. Murray found himself having to elucidate the fundamental principles of descriptive linguistics in which culturally based notions of 'good' and 'bad' in relation to the sources used for the dictionary were simply untenable. 'To the philologist & historian of language – newspaper quotations are the *most valuable* of current instances', he explained. For example, 'they show how the language grows – they make visible to us the actual steps which for earlier stages we must reconstruct by inference'.[71] In a historical dictionary, the insights such usages gave into the mechanisms of change and diffusion were incalculable. For that reason alone they could not be excluded. Murray firmly dismissed such opposition to their presence as the product of mere 'prejudice'.[72]

Prejudices of a variety of kinds nevertheless emerged from the meeting of the Delegates' Dictionary Committee on 10 May 1883. Having scrutinized Murray's partial draft of the dictionary's first part, the Delegates presented their verdict. Surely 'there were too many new scientific words', they opined; similarly 'should not the quotations illustrative of modern literary words be taken from great authors, and the language of newspapers banished?'[73] Murray's earlier reassurances to Bartholomew Price of the linguistic validity of popular usage had clearly met with little success. The meeting resulted in a new set of draft guidelines, formalized by the Delegates and headed *Suggestions for Guidance in Preparing Copy for the Press*. Science, the terms of modern popular discourse, slang, Americanisms, and the curbing of what seemed to be unnecessary sense-divisions, were all pointed out for Murray's consideration. Openly engaging with evaluative issues of usage, they queried 'whether bad English should be inserted'. Derivative words too prompted negative comment. 'Is there any use in giving examples of derivatives unless the meaning of the word is changed?' the Delegates asked, pointing out what seemed to be the excesses in words of this kind related to *abandon* and *abate*. Murray's copy of the *Suggestions*, covered with apoplectic annotations, remains in the Murray Papers in the Bodleian Library. Alexander Ellis was equally enraged. 'The delegates contracted to *print* the dictionary – not to edit it . . . there is not one word in the whole contract which authorises the delegates to interfere with the editing', he expostulated.[74] The Delegates placed the literary above the technical, and the canonical above the potentially ephemeral. Almost six whole pages could be excised, they declared, if Murray followed the proper course of cutting scientific words from the text. 'The words treated belong to a scientific dictionary', the *Suggestions* insisted.[75]

The gaps in understanding – and the divergent set of ideals – which this document reveals are important, not least perhaps in stressing just how radical an enterprise the *OED* was when work on it first began. Trench's descriptive manifesto had, for instance, provoked outright dissent from some quarters. 'What is this but to throw down all barriers and rules, and to declare that every form of expression which may have been devised by the humour, the ignorance, or the affectation of any writer, is at once to take rank in the national vocabulary', the Cambridge-educated writer John Marsden publicly declaimed in the pages of the *Edinburgh Review*.[76] Disagreement could be heard even in the Philological Society.[77] As various members pointed out, dictionaries were conventionally repositories of 'good' usage, offering prescriptive rulings on correctness. As in Johnson, examples were properly derived from 'polite authours' and the 'best writers'. Moreover, as Johnson had stated in his *Preface*, 'tongues, like governments, have a tendency towards degeneration'.[78] A dictionary could 'retard, if not repel' such processes. Many of the Delegates agreed, alarmed by a work which, as the first fascicle of the *OED* would prove, overtly sought to include modern coinages such as *academize* ('to form into an Academy'), illustrated only by an 1868 quotation from the *Daily Telegraph*, or recent scientific 'jargon' such as *abietene*, which was meticulously defined by Murray as 'A hydro-carbon obtained by distillation of the resin or balsam of the nut-pine of California (*Pinus sabiniana*), analogous to oil of turpentine' and dated to 1875. For all their scholarly standing, the Delegates responded to the pull of a range of popular antipathies about language and the nature of the English dictionary. To see the beginning of the *OED* in its own time is therefore to apprehend something of the revolution in English lexicography that it strove to create. And as the missives of the Delegates from this time record, many were not in the mood to see themselves as revolutionaries even if this activity came under the formal heading of 'a new Dictionary . . . worthy of the present state of Philological science', as the 1879 *Appeal* had proclaimed.

After the eventual appearance in 1884 of *A–Ant*, Sir William Markby, one of the Delegates (and a key member of their Dictionary Committee), as well as Oxford's first Reader in Indian Law, wrote privately to Price. In his letter, he set up his own hidden history for the making of the *OED*. 'I think we ought to be free to *discontinue the enterprize* if in *our* judgement it is likely to be unsuccessful', he advised; if 'we find that it must end in a heavy loss, the Society could hardly compel us to go on with it'.[79] Finance proved the real imperative here. From the point of view of purely academic criteria, the dictionary had been spectacularly well received. It was 'a work of the utmost importance to the scientific study of the English language', the *Times* had stressed;[80] it possessed 'manifold excellence', a review in the *Athenaeum* concurred, praising in particular the voluntary labours of the nation by which 'materials [had] been for the first time collected systematically by an army of readers'.[81] Admittedly some of the Delegates' concerns had been echoed in publications such as the *Church Times*. Words 'which have no earlier or higher source than the *Daily Telegraph* and *Daily News* . . . if not actually excluded, ought to have been marked as bad English', the reviewer had contended, disconcerted at the presence of a whole range of usages emanating from the popular press. 'If the daily papers use "bad English", they fortunately leave to others the use of bad nonsense', Murray countered before the Philological Society in 1884. This kind of criticism was 'by far the silliest the dictionary had elicited', he averred,[82] sure that posterity would agree. The vast majority of reviews were sympathetic to what he was trying to achieve, recognizing the significance which this new dictionary promised in both national and lexicographic terms. Nevertheless, as Markby also pointed out to Price, rather than the 'certainty of large returns' promised by Sweet, the Delegates found themselves burdened with a work which had no hope of being finished within its designated time limit. Five years had seen the publication of less than a single letter. On the same scale the complete work could conceivably take almost three centuries. Even if some of the current delay was attributable to the need to sort the accumulated material and to establish working practices (as well as the vital details of presentation), the Delegates were rightly concerned. On the evidence of the dictionary's first part, as the *Athenaeum* had already remarked, the revised scale of the project must 'be raised to about . . . six very thick quarto volumes'. The reviewer 'earnestly hoped that the whole time required for the completion of the work has not been similarly underestimated'.[83] Back in Oxford, the Delegates discussed the urgent need to consider 'the future management and more speedy publication of the dictionary'.[84] Lexicography, even that formed on wide-ranging historical principles, came with commercial constraints. Ideals had to be tempered by pragmatism. If the dictionary did not appear, then it could not be sold, and losses were inevitable.

Benjamin Jowett, Master of Balliol, Regius Professor of Greek since 1855 and *ex officio* chair of the Delegates from 1882, was inspired by the need for economic restraint. The reforms which he had put in place at Balliol had transformed the college; Jowett saw potential at the Press. Frederick York

Powell, the Regius Professor of Modern History at Oxford who became a Delegate in 1885, would later recall Jowett carefully explaining that 'money profit rather than advancement of learning must be first regarded in the policy of the institution'.[85] The same enthusiasms were in evidence in the early days of the dictionary. Under Jowett's leadership, the Delegates' Dictionary Committee strove to impose stringent measures on Murray, demanding that he pledge himself to produce a minimum of 300 pages a year (and ideally two parts of 352 pages each), with financial penalties to be imposed if the targets were not reached. Informed of this by Murray, Henry Hucks Gibbs reacted with anger, writing directly to Price to stress that, in his opinion, 'no honourable man would take such an engagement, and that if he did it would hang like a weight round his neck, paralyse his energy, and go far to defeat the end which the Delegates have in view'.[86] As so often in the spats between dictionary and Delegates, Gibbs's diplomatic firmness prevailed. Whilst this particular pressure was therefore resisted, the reality of the dictionary ideal was already beginning to dawn for all concerned. In marked contrast to the neutrality of Trench's metaphor of the inventory, Murray had already come to see the dictionary as an anthropomorphized 'abyss', voracious in its appetites and capable of swallowing weeks and months in the attempted elucidation of a single word. It 'will never cry "Enough"!' he declared to Gibbs in 1882.[87] Other metaphors too would gradually come to the fore. Letters were 'enemies', needing to be faced and defeated. Murray was the dictionary's 'slave', as he informed Fitzedward Hall,[88] bemoaning the fact that for days he had been effectively housebound as a result of its insatiable demands. In the new levels of information which were required for definition, for the division of senses, in the transcription of pronunciation (for which an entirely new alphabet had to be devised), and in accurately establishing the historical record, Murray was pushing through uncharted territory, often spending 'hour after hour' in trying to elicit 'a logical chain of development' from what was merely the 'fragmentary evidence' of the 'incomplete historical record' he had before him.[89] In striving to create an ideal dictionary he was compelled to venture into areas in which 'simply nothing whatever has been done in English'. And the time which this demanded was enormous. Murray's intellectual convictions about the nature of a new dictionary remained unchanged, but it is scarcely surprising that by 1884 he could describe himself as both 'weary' and 'embittered'.[90]

Against the ambitious ideals on which the dictionary had been founded there came to stand the daily rigours of making the dictionary. Murray too was forced to admit to Bartholomew Price that 'the slowness of the actual pace at which we have been able to produce the Dictionary is a source of deep disappointment to me'. And, as he also conceded, '*I* cannot, I am sorry to say, put more work or more effort into it, than I am doing'.[91] His own physical limits came into play too. While *Ant–Batten*, the second part of the dictionary, managed to make a relatively swift appearance, being published in November 1885, this merely provided a temporary respite from the underlying difficulties. By the following January the Delegates were already calling attention 'to the slow progress of the third part'. Henry Frowde, the Press's most senior official, was also displeased. 'The prospects of the Work' as a whole had, in his opinion, already been 'seriously injured' by the lengthy gestation of its first two instalments. Moreover the fact the Press had given 'great prominence to an announcement that subsequent parts would be issued at intervals of six months' rendered the current situation one of significant – and public – embarrassment.[92] The Delegates shared his opinion and sent a series of reproachful letters to Murray, stressing their 'consternation' at the 'present rate of progress', not least given the 'substantial financial resources' they had already allocated to the dictionary.[93] They had, for example, supplied a further £1,250 in 1885 to facilitate the employment of additional dictionary assistants, and confessed themselves perplexed by the fact that, in spite of this, Part III seemed as remote as ever. Murray had also given up his position at Mill Hill and had moved to Oxford to edit the dictionary full time, erecting another Scriptorium in the grounds of his house on Banbury Road. Yet progress – at least in terms of formal publication of results – still seemed a misnomer. A tally of fifty-six sheets of the new part of the dictionary had been passed for press in the first half of 1886. Three years before the dictionary had originally been expected to be finished, not even the second letter of the alphabet had been completed. The Delegates' despair was understandable – as indeed was that of Murray himself, subject as he was not only to the pressures which the Delegates imposed but also to the daily toil of trying to write the dictionary against what seemed impossible expectations. Even with a regular working day of some thirteen hours (and often longer), the dictionary did not make the advances that the Delegates required.

The appointment of Henry Bradley as the *OED*'s second editor in 1888 served in some ways to lessen the individual responsibility which Murray bore for the fortunes of the dictionary project. It did not, however, expedite progress in the ways the Delegates had hoped. Price's successor as Secretary, Philip Lyttelton Gell (a close friend of Jowett), sent a frantic letter to Murray in March 1887 to inform him that 'the Delegates will be appalled to learn that the whole *completed* result since Feb. 1st is two sheets'.[94] They were presumably no less dismayed by the single sheet which appeared between May and June of that year. Even if Bradley had professed himself more willing to compromise than Murray seemed to be, he would in fact regularly prove to be a much slower editor, often producing significantly smaller amounts of finished work than his senior colleague.[95] Bradley's early correspondence with Bartholomew Price on the subject of the dictionary had nevertheless seemed encouraging, at least from the Delegates' point of view. One can imagine them nodding enthusiastically as they read comments such as 'it is clear that it may be possible to pay too high a price even for perfection of execution' or as they scrutinized his statement that 'the sacrifice, to some extent of completeness & accuracy is after all preferable to the alternative of causing, if not the collapse of the undertaking, at least the postponement of its completion to an infinitely remote future'.[96] Such apparent pragmatism agreed with their sentiments entirely. 'If I am entrusted with a share in the work', Bradley vowed, 'my principle . . . will be to aim at the greatest excellence within definite limits of time'.

Yet as the history of the dictionary repeatedly affirmed, principles and practice would often assume a markedly uneasy relationship. Bradley's role as editor proved no exception. The easy confidence of his early letters to the Press disappeared. Within a year of beginning editorial work on the dictionary he had realized that Murray's methods – and his meticulous search for detail – were in essence right. 'I am bound to say that in the great majority of cases the alterations which [Murray] had made in the articles as prepared by me are decidedly for the better', he wrote, resisting the compromises he had at first seemed to advocate.[97] Like Murray, he was seduced by the desire to create the ideal dictionary, whatever the cost. He delved into etymological cruces with vigour, tracking elusive chains of development and philological nuances that might illuminate the entries he sought to write. He rephrased and redrafted, proving himself Murray's true disciple in his endeavours to craft the perfect entry, to secure the precise shades of meaning he desired.[98] By 1896 the Delegates would be imposing stringent requirements on his productivity. As they resolved early in February of that year in the midst of the dictionary's most serious crisis, Bradley was to 'be informed that it will be necessary that his connexion with the Dictionary should close unless he keeps within due scale on the remaining portion of this letter'.[99]

Looking back at the early history of the dictionary, it is remarkable how fragile its continued existence at times seemed. While its scholarly ideals were impeccable, their compatibility with commercial publication repeatedly caused concern. 'The dictionary is *wanted* by students *now*', the Delegates exhorted, self-evidently frustrated at what they often regarded as an unrealistic commitment to document the history of the language in each and every detail.[100] Johnson had managed to devote less than a third of a column to his entry for *black*. Noah Webster, regarded as a similarly canonical authority for many in the nineteenth century (especially in America), had needed only sixteen lines (excluding the etymology). The Delegates repeatedly held him up as an example of lexicographical economy to the recalcitrant Murray. Murray's entry for *black* instead encompassed twenty-eight divisions of sense and sub-sense for the adjective alone. *Candle* was similar. Johnson had required fourteen lines and two senses for this apparently easy word. Webster's entry had covered twenty lines within a single column of text. *Candle* in the *OED* conversely occupied four columns and 376 lines. Exhaustiveness of this kind was expensive, requiring seemingly infinite amounts of money and time – even if it did manage to transcend the achievements of all other dictionaries. Between 1888 and 1893, for example, Murray had painstakingly edited 29,295 words and phrases beginning with C. Before that, he had covered 10,049 words beginning with B and 12,183 which began with A. Philologically the achievement was undeniable. Financially, the position was somewhat different. Ideals on each side failed to match up. The cost of the *OED* surpassed all expectations. Even the corrections made in proof had reached a total of just over £1,268 for the first volume alone.

'The point of view creates the object studied', as Ferdinand de Saussure would later write in setting out the fundamental principles of structural linguistics. His words are entirely apposite to the dictionary throughout the troubled period of the 1890s. What the dictionary was differed markedly depending on how one chose to look at it: the *OED* often seemed to assume a set of mutually irreconcilable identities on which Delegates and dictionary-makers failed to agree. The accumulation of material – and the philological advances thereby achieved – clearly made the demands of the dictionary worth while from the point of view of abstract knowledge. 'It pleases me, at any practicable amount of work, to get at the facts, and force them to yield their secret', Murray later wrote to his close friend Edward Arber, Professor of English Language and Literature at Birmingham University.[101] Skeat sent a celebratory poem to Murray:

> Wherever the English speech has spread,
> And the Union Jack flies free,

The news will be gratefully, proudly read,
That you've conquered your A. B. C ![102]

His jubilation was not echoed by the Press. The Delegates calculated that expenditure on the dictionary totalled £32,400 by 1892, with a net loss of some £22,400. They understandably declared themselves 'profoundly dissatisfied', not least with the 'steadily growing disproportion between the money spent upon the "Dictionary" and the work done'. Paradoxically it seemed that the more money they spent, the more time the dictionary took. They looked back with apparent nostalgia to the early days of Mill Hill when Murray had edited the dictionary alongside his teaching and when, perversely, it now seemed that the dictionary 'had never advanced so rapidly'.[103]

The years between 1892 and 1896 were some of the hardest in the dictionary's history. The Delegates appointed a new dictionary committee, which made a formal report in 1893 and another (far more stringent one) in 1896, setting out a new series of suggestions for the future of the dictionary. Like their counterparts in 1883, these lists of desiderata stressed the Delegates' continued opposition to the words of science and technology, to the incorporation of modernisms (such as those words which had arisen since *c.*1880) and to the presence of slang and Americanisms (in spite of the valuable contributions which, as Murray asserted, the American people were making to the dictionary as a whole). Unlike the 1883 *Suggestions*, however, the requirements of the 1890s were far more autocratic, often – as in 1896 – forcibly seeking to revise the ideals with which the project had set out. The aim was now explicitly 'curtailment' in the scale of the dictionary, a word which Murray had in fact recently defined. 'The action of curtailing, shortening, diminishing; abridgement', he had written, perhaps taking a quiet pleasure in the 1878 quotation from John Morley's *Diderot and the Encyclopaedists* with which he had concluded the entry: 'The copies were returned to their owners with some petty curtailments'. Not content with issuing edicts, the Delegates were by this stage reading preliminary drafts of the dictionary and pointing out words, senses, and citations which, in their opinion, did not need to be included.[104] They recommended strict adherence to a fixed scale for the dictionary, based on the unabridged edition of Webster's *American Dictionary of the English Language* of 1864.[105] While this scale had been in existence before,[106] it was, they decreed, now to be implemented far more rigorously. As the Delegates belatedly realized, in practice this had hitherto operated as a notional rather than practical norm. Murray 'has never at any time observed the conditions laid down in his agreement', the Regius Professor of Greek, Ingram Bywater, noted with alarm. Bywater had been appointed as a Delegate in 1879 and was, as Herbert Warren (Master of Magdalen and a Delegate himself) later noted, 'peculiarly in his element' in this role. In terms of the dictionary, Bywater's concern intensified when he realized that the contractual limits of the dictionary had been 'systematically neglected by both Dr. Murray and Mr. Bradley'.[107] Henceforth, as both Murray and Bradley were informed, they were not permitted to exceed a scale of six pages for each one of Webster's *Dictionary*; an increase to 7:1 might be allowed in 'exceptional cases' – though only if explicitly agreed in advance. The image of the inventory disappeared. The dictionary could encompass language only within the limits imposed. Contrary to the tenets expressed by Trench, the new imperatives of the Delegates meant that the lexicographer was indeed once more to be partial and selective, interposing his judgement on which words were worth recording. Philology itself was also under threat. 'In the . . . purely philological part of the work . . . fewer parallels to be given from cognate languages', Murray and Bradley were told.[108] Rather than advancing philological science in line with what now seemed a naïve faith in the virtues of scholarship, such information could be excluded since it was 'superfluous to the learned, and confusing to the unlearned'.[109] The value of historicism – and the 'historical principles' vaunted on each and every title page of the dictionary – were likewise thrown into doubt. Too much time had been wasted on trying to trace obsolete words, the Delegates declared. The fact that history is an ongoing process – not least as it concerns the manifold forms of language – was cast aside. As the Delegates categorically averred, 'it is a waste of time and brain to give . . . any serious attention in an historical dictionary' to 'the latest specimens of Journalese, or the newest Americanisms'.[110]

As discussions about the untoward scale of the dictionary began in 1892, Murray wrote to Furnivall in despair, setting out his own despondent resolutions for ways in which the dictionary might reach completion. 'Aim at doing everything less fully & exhaustively', he noted; 'Draw the line *against* all doubtful candidates for admission'.[111] Was he wrong, he wondered, to try and include the diction of science? His own role as a 'self-professed scientist of language' inclined him to include such terms – yet popular sympathies, as he was well aware, were against him. 'Nothing is gained by the insertion of such items of scientific jargon' as *eclampsy*, *edripthalmian* or *ekbergite*, as a review in the *Athenaeum* had stressed two years earlier.[112] Murray contemplated casting his image of an ideal dictionary aside. Yet to do so would, he realized, be to betray what he came to see as his destiny, a duty to the language and the nation. 'I am doing what God fitted me for, & so made my duty', as he later wrote to James Bryce.[113] It was this, in part, which inspired his unwillingness to implement in full the kinds of compromise which the Delegates wished to impose. 'I am fully alive to all the difficulties, financial and other, of the situation', he wrote to Gell in 1896 in the midst of the continued spat on the dictionary's scale. He was, he affirmed, likewise 'willing to try any practical plan to diminish these difficulties'. What was 'practical', however, did not necessarily include anything that might change the very nature of the dictionary. Here Murray could prove just as intransigent as the Delegates. 'Rather than see the Dictionary deprived of the characters which constitute its only justification, I should prefer to see it stopped altogether', he stated. The work of the dictionary was 'original work'. It could not be cut short without sacrificing the justification of the work as a whole. In this respect the ideals remained intact. 'The only satisfaction I personally have in it', Murray stressed to Gell, 'is that which comes from the feeling that the best possible has been done to realize, within the narrowest limits possible, the ideal of a dictionary on historical bases.'[114]

Words that Begin with D

D, which Murray began editing in 1893, contained a selection of words which came to seem well suited to the experience of these years. *Desperation*, *depression*, *despair* – as well as *delegate* – would all occupy Murray's attention.[115] *Dictionary* too would make its appearance. Murray deftly reasserted Trench's canonical insistence on inclusivity in illustration. 'A Dictionary, according to that idea of it which seems to be alone capable of being logically maintained, is an inventory of the language', the entry averred. Later quotations insisted on the historical principle too. 'A dictionary is not merely a home for living words; it is a hospital for the sick; it is a cemetery for the dead', R. W. Dale had stated in 1878. Murray included entries for *dictionary work* ('The main difficulty in the Dictionary work is to trace the history of the development of the meanings of a word', illustrated by a quotation from the *Transactions of the Philological Society*), *dictionary word*, and *dictionary-maker*. The entry itself would be 168 lines long, occupying a column and a half in the printed text. The corresponding entry in Johnson had been fourteen lines, that in Webster merely ten.

The disparities yet again confirmed the irreconcilable demands made by the *OED*. Relentlessly it moved beyond its predecessors in scale and scope, providing a source of both congratulation ('No one can examine the "Dictionary" without being impressed by the patience and genius for detail to which every page bears witness', the *Manchester Guardian* declared in 1895)[116] and concern. Charles Doble had, for example, written to Murray from the Press to alert him to 'the abnormal development of the early part of F' under Bradley's editorship. But what was abnormal for a dictionary such as the *OED*? 'Deviating from the ordinary rule or type; contrary to rule or system; irregular, unusual, aberrant', Murray's own definition in 1884 had stated. Bradley's work conformed to the original expectations of the dictionary in terms of abstract scholarship. 'We find ourselves less and less able to supply omitted words', as the philologist Charles Fennell commented in the *Athenaeum*, drawing the logical inference that 'the quality goes on improving at a greater ratio than might be expected'.[117] Yet its scale and liberality went against the revised expectations of the Delegates, especially in relation to those categories of words decried in their dictates of 1893 and afterwards. 'Technical and scientific words' were particularly in evidence in Bradley's drafts of the first part of F, as Charles Doble pointed out on behalf of the Press; similarly the provision of citations, especially from non-canonical sources, erred towards the unduly generous – not least given the earlier promises by the dictionary editors 'to take energetic measures to save space'.[118] Bradley redoubled his efforts, monitored by Murray. Curtailment acquired a variety of synonyms in the day to day workings of the dictionary. Terms such as 'reduction' and 'compression' frequently appear. While they had of course been used before, their application took on a new urgency. 'If the publication cannot be accelerated, the Delegates will proceed to question the continuance of the work', Murray had been warned in 1892. The threat remained over the following years.

Ironically, it was Murray himself who pre-empted the most serious part of the crisis in 1896, as well (as events proved) as the means to its resolution. His prognostications about his own progress were positive. 'Unless our course is arrested by some unforeseen loss or accident', he would finish the third volume of the dictionary – that covering C – before the end of the year, Murray wrote to Gell.[119] His opinions on Bradley's part of the work were less hopeful. While Murray finished C, Bradley was at work on F, a letter which, as we have seen, had already been causing concern. Murray's letter to Gell merely heightened this – and with it focused anxieties for the future of the dictionary as a whole. Murray's admission that even *fa* to *florin* exceed the notional scale of the *OED* to Webster by some sixty-six pages was startling. Still worse was Murray's assessment that, since Bradley had spent '3 years & 4 months' on this section alone, it was likely that 'it will take about 15½ years to finish the volume'. Abdicating responsibility for the part ('the scale to which it is done is entirely opposed to my wishes as Editor-in-chief . . . I desire to wash my hands entirely of Vol. IV'), Murray urged the Delegates to action.

Murray's own lack of caution in this matter is striking. As he stressed to the Delegates, he was indeed 'Editor-in-chief', a role which he would constantly differentiate from that of his co-editors. Murray's own role was that of 'Editor of the whole work', as he affirmed to the Vice-Chancellor of Oxford, John Magrath, in the following year. Murray demanded 'the continuance and recognition' of his 'position and status' in this respect.[120] Bradley and later William Craigie (appointed third editor in 1901) were conversely designated 'collaborators'. They were merely the 'authors' of their own sections, Murray stressed. So it was of course clear that responsibility for F could not, in effect, be abdicated so lightly. In the ensuing conflict over Bradley's work, Murray was caught in the cross-fire. Subsequent missives from the Delegates on the need to curb the dictionary's size are, for example, addressed to Murray and Bradley alike. Both were 'requested to give an explicit undertaking' that they would henceforth observe the 'rules' of the Delegates on both scale and contents.[121] Moreover Bradley's careful responses to the Delegates inadvertently confirmed that, if the dictionary were indeed moving beyond its designated limits, then it was not entirely due to him. Between *afounder* and *againwards*, for instance, which had been edited entirely by Murray, the proportion of the dictionary in relation to Webster had been 17:1. Throughout Murray's editing of B, the average scale had been 7.85 to 1.[122] As a result, rather than Bradley's work on F being awry, his calculations confirmed that only rarely had the dictionary attained its intended scale. Yet, as Bradley continued in defence, this was inevitable. 'Uniformity of "scale" . . . throughout the work would necessitate constant fluctuation of method', Bradley pointed out. As his own experience with F had proved, if this form of rigid accountability were to be adhered to, then attempting to do justice to the resources of the language in one part of the dictionary would mean conscious (and damaging) compromise in others. Not all sections of the alphabet were similar. If it had indeed been possible in certain parts of A to achieve a ratio of 6:1, the same was unlikely to be true for, say, S, for which many more words would need to be included given the structure of the English lexicon. With irrefutable lexicographical logic,

Bradley carefully set out his opposition to the Delegates' proposals, emphasizing above all 'the special characteristics' of the dictionary which 'constitute its chief claim to superiority over all possible rivals'. Were the Delegates' recommendations to be carried out in full, this would render the *OED* a very different work, utterly divesting it 'of those qualities to which its unique value and reputation are chiefly due'.

In this the editors were united. After all, as Bradley's private letters to Murray stressed, had a rigidity of scale of this kind been imposed throughout Murray's editing of B, 'there would have been a unanimous and well-founded outcry from competent critics that the quality and value of the work had declined greatly from the original standard'.[123] Murray's own attempts to identify where the cuts could be made from F brought him to the uncomfortable realization that moving to the Delegates' desired scale would in effect mean cutting forty-five lines from every single column of Bradley's recent work. Yet even after having spent hours scrutinizing the sheets with his assistants, he had failed to find more than a fraction of quotations that could perhaps be omitted without substantially reducing the quality of the work. While it was clear that 'a *Dictionary* certainly could be made with such limits', such a task would, Murray admitted, create 'a new work, different from our Dictionary'.[124] Like Bradley, he came to insist that the Delegates' limit of one page of Webster to every six of the *OED* was '*entirely impracticable*, without so changing the character of the Dictionary as to make it not worth doing'. As he informed the Delegates, his own recent experience with Bradley's proofs had made him aware that 'it is not possible to do the work on a scale less than that of eight times Webster's Dictionary'. Even this, he added, ought to function as a general scale rather than one to be applied on each and every page. The conclusions of the Philological Society, where the matter had likewise received extensive debate, were similar. As Fitzedward Hall insisted, a rigidity of treatment of the kind proposed would 'seriously impair the commercial value of the dictionary'.[125] It was an argument which, he felt sure, the Delegates would understand.

The situation seemed insoluble. After all, as Gibbs had pointed out to Murray in 1892, as he once more assumed his role as peacemaker, the Delegates had been 'very long-suffering'. They too had had ideals and expectations. A loss of over £20,000 was scarcely negligible. As a result, they 'must of course be expected to take to heart the slow and inadequate return for their expenditure'.[126] Gibbs too had ventured to make suggestions for omission – perhaps the technicalities of art or some 'foreign' words could be excluded. He gave the example of *chaston*, which Murray had included as an obsolete and rare word in the fascicle *Cast–Clivy* (published in November 1889). 'The broad part of a ring in which the stone is set; the collet', stated Murray's definition. 'A looking-glasse of golde, shining and well burnished . . . They called this glasse or chaston of golde "Irlacheaya"' read the accompanying quotation. Yet, as Gibbs suggested to Murray, though 'the information you give is very interesting . . . if you are to curtail, that's the sort of thing to cut out'. As here, Gibbs came to adopt the Delegates' own idioms of curtailment, using it as the basis for possible compromise. Bradley's letters to the Press in 1896 adopted a similar tenor. As he recognized, for all the autocratic rhetoric which could be displayed, there was 'a desire on both sides to act reasonably'. What would now be ideal was for 'some compromise [to] be arrived at, which may to some degree relieve the Delegates of their anxieties, without destroying the character of the Dictionary'.[127]

Compromise had, however, been involved in the writing of the dictionary from the beginning. While the popular image of inclusivity remained intact (the dictionary 'seeks not merely to record every word that has been used in the language for the last 800 years . . . but to furnish a biography of each word', as Murray would declare in 1900),[128] notions that the *OED* might include all words had long been open to debate.[129] The lexicon could not, in practice, be encompassed by the lexicographer. As Murray had already indicated in his prefatory 'General Explanations' for the dictionary in 1884, the activities of the lexicographer were, in essence, like the drawing of a line which, even as it includes some words, must simultaneously exclude others. If Murray at this point was unaware of the full implications of the tensions that would result, he was nevertheless entirely clear that there was some latitude between language *per se* and what lexicography might be able to achieve. While the dictionary strives to pin words down, to delimit them at a specific point in time merely by virtue of the act of publication, the language itself knows no such stasis. Words would be coined of which the lexicographer has no knowledge. Even the evidence on which he depended for the words which he did know would often prove faulty. The surge of fresh information on dates, citations, and senses which was prompted by the appearance of the dictionary's first fascicle was, as he had warned the Philological Society in 1884, 'a mere nothing . . . in comparison with what the experience of future times will suggest'.[130] As the evidence of the proofs furthermore confirms, compression had in reality been an ongoing task since the first pages of the text. Murray stressed to the Delegates in 1896 that it was indubitably true that 'all the literary helpers who read our "proofs" . . . know that the economizing of space is in my eyes of the first moment'. Indeed, he added, 'I am ten times more thankful for criticism that cuts out anything, than for that which necessitates additions'.[131] Bradley agreed. He too had been making 'laborious efforts after compression' throughout the making of F. In this respect, Delegates and dictionary-makers were at one. The only difference was on the precise limits which such economies were to observe. What gradually became apparent to all concerned was that the stringent requirement that the dictionary should maintain a consistent scale of six pages to every one of Webster, enshrined by the Delegates in their meetings as the prime desideratum for the remainder of the *OED*, would require a level of excision which was by no means compatible with the scholarship – and particularly the scholarly standing – of the work.

Pragmatism resolved the inevitable stalemate. As Fitzedward Hall had astutely perceived, the Delegates had no desire to publish an inferior work. The reputation of the dictionary rested on its impeccable scholarship, its extraordinary detail, its etymological rigour. To compromise on any of these would lessen not only its quantity but also its quality. And the reputation of the Press would suffer in turn. Newspaper reports that the Delegates were considering suspending publication of the dictionary 'except on the condition that its scale is greatly reduced' had already caused damage. To read in the *Saturday Review* that this contemplated action was 'a national calamity and an indelible disgrace to the University' had by no means been pleasant.[132] The article explicitly invoked Trench's image of 'the ideal dictionary' as 'the complete inventory and a complete history of our language'. It continued: while 'retrenchment may, for all we know, be necessary in the economy of the Press', the notion that it 'should take this particular form is most strongly to be deprecated'. The rumours were swiftly countered. The Delegates continued to express their desire to limit 'the extent of the work to the narrowest bounds', but these bounds, as they came to realize, had to be 'consistent with its thoroughness and historical character'. As Murray and Bradley had wished, the earlier desideratum of six times Webster was relaxed. Eight pages of the *OED* to one page of Webster became the new (and explicit) norm, affirmed in the Delegates' Order of 27 March 1896. The collective argument – and irrefutable reason – of Murray, Bradley, and Hall had won the day, aided by the fact that, as the Delegates' experience with Bradley's proofs revealed, the ideals which they too had proclaimed were not so easy to achieve when it came to actually making the dictionary. Even given their own remit to cut and condense, the Delegates found that they too failed to reach the notional scale of six (or even eight) pages of the *OED* to one of Webster. Oxford University Press committed itself to ways of finding 'more fitting support' for what was now proclaimed the 'truly national work' of the dictionary. Funding for a new appointment appeared in the following year and William Craigie joined the staff of the *OED*. He maintained the tradition of scholarly self-help and determination which had been established by Murray and Bradley. The son of a jobbing gardener, he displayed the same zest for languages, acquiring Gaelic from his maternal grandfather, and learning German and French (and making a start on Danish and Icelandic) while reading for a degree in classics and philosophy at St Andrews. Demonstrating an early affinity with lexicography, he had started annotating a copy of Jamieson's *Scottish Dictionary* when aged thirteen. Craigie began work at the *OED* in 1897, becoming a fully independent editor in 1901.

Nevertheless, if it seemed that the dictionary-makers had triumphed, it still has to be remembered that adopting a ratio of 8:1 in the making of the dictionary would inevitably involve sacrifices. After having examined Bradley's work on F, Murray had, for example, concluded that if the 6:1 ratio was impossible, 8:1 could be achieved only '*with difficulty*' and '*with daily stringent application of the screw*'.[133] This image of lexicographical torture proved apt. 'No one knows as well as I do, how it grieves one to have to do this', Murray would later write to Craigie; 'I have had to steel my heart & clench my teeth & do it, for years'.[134] Cutting words or senses or citations would not be without cost, even if it undoubtedly contributed to the publication of the dictionary. As later chapters explore, the printed page does not always reflect the liberality of the dictionary's first versions; excisions and deletions litter the extant proofs, often changing the balance of evidence, the possible range of non-canonical writers, as well as the relative presence and absence of the words of science and technology, or the various usages and citations deemed potentially ephemeral. The *OED* would not, in the end, proffer 'the meaning of everything' as the title of a recent book on the dictionary avers.[135] And, perhaps predictably, this attrition would be most noticeable in the years during and after the crises of the 1890s.

For a complex of reasons of this kind, the dictionary manifested some shifts within its attempted realization. The forty-four years which cover its publishing history alone mean that change was of course inevitable. 'Seen in this context, the commonly received idea of the *OED* as a monolithic scholarly edifice must be modified', as Roderick McConchie has rightly noted. 'Limited by the activities of its workers, to some extent hamstrung by its own policies, and evolving further policies as the project grew', the *OED* would inevitably engage in metamorphosis, even if its essential identity remained intact.[136] Its making was, however, far more complex than anyone had initially envisaged. Readers, editors, and publishers were all forced to reassess the nature of what could be achieved, and the means of achieving it. As the nineteenth century ended and a new century began, the dictionary marched slowly towards completion, aided by the promotion of Charles Onions – a protégé of Murray's friend Edward Arber – to fourth editor in 1914.[137] Only in 1928 would its final word be published, thirteen years after Murray's death. If Murray had begun publication with *A*, it was Onions who, as he afterwards liked to recall, had literally the last word in the history of the first edition of the *OED*.[138]

'Even the most insignificant enterprizes . . . have the sense of an unattained ideal', Henry Sweet had written to Murray early in 1882. 'You are engaged in one of unexampled magnitude, on very insufficient foundations', he continued.[139] Although Sweet's claims in an earlier letter to the Press had proved strikingly unfounded (the dictionary had not been remunerative, the citations collected by the Philological Society had not proved invaluable), his prescience in this respect was undoubted. Throughout the making of the dictionary Murray (and his co-editors) would be haunted by the sense of the ideal – and its elusiveness. The original *Notice of Publication* for the dictionary, drafted in late 1883, had eloquently stressed what the dictionary hoped to attain. Based on 'new methods of knowledge', the work was 'the fuller development of the ideal which floated before the mind of Dr. JOHNSON when he first conceived the intention of becoming a lexicographer'.[140] The dictionary's originality, its philological rigour, its deployment of authoritative evidence (all to be precisely dated and accurately attributed) were justly displayed. Even here, however, a sense of reality coexists with the descriptive rhetoric by which a new era within English lexicography was announced. 'It is certain that the ideal cannot be fully realised', Murray admits. He returned to the same point in 1884 after the first part of the dictionary had been published. 'Our efforts to realize that ideal, imperfect in many respects as we know them to be, have not been entirely unsuccessful', he stressed in his Presidential Address to the Philological Society.[141] The dictionary was, and would be, more than a set of abstract principles. It was underpinned by human endeavour and human institutions – and the fallibilities which such institutions can bring.

CHAPTER 2

Palimpsests

Palimpsest, like many other word-entries in this new dictionary on historical principles, conspicuously revealed the inadequacies of previous lexicographic investigation. While, as Murray confirmed, it had existed in English since 1611 (in the now obsolete sense 'Paper, parchment, . . . writing-material prepared for writing on and wiping out again, like a slate'), *palimpsest* had passed unremarked by both Johnson and Bailey. The former had instead moved seamlessly from *palification* ('The art or practice of making the ground firm with piles') to the more familiar *palindrome* ('a word or sentence which is the same read backward or forwards'). Nathaniel Bailey had earlier made a similar leap in his *Universal Etymological English Dictionary* of 1721, though here it was *palilogy* ('a Figure in Rhetorick in which the same Word is repeated') with which *palindrome* had instead been preceded. Only in John Kersey's revised edition of Edward Phillips's *New World of English Words* in 1706 had the word previously appeared, albeit in a slightly different form: *Palimpseston*: 'a sort of Paper or Parchment, that was generally us'd for making the first draught of things, which might be wip'd out, and new wrote in the same Place'.

Murray carefully included Kersey's definition in his own account of *palimpsest* alongside the additional sense-developments which the word had seen over the nineteenth century. 'A parchment or other writing-material written upon twice, the original writing having been erased or rubbed out to make place for the second; a manuscript in which a later writing is written over an effaced earlier writing', Murray noted, tracing this particular usage back to 1825. He added evidence of its recent figurative extension too. As the data files of the dictionary revealed, the human brain, the soul, and history itself were all variously figured in this way. 'What else than a natural and mighty palimpsest is the human brain?' asked De Quincey in 1845, illustrating the shift to the metaphorical richness which uses of the word were henceforth to display. 'History unrolls the palimpsest of mental evolution', states a quotation from G. H. Lewes's *The Study of Psychology* (1879) which had also memorably been selected for inclusion. In the images thereby generated, history becomes not a single and sequential narrative but a layered text, one in which alternative versions – or other tales entirely – may be concealed beneath its apparently pristine surface. 'All history was a palimpsest, scraped clean and re-inscribed exactly as often as was necessary', as George Orwell was later to proclaim in *Nineteen Eighty-Four*,[1] documenting as part of his dystopian vision the multiple ways in which history could be rewritten and revised, eliminating what had gone before.

As the Preface to this volume has already indicated, the same holds true for the history of words in the *OED*, and indeed for the history of the dictionary itself. Behind the finished text of the first edition stands a complex history of other textual variants which explore alternative ways of presenting the same material – or, indeed, of including different material (and different words) entirely. In these underlying versions which the seemingly immutable forms of the final fascicles conceal, the figurative deployment of *palimpsest* was to receive one of its most apposite illustrations. In effect, the making of the dictionary was a densely accretive process, sequentially combining the work of readers, sub-editors, dictionary assistants, critical readers such as Fitzedward Hall and Walter Skeat, as well, of course, as that of the editors themselves. It was, for example, voluntary sub-editors such as the phonetician Richard Lloyd who undertook the preliminary stage of editing, sorting the slips which had been generated by the various reading programmes and generating a provisional set of entry words and sense-divisions.[2] Lloyd's work on sub-editing the adjective *high*, for example, led to a preliminary distribution of sixty-eight different meanings which he duly forwarded to Murray's Scriptorium. Possible definitions were also added at this stage, while a cross added on the upper right-hand corner of slips already marked out those illustrative quotations which, in the opinion of the sub-editor, seemed best to reveal the requisite sense. The material as thus ordered was then dispatched to the dictionary staff, who subjected the careful work of the sub-editors to further detailed scrutiny, resulting perhaps in a different arrangement of senses and sub-senses, as well as a different set of definitions. The sixty-eight senses of *high* which Lloyd had identified were stringently condensed by the time the fascicle (here *Heel–Hod*) appeared in proof. The end product at the sub-editing stage was an ordered bundle of slips, together with their suggested mode of organization. This was passed to the editor of the relevant section who added a further level of revision to the assembled material, reassessing the available quotations (even those which might provisionally have been rejected), and introducing further refinements to both definitions and sense-distribution. As Murray later confirmed, revising the 'defective' versions provided by 'imperfect helpers' could be a time-consuming task.[3] The etymology might at this stage also be revised or completed, depending on the complexity of the individual entry (and the levels of knowledge of the dictionary assistants on this matter). Only at this point would the material be set in printed form, generating the proofs on which so much work was later to be done.

These stages of making the dictionary were critical. 'In first proof, first revise, and in page form, every statement, every quotation, every date must be controlled by the editor and one or more of his staff', an in-house account of the dictionary process explained.[4] Murray's canonical insistence that 'the perfection of the Dictionary' must be 'in its *data*' was fully reflected in the proofs.[5] Even the smallest slip could compromise the scholarly standards on which the dictionary's reputation was based. While *proofreading*, as already indicated, would fail to be included as a lemma in the first edition, its practice was widely implemented. After all, what in other contexts might be judged to be a minor typographical error could have serious consequences here, not least since spellings and dates were crucial aspects of the historical record. The physician William Sykes, for example, assiduously read Bradley's proofs in his own role as a critical reader. Encountering the word 'Chysiologist' in a 1664 citation from Henry Power's *Experimental Philosophy* in the proof entry for *gather*, he was transparently puzzled. 'The Chysiologist also may gather from the former Observations, touching the nature of Colours', he read. Surely the quotation was unduly enigmatic. What or who was a chysiologist? Earlier parts of the *OED* offered no illumination and Sykes signalled the crux in the margin before returning the sheet to the dictionary. His sense of the language, however, proved entirely right. *Physiologist* displaces the typographically errant form in the revisions which were duly made. In a similar way, Gibbs picked up the distorted definition which accompanied the entry for *fork* in the first proof: 'The forked tongue (popularly supposed to be the sling) of the snake'. He supplied a corrected version in the adjacent margin. The definition of *glossologist* in the first proof revealed further inadvertent error. 'One versed in comparative physiology', it stated. 'Philology', Skeat pertinently corrected.[6]

As this indicates, merely 'routine' corrections could become far from routine in their implications for the historical record which the dictionary unremittingly sought to verify. Errors in the first proof of *Glass-coach–Graded* by which one of the quotations for *goll* (defined as 'a hand, esp[ecially] a large or ill-shaped one, a "paw"')[7] unaccountably appeared under *golion* (a kind of gown or tunic), or in which various entries manifested an order which was by no means alphabetical (*grumphy* preceding *grumphie*, *glosser* preceding *glossal*) or, still more worryingly, in which a reference under *griddle* based part of its explanation on an 1881 citation which was in fact nowhere to be seen, combined to signify the kind of relentless attention to detail which was necessary to secure the factual perfection at which Murray and his co-editors aimed. The fact that in these and thousands of other instances the relevant problems were remedied stands as further testimony to the dedicated efforts of that community of scholars who assiduously minded the dictionary through these early and provisional stages.[8] This underlies in part the gratitude which Murray repeatedly affirmed to readers such as Fitzedward Hall who diligently read three sets of proofs a week during the hard-pressed production of the fascicles which made up D. The daily stint of some four hours which Hall devoted to the tightly printed proof sheets was, as Murray unerringly acknowledged, 'the most generous literary assistance which the annals of literature can show'.[9]

Corrections on the proofs were, however, often far more extensive. Providing compelling evidence of the textual evolution of the first edition, work at this stage often entailed detailed patterns of writing and rewriting, critical revision, and the deliberate culling of that which, for one reason or another, was deemed unnecessary or unwanted in the final form of the text. Unlike the visual excellence which Henry Bradley singled out for especial praise when reviewing *A–Ant* for the *Academy* in 1884,[10] the surviving proofs are often overlaid with dense annotations or pierced by pins which attach batches of newly received material. While the latter aptly confirm the flux of language which was at the heart of the *OED*'s enterprise as a dictionary on historical principles, it also reveals the difficulty of the editorial role as well as explaining in part the level of correction that the proofs often show. *Luthern* ('a dormer window') was, for instance, not in the dictionary at all until the first proof of May 1903 when a pile of slips generated by the further activities of the reading programme suddenly appeared, pinned to the top left-hand corner of the sheet with instructions for their inclusion. *Legatess* ('a female legate') likewise failed to materialize until the first revise when Bradley had to draft an entry in the bottom margin of the relevant sheet based on another influx of data. An antedating for *forefront* ('The principal face or foremost part of anything') made its appearance when the entry was in the relatively fixed state of the page proofs. It had to be incorporated nevertheless, especially since it established usage of the word one century earlier than had previously been thought.[11] Even *lexicography* was subject to similar shift. Only when the entry had been set in type did the dictionary's evidence of its earliest use appear, written by hand on the first proof: 'I shall therefore only make some few reflexions upon Etymology and Syntax, supposing Orthography to belong to Lexicography', George Dalgarno had stated in his *Didascalocophus, or, The Deaf & Dumb Man's Tutor* of 1680.[12] Such changes in available information were all too common.

From the point of view of completing the record of the language, additions of this kind were always welcome, providing crucial revision before the entry reached the finality of publication. A newly arrived citation could relocate the origin of a word by a century or more. This, for instance, was the case with *gaucherie* ('Want of tact or grace of manner, awkwardness') which was dated to the eighteenth rather than the nineteenth century by means of the opportune appearance of a new piece of evidence from Charlotte Smith's *The Young Philosopher* of 1798. At other times, editorial convictions that a word or sense was in current use were only supported at the very last minute by the appearance of the vital evidence. The now dominant sense of *glass* ('The substance considered as made into articles of use or ornament . . . things made of glass: e.g. vessels or ornaments of glass, window-panes or lights') had, for example, been distinguished by an entire absence of citations in the first proof, a fact which yet again serves to illustrate the real problems which could and did attend a volunteer reading programme. No examples of this use had been sent in to the dictionary. Bradley as a result had felt compelled to invent his own. '*Mod.* The glass is kept in one cupboard and the silver in another', he wrote in a practice which remained a last resort for lexicographers throughout the writing of the *OED*.[13] 'Slip sent in', a note in the margin of a later proof triumphantly records. A citation from Thackeray's *The Newcomes* ('A waggon full of fenders, fire-irons, and glass, and crockery') had arrived to supplement the record of the language and thereby substantiate a usage so ordinary and everyday that it had paradoxically escaped everyone's notice.[14]

Reassessment of other entries was prompted by the activities of the critical readers. Gibbs, for example, subjected Murray's original version of *cheque* to a thorough review in the margins of the relevant sheet.[15] 'I doubt this', he commented alongside the conjectures by which Murray had attempted to explain its specific sense-development. 'It looks as if the Bank retained the counterfoils as a "check" against them when they came in as drafts for payment', Murray had written. Gibbs dismissed this as a species of folk etymology and the material was subsequently cancelled. Murray's various discriminations of sense in his draft of this entry, however, fared no better. Gibbs's expertise in his professional capacity as a director of the Bank of England (1853–1901) proved him a more than able critic in this respect. 'How is this obsolete?' he demanded in the margin alongside Murray's first sense ('The skeleton form with a counterfoil, supplied by a bank to a customer for making out his draft or order on; a cheque form'). A cheque in the sense of a skeleton form was indubitably current and Gibbs adduced further examples to prove it. Murray submitted to correction and changed the sense. 'The counterfoil of a bank bill, draft, etc. *Obs.*', he wrote in a version which remains intact in the finished text. 'Wants careful emendation', a handwritten instruction from Murray had stated at the head of the sheet in question. This was duly achieved. The entry was comprehensively revised in the light of Gibbs's detailed remarks with evident gains in both accuracy and precision. Parallel examples can be found in the revisions, again prompted by Gibbs, in the original entry for *alameda*, a Spanish loan used in English since 1797. Murray's conviction that it was an avenue lined with poplars was entirely awry, Gibbs averred on reading the relevant proofs. This 'is *not* an avenue (i.e approach) and has I think nothing to do with poplars but may be of any trees', he wrote, basing his information on a comprehensive general knowledge which often stood him in good stead in his varied duties as a critical reader for the dictionary.[16] The published entry as a result reflected Gibbs's sense of the word: *Alameda*: 'A public walk or promenade with a row of trees on each side'.

While instances of this kind were often to lead to a process of significant revision, editorial rewriting on the proofs did not always occur as a result of the comments of the critical readers or in response to the arrival of some new piece of information. It was at this point in the textual history of the *OED* that a new level of analysis often begins, involving wholesale re-engagement with the core of a word and its meanings. It was a working practice which Murray had established in the very early days of the dictionary. As he informed the Philological Society in May 1881, he had just sent to press an extensive section of the dictionary covering the word *all* (with its accompanying combinations and derivatives) and the word *alms*. This was, however, not to imply that any final conclusions had been reached. Instead, Murray stated, his hope was that by practically trying these entries and submitting the printed results, perhaps in more than one form, to scholars and critics, he would in turn be able to settle many details of typography and mechanical arrangement, as well as the relevant limits of inclusion for combinatory forms.

Long after these necessary decisions on presentation had been made, however, Murray continued to use the proofs as a means of putting word-entries to the test. *Art*, for instance, had been an entry with which Murray had struggled extensively in 1884 before finally managing to send it off to the compositors. Nevertheless, as soon as he was in possession of the relevant proof sheets, Murray comprehensively demolished his earlier work, engaging afresh with the material and the ways in which it might best be arranged. 'The renewed consideration of it in print, with the greater facility of reading and comprehension which this afforded, led to the entire pulling to pieces and reconstruction of the edifice', he later explained.[17] *Do* offers an excellent example of this process. This was one of the most difficult words in the dictionary, having fifty-four divisions of sense in its final form and occupying seventeen columns of text. Unseasonably, Murray began work on it over Christmas in 1895: it would take almost three months before he was ready to see it put into type. The stability so laboriously achieved again proved transient. In real terms it was almost July before Murray finally felt satisfied with his representation of the word and its manifold meanings. The intervening time had been spent on the various proofs and revises which were changed, emended, rephrased, and changed again. Peter Sutcliffe's estimate that these preliminary versions of the dictionary are 'possibly the most heavily corrected proofs ever known' is scarcely an exaggeration.[18] They were, in consequence, also to be extraordinarily expensive.[19] Perhaps predictably, complaints about the 'cost of corrections' became yet another recurrent feature in the Delegates' discussions of the dictionary. Moving far beyond the remit which Murray had formally indicated in 1881, the proofs became an invaluable part of the methods of critical lexicography which he established in the making of the *OED*.

While Murray constantly resented the amount of time which the proofs demanded ('there are 6 hours every day absorbed by the work after it gets into print', he wrote to Price in 1884, complaining that this left little time for the 'real work' of the dictionary),[20] it is nonetheless evident that considerable amounts of 'real work' were indeed done at this stage, not only by Murray but by his co-editors. Bradley, for example, readily adopted Murray's habit of extensive revision on the proofs. The first proof of *library* provides a comprehensive illustration here as Bradley wrote and rewrote his definitions on all available space, finally resorting to pasting a further sheet of notes along the left-hand margin. The original definitions on the proof are firmly crossed through. 'A room or building set apart for the reception or storage of a collection of books' had, for instance, initially been given as

Bradley's first selected sense. Yet, like Murray, Bradley seemed to see new potential in an entry once it reached the temporary stasis (and clarity) of the proofs. Drafting a new definition to the right of the original entry – 'A place set apart to contain books for reading, study, or reference. (Not applied, e.g. to the shop or warehouse of a bookseller.) In various applications more or less specific' – he decided that two further sub-senses were necessary. These appear, with considerable evidence of further revision, on a sheet pasted to the left-hand margin, and reflect the distinctions that the entry bears today: '1a. Applied to a room in a house, etc.; also, | a bookcase. In mod. use, the designation of one of the set of rooms ordinarily belonging to an English house above a certain level of size and pretension'; '1b. A building, room, or set of rooms, containing a collection of books for the use of the public or of some particular portion of it, or of the members of some society or the like; a public institution or establishment, charged with the care of a collection of books, and the duty of rendering the books accessible to those who require to use them'. Other new distinctions of sense appear for subsequent parts of the entry, reflecting the kind of comprehensive re-engagement which Murray regularly practised in his own sections of the text. While Bradley, like Murray, therefore protested to Philip Lyttelton Gell that his chief work was done on the revises rather than these initial versions of the text, the evidence of the first (and second) proofs regularly suggests otherwise. Editorial crafting of the dictionary took place at all stages of the text, often resulting in wide-ranging changes to the substance as well as the style of individual entries.

Perhaps still more telling is the fact that it was not always the individual editors who independently imposed such changes in their own sections of the text. Bradley, as we have seen, did indeed meticulously rewrite definitions which, in the cold light of the printed proof, he no longer found satisfactory. The uninspired 'Rather light; not heavy' was, for example, rejected from the first proof of *lightsome* in favour of a far more detailed handwritten replacement which Bradley supplied in the margin: 'Having the effect or appearance of lightness; now chiefly with reference to form, light, graceful, elegant'. *Looseness* provides a further example as Bradley was apparently struck by the ways in which the original definition provided an entirely apposite illustration by means of its own diffuseness of style. The earlier 'freedom or laxity of manner, custom, constitution, or opinion' was decisively crossed through and a new definition appears in the margin in Bradley's careful script, giving the much improved 'Lack of strictness; laxity of principles or practice'.

The successive versions of *grotto* in the preliminary versions of the fascicle *Green–Gyzzarn* tell a different story. This was, one might imagine, a relatively 'easy' word. An earlier – and markedly evocative – definition already existed in Johnson's *Dictionary*: 'A cavern or cave made for coolness. It is not used properly of a dark horrid cavern', Johnson had written, citing Dryden in illustration: 'Their careless chiefs to the cool grotto's run/ The bow'rs of kings, to shade them from the sun'. Other dictionary-makers too had itemized its salient semantic properties. 'A cave or den', Nathaniel Bailey had economically stated in 1721. 'A cavern or cave made for pleasure', James Barclay elaborated in his *Complete and Universal English Dictionary* of 1774. Such attempts were of little use to Bradley, bound to the track of what was emphatically established as a 'new' English dictionary. The various 'acts of piracy' which earlier dictionaries had tended to commit upon their predecessors were deliberately abandoned in the making of the *OED*.[21] 'The Philological Society's Dictionary will . . . insert no word because it is in another Dictionary', Murray had vowed in his 1880 Presidential Address.[22] *Grotto* had to be considered from scratch.

This principle of determined independence underlies in part the quest for perfection which the proofs of the *OED* record, as well as motivating in many cases the layers of changes which contribute, palimpsestically, to the dictionary's final form. The first version of *grotto* was, for instance, apparently detailed as well as clear, its four enumerated sense-divisions far exceeding the seventeen words that Johnson had deemed sufficient for definition of the whole entry. 'A cave or cavern, whether natural or artificial', Bradley stated, elucidating his first sense. He added a series of examples to illustrate what he judged to be the relevant nuances in this context. A *grotto* could consist of 'an arched tunnel; e.g. *the grotto of Posilipo*' or, he further elaborated, it could also be used to denote a formation such as '*The Dog's Grotto (Grotto del Cano*); a cave near Naples where the mephitic vapour, lying near the ground, stupefies dogs'. For all the vividness and incidental interest of the latter, it was nevertheless to disappear from the final wording of the sense, as indeed was everything else with the exception of Bradley's first four words. 'A cave or cavern' was alone deemed acceptable by Murray who, casting a critical eye over the first proof, decided to intervene, writing a new definition in the margin and firmly deleting Bradley's previous attempt. It was, in consequence, Murray's words which went on to form the text of the final version. This, losing all mention of mephitic vapour and its untoward effects upon the canine species, now simply – if less strikingly – reads 'esp[escially] one which is picturesque, or which forms an agreeable retreat'.

Though Bradley was ostensibly the sole editor of G, Murray's proprietary hand on the dictionary could, as here, regularly be discerned. As Murray often reminded his co-editors and the Delegates alike, his role was that of editor-in-chief.[23] With this came a sense of lexicographical responsibility which was often to include having what was quite literally the last word on the phrasing of innumerable entries. *Grotto*, as a result, bears the definitive stamp of Murray's sense of the word rather than that which Bradley and his assistants had originally proffered. Murray's interventions continued in the proofs of Bradley's second sense. 'An apartment serving as a cool retreat in summer, either excavated, or erected above ground; in a garden or pleasure-ground; often adorned with shell-work', the proof had stated in a form of words which again appears unexceptionable in the analysis it provides. Murray, however, was not persuaded. Though 'a cool retreat' and 'often adorned with shell-work' met with his approval, the rest was firmly excised. A new version, again courtesy of the *OED*'s most experienced editor, was written in his neatly angled hand in the adjacent margin: 'An excavation or structure made by imitating a rocky cave, often adorned with shell-work, etc, and serving as a place of recreation or a cool retreat.' It is this which was to stand in the published fascicle, remaining intact through the revisions of the *Supplements* and *OED2*.

Such revisions are further evidence of Murray's abiding perfectionism. As he had already admitted to Bartholomew Price in 1884, 'the more I have to leave over to others . . . the less satisfactory will the results be to me at least, and perhaps to others also'.[24] When Bradley began work first as an assistant in 1886 and then as an independent editor two years later, it had been natural for Murray to monitor his proofs, making such changes and refinements as he considered necessary for the greater good of the work. After all, it was consistency of treatment over the dictionary as a whole which mattered most. Concerns of this kind presumably influenced the substantial rewording which Murray made in Bradley's early versions of words such as *exquisite*. The fifth sense of this word was, for example, entirely rewritten in page proof, displacing Bradley's original version ('productive of intense and refined pleasure; exciting delight or admiration by faultless and delicate beauty') in favour of a new version by Murray himself. 'Of such consummate excellence, beauty, or perfection, as to excite intense delight or admiration', as the relevant sense still states in the published *OED*.

The proofs from this period confirm a markedly interventionist role for Murray in ways which, further increasing the Delegates' anxieties, often served to impede rather than accelerate the pace of production (as well as considerably increasing the costs). While the Delegates, as we have seen, had hoped that the appointment of a second editor would increase productivity, Murray's zealous work on Bradley's proofs could in effect serve to create a bottleneck for the dictionary. Gell, for example, had to write to Murray in June 1887 to request that the large amounts of Bradley's copy which remained in Murray's possession be delivered to the Press. 'Would it be possible for you to finish all this up?' he asked. The Long Vacation for the university was approaching and the Delegates expected 'definite information as to the progress of the Dictionary'.[25]

Even if Murray had solemnly promised the Delegates that, once the volume covering F was complete, he would henceforth devote his energies to his own sections of the dictionary in the attempt to expedite production,[26] the evidence of the proofs suggests otherwise. Even in L, when Bradley had been working as an independent editor for some three years, Murray's editorial pen is still at work, emending Bradley's version of *leading article*. Bradley's decision to provide a cross-reference which simply directed users of the dictionary to the entry for *leader* would, Murray decided, not do at all. This was far too cursory. Three attempts later (having comprehensively deleted the information already provided), Murray had finally arrived at a form of wording with which he felt satisfied and which justified the right of *leading article* to be considered, and analysed, as an independent sense. 'One of the longer large-type articles in a newspaper, appearing as the expression of editorial opinion on any subject; a leader', Murray dictated. The amount of crossing-out which the extant proof sheet bears, together with the cumulative rejection of earlier versions – such as Murray's first attempt ('A principal editorial article in a newspaper') – provides a concise picture of the real difficulties which would regularly surround the writing of entries in the dictionary. Version by version the final text was built up, a process of dispute and negotiation, accretion and dissent.

It is scarcely surprising that the burden of the proofs becomes a frequent refrain in Murray's letters. Like a shadow, they followed him 'to holiday haunts or friendly visits' where their presence, as well as being uncongenial, usually also served to generate further anxiety.[27] There was, for instance, always the worry that a sheet might somehow be lost, as indeed happened in 1901 when Murray was visiting Fitzedward Hall's son, Richard. This was a 'disaster', Murray wrote in a frantic letter once he realized what had happened. Somewhere in Hall's house, maybe on the table at which Murray had been working or perhaps in the bedroom, lay the copies of all the proofs from *Jute* to the end of J.[28] They had to be recovered. Yet even if this danger was obviated by leaving the proofs safely locked up at Oxford in his new Scriptorium, the enormous and accumulated workload they presented on Murray's return made any real sense of respite impossible. 'I feel inclined to sit down and weep, and vow that I will never go again', he wrote as he faced an enormous pile of proofs, together with other arrears of work, which had accumulated during two weeks away from the ardours of lexicography.[29] Within a few days, it was guaranteed to dispel any sense of well-being that his holiday might otherwise have brought.

The Practice of Criticism

Criticism, under a variety of guises, remained an essential element of the lexicographical process, leading to the time-consuming collation of countless individual remarks and possible emendations in the making of the individual fascicles. Walter Skeat, for instance, drew careful illustrations of lacrosse sticks on the relevant proof in the aim of convincing Bradley that the etymology of *lacrosse* (as French *la* + *crosse*, 'a hooked stick') was mistaken. This couldn't be right, Skeat argued. Surely it was based on 'crosier' (the staff or crook of a bishop or abbot). The old form of a lacrosse stick with its curved neck was, he added, '*remarkably* like a crosier' in appearance. Clearly better as a medievalist than an artist, Skeat was transparently frustrated in his attempts to prove this visually, despite the several versions which appear in the surrounding margins. 'I *can't* get it right', he exclaimed, desperate in his attempts to convert Bradley on this point. Bradley remained unmoved. The etymology which he had originally determined as correct remains intact in the published version of the text.

It was Skeat too who, in proof, regularly provided evidence from unlikely sources and certainly those likely to have been missed during the reading programme. A riddle from an early edition of the *Boy's Own Book* is scrawled alongside the entry for *lichen*, for example, corroborating by its laboriously punning resolution the pronunciation (as /laikən/ rather than /lɪtʃən/) which Bradley had recommended in the dictionary. 'I remember a riddle, 40 years old', Skeat wrote in the adjacent margin: 'Why is a rare moss like falling in love with your grandmother? – Because it is a curious lichen (a liking)'. It was a pronunciation which other users of the dictionary were nevertheless to regard with suspicion. 'Some of our readers will be startled to find that they are to pronounce the *ch* of "lichen" as a *k*, as the alternative "is now rare in educated use"', a later reviewer noted.[30] The diversity of information which could be included on the proofs is striking. Skeat provides a rhyme alongside *gift* in the sense 'A white speck on the finger-nails, supposed to portend a gift'. 'A gift on your thumb/ Is sure to come;/ A gift on your finger/ Is sure to linger', he wrote, inscribing a piece of proverbial knowledge which did not, however, find its way into the published entry. Annotations alongside *goose* on the other hand served to reveal a surprising familiarity with the symptoms of venereal disease. 'A certain venereal disorder', Bradley had primly written as his chosen definition for *(Winchester) goose*, an idiom which he traced back to Shakespeare.[31] 'One who has it walks like a new born calf', Skeat added in the margin. 'So the French dictionaries', he verified, careful to establish the source of his information. Elsewhere, however, countless other references and suggestions with which Skeat annotated the proofs were indeed added to the individual entries and senses, incomparably swelling the evidence at the dictionary's disposal.

Pronunciation, etymology, meaning, and quotations could all provide material for critical suggestion. Gibbs, for instance, tackled Bradley on the pronunciations which had been given in the dictionary for words beginning with *gyno-*. Bradley had uniformly recommended the soft /dʒ/ as their opening sound. No other possibilities were acknowledged. Yet, as Gibbs wrote on the relevant proof sheet, 'the pronunciation surprises me'. He had always used – and heard – 'hard g'. 'I think you should at least give an alternative pronunciation', he advised, even though his own feelings were that Bradley's sense of the language here was misplaced.[32] Skeat's comments on Bradley's selected pronunciation of *golf* as /gɒlf/ were more outspoken. 'I think golf is going *out*, & gof becoming more general', he countered; 'the former is often received with *derision*'. As Gibbs had earlier warned Murray, the marginal annotations of the critical reader often had to be forthright in style. 'When I speak my mind on the margin of a proof', he cautioned, 'space demands that my remarks be short and sharp, & not as gentle as they would be if I had more room on which to smooth them out'.[33] His reactions to the enunciation of *gala* as specified in the dictionary provide an apt illustration. 'I have *never* heard it so pronounced', Gibbs wrote, flatly denouncing Bradley's /geɪlə/ as given in the first revise. Instead he recommended /ga:lə/ with a '*long* a', precisely as in modern enunciations of this word.[34]

Critical practice here brought its own compression to the text. The questions that Gibbs posed in the margins signalled potential problems and cruces which demanded resolution before the dictionary went to press. 'An intercalary day in the calendar, esp. that of leap-year', the first proof of *leap day* had stated, for example, stating further 'now February 29th'. Gibbs pounced on what he deemed to be the extraneous 'now'. 'Was any other day but Feb. 29th a Leap-day in our Leap-Year?' he challenged. 'Your "now" reads as if there had been'. The wording was duly changed. He cavilled too at the infelicities he detected in the original entry for *linarite*, a sulphate of lead and copper. 'Named . . . after a supposed locality *Linares*, Spain', the entry had stated in a form of words which, as Gibbs pointed out, 'makes it sound as if Linares were an imaginary place'. The necessary changes were once more incorporated. 'Named by Glocker, 1837, from *Linares*, Spain, where it is alleged to be found', the entry now states. Skeat too could take issue with infelicities of wording which, to his mind, were incompatible with the intended authority of the dictionary. 'I could not bring myself to write this', he commented with distaste alongside the definition which appeared in the first proof of *lack* in September 1900. 'The fact of a person or thing not being at hand', the entry had stated for its fifth sense. Skeat's comments prompted the stylistic reappraisal he had deemed essential. 'The fact that a person or thing is not present; absence', as the entry now states in the far more successful wording of Bradley's emended text. Skeat's role as a critic of words often extended to subjective appraisals of correctness (or otherwise). He carefully changes the placing of *only* in Bradley's original entry for *lade* ('To burden, load oppressively; chiefly in immaterial sense'). Bradley's additional point that 'in this sense, now only used in past participle *laden*' received a note in the margin of the first proof, instructing that 'only' and 'used' should be transposed, precisely in line with emerging shibboleths on the 'incorrect' placing of sentence adverbs.[35] 'I dislike this English', Skeat likewise averred alongside the proof entry of *fox* in December 1896. 'It has been conjectured that this use arose from the figure of a wolf, on certain sword-blades, being mistaken for a fox', the entry stated in further illumination of sense 6 ('A kind of sword'). In this instance Skeat's scruples were simply dismissed. In *OED1* (and *OED2*) the entry remains intact in the form it had originally assumed.

Comments such as these evidently allowed subjectivity to intervene, especially when notions of 'proper' English seemed at stake.[36] Others, however, resoundingly confirmed Skeat's role as a critic well grounded in the concern for factual accuracy and the historical imperatives of the dictionary. 'What inaccuracy', as he commented alongside the original entry for *landing-net*. The illustrative quotation from Thackeray's *Book of Snobs* had been provided with an entirely erroneous page reference.

'Here you are', Skeat wrote, supplying the correct information in the margin. If issues of right and wrong are entirely unambiguous here, the presentation of the facts at the dictionary's disposal was at other times far more complex. The dictionary had, after all, assembled vast amounts of facts by virtue of the collective input of the reading programmes. This was the essence of the 'fabric of fact' on which Murray declared the dictionary to be built.[37] 'That which is of the nature of a fact; what has actually happened or is the case; truth attested by direct observation or authentic testimony', as the dictionary in turn attested for *fact* itself. Yet, as the experience of editing the dictionary repeatedly confirmed, the information sent in and drafted into entries could at times deceive, suggesting the existence of words or senses which were in reality illusory or non-existent. Apparent facts had to be treated with caution. An entry for *gentianellar* was, for instance, included in the first proof of the fascicle *Gainscope–Germanizing*. Bradley had carefully drafted the entry based on the information he had before him. 'Eyes of gentianellar azure', read the slip which the contributor had sent in, giving a quotation from Elizabeth Barrett Browning's 'Hector in the Garden'. 'Of or pertaining to a gentianella', stated the accompanying definition in the dictionary. However, Mrs Browning had written something slightly but significantly different. Her poem eloquently described the quality of 'gentianellas azure' in her garden at Hope End. 'Gentianellar' had not been used at all. In this instance, a hunch that something might be amiss evidently led to the slip being rechecked, a process which managed to obviate a potentially embarrassing error. *Gentianellar* swiftly disappeared from the proofs, its pretensions to the status of a 'real' word having conclusively been dispelled. *Lustricity* was similar. This had been given in the first proof of May 1903 as an obsolete and rare form of which only one example had been found. 'He may not have heard of our Lustricity at the Pantiles', read the single citation, based on a letter from 1737 which had recently been reprinted in *Blackwood's Magazine* (1891, p. 516). Yet the form was still rarer than Bradley had supposed, having in reality never been used at all. 'In the letter the word is il-lustricity', one of the dictionary assistants notes alongside the entry on the proof. It was the hyphenated form, caused by the line-break in the original layout, which had presumably given rise to this particular illusion. Even if it deceived the original reader who had sent in the slip – and indeed the sub-editors and dictionary staff too for a time – it was, like *gentianellar*, firmly to be dispatched from the dictionary before it reached the finished text.

Entry-words such as these are the bane of all lexicographers. 'We should zealously guard against all chances of giving any undeserved record of words which had never any real existence', Walter Skeat had declared at a meeting of the Philological Society in 1886, formulating further resolutions for the exemplary status of the *OED*.[38] Such words were 'mere coinages due to the blunders of printers or scribes' or the products of 'the perfervid imaginations of ignorant or blundering editors', he stressed. They were forms which took on the external shape of words but, having never been used in genuine communication, possessed none of their substance. They were mere illusions to plague the dictionary-maker as he set about his work. It was Skeat who coined the term by which such apparitions are now known. They are, he stated, *ghost-words*, a term which all too evocatively describes the lexical figments with which the dictionary at times had to deal. 'Like ghosts we may seem to see them or may fancy that they exist', Skeat declaimed, yet 'we cannot grasp them' and 'when we would do so, they disappear'.[39]

The real challenge for the *OED* was to lay such ghosts to rest while the dictionary was still in proof rather than, as was common in a number of the dictionary's predecessors, perpetuating the illusion that various words of this kind had a legitimate existence in the language. *Abacot*, for example, was decisively dismissed by Murray in the very first fascicle of the *OED* as an illusory form of precisely this kind. 'A Cap of State, made like a double Crown, worn anciently by the Kings of *England*', Nathaniel Bailey had stated with conviction in his dictionary of 1721. Murray proved to be an adept ghostbuster, revealing *abacot* to be based on an early misprint of *bycoket* (a cap or head-dress) after which, bizarrely, it had taken on an entirely independent life and meaning in the pages of various dictionaries, being passed down 'like a precious heirloom' from Phillips to Bailey, Ash and Johnson, as well as to the canonical Webster.[40] This alone was a clear demonstration of the virtues of scientific philology and empirical investigation. 'There is not, never was, such a word', Murray triumphantly declared. Its existence in previous dictionaries merely proved the defects which a lack of 'independent study' could bring.[41]

Elsewhere, however, it could be more difficult to identify such spurious words. Though Skeat had optimistically envisaged a process in which these lexical impostors would obligingly disappear when faced with the cold gaze of the lexicographer, the experience of those who worked on the *OED* tended to be somewhat different. 'Ghosts' could be elusive, difficult to distinguish from the genuine words which indubitably required inclusion.

As Murray recorded in 1903, some dictionaries that he had examined contained almost one hundred such words.[42] These precedents emphasized the need for vigilance on behalf of the *OED* and its own compositors. Whether these words crept in as spurious entry-words or occurred as elements disconcertingly concealed within other citations, editors and dictionary staff needed to be constantly aware of their potential presence. *Cairbow*, for example, stood prominently near the beginning of a quotation used in the first proof illustration of *glare*, an adjective used in the sense 'slippery, glassy'. 'It [the Cairbow] then suddenly squats upon its haunches, and slides along the glare-ice', the citation stated, producing images of an unknown and certainly unidentified beast inhabiting icy realms. Demonstrating his value as a critical reader of the proofs, it was Frederick Pollock who spotted a problem. 'No such word in N.E.D.', Pollock authoritatively declared by the side, underlining *cairbow* as he did so. He had checked his facts; certainly no such creature as a cairbow had so far appeared in the dictionary. Its presumably rightful place in *C–Cass* was empty. Murray, editing this in 1888, had merely passed from *cair* (a poetic word for 'to go') to *caird* (a Scottish designation for a gypsy). Like the unicorn, the 'cairbow' was also to prove less real than might initially be supposed. Further investigation led to the original slip, and the citation which it contained, being rechecked. In the process, it fortunately became clear that, though the 'cairbow' might be illusory, the *caribou* was not, a word whose legitimate existence the *OED* had already carefully substantiated. Bradley deleted *cairbow*, and another puzzle in the history of the language was solved.

Pollock was particularly adept at spotting potential anomalies of this kind, his emphatic 'Not in N.E.D.' or 'What is this? *Not in Dict*' regularly alerting editors and dictionary staff to the fact that some difficulty had once again surfaced in the proofs. *Aplaintife* was another unrecorded form spotted by Pollock at an early stage of the dictionary. 'The defendant by his false plea maketh himself chargeable both to the aplaintife & to the garnishee', Sir Henry Finch had stated in his *Law, or, a discourse thereof* of 1613, providing, for the purposes of the *OED*, a quotation which aptly illustrated the first recorded use of *garnishee* in English. This was a legal term which Bradley had painstakingly defined.[43] Nevertheless, if the utility of the quotation was incontestable in this respect, in terms of *aplaintife* it proved deeply disturbing. *Aplaintife*, as the dictionary staff found when checking the material in this case, was anything but a ghost. This was a real word which had inadvertently been missed during the earlier reading programmes. Bradley found himself in a real dilemma. Were he to include the quotation in the form in which it had appeared in his first proof, then it would necessarily foreground the absence of *aplaintife* from Murray's earlier work on *Ant–Batten*, and this, from a number of points of view, would be unacceptable. Moreover, because of the serial publication of the *OED*, it was impossible to insert *aplaintife* where it should rightly have appeared – in spite of its undoubted legitimacy. After all, this section of the dictionary had been published thirteen years previously, in 1885. Another solution must be found. It was for these reasons that Bradley evidently decided to delete the quotation, together with all evidence for the existence and use of *aplaintife* in English. Another example of *garnishee* from the same year and the same text was located ('If they were deliuered vpon other condition then the defendant alledgeth, the garnishee is at no mischiefe but the defendant') and it was this which Bradley inserted in the fascicle as finally published. His action preserved the integrity of the entry and also managed to resolve the anomaly that Pollock's ever vigilant eye had spotted. But it was undeniably at the expense of a word which was – and still is – entirely unregistered in lexicographical terms.

Editorial responsibility, as here, could also mean taking responsibility for actively editing out, a worrying agenda in a dictionary which publicly prided itself on its completeness. Decisions of this order were evidently neither ideal nor easy to make. Certainly they tend to be concealed in the proofs rather than discussed in the annals of the Philological Society or in the reports which the editors regularly made to the Delegates of Oxford University Press. This aspect of the *OED*'s history does indeed tend to be a hidden one, an element which of course further increases the scholarly value of these early stages of the text. Writing the *OED* was, however, full of hard realities. Lexicography could seem a life full of incidental frustrations as editors battled against words which refused to yield up their meaning, or attempted to decipher the illegibility of some of the many handwritten slips which had been generated during the years of volunteer reading for the *OED*. The latter was a constant problem in the early stages of the dictionary. The dictionary was at the mercy of its data – but if these couldn't be read, then still other problems emerged to surround the beleaguered editors and dictionary staff. 'Slip illegible', 'bad writing again'; such comments constitute a litany of despair acted out in the margins of the proofs, potentially necessitating other problematic decisions from an editorial point of view since that which was illegible could not, by definition, be included in the record of the language which the dictionary strove to represent. Still other slips were simply inadequate in what the reader had chosen to include. A quotation from Thomas Fenby's *On the Wild Rose* of 1824 was, for instance, used in the first proof as the sum of evidence for the phrase *gay-moving*. 'So blooms in life's gay-moving scene', the reader had recorded before sending the slip off to the dictionary. But this, as Skeat pointed out, was just too elliptical to be useful as it stood. 'Go on, to give subject of verb', he urged. This, however, was impossible. The quotation he criticized had in fact utilized all the information which the dictionary had at its disposal. 'All the reader condescended to give is quoted', a comment in the margin caustically replies. The dictionary staff conceded defeat. Casting a supervisory eye once more over the proofs, Murray gave his own – and final – verdict. 'We can perh[aps] omit this quot.', he decided, though, with the loss of the quotation, the entry as a whole was to be the next casualty. The final text preserves a record of neither, since rechecking the material – and thereby compensating for the inadequacies of this particular reader – was evidently judged to be too costly in terms of both the time and effort required. The pragmatic was, as we shall see, an issue which on countless occasions would bring its own imperatives to the making of the dictionary.

Disturbingly, instances such as these suggest that the facts were at times open to overt manipulation, their selective presentation capable of changing the record of the language as it would publicly appear. Formally of course Murray retained his almost Gradgrindian reverence for the objectively verifiable. This, after all, was fundamental to the historicism on which the dictionary was based, not least in displacing the evident subjectivities of earlier lexicographical work in English. Nevertheless, at various points in the making of the dictionary, facts were often less solid, less certain, than they might at first have seemed. 'History consists wholly of facts and inferences from facts', Murray declaimed in a lecture which he delivered to the Royal Institution in 1903.[44] Taken as a whole, however, it was a statement which contains a worrying dichotomy. As the *OED* itself would confirm, 'inferences' and 'facts' can scarcely be said to be synonymous. A *fact* is 'something that has really occurred or is actually the case; something certainly known', as Bradley wrote in his own entry for *fact*; it is 'a particular truth known by actual observation or authentic testimony'. Moreover, he continued, it is necessarily distinguished from 'what is merely inferred, . . . a conjecture or fiction'. In the multi-layered history of entries which the proofs attest, this is clearly the crux. To return to *grotto* and its own history in the proofs, for example, it is clear that Bradley's own 'inferences' from the 'facts' which he had at his disposal were not shared by Murray. Similarly, reading through Bradley's first attempt at *exquisite*, Murray retained the right to insist on his own – somewhat different – inferences from the facts which Bradley and his assistants had carefully assembled. As the proofs affirm, even where the same information is shared, the inferences drawn by different editors (or different critical readers) will vary significantly, raising the problem of subjectivity in a domain in which objectivity was prized as a lexicographical prerequisite of the first order.

That there should be differences in such matters is, however, perhaps inevitable. Language is perpetually open to new readings, involving 'matters of opinion in which no two men will ever spontaneously see alike', as Murray had stressed to Benjamin Jowett in 1884. The consequences of this difference ineluctably pervade the dictionary in both its writing and its reception. Only if equipped with precisely the same 'mental eyes', Murray admitted, would the interpretation of one reader or one editor coincide precisely with that of another. 'I do not expect that my treatment of words, especially difficult words, will strike people as that which they would have adopted', he carefully explained to Jowett. As he concluded, 'the most that can be expected' in any circumstance is the verdict: 'This is not an unreasonable way of interpreting the facts.'[45]

What was 'reasonable' (or, conversely, unreasonable) could also remain open to debate. 'You will, I hope, believe me to write in perfect friendship, and with no interest but that of the credit of the Dictionary', Murray assured William Craigie, affirming the wider interests of lexicography as the prime factor behind the changes he desired to see in Craigie's proofs. Murray's accompanying criticism, here with reference to Craigie's definition of *Roman Catholic*, nonetheless has little that is overtly friendly about it. The entry was, Murray declared, 'quite unsatisfactory'. Facts and inferences again failed to coincide. No doubt further wounding Craigie's professional pride (he had, after all, been working as an independent editor on the dictionary for some eight years by that point), Murray had chosen to confirm his opinion by showing the proof to his 'friend and neighbour Sir John Hawkins' who likewise 'thinks it would be very unfortunate if the matter were to be so left'. A mere three weeks before the publication of the relevant fascicle, Craigie was told that the entry would have to be completely rewritten. And if it were not rewritten to Murray's satisfaction, the letter continued, Murray would have no choice but to dissociate himself publicly from that part of the dictionary. The threats went further. Should Craigie fail to comply, the issue might even result in an appeal to the Delegates of the Press on the wider acceptability of Craigie's work.[46] This was the other side of editing the *OED* as editorial tempers flared and an autocratic show of strength was paraded by the dictionary's senior editor.[47] Craigie submitted, rewriting *Roman Catholic* precisely as Murray dictated. The revised wording which Murray provided in his missive would, as he further assured Craigie, 'satisfy Sir John Hawkins, and would be approved of by all the Delegates before whom I have quite unofficially brought the matter'. Craigie learnt more than one lesson from the experience. In after years, he was to become markedly more cautious in his editorial tactics and, while still sending his proofs out for critical comment to readers such as the surgeon and naturalist, Joseph Fowler, he wrote prominent instructions that the sheets were not to be sent for a similar critical perusal to Murray himself. Too much criticism, he had decided, could be distinctly counter-productive at times.[48]

The Indefinable Something

In terms of the definitions that Murray and his co-editors strove to provide, the proofs confirm the fact that arriving at the intentionally watertight clarities of the published fascicles was by no means an easy process. Behind the precise enumerations of sense and sense-division, or the careful delineations of semantic nuance with which the modern user of the *OED* is familiar, lie other attempts, often far less successful, at condensing meaning into the economical and unambiguous expression which was required. If the final version of the dictionary gives the illusion that such definitions were a foregone conclusion, easily achieved from the mass of material with which the dictionary-maker had at first been presented, then this illusion too is rapidly dispelled in the proofs. Annotations by William Sykes often comprehensively refine the provisional meanings assigned to words of science and technology;[49] Skeat and Gibbs, as we have seen, regularly proffer more wide-ranging assistance. The extant archives are in turn filled with countless editorial letters which request assistance in ascertaining the relevant nuances of meaning. Murray, for example, wrote to Dr Patrick Fairbairn in 1898, asking for help in defining *High-Churchman* in a way which 'would be accepted by High and Low, or at least would give them no reasonable cause of offence'.[50] Attaching the proof of his own 'not very successful attempt', he also enclosed the 'volume of comment' which his provisional version had already elicited from the critical readers. This alone provided all too telling confirmation of the difficulties he faced. Words such as *High-Churchman* (and Craigie's *Roman Catholic*) seemed prone to raise religious hackles in matters relating to the proper nuances which the dictionary should convey. *Chasuble* was similar. 'I don't think your definition of Chasuble a good one', Gibbs intransigently informed Murray after reading the relevant proofs. 'I have put beneath it what I think it ought to be', he stated, stressing in particular that the entry had to avoid 'controversial points'.[51] Murray carefully revised the original, aiming at a neutrality which might defuse criticism from the range of religious groups

What one conceives of as eminently 'ordinary' words could also prove problematic. '*Handsome* . . . is a desperately difficult word to grasp', Murray declared to Hall, for example. Indeed, he confessed, he found it 'impossible to formulate the differences between current & many obsolete uses, and between British and many American uses'. He had resorted to the testimony of individual experience, basing judgements on the entirely subjective matter of whether he would or would not use a given sense of the word. Moreover, after having discussed the matter with the Scriptorium staff, he was forced to conclude that 'I fancy we none of us quite agree in our notion of the actual sense of "handsome"'.[52] He wondered whether Hall might be more successful. 'If you can send us a definition, it shall be lovingly considered', he wrote. Bradley battled in a similar way with *grin*, deciding to engage upon a completely new process of revision in the relative finality of the page proofs. 'To show the teeth in smiling; to distort the features so as to produce a merry, scornful, or stupid smile', the original version had stated. 'By way of a forced or unnatural smile, or of the broad smile indicative of unrestrained or vulgar merriment, clownish embarrassment, stupid wonder or exultation, or the like', stands the rewritten version drafted in the adjacent margin. Last-minute reassessment, as here, could significantly change the tone of an entry. Bradley's rewritten text was far more negative in its embedded connotations, certainly suggesting the kind of activity with which he himself would not be happy. Alongside the objective evidence of the accompanying quotations, a certain subjectivity again potentially intervenes. Bradley's sympathies with the 'vulgar herd' were not evident.[53]

Yet, as Murray's comments on *handsome* have illustrated, editors were in many cases ultimately forced to rely on their own sense of a word in order to elucidate the evidence they had before them. Citations certainly provided empirical evidence of usage. Nevertheless, the factual had to be interpreted by means of practical lexicography and resulting acts of interpretation could differ significantly. How, after all, did one reduce the act of grinning to the printed page in a form of words which, of necessity, had to be as economical as possible? Bradley's difficulties seem entirely understandable. Johnson's definition in the first edition of his own dictionary had, for instance, been far from satisfactory. 'To set the teeth together and withdraw the lips', he had stated in a form of words which clearly fails to capture the realities involved. Johnson too rewrote this entry. 'To set the teeth together and withdraw the lips in either anger or mirth', the fourth edition of his *Dictionary* states. Gibbs's annotations on the first proof of *lay* offer further examples of such flux in what might be considered the appropriate wording to be employed. Scrutinizing the definition which accompanied an illustrative quotation from Defoe's *Robinson Crusoe* ('I perceived . . . two miserable wretches dragged from the boats, where, it seems they were laid by, and were now brought out for the slaughter'), he found himself unable to agree. 'To put away out of use or for safety', the entry stated. Yet, as Gibbs rightly argued, surely evidence and editorial judgement had in this instance failed to accord. The 'two wretches' in *Robinson Crusoe* had by no means 'been put out of use' while 'laid by'. Gibbs rewrote the original definition in the margin, providing the far more accurate 'To put away for future disposal'. Reading through Gibbs's lengthy annotations, Bradley later concurred. 'To put away for future disposal or for safety', the revised entry of the published fascicle states. Synthesis offered the best course.

Neutrality and impartiality remained the aim. While both could at times slip in the published text, the surviving proofs show that attempts were regularly made to edit out the overly subjective as it pertained to the art of definition. The entry for *jumbo* had, for instance, once engaged wholeheartedly with nineteenth-century childhood experience. 'A big clumsy person, animal, or thing; popularized, esp., as the individual name of an elephant, famous for its size, in the London Zoological Gardens, subsequently sold to Barnum; when applied to any individual that is big of its kind or to a person of great skill or success', the first proof had stated, already revealing some latitude between the stated territory of a dictionary and that of an encyclopaedia. This too was an area in which drawing the line could be difficult. Subsequent handwritten annotations, however, confirm a slippage for *jumbo* which is still more conspicuous. Suggesting as it does the very real pleasure of the Victorian child in the presence of the original Jumbo, we are told that the latter 'had endeared himself to the hearts of many thousands of dear little Britons, who had so often ridden on his broad, comfortable back for the smallest of considerations'. Historical principles are transmuted into the history of one particular elephant as further annotations state that 'essaying a trial of strength with a locomotive, [Jumbo] gave the latter best, and only his poor old bones returned to the "Greatest Show on Earth"'. Meanwhile, the annotations continued, 'his dear wife "Alice" remained in the Zoo for some years'.

Perhaps predictably, this set of emendations did not find its way into the finished fascicles, even if it does provide a compelling insight into one aspect of cultural history. If the entry for *Jumbo* offered too much information in the revisions as suggested in the proofs, other entries as originally drafted offered too little, allowing too much latitude for the fallible interpretation of words. Those individuals unfamiliar with letter-boxes might, for example, have been somewhat confused by the definition which originally appeared in the first proof. This was, it stated, to be understood as 'a box in which letters are kept' or alternatively 'one in which they are deposited for transmission by post'. 'I believe some people have letter-boxes in front doors etc', Murray laconically noted in the margin as he read over this section of the text, mindful once more of his own role as editor-in-chief. He left Bradley to sort out the obvious omission. *Greasy pole* presented other ambiguities to Murray's mind, even if they had originally been unperceived by Bradley as he sent the relevant sheet off to the Press to be set in type. 'A pole rubbed with grease to make it harder to climb or cling onto', the first proof states. Again, Murray's meticulous attention to detail led him to take a more critical view. 'Used as a frequent object of diversion at sport etc.' should be inserted, he suggested, not least since 'if something of this kind is not added it looks as if people were so keen on climbing poles that they had to be kept at a distance by the use of grease'. This was clearly not what Bradley had intended and the entry was swiftly changed in line with Murray's recommendations: 'a pole rubbed with grease to make it harder to climb or walk upon (commonly used as an object of diversion at fairs or village sports)'. The clear specification of context no longer suggests a national fascination with the climbing of poles.

The quest to eliminate semantic loopholes of this order was a long and painstaking one in which the critical readers once again played an important part, regularly picking out infelicitous or indeed simply erroneous elements in the proofs. Bradley's apparent conviction in his first definition of *ground-floor* that it could be summed up by 'The lowest set of rooms in a building, having their floors more or less level with the ground outside' was, for instance, rapidly countered by Gibbs. 'The basement rooms are lower', Gibbs stated in the adjacent margin. His point was duly taken. 'The floor in a building which is more or less on a level with the ground outside', the entry now states, the early critical reception having obviated the risk of a more public form of censure once the fascicle emerged in its published form. Skeat could be similarly to the point – as well as remarkably restrained – even when picking up howlers such as that which he found in Bradley's first version of *furry*. This was a word which Bradley had chosen to analyse by means of a number of interlinked sense-divisions, the second of which specifically referred to animals. 'Covered or provided with fur; furred', he noted in this context. Surveying the evidence before him, Bradley came to the decision that a further sub-sense was required in which *furry* took on slightly different nuances when applied to caterpillars. In this respect, he added, *furry* was to be understood as signifying 'covered with short hairs, resembling fur'. A single citation (from the *Chicago Advance* in 1893) was given in appropriate illustration: 'The furry, striped beauty [chipmunk]'. As Skeat swiftly realized, however, here Bradley was indeed in error and seriously so. This was an entry which had to be rectified before this part of the dictionary reached publication. 'The *chipmunk* is the smallest of the four American varieties of the *squirrel*', Skeat hastily wrote in the margin, underlining *squirrel* as he did so. Rather than a particularly ornate (and hairy) variety of caterpillar it was, he realized, the 'striped beauty' of the chipmunk to which the citation referred. On receiving the corrected proof, Bradley swiftly – and humbly – removed all reference to caterpillars and the nature of the fur covering them. No trace remains in the version published in January 1898.

Even the tireless critical readers could, however, occasionally find themselves at a loss when it came to the attempt to clarify meaning in the dictionary. Gibbs, for example, conscientiously pored over Bradley's first proof of *leary*. His annotations merely stated the obvious as he observed that Bradley seemed to have omitted the definition. He turned instead to the quotations – both from *Rural Economy in Yorkshire* (1641) by the Renaissance landowner and farmer, Henry Best, which Bradley had provided to illustrate the word. But even these did not help. 'I have not my Best here to learn his meaning', Gibbs lamented, clearly baffled. 'The shortest and most leary hey is allwayes accounted the best', the quotations stated; 'Shepheards are to have an especiall eye to their hogges, and allwayes to give them the shortest, learyest, and best hey'. The problem was that here Bradley was baffled too, his omission of the definition being entirely intentional in the hope that Gibbs, or one of the other critical readers, would be able to help. But collective endeavour failed. 'Origin and meaning obscure', Bradley was forced to conclude in a declaration which still stands intact in

OED2. *Landon* presented parallel problems. 'But what does it mean?' Skeat demanded in the inner margin of the first proof in November 1900, clearly made none the wiser by an examination of the single quotation (from the *Alliterative Morte Arthur*) which Bradley had supplied. Obscurity here led to excision, *landon* joining the ranks of lost words to be discussed in Chapters 3 and 4.[54] These were problems which, to some extent, had been foreseen by Murray. 'Nobody exc[ept] my predecessors in specimens of the Dict^{y}. has yet *tried* to trace out historically the sense-development of English words . . . I shall have to do the best I can at defining probably 80,000 words that I never *knew* or *used* or *saw* before', he had written to Henry Sweet in the early days of the dictionary.[55] Definition was difficult, with ambiguities and semantic loopholes littering its path, some of which – as for *leary* and *landon* – simply proved insurmountable.

In the abstract, the construction of meaning remained, for Murray, one of the most important aspects of lexicography.[56] Yet, as Chapter 1 has already illustrated, commercial constraints constantly intervened in the material which could be included in the finished text. The same imperatives came to influence the art of definition. From the beginning the Delegates had cavilled at the number of senses which Murray often deemed necessary for the due elucidation of a word. 'The sub-division of articles' was 'not to be too numerous', they had stated in the 1883 *Suggestions*, picking out the drafted entry for *agitation* in which 'the first three senses (or at all events the 2nd and 3rd) seem needlessly distinguished'.[57] 'There is a growing tendency to expansion', they stressed in 1896, once more affirming the need to curb what they perceived as the unnecessary 'sub-division of meanings'. 'Time and expense seem to them to be more wasted in this than in any other direction', they informed Murray and Bradley in the hard-line resolutions for the future of the dictionary which featured in the discussions of this time.[58] In the need to compress the dictionary's scale, the level of analysis which any one entry might receive also came under active consideration, likewise eliciting the dictate of compression. 'We have been both omitting & compressing greatly during the last 3 months', Murray had already sought to reassure Price in early 1884.[59] 'I see what you mean about compression', Gibbs wrote in a later letter to Murray. Acknowledging that 'the question of space is an imperative one', the division of senses came to seem an entirely appropriate target. 'I . . . will apply the press', as Gibbs resolved, noting that 'I have not infrequently observed distinctions of sense . . . where the distinction is not real though apparent'.[60]

It was this, for example, which motivated Murray's stringent criticism of Craigie's proofs of *railroad* and *railway*. Here, he noted, 'much valuable space appears in consequence to be consumed on what is of no practical value'. While Craigie had, in Murray's opinion, also seen fit to include unwarranted collocations (such as *railway porter*) which had to be cut,[61] the proliferation of unnecessary senses was also of concern. Compression is necessary in 'nearly every direction', Murray stressed. 'Reduction in the number of senses and sub-senses' was especially important, not least in 'the abandonment of the contextual distinctions' generated by the differentiated use of given forms. If Murray's ideal remained the detailed elucidation of words, the pragmatic realities of commercial lexicography had led to a certain readjustment in this context too. 'It is the *lexicographer*'s business to make broad definitions . . . the synthetic power is far above the analytic', he reminded Craigie. The overworked editor-in-chief once more comes to the fore, his work evident again and again in the proofs, which are littered with suggestions for saving half a line here or a few words somewhere else. 'Is space wanted?' he suggested by the side of *gravidness* ('gravidity'), suggesting a possible amalgamation of two lines into one in the first revise. 'If space is wanted say "A grave speech"', he similarly advised alongside *graviloquence* ('1656 Blount *Glossogr.*, *Graviloquence*, a grave speech, or a speaking gravely'). Bradley's proofs of *go* are likewise densely annotated with recommendations for excision. 'Too much sub-divided', 'not wanted', 'absolutely superfluous', he writes alongside Bradley's scrupulous attempts to do justice to the manifold meanings which *go* might be said to possess. Bradley readjusted his work on *garish* in response to similar injunctions from his senior colleague. 'Too much sub-divided' had been Murray's verdict on the first revise. Bradley duly reduced the length of the definitions which survived, cut specific senses which referred to architectural applications or to individual decoration, and provided a more economical format for the entry as a whole. *Guider* received similar treatment as Bradley rewrote the entry in the right-hand margin of the proof, cutting a sense and observing greater stringency in the selection of quotations and meanings. Murray himself actively intervened in the scale of the original entry (and definition) of *lightsomeness* ('The quality of being lightsome, luminous, or well-lighted; brightness'), giving a single sense instead of the three which had originally been specified in Bradley's text. 'We are tied to finish the work in a definite number of volumes', Murray reminded Craigie in 1902. Every saving of space, however insignificant it might seem, contributed to this aim.

Culling Quotations

The deletions and excisions with mark these early stages of the dictionary provide incontestable evidence of the culling which, in various ways, was also to become a vital part of the making of the *OED*. While sense-distribution remained an obvious target for editorial intervention, the number of quotations had also early been identified by the Delegates as an area in which there seemed to be undue liberality. If maintained, this would, they argued, certainly increase the scale – as well as the expense – of production. 'On every page there are unnecessary examples', the 1883 *Suggestions* complained. Members of the Philological Society at times also ventured to agree. Benjamin Dawson had, for instance, been consulted by Murray during the discussions about the form and scale of the dictionary. 'Occasionally the quotations are unnecessarily long . . . & sometimes they are needlessly many', Dawson had responded, adding further that 'I think the Delegates are right in suggesting that the quotations from newspapers should be as few as possible.'[62]

Dawson's words, like the Delegates' own edicts, explicitly raised the question of a form of qualitative discrimination which might come into operation between different kinds of quotations. As we saw in Chapter 1, while citations which derived from 'great authors' and 'writers of repute' appeared unexceptionable, the Delegates repeatedly cavilled at the inclusion of non-canonical citations. Reviewers too often affirmed the same predilections. 'A sentence . . . from "Punch" does not strengthen the evidence, and is unwarranted', as a review in the *Scotsman* categorically declared.[63] The disputes of the 1890s merely served to harden already established sympathies. Bradley promised 'to take energetic measures to save space, chiefly in the direction of cutting down illustrations'.[64] As issues of space grew more and more imperative, certain vulnerabilities came to attend the range and extent of the quotations which could be included. 'The number of quotations need seldom exceed one for each century, unless there is some noteworthy variety of meaning of syntax to be illustrated', the Delegates decreed in 1896. Given a citation file which would ultimately extend to some six million quotations, it was clearly impossible for all available information to be included. The aim was to establish the historical record, rather than recording every possible instance of use.

The assiduousness of, for example, Fitzedward Hall in searching out citational evidence led to an overwhelming mass of detail which simply could not be used. 'As to your remark that you have upwards of 200 quotations for

Hand we have to consider the question of space', as Murray reminded Hall. 'We have not printed more than 1/7 of our material, leaving out innumerable good things that we should have liked to give.'[65] The rhetoric of 'condensation' and 'compression' had to be kept in view. In the difficult days of 1896, the 'revising committees' of the Delegates 'are severe upon "mere verbal & syntactical curiosities"', as Murray informed Hall in another letter, adding further that 'this demand for condensation has prevented me of late from using your additional quotations as fully as I had done before'. Selection was vital. As Skeat pointed out on the relevant proofs, a generosity which led to three citations from the sixteenth century for the second sense of *leisure* ('Opportunity afforded by freedom from occupations') was surely unnecessary. The evidence originally given in the first proof of *lop-sided* (in the figurative sense 'inclining towards or favouring one side more than the other; partial') was similar, presenting an abundance of citations no means in keeping with the 'definite limits' which Murray felt impelled to impose. Nine appeared for a single century, as Skeat noted in the margin. These would be reduced to three in the published text. Excesses such as these display a latitude which could rarely be maintained in the final fascicles. Even if Bradley resisted such pressures in *leisure* (in which he determinedly retained his trio of Renaissance citations)[66] or indeed in *level-coil* ('A rough, noisy game, formerly played at Christmas . . .') where ten quotations appear for a time span of ninety years, the recommended direction of change was clear. Cutting quotations became part of the fixed practice of the dictionary. 'You must steel your heart a good deal more against innocent quotations', Murray advised Craigie in 1901 after reading through some of the latter's drafts of Q. 'I well know the difficulty', he added, noting that 'I . . . am glad myself when any of my readers suggests "This could be done without".' Such advice on omission was paradoxically, as Murray concluded, 'perhaps the most valuable help that they can give'.[67]

It is a process which affects both canonical and non-canonical. De Quincey and Smollett disappear from the first proof of *glancing*, Wordsworth from *leader*, Addison from *loquacious*, and Sidney from *lightsomeness*. Hardy was deleted from *lathe*, and George Eliot from *leafy*. Even Scott, still one of the most heavily represented writers in the *OED*, originally had a tally far in excess of that which he now possesses. The proofs of *gross*, *grimalkin*, and *loop*, for example, had all included relevant citations from his works, each of which was excised in the continued editing which the proofs attest.[68] A quotation from Furnivall himself was excised from *gradual* ('an antiphon sung between the Epistle and the Gospel at the

Eucharist'). Three nineteenth-century citations appeared in the first proof. Given the edicts of the Delegates, it was unlikely that all three could survive. Furnivall's evidence (embedded in a citation from his EETS edition of the *Digby Mysteries*) was evidently adjudged the most suitable candidate for loss. It is, however, the eliding of the non-canonical which is most striking. In entries such as that for *laughing*, quotations from Pope, Carlyle, and Shelley remain while an apparently equally valid example from the *Society* ('The laughing girl romping down a country dance at a village inn') is deleted. *Lazzarone* ('One of the lowest class at Naples, who lounge about the streets, living by odd jobs, or by begging') is similar, so that an 1814 citation from the *Sporting Magazine* is excised while quotations from George Eliot and Disraeli are preserved intact (though under renewed pressures of space Disraeli too was to fall victim to this process in the first revise). Macaulay and Ruskin are used to provide evidence for the seventh sense of *grant* ('to admit, confess'), both moreover in citations dated to 1849. Nevertheless, in a vivid illustration of the processes at work, both Macaulay and Ruskin are retained in evident preference to an 1831 citation from the *Society* ('You hold me already in your chains; though I grant you, they seem "padded with cotton"') – even if one might think that the duplication of date would logically have rendered Macaulay or Ruskin a more suitable candidate for loss. However skewed such selectivity appears to be, it is a pattern which is repeated on many occasions. '"Gloves off! Gloves off!" shouted one voice after another' had, for instance, originally concluded the entry for *glove*. Deriving from the *Westminster Gazette* of 1896, it had attested usage almost up to the date of publication, giving a striking sense of contemporaneity to this dictionary on historical principles. But this too was to disappear in the second revise of the relevant sheet. In the published fascicle (and still in *OED2*) the last attested instance would be located half a century earlier in the far less colloquial circumstances of Daniel Rock's *The Church of our Fathers, as seen in St. Osmund's Rite for the Cathedral of Salisbury* ('This form of the episcopal glove, with its tassel, or tuft of silk, is well seen on Archbishop Chicheley's effigy, in Canterbury Cathedral'). Such examples can be multiplied indefinitely, as in *libeller* ('One who libels another; one who publishes a libel or libels') in which citations from Byron and the historian Henry Buckle are retained as evidence of nineteenth-century usage while that from the *Daily News* of 1896 is excised. 'If a person, under the pretence of criticizing a literary work, defames the private character of an author . . . such a person is a libeller', the entry had once pertinently concluded.

A still more striking pattern of loss is revealed if one examines the attrition of quotations from one specific position – that in which they happened to occur in proof in final position within the entry for a word or sense. As the changes made in the proof versions of *libeller* and *glove* have already illustrated, this was a position of some vulnerability. Looking at the first proof of the fourth sense of *languor* ('Tenderness or softness (of mood, feeling, etc.)'), the decision to retain intact Swinburne's 'The lilies and languors of virtue' of 1865 but to excise the originally concluding citation from the *Century Magazine* in 1885 ('Here in vogue long after German dreams, Italian languors') is clear in the deletions which the handwritten emendations on the proof display. Likewise, in *lap* used in the sense 'to enfold, surround', the once final citation from *Harper's Magazine* in 1883 ('He goes to be lapped . . . in soft Lydian air') is pruned in the first proof, leaving the philosopher (and first editor of the *DNB*) Leslie Stephen to provide the most recent evidence of usage. Other 'canonical' sources such as Swinburne's 'The joy that like a garment . . . lapped him over and under' from his *Songs of the Springtides* (1880) were later added to supplement the entry in a fashion which was evidently judged more fitting. *Larval* revealed losses of a similar kind, losing final citations from both the *Daily News* and the *Scotsman*. *Gambling* too presents an identical situation, the first proof showing Bradley's entirely motivated decision to retain Darwin in 1845 in what thereby became the most recent attested evidence for the word: 'Robberies are a natural consequence of universal gambling'. He conversely deleted a citation from half a century later which instead derived from the *Daily News*: 'That contemptible method of appropriating other men's money, which is known as gambling and betting'. A quotation from *Christian Aspects of Life* (1897) by the eminently scholarly Bishop of Durham, Brooke Westcott ('The State . . . must deal in some way with gambling'), later replaces it. *Grand* ('that which is grand; the lofty, magnificent; sublime') presents another disparity in the evidence which was selectively allowed to remain in the proofs. An 1885 citation from the *Academy* is deleted, leaving an 1821 quotation from the *Lectures on Drawing, Painting, and Engraving* by William Craig (drawing-master to the Princess Charlotte of Wales) in final position in the entry as it now stands.

Innumerable other entries present evidence similar in kind. In each case the proofs record the decision to edit quotations out in ways that confirm the prioritization of some forms of writing above others in the active processes of making the *OED*. Such processes also, of course, implicitly deferred to the sensibilities of the Delegates. 'No special effort need henceforth be made to find quotations for *words believed to have come into use since 1880*', the Dictionary Committee of 1893 had stressed.[69] 'This principle should be rigorously adhered to', its 1896 counterpart echoed. Since the final citation of each sense was, of necessity, also the most recent, excision in circumstances such as these could satisfy two desiderata simultaneously – even if it also rendered the dictionary far more historical than it had appeared in its underlying versions. More tellingly perhaps, it also provides an explanation for some of the absences in the *OED* that Marghanita Laski pointedly observed in the later twentieth century. 'Most "latest examples" in *OED*', she wrote, 'even in the later volumes, are nineteenth-century, often early-nineteenth-century'.[70] The same, however, cannot be said of the proofs where, if only temporarily, recent instances of usage – as well as non-canonical illustrations – did indeed engage with the wider realization of the *OED*'s founding principles.

Though such policies of selection were never consistently implemented, they do have an explicit foundation in the early days of the dictionary. Henry Hucks Gibbs in 1882 wrote privately to Murray on the ever pressing problem of space, focusing in particular on the ways in which the dictionary might be rendered more economical without suffering any corresponding reduction in its standards of scholarship. It was a natural transition for him to consider the use of quotations from a range of sources. 'You know I have always shared the dislike of the delegates to the newspaper quotations', Gibbs remarked, harking back to a topic which often surfaced in discussions of the dictionary. Given this problem, one possible solution occurred to Gibbs. 'You would please them and do the work no harm, if supposing you had a good quotation of 1860 you refrained from a D[aily] T[elegraph] quotation in 1883',[71] he wrote, describing one way in which the length of the dictionary might indeed be curtailed without undue sacrifice in other respects. Gibbs's words seem to have made their mark. Pragmatics and production yet again enforced a certain stringency which, left to their own devices, Murray and his co-editors would not have felt it necessary (or desirable) to implement. Fascicles had to end at one point rather than another; entries must be curbed to fit their reduced circumstances. Quotations were often simply the most expendable element when there were editorial pressures to save space – not least since it was easier for a final citation to be excised rather than one from the middle of an entry with all the adjustment of type that this would have involved. It was, just as Gibbs had advised, this particular set of quotations which seems overall to have borne the brunt of this pragmatic culling. In consequence, the dictionary was to become far more dependent on the canonical and classical among those published writings which survive into the finished forms of the text. The proofs, and the palimpsestic history they contain, are, uniquely, able to make this process of selective excision explicit, and entirely unmistakable.

CHAPTER 3
Lost Words

The image of inclusiveness gave direction to the *OED* from its first inception. The lexicographer was a historian, not a gatekeeper of language, Richard Chenevix Trench had declared to the assembled members of the Philological Society in 1857. He firmly rejected notions that a dictionary should be the product of a discriminatory sifting through language. In no way was the dictionary-maker to 'pick and choose', leaving this and taking that as Johnson had, for example, done in his wholesale rejection of the language of the philosopher Thomas Hobbes.[1] In the brave new world of lexicography which Trench foretold, such policies of selection were cast aside as anachronisms, emblematic of the deficiencies of the past.

In some ways of course, this diction of 'completeness' was all too familiar in the history of lexicography. *The Complete English Dictionary* proclaims the title page of Frederick Barlow's dictionary of 1772; *A Complete and Universal English Dictionary* echoed James Barclay two years later, closely followed by John Ash in 1775 with his own *New and Complete Dictionary of the English Language*. In the nineteenth century the same trend continued with the publication of works such as John Boag's *Popular and Complete English Dictionary* (1848) and *Dr. Webster's Complete Dictionary of the English Language*, 'thoroughly revised and improved', by C. A. Goodrich and N. Porter in 1864. Yet, as William Craigie and C. T. Onions later affirmed, such dictionaries were like acorns against oaks, their scale dwarfed by the new and far more genuine sense of completeness which the *OED* would confer upon English lexicography.[2] The 125 fascicles and 414,825 words of the first edition of the *OED* would, for example, immediately place the single octavo volume by Barclay in an entirely different perspective, rendering its claimed inclusiveness visibly untrue. Agendas by which 'hard' words or 'good' words are prioritized compromise the dictionaries of the past. Johnson, for example, castigates *slippy* ('A barbarous provincial word') as against *slippery*, or declares *cheery* to be 'ludicrous' when compared with a favoured form in *cheerful*.[3] As Robert Burchfield eloquently notes, dictionaries of this kind take on the appearance of 'herbaceous borders in a private garden, filled with well-cultivated flowers that had been planted with reasonable deliberation'.[4] Language as represented in Johnson's *Dictionary* had been pruned and weeded, trimmed to meet the desires of the individual lexicographer. It was against preconceptions of this kind – for both dictionary-makers and dictionary-users – that Trench defined the new dictionary of the Philological Society. This would be a vast '*lexicon totius Anglicitatis*' which, he added, we 'ought not to rest satisfied until we possess'.[5]

Completeness was duly formalized as the first and axiomatic principle of the 1859 *Proposal for a New Dictionary of the Philological Society* ('The first requirement of every lexicon is that it should contain every word occurring in the literature of the language it professes to illustrate'), later being inherited and endorsed by Murray himself. 'The design of the NEW DICTIONARY is to furnish a complete account of the present meaning and past history of *every English word whatsoever* now in use, or shown to have been in use', Murray averred in 1883, drafting the prefatory matter for the first part of the *OED*. 'The DICTIONARY aims at being *exhaustive*', he confidently declaimed.[6] The agenda of inclusiveness was grasped with enthusiasm. Yet such an ideal was, in reality, deeply problematic, a fact which was swiftly brought home to Murray as he sent out proofs of the Preface to a variety of other members of the Philological Society. 'This *exhaustive* must be limited somehow', Frederick Furnivall immediately wrote back in reply, clearly uneasy at the claims publicly being made for the dictionary – in spite of his own earlier protestations in the same vein.[7] Annotations on the proofs returned by Alexander Ellis reveal similar reservations. 'You omit "slang" & perhaps obscenities thus are by no means exhaustive', Ellis pointed out elliptically in the margin, providing an all too logical refutation of the lexicographic hyperbole into which Murray had crept.[8] Linguistic and lexicographical actualities were, it seemed, already at odds. By the next proof, dated 17 September 1883, some critical revision has taken place. No longer did the Preface claim that the *OED* would contain '*every English word whatsoever*'. Instead Murray's earlier rhetoric of exhaustiveness was itself marked for excision (see fig.2). The restated aims were now 'to furnish a complete account of the meaning and history of *English Words* now in use, or shown to be in use'.[9] By the time the fascicle went to press, this had been subject to still further modification. 'The aim of this Dictionary is to furnish an adequate account of the meaning, origin, and history of English words now in general use, or known to be in use', as the published text modestly explains. Even before the first fascicle had been published, it was evident that words would have to be lost from the dictionary, its democracy constrained by the complex realities of dictionary-making in a language which was, as Murray stressed, virtually infinite.

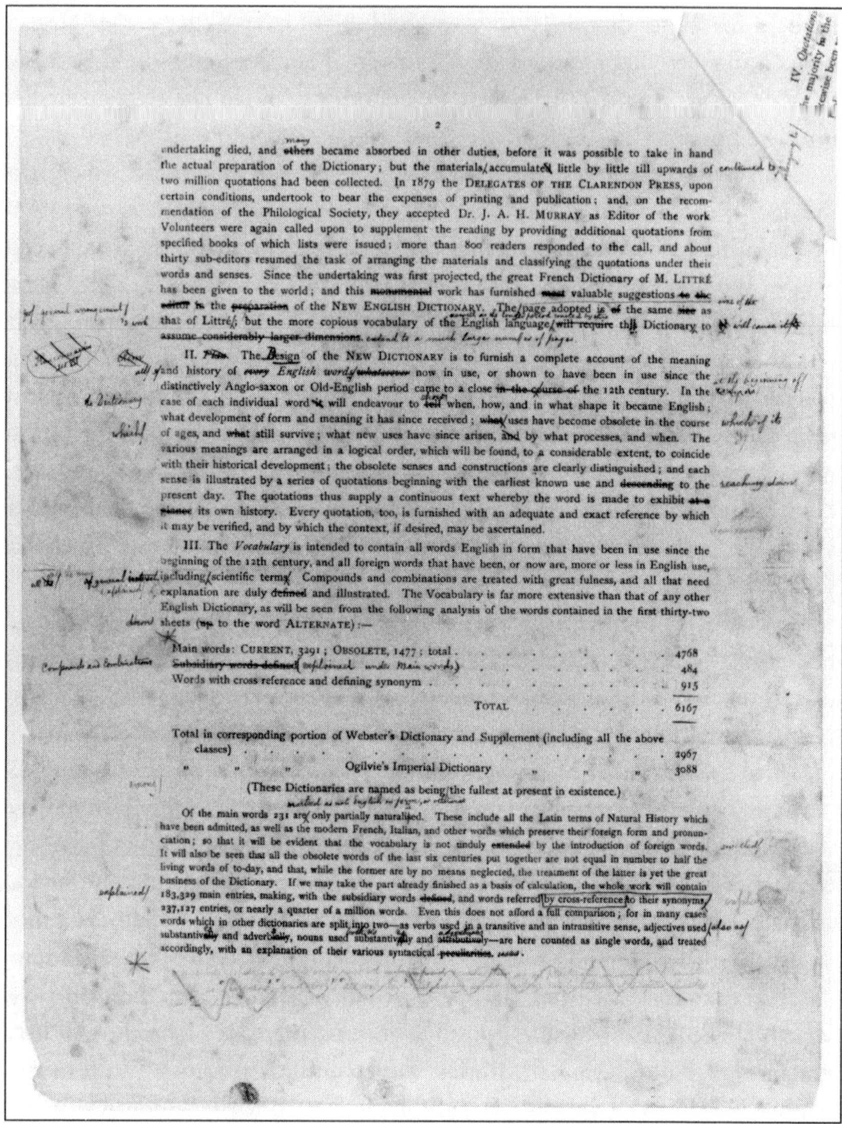

2

undertaking died, and others became absorbed in other duties, before it was possible to take in hand the actual preparation of the Dictionary; but the materials accumulated little by little till upwards of two million quotations had been collected. In 1879 the DELEGATES OF THE CLARENDON PRESS, upon certain conditions, undertook to bear the expenses of printing and publication; and, on the recommendation of the Philological Society, they accepted Dr. J. A. H. MURRAY as Editor of the work. Volunteers were again called upon to supplement the reading by providing additional quotations from specified books of which lists were issued; more than 800 readers responded to the call, and about thirty sub-editors resumed the task of arranging the materials and classifying the quotations under their words and senses. Since the undertaking was first projected, the great French Dictionary of M. LITTRÉ has been given to the world; and this monumental work has furnished most valuable suggestions to the editor in the preparation of the NEW ENGLISH DICTIONARY. The page adopted is of the same size as that of Littré; but the more copious vocabulary of the English language will require this Dictionary to assume considerably larger dimensions.

II. Plan. The Design of the NEW DICTIONARY is to furnish a complete account of the meaning and history of every English word whatsoever now in use, or shown to have been in use since the distinctively Anglo-saxon or Old-English period came to a close in the course of the 12th century. In the case of each individual word it will endeavour to tell when, how, and in what shape it became English; what development of form and meaning it has since received; what uses have become obsolete in the course of ages, and what still survive; what new uses have since arisen, and by what processes, and when. The various meanings are arranged in a logical order, which will be found, to a considerable extent, to coincide with their historical development; the obsolete senses and constructions are clearly distinguished; and each sense is illustrated by a series of quotations beginning with the earliest known use and descending to the present day. The quotations thus supply a continuous text whereby the word is made to exhibit at a glance its own history. Every quotation, too, is furnished with an adequate and exact reference by which it may be verified, and by which the context, if desired, may be ascertained.

III. The *Vocabulary* is intended to contain all words English in form that have been in use since the beginning of the 12th century, and all foreign words that have been, or now are, more or less in English use, including scientific terms. Compounds and combinations are treated with great fulness, and all that need explanation are duly defined and illustrated. The Vocabulary is far more extensive than that of any other English Dictionary, as will be seen from the following analysis of the words contained in the first thirty-two sheets (up to the word ALTERNATE):—

Main words: CURRENT, 3291; OBSOLETE, 1477; total	4768
Subsidiary words defined	484
Words with cross reference and defining synonym	915
TOTAL	6167
Total in corresponding portion of Webster's Dictionary and Supplement (including all the above classes)	2967
" " " Ogilvie's Imperial Dictionary " " "	3088

(These Dictionaries are named as being the fullest at present in existence.)

Of the main words 231 are only partially naturalized. These include all the Latin terms of Natural History which have been admitted, as well as the modern French, Italian, and other words which preserve their foreign form and pronunciation; so that it will be evident that the vocabulary is not unduly extended by the introduction of foreign words. It will also be seen that all the obsolete words of the last six centuries put together are not equal in number to half the living words of to-day, and that, while the former are by no means neglected, the treatment of the latter is yet the great business of the Dictionary. If we may take the part already finished as a basis of calculation, the whole work will contain 183,329 main entries, making, with the subsidiary words defined, and words referred by cross-reference to their synonyms, 237,127 entries, or nearly a quarter of a million words. Even this does not afford a full comparison; for in many cases words which in other dictionaries are split into two—as verbs used in a transitive and an intransitive sense, adjectives used substantivally and adverbially, nouns used substantively and attributively—are here counted as single words, and treated accordingly, with an explanation of their various syntactical peculiarities.

Figure 3 Murray's annotated copy of the Preface to Part I.

So ideal and reality assumed a transparently uneasy relationship as Murray was forced to reassess his early ideas on just how complete the dictionary could be. Even the inaugural exposition of Trench's *lexicon totius Anglicitatis* in 1857 had been noticeably less than total in some respects. Trench's expressed decision to relegate words of science and technology to a separate sphere – on the grounds that they regularly constituted an 'abuse' of language – already served to raise qualitative issues of entitlement.[10] Murray firmly rejected such rigid demarcations in vocabulary, often spending many hours tracking down the precise meaning of recent scientific coinages.[11] Nevertheless the 'General Explanations', which he wrote and rewrote in late 1883, reveals the tensions which, as Murray came to recognize, would inevitably surround the attempt to encompass the whole of English in a single work. If images of inclusiveness remain, they are tempered by caveats which were rendered necessary by the very nature of both language and lexicography. Murray was, he realized, bound by the physical limits which a dictionary must observe, and by the irreconcilable tensions which exist between the indeterminacy and open-endedness of language and the all too definite confines of the printed page. The two could never exist in perfect concord; always the former would be greater than the latter, and the latter would always be the result of a line drawn, arbitrarily, around what is 'English' and what is not.

'English' in these terms became not a fixed reality, a neatly segmented entity lying ready to be recorded by the willing historian of language. Instead it was more accurately seen as a construct or a theoretical proposition, something which was perhaps easily identifiable in the common core of usage[12] but which invariably remained hazy and indistinct at its margins, the borders which the lexicographer must impose. Murray redrafted and rephrased the 'General Explanations' as he battled with this problem. English is 'a central mass' with 'no discernible circumference', he stated;[13] it is 'not a fixed quantity circumscribed by definite limits'; it is a 'vast assemblage of words and phrases' suggesting 'the aspect of one of those nebulous masses familiar to the astronomer, in which a clear and unmistakable nucleus shades off on all sides, through zones of decreasing brightness, to a dim marginal film, which, without ending anywhere, loses itself in the surrounding blackness'.[14] In these terms, it is a construct upon which the lexicographer, like a naturalist classifying species, must merely draw a line 'inside or outside of a particular form'. The image of arbitrariness which results is striking. As in the compass diagram with which Murray also sought to image forth the complex reality of a national language (see fig. 4), there is therefore no real dividing line which demarcates 'English' or – in Murray's terms – 'Anglicity', a word which he himself coined and duly added to the word-stock.[15] Instead there is merely a series of directions along which the language continues. In a dictionary intentionally founded on scientific principles, this absence of 'mathematical accuracy' was problematic. Attempts to resolve it preoccupied Murray during the early 1880s. As in the Presidential Address which Murray delivered to the Philological Society in May 1880, he returned again and again to the affinities which analogies of language and science suggested while at the same time being forced to acknowledge their ultimate irreconcilability. 'The English language is not a square with definite sides containing its area', he explained; 'it is a spot of colour on a damp surface, which shades away imperceptibly into the surrounding colourlessness'; 'it is an illuminated area in a midnight landscape . . .'. Even if the image of the circle suggested mathematical affinities with Euclid, the circle of language – diffuse, unbounded, and lacking a circumference altogether – was, he continued, a form such as Euclid had never seen and had certainly never contemplated.[16]

Murray's repeated metaphorical forays express the conflicts in which he found himself. Faced with the past and present of a language which could not be pinned down in its entirety, he was still committed to recording the 'English language' on 'historical principles' in a dictionary which had publicly aimed at giving a 'complete biography of every English word'. Compromise was inevitable, not least since history – together with new words and senses – accumulates each day. English is in a 'slow but incessant dissolution and renovation', Murray acknowledged; it is no 'more permanent in its constitution than definite in its extent'.[17] Outside the dictionary with its precisely enumerated senses and definitions lay the flux of language which, as Johnson had already lamented in 1755, was constantly 'budding' and 'falling away'. Given the nature of the serial publication of the first edition of the *OED*, and the forty-four years which divided *A–Ant* and the appearance of its final part, this was moreover an issue of great concern. While evidence from the early twentieth century might appear in the fascicles which recorded the second half of the alphabet (see, for example, the quotation from 1910 which Murray included under *totem*),[18] the evidence of the first fascicle was necessarily limited to words which had been gathered before work on it finished in late 1883. For this reason alone the 'exhaustiveness principle' could not hope to be achieved. Language would always move beyond the apparent fixity which the dictionary might impose upon its forms.

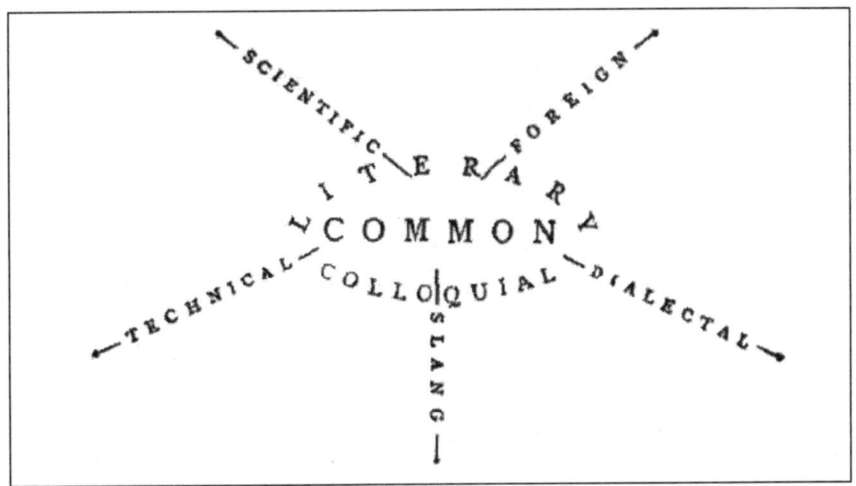

Figure 4 The compass of the language.

Even words that had long been in existence could, however, prove problematic. Completeness here was regularly frustrated by the fallibilities of the linguistic information which Murray had at his disposal. *Aged* was typical; used in the sense 'of such an age', it was, for instance, located only at the last minute by a diligent (and desperate) search of the inscriptions in Kendal Church by Murray's second wife, Ada. In partial compensation Murray and his co-editors were forced to invent quotations themselves for words which they knew to be in existence but for which the necessary evidence remained absent. 'Such responsibilities are not abdicable at will', Murray wrote in illustration of *abdicable* ('Capable of being abdicated'); 'He gives very good dinners, but I don't think much of his cellar' likewise appeared in illustration of *cellar* in the sense 'wine-cellar'. For the historian of language, these weaknesses in the assembled evidence were troubling, not least because individual invention at times had to take the place of empiricism. Yet in other ways too the very nature of language meant that the realities of usage might conceivably elude the dictionary-maker's grasp. 'The word was *spoken* before it was *written*', as Murray stressed to the Philological Society in 1884.[19] As a result, the real – and unavoidable – problem was that senses or words were regularly used for twenty or thirty years before they emerged into print. Some would never be located in the published evidence on which the *OED* was primarily to depend. This is the fundamental linguistic problem which underpins the linguist Roy Harris's later censure of the *OED*. It was 'black-and-white lexicography' of this kind, he cavilled, which led to an undue focus on the 'language of the literate strata of society'.[20] Though Murray was all too aware of the potential repercussions which this bias might have, the fact remains that an inevitable dependence on print culture would, throughout the dictionary's making, further serve to underscore the disjunction between the rhetoric and the reality of an all-inclusive dictionary.[21]

Yet even such completeness as might be achieved could present problems of an entirely different kind when seen from the point of view of those who read and used the dictionary. If admirable as a descriptive ideal, the drive to document English in use could, it seemed, emerge as distinctly disturbing when translated into lexicographic practice. Murray's zeal in recording recent usage – the coinages of ongoing change – was sometimes met with outright censure. 'How can he excuse the fourteen lines expended on *amphiarthosis* and the nine lines on *aecidium*?' a reviewer in the *Athenaeum* demanded, viewing certain entries in the first fascicle with distaste.[22] Trench was clearly not alone in his antipathy to scientific lexis and, as we shall see in Chapter 4, Murray's judgements in this respect were regularly deemed incorrect. Other responses to the image of inclusivity as revealed in this first part of the dictionary were similarly critical, further illustrating the problems which 'completeness' – even in modified form – could bring. Entries such as those for *absinthiate* ('to impregnate with wormwood'), *accommodated*, or *advertisemental* provoked strong reactions. *Accommodated* should be cast aside entirely, Henry Hucks Gibbs urged Murray. Evidence for its use came from the *Daily Telegraph,* a scarcely valid authority in Gibbs's opinion. Like the Delegates of the Press, his linguistic sensibilities were affronted by the way words of such dubious origin were apparently legitimized by being included in the dictionary.[23] Yet, as Murray repeatedly countered, the subjective opinions which Gibbs and others ventured to express were irrelevant. A descriptive dictionary must be impartial, as should the lexicographers who contributed to its making. '*You* don't like *advertisemental*: I like it as well as *testamental*, *monumental*, *ornamental*, *governmental*, *fundamental*, *instrumental* or any other *-mental*', he wrote to one reader who had ventured to complain about the excessive liberality of the first fascicle. 'The Dictionary does not advise *you* to say so, it merely records the fact that such has been said'.[24] Murray was bound to the historian's respect for data and, by extension, to their proper – and objective – understanding. This alone provided the necessary justification for the inclusion of such terms. *Advertisemental* and *accommodated* (as well as a variety of other words which Gibbs condemned) had to be included if descriptivism were indeed to find a true basis in lexicographic practice. The same was true of *aecidium*, which Murray defined with scientific precision as 'The cup-shaped fruit borne on the mycelium of certain parasitic fungi'. The claims of linguistic history in such ways regularly took precedence over the preferences of the individual in an argument which, at least in part, Gibbs could understand. 'There is a great deal in what you say about its not being the business of the Editor to sit in judgment on words & decide on their merits', he conceded, acknowledging the theoretical validity of Murray's descriptive ideals. Yet Gibbs remained not entirely convinced. Notions that the lexicographer might even-handedly seek to include all words and all usages were ultimately untenable, he argued. Gibbs in turn demanded recognition of what he already saw to be the more complex realities of dictionary-making. Theory had to be translated into practice, a domain in which, he countered, the lexicographer must 'necessarily sit in judgment to some extent'. In this respect it was surely impossible for the lexicographer invariably to assume the passivity of Johnson's 'harmless drudge'. '[You] do and must reject some rubbish which passes for words', Gibbs pointed out.[25] Even in a descriptive dictionary, selection must come into play. Murray's linguistic idealism is here set in sharp contrast to Gibbs's enduring pragmatism. Even though Murray would never – at least explicitly – allow himself to countenance the idea that any word might be deemed 'rubbish' while others had value enough to be 'saved', Gibbs would nevertheless essentially be proved right. The line must be drawn even if 'Nature has drawn it nowhere', Murray had written in the 'General Explanations' as he described the policy of inclusion – and its converse. It was moreover Murray and his co-editors who were of course variously responsible for drawing it, a fact which, as Gibbs already recognized, let subjectivity in by the back door even as it was formally excluded by the front.

Drawing the Line

Outside the rhetoric of 'completeness', the reality of practical lexicography in the making of the *OED* meant that decisions on exclusion and inclusion had, in effect, to be made each day, as indeed did decisions on exactly where the dividing line of the language could, in each individual instance, be said to lie. 'Common' words such as *indicate* and *cupboard*, *church* and *chimney* must be included, yet, on the margins, decisions were less certain and were endlessly open to criticism and debate. Since English in practice has no limits and is endlessly created anew by its users who coin words such as *gymcrockery* or *bite-beast*, *ironworky* or *jog-trotty* according to the whim of the moment,[26] the lexicographer must exclude some words that he knows to be in existence but of which the claims can, for one reason or another, be judged to be less pertinent than those of other words. If the American poet and philosopher Henry Thoreau's *indian-summerish* (given, without a definition, as a nonce-word) and the Victorian novelist Trollope's *manger-doggishness* ('the character of a dog-in-the-manger') went on to the final stages of the text and the record of the language which we can still read today, it can be seen from the proofs of the first edition of the *OED* that entries made for other words were noticeably less secure. In the pragmatic processes of dictionary-making, Murray and his co-editors were indeed forced to select, and to reject. *Longishness* and *landlord*, the latter used as a verb ('To play the landlord'),[27] were both, for example, excised at proof stage. Words as disparate in origin as *listiness* ('readiness, quickness') which had been used by the Renaissance writer and translator Richard Stanyhurst in 1582 and *glideness* ('the quality of being a glide'), used by the phonetician Henry Sweet some three centuries later, shared the same fate, being excised from the dictionary as the line was drawn more tightly. *Litotetical*, providing an adjective for *litotes* ('Of or pertaining to the figure *Litotes*'), disappeared in a similar manner along with the only dictionary citation from the nineteenth-century philologist, Julius Zupitza. Editing the various proofs, Bradley found himself deliberately cutting entries which he and his assistants had earlier drafted with meticulous care. The strikes of his pen hence dictate the exclusion of words such as *light-brain* ('A trifling, empty-headed person', dated to 1554) even if he chose to retain its corresponding adjective (Marlowe, *Edward II*, v. ii. (1598): 'The proud corrupters of the light-brained king'). Even the provision of memorable citations was no guarantee of survival. 'All latch-keyed daughters, knicker-bockered maidens, and discontented people generally', the now excised citation (from the *Daily Telegraph* in 1895) had quoted for *latch-keyed*, placing the advances of the 'New Woman' of the late nineteenth century in a distinctly negative light. Such evocative forms as *lericompoop* (a verb with the meaning 'to hoax' or 'delude' used by the poet and dramatist, Thomas D'Urfey (1653–1723)), *lip-lip* ('Of water; To make a sound as of touching gently with the lips'), and *lip-ringlet* (used for 'moustache' by the popular nineteenth-century novelist George Meredith) are similarly no longer to be found in the pages of the *OED*, in spite of their prominence in the proofs. Words such as *graiomania* ('a mania for what is Greek') and its accompanying antonym *graiophobia* likewise disappeared, their existence henceforth condemned to oblivion as far as the public face of the dictionary was concerned. The terms of lexicography could be affected too. *Lexicographing* ('The writing of dictionaries') was excised from the first proof, in spite of the eloquent citation by which it was illustrated. 'Lexicographing, like other pursuits . . . routs out things remote', as William Henry Pyne had aptly declared in *Wine & Walnuts* in 1824. *Lexicographically* ('with reference to lexicography') disappeared, too, along with an accompanying citation from Murray himself ('He compared the Awai grammatically as well as lexicographically with the other languages'). The fact that the latter was specified as potentially catachrestic (by dint of Murray's use of 'lexicographically' where 'lexically' was intended) may of course have helped to hasten this particular departure from the text. As in the revisions which attended Murray's prose in writing the various prefaces, correctness was deemed to be important.[28] Even if *lexicographically* was later restored, aided by an entirely apposite citation from Furnivall ('To place English lexicographically in a position abreast of any modern language'), thousands of other words vanished for ever from the published fascicles.

As a result, though Murray, like Trench, had initially sought to set up the roles of historian and judge as antithetical for the lexicographer, the practice of dictionary-making was at times to enforce their synthesis, however reluctant – and painful – this must have been. As for *latch-keyed* and *lericompoop*, the metaphorical line would be redrawn at one point rather than another, denying entrance to some words even as it admitted others. As Chapter 1 has already indicated, Murray and his co-editors were increasingly forced to keep within the 'practicable limits' rendered necessary by the nature (as well as the expense) of publication.[29] And in the decisions on inclusion which had to be made, the 'practicable' often caused still further attrition of the ideals with which the project had begun. The process of loss could become peculiarly overt, problematizing the earlier rhetoric of the dictionary as inventory and the lexicographer as historian. According to the claims of both, for example, a word such as *cultoist*, for which Murray had 'a goodly bundle' of slips, should undoubtedly have found admission. Yet, as an interview with Murray in 1893 revealed, this was not necessarily to be the case. 'It is probably new to you, as it was to me yesterday', he informed his interviewer. As a result, 'no one would be called rash who, in an ordinary way, condemned it as a superfluous word'. While Murray again sought to distance himself from subjective considerations of this kind ('I cannot act half so hastily with such a pile of evidence as this before me'), notions of judgement were nevertheless to intervene. 'I have to think very carefully before rejecting any word, however faulty it may be at sight', Murray admitted. Evidence did not provide an automatic guarantee of entry.[30] *Cultoist* demonstrably failed the criteria which Murray felt forced to impose. As he had found to his cost, Murray was engaged in a tripartite role as historian, linguist, and lexicographer, a trio of identities which were by no means always compatible. And as communications from the Delegates regularly reminded him, if the dictionary was to be published at all it was essential for commercial as well as linguistic expedients to be considered. This too was part of practical lexicography.

The wealth of material accumulated by the dictionary could therefore be a source of disquiet as well as congratulation. Presumably much to their alarm, the Delegates were informed that Murray was in possession of twenty yards of material for H, another seventeen yards for I, and seven more for J and K, all of which occupied 260 pigeonholes in Murray's Scriptorium.[31] Yet the very pragmatics of publication meant that this vast tally, over forty metres in all, would have to be condensed into five fascicles – a single volume – of the dictionary. More space was not forthcoming. Self-evidently the line had to be drawn for this reason too, curbing the abundance of words which might be included (and for which evidence existed) in favour of a pragmatic compromise by which the dictionary itself might reach completion. 'What the Delegates desire is shortening of *time*, and diminution of *bulk* i.e. of expense of printing', as Murray was frequently reminded.[32] The 'safe and remunerative undertaking' which Henry Sweet had promised the Press in 1877 was constantly threatened by what the Delegates at times came to see as the excesses of language as reflected in the dictionary. 'Superfluity should be avoided', Benjamin Jowett as chairman of the Delegates' Dictionary Committee dictated,[33] though deciding on what was 'superfluous' or not was, like the vanishing borders of the language itself, open to some differences of opinion.

As they advised on the economies which must be practised the Delegates relied on one fundamental equation: that saving space in the dictionary meant saving time for the editors and that this, in turn, meant saving money for Oxford University Press. That this equation was not wholly without exception was a further problem which dogged the dictionary through its many years of production. Even before publication of the first fascicle, Murray himself was explicit on the underlying fallibility of this time/money/space correlation. As he informed Bartholomew Price, Secretary of the Delegates of Oxford University Press in 1883, he had already been doing his best to implement the Delegates' suggestions for compression. He had tried to subdivide senses less minutely, to cut down where he could on derivative words, a principle which would be implemented throughout the dictionary, triggering the loss of words such as *libational* ('pertaining to libation', used in 1880 in Wallace's *Ben-Hur*) or George Meredith's *liquorly* from the proofs and revises.[34] He had likewise striven 'to draw the line more closely in the direction of scientific, technical, and other diverging senses of words'.[35] This had, Murray thought, led to some saving of space though it had not, he pointed out, as yet been matched by a corresponding reduction of time. On the contrary, as Murray tried to explain, it was often easier (and much quicker) simply to insert words, especially since at this early stage of the dictionary he often preferred to get external advice on whether a word should be cut. A second opinion certainly seemed desirable in such weighty matters. And even if a second opinion was not forthcoming, then cutting words was a matter which, he stressed, required much consideration. Murray made the same point, again to Price, in the following year, once more emphasizing the fact that though he had been both 'omitting & compressing greatly', the time which had been lost in doing so was as great as the space he had managed to save.[36] In a paradox that Price and the Delegates repeatedly failed to heed, losing words in fact regularly led to losing time and hence of course, from the Delegates' point of view, to losing money. It is this complex interplay of factors which, as we will see, serves to underscore the real arbitrariness of the dictionary and the words it eventually came to include – as well as those it did not.

The Sense of Loss

'Loss', as the relevant entry in the *OED* states, is to be deprived of or to fail to keep something which has originally been in one's possession. This can be a physical object or an abstract quality. It can partake of the accidental or, conversely, it could be both deliberate and intentional; it can signal disadvantage as well as simply absence. As in the loss of the dictionary's first editor, Herbert Coleridge, it can signify death as well as a range of separations of other kinds. Like many words which Murray and the other editors were forced to contemplate, *loss* was densely polysemous, its sense-divisions and citations eventually occupying two and a half columns of the printed dictionary. *Lose* as a verb was even longer, covering five and a half columns of text and being equipped with ten main sense-divisions and abundant examples. Sense 5a of *lose*, for example, deals with inadvertent loss: 'To become, permanently or temporarily, unable to find in one's own possession or custody; to cease to know the whereabouts of (a portable object, an animal, etc.) because it has strayed or gone unawares from one's possession, or has simply been mislaid'. Much to Murray's discomfiture, it was a sense for which the history of the dictionary could also have appeared as adequate illustration. 'I am afraid it is quite true that the word *bondmaid* has been omitted from the Dictionary, a most regrettable fact', he was forced to admit in 1901, fourteen years after the publication of the fascicle (*Batter–Boz*) in which it should have appeared. The admission was prompted by a letter from a perplexed user of the dictionary whose search had in this instance been a fruitless one. Murray's reply was deeply apologetic. He could offer no 'rational account', he wrote. This word was indeed 'lost': 'One can only surmise that the "copy" for it was in some unaccountable way lost either here or at the press'. Either way it was inexplicable and, he added, 'absolutely unparalleled'.[37]

A loss of this nature was indeed unusual, though suggestions from Murray's co-editors that other materials might have met with the same fate received typically short shrift. 'There are no holes in the Scriptorium floor through which such portions could slip', Murray berated Bradley five months later, demonstrating a remarkably short memory as well as a marked change of tone from that of the earlier letter. The irascibility of the over-stretched editor-in-chief once more came to the fore and Bradley's temerity in commenting on the putative absence of some of his own prepared copy for the dictionary met with an emphatic denial. Every table was periodically cleared, every slip filed, Murray stressed; permanent loss was 'inconceivable'.[38] Perhaps wisely, Bradley decided not to pursue the matter.

With occasional exceptions, this may well have been true as far as simply mislaying material was concerned. Other aspects of loss could, however, have the more permanent consequences which Murray had explicitly denied in his intemperate letter to Bradley. Loss could, for instance, mean deliberate removal, as indicated in Bradley's third sense of *lose*: 'To cease to have, to get rid of', a sense bound up in the shedding of that which is 'undesirable and unwanted'. This, for example, was true of the word *okonite* which was indeed both permanently and intentionally eliminated in the course of further research for the dictionary. Drafting the relevant entry in the course of editing the fascicle *O–Onomastic*, Murray was hampered by distinct gaps in the evidence he had at his disposal. As with many words in technical registers, he felt compelled to seek outside help in the quest to elucidate the word and its precise meaning. After all, merely having evidence of a word's existence was by no means adequate in a dictionary which aimed at impeccable thoroughness in each recorded entry. In this instance therefore, Murray's own knowledge would not do and nor would the data files of the dictionary. Murray accordingly wrote to the engineer, Sir William Preece, in search of further assistance. Preece's prompt reply was helpful in the extreme, though it also contained the categoric recommendation that lexicographic completeness was not desirable in this context. *Okonite* was 'not a term of importance', Preece confidently announced. Demonstrating the remarkable dedication which was so often shown by the dictionary volunteers, Preece had in fact managed to track down okonite's inventor, thereby eliciting a detailed – if surprising – etymology for the word. It was, he had determined, 'merely a trademark', testimony to the linguistic inventiveness of its creator as much as to its utility as a product. 'The inventor told me he had to make a name for his new stuff', Preece informed Murray; as a result, he had taken 'O.K. "slang" for "all correct" and as nearly all insulating material ended in "ite" he thought "okonite would just fetch the market"'.[39] The entry for *okonite* duly disappeared from the draft of the dictionary, its status as a trade designation clearly pointing to its rightful place outside the borders of the language as formulated in the *OED*.[40]

This is not, however, to imply that all such words were lost from the first edition of the *OED*. Accidents could happen here too and the inadvertent inclusion of words such as *delta-metal* was to be regarded as a lapse on almost the same level as the omission of *bondmaid*. Defined in the fascicle *Deject–Depravation* as 'an alloy of copper, zinc, and iron introduced about 1883, and named in allusion to its *three* constituents'), *delta-metal* proved in fact to be another commercial designation. Murray found himself the author of another apologetic letter to a reader of the dictionary, expressing his regret at the inaccuracies of both derivation and explanation. He was, however, still more sorry that *delta-metal* had been included at all. 'If we had known that the name was a registered proprietary name, we should have either stated this, or, more probably, excluded it from the Dictionary', he wrote.[41] Unwarranted inclusion could, as this indicates, complicate still further the nature of that 'Anglicity' which Murray strove to encompass within the pages of the *OED*. Completeness was double-edged. All decisions were potentially fraught with untoward difficulties, many of which would become apparent only with hindsight.

Murray's 'Anglicity' – or perhaps rather 'Englishness' – presented other problems too for the lexicographer who, as well as trying to record the facts of usage, might find himself enmeshed in a set of cultural assumptions regarding which facts should – and should not – be recorded in the dictionary, irrespective of their historical validity. This was particularly the case with words deemed 'obscene' for which a marked set of cultural filters came into play. The surgeon James Dixon (another assiduous critical reader for the dictionary) wrote, for instance, with evident caution to Murray about his researches into the word *condom*. 'I am writing on a very obscene subject', he announced, a circumstance reinforced by the 'Private' conspicuously written on the envelope.[42] 'There is', he went on, 'an article called a Cundum [illegible] a contrivance used by fornicators, to save themselves from a well-deserved clap; also by others who wish to enjoy copulation without the possibility of impregnation'. Dixon's deployment of the highly negative 'fornicator' is a telling indication of his moral censure, as indeed is his conviction that gonorrhoea or 'clap' is an entirely appropriate retribution for those who engage in such extra-marital activities. Victorian respectability evidently compromised Dixon's search for intentionally objective data to send on to the dictionary. *Condom*, he averred, was surely 'too utterly obscene' for Murray even to contemplate its inclusion.[43] Dixon's surmise here was to prove correct. The evidence was provided and historical (as well as contemporary) usage duly verified,[44] but the word was 'lost' from the first edition of the *OED* as part of a policy which, as Ellis had noted as early as 1883, would undeniably serve to compromise the images of inclusiveness with which the dictionary had formally set out.[45] Even the 'clap' which Dixon isolates as the just deserts of those who act with such profligacy is, though recorded in the *OED*, ostensibly consigned to the past of language. '*Obsolete* in polite use', Murray emphatically declared in the fascicle *Cast–Clivy*, published just one year after Dixon had used *clap* with a politeness which was entirely indisputable.

Cunt was to offer dilemmas similar in kind as historical principles and socio-cultural sensibilities once more failed to accord. Interestingly, here Dixon was to urge inclusion, albeit in a modified form. 'The thing itself is not obscene', he stressed; moreover 'it will look cowardly to shirk it'. His suggested solution – to list the word in its rightful place but to avoid any illustrative citations, as well as any definition which ventured beyond the (highly ambiguous) 'obscure term applied to the private parts of a woman' – was nevertheless not without its own elements of lexicographical cowardice.[46] The recommended obscurity would, for instance, be culturally determined rather than linguistically true. The classical scholar Robinson Ellis likewise urged inclusion. It 'must in *any* case be inserted', he wrote to Murray. The fact that 'it is a thoroughly old word with a very ancient history' was entirely in accordance with the stated principles of the dictionary.[47] As for *condom*, however, omission was again felt to be best though, just as Dixon had warned, Murray was later called upon to justify the dictionary's evasiveness on this matter. The loss of *cunt* occurred 'after wide consultation and much discussion', Murray wrote in attempted explanation to another critic of what the dictionary had or had not done. Readers of the *OED* seemed endlessly vigilant and endlessly willing to communicate the results of their vigilance to the dictionary's editors. Here Murray mounted a careful defence. The omission had not been undertaken without 'regret' at the evident sacrifice of historical principles; it was merely that, as yet, the word was inappropriate in the lexicographical context of the *OED*. The compromise was only partial, Murray added in further attempted reassurance; after all, the data files of the dictionary would retain the historical evidence intact. The facts were not denied but simply suppressed. Victorian society was not yet ready for descriptive explicitness of this kind.[48] Whether the recipient of the letter – John Hamilton, headmaster of Minto school in Roxburghshire in Scotland (which Murray had attended between the ages of twelve and fourteen) – was satisfied with this explanation remains unknown. Hamilton's own robust argument for the legitimate inclusion of the word ('The mere fact of its being used in a vulgar way, does not ban it from the English language') remains in the archival collection of Murray's letters in the Bodleian Library. 'It is an old English word of Teutonic origin, & is just as good English (though by the nature of things not so much used in polite society) as the words, leg, arm, heart, stomach, & other parts of the body', he rightly pointed out.[49] Its historical credentials were impeccable and its 'Anglicity' undoubted. In spite of Murray's carefully worded reply, the sense of compromise was clear.

Earlier dictionaries had ironically often been more rather than less complete in this respect. Such words were English and as such they merited a place in an English dictionary. Giovanni Florio's *Worlde of Wordes* of 1598 included *fucke*, as did Nathaniel Bailey's *Universal Etymological English Dictionary* of 1721, albeit with a definition which was itself veiled in the obscurity of Latin ('*fæminam subagitare*'). Bailey also included *cunt*, for which he gave the similarly oblique definition of '*Pudendum muliebre*', a solution which Murray seems to have gratefully adopted in defining *twat* in the *OED*. He embedded Bailey's definition as an illustrative citation within the entry, thereby avoiding having to give a definition himself.[50] *Piss* and *fart* were widely included in earlier dictionaries, Johnson even deciding to incorporate an illustrative poem by Sir John Suckling for the latter ('Love is the fart/Of every heart;/It pains a man when 'tis kept close;/And others doth offend, when 'tis let loose'). Nevertheless, a sense that the English dictionary should maintain certain decorums tends to become apparent from the mid-eighteenth century onwards, precisely in line with the increasing emphasis placed upon its role as a domain of 'proper' and normative usage. Even if he chose to include *fart*, Johnson, for example, had excluded other areas of lexical taboo from his *Dictionary*, a situation which apparently prompted a number of frustrated searches though its pages. 'I hope I have not daubed my fingers', Johnson is reputed to have replied to one such query on the absence of entries of this kind. As Johnson's words indicate, however, editing a dictionary had already become a process of consciously editing out, the picking and choosing which Trench would later decry. This was to be intensified still further in the context of Victorian England, a period in which language was regularly to engage in the art of euphemism to conceal what were regarded as the 'baser' aspects of life. In what G. L. Brook has referred to as 'one of the strongest taboos in Victorian times',[51] trousers (as well as undergarments of various kinds) were frequently referred to under covert designations such as *unmentionables*. This was included in the *OED*, as in the 1823 citation from the *London Magazine*: 'Liston, in a pair of *unmentionables* coming half-way down his legs'. Such niceties form a frequent target of Dickens's linguistic satire, his *Sketches by Boz* likewise being cited under this head in the *OED*: 'The knees of the unmentionables . . . began to get alarmingly white'. Dickens's acuity in relation to popular cultural sensibilities even extends to the similarly euphemistic use of *shoes* in *Oliver Twist*. Forced into a situation in which the unmentionable must apparently be mentioned – and in female company too – Giles the butler is hence made to resort to indirection of a particularly conspicuous form: '"I tossed off the clothes", said Giles . . . looking very hard at the cook and housemaid, "Got softly out of bed; drew on a pair of –". "Ladies present, Mr Giles," murmured the tinker. "– of *shoes*, sir," said Giles . . . laying great emphasis on the word.' Given such sensitivities, the *OED*'s reticence about *cunt* and *condom* is perhaps entirely predictable, even if it thereby abdicates a crucial aspect of its own descriptive principles.

Though the prudishness which is prominent in these popular Victorian stereotypes has been contested and its potential fallibilities revealed,[52] such issues do make plain the fact that the cultural climates in which dictionaries have their being can play a significant part in the ideological codes which, implicitly as well as explicitly, are revealed within their pages. However objective dictionary-makers proclaim themselves to be, it is in many ways virtually impossible to secure entire liberation from contemporary mores. These have an insidious habit of creeping in, whether in the choice of entry words or the phrasing of definitions.[53] That Murray viewed both himself and the dictionary as essentially 'Victorian', with the cultural as well as linguistic legacies which this involved, has of course its own significance. His view of his own identity was firmly embedded in the time in which he lived. He was by no means a 'modern', he stressed to Edward Arber in 1905. 'You & I are of Victorian era, and History, if it remembers us, will so describe us'.[54] Murray was born in, and deeply bound to, an era that was marked both by its advances (as Chapter 4 explores) and by a set of decorums that now appear unduly restrictive in their implications. The latter inevitably contribute to the cultural sensibilities to which the dictionary at times pays deference, as in the morally charged definition of *masturbate* ('To practise self-abuse') or the obfuscation which attends the entry for *orgasm* ('Excitement or violent action in an organ or part, accompanied with turgescence; *spec.* the height of venereal excitement in coition'), a usage which is further specified as restricted to the scientific domain of physiology. *Self-abuse* itself offers little elucidation in this sense as originally defined in the *OED*. 'Self-pollution', it states in an entry which (accompanied by precisely the same evidence) has now received the more explicit definition 'masturbation' in *OED2*.

The *OED*'s silence on words such as *condom*, *cunt*, and the profane use of *bastard*,[55] or its proscriptive and on occasion unduly class-orientated prohibitions that define – at least in theory – *shit* as 'not now in decent use' or *bloody* as a term favoured only by the lower orders, all stand as further manifestations of this fact. 'Now constantly in the mouths of the lowest classes, but by respectable people considered "a horrid word", on a par with obscene or profane language', as Murray stated in the entry for *bloody* in 1887.[56] As in the deployment of 'vulgar' as a label for words such as *pram* and *person*,[57] class – together with the 'ears polite' that Murray holds up as a linguistic standard in this entry for *bloody* – could fracture the representativeness of the dictionary. Neutrality was, it seemed, an almost unattainable ideal.[58]

Fixing the Borders

Loss could be motivated in other equally conscious ways. If ideological considerations impelled the exclusion of certain key words with reference to the various sensibilities of readers, editors, and publishers then, at the other end of the scale, hard pragmatism demanded the excision of others. Here it could simply be a case of a word being in the wrong place at the wrong time, as Murray and the other editors were forced to juggle the contents of each fascicle in order to secure a neat end to its concluding page. The *OED* has of course memorably (if erroneously) been described as the longest serial publication in existence but, as with all serial publications, it was a form which could bring its disadvantages. As Victorian novelists also found, writing for a monthly or weekly journal could put severe strains on the creative process since they were bound not only to the need to produce copy by a certain date but, more specifically, to produce exactly the right amount of copy at the right time. Dickens regularly found himself in the position of having written too much material for a given instalment or 'number' and hence having to excise what was termed 'over-matter' while the part in question was still in proof. In *David Copperfield*, for example, all but seven of the nineteen parts were too long in the form in which they were first written, the sixth part being almost a hundred lines over its formal limits when first submitted. Loss was inevitable and Dickens managed to remove almost half of the surplus in the latter as well as cutting forty excess lines in Part X. As in his instructions to the printer with respect to the additional material which still remained in Part IX, Dickens, however, had the advantage of being able to insist on the artistic imperative. 'The over-matter must be got in somehow – by lengthening the page', he dictated, his authority in this matter incontestable.[59]

While this was not an option open to the lexicographers of the *OED*, 'over-matter' was nevertheless a condition which regularly affected the making of the dictionary. The limits of inclusion and exclusion were in consequence often made to observe the desiderata of printing rather than those of the language – or indeed the lexicographer – *per se*. Editorial responsibility in this context, just as in the revisions enforced on Dickens by the constraints of space, required a further level of correction or of what, in a euphemism of the editorial process, usually came to be referred to as 'adjustment'. While the proof sheets of the *OED*, as we have seen in Chapter 2, abundantly attest the minute attention to detail which was involved in crafting the dictionary towards its final form, they can at other times reveal with striking clarity the strategic manipulations of space rendered necessary by the very act of publication. 'The sheet . . . must end with the termination of an article', Bradley wrote on the revises of what was to become the fascicle *Germano–Glass-cloth*, adding, 'Please let me know precisely where the end will come as the corrections stand at present, that I may know what further adjustment to make'. 'To adjust', as the relevant entry in the very first fascicle of the dictionary affirms, is, in part, to arrange, compose, settle, or harmonize. It is, however, its fourth sense which bears most precisely on the processes of 'adjustment' which the proofs reveal: 'To arrange or dispose (a thing) suitably in relation to its parts; to put in proper order or position; to regulate, systematize'. In terms of the proofs therefore, regulating could in reality come to mean rejecting while disposing could in turn signify identifying the disposable – or indeed the 'losable', a word which the *OED* would in fact later retain.

As Murray wrote to Gibbs in December 1900, it was 'adjustment' – and its time-consuming and onerous demands – which lay behind the failure to send any new proofs during recent weeks. 'The finishing of I and beginning of J required a number of technical adjustments which took up much time', he explained; 'one must contrive to end near the bottom of the second p[age] of a leaf, and that requires usually much measuring, adjusting, contracting & expanding'.[60] The image of the lexicographer physically measuring out available space here offers a disturbing corrective to the ideals of exhaustiveness which had earlier been expressed with such confidence. As Murray's words show, writing a dictionary in this sense could become not so much an act of registering the words used in the past and present of language, as of registering which ones might be deemed expendable and hence able to be excised. The constraints which 'adjustment' came to enforce underlie the patterns by which, over and over again, certain categories of words prove vulnerable to loss. In effect the dictionary became a complex balance sheet over which the lexicographer must keep tight control. Any late additions of words – such as the nonce-word *glossomachiall* ('Given to wordy strife') for which evidence suddenly appeared in a handwritten addition in the margin when the relevant fascicle was in the first revise – had to be compensated for by the excision of other material. In this instance, the nonce-word *glossocracy* ('Government by the tongue') was promptly marked for deletion on the same sheet. The fact that the latter derived from *Blackwood's Magazine* in 1841 while the former had been traced to the poet Gabriel Harvey was presumably not irrelevant in this choice.[61] As here, loss and gain frequently existed in precarious symbiosis, though it was always made clear that any unnecessary expenditure in terms of space was to be curbed. Conversely, 'debits' – in view of what the Delegates regarded as the inordinate size of the dictionary – were to be positively encouraged, especially since such reduction would, they hoped, bring about a similar reduction in the rather more literal debits which continued to be made by the dictionary. 'Adjustment' in the proofs thus becomes a process with explicit and immediate consequences. 'The sheet is required to end before the article *Frankish*', Bradley instructed the printers with reference to what was to become the final part of *Foisty–Frankish*. The necessary losses – here of the entry for *frankify* ('To give a frankish appearance or form to') which Bradley deleted in order to secure the space he needed – had to be made. With evidence from the letters of Lord Strangford ('As for Frankifying their own names, the Greeks do it worse than we do'), *frankify* here merely seemed a 'better' candidate for omission at this point than, say, *frank-ferm* (an obsolete legal term) and *frankfort black* ('a fine black pigment used in copper-plate engraving'), both of which were retained. Its loss was, however, entirely arbitrary, a sacrifice made in terms of the need to secure a specific ending to one specific sheet.

Other proof sheets illustrate that adjustment could at times go far beyond the simple removal of isolated words. These wider patterns of loss were often motivated by the sheer scale of material which had been generated for possible inclusion in the dictionary. Even in the early days, this had been a source of some concern. It had, for example, been openly troubling Walter Skeat in 1876. Surveying the mass of evidence which more than twenty years' work by the voluntary readers for the Philological Society had already generated, Skeat posed what he identified as the chief question. 'Can it be cut down?' he demanded. His own response was an unconditional one: 'I answer – most certainly it can', though, as he afterwards acknowledged, 'to know what to leave out, & what to put in, is very difficult'.[62] This, however, was the crux. If it was impossible to include everything, then selection was imperative. But selection on what grounds? And for what reasons? These were questions which dogged the realization of the *OED* over the coming decades.

Murray initially appears to have been resistant to comments about the need to secure a 'reasonable' scale for the dictionary. Skeat's detailed suggestions for losing what he regarded as 'useless or unimportant words' in the proofs of the first fascicle were, as we have seen, rejected out of hand.[63] Murray comprehensively disregards the deletions on the drafts of the dictionary which Skeat returned to him at this point. Nevertheless, as the dictionary advanced, this resistance was gradually eroded. While, as we saw in Chapter 2, editorial responsibility readily came to involve the culling of individual citations, far more disturbing was the practice by which culling came to operate on entire entries. Against his natural inclinations as both scholar and lexicographer, Murray was forced to contemplate – and indeed to formulate – policies by which the extent of the dictionary might be reduced. In another set of terms which came to be favoured by the Delegates, the dictionary had to be 'pruned'. The organic imagery often deployed by Murray and by Trench in their descriptions of language ('a language has a life, just as really as a man or as a tree', Trench had asserted in his early lectures on the study of words)[64] here evolved into a pervasive metaphor in exchanges between dictionary-makers and Delegates. The dictionary was, for instance, regularly figured as an unruly plant which had exceeded its allotted space. What Murray angrily referred to as their attempt to 'guillotine' the dictionary was thus rephrased by the Press as a process which was, at least superficially, far less violent. 'I must demur to the word "guillotining" as applied to the reduction of scale which we think the Dictionary requires', Philip Lyttelton Gell countered. The aim was, he continued, merely 'to remove superfluous foliage but none of the essential parts of the tree'. As for plants, pruning was an essentially beneficial activity, keeping unwarranted growth in check. It was therefore 'distinctly for the good of the Dictionary'.[65]

Certainly pruning was not inherently negative. As Murray would later state under the relevant entry in the fascicle *Prophesy–Pyxis*, pruning was in essence merely an act in which branches, boughs, or shoots are cut or lopped off. As a possible consequence of Murray's own experience in this context, however, figurative uses of pruning attract a somewhat less neutral interpretation, especially where they concern the written word. 'To "cut down", mutilate . . .; to rob, spoil . . . *esp.* to cut down or reduce by rejecting superfluities; also to rid or clear *of* what is superfluous or undesirable', Murray declares. The evidence he chose to provide as appropriate illustration is, if anything, still more telling. 'It is neither indifferent, nor true dealing, thus to nip, and to proine the Doctours sayings', the accompanying quotation from the sixteenth-century theologian Bishop John Jewel avers.[66] The message for the Delegates was clear.

Pruning was nevertheless both easy and (relatively) uncontroversial in some cases. Evident inadequacies of data prompted the cutting of a number of words for which draft entries had appeared in the early proof sheets of the dictionary. The semantic opacity of *loretto*, defined by Bradley as 'App[arently] a game of some kind', or *grill* ('Some kind of stone') clearly rendered them suitable candidates for omission. Entries such as that for *langa*, deleted in the first revise of *L–Lap*, further illustrate the problems of lexicography. Bradley here had evidently tried – and failed – to find a definition at all. 'The Langa . . . skimming (as it were) The Ocean's surface, seeketh everywhere The Hugy Whale; whence slipping in (by Art) In his vast mouth, she feeds upon his heart', states the evocative citation from the poet Josuah Sylvester in 1591. The precise identity of the langa was unknown and apparently unknowable. Bradley here confessed defeat and simply cut the word. Losses of this order tend to constitute part of that 'natural wastage' which, as Robert Burchfield notes, is common practice in the making of dictionaries. Simple criteria of editability thus become a significant factor in the retention – or otherwise – of words.[67]

A more problematic target for such pruning was the category of words illustrated not by the eloquence of writers such as Scott and Shelley but by the usage of 'popular' writers or, still worse, by what Gibbs tended to term the 'slip-slop and hasty' forms of journalists.[68] True here to his descriptive principles, Murray could be scathing about such unfounded antipathies. The Delegates' repeated preferences for 'great authors' met with short shrift; likewise reviews which dwelt on the dictionary's non-canonical departures were publicly castigated in the Philological Society.[69] Nevertheless, words for which the sole evidence lay outside the confines of what might be deemed 'canonical' also found themselves subject to a critical scrutiny under which they could be found lacking. While their excision served to make a positive contribution to the internal economies of the text, it also contributed to those perceptions of under- and over-privileging which have become a recurrent topos in comment on the *OED*.[70] The difference in this context, however, is that, via the proofs, one can again see the critical processes of loss – and selection – at work.

Words such as *guidecraft* (cited from the *Academy* in 1888), the evocative and onomatopoeic *glou-glou* ('the sound made by a liquid when being poured out of a bottle', used in *Good Words* in 1883: 'Aha! The bottle! – the glou-glou of the bottle!'), *grogging* (originally cited from the *Daily News* in 1891), *grogless* (from the *Daily Telegraph*), *griddled* (from an article in the *Westminster Gazette*), *governmentless* (from the *Pall Mall Gazette* in 1885), and *grigginess* (from the *Cornhill Magazine* in 1890) were just a few of the entries to disappear from the various proofs and revises over the 1890s. 'If we know little about the paternity and maternity of eels, we know a great deal about their grigginess and elverhood', the citation for *grigginess* ('of or pertaining to a small eel') had averred. Yet if well known in 1890 when this particular number of the *Cornhill* appeared, it was a quality which was henceforth to be forgotten as far as the *OED* and its eventual readers were concerned. In a similar way, *gimpy* ('Resembling gimp, gimp-like. *Rare*'), illustrated by a single 1893 citation from the *Birmingham Weekly Post* ('a bonnet . . . of black open-work gimpy sort of straw'), was doomed to become still rarer by virtue of its departure from the first revise of this part of the *OED*, even though it had managed to survive intact in the proofs up to that point. Similar casualties were the entries which had originally been drafted for *fortificational* (from the *Pall Mall Gazette* in 1889), *lasso-wise* (from an 1894 article in the *Daily News*), and *frogginess* from the *Fortnightly Review*. All in various ways illustrate the sense (as well as the consequences) of intentional loss, the semantics of which were later carefully anatomized by Bradley in his own entry for *lose*.

The ephemeral nature of the publications in which words of this kind appeared could, it seemed, lead to a similar ephemerality for the words which they contained. While *lin-lan-lone* ('an echoic formation intended to suggest the sound of a chime of three bells') appears in the more permanent printed form of Tennyson's poetry (duly becoming a permanent accession within the pages of the *OED* too), similarly onomatopoeic words such as *glou-glou* tended, as we have seen, to disappear, vouchsafed only by their usage in journals such as *Good Words*. A similar set of contrasts can be located in, for instance, the excision of *lynchable* (from the *Nation*) and *levantwise* ('after the fashion of the Levant', used in *All the Year Round* in 1860). While derivative words such as these had, as we have seen, constituted a recurrent target for compression in the dictates of the Delegates, it is nevertheless plain that some derivative words were adjudged of more value than others. Dickens's *fireworkless* and Browning's *feloness* – as well as Coleridge's *friendism* – are, for example, all retained in the published fascicles, unlike their less privileged counterparts from the *Nation* and *All the Year Round*. Precisely parallel is *greenable* ('able to be made green') for which evidence derived from the *Athenaeum* in 1892. While this entry disappeared during the rigours of the proof stage of the dictionary, it remains worthy of note that Samuel Taylor Coleridge's *gardenable* ('able to be gardened') was unthreatened by the process of excision: 'Above the town, little gardens . . . are scattered here and there, wherever they can force a bit of gardenable ground', as he wrote in a letter in 1804, providing a citation which in turn found a permanent home in the pages of the *OED*. In the absolute terms of linguistics, such forms are precisely the same weight and value. If derivative words had indeed been identified as an area in which space might be saved, the wider implementation of this policy came to depend not upon the existence of a given derivative word *per se*, but on who had happened to use such a word as attested in the citation files of the *OED*, and on the pressures which came into operation in specific fascicles.

Gladstone's *guestship* thereby remained while *guesthood* (attested only from the *Pall Mall Gazette*) disappeared. 'The condition of being a guest', the definition of the latter had stated in the proofs; 'The condition or position of being a guest', the definition of the former still affirms in the published text of the dictionary. Words of this type transparently failed to achieve the descriptive equality which had been vaunted since the early days of the dictionary.

Nevertheless, in keeping with beliefs in the fundamentally descriptive nature of linguistics (and, by extension, of lexicography too), Murray and his co-editors did not operate a consistent policy of discrimination. Furnivall's regular clippings from his morning newspaper which so pleased Murray's children swelled the citation files and in turn the evidence of the dictionary.[71] The *Daily News* still provides over 10,000 quotations in the published text, even if not all can be attributed to Furnivall's own assiduousness. Similarly, words such as *featherdom* (attested in *Harper's Magazine* in 1885) found a permanent home in Bradley's editing of *Fanged–Fee* in 1895, as did *frockless* from the *Daily News* (1880) which appeared in *Frank-law–Gain-coming* three years later. Bradley's liberality here should of course perhaps also be seen in the context of that 'abnormal' development of F which Murray as well as the Delegates decried.[72]

These processes of attrition as revealed by the proofs lead at times to what can now seem surprising decisions on where the lexicographical 'line' was to be drawn, especially after the trenchant discussions of the 1890s. Words which now seem incontestably 'core' items of vocabulary such as *landscaping*, *limeade*, and *lunching* were, for instance, all excised at various stages of the proofs. 'The lookers on . . . devote very little time to lunching', the *Saturday Review* had stated in 1880. 'The action of taking lunch' had been duly proffered as its definition in an entry which appeared in both the first and second proofs of the relevant fascicle. Renewed pressures of space in the first revise, however, prompted a fresh look at the material which had been included in this section of the text. Under the critical scrutiny which resulted, *lunching* suddenly appeared vulnerable, especially given its relative 'newness' as a lexical form (against, for example, other comparable forms such as *forgetting* and *forging* which were included in the text as finally published). Joining the other 'lost' words of the *OED*, the entry was excised in June 1903, evidently being declared outside the borders of 'Anglicity' for the purposes of the first edition. *Limeade*, attested in 1894 in the *Popular Science Monthly*, failed to survive beyond the first proof. 'Not in Dicts' states a handwritten annotation alongside this entry in the margin of

Bradley's proofs. It was a form of words which by no means operated as a commendation of originality. Even though one might have thought that this was a reason to include rather than exclude the form, the intent was instead to signal that the entry could be cut. Bradley obliged. Proving the truth of the lexicographical axiom that 'all decisions are reversible: a term may be too out-of-the-way one year, and yet demand inclusion the next',[73] motivated losses such as these, which could later be reversed in the *Supplements* of the twentieth century. *Lunching* was therefore included in the published dictionary in 1933 with a definition which provides a precise echo of that which had been deleted by Bradley so many years before: 'The action of taking lunch'. Given the temporal hiatus between these entries, it is perhaps only to be expected that similar continuities fail to extend to the accompanying citations. From a lexicographical (and linguistic) viewpoint, the difference is, however, significant. While 1920 stands in the 1933 *Supplement* (and hence *OED2*) as the date at which *lunching* was first used, the hidden history which the proofs reveal confirms a far earlier date, locating the word in a different century and antedating it by forty years – merely by means of that 'ephemeral' citation from the *Saturday Review* which had presumably in part contributed to its downfall.

Such disparities between different editions of the dictionary are common, further underscoring the continued validity of the proofs as evidence not merely for the history of the *OED* but equally for the history of the language in itself. *Landscaping* was another word which was to be restored to the record of the language by *OEDS*. Here Burchfield traced its first use in English to three years after the first edition of the *OED* had been completed. The proofs and revises once again tell a different story. Before pressures of space compelled Bradley to excise the word, he had assembled evidence which traced usage back to 1822, as in the citation from *Blackwood's Magazine* which had originally accompanied the entry: 'to those, into whose notions of interesting landscaping, trees and cultivated fields, and frequent cottages, invariably enter'. Under the reiterated demands to prune the dictionary more and more drastically, it was inevitable that some words would disappear where, with hindsight, ideally they should have been kept. Murray and his co-editors came to feel that the choice to include all words – formulated in the very *Proposal* on which the dictionary was based – was a luxury which was no longer open to them. 'Draw the line *against* doubtful candidates for admission', Murray had vowed, for example in 1892; undue latitude could no longer be afforded.[74] In a domain in which the authority of the dictionary was often popularly deemed to be authority for the existence – or otherwise – of words *per se*, the consequences of this practice could be serious. To *lose*, as a further sense of Bradley's definition states, could also mean 'to cause to be forgotten'. Though this was demonstrably not the case for words such as *lunching* and *landscaping* (the increasing currency of which made their absence from the dictionary a cause for comment), collective memory has no such record of words such as *life-preserving* (originally evidenced from the catalogue of the Great Exhibition of 1851 with reference to a prototype of the life-jacket) or of the adjectival uses of *gesticulate*. 'An eye unduly oppressed with gesticulate display is an evil in the same way', the writer on education Alexander Bain had maintained in 1855. The inventive use of *gossipiana* by which the *Sporting Magazine* in 1813 collectively designated 'items of gossip' has likewise been forgotten. Only the proofs (and the original texts from which such citations derive) record the existence of such words, just as they do that of *laconium*, used by the parliamentary orator and political thinker Edmund Burke to denote 'A laconic or pithy speech', or the ways in which *froudacious* took on a topical currency in the late nineteenth century as a synonym for 'lying'. For the reader who consults the *OED* today, the definitions, citations, and etymologies with which words such as these were once supplied have disappeared. Nothing remains to show the effort with which such entries were once researched and written – or the deliberation with which they eventually came to be excised.

Motivated attrition is, however, not restricted to entries which derive from popular journals and newspapers. While the usages of the 'best' writers were enthusiastically endorsed by the Delegates – and by Gibbs – certain reservations could attend those of writers who were, in various ways, considered as outside the canon of the great and good. The qualities – both linguistic and literary – of the popular Victorian novelist, Rhoda Broughton, were, for example, viewed with marked scepticism by Gibbs. Author of some thirty novels, she was, by definition, a 'hasty writer', Gibbs advised Murray. Surely this alone gave ample grounds for the exclusion of her 'slovenly' use of words such as *accentedest*. This was 'horrid', Gibbs declared: a 'solecism which should not find entrance'. The proper role of the dictionary was, he argued, to filter usage, discriminating between that which could be commended and that which was self-evidently 'inferior'.[75]

Murray's descriptive credentials in this instance were impeccable and he implacably resisted Gibbs's advice. The citation from Broughton's novel *Nancy* (1873) appears in the relevant entry without a trace of that subjective censure which Gibbs had desired to see: '"Algy!" repeat I, in a tone of the profoundest, accentedest surprise'. This, however, was in the relative liberality of the first fascicle. As pruning intensified in later sections of the dictionary, a certain pattern of selection does become apparent in the losses which are evidenced in the proofs. Nonce-words coined by Samuel Taylor Coleridge such as *literata* ('A learned or literary lady') are, for example, retained in the final form of the text. The underlying proof sheet nevertheless reveals the deletion of other words such as *literately* ('learnedly'), illustrated by a single citation from the minor eighteenth-century novelist, Elizabeth Griffiths. Comparisons may indeed be odious but they evidently came into play in instances such as these, placing Coleridge against Griffiths, and finding the latter wanting. *Forgivenness*, used by Adeline Whitney in her novel *Sights and Insights* of 1876 ('A soul . . . would feel blessedly its own redemption and forgivenness'), was similarly marked by Bradley as a suitable candidate for excision, although comparable words such as *lazarousness* and *likewiseness* are retained elsewhere in the dictionary. *Fringant* ('Of a horse; Springing about, capering, curvetting') exits in a similar way (1883, Lady Waterford in A. J. C. Hare, *Two Noble Lives*: 'There was her portrait – gallopping on a fringant horse, as I can remember her') yet *fringent* ('Exercising friction'), likewise illustrated by a single citation, remains. The fact that the latter was from the irreproachably canonical Emerson ('A shower of meteors . . . lit by fringent air, Blaze near and far') was again presumably not irrelevant. 'Mere silence – omitting a word or a meaning – is itself a kind of condemnation', as Roy Harris later contended.[76] Silence was, however, to be the allotted portion of many such casualties in the proofs. Words such as *grinny* ('full of grinning), *levify* ('to relieve'), and *lickersome* ('lecherous') were all excised, deriving from (respectively) Frank Stockton's *Pomona's Travels* of 1894 ('He looked as proud and grinny as if the rocks had been his own baby'), Richard Tomlinson's *Medicinal Dispensatory* of 1657 ('Conserve of violets . . . dilates and levifies [relieves] the jaws and asper artery'), and the Cambridge Platonist Henry More in 1656 ('Men of shallow minds and lickersome bodies, cleaving to the pleasures of the flesh').

Of course, even the so-called 'best' writers could experience rejection by the *OED*. *Grumble* as used figuratively by Ruskin in 1894 ('One never felt that one had got such a nasty thing as a conscience rustling and grumbling inside') was firmly marked for deletion by Bradley, and duly disappeared from the finished text. *Lecturation*, used by Dickens in a private letter in 1850, made a similar exit as did entries for *gloriful* (used by Meredith in his *Adventures of Harry Richmond* of 1871 to mean 'full of notions about glory') and *lightful* from John Bunyan's *Pilgrim's Progress* ('Tho' my heart was lightful and joyous before, yet it is ten times more lightsome and joyous now').[77] Losses such as these illustrate the general vulnerability that came to surround certain categories of words in the making of the dictionary. Figurative uses of words, given the infinite creativity of writers and speakers, could not hope to be treated exhaustively, though in the absences which become obvious when one compares proofs and final versions of the text, it is impossible to avoid regretting some of these decisions. The prominence of the railway as metaphor in nineteenth-century novels was, for instance, admirably extended in the figurative uses of *locomotive* illustrated only in the first proof of *Lock–Lyyn*. 'It takes a tremendous pull from the locomotive of circumstances to remove you from the roadside station which you had taken for the terminus', as the Scottish writer Andrew Boyd memorably declared in his *Lessons of Middle Age* of 1868. The original entry for the verb *lasso* offered similarly vivid illustration. Here nineteenth-century figures such as Oliver Wendell Holmes and the celebrated travel writer Mary Kingsley conspicuously antedate the figurative usage of this word which, according to the evidence of *OEDS* and *OED2,* is formally attested only in James Joyce. The evidence which the proofs provide is significantly different. 'Dr Henry Guillemord . . . has most kindly gone through the proof sheets, lassoing prepositions which were straying outside their sentence stockade', as Kingsley noted of the curbing of her own linguistic excesses in the prelude to the publication of her *Travels in West Africa* of 1897. Such figurative extensions of senses were, however, another category which Murray had been made to consider omitting entirely in the troubled discussions between Dictionary and Delegates over the 1890s. Even if undoubtedly interesting, such uses were, Murray conceded, 'merely matters of rhetoric, always possible and not needing special mention'. If words had to be cut, these were obviously prime candidates.[78] Given this policy, we should perhaps be grateful that any survived at all.

Creative Vulnerabilities

Words given as 'nonce' formations in the dictionary could reveal a corresponding vulnerability. Like 'Anglicity', the notion of the 'nonce-word' ('the term used in this Dictionary to describe a word which is apparently used only for the nonce') was itself invented by Murray. It was one to which he often had recourse throughout its many pages. First appearing in the entry for *anotherness*, it was used to signify deliberate and *ad hoc* creations, lexical coinages which are confined to the contexts for which they were originally devised. Here, for example, belong Mary Braddon's *Cinderella-ship* and Tobias Smollett's *goutification*, freshly minted by their respective authors for particular literary purposes, and conveying shades of meaning which existing English words evidently failed to signify. Such formations were justly considered as lying on the borders of the language, their very nature as uniquely individual uses rendering them far from that 'common core' which Murray and his co-editors were above all committed to recording. This was certainly the view of the Delegates. 'Words coined for the nonce can hardly be worth recording unless the writer's authority is so great as to lead to the permanent adoption of any word he uses', Murray was informed in 1896.[79] 'It appears to the Delegates that it has become necessary to lay down more definitely the principles on which the compilation of the Dictionary ought to proceed', the letter autocratically dictated, stressing once again the need for compression. In the various trials and difficulties which surrounded the *OED* in the 1890s, both editors were forced to consider such objections as the basis of an explicit policy of exclusion. 'Omit curiosities of sense & accidental or peculiar senses used by single writers', Murray wrote to Furnivall, expounding another new lexicographical resolution for the future. 'Aim at doing everything less fully & exhaustively', he added. 'Always consider whether any particular thing is worth the time it would take'.[80]

Such maxims reveal the line which Murray felt himself up against as well as – in terms of the practical realities of the dictionary – that other line which, with far greater restrictiveness, he and his co-workers henceforth had to draw. In terms of words deemed *nonce*, it is these maxims which, at least in part, underlie the loss of Meredith's *gloriful*, Dickens's *lecturation*, and Robert Surtees's *liegeous*. 'The Queen she is my liegeous queen', as Surtees had written in his poem 'Claxton's Lament'. Though Robert Burchfield in the twentieth century has contended that nonce-formations of this kind were admitted into the dictionary in a pattern of inclusion which was ultimately determined 'as much by the choice made by the readers as [by] an abstract principle adopted by the editors', arguing further that if a reader made a slip for a given word of this kind, it was, as a result, 'likely to be included', the evidence of the proofs again suggests otherwise.[81] Nonce-words instead emerge as highly vulnerable to the processes of editorial pruning. Nothing, for example, remains in the published text of earlier entries such as *loftify* ('to make lofty') or *latinically*, invented respectively by the anonymous author of a 1669 *Address to the English Gentry* and an early nineteenth-century writer in *Blackwood's Magazine*, or of *lagster* ('One who lags behind', used in 1837 by Capel Lofft in the first volume of his *Self-formation; or, The History of an Individual Mind*). The use of *goddess* as a verb ('to make a divinity of, to call "goddess"') provides a further example of such attrition in the proofs, here in the work of the minor poet, Alexander Rodger. Losses of this kind further confirm that form of literary privileging which, as Jürgen Schäfer and others have argued, often seems to pervade the dictionary's evidence. The omission of words is, for Schäfer, 'one of the most salient examples of literary bias', constituting a pattern of 'preferential treatment' which undermines the kind of linguistic even-handedness which one theoretically expects from a dictionary such as the *OED*.[82] As with the lexis of taboo, a further set of cultural filters could evidently be applied in this context. And as the proofs reveal, it was on the whole the verbal inventiveness of authors regarded as being outside the spectrum of 'greatness' that bore the brunt of this process. *Lanarian* ('Wool-clad') used by Edward Ward, a tavern-keeper as well as the writer of *Vulgus Britannicus; or, the British Hudibras* (1710), was, for instance, excised at proof stage,[83] along with *formicologist* ('One who makes a study of ants') from E. H. Aitken's *A Naturalist on the Prowl* of 1894. R. D. Blackmore's *legsome* likewise disappeared before publication of the finished text. 'Convenient for the legs', the accompanying definition had originally stated alongside a citation from Blackmore's *Christowel* of 1881: 'They spread out their own noble bodies on the handy, or perhaps rather legsome, height of the low wall'. Charles Russell Lowell's sceptical coinage of *lazyship* (on analogy with *fellowship*) likewise failed to survive the pressures of editing at this stage, in spite of the carefully crafted definition which it had originally possessed: 'a position in a college endowed with certain emoluments on the condition of being lazy'. *Forestian*, deployed with deliberate creativity by the writer Anna Seward ('the images . . . so truly forestian, if I may be allowed the . . . coinage'), and *leather-jacket*, used in the journal *Lights and Shades* in 1828 to mean 'a covering of skin' ('Features which fitted their leather-jacket so tightly that one would have thought that it had shrunk from washing'), were other casualties of the need to curb the dictionary's scale. None of these could be said to come into the category of those 'giants of literature who formed our language', as Marghanita Laski described the dominant impression gained from reading the final form of the *OED*.[84] The Renaissance coinage of *leathern*, for instance, was evidently deemed to possess qualities which the excised *leather-jacket* lacked.

Supported by a 1596 citation from *Edward III* ('Since leathern Adam till this youngest hour'), the former had a validity which accorded well with the desires of the Delegates and the historical principles of the dictionary. Yet alongside the continued presence of, say, *gipseian* ('belonging to gipsies') as used by Fielding or Thomas de Quincey's *gluttonism* ('The practice of being a glutton') stand the rejected verbal ingenuities of those whose canonical status was far more open to question. The paucity of the twenty-one citations from Richard Blackmore which appear in the published text of the *OED* – in spite of the contemporary popularity of his fourteen novels, including *Lorna Doone* (1869) – is in itself a telling illustration of the imbalances in evidence which can occur, exacerbated, as here, by the losses which editing was additionally forced to impose. Blackmore's popularity was regularly set alongside stylistic traits which were less positively received. Charges of 'obscurity, want of proportion, involution of diction, and prolixity' attended the initial reception of his novel *Cradock Nowell*, prompting Blackmore to issue the second edition with a title page which announced that the work had been 'diligently revised and reshaped'.[85]

The lost words of the proofs here tend to bear out the somewhat trenchant criticisms of the linguist Roy Harris. Writing in the *Times Literary Supplement* in 1982 of the ways in which the originally 'radical initiative' of the *OED* had, over time, been forced to succumb 'to compromise and Establishment assimilation', Harris was eloquent on the binarisms which could emerge. Creativity was, he contended, Janus-like in terms of the variable attention which could be paid to it in the pages of the dictionary. 'If you happened to be a famous author, you could take the liberty of inventing a word, or cribbing one from a foreign language, and your boldness was likely to be held to "enrich" the English language', Harris argued. On the other hand, 'if you were just a reporter writing for the local paper, or a civil servant drafting a document, you apparently had no business introducing new words at all, however useful.'[86] Though this may be to overstate the case, Harris nevertheless has an undeniable point and one which is supported over and over again by the proofs. *Greyhoundy*, a nonce-formation from the popular weekly journal *Black & White* ('A wiry, light-fleshed filly of the greyhoundy type'), is deleted while Coleridge's *linguipotence*, though tentatively defined ('? Mastery with the tongue, or of languages'), is decisively included. *Longhander,* used with deliberate verbal ingenuity in William Hanna's biography of the theologian Thomas Chalmers, and *grannyism*, evocatively deployed by Henry Hudson as he took Polonius to task in his critical analysis of Shakespeare's *Hamlet* in

1879 ('What a precious, characteristic specimen of unconscious grannyism he blunders out'), were both to disappear. From the point of view of the purely descriptive, such words are – linguistically – equal to the thousands which were retained. A sense of verbal hierarchy and differential value, based on ideological notions of culture and canonicity, instead, at times, informed the pragmatically necessary processes of loss in the proofs.

Yet, if we look more closely at Harris's words as they relate to the making of the dictionary, we find that words such as these were not regarded as inferior *per se* by Murray, Bradley, or the other editors, even if Trench in the early history of the dictionary may have had his doubts on this score.[87] On the contrary, usages of this kind – and from these sources – appear in considerable numbers in the early versions of the dictionary. Charles Mansfield's *learnerhood* and the *luniversary* of Oliver Wendell Holmes's popular *Autocrat of the Breakfast Table* (defined as 'the day of the month on which something recurs') here take their place alongside the creative forms of writers such as Coleridge and Carlyle. But under the constant pressures to cut and 'prune', the former rather than the latter came to be viewed as more expendable. Yet countless examples do remain. It is, in this sense, a relative estimation of worth rather than an absolute, and one which tended to come into play at specific points in the dictionary's making – especially when the pressures of available space and available material seemed particularly irreconcilable. It was, however, a process that was endorsed by the Delegates as well as by a significant number of those who read and reviewed the dictionary. Picking and choosing again came to be an essential part of the editorial process. That the end result is skewed in terms of the written evidence which remain is undeniable, obscuring in the published pages of the dictionary that greater liberality that the first versions of the dictionary originally maintained.

Aliens and Englishness

As the dictionary advanced, it seemed that words increasingly had to merit inclusion, to earn their place within the borders of what was to be designated 'English'. 'Worth the space?' Murray queries in the margin of Bradley's entry for *loosening-bar* ('a stiff iron bar used in metal founding and moulding, which serves to loosen the pattern slightly in the sand'). His comment no doubt influenced its subsequent deletion. 'The word is good enough, but the quot. is absurd', Murray had similarly noted on the first revise of *gorgonesque* ('Having the characteristics of a gorgon: hideous, repulsive').[88] 'Very ugly', he commented against *glideness*, coined by Henry Sweet in his *History of English Sounds* in 1888 ('Glideness and nonsyllabicness generally go together'), a word which in response was to make an all too fleeting appearance in the text. Those who acted in the capacity of critical readers for the dictionary sometimes shared these evaluative considerations: 'This is the sort of word which one should save on', Skeat wrote alongside *opossum*, although in this instance Murray chose to disregard his advice. As such comments indicate, the principles at stake increasingly came to be not inclusiveness *per se* but instead what Henry Bradley referred to as 'entitlement' – the essentially relative claims of a word to merit a place in the *OED*. 'It has sometimes happened that Americanisms, and also slang words, have found a place in the Dictionary to which they were not entitled', he wrote as part of the renegotiations on the contents of the dictionary which occupied so many letters and discussions with the Press in 1896. 'Against the occurrence of such oversight I will try to be more watchful', Bradley resolved, striving to reassure the Delegates of his future diligence in this respect.[89] *Entitle*, formally defined in *E–Every*, informs his own usage here. 'To give (a person or thing) a rightful claim *to* a possession, privilege, designation, mode of treatment, etc', Bradley's earlier definition had stated. It is this which underpins his comments on the limits of lexicographical inclusivity, and not least as they came to apply to determining the precise nature of 'Anglicity'. Words had to deserve recording; entry into the dictionary was a privilege which not all would receive.

Yet conceptions of 'Anglicity' were challenged by the very nature of English and its traditional hospitality to words from other countries and other lands. The Norman Conquest had led to thousands of words transforming the native word-hoard, not merely adding to its nuances with loans such as *courteous* and *virtue*, *inspire* and *courage*, but also displacing items of core vocabulary so that, for instance, long-held concepts of *kynde* transformed in favour of *nature* (deriving from Latin *nātūra*, and borrowed from French, with usage attested in English from the thirteenth century). Such shifts were merely part of a general pattern of borrowing which henceforth characterized English. *Dedicate*, *encyclopaedia*, and *mature* are recorded from the sixteenth century; loan words such as *devote*, *castigate*, and *restoration* emerge in the next. In the eighteenth century terms such as *casserole*, *bouquet*, and *coterie* come to the fore, all courtesy of French. The nineteenth century was no different. Yet here again the dictionary-maker would be called upon to judge, trying to discriminate between the claims of recent loans such as *grès* and *gros de naples*, *guimpe* and *gros-bleu*, all of which were attested and used in nineteenth-century English. Hence while time had dignified borrowings such as *people* (from Old French and Anglo-Norman *peuple*) and *famous* (from Old French *fameux*), duly conferring the quality of undisputed 'Anglicity', other – more recent – loans presented real problems. Was *grillo*, which had been defined in the first proof of *Green–Gyzzarn* as 'A grasshopper', to be seen as 'English' or not? It had been used by Southey who, being born in Bristol (and educated at Westminster School and Oxford), was himself undeniably English – but did this make *grillo* 'English' as a result ? What about *grillino* ('A little cricket'), deployed by Elizabeth Barrett Browning whose native descent was similarly incontestable? And what about *fräuleincy*, used with panache in an early nineteenth-century edition of *Fraser's Magazine*?

As the proofs reveal, such questions had no easy answers. *Fräuleincy*, *grillino*, and *grillo* all had entries drafted for them, appearing in print in the early stages of the dictionary. All, however, subsequently disappeared from the final versions of the text. The *Pall Mall Gazette* similarly commented on the 'omnipresent' *guimpe* in 1896. As a kind of chemisette with a low or square-necked dress, it was 'an incomparable item', the paper declared. Assumptions about its omnipresence were nevertheless presumably challenged by Bradley's decision to exclude the entry (together with the eloquence of the *Pall Mall* citation) in the first revise of *Green–Gyzzarn* in July 1900. Of the entries for *gros-bleu* ('Of a dark blue', attested in the *Daily News* in 1894 and 1899), *gros de Naples* ('A heavy silk fabric, made originally at Naples', attested since 1828), and *gros-grain* ('A strong corded silk fabric', for which citations were available only since 1900), only *gros de Naples* survived: while all had originally appeared on the same sheet in proofs, *gros de Naples* alone made its way into the published fascicle. Nevertheless, confirming the continual flux of both language and lexicography once more, William Craigie and Charles Onions would reinsert *gros-grain* (and indeed *guimpe*) in the *Supplement* to the *OED* published in 1933; Robert Burchfield later reinserted *gros bleu* in his own *Supplement* published in 1972. *Grès* ('grit, sandstone') experienced a similar about-turn as Bradley again changed his mind at proof stage on where 'English' might be said to end. Citations which had spanned half of the nineteenth century were suddenly deleted as *grès* was forced outside the margins of the language set by the first edition of the *OED*. The process which Bradley referred to as 'legitimate reduction' was evidently once again at work.

Yet again a marked sense of arbitrariness seems to govern the losses which were being made. Words which in one version of the text are declared to be part of the language are excised at the next. Glimpses of the 'completeness' which could have been are undermined by the compromises being enforced. In the peculiarly nationalist rhetoric which Murray deployed in this context, loan words came to engage in a tripartite division of 'aliens', 'denizens', and 'naturals'. Aliens in this sense were words 'from one language used but not naturalized in another language', a meaning parasitically illustrated in the *Dictionary* by Murray's own 'General Explanations' (1884, *New Eng. Dict.* p. ix: '*Aliens* are names of foreign objects, titles, etc., which we require often to use, and for which we have no native equivalents'). 'Naturals' signified the converse, suggesting complete assimilation into the native language and a level of integration shared only with those words which have always – and naturally – been 'English'. 'Denizens' were deemed to occupy an intermediate position, being naturalized in terms of their use in English yet – as with words such as *table d'hôte* or *tête-à-tête* – still retaining traces of 'otherness' in their spelling, pronunciation, or form. The notion of 'naturalization' was crucial to all three. *Naturalize*: 'To admit (an alien) to the position and rights of citizenship; to invest with the privileges of a native-born subject', as William Craigie defined the word in the fascicle *N–Niche*. Words not naturalized thus have no such privileges and, as *grillo* and *grillino* confirm, even their rights as 'aliens' within the language – as least as represented in the dictionary – were likely to be withdrawn with scarcely a moment's notice. Naturalization could appear similarly arbitrary in its operation. *Lugubre* ('lugubrious') was naturalized according to the first proof, received a]] (the marker used in the dictionary to designate 'alien' status) in the first revise, yet had apparently been naturalized once more by the time the fascicle went to press. As the final entry states: '† **lugubre**, *a. Obs.* [a. F. *lugubre*, ad. L. *lūgubris*, f. *lūgēre* to mourn]. Lugubrious. **1727** Lady M. W. Montagu *Let. to C'tess Mar* July. You see my philosophy is not so lugubre as yours.'

Though the rhetoric of naturalization in the *OED* can operate in ideological constructions which may now seem disturbing in their wider implications, its basic premisses were in some ways sound. As Henry Hucks Gibbs insisted on the proofs of *frotteur*, a word to which Bradley had originally devoted nine lines of text as well as two sense-divisions ('One who rubs a patient after a bath'; 'One who waxes and rubs floors with a brush'), for such words to be included one had to be sure that they really were being used as an integral element of the language – and not just providing a spot of 'local colour' in ways that rendered them explicitly (and intentionally) 'non-English'. In Gibbs's view, the latter applied to *frotteur*. 'All foreign words used in description of their own country should vanish', as he dictated, setting out another general principle for the further compression of the *OED*.[90] Bradley, after reconsidering the entry for *frotteur*, concurred. He excised the word and cast it beyond the line of the native language. The same was true of Southey's *grillo* and Elizabeth Barrett Browning's *grillino*. Both were deemed merely lexical souvenirs of residence abroad and did not as a result survive their respective proofs. *Lomi-lomi* (enigmatically defined as 'The shampooing practised among the Hawaiians') and, say, *liang* ('A Chinese weight, about 1⅓oz. avoirdupois; this weight in silver as a money of account') were presumably in some sense felt to be different since both were retained – even if one could perhaps conceivably argue the same kind of 'difference' for *gros-bleu* which, as we have seen, failed to survive the process of editing. Other entries which are still present in the dictionary, such as that for *likin* ('a Chinese provincial transit duty'), can likewise seem anomalous (1876, *Agreement of Chefoo*: 'The amount of likin to be collected will be decided by the different Provincial Governments'). Absolute consistency in a work of the size of the *OED*, like the image of inclusiveness, was a domain where ideal and reality would often diverge.

Feelings about the inclusion of words of this kind could run high. Gibbs was overt about his own antipathies, denouncing *cahier* and *ça* as 'vermin' which should deservedly be eliminated from the dictionary.[91] Similar instances of linguistic xenophobia could emanate from the Delegates as well as from the popular press. Such proscriptions were often deliberately ignored in the making of the dictionary. *Cahier*, Murray decided, merited not extermination but a five-line entry in the relevant fascicle (even if this included the statement 'Hardly in English use'). *Garçon*, likewise proscribed by Gibbs ('I don't think this is admissible unless you have a true *English* example. This one is French'), was granted a similar format in spite of Gibbs's censure of the only citation which Bradley was able to provide: 'Here we dined, and were charged four francs for dinner, besides sous to the garçon' from a letter in 1839.[92] Words of this order were often literally on the margins of the language and their lexicographical vulnerability was particularly evident when they had been borrowed in the final decades of the nineteenth century or, with reference to later fascicles, in the early years of the twentieth. Who, after all, could be sure that these were not merely transient transfers, briefly used in English and then – at some later stage – simply excluded once again? In the practical realities of editing the *OED*, this became the criterion according to which non-native words did indeed regularly become subject to loss. The record of what might initially have been declared 'English' tended to shift as the dictionary advanced, in favour of a more restrictive process governed not by the borders of the language but, once again, by the ever-rigid boundaries of the printed page. The liberalities whereby *greeven* ('A Russian coin') and *groot* ('A silver coin worth something more than the English groat') were initially accepted – if as 'aliens' – into the proofs and revises are thus not mirrored in the final forms of the text, even if other, seemingly parallel terms such as *angelot* ('A French gold coin struck by Louis XI'), *bajocco* ('A small Italian copper coin (now obsolete)'), or *crusado* ('A Portuguese coin bearing the figure of a cross'), had survived in earlier fascicles. Similar losses can be traced in the first revise of *L–Lap*, reversing the linguistic citizenship originally conferred on *lagniappe* ('Something given to a purchaser; a present from a tradesman to a customer') or, in the revises of *Lief–Lock*, that once accorded to *liquidogenic* ('That produces a liquid') which derived from French.[93] Again the lexicographer was forced to pick and choose, to select and to reject – even if such activities were antithetical to those which Trench had originally proposed.

As Rosemarie Morgan has written of the changes which the novelist Thomas Hardy was compelled to make at the proof stage of *Far From the Madding Crowd*, it is not always easy or indeed even possible to distinguish between the 'willing' and the 'unwilling' revising hand.[94] The same is of course equally true of the revisions which were made in relation to the cancelled words of the *OED*. That many such changes were 'unwilling' – or willed by external pressures rather than the internal desiderata of the language or the dictionary-maker – is evident in Murray's own comments on the pain which loss of this nature caused him. 'No one knows as well as I do, how it grieves one to have to do this', he confessed.[95] As Murray explained to Fitzedward Hall, 'we are compelled to save in every possible direction, & omit whatever we can'.[96] This was the refrain which accompanied much of the making of the dictionary, driving Murray to alternate outbursts of anger and despair. His frustration could be tangible as he set in motion those compromises which the very editing of the dictionary forced him to make, irredeemably changing his vision of what the dictionary, in other and better times, might perhaps have been. Regional words, in relation to which he had once declared his intention to be '*as liberal as possible* in their inclusion', thus came to be treated with greater stringency as the dictionary advanced.[97] Loss rather than gain was to be encouraged in this respect too in spite of the conflicts thereby introduced with the founding principles of the dictionary.[98] Craigie had to be instructed to exercise due caution here just as he did with the treatment of Scottish words. Only the 'bare minimum' could henceforth be included, Murray instructed in 1901, noting that he was now excluding them 'rigidly' in his work on K, in contradistinction to the 'laxity' evident in earlier parts of the *OED*.[99]

While Murray strove to cut the excesses of K, Bradley worked in parallel at G. Words such as *glowbason* ('a glow-worm'), *grohman* ('a sea-bream about two thirds grown'), *glammach* ('a voracious bite), and *gosky* ('rank, luxuriant') disappeared from the drafts of the dictionary. *Glock* ('To gurgle, of liquid escaping from a bottle'), *goody* ('to thrive'), and *gluther* ('a rising or falling of the throat, a guggling sound in it') provide further examples. American words came under the same edict, leading to the loss of such distinctive words as *funkify* ('to frighten', used in Haliburton's *Sam Slick in England* of 1844: 'He might have knowed how to feel for other folks, and not funkify them so peskily'), *giggobble* ('To make a noise like a turkey-cock'), and *lap* ('Of a bear: To gather berries while seated in the lap or fork of a tree'). Even obsolete words could feel the cut of the editorial pen, in spite of the historical principles on which the dictionary was founded: *groundle* ('fundamental, chief, main', used by Cardinal Reginald Pole in 1538), *forgement* ('Something forged, a forged statement') used by the Royalist poet Alexander Brome, and *ligement* ('An alleviation, a lightening') used by Malory were all lost in similar ways. *Lie-child* used by Charles Lamb in his *Essays of Elia* (1823) as a further synonym for illegitimacy ('The devil . . . jealous possibly of any lie-children not his own'), *godele* ('to slander', from the *Ayenbite of Inwyt* in 1340) and *loathed-loving* used by Sidney in his *Arcadia*, as well as *forelie* ('To lie or be placed in front') used by Spenser in the *Faerie Queene*, suffered the same fate. The ideals by which the dictionary was 'intended to contain *all* words English in form that have been in use since the beginning of the 12th century', as Murray stated in early versions of his Preface to the first part of the dictionary, were again subject to reassessment. Even historical principles would not invariably hold firm.

It was in this way that the image of exhaustiveness faded into the past, a consequence of the manifold difficulties which attended the writing of a dictionary on the scale of the *OED*. Fascicles had to be finite even if the language was not; each time some words would be selected and others excluded. 'One of the most serious difficulties was to know which words should be put in and what should not', as Murray informed his audience in the speech he gave after the celebratory dinner in honour of the dictionary's dedication to Queen Victoria in 1897.[100] If the rhetoric of completeness remained, it was therefore in an inevitably restated form. It was this which Stanley Baldwin, Conservative Prime Minister of His Majesty's government, celebrated upon completion of the first edition of the *OED* in 1928, lauding the national achievement of England and English in a work 'unrivalled in completeness and unapproachable in authority'. It is this which in turn appears in modern accounts of the dictionary that once impossibly promised to be a 'complete inventory'. It presents a 'comprehensive history of the English language', Berg notes;[101] it is 'sufficiently complete', Burchfield affirms.[102] 'Characterised by comprehension; having the attribute of comprising or including much', Murray stated in his entry for *comprehensive* in 1891, little knowing that it was this which, in one sense, would stand as the final accolade for the dictionary on which he spent his life.

CHAPTER 4

Science and the Principles of Selection

It was, James Murray wrote in 1900, the 'scientific spirit' of the nineteenth century which had both 'called for and rendered possible the *Oxford English Dictionary*'.[1] Science was in this sense made central to the *OED*'s achievements and execution, as is evident in the tenor and content of its entries and explicitly stated on its title pages ('edited by James A. H. Murray . . . With the Assistance of many Scholars and Men of Science'). Whereas Johnson in 1755 had seen the writing of dictionaries as an art and his own role as that of 'a poet doomed . . . to wake a lexicographer',[2] Murray firmly disclaimed the relevance of non-scientific knowledge for the aspiring writer of dictionaries. As he searched for a new assistant in 1889, he stressed that what was needed was 'a *logical* man accustomed to *scientific* accuracy of method'. Literary attainments were dismissed as peripheral. These 'give no special preparation', Murray stated – someone who had studied with the philologist Eduard Sievers in Leipzig would be much better, as would a scholar who had worked on comparative linguistics with Julius Zupitza in Berlin. His own opinion was clear: 'if a man has studied *language*, and knows something of Germanic and Romantic philology he is much more promising'.[3]

Earlier lexicography was brushed aside as merely 'pre-scientific' with all the failings which this implied. Much to its demerit it was, for instance, as 'pre-scientific philology' that Murray chose to dismiss Johnson's *Dictionary*. Written in an era when 'real analogies were overlooked, and superficial resemblances too easily seized',[4] it was this which underpinned its weaknesses and set a pointer for the scientific reorientation of the *OED*, a lexicographic enterprise in which empirical observation would take the place of *ipse dixit* leaps into the dark. No longer would it be tenable to suggest an etymology for *peacock*, as Johnson had done, based on the belief that it might be explained as 'peak cock, from the tuft of feathers on its head; the peak of women being an ancient ornament'. Instead, as the *OED* scientifically confirmed, *peacock* can be traced back through the diachronic stages of English into its origins in other languages: *páwa* in Old English, deriving from *pāva* ('pea-hen') in Latin, in an entirely objective and verifiable account of its forms. Similar was Johnson's entry for *caterpillar*, the etymology of which displayed obvious weaknesses. 'It seems easily deducible from *cates*, food, and *piller*, Fr[ench] to rob; the animal that eats up the fruits of the earth', Johnson had emphatically declared. The *OED* again tells an entirely different story in which density of philological discourse displaces the conjectures of the past. In the scientific exactitude which results, *caterpillar* is instead 'generally compared with the synonymous Old French *chatepelose*, lit. "hairy or downy cat" . . . of which the Old Norman French would be *catepelose*. This is a possible source, though no connexion is historically established: the final sibilant might be treated in English as a plural formative, and the supposed singular *catepelo* would be readily associated with the well-known word *piller*, *pilour*, pillager, plunderer, spoiler . . .'. If the incidental charm of Johnson's entries disappears, then so too does their inaccuracy, their etymological fallibility. 'One does not look in Johnson for Etymology, any more than in 18th c[entury] writers for biology or electricity', Murray averred.[5]

As the selected terms of Murray's analogy suggest, both biology and electricity offered conspicuous examples of the kind of intellectual transformation which had been taking place over the nineteenth century. *Biology*, for instance, had formally come into existence in 1819. Its inception was precisely located in the relevant fascicle of the *OED* in William Lawrence's *Lectures on Physiology, Zoology, and the Natural History of Man*. 'A foreign writer has proposed the more accurate term of biology, or science of life', Lawrence had written, discussing the generic status of his subject. 'The term Biology . . . has of late become not uncommon, among good writers', confirmed the great scientist William Whewell of Trinity College, Cambridge, some thirty years later. Like many other expanding areas of research, biology was a new branch of knowledge requiring new lexical recognition as well as a new vocabulary in which its discoveries could be formulated and its discussions carried on. As the *OED* confirmed, the same was true of *ethnology* (1819), *palaeontology* (1838), *embryology* (1859, in Darwin's *Origin of Species*), *gynaecology* (1867), *fungology* (the science of fungi, 1860), and *anthropology* (in its more specialized scientific sense from 1861). All are precisely dated and verified in the new dictionary of the Philological Society. Dickens, with characteristic acuity, was to depict the nineteenth century as one dominated by *ologies* ('any one of the various sciences or departments of science', as the *OED* in turn specified). Like *biology* or *petrology* ('the science of stones', dated to 1811 in Murray's fascicle *Pennage–Pfennig*), *ology* was itself to stand as a significant creation of the time. 'Ologies of all kinds from morning to night', Mrs Gradgrind duly states in Dickens's *Hard Times* of 1854, commenting in despair on their omnipresence in the early education of the Gradgrind children: 'If there is an Ology left, of any description, that has not been worn to rags in this house, all I can say is, I hope I never hear its name.'[6] *Morphology* (1830), *glaciology* (1892), as well as the nineteenth century preoccupation with *phrenology* (the study of the mental faculties based on the external formation of the cranium), prove other examples of this trend. All would be meticulously recorded in the *OED*. As here, scientific and lexical developments often operated in parallel and the speed of change could be remarkable. 'In a morning's work I turned out ten genera of vertebrate animals of which five are certainly new,' wrote Darwin's contemporary, the wide-ranging scientist Thomas Henry Huxley; 'of these four are Labyrinthodonts, amphibia of new types . . . baptised *Ophiderpeton*, *Lepterpeton*, *Ichthyerpeton*, *Keraterpeton*.'[7] As Huxley proved, even a few hours could stretch the resources of the language, stretching too the data open to lexicographers and the decisions on inclusion or exclusion that had to be made.

In the nineteenth century, the potential reverberations of this interweaving of science, labelling, and language were immense. Scores of seminal scientific advances – and the new designations by which they were to be known – are observable. Faraday's discovery of *electromagnetic induction* is dated to 1831, *thermodynamics* had its beginnings in the 1850s; Edison invented the *phonograph* in 1877 and began work on the *electric light* in the following year. Alexander Graham Bell's 'Electrical Speaking Telephone' was introduced in 1876, gradually transforming the nature of what could be achieved in terms of communication. Darwin's own work on evolution and natural selection began its published history in 1859 (though the first formulations of his ideas can be traced to the late 1830s). Like countless others, he too was 'telling a new story against the grain of the language available to tell it in',[8] changing that language irretrievably as the story itself evolved. Moreover, as other discoveries served to confirm, there were innumerable 'new stories' which needed to be communicated. 'I must beg leave to propose a separate technical name "chromosome"', as the German anatomist Heinrich Waldeyer stated in 1889. In this instance, however, the advance thus announced proved fractionally too late for the first edition of the *OED*. In yet another of the hazards which could attend serial publication, the relevant fascicle *Cast–Clivy* had been published earlier in that same year. In spite of its nineteenth-century foundations, over forty years would intervene before it gained a place in the *Supplement* of 1933. The fascicle *X–Zygt*, published in 1921, was, however, late enough to be able to include *X-rays*, discovered and duly named by Wilhelm Röntgen in 1895; similarly *radioactivity*, discovered by Henri Becquerel one year later, appeared in *Q–Ree* in July 1904. *Radium* as a new radioactive substance was christened in 1899. According to the *Daily Mail* four years later, its advent opened the door 'to something like a new world of science' even if it was one which, in this instance, failed to be reflected in the dictionary. William Craigie wrongly judged it (on Murray's advice) to be a potentially ephemeral coinage, making it yet another of the 'lost words' of the first edition.[9]

Scientific discourse was evidently prolific, and its dominance was affirmed by its refusal to be consigned to the abstruse proclamations of journals or learned bodies. Instead, in a term which itself derives from Darwin (as Murray would meticulously verify in *Consignificant–Crouching* in 1893), science engaged in a productive series of 'cross-fertilizations' with literary and popular culture,[10] its debates and discoveries filtered into the pages of nineteenth-century novels or the topics covered in working men's clubs. It is, for example, contemporary advances in medicine which provide the context for Lydgate's initial triumphs as a doctor in George Eliot's *Middlemarch*. Lydgate's adoption of the stethoscope (invented in 1820 and so dated in *OED*) carefully sets him apart from traditional Middlemarch practitioners who, as Eliot stresses, continued to rely on the doubtful (and ultimately unscientific) efficacy of 'bleeding and blistering and starving'.[11] In a similar emphasis, the zoological expeditions and discoveries of 'the famous traveller – the scientific Mr Hamley' provide a fictional version of Darwin's early life in Elizabeth Gaskell's *Wives and Daughters*, serialized in the *Cornhill Magazine* from August 1864. The original audience of the novel gained a new familiarity with the terms of comparative osteology and anatomy, as well as an entirely contemporary emphasis on the 'classification of facts'.[12] One year earlier, the new evolutionary principles had found a home in Charles Kingsley's *Water Babies*. 'I am not going to trouble myself to make things . . . I sit here and make them make themselves', Mother Nature is made to declare.[13] Thomas Hardy meanwhile invested geology with similar significance in *A Pair of Blue Eyes* (1873). 'The eyes, dead and turned to stone, were even now regarding him. It was one of the early crustaceans called Trilobites. Separated by millions of years in their lives, Knight and this underling seemed to have met in the place of death', Hardy wrote in his memorable account of Henry Knight's encounter with a fossilized trilobite as he clung to the precipice on the 'Cliff without a Name'.[14] It was geology too, and its wide-ranging implications for the human understanding of time and faith, that infused George Gissing's *Born in Exile* of 1892 and the crises of doubt and religious hypocrisy which it records. As its central character, Godwin Peak, demanded: 'What could be said of a man who had devoted his life to geology, and still (in the year 1884) remained an orthodox member of the Church of England?'[15] Science in this sense clearly had a significance which went beyond the formal principles of discovery and the language in which it was framed. As in the recent discoveries of palaeontology – or Richard Owen's formulation of the term *dinosaur* in 1841 – science had the potential to disturb the traditional paradigms of the past, giving history itself an extended scope which could no longer be encapsulated in Archbishop Ussher's biblically truncated time-scale of 6,000 years since the creation of the world.[16]

Apart from the seemingly endless flow of nineteenth-century neologisms such as *magneto-electricity* (going back to Faraday in 1833), *genetic* (dated to 1831), or *gersdorffite* (a mineral named in 1842), it was perhaps these new understandings of time and change which were to link language and science most closely, providing an obvious relevance for the newly articulated principles of the dictionary. 'Language is fossil poetry', Emerson had written in 1844,[17] providing a figurative extension for those palaeontological discoveries which inspired Dickens (as in his celebrated opening of *Bleak House*)[18] and, in different ways, preoccupied scientists such as Owen, Darwin, and Huxley. Philology demonstrated unmistakable affinities with the new paradigms of evolutionary thinking. 'We cannot doubt that language is an altering element', as Darwin himself wrote, musing on the apparent flux of verbal form; 'we see words invented – we see their origin in names of People – Sound of words . . . often show traces of origin.'[19] Changes of this kind provided a recurrent topic of conversation between Darwin and his cousin, the etymologist Hensleigh Wedgwood who, as a prominent member of the Philological Society, was also involved in the early years of the *OED*.[20] Words in 'everyday use', Darwin reflected, 'have been worn, until, like pebbles on the beach, they have lost every corner and distinctive mark, & hardly a vestige remains to indicate their original form'.[21] As Darwin realized, comparative philology tracked missing links between languages, tracing hitherto undiscovered linguistic relationships, just as – in geology – the discovery of fossils such as *archaeopteryx* (a bird with teeth and a long vertebrate tail, first recorded in the *OED* from Darwin's *Origin of Species*) provided other 'missing links' in the history of physical forms. The wider implications in the case of archaeopteryx were disturbingly clear. Like language, it appeared to confirm an evolutionary past in which change and flux were undeniable, unsettling traditional beliefs in the divinely created immutability of all living forms.

The historical thrust of the new dictionary was to prove responsive to these wide-ranging shifts in scientific thinking and its expression. After all, each and every entry in the dictionary imaged forth the effects of time and the very absence of immutability which attended the forms of speech. Even a word such as *silly* could be shown to display a complex linguistic history, the apparent stability of its modern spelling merely serving to conceal the diversities of the past. As Murray stressed, the lexicographer was an archaeologist of language whose research served to uncover these hidden strata: Old English *sælig*, later *seli(e)*, *sely*, *sele*, *celly*, *selli*, *syly*, *sylie*, *silie*, *sily*, *cillie*, *sillie* (among others). The range of meanings observable through these historical layers was, if anything, still greater: 'happy, blissful; fortunate', 'spiritually blessed', 'pious, holy, good', 'innocent, harmless', 'pitiable, miserable', 'unlearned, unsophisticated, simple, rustic, ignorant', 'lacking in judgement or common sense; foolish, senseless, empty-headed'. For the *OED*, this engagement with the past provided empirical evidence of linguistic evolution, with the obsolescence of older forms and the rise of newer, more successful, variants. Fresh adaptations of form and meaning repeatedly developed as the lexical units of the language entered into new relationships, new modes of organization and use. After the Norman Conquest, for example, and the lexical (and cultural) invasions which accompanied this new period of rule, French loan words such as *voice* (deriving from *voiz*) or *poor* (deriving from *povre* > *poure*) ultimately marginalized and displaced respective native equivalents such as *steven* and *earm*. *Science* itself would change its semantic borders over the course of the nineteenth century. Johnson's *Dictionary* of 1755 had, for instance, isolated 'knowledge' as the primary meaning of the word, based on its etymological derivation from Latin *scientia*. Accompanying citations emphasized the religious affiliations of its use, as in that which Johnson chose to give from the theologian, Henry Hammond: 'If we conceive God's sight or *science*, before the creation of the world, to be extended to all and every part of the world, seeing every thing as it is . . .'. Here too the *OED* would necessarily transcend its predecessor, affirming instead the radically new configurations of meaning which *science* had assumed by the second half of the nineteenth century. 'Modern use', as Henry Bradley confirmed in the fascicle *Sauce-alone–Scouring*, meant that *science* had come to be synonymous with 'Natural and Physical Science . . . restricted to those branches of study that relate to the phenomena of the material universe and their laws'.

Scientist provides a concise reminder of the differences in intellectual context which underpin these two contrastive stages in lexicographical history. A term entirely unknown to Johnson, it had explicitly been called for by the foundation of the British Association for the Advancement of Science in 1831. Those who attended its meetings found themselves in need of a collective designation, the absence of which, as contemporary journals reported, was 'felt very oppressively'.[22] Of the various solutions that were proposed, such as 'philosopher' and 'savant' (the former rejected as being 'too wide and too lofty a term' while the latter was 'rather assuming'), it was *scientist*, formed on analogy with *artist*, which gradually came to seem most suitable. 'We need very much a name to describe a cultivator of science in general. I should incline to call him a Scientist', William Whewell agreed in his *Philosophy of the Inductive Sciences* in 1840, a year before he took over as President of the Association. By the time of the relevant fascicle of the dictionary, the new word was both established and unquestionable. 'A person with expert knowledge of a science; a person using scientific methods', Bradley's definition states in 1910. Its implications had, however, long been evident in the making of the *OED*. 'I know philology . . . and enough of nearly every other science and subject – chemistry, botany, entomology . . . to treat their terminology without help', Murray had proclaimed of his own task in editing the dictionary; 'I can at least write as a geologist to Prof[essor] Geikie, as a botanist to Sir Thistleton Dyer, as an anatomist to Sir J. Burdon Sanderson, as a chemist to Roscoe or Thorpe.'[23] Science provided a language – and a methodology – to which Murray often had recourse. Still more to the point were the lectures which Murray gave to the Ashmolean Natural History Society in Oxford in which he stressed that in his dictionary activities he was not to be seen as 'a literary man'. Instead, he declared, 'I am a man of science, and I am interested in that branch of Anthropology which deals with the history of human speech.'[24] For Murray, lexicography too was emphatically a domain where the scientist must prevail.

To turn to the history and evolution of the *OED* is, however, to confront the fact that the projected plan of the dictionary had by no means always included a direct engagement either with science or with its linguistic legacies. Trench delivered his lectures to the Philological Society in

November 1857, two years before Darwin's *Origin of Species* made its appearance. Nevertheless, while the entire spectrum of English society seemed to be demonstrating a compelling enthusiasm for the scientific advances being made ('I want the working classes to understand that Science and her ways are great facts for them', Thomas Huxley declared in 1855 as he began what was to be the first of many popular lectures to working men),[25] Trench, on the other hand, was notably critical of the claims of science, especially in relation to its putative inclusion in the dictionary. There were of course exceptions. Scientific words which were validated by long usage or, better still, by their adoption by significant writers in the history of the language should be sanctioned. Here might be included *spagyrist* ('an alchemist') which had been deployed by the seventeenth-century divine, Jeremy Taylor. But overall Trench advocated a general policy whereby the incorporation of technical terms *en masse* into the dictionary was to be avoided. These, he said, were not 'for the most part, except by an abuse of language, words at all'. They were merely 'signs', lexical elements which had been deliberately 'invented as . . . nomenclature'. As such, he argued, they were less than 'real' words. 'Tokens' might be a better designation since lexical elements of this kind operated solely within specialized domains and 'never mingled with the general family of words'. To include the coinages that littered modern scientific works on chemistry or electricity would, Trench concluded, inevitably 'crowd and deform the pages of a Dictionary',[26] betraying what he conceived as its true purpose.

For a writer who was overtly concerned with redefining the role of the lexicographer in a way that prioritized historical objectivity above the evaluative (and subjective) criticism of words, the emotive thrust of Trench's linguistic diatribe is disturbing. 'Half a dozen genuine English words recovered from our old authors would be a greater gain, a more real advance', he declaimed, setting images of a 'genuineness' legitimized by literary authority against the implicitly spurious formations which science might create. Trench's negative diction was marked. The coinages of science were 'mere encumbrances' and 'disfigurements' in a dictionary, the 'labour' of their inclusion being 'little more than that of transcription' while 'the gain is nought'. Indeed, Trench added, the lexicographical benefit may be 'less than nought'.[27] In the exposition of such concerns, the ideal of the *lexicon totius Anglicitatus* again fragments, as does the neutrality of the 'complete inventory of our English tongue' with which Trench sought to inspire the members of the Philological Society. Completeness was, it seemed, not necessarily to include science; likewise the 'inventory' was once again to prove partial and selective.

Trench's proposed solution to the linguistic anomalies with which science apparently presented the lexicographer was the creation of a subsidiary lexicon outside what came to be referred to as 'the Main Dictionary'. So it was with this principle of division that the *OED* first began. The *Canones Lexicographici* of 1860 makes this divide still clearer. Setting out the formal structures of the proposed work, it stressed that all words used in English books were to be recorded, however 'worthless' they might seem to be. Science again proved the exception, being constituted as a domain in which 'worth' was a qualitative consideration of a somewhat different order. Aside from those forms which had passed 'out of their peculiar province into general use', the vocabulary of science, especially that deriving from treatises on specifically scientific subjects, would be literally marginalized, appearing in a separate 'Vocabulary of Technical and Scientific Terms'.[28] Paired with a 'Vocabulary of Proper Names of Persons and Places', this was to be distinct from the main work in both design and content, not least since the explanations accompanying the word-entries in this part of the dictionary were to be deliberately truncated – 'a line or two . . . in the shortest possible form', the *Canones* prescribes.[29] It was a framework which, in essence, set out a hierarchical model of language, disturbing the foundations of objective impartiality on which the visions of a new dictionary ostensibly rest. As in the 1859 *Proposal* for the dictionary, the division was clear. 'We admit as authorities all English books, except such as are devoted to purely scientific subjects, as electricity, mathematics', as the latter had decreed.[30]

Such attitudes reflect a popular form of cultural censorship in which the real inventiveness of nineteenth-century scientific lexis was habitually dismissed. It was merely 'nomenclature' or, in another contemporary coinage, it was 'terminology'. 'I designate as Terminology the system of terms employed in the description of objects of natural history', William Whewell had written, setting out the fundamental principles of scientific discussion in his *History of the Inductive Sciences* (1837).[31] 'Every calling has its technical terminology', Thomas Huxley later stressed.[32] To dismiss terminology was nevertheless demonstrably to underestimate its significance. As Huxley strove to make 'order out of the chaos of invertebrate zoology',[33] it was language – the lexical creation of new terminology, new systems of nomenclature – which underpinned and located the advances in knowledge which were being made, here reflected in his introduction of words such as *amphicoelous, amphipodan*, *amphistylic*, and *pholidogaster*.[34] In a similar way, it was the discovery – and categorization – of new genera, and new anatomical nuances, which preoccupied Darwin in his multifarious discoveries regarding cirripedes, barnacles, or spiders. Accuracy in research was founded on the need for a precise and substantiated language. As Thomas Huxley wrote to the botanist Joseph Hooker in 1858, 'with animal morphology in the state in which it is now, we have no terminology that will stand'.[35] Creativity was vital. Literary writers happily coined words to suit their purpose as in Thackeray's use of *embracive* in his novel *The Newcomes* (1855), a word which Bradley duly included in the *OED* ('Given to or fond of embracing; embracing demonstratively'). It was creative necessity of a different kind which prompted other neologisms in many domains of science, leading to the appearance of forms such as *cirripede* in 1828 ('. . . a class of marine animals of the Sub-kingdom Annulosa, closely related to the Crustacea, but in the adult state much less developed . . .'), *Cambrian* as a geological designation in 1842, or *ceratodus* (again courtesy of Darwin) in 1874. The naming of *ceratodus* alone – a fish with lungs and with fins which could be used as legs – self-evidently served to confirm another significant discovery in the narrative of evolution. Its existence – and its import – were moreover simultaneously consolidated by Darwin's addition to the word-hoard, and later added by Murray to the *OED*.[36]

Given the peculiarly wide-ranging ramifications of scientific lexis in this context, especially given the consequences of such advances for belief in a divine and immutable creation, Trench in his public role as Dean of Westminster (and later Archbishop of Dublin) could perhaps be forgiven for his suspicions about seeming to legitimize certain aspects of language of this order by their inclusion in the dictionary of the Philological Society. Genesis and geology were, for instance, regularly at odds in the nineteenth century, their dissonance evident in the pointed questions which the geologist Mr Gunnery directs at the young Godwin Peak in Gissing's *Born in Exile*. '"*What* deluge? *Which* deluge?"' Mr Gunnery demands, his words entirely in keeping with the 'immoral theories concerning the date of creation' which accompany his understanding of the fossilized records of the past.[37] Trench's own metaphors of fossils and geology were given somewhat different resonances. Here 'the region of nature' is 'the region of God's wonders' and geology carries implications for moral investigation and the truth of God's purpose.[38] Where geologists identify different strata and hence verify the 'successive physical changes through which a region has passed' so, Trench argued, in the strata and deposits which form the history of human words, God has 'impressed such a seal of truth upon language, that men are continually uttering deeper things than they know'.[39]

Trench's views allied him closely with the geologists of the first half of the nineteenth century, men such as William Buckland, Reader in Mineralogy at Oxford (and one of Trench's predecessors as Dean of Westminster) whose inaugural lecture at the university was entitled *Vindicae Geologicae; or, the Connexion of Geology with Religion Explained.* Buckland's *Reliquiae Diluviae; or, Observations of the Organic Remains . . . Attesting the Action of a Universal Deluge* (1823) likewise indicates his concern to explain observable phenomena by recourse to biblical truth. For writers such as Buckland and Trench, nature and language were evidence for a superintending power, a rejection of those evolutionary principles which, even before publication of the *Origin of Species*, had gradually been gaining ground. Science – especially biology, zoology, geology, and their associated terminologies – held implications which disrupted accepted paradigms, raising, as Darwin himself was to admit, a set of new and dissonant 'doctrines' and, by extension, a new – if radically different – set of 'converts'.[40] So Trench's personal antipathy to the inclusion of science in the dictionary, as well as to the abuses of language he held it to constitute, was perhaps understandable.

Nevertheless, this attempted segregation of scientific and 'genuine' words, endorsed by the dictionary's first editor, Herbert Coleridge, could not change either the popularity or the significance of science and its accompanying linguistic forms. Darwin's *Origin of Species* sold out within a day, necessitating the immediate preparation of a second edition of 3,000 copies. A Victorian best-seller, 24,000 copies had been purchased by 1872. Likewise, even as the *Canones* were issued in 1860, Huxley was lecturing to packed audiences of working men on the topic of 'The Relation of Man to the Lower Animals', a subject on which Darwin had by this point ventured only to hint. From February to May of the following year Huxley held weekly sessions in London on 'The Relation of Man to the Rest of the Animal Kingdom', an area which placed human history in a new light altogether. As Huxley wrote with evident delight to his wife, 'My working men stick by me wonderfully, the house being fuller than ever last night. By next Friday evening they will all be convinced that they are monkeys.'[41] The receptivity of Huxley's audiences confirmed his central thesis. It was, Huxley observed, a time of revolution which could not be ignored.[42] Though objections continued to be made, the direction of change was clear. 'In its widest application, an animal of any species of the group of mammals closely allied to and resembling man', Bradley would confirm in 1907 in the scientifically validated entry for *monkey* which he crafted for the *OED*.

The linguistic apartheid of these initial plans of the dictionary could not be sustained – at least not unless the dictionary was to be an anachronism before a single word had been published. Murray's own lexicographical inclinations in this proved truer to the temper of the time, and to those images of ongoing revolution which continued to pervade popular comment. His early fascination with botany, entomology, and geology is well documented and his drive for self-education through the medium of works such as Cassell's *Popular Educator* led to a working knowledge of both mathematics and mechanics, as well as chemistry and electricity.[43] In Murray's hands, the *OED* was itself to evolve from the early paradigms set out by Trench and Coleridge. While formally aligning himself with principles of data collection which excluded 'purely scientific subjects' (as in his *Appeal to the English-Speaking and English-Reading Peoples* of 1879), Murray's accompanying list of books to be read in order to gather quotations for the dictionary already includes the geological works of Charles Lyell and the Irish naturalist (and physicist) John Tyndall's works on glaciation, as well as (among others) Michael Faraday's published researches into electricity. Faraday's work alone eventually yielded almost 500 citations in the published fascicles. Murray's desiderata also conspicuously included 'early treatises on any of the sciences' while a later list of books adds contemporary works of science too. Accum's *Chemical Tests*, Salmon's *Synopsis Medicinae*, Pennant's *Zoology*, Darwin's *Voyage of a Naturalist*, the works of Humphry Davy and Joseph Hooker (as well as those of Lyell) are, among others, all specified on the 'Third List of books for which Readers are Wanted'.[44] In 1880 Murray moreover made a specific appeal to 'Members of various Scientific Societies' to engage in the lexical documentation of the terms of their own disciplines, stressing that this was a domain of usage to which the new dictionary intended to 'do full justice'. An appeal in the *Journal of the Linnean Society*, for example, asked for 'early instances of every word of the special terminology of the biological sciences'. Words as diverse as *armadillo* and *wombat*, *achene* and *mesoblast*, as well as 'all other words of scientific nomenclature', were in need of collection and elucidation.[45] The scientific component of the word-hoard was, it seemed, indeed to be given its due.[46]

Murray's deliberate reorientation of the *OED* is evident in other ways too. Science would in effect transmute the very presentation of the dictionary. Images of biology and astronomy dominate the opening of the celebrated 'General Explanations'. In Murray's chosen analogies, just as the naturalist strives to identify and demarcate the nuances of different species, so was the lexicographer to act as a scientist engaged in classifying the phenomena of language. In this light, he wrote, English 'may be compared to one of those natural groups of the zoologist or botanist, wherein typical species forming the characteristic nucleus of the order, are linked on every side to other species, in which the typical character is less and less apparent'. The visual 'compass' of the language which illustrates his words further confirms the new and explicit significance of science (see p. 75). Scientific lexis metaphorically stretches away to the borders of the language in a north-westerly direction while technical domains of usage do the same in the south-west. Even the system of labelling to be deployed within the dictionary reflects these new preoccupations, and their inevitable rise to prominence in the dictionary's history. A proof sheet from 11 November 1883 which details the list of abbreviations to be used in the dictionary notes the addition of terms such as 'Conch.' (conchology), 'Cryst.' (crystallography), 'Min.' (mineralogy), 'Opt.' (optics), 'Palaeont.' (palaeontology), as well as 'Philol.' (philology).[47] A still later listing adds 'Zool.', designating zoology.

Against the restrictions which Trench had sought to impose, Murray thus deliberately adopts a new language of inclusiveness. The dictionary will, he writes, include all scientific and technical lexis which is English in form 'except those [words] of which an explanation would be unintelligible to any but the specialist'.[48] Other more familiar (and non-English) words such as *lepidoptera*, *invertebrata*, or *stratum* were also to find a place if they were considered to be in general use or if they were deemed to 'belong to the more familiar language of science'. It was a formula which allowed for considerable latitude in its implementation. Words such as *alcyonarian* (1878, 'a sub-order of Actinoid Zoophytes'), *amenogram* ('An automatically-marked record of wind-pressure', first deployed in 1876), and *actinium* (a metal discovered in 1881) hence triumphantly appear in the first fascicle of 1884. New minerals such as *allogonite* (1878), *allomorphite* (1837), and *allophite* (1880) are defined alongside newly identified genus types. *Alfalfa*, *alerce*, and *algarroba* were, for instance, all given their first description in English by Darwin in his journal of his voyage on the *Beagle*, published in 1839. Entries in the dictionary could take on a striking contemporaneity. Forms arising in 1881 (*ablastemic*, *acanthological*, *abrader*) are documented with lexicographical precision three years later in the dictionary's first published part.[49] Other words such as *adiabatically* ('In an adiabatic manner; so that heat neither enters nor leaves (a substance)') and *amperometer* (a device for measuring electrical current) are recorded from 1882. A mere two years elapsed before they received linguistic recognition in the *OED*. Words such as *abiogenesis* ('The (supposed) origination or evolution of living organisms from lifeless matter without the action of living parents; "spontaneous generation"') and *agnostic*, both coinages of Huxley, touch more disturbingly on the controversies of the time, while entries such as *anepiploic* (1879) and *acanticone* (1804) openly seem to contravene the principles of commonness and comprehensibility which had been stated in the 'General Explanations' as a guide to the limits of inclusion. 'Having no epiploon, or omentum'; 'A synonym of Arendolite, a kind of epidote', their respective definitions state. The conditions of serial publication for the first edition merely compounded these problems since key elements within definitions of this kind (*epiploon*, *epidote*, *omentum*) would of necessity only be elucidated at a later date. *Omentum*, for example – 'A fold or duplication of the peritoneum connecting the stomach with certain of the other viscera, as the liver, spleen, and colon' – was not to be defined until twenty years later when the fascicle O–*Onomastic* appeared in 1902. Readers would have to wait a further three years before the definition of *peritoneum* appeared. Innumerable examples of a similar kind can be located throughout the dictionary, betraying a certain inconsistency of approach[50] – if a compelling enthusiasm for the dictionary's own place in the scientific revolutions of the nineteenth century. In the elucidation which is offered by its definition, the entomological term *glossotheca*, for instance, defeats all but the specialist ('The tongue-case, or that part of the integument of a pupa which encloses the haustellum'). Nor is the illustrative citation of much help: 'The glossotheca covers both the legs and tongue in some of the sphinxes'. As here, criteria of 'familiarity' and 'general use' are abandoned as part of the abiding zeal for that 'classification of facts' which remained characteristic of the *OED* throughout its making. Murray, in his self-proclaimed role as a scientist of language, sought to seize available opportunities to record a new and often hitherto unassembled lexis. In his first published fascicle – as well as elsewhere throughout the dictionary – countless entries attest a commitment to the vocabulary of a new era, and the insights and advances which such newly formalized words record.

The Struggle for Existence

This is not to suggest that the fortunes of science in the *OED* were without problems, even after Murray took over as editor in 1878. Reactions to the first fascicle as it was being prepared give interesting insights into the dilemmas of inclusion in which Murray must often have found himself. Where his own inclinations led him to engage wholeheartedly with the scientific domains of usage already discussed, other views could differ markedly. 'The chief object of the Dictionary is surely literary', Henry Liddell, the Dean of Christ Church, Oxford (and one of the Delegates appointed to the Dictionary Committee), wrote to Henry Hucks Gibbs in 1883. If introduced at all, technical words 'ought to be reduced to a minimum of space', he advised.[51] Trench's earlier visions of the proper role of the dictionary were evidently not without their advocates. Crucially, Liddell's personal views concurred with those more formally expressed by the Delegates in their printed list of *Suggestions for Guidance in Preparing Copy for the Press*. As we have seen, this regarded scientific neologisms with suspicion.[52] Like Trench, the Delegates put their reservations aside if such words had 'been found in literature' but otherwise they advocated a policy of wholesale exclusion. 'There are too many new scientific words', they complained after reading the preliminary versions of the text. *Abactinal*, for example, should definitely be excised; they failed to see sufficient justification for Murray's lengthy and detailed entry ('Remote from the actinal area; pertaining to that part of the surface of a radiated animal which is opposite to the mouth, e.g. the apex of a sea-urchin, or upper surface of a star-fish . . .'). 'The TECHNICAL terms of Chemistry etc. may well be omitted', the Delegates further recommended. Such attitudes exemplify another side of the conflict between Murray and the Delegates in the writing of the *OED*, with science as yet another battlefield on which disagreements had to be resolved.

'The writers of this did not at all understand the dictionary', Murray expostulated in the margins of his own copy of the *Suggestions*.[53] His acerbic annotations underlined the problems at stake. If the Delegates would accept words of science which were provided with literary authority, then the logical (or indeed illogical) consequence was that all literature would have to be read. But this was impossible. 'I will take *much* counsel on this', Murray vowed, alert to its potential ramifications: 'omission is not always nor often a shorter process than admission: it means scanning every scientific or technical [word] . . . with the proverbial difficulty of establishing a negative'. And moreover, he demanded, much in the manner of a modern theorist, what *is* 'literature'? Did it include journals such as the *Nineteenth Century* or the *Contemporary Review*? Did it include works such as Max Müller's own *Lectures on the Science of Language* or the scientific articles which often appeared in popular journals? An essay on 'Aniline Dyes' had, Murray noted, recently featured in the *Fortnightly Review*. Was *aniline* therefore 'literary' – and hence admissible according to the Delegates' criteria? Thomas Huxley had similarly written a detailed article on glaciation for the *Saturday Review*. What then was the status of the terms it had used? Were they 'literary' – or not? 'In an age when everything written is expected to have a literary form', Murray protested, 'and every department of the known and unknown is ransacked to afford material for "articles", I confess to inability to say what is literature, and utter inability to say whether any given "scientific" word has or has not been used in literature.'[54]

Canvassing members of the Philological Society, he was dismayed to find that some opinions on this matter accorded with those of the Delegates. While the amenable Alexander Ellis was gratifyingly affronted by what he saw as the untoward assumptions of the Press ('What business have the delegates as such to edit the dictionary? This is what it amounts to. Edited by Jowett! No!'),[55] others such as Benjamin Dawson, the long-standing Treasurer of the Philological Society, and the barrister Edward Brandreth (another Philological Society stalwart who sub-edited large sections of the *OED*), expressed similar reservations about the role of scientific vocabulary in the forthcoming dictionary. 'From my point of view the Dict·y will be improved by curtailment in the purely Scientific and Technical department', Dawson wrote, convinced that the proper place for such words was within specialized dictionaries.[56] 'I should think you ought to meet the wishes of the Delegates if such really are their wishes by omitting the scientific words', Brandreth concurred.[57] Skeat too, as we have seen, liberally annotated the early proofs which Murray sent on to him, condemning the inclusion of words such as *anginous* (used in pathology) and *aneurysmatical* ('Of, pertaining to, or due to aneurysm; affected with aneurysm').[58] The proof sheets returned by Fitzedward Hall told the same story. *Abiogenietic* and *abiogenous*, both of which derive from Huxley's own coinage of *abiogenesis* – or as Murray defined it 'The (supposed) origination or evolution of living organisms from lifeless matter without the action of living parents; "spontaneous generation." (Introduced by Prof. Huxley in addressing Brit. Assoc. at Liverpool, Sept. 1870)' – are, among others, firmly crossed out. Later proof sheets from the first fascicle of the dictionary record the suggested excision of *ampelography* ('the scientific description of the vine') and *amperometer*, the latter criticized on the grounds of its undue technicality. That Murray ignored all such advice on scientific omission at this stage of making the dictionary is merely confirmation of his own determined instincts that the language of science should and would be included in the *OED*.

Cultural stereotypes of what a dictionary ought to be obviously play their part here, as do similar cultural stereotypes which had come to surround the language of science in itself. As we have seen, Johnson's prioritization of the language of the 'best writers' still cast its shadow over what the Delegates – together with some members of the Philological Society – expected a dictionary to be. Though Johnson had included some technical terms (as in the specifically chemical senses which he provided for *precipitation* and *analyse*), the thrust of his own *Dictionary* had undoubtedly been towards privileging the literary and canonical. If he had, as he proclaimed, 'extracted . . . from chymists whole processes' in the making of the dictionary,[59] citations which derive from writers such as Shakespeare, Milton, and Dryden clearly dominate in the published text. The *Lexicon Technicum* of John Harris (1704) had also publicly endorsed the idea of separate spheres. While other contemporary dictionaries often chose to concentrate on hard words, Harris's dictionary dealt in the 'Explication of the *Technical* Words' to the exclusion of the ordinary and everyday. *Opposite* was hence defined only in terms of angles, *oil* in terms of its chemical properties and behaviour.

Perhaps more to the point, even outside the realm of the dictionary the diction of science was often laden with negative associations. Trench was by no means alone in his rejection of 'terminology'. Science and culture, as Thomas Huxley regretfully admitted, were all too often regarded as antonyms in nineteenth-century society. Though he sturdily argued to the contrary ('Science and literature are not two things, but two sides of one thing'),[60] it was nevertheless clear that even those well versed in science might feel uneasy about the validity of the discourses in which they conducted their experiments or gave shape to their observations and conclusions. The discourse of science was often dismissed as 'jargon', 'cant', or, in another nineteenth-century usage, as *grimgribber*, a word used to signify educated gibberish. 'Medical writers, whose grimgribber is seldom much . . . read', as the *New Monthly Magazine* stated with disdain in 1824, duly being cited under this head in the dictionary itself. 'He who fears to speak a language too well will speak a jargon', Samuel Oliver similarly averred, his words redolent of the contempt which such appellations could evoke.[61] In the metalanguage of prescriptivism, 'jargon' operated as a term of abuse, its ramifications apparently still institutionalized in popular collocations such as 'scientific jargon'. 'Nobody has a good word for jargon', Walter Nash declares.[62] 'Surely you will not attempt to enter all the crack-jaw medical and surgical terms', the surgeon James Dixon had earlier asked Murray, his long service as a contributor to the dictionary clearly granting him a certain temerity in this matter.[63] Dixon's reluctance to see such words admitted within the apparently hallowed sphere of the dictionary is transparent in his selection of the evocative *crack-jaw* ('Fit to crack the jaws; difficult to pronounce') as an appropriate term of description. It was evident too in his grudging acceptance of Murray's own wishes in this context. 'If you *insist* upon surgical terms . . . I will send them', Dixon concedes. 'But I think that you are better off without them', he felt compelled to add.[64] Murray's voice could at times seem a lone one.

The imperatives consistently urged upon Murray were those of judicious (and deliberately restrained) selection. In this context, however, selection tended to operate in a distinctly different way from the *natural selection* which had been used by Darwin to characterize the underlying mechanisms of evolution. This, as Darwin explained, can be seen to act 'through one form having some advantage over other form in the struggle for existence'. The spread of mistletoe provided an apt illustration: 'it may metaphorically be said to struggle with other fruit-bearing plants, in order to tempt birds to devour and thus disseminate its seeds rather than those of other plants'.[65] Appropriate metaphors of selection for the dictionary instead seemed to incline to the workings of *artificial selection*. It was, as Darwin stressed, man who acted as the controlling force for the latter, deliberately preserving some features or varieties while those less favoured were, with equal deliberation, weeded out. As Darwin explained to the American botanist Asa Gray, 'man, by this power of accumulating variation, adapts living beings to his wants – he *may be said* to make the wool of one sheep good for carpets, and another for cloth &c.'[66] It was an essentially evaluative process as individual variants were appraised – and accordingly rejected or retained – in the attempt to craft the standards desired.

Darwinian models of evolution provided entirely apposite analogies for the crafting of the dictionary too. In effect, similar principles of motivated selection were urged upon Murray, with the language of science ironically itself being proposed as a regular candidate for such 'weeding-out'. In another image of the late nineteenth century, it was the survival of the 'fittest' which was seen as dominantly coming into play, raising wide-ranging questions about the appropriateness of various types of evidence, and the inherent inferiority or superiority of different kinds of discourse. Notions of the 'fittest' as used by Darwin of course referred specifically to the continuance of those forms which, in various ways, were best adapted to survive. 'Fittest' here pertained to adaptation, the degree of consonance with climate or surroundings which might in turn ensure a greater chance in the struggle for existence. In terms of the metaphor of artificial selection, however, the 'fittest' applied to those forms which, for one reason or another, were judged to be more in keeping with the chosen 'adaptation to man's need or fancy'. It was this which Darwin perceived at work in the activities of pigeon-fanciers or horse-breeders as, through successive generations, they crafted a better plumage or a faster horse. Adaptation here was engineered, open to the whims and aesthetic predilections of individuals. 'Fittest' became polysemous. On one hand it was neutral in the adaptive operations of natural selection. On the other it became consciously evaluative, selecting the forms perceived as 'best'. There is 'an unfortunate ambiguity of the term', as Thomas Huxley had rightly warned.[67]

The selection of those words deemed 'fit' to be in the dictionary inevitably took on special resonances in nineteenth-century culture, openly trading on notions of appropriacy (what words should be included in a dictionary) as well as aesthetic merit, those popular evaluative hierarchies by which Johnson, for example, had already excluded whole tranches of the vocabulary from his dictionary.[68] For the Delegates moreover (particularly given the Darwinian thrust of much scientific thinking in the latter part of the nineteenth century), it is of course possible that other considerations may also have intervened. Most of the profits of the Press derived from the sale of bibles, a fact which had already given rise to public censure because of the use of revenue 'from a very sacred source' to support the building of the Science Museum in Oxford. This was misuse of 'the profits upon the printing of God's word', the detractors of the Museum decreed.[69] The *OED* could conceivably attract similar charges, especially given Murray's determined principles of inclusivity. Darwin, for example, would feature prominently in the first fascicle of the dictionary, used in salient illustration of words such as *abnormal*, *abortion*, *acquiescence*, *adult*, *aggregate*, *albatross*, and, of course, *adaptation* (among many others). Oxford had not been a natural home for scientific advances in this context. Evolution and theology had clashed spectacularly at a meeting of the British Association for the Advancement of Science in 1860, in an exchange between Huxley himself and the Bishop of Oxford, Samuel Wilberforce. Four years later, Oxford had witnessed the signing by 11,000 clergymen of the Oxford Declaration, a treatise which explicitly insisted on the literal interpretation of the Bible.

Nevertheless, by the 1880s and the early days of the *OED*, matters had largely moved on. The value of Darwinism could even be endorsed by the Delegates, as in Max Müller's own enthusiastic commendations.[70] Rather than intellectual conviction (or theological scruples), it seemed that simple prejudice alone accounted for the continued opposition to the role of scientific lexis. Trench's legacy lingered on. Such words were 'mere incumbrances' to the real task of the dictionary, he had asserted. The Delegates evidently agreed. Murray hence faced the task of trying to reconcile these conflicting viewpoints with reference to the actual editing of the dictionary. Compromise yet again seemed inevitable. As his letters to Bartholomew Price in late 1883 indicate, Murray had evidently attempted to put some of the Delegates' suggestions into practice in the weeks before publication of the first fascicle. In spite of his own reluctance to see the deliberate editing out of vocabulary in this way, he had drawn the metaphorical line of inclusion and exclusion more closely in the later sheets, especially 'in the direction of scientific, technical, and other diverging senses of words'.[71] In the lexicographical struggle for existence, science was already starting to lose out as the needs and fancies of artificial selection took their toll. As a later editor of the *OED* has stressed, lexicography for Murray necessarily involved the interplay of various 'cultural filters' which, while bringing some linguistic phenomena into close focus, would conversely obscure and suppress others.[72] Certainly the desire to 'filter' scientific words out of the dictionary was transparent in the Delegates' wishes and inclinations, just as it was in the reviews which various fascicles went on to receive. 'Many pages and columns of the present part are largely filled up with words of uncouth aspect which none but scientific experts ever require to use', criticized the *Manchester Guardian* in 1891 after having scrutinized the first part of the *Dictionary* under Bradley's independent editorship.[73] 'Nothing is gained by the insertion of such items of scientific jargon as . . . enostosis, entellus, epicorocoidal, ethene', the *Athenaeum* echoed in the same year.[74] Some individual users of the dictionary manifested the same distaste. 'It looks as if you would even countenance such inexcusable barbarisms as . . . *mimeograph*', one reader noted censoriously in 1899,[75] eventually being proved right in this surmise in the entry which Bradley included seven years later in *Mesne–Misbirth*. *Mimeograph*, the dictionary stated: 'A duplicating machine for producing copies from a stencil'. Murray and his co-editors were constantly caught in the cross-fire which surrounded the inclusion of words. If they never entirely succumbed to the pressures placed upon them, they did, as we shall see, undoubtedly cull a number of entries that the dictionary might well otherwise have chosen to retain.

As reviews such as that in the *Manchester Guardian* suggest, the debate surrounding the legitimacy of scientific lexis for inclusion in the dictionary was by no means to end with the publication of the first fascicle. But disputes with the Delegates on this matter did abate for a few years at least. Murray abided by his promise to Price, consciously striving to draw the line more tightly than he would have done if left to his own devices. Nevertheless he still managed to include words such as Darwin's recent coinages of *aphe-liotropic* and *apheliotropism* from 1880 (both of which referred to the habit of plants to turn away from the light), just as he also provided entries for conspicuously new terminology such as *anthotaxy* ('Arrangement of flowers according to their inflorescence') and the zoological *anthozooid* ('An indi-vidual animalcule of a compound Zoophyte'). He likewise happily invented additional examples for *acephelan* and *alation* where he deemed existing evidence to be inadequate.[76] In similar ways the prefaces to the individual parts continued to record thanks for the range of specialist scientific assis-tance which was regularly given to the dictionary – to Professor Geikie in Edinburgh with reference to geology, to Sir Henry Roscoe for chemistry, to William Sykes for medicine and anatomy, to Professor Albert Chester for mineralogy, amid a range of others. This solved a further practical problem for science and its representation in the *OED*. As Bradley had admitted to Murray in 1886, 'I find a good deal of embarrassment with the technical words: the quots. from scientific books seem to have been made in many cases by readers who cannot have been well-acquainted with the subject'.[77] Despite this, as the time scale of publication was formally extended, along with the number of volumes needed, renewed anxieties about the dictionary – and its potential to include the language of science – emerged.

The Order Book of the Delegates for these years makes revealing reading. Subcommittee after subcommittee was appointed to 'consider the execution of the Dictionary', with various attempts being made to impress upon dictionary staff the need for increased productivity. Seen from the Delegates' point of view, the dictionary was indeed proving troublesome. 'To write dictionaries is dull work', Johnson had declared in 1755, providing an apposite illustration for *dull*. The Delegates would more accurately have substituted 'expensive' in view of their own experiences. The losses were immense and their impact all the greater in the economic depression which hit the Press in the early 1890s.[78] Another dictionary subcommittee was formed. Early in 1893 it reported back to the Delegates that limits must be imposed on the dictionary, especially by paying 'less attention . . . to *purely technical and scientific words*'.[79] If these recommendations were originally framed by a liberal acknowledgement of the ultimate authority of Murray and Bradley in this matter ('we think that the utmost discretion and judgment would be required on the part of Dr. Murray and Dr. Bradley in carrying them into practice, remembering that the permanent standing of the Dictionary does not so much depend on its subsidiary advantages as upon its historic character'), this too would swiftly change. Realizations that the true scale of the dictionary would, on then current projections, necessitate a work of some 12,885 pages (rather than the 8,400 which had actually been agreed) led, as we have seen, to stringent demands for curtailment. The lexis of science and technology (and its contested admissibility) explicitly came to the fore in the disputes which were to follow.

To look at the proofs of the dictionary from these years is often demonstrably to see the struggle for existence in action. It is especially conspicuous in Bradley's work on F. His relative slowness in editing the dictionary had already been cause for negative comment.[80] As 1893 began, for example, Bradley had produced 26 pages against Murray's 56 in the same three-month period. Three months later, the relative proportions were 42 to 106. Not only was Bradley's speed of production at issue but the scale of his work was a subject of explicit concern. F was causing huge problems. At the meeting of the Delegates in January 1895, Gell stressed the practical problems being experienced in the printing house as a result of 'the excessive amount of type locked up' in the making of F. At the meeting in May, Gell was officially required to 'remonstrate with Mr Bradley on the subject'.[81] Such remonstrations evidently failed to have the desired effect and, at their first meeting in 1896, the Delegates made a collective resolution 'that Mr. Bradley be informed that it will be necessary that his connexion with the Dictionary should close – unless he keeps within due scale on the remaining portion of his letter'. F thus becomes a volume in which the struggle for existence with respect to scientific and technical words is marked, following not only the Delegates' specific edict of 1893 but also their continual monitoring of Bradley's output. The consequences of this are clear. To compare Murray's first fascicles with Bradley's eventual version of F (and especially its second half) is to enter a different lexicographical world, one in which the need to keep within limits is clearly at the forefront. This is not to say that scientific lexis does not appear. Words such as *fossiliferous* and *formaldehyde*, or new chemical terms such as *fumarin* ('An acid isomeric with maleic acid') duly take their place, as befitting their status as key items within the scientific advances of the nineteenth century. But the sheer abundance of scientific terminology of *A–Ant* which Murray had maintained, even in light of the Delegates' wishes to the contrary, is missing. The second half of F is pared down to its essentials in line with the Delegates' specific instructions, recorded at their meeting of 6 March 1896, that the *OED* was henceforth to be 'advantageously condensed'. To make their point still more strongly, they marked up a set of F proofs for Bradley's benefit, deleting and excising elements they deemed unnecessary.

Bradley submitted to correction, diplomatically asking the Delegates for further help with his proofs, and for further recommendations of words it would be best to excise. In the surviving proofs of the later parts of F, this new stringency is widely apparent. Entries for botanical terms such as *forsythia* and *fragilis* were, for instance, firmly deleted (the former only to be reinserted in the *Supplement* of 1933).[82] Bradley's careful revisions on the proofs of *forsythia* as he strove to find an apposite definition hence failed to materialize in the finished text. Paradoxically, however, this new lexical stringency is particularly marked in the *absence* of that plethora of deletions which, throughout earlier parts of the dictionary, had habitually littered the proofs. In this part of F it is as though the proofs already reflect a hard-line filtering of language through the selective principles which the Delegates had outlined. As Charles Doble had stressed in 1894, Bradley 'aims at bringing the letter within its limits by giving what is merely indispensable in the remaining portion'.[83] Conversely, that which was dispensable was to be omitted. 'That can be dispensed with or done without; unessential, omissible; unimportant', as Murray's definition for the latter had stated one year earlier. In this particular context, as Doble's letter went on to confirm, it was a process which explicitly required the 'energetic measures' that Bradley henceforth adopted with reference to cutting 'technical and scientific words'. The marked attention to new discoveries so perceptible in the dictionary's first fascicle would become one of the resulting casualties. Further letters from the Press endorsed the need for the strictest economy, stressing that, in the face of 'the steadily growing proportions of the Dictionary', recent usages were to be avoided. 'This principle should be rigorously adhered to', Murray and Bradley were informed.[84] In the dictionary the principles of selection would, of necessity, be made to change.

Evolution in Action

F represents a low point for the history of science in the *OED*, a moment of crisis when lexical over-population led to renewed zeal in the need to circumscribe what the dictionary could, or should, admit. As in Darwin's 'oeconomy of nature', and the Malthusian checks he detected at work once the pressures on natural resources had become too great, so too in the dictionary were similar perceptions of over-population to take their toll. 'As more individuals are produced than can possibly survive', Darwin noted, 'there must in every case be a struggle for existence'.[85] The same came to be true of words. More were invented than could be included within the microcosm of the dictionary. As Chapter 3 has already illustrated, the continued increase in the number of words which might potentially inhabit the dictionary was checked by conscious and entirely deliberate control. In the practical terms of dictionary-making (and especially dictionary-publishing), the linguistic climate would be less receptive to the survival of some, more conducive to the continued existence of others. Darwin's *fumariaceous* ('Professor Braun mentions a Fumicareous genus'), which he deployed in his *Origin of Species*, was duly excised from the drafts of *Frank-law–Gain-coming*.[86] Similarly, the extensive scientific compounds involving, for example, the prefix *gymno-* were painstakingly pruned in the first revise. The adjacent *gymnologize*, with its striking definition of 'to dispute naked like an Indian philosopher', was retained without question. 'Omit most?' Murray likewise later queried by the side of a column of recent scientific lexis involving compounds with *lampro-*. Bradley duly complied, consigning forms such as *lamprocarpous* ('having shining fruit'), *lamprophyllous* ('a term applied to plants remarkable for their smooth and bright leaves'), and *lamprospermous* ('having bright shining seeds') to the piles of rejected words.

Once again the proofs provide a vivid record of evolution in action, revealing as they do the original inhabitants of fascicles as against those which survived into published form. From F onwards, the consciousness of selection in relation to scientific and technological lexis clearly played a renewed part, curbing the words of zoology in the excision of *lepadite* (a kind of barnacle), *lophopodous* ('with tufted or feathered feet'), and *globiocephaline* ('having a globose head'), while also culling those of chemistry, with the loss of *glycosine*, *lactam*, and *guiaiaconic*. 'Not in dicts', Murray records by the side of *guiaiaconic* (a kind of acid) as he monitored Bradley's proofs. Though the absence of this form from the other dictionaries might lead one to think that this was precisely the reason why the *OED* should wish to record it – especially given the inspirational agenda of the all-inclusive inventory with which it had begun – this was not to be the case. *Guaiaconic* duly disappears, lost from the record of the language, as was *glyceramic* (a term for a different acid) on similar grounds. 'Not f[oun]d. Omit', states a marginal instruction for the latter, discounting the evidence from *Cassell's Encyclopaedic Dictionary* of 1884 with which the entry was provided (even though this was used as a major source of information for countless other entries that did survive).

Such losses could have serious consequences for the understanding of the past. *Lactam* ('One of a series of anhydrides of an amido type, analogous to the lactones') was, for instance, one of the words excised from the first proof in the interests of lexicographical economy. Some seventy years later the entry reappears, included by Robert Burchfield in the second volume of the *Supplement* (1976) in an attempt to remedy the perceived omissions of the past. Yet the sense of absence remains. According to the information at Burchfield's disposal as he edited this entry, *lactam*'s own past extended merely to 1883. Yet in the entry as it originally appeared in the proofs, usage had been attested a quarter of a century earlier, in 1858. The disparity is significant for a dictionary which publicly insists on the salience of its historical principles. Similar is *giraffid* ('One of the *Giraffidae*, the animal family of which the giraffe is the only representative') which was recommended for excision from the first revise of Bradley's *Germano–Glass-cloth* in common with scores of other words denoting the distinctions of genus and species. 'It seems a very useless word', a marginal annotation declares. *Giraffid* was therefore deleted though it too was to reappear in the *Supplement* of 1976, assessments of its utility evidently having changed. As Peter Gilliver has recently noted, such decisions on inclusion and exclusion tend – as different versions of the dictionary in this instance confirm – to partake in a marked sense of provisionality in which 'an item is not so much omitted, as postponed pending the appearance of further evidence'.[87] While the evidence of the proofs suggests that the presence of adequate citations (or otherwise) was not always the point at issue, this process of loss and reinstatement is a common one. *Forsythia* and *foussa*, for instance, reflect precisely parallel processes. Problems of space led to their loss within the textual evolution of the first edition of the *OED* while, given greater freedom – and an explicit agenda of supplementing the deficiencies of the past – the *Supplements* of the twentieth century later rescind such rejections. *Foussa* was hence a word which Bradley found himself excising from the first revise of *Foisty–Frankish*, in spite of having carefully crafted it into shape as an entry in previous stages of the text. A 'fierce weasel-like quadruped . . . found in Madagascar', it was an 'alien' in the dictionary's terms,[88] even if it was also one popular enough to be described in the newspapers of the day, as in the citation from, say, the *Standard* in 1890 which had accompanied the original entry. Robert Burchfield in the twentieth century instead deemed *foussa* a word which the *OED* should record, and he duly wrote another entry for the *Supplement* of 1972. Happily in this instance *foussa* (unlike *lactam*) was equipped with citations which managed to antedate by some fifty years the information which Bradley had earlier had at his disposal.

As these examples combine to suggest, the loss of scientific words was in fact to become acute in the revises of the individual fascicles. It was at this point that entries which had previously been drafted in longhand, set in type in the first proof, and which had moreover managed to survive intact through the rigours of the second proof, were suddenly liable to be declared redundant. Entries for plant names such as *fragilis* could become vulnerable to more critical assessments, now being excised in spite of the detail with which the drafted entries were supplied. The evocative citation from Harriet Parr's *Basil Gadfrey's Caprice* of 1868 ('in moist shaded chinks . . . sprang pale tufts of fragilis') was decisively crossed through in the drafts of the first revise. The same was true of other designations of genus and animal types such as *glareole* ('a bird of the genus *glareola*'), *grewia* ('a tillaceous genus of shrubs or small trees . . .'), or *lane-snapper*. The last of these (designating a North American bird) presumably also offended the Delegates' principles on the unnecessary and excessive use of Americanisms.[89] All disappeared in the critical scrutiny afforded to the revises. While genus types were not formally a major object of the *OED* (especially in light of the stated desire to discriminate between the proper territory of a dictionary against that of an encyclopaedia),[90] they are abundantly recorded in many parts of the dictionary as in the entries made for *acacia* (a genus of shrubs), *habracome* (a genus of small South American rodents), or *meconopsis* (a genus of plants).[91] Yet when it came to the pressure to save space in particular sections of the text, such entries could, to their cost, evidently find themselves in the wrong place at the wrong time. Although corresponding forms such as *abelmosk* (a genus of plants), *neossine* (a genus of swifts), and *lobfish* ('a kind of stockfish') continue into the published fascicles, countless others – such as *galeodes* (a genus of spiders) or *gadus* (a genus of fishes) – do not. While displaying a randomness of survival which accords well with the Darwinian mechanisms discussed elsewhere in this chapter, this is nevertheless potentially disturbing within the editing of a dictionary and the principles of consistency that were explicitly invoked in its inception. *Galeodes*, for instance, had been meticulously documented, equipped with two careful citations which traced usage through the nineteenth century, as well as being provided with accurate details of pronunciation and etymology. As Robert Burchfield would later confirm with reference to the making of *OEDS*, there is a 'need for constant decision-making at the boundaries of many word-classes'.[92] In this respect the continuities with *OED1* are clear.

This apparent arbitrariness is noticeable in other domains of scientific usage too, as in Bradley's evident decision to excise *glycosine*, *glycuronic*, *glyceramine*, *glyoxylate*, and *glyoxylic* but to retain – on the same sheet – other chemical terms such as *glycollide*.[93] 'Glycuronic acid, uric acid . . . are well-known', the entry for *glycuronic* had originally stated. It was supported by an 1897 citation from Thomas Allbutt's *System of Medicine*, another popular source of evidence for the dictionary. Well known or not, it was a word which Murray, once more casting a critical eye over Bradley's proofs, was to recommend for deletion, a factor which presumably influenced its demise. The fact that another non-scientific word was also added at the same stage was, however, presumably not an entirely irrelevant factor in relation to this excision. A drafted entry for *glycypicron* ('Something composed of sweet and bitter') heads the relevant sheet, providing evidence from texts such as Burton's *Anatomy of Melancholy* of 1621 to support what was evidently deemed to be a far more necessary part of the word-hoard. 'He saith our whole life is a Glucupicron, a bitter sweet passion', Burton had written.

Contravening the decisions of the past once more, Craigie and Onions were, however, to restore the dictionary status of *glycuronic* in the 1933 *Supplement* in yet another instance of the flux of evidence and admissibility which surrounds the record of English in the *OED*.[94] Of similar prominence are the transparently fluctuating fortunes of other words in the first edition, their fate hanging in the balance in the course of revision, evidently pending decisions on the inclusion or otherwise of further lemmas or citations which might necessitate the sudden requisition of space. *Leucol* as a chemical designation ('An organic base derived from coal-tar, identical with quinoline') was, for instance, emphatically recommended for deletion in the first revise of *Leisureness–Lief* and Bradley crossed out the entire entry. It was evidently later reprieved. The fascicle as finally published in March 1902 instead affirmed its existence and use, as well as its renewed validity as a term to be included. Precisely the same process of lexicographical uncertainty attended chemical terms such as *lactimide* and *leucoline*, the mineral designation *leucopyrite*, and *lathyrus* (a genus of plants) or, in an earlier fascicle, *gymnopterous* (an entomological term referring to the condition of having wings without hairs or scales). All appeared, were crossed through, and later surfaced intact in the final version of the text. Other words, such as the zoological terminology of, say, *lophosomatous* (having tufts on the body), or *lophocerous* (having tufted antennae), manage to survive unscathed even through the vicissitudes of the first revise only to disappear in the relatively rare circumstances of the second revise (a point at which only very minor changes tended to occur). The processes of attrition in this particular fascicle (*Lock–Lyyn*) obviously required yet another round of pruning in the attempt to reduce it to the required size. Murray and his co-editors were forced to scrutinize scientific entries carefully, rejecting words on grounds which in other circumstances might have been able to secure their continued presence in the dictionary.

Patterns of conscious symbiosis were moreover evidently forced into play. If Bradley, on reconsidering his entry for the chemical term *lobelic* (an acid obtained from the plant *Lobelia inflata*), realized that he needed more space – here for an additional quotation which would allow a date of first use in 1840 rather than 1874 to be confirmed – then he was also forced into the corresponding realization that this space would have to be acquired from somewhere else. In this case, the following (and related) word, *lobelliin* would have to be excised. Gain could not exist without loss, a pattern which countless other sheets also attest. *Glochidial* (an adjective describing the offspring of certain fresh-water mussels) and *larvivorous* (devouring larvae) stand among innumerable scientific entries which failed to survive the pressures of the proofs. Even Darwin's coinages could be lost in the struggle for existence. *Gossipaceous*, deployed in the course of a letter to Joseph Hooker in 1849 ('I received your two interesting gossipaceous and geological letters'), is, for example, deleted from the first revise though other nonce-words – as in Thomas de Quincey's use of *gimlet* as a verb ('very soon he had gimleted himself down amongst the family rats') – are conspicuously retained. Darwin was not to be regarded as 'an authority for correct modern prose', Gibbs had informed Bradley on reading the proofs of *like*. While Darwin would probably have agreed that he did not deserve to be ranked among the world's greatest prose stylists ('I had no idea of the trouble which trying to write common English could cost one', as he lamented),[95] this was not in reality a legitimate argument for the elimination of words. Data could not be discarded on the grounds of inconvenience, just as Darwin argued in his own research. In the pragmatics of production which attended the *OED*, this is nevertheless what regularly seemed to happen as words, and particularly scientific words, were lost in response to the need to create space on individual pages in the proofs.

Yet in terms of the wider concerns which informed the making of the *OED*, the picture is more complex. Even as Murray and his co-editors felt compelled in a variety of ways to truncate the dictionary, excising elements which, in an ideal lexicographical world, they would have preferred to see in the published text, so too did they continue gathering and monitoring the new words of science. 'The only quotations we now want seem to be from modern scientific and technical works. We seem to have the *ordinary* words of the language as fully as the reading of books can gather them', Murray informed a potential volunteer in 1911.[96] Compromise could only go so far. In this respect, the data files of the *OED* would present the complete history (in so far as it could be told) even if, in the end, this was not always reflected in the dictionary itself.

Especially telling in this context were the unremitting efforts of various contributors who dedicated themselves to the cause of science within the dictionary. One of the most prominent was William Sykes, the physician and antiquarian whose work as a critical reader for the dictionary has already been mentioned in Chapter 2.[97] 'Pray make me as useful as you can', he had written to Murray in 1888.[98] His zeal rarely flagged over the next eighteen years, even when illness made him virtually prostrate. 'Owing to a gastric ulcer and a violent loss of blood, which nearly killed me', Sykes had been obliged to give up his medical practice, as he told Bradley in 1902,[99] adding in the same letter that he had still managed to send his regular batch of scientific quotations to Murray. He announced that henceforth he was willing to devote still more time to the dictionary: 'If I can be of use to you, pray command me', he urged Bradley. A meticulous contributor, Sykes was to prove vital in tracking down the often elusive information which was required on the specific history of medical terms, sending lengthy letters to both Murray and Bradley on subjects such as bronchitis, the properties of castor oil, the anatomical definition of the ear, or the nature of compound fractures, each of which further attested to the productive fusion of his lexicographical and medical zeal.

Sykes's attention to detail is perhaps most in evidence on the surviving proof sheets. Here his careful annotations provide a densely written commentary on the text as originally drafted, spotting omissions and potential antedatings, alternative senses, and unrecorded compounds in the scientific and technical vocabulary of the *OED*. He antedates *gastralgia* ('pain in the stomach') and *galvanization* ('The process of subjecting (a person, nerve, etc.) to the action of galvanism'), *galago* (a genus of lemurs), and *Brownian motion*, and carefully rephrases existing entries to eliminate possible problems.[100] He offers moreover innumerable new words for editorial consideration: *funic* ('pertaining to the funis, or umbilical cord', as Bradley duly defined it in the relevant fascicle), *gastricism* and *gastricity*, *glucate* ('A salt of glucic acid'), *gastro-catarrhal*, *gastro-bronchitic*, *gastro-enteralgia, gastropathy* (a general term for disease of the stomach), in a medical litany which often served to provide an ironic counterpoint to his own continuing gastric illness. *OED* entries such as that for *furfuramide* ('A white crystalline substance produced by the action of ammonia on furfurol') and *genupectoral* ('Of posture: Resting on the knees and breast'), the latter dated to 1889, depend almost word for word on the information provided by Sykes, neatly inscribed along the margins of the first proofs. The same was true of *germ-particle*, the absence of which Sykes spotted on his copy of the first proof. The citation he provided ('The slightest dislocation of the ultimate germ and sperm-particles will modify the entire future development of the embryo') was adopted by Bradley as the substance of the relevant entry as it later appeared in the dictionary.

Compounds such as *galvano-puncture* and *galvano-caustic* (both duly inserted into the text in its published version) or *glosso-epiglottic* are crowded into any available space on the proofs which Sykes returned to the dictionary, often being accompanied by extra loose sheets of notes if space on the proofs proved inadequate. Words such as *genyplasty* ('An operation for restoring the cheek when it has been destroyed or is congenitally imperfect') or the lexical recognition of new forms of disease such as *geophagism* (the eating of earth) are precisely set down on the proofs he read, attesting new formations and fresh developments in both language and science. 'A forcible bending of the knee as a curative method', he noted in possible definition of a new surgical sense of *genuflexion* which he had observed ('*Surg.* A forcible bending of the knee as a curative measure in popliteal aneurysm', the dictionary later echoed). New scientific vocabulary such as *germatic*, deriving from Campbell's *Causation of Disease* in 1889 ('We have seen that the spermatic and germatic environment cannot be the same for any two germs'), is set down with appropriate citations in line with Sykes's expressed belief that the dictionary in this respect must remain up to date. 'I think the rule about not including quotations after 1900 a foolish one', he censured, warning that by the time the dictionary was complete, the absence of 'modern new scientific terms' would make the work even more historical in realization than had originally been intended.[101] Against all the Delegates' inclinations, Sykes repeatedly defended the role of science in the *OED*. Though he acknowledged that 'to insert words in a historical dictionary which have no history and little if any actual use seems rather absurd', nevertheless, he continued, 'every man rightly expects to find in a dictionary such as the N.E.D. such technical words.'[102]

That Sykes's judgement was not awry on this matter is borne out by the number of letters that Murray received from those who had looked up such technical lexis in the published fascicles only to find it absent. Words such as *anaerobic*, *nitrary*, or *appendicitis* were nowhere to be found in the first edition of the *OED*.[103] *Appendicitis* alone made Sykes's point. Dated to 1886 in the 1933 *Supplement* (the point at which it entered the *OED* for the first time), *appendicitis* had naturally not found a home in the relevant fascicle of the dictionary (*Ant–Batten*) which had been published in 1885. The mere facts of ongoing history made the claims of new words of this kind a matter for imperative consideration. Though James Dixon expostulated against the very idea of including *appendicitis*, here in another outraged letter on the barbarous productivity of medical lexis ('such jargon as they are! Only yesterday I met with "appendicitis" – to mean an inflammation of the Appendix. You know doctors think the way to indicate any inflammation is to tack on "itis" to a word'),[104] other users of the dictionary were quick to notice its absence. 'We received two letters today from America, one stating the fatal ending of an operation for Appendicitis, the other, what I hope will prove a cure after Appendicitis', Max Müller wrote to Murray in 1894. He had immediately sent his wife to look the word up in the *OED* 'but there it is not', he complained. Given its prevalence ('like that of influenza', he remarked), surely it should have been included? [105] In 1902, following the delay of Edward VII's coronation as a result of a royal case of appendicitis, the word was indeed to become one of the most famous omissions of the dictionary. But although Murray could not predict which words were to come into widespread use, Sykes's wider thesis was that where the evidence did exist for such neologisms, they should receive their due within the dictionary. 'I can't help thinking you will be astonished at the fertility and rapidity of growth of this new department of terminology', he stated in a letter to Murray,[106] celebrating the inventiveness of clinical medicine as attested in the comments and additions which he had liberally written on the accompanying proofs.

Sykes was indeed an expert witness in the history of scientific lexis. He tracked down elusive citations, providing, for example, the supporting evidence which the dictionary now records for scores of technical words. Yet editorial deployment of this wealth of information again seems to betray the problems of selection which we have already seen in action. Sykes's recommendations of *glosso-laryngeal* and *glosso-pharyngeal* are accepted yet *glossopalatine* is not, even though the evidence for all three is similar in kind. Details on *glosso-epiglottic* ('pertaining to the tongue and to the epiglottis') gain entry in the dictionary (yet, in Sykes's careful annotations, this is again based on precisely comparable evidence). Similar dichotomies can be seen in the decision to incorporate, say, Sykes's suggested *gastro-enteralgia* yet to ignore *gastro-bronchitic*. Images of arbitrariness are impossible to avoid in the surviving proofs. Words such as *galactophorus* ('An instrument intended to facilitate suckling') or the memorable *galeanthropy* (a variety of melancholy in which the patient believes himself changed into a cat) are carefully provided with appropriate evidence (and painstaking definitions). Set down on the proofs in Sykes's commendably neat script, they were nevertheless crossed out with equal neatness as surplus to requirements once they reached the offices of the dictionary. Similar were Sykes's careful annotations on the lexical record of *gastroptosis* ('a downward displacement of the stomach'). While the term was later to be included by Craigie and Onions, being dated to 1893, Sykes's original evidence had traced usage to some four years earlier (and had provided a definition which still remains absent in the published *OED*). All too often Sykes's meticulous additions and emendations are covered by a layer of unambiguous deletion as hours of carefully expended effort disappeared at the stroke of a pen.

Of course it remains undeniable that not all Sykes's suggestions could be included. Selection, as we have seen, was imperative, especially in the years during and after the crises of 1892–96. Sykes's efforts thus simultaneously reveal the sheer inventiveness of nineteenth-century vocabulary in the service of science – and the real impossibility that all could appear in the dictionary. Editing out was vital, however much this might run counter to the descriptive inclinations of its editors. Against the finite dictionary stood an indefinitely extending language and the rapidly expanding horizons of modern science. The two could never be entirely compatible. Science merely came to stand as another area in which such incompatibility was put to the test. Nevertheless, the artificial selection which Murray and his editors were forced to impose in order to try and limit the scale of the *OED* was not the end of the matter. 'How fleeting are the wishes and efforts of man!' Darwin wrote of human endeavours to constrain the variety and flux of nature; 'how short his time! and consequently how poor will his products be, compared with those accumulated by nature'.[107] While the first edition of the *OED* eventually came to a close in 1928, language, and especially scientific language, did not halt. In successive *Supplements* the words of science and technology have increasingly made their mark: *radium*, omitted by Craigie in 1904, was finally admitted to the dictionary in 1933, along with associated words such as *radiumize* and *radium therapy*. Adjacent pages contain scores of similarly scientifically oriented lexis such as *radiometallography* and *radiothorium*, *radiobiology* and *radioatom*. Still later, as Edmund Weiner has noted, the 'severely scientific' (such as *spirogyra*, *sirolactone*) took its place in Burchfield's *OEDS* along with the 'pungently demotic' and the democratized lexis of a new age.[108] *OED2* added still further selections, incorporating the diction of computing in new senses added to words such as *editor* ('A program that permits the user to alter programs or to alter or rearrange data or text held in a computer') and *disc* ('A rotatable disc used to store data in digitally coded form') as well as scores of individual entries (*computer-literate*, *computer-literacy*, *floppy*, *software*). Other scientific discourses too were extended. As *OED Online* is gradually brought into being, the same trend can be detected: *cookie* and *MFLOPS* (both from computing),[109] *magnetic resonance imaging* and *magstripe* (a strip found on swipe cards), *mycobacteriophage* ('Any bacteriophage that infects mycobacteria') and *nannandrium* ('The single-celled male plantlet (dwarf male) of nannandrous green algae') can all be found in a record of the language which, by dint of its status as an on-line edition, is no longer confined by the immediate constraints of printed publication.[110]

CHAPTER 5

'I am not the editor of the English language'

Even before formally signing the contract to edit the *OED*, James Murray had found himself catapulted into unwelcome discussions of the ways in which the new dictionary might endeavour to standardize the language. 'I learn with pleasure that you are appointed to take the lead upon the question of "an English Dictionary"', commended Dr Ancell Ball, writing from Spalding in Lincolnshire in April 1878. The forthcoming work would, he hoped, be synonymous with an English Academy, providing definitive edicts on matters such as spelling and pronunciation as well as curbing unwarranted (and certainly deleterious) changes in current English usage. A dictionary produced under the auspices of Oxford University Press surely could not sanction the wilful changes he had recently observed, especially what he deemed to be the evident errors of modern pronunciation. 'Harsh and offending sounds' seemed to be displacing the euphonious habits of the past, being 'taken up by the unreflecting many, simply because it is fashionable to do so'.[1] The dictionary could take a stand against such mutability, Ancell Ball concluded. It would be an indubitable authority, providing linguistic laws by which the language would be regulated and refined.

This was the first of many such letters which Murray received over the next few decades. While he resolutely insisted on the validity of usage, and the duty of a descriptive dictionary to record and observe this ('The first aim of the dictionary is to exhibit the actual variety of usage', as the Preface to *Ant–Batten* declared), popular perceptions of the role of both lexicographer and lexicography could be very different. 'Instead of giving and thereby authorizing the blunders of ignorant and irresponsible writers, the great Dictionary should give only inherently correct definitions', Murray was, for instance, informed in another unsolicited missive, this time from Jasper Davidson.[2] The autocratic proclamations of Dr Johnson clearly continued to influence popular assumptions about the nature, and the intended role, of the dictionary. As Davidson's words indicate, it could seem paradoxical for the new dictionary simply to defer to the fallibilities of ordinary individuals. Along with many others, he believed that the dictionary ought to dictate what they *should* have written, setting a standard of 'good' usage to be followed by the populace. Dr Johnson had, after all, famously felt few scruples in declaring *fuss* to be 'a low cant word' or in castigating *volunteer* (again on the grounds of 'cant'), in spite of the evidence he presented for these forms from writers such as Dryden and Swift. Many felt that Murray's role should be similar, based on judicious discrimination rather than a descriptive subservience to language in use. 'I have come to regard the function of a Dictionary to be not merely to record popular usage in its greatest licence but rather to restrict licence and to correct abuses by insisting on well-defined and recognised principles of language', Davidson therefore continued, setting out a further series of prescriptions for Murray to follow in future parts of the dictionary.

By extension, and much to his discomfiture, Murray was often regarded as a kind of public linguistic oracle to be consulted at will on matters of semantic nicety or phonetic indecision. Few, it seemed, were prepared to wait for the publication of the relevant fascicle for the answers to their questions. Instead they wrote directly to Murray, requesting conclusive opinions on the 'correct pronunciation' of *isolation* or whether '*run slowly*' could be considered 'correct English' or how best to pronounce *laboratory*.[3] 'I do not know where I can get a more authoritative reply than from you', as William Read stressed in 1913, requesting information on the 'proper' pronunciation of *Cheyne* as in *Cheyne Walk*.[4] This, however, was the crux. Like the dictionary he was editing, Murray had no qualms at all about being authoritative. He willingly dispensed information on the ways in which various words were actually used in the language. Being authoritarian was, however, a different matter entirely and Murray's replies tended therefore to reveal an almost scandalous disregard for the prescriptive proprieties which were desired by many of his correspondents. Keith Harrison, for example, wrote to Murray in 1906 requesting a verdict on 'the correct spelling' of *whisky*.[5] Should he write *whisky*? Or was *whiskey* better? Which one was right? Murray's response conspicuously avoided the issue from Harrison's point of view. 'Both forms are current and equally correct or incorrect', Murray instead stated with dispassionate objectivity. As a result, 'when in a hurry you may save a fraction of time by writing *whisky*, and when lingering over it you may prolong it to *whiskey* . . . in matters of taste there is not "correct" or "incorrect"; there is the liberty of the subject'.[6] This remained his central thesis. 'I am not the editor of the English language', he would insist. 'I am too busy to set up as a general referee on English words'.[7] The dictionary would register the realities of usage, including variations in such usage, precisely in line with Trench's visions of an empirically substantiated English lexicography. Variability, as in the four different pronunciations which the *OED* provided for words such as *vase* or *hegemony*, had to be seen as a salient part of language, even if its presence disconcerted those who searched in vain for categoric proclamations on 'good' or 'bad' in usage. The same was true, as Murray assured another anxious correspondent, of the ongoing variation in the pronunciation of *either*. This 'picturesque variety' was discernible even in his own family. 'I say *eether*, my children all say *īther*', Murray confirmed – yet this was not an issue of concern. 'It is a matter of taste', he asserted. 'No wise person would wish to impose his or her taste on others'. A normative response was inappropriate. After all, Murray added, variation 'gives life and variety of language', proving its vitality and its status as a living and mobile tongue.[8] 'Some people wear turned-down collars, & some wear stand-up collars; why should they not? Is not speech as free as dress, when the pronunciations are equally well-grounded?' he declared in yet another letter on this subject.[9] The integrity of descriptivism was, as here, resolutely maintained.

The fact that popular linguistic culture in the late nineteenth century had in many ways remained determinedly prescriptive tended, however, to problematize both the writing and the reception of the dictionary. After all, even if the *OED* strove to reject the subjectivities of the past, other current works on language regularly adopted a far less impartial stance, vigorously engaging in the politics of correctness. Attitudes to the contemporary vacillation of *different to/from* provide a case in point. Whereas this was scrupulously described in Murray's entry in the fascicle *Development–Diffluency*, Henry Alford's *A Plea for the Queen's English* (in its seventh edition by 1888) instead polarized notionally 'good' and 'bad' variants. Those who use *different from* were commended; the use of *different to* conversely attracts outright censure in Alford's prose, being condemned as 'a combination . . . entirely against all reason and analogy'.[10] The authority of usage was regarded as distinctly specious. As Alford continued, although *different to* was undeniably 'very common of late', it was nevertheless to be avoided by all who wished to class themselves as 'good' speakers. From this point of view, Murray's later entry in the *OED* could be seen as betraying a striking laxity, not least in his deliberate avoidance of any impulse to condemn one form at the expense of the other. Instead 'the usual construction' is given as *different from* while, with impeccable impartiality, we are informed that *different to* is also to be 'found in writers of all ages'. It is the egalitarian image which dominates. William Thackeray's use of 'The party of prisoners lived . . . with comforts very *different to* those which were awarded to the poor wretches there' in his *History of Henry Esmond* (1852) is carefully placed alongside *different from* as deployed nine years later by Mark Pattison, the Rector of Lincoln College in Oxford. 'Warehouses and wharves no way *different from* those on either side of them', Pattison had written. Alford's text is in contrast littered with an array of published partialities, actively proscribing usages such as *in our midst* ('objectionable'), *desirability* ('a terrible word'), and *evince* ('one of the most odious words in all this catalogue of vulgarities').

Such views are by no means restricted to Alford. *Don't. A Manual of Mistakes & Improprieties More or Less Prevalent in Conduct and Speech* serves to make this persistent dichotomy of prescriptive and descriptive principles still more overt. Published anonymously by Oliver Bunce in the same year as the first fascicle of the *OED*, the book provides a lengthy list of linguistic edicts, all of which are governed by the imperative which heads its title. 'Don't say that anybody or anything is *genteel*. Don't use the word at all', Bunce dictated. 'Don't say "It is *him*," say "It is *he*"; Don't use a plural pronoun when a singular is called for. "Every passenger must show *their* ticket" illustrates a prevalent error'.[11] Even in the academic circles of Oxford, the same assumptions could prevail. Thomas Kington-Oliphant, a Fellow of Balliol College during Jowett's period as Master (and a member of the Philological Society during the early years of the *OED*'s making and discussion), sought, for instance, to impose similar linguistic strictures in his own work on language. While the dictionary of the Philological Society stressed the need for objectivity in linguistic investigation, for Oliphant it was imperatives of a rather different kind which were made to govern the practice of linguistic criticism. The latter is compared to the rightful actions of 'a sharp-eyed gamekeeper' who 'nails up rows of dead vermin on a barn door'.[12] Contemporary uses of *solidarity*, *egoism*, *acerbity*, *donate*, and *banalities* were duly constructed as verbal 'vermin' under this head though, as Oliphant admitted, these (unlike the victims of the hypothetical gamekeeper) were 'unhappily . . . not yet dead'. In a nineteenth-century version of the kind of linguistic censorship regularly practised by the Académie Française, he urged the editors of newspapers and journals to assist in the active processes of linguistic control, heading their columns 'once a month or so . . . with a list of new-fangled words, the use of which should be forbidden to every writer'.

While even Johnson had gradually come to distance himself from the reality of such processes – as he acknowledged, 'to enchain syllables, and to lash the wind, are equally the undertakings of pride, unwilling to measure its desires by its strength'[13] – those descriptive precepts by which the lexicographer abdicated even the illusion of control could make the *OED* seem distinctly out of line with many prevalent linguistic sympathies. 'Under present conditions erudite but irresponsible persons issue dictionaries', as Heald declared with scarcely veiled disparagement of the activities of the Philological Society. The result was that 'on the particular points on which he desires instruction, the inquirer finds himself left in a state of uncertainty'.[14] In determined opposition, Heald maintained a firm line on such matters in his own work on language, openly denouncing disfavoured forms such as *twin*. 'This is erroneous', he categorically stated. '"Twins" is a plural noun like scissors, tongs, tweezers . . . the fact that the word terminates with an "s" is an accident, which in no way warrants its transformation into a bastard singular noun'.[15] The *OED*'s entry for the same form contrasts sharply. Historical principles meant that usage was traced into the fifteenth century while strict impartiality meant that value-judgements did not intervene. 'One of two children or young brought forth at a birth', Murray's definition stated. No more was necessary. *Twin* was legitimized by the facts of history and the undeniable continuities of usage.

Yet for Heald and others of the same bent, descriptivism of this kind could merely seem like neglect, providing apparent sanction for words which were logically 'wrong'. 'It is a great pity you are so diffident about suggesting or advising the correct spelling or pronunciation of words', as the writer of another private letter complained to Murray; 'surely it would be better for you to be in advance of the times rather than behind it'.[16] The *OED*'s carefully assembled evidence on the coexistence of assorted forms could, as here, be perceived as regrettable evasiveness or a wilful rejection of the responsibilities which the dictionary-maker should properly adopt. 'Reticence of this kind is undesirable', a later review likewise concurred, censuring Henry Bradley for his failure to condemn the use of words such as *leisureness* in the course of editing *Leisureness–Lief*. The reviewer himself felt no such scruples. Compensating for the perceived deficiencies of the *OED*, he informed his readers that *leisureness* 'is not correct English'. It should have been 'branded' as both 'erroneous and superfluous'.[17]

The Clash of Cultures

Such iterated sensibilities act as eloquent testimony to the marked cultural gap that existed between dominant language attitudes and the somewhat different intellectual credo which informed the making of the *OED*. The tensions were self-evident. As in the laments and aspirations of Davidson and Ball, the descriptive revolution of which the *OED* was part could leave ordinary users behind, clinging to assumptions about language and 'correctness' – as well as to assumptions about the wider role of dictionaries in instituting such correctness – which had, as we have seen, been deliberately abandoned in much contemporary linguistic scholarship. This became the theme underlying countless criticisms of the *OED*. While its entries and evidence continued to vaunt the brave new world of philological science, letters and reviews repeatedly brought Murray face to face with the disturbing (and deeply frustrating) fact that, at least in popular terms, readers continued to crave a simplified version of linguistic reality where once more the lexicographer would opine from on high on preferred variants and proscribed forms. And still more worrying was the fact that even when individuals were able to appreciate in theory what the new dictionary was trying to achieve, the old ideals could still remain intact. Edward Parry, for instance, wrote a remarkably perceptive letter to Murray in 1907 which revealed a flawless understanding of the principles and practice of the *OED*. Against the controversies of usage in which ordinary speakers found themselves enmeshed, Parry placed the 'philosophical calm' of the dictionary-maker. Anxieties about usage, and the conflicting claims of coexisting variants or ongoing change were, he recognized, simply '"fish" for the lexicographer's net'. Where earlier lexicographers would have sifted and selected, endeavouring to eradicate forms deemed undesirable, the modern maker of dictionaries merely caught and observed the variabilities of usage before returning them intact to the flow of language. 'That things are what they are is a matter to be faced', Parry concluded.[18] Yet alongside this stands the admission that, at heart, he still could not dispel the sense that it would 'be better that [things] were what they *ought* to be'. Intellectual understanding and personal predilection failed to coincide. If the lexicographer could be philosophical, this was, Parry stressed, something which the 'unsophisticated layman' might find impossible. Behind the latitude of descriptivism lurked the 'uneasy feeling that the English language, & its history have some rights as against custom, which is often only a name that covers undesirable things like ignorance [and] mental sloth'. Deprived of the intentionally controlling hand of the lexicographer, as Parry admitted, usage alone could seem a somewhat insecure foundation on which to construct a dictionary.

Such problems had, in part, been foreseen by Richard Chenevix Trench. His 1857 lectures had dealt stringently with the pervasive – if misconceived – belief that the lexicographer was properly some form of linguistic dictator, ruling over language by means of the assembled entries of the dictionary. 'There are many', he had warned, who 'conceive of a Dictionary as though it had this function, to be a standard of the language'.[19] Nevertheless he was resolute that, in this respect, the weight of popular opinion had to be discarded. 'A dictionary is nothing of the kind', Trench affirmed. If the new dictionary he envisaged was to represent a 'standard' at all, then it would be a standard of actual rather than merely theoretical usage, and of the past as well as of the present. Yet even in 1857 such categorical statements existed alongside Trench's admission that a state of 'constant confusion' undeniably prevailed on this matter. A new prescriptivism ironically seemed to be the only solution – inculcating a new and more enlightened way of thinking in those who used the dictionary. In the dictionary itself compromise was declared to be out of the question.

Almost thirty years later, however, as Murray and his co-editors repeatedly found, such confusion remained intact. Indeed a paradoxical process often came into play by which descriptive facts were translated into prescriptive edicts by the very act of using the dictionary, rendering Murray's intended objectivity awry. 'Recent events . . . have shown that people will not be content to let me be purely historical', he lamented to Herbert Warren, President of Magdalen College in Oxford.[20] Instead, aptly illustrating the interpretative problems of which Trench had warned, entries which had been written in perfect accord with descriptive principles, presenting empirical data on the dating and use of given words, were perversely read as though they were prescriptive rulings on correctness. In consequence, as Murray confessed, he was often 'made a king orthographically', with his attempts to describe usage being received as though they had the status of royal proclamations. How then, Murray asked Warren, should he venture to spell *disyllable* in the dictionary? Should he use *disyllable* (which was his own preferred form) or did Warren consider *dissyllable* a 'better' spelling for lexicographic purposes? The problems of transmission in this sense seemed insoluble. As Murray admitted, 'I have no desire to pass an Act of Uniformity' but nevertheless 'feel that if I give a preference to *Disyllable*, multitudes will follow the standard'.[21] Murray here found himself trapped in the discourse and processes of standardization, forced to consider the prescriptive consequences of what were, in both essence and intention, merely statements of descriptive truth.

The effects of this 'confusion' were still more serious since they were by no means restricted to the ordinary users of the dictionary. Assumptions that descriptivism was the only logical route for the new dictionary had in fact been vehemently disputed. Derwent Coleridge had, for instance, made a determined stand against its stated policies, revealing dissent even among the supposedly enlightened members of the Philological Society. As he had argued, the subservience to usage which was affirmed by Trench's specified role of the lexicographer as witness rather than judge was surely amiss. Instead a work of this kind ought to 'set up a continual protest against innovation', Coleridge informed his own audience at the Society in May 1860. Even 'in the rare event of some change being at once possible and desirable', he added, it was in many cases better for the dictionary to indicate 'the laws to which the novelty can conform'. Like later writers such as Kington-Oliphant and Heald, he drew favourable analogies between the ideal dictionary as thus conceived and the activities of the Académie Française. 'Would it be desirable, even if it were practicable', Coleridge demanded, 'to record all the clumsy derivatives, false inflexions, and unauthorized connections supplied by the current literature of the day?'[22] The distance from his nephew on this matter seemed insurmountable. While Herbert Coleridge, as we have seen, insisted on the lexicographical virtues of impartial historicism, Derwent Coleridge recommended a firmly normative role for the projected work, not least since to his mind it was clear that usage *per se* was often flawed. As he averred, in matters of lexicography – just as in Johnson's earlier and canonical work – 'a liberty of selection must be allowed'. By extension, even if the fundamental aim of the dictionary was to be 'declarative', this did not necessarily mean that its 'regulative' function should be abandoned. Control was necessary, he continued to insist. There was a sense, as for modern words such as *telegram* and *eventuate*, in which undue liberalism would surely be misguided. 'Here, I think, the lexicographer must exercise his own judgement', Coleridge stressed, especially since the language, secure in its dynamism, was 'still capable of misgrowth'.[23] There was, he contended, no reason for the lexicographer simply to succumb to what was erroneously perceived to be inevitable. This was an area where the dictionary could (and should) beneficially intervene.

While Coleridge's dissenting voice had its advocates, the linguist Edward Nicholson, a friend of Benjamin Jowett (under whose vice-chancellorship

Nicholson was appointed Librarian of the Bodleian in Oxford), held still stronger views. 'Phonetic change is due to no unalterable causes but simply to laziness and want of instruction', Nicholson told Murray, urging the principle of lexicographical resistance. Like Derwent Coleridge, he believed it was of paramount importance that the dictionary should not weakly accede to such shifts. In the phonetic transcriptions with which each entry would be supplied, proper norms should be established and infelicities indicated. 'A standard has to be fixed', Nicholson stressed, noting the opportunities thereby presented for linguistic reform. His words hypothetically transform the *OED* into the legitimate descendant of works such as Thomas Sheridan's *General Dictionary of the English Language* of 1780, a work which, as its title page declared, had expressly been written with the intent to define 'a plain and permanent STANDARD of PRONUNCIATION'. 'It seems to be quite possible that whatever pronunciations you give in your dictionary would be gradually accepted', Nicholson urged. Like Sheridan, Murray could perhaps make the dictionary a tool for the acquisition of elocutionary propriety, a means by which the 'disgrace of dialect' might be avoided and an elegant accent secured.[24]

While such suggestions were politely – if firmly – resisted, more disturbing was the fact that even the crucial data on which the dictionary was based could be infused by the prescriptivism of popular linguistic culture. Ideological agendas of correctness are, for instance, transparent in the information supplied by the civil engineer Alexander Beazeley on contemporary semantic developments in *arcade*.[25] 'The meaning – the correct meaning – appears undoubtedly to be "a series of arches"', Beazeley informed Murray, submitting a set of citations which were to be sifted and interpreted as an intentionally objective record of the language. 'All applications of the word to the *space* or *passage* enclosed by an arcade or wall, or by two arcades' were denounced, in spite of the plentiful evidence he provided for their existence.[26] As here, Beazeley's work as reader for the *OED* can play on an assumed morality of usage which, at least in theory, denies any legitimacy to the disfavoured change. Murray's entry for *arcade* in the dictionary nevertheless systematically filters out such preoccupations, carefully reasserting the role of the *OED* as witness rather than judge. The sense decried by Beazeley as 'incorrect' appears as the dominant and unmarked meaning ('a passage arched over . . .'). Conversely the meaning which Beazeley had commended for its superior proprieties is restricted to purely architectural applications, appearing as a third and minor sense of the word. Similar were Hall's prescriptively orientated annotations alongside the supporting evidence that Murray had included in his draft entry for *abhorrence*. 'Abhorrence *for* a thing is, I think, *not English*: the example is better away', Hall declared in the margin by the side of the selected quotation from the nineteenth-century scientist John Tyndall ('A wrench, for which I entertain considerable abhorrence . . .'). In both entries as eventually published, the erroneous claims of purism disappear in favour of Murray's resolute appreciation of descriptive principles – and the realities of linguistic practice – in the late nineteenth century.

Such conflicts confirmed, on an almost daily basis, the real difficulties which surrounded the attempt to realize the *OED* in terms of the descriptive ideals by which it was fundamentally inspired. As Fitzedward Hall declared, the prevalence of such 'peremptory and unreasoned pronouncements as to what is bad English' were 'not the least of the minor pests which vex our enlightened age'.[27] Descriptive scholarship could seem remote from such concerns, standing as a noble – but largely irrelevant – ideal when faced with the kind of linguistic insecurities generated by writers such as Alford or Heald. Against the intended neutrality of the dictionary stood evaluative frameworks in which the use of *allude* (instead of *mention*) or constructions such as *frightened of* were regularly declared to be wrong.[28] An all too conspicuous irony therefore attends the fact that normative impulses of a similar kind had an impact on the published form of the Prefaces and 'General Explanations' of the *OED*, influencing the very wording in which Murray strove to set out the descriptive manifesto on which the work was based.

Murray had started the task of writing the 'General Explanations' in the autumn of 1883, crafting a document which aimed to set out the guiding principles (and methodology) of this new dictionary of the English language. Usage, variation, and the legitimacy of coexisting forms all emerge as significant concerns. Problems of dating, evidence, obsolescence, and appropriate conventions of labelling are discussed with entirely objective rigour. Murray duly sent the proof sheets containing his first attempts to the critical readers, inviting comment as well as criticism. The markedly prescriptive nature of the latter must nevertheless have been surprising. 'Their use is too occasional to allow us with certainty to infer their disuse', Murray had, for example, written as he sought to explain the problems which inevitably surrounded lexicographical decisions on whether certain words were to be deemed obsolete or merely rare. 'Too occasional' drew Fitzedward Hall's attention. *Occasional* does 'not admit of degrees', he declared, firmly annotating his own proof sheet before returning it to

Murray.[29] Skeat agreed. 'I doubt the existence of any good authority for such an expression', his own annotations record.[30] Murray was convicted of error in ways of which Alford would have been proud. 'More absolute' in the draft of the Preface to Part I of the dictionary had drawn similar censure. 'The further back we go, . . . the more absolute the impossibility of distinguishing certain from doubtful elements', Murray had noted in his endeavours to elucidate the historical limits of inclusivity. If the underlying facts were undisputed, the combination of *more* and *absolute* again provoked swift condemnation on the grounds of 'good' English – and its converse.[31] Absolute adjectives were in theory incapable of modification – though as Murray's original wording aptly illustrates, the realities of linguistic practice evidently told a different story.[32] Murray's unwitting use of *due to* was also singled out as another prescriptive shibboleth,[33] in this instance by Jowett who, scrutinizing the proofs of the 'General Explanations' in September 1883, decided to revise what he judged to be Murray's evidently shaky grammar. 'The reader will understand that 'g' and 'ȝ' represent the same Old English letter, and that the distinction made between them is due to the Editor', Murray had written in explanation of editorial policy and the intricacy of textual representation. Jowett helpfully emended it on the proof sheet he had been sent, firmly crossing out the final four words of Murray's sentence and supplying a corrected (and 'correct') version: '. . . the distinction made between them is editorial', he wrote.[34] *Due to* was eliminated, though Murray must later have taken particular delight in providing a citation for *due* in precisely this sense from Jowett himself. 'The . . . difficulty in the Philebus, is really due to our ignorance of the philosophy of the age', Jowett had written in the introduction to his *Dialogues of Plato*. Murray incorporated it into the relevant dictionary entry in a form which henceforth became part of the permanent printed record for all to see.

Murray was to become the recipient of scores of suggested emendations of this kind. 'I cannot see good grammar in what is printed', Skeat declared, his own prescriptive sympathies to the fore as he scrutinized Murray's attempt to elucidate the importance of descriptivism in the English dictionary.[35] Evaluative notions of 'good' and 'bad' ironically came to affect the very words in which descriptive linguistic practice, and the duty of the lexicographer to record what he saw before him, were discussed. Ellis attacked Murray's use of *substantivally* ('a vile word'); Murray's phrasal verbs were likewise found wanting in a proof of the Preface to Part I from September 1883. 'To *approve of*, but *approved by*', the marginal annotations state in the manner of a textbook on prescriptive grammar: 'This is according to the best usage'.[36] Murray's original construction ('In 1879, specimens were prepared by me . . . and approved of by the Council of the Philological Society') was regarded with distaste. Descriptive theory and prescriptive practice would, as a result, often assume an uneasy coexistence. The function of philologists, as Hall had stressed in his *Modern English* of 1873, 'is, chiefly, to record, and never to legislate'.[37] Yet Hall's attempted legislation against the rights of usage – and in favour of specified norms of correctness – is nevertheless all too common in the annotations which litter the proofs he sent back to the dictionary. 'Our best writers very rarely use *ere* in prose. I hate it', he wrote, for instance, in April 1888, censuring Murray's selection of the despised *ere* in a draft of the Preface to the first completed volume of the dictionary.[38] And he too attacked Murray's use of *due to*. 'I would not use "due" too often', he cautioned, inserting 'owing' in its stead.[39]

What is perhaps surprising is Murray's meek submission to such normative dictates. Hall's disfavoured *ere* was edited out and Murray's original version ('Some of these ere long pass from conversational, into epistolary, journalistic, and finally into general literary use') was revised. 'Sooner or later' replaced the offending form. Murray similarly redrafted the adjectival constructions which had raised the linguistic hackles of Skeat and Gibbs, moving his prose into forms that adhere to the prescriptive commonplaces of 'good' usage with which he often found himself confronted. If his private letters insist upon the 'impropriety of applying *right* and *wrong* to mere matters of current usage',[40] he would repeatedly find evaluative notions of precisely this kind affecting the words he wanted to use and the ideas he wanted to convey. Popular linguistic prejudices meant that the editor of the *OED* could not be seen to be mangling his verb forms or misusing his adjectives, even if such structures did indubitably constitute part of that complex linguistic reality which the *OED* sought to present to its readers. The clash of cultures, as this indicates, came to operate at the very heart of the dictionary.

Even the title of the dictionary was transformed under similar convictions of 'impropriety'. Its working title, as an early proof of September 1883 confirms, was *A New English Dictionary Showing the History of the Language from the Earliest Times*. This, however, had met with marked antipathy, not least from Jowett. In line with the markedly interventionist role which the Delegates could assume (especially in the early days of the dictionary), he decided to correct the proof he had been sent, providing instead an emended version: 'A New English Dictionary Arranged so as to

Show the Continuous History of the Words from Materials Collected under the Authority of the London Philological Society' (see fig. 5).[41] Whilst this was rejected out of hand by Murray, the marked lack of enthusiasm for the original title among other members of the Philological Society meant that a new title altogether might be advisable. The various drafts of the Preface and 'General Explanations' from late September and October 1883 appear under the heading *A New English Dictionary on a Historical Basis Founded Chiefly on Materials collected by the Philological Society*. Yet this too was to trigger prescriptive scruples about the nature of 'proper' English. Skeat queried Murray's choice of the construction *a historical*. 'Does any one ever say *a his*?' he asked, revealing sensibilities precisely in line with those articulated by writers such as Alford on this subject.[42] 'We cannot aspirate with the same strength the first syllables in the words *history* and *historian*, and in consequence, we commonly say *a history*; but *an historian*', Alford had affirmed. The preferred form was hence *an historical*. Fitzedward Hall agreed. The combination of *a* and *h* 'grates on my ear painfully', he informed Murray in another marginal annotation on the proof sheet he returned to the dictionary in October 1883.[43] Notions that 'Basis' and 'Founded on' could not coexist within the same construction provoked censure of a similar kind, and the Delegates seem to have sympathized with this belief. Their argument was based on a conviction of semantic logic – or what they felt to be an absence of such logic in Murray's selected phrasing. *Basis* was derived from *base* and this, in terms of etymology, meant 'the lowest or supporting part of any item'. As a result it was inconceivable for a basis, whether historical or otherwise, to be 'founded' on anything else. The Delegates rested their case. Murray reacted with habitual anger, resenting what he again perceived as the Delegates' attempt to edit the dictionary rather than merely being content with publishing it. The fact that here they were attempting to censor his own usage – and with reference to spurious notions of correctness – made the matter still worse. Yet the objections had to be taken seriously. Murray took a straw poll on the legitimacy of the form, consulting 'scholars and practical men of all kinds on the matter'. Without exception, he informed Bartholomew Price, these had taken a dim view of the linguistic niceties of Jowett and the other Delegates. '*Not one* has seen any objections to the words', he stated. Moreover 'when I proceeded to point out the possible objection to *Basis* followed by *Founded on* (which nobody saw himself) it was considered purely hypercritical.'[44] Murray's sense of validation was clear although, in terms of the (often strained) relations between dictionary and Delegates, the problem

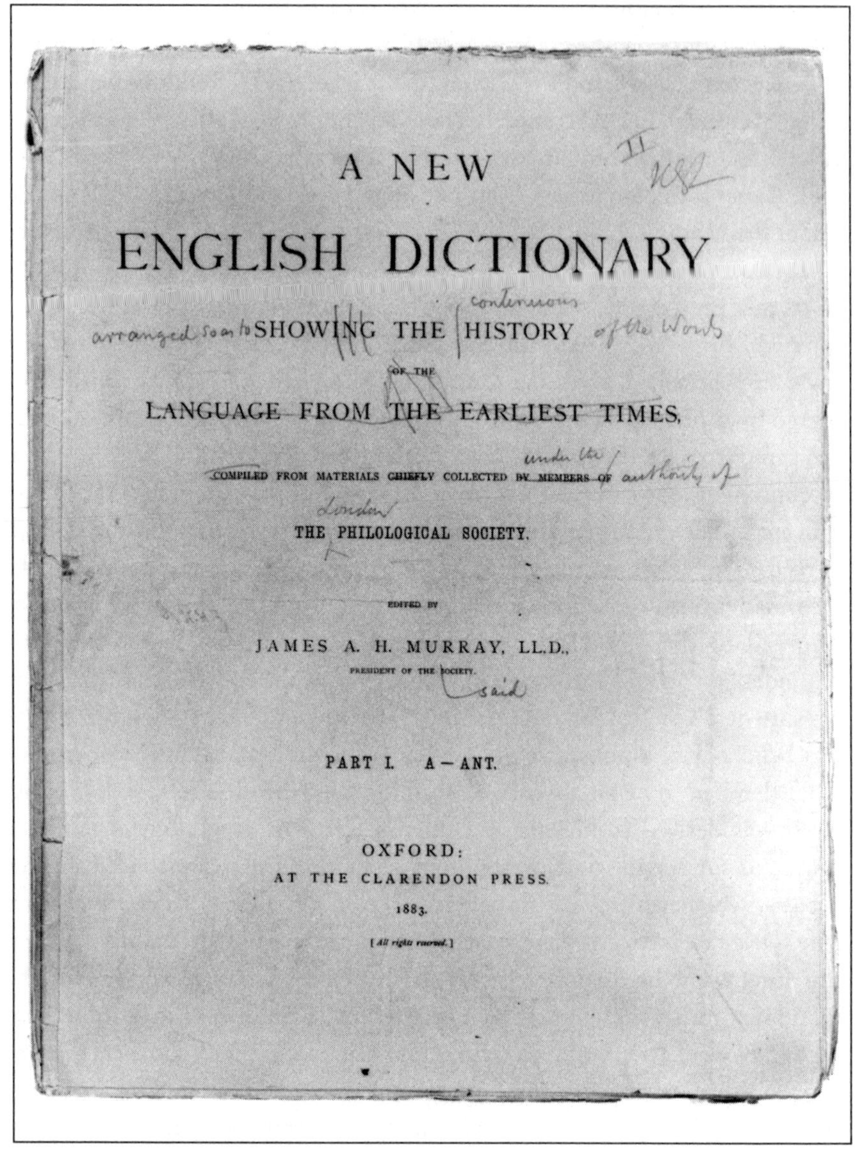

A NEW

ENGLISH DICTIONARY

SHOWING THE HISTORY

OF THE

LANGUAGE FROM THE EARLIEST TIMES,

COMPILED FROM MATERIALS CHIEFLY COLLECTED BY MEMBERS OF

THE PHILOLOGICAL SOCIETY.

EDITED BY

JAMES A. H. MURRAY, LL.D.,

PRESIDENT OF THE SOCIETY.

PART I. A – ANT.

OXFORD:

AT THE CLARENDON PRESS.

1883.

[All rights reserved.]

Figure 5 Jowett's suggested revisions on the title page of the dictionary.

remained. The title had once more been vetoed and another must be found.[45] It was for reasons such as these that the proof of the title page of the first part of the dictionary, dated 28 November 1883, took on the new identity of *A New English Dictionary on Historical Principles*, confirming a handwritten annotation of the revised title that had been made by Murray on a proof from 16 November. As in so many other instances in the making of the *OED*, compromise proved to be the safest course. *A New English Dictionary on a Historical Basis* was formally consigned to history – even if such history (for the first edition at least) refused to stay in the past. In an all too significant oversight, while *Historical Principles* were thereby undoubtedly affirmed on the title page, the first page of the dictionary would continue to reflect a different, and earlier history, in its own heading of *A New English Dictionary on a Historical Basis*.

Historians and Critics

As the various emendations made in the Prefaces and the title of the dictionary already illustrate, the optimistic vision that the new dictionary would emerge into being entirely untrammelled by the prescriptive convictions of the past could at times seem somewhat naïve. Trench's rigorous separation of the roles of historian and critic for the lexicographer had, after all, intentionally precluded the influence of prevailing language attitudes, envisaging instead a pure engagement with the realities of usage. 'The *delectus verborum* . . . on which nearly everything in style depends, is a matter with which *he* has no concern', Trench had stressed; the dictionary-maker's task was, as a result, simply 'to collect and arrange all the words . . . whether they do or do not commend themselves to his judgement'.[46] But judgement could not be entirely forgotten. Each and every entry can in practice be seen to reflect the process by which evidence was sifted and selected, initially by the sub-editors and dictionary assistants, and then by the various editors themselves. Definitions similarly were written and rewritten, prioritizing certain nuances even as others were ignored.[47] Moreover even if normative judgements in the style of Johnson were to be avoided, the lexicographer still had to decide on what could legitimately be given as the consensus norms of usage – the forms, in other words, which were really being used in the language at any given time and which it was the acknowledged duty of the dictionary to record.

This too could be deeply problematic. Consensus was, for instance, rarely as distinct as it appeared in Murray's definition of the word ('agreement in opinion; the collective unanimous opinion of a number of persons'). Indeed, as an early exchange between Ellis and Murray revealed, members of the Philological Society at times found themselves distinctly out of sympathy with current trends in the language. Ellis, for instance, confessed that he could not help but object to the use of *reliable*, a word which had become a frequent target of popular prescriptive censure in the late nineteenth century.[48] As Henry Alford had argued in 1864, for instance, 'we do not *rely a man*, we *rely upon a man*; so that reliable does duty for *rely-upon-able*'. On these grounds, Alford concluded, its use was 'hardly legitimate'.[49] Yet, as the evidence at the *OED*'s disposal was to prove, the word was indeed in frequent use in nineteenth-century English, a fact which once again served to place consensus on usage and consensus on perceived correctness at odds. Ellis, however, retained a clear grasp of descriptive priorities. In spite of his own inclinations, it was the consensus norms of usage – in which *reliable* had to be included – which were to take precedence in the dictionary. Even if not part of his – or Murray's – individual lexicon, the place of *reliable* in the wider inventory of the language was clear. 'You (like myself) may object to the use of the word *reliable*, but there is no doubt it is used', he wrote, setting up what was to be an important desideratum in the recording of words.[50] Consensus had to rest with the majority even if, from Ellis's point of view, it might at times appear to be a largely unenlightened one.

Other instances of linguistic dissent were less clear-cut in their resolution. Consensus could often prove difficult to establish, fraught with conflicting opinions. Bradley, for example, sifting the evidence at his disposal, decided that *gad* (given as a 'minced pronunciation' of *God* in various exclamatory phrases) merited the labels *obsolete* and *archaic* in the dictionary. Henry Hucks Gibbs, reading through the proofs of the relevant entry in the late 1890s, conversely argued in the adjacent margin that 'I have often heard By Gad . . . in schoolboy mouths where there has been no thought of archaism'. Which of these two conflicting versions of linguistic reality was right? Was *gad* obsolete or current? Where did the consensus norm lie in the demonstrable lack of consensus which the proofs reveal? Both views were after all demonstrably based on usage. Similar to this was *full* in the sense of 'quite, thoroughly'. '*Obsolete*', Bradley had declared, only to find himself in conflict with Gibbs once again when the latter came to examine the proofs. 'I should not think myself speaking archaically, if I said to any one who had kept me waiting "you are full late this morning" ', Gibbs countered. While Bradley was to effect a partial compromise in the published entry for *gad*, replacing *obsolete* with *rare* in deference to Gibbs's objections, he chose to maintain the validity of his original viewpoint for *full*: 'Now *archaic*, chiefly in **full well**', as the entry still reads.

Even if not all his suggestions met with editorial approval, Gibbs took his role as critical reader seriously, especially when it came to criticizing where the boundaries of current usage might be said to lie. 'I have often heard in my youth "Get you gone" without any suspicion of archaism', he objected, for example, alongside what he evidently regarded as Bradley's misguided restriction of such forms (as in 'to get oneself gone') to the English of the past. Bradley's conclusions on *glister* ('to sparkle; to glitter') were similarly judged open to question. 'The word is obsolete in ordinary use', Bradley had decided, sending his decision off to be set in type. 'Is it?' Gibbs immediately wrote next to the entry on the first proof: 'I should certainly have used it without conscious reminiscence', he added. Gibbs's dissenting voice once again prompted a slight but significant change in the wording which Bradley eventually chose to provide. 'The word is obsolete in ordinary colloquial use (though preserved in dialects)', Bradley's revised entry states, formally allowing – just as Gibbs had urged – the possibility of non-colloquial usages in which *glister* might indeed still feature in the contemporary English of the late nineteenth century.

Skeat too annotated the margins of the proofs with comments which confirm a pervasive lack of consensus within the intentionally descriptive accounts of English in the dictionary. 'Can that be obsolete which would be perfectly intelligible if used now?' he queried, disputing Bradley's verdict that *forth* in the sense 'forwards, as opposed to backwards' was no longer in use. Likewise, could *glass eye* used to mean 'eye glass' really be confined to the past rather than the present of language – especially given the fact that Thackeray had made use of it in this very sense. 'It seemed to me that there shot a flame from his eye into my brain, whilst behind his *glass* eye there was a green illumination as if a candle had been lit in it', as Thackeray had written in his *Roundabout Papers* of 1862. Bradley's assessment that this was obsolete was simply mistaken, Skeat contended. He was, however, presumably unprepared for the solutions which Bradley could choose to adopt in defending the integrity of his original labels. '*Obs[olete]* except in *back and forth*, now only *U.S.* (? or *dial.*) = "backwards and forwards"', Bradley insisted for *forth*, maintaining the integrity of his earlier editorial judgement and discarding the criticism that Skeat had ventured to make. For *glass eye*, however, Bradley simply deleted the inconvenient evidence of Thackeray's usage. In the entry as eventually published, the quotations neatly come to an end in 1721 in a change which renders his verdict of 'obsolete' entirely incontrovertible – even if one might argue that the editing of the dictionary in this instance had exceeded its expected remit.

If descriptivism appeared a difficult ideal to maintain in instances such as these, the problems could be still more far-reaching when it was the consensus norms of different editors which failed to coincide. Bradley's original decision in the first proof of *Glass-coach–Graded* that the verb *goodfellow* ('to call (a person) a good fellow') was obsolete was, for instance, rapidly to come into conflict with Murray's own assessments of usage once the latter came to read through Bradley's proofs. In Murray's opinion, as he noted in the margin alongside the word in question, *good-fellow* was merely *rare*. Bradley here chose to defer to Murray's neatly written corrections and it was as *rare* rather than *obsolete* that *goodfellow* went on to appear in the final printed version of the text. As the proofs repeatedly confirm, the appropriate labels for words and senses could participate in a marked flux – and not a little arbitrariness depending on the variable susceptibilities of different editors. Both *furied* and *furify* (respectively 'having fury', 'to render furious') came, for example, to be declared *rare* rather than being seen as an unmarked part of ordinary usage again as a result of the existence of conflicting viewpoints. While Bradley had at first chosen to see – and represent – them as ordinary and everyday, Murray's preference for the more restrictive category of *rare* was instituted in the corrections he made on Bradley's proofs in the summer of 1897. *Garlandry* (a collective term for garlands) underwent an identical shift in January of the following year, again following Murray's editorial interventions. In a similar pattern of emendation and change, *grained* (an adjective meaning 'having tines or prongs') was confined to dialectal rather than general use. 'Now *dial.*', Murray added to Bradley's entry in the first revise.[51] Still more telling, however, was the dispute which arose over *fray*. Here the demonstrable lack of consensus between Bradley and Murray was to bring the real problems of descriptivism and the dictionary into sharp focus. *Fray*, a verb used to mean 'to frighten or scare away' had, for instance, unambiguously been declared obsolete by Bradley in the fascicle *Frank-law–Gain-coming*. According to the facts at his disposal, this incontrovertibly seemed to reflect the linguistic situation of the day. The only nineteenth-century citations he had managed to locate were distinctly (and deliberately) archaic, as in Sir Walter Scott's 'It is enough to fray every hawk from the perch', spoken by 'old Raoul the huntsman' in *The Betrothed*.[52] As Bradley later found out, however, he should have taken Murray's own usage into consideration in making such a judgement. Indeed, when Murray was later drafting the entry for *huff*, it was 'fray' that Murray used to convey the semantic nuances he required. 'To fray by calling *huff*', his original definition stated. 'My impression (subject to correction) is that [fray] is the ordinary word for "to frighten away birds by shouting or with a rattle" all over rural England', he noted in evident opposition to Bradley's previous assumption of its obsolescence. 'It is *my* natural word for this', Murray emphasized. As a result he had 'naturally used it to explain *huff*'.[53] Consensus here moved in two mutually incompatible directions, not least since *fray* was obsolete according to the evidence of Bradley's entry, yet simultaneously part of current usage according to Murray's linguistic practice in the drafts of a later fascicle. Compromise yet again won the day, with Murray finding himself compelled to change the way he had originally defined *huff*, thereby eradicating *fray* from its conspicuously non-obsolete role within the dictionary. The decision was, however, taken on the grounds of practical consideration rather than his own apprehensions of linguistic truth. The lexicographical anomaly had to be resolved and, since Bradley's fascicle was at the point of publication when the problem was discovered, it fell to Murray to make the change. *Huff*: 'to scare away by calling *huff*', the dictionary now states.

If the lexicographer was therefore to be a historian, then several (possibly irreconcilable) versions of history could at times be present to his view. History had to be constructed and, as in *fray*, personal sensibilities could and would intervene in the conclusions which were drawn, enabling individual predilections and perceptions to influence presentation in what formally remained an objective domain of fact.

As such instances confirm, any dictionary is ultimately an all too human product. It is, like language, 'the work of man, of a being from whom permanence and stability cannot be derived', as Johnson eloquently declared in his Preface.[54] Outside the rhetoric of pure descriptivism, it could be an almost insurmountable task to divorce personal predilections – or one's own sense of the language – from the realm of words which had to be constructed in the dictionary. Johnson's own *Dictionary* provides ample evidence of the ways in which such partisan practices can come into play. Individual allegiances, rather than an objective assessment of the relevant linguistic (and semantic) facts, underpin his definition of *Tory*, for instance. 'A cant term, derived, I suppose, from an Irish word signifying a savage', he stated in the seemingly authoritative sphere of the dictionary. Scores of other entries such as *oats*, *patron*, or indeed *lexicographer* ('a harmless drudge, that busies himself in tracing the original, and detailing the signification of words') do the same. The *OED*, if less overtly, displays similar indications of the human factors which influence a dictionary's production. Absolute neutrality is perhaps impossible. The lexicographer is inevitably bound to time and place, embedded in his (or her) own cultural preoccupations. The inventory of the language is framed by ideologies of various kinds, ineluctably revealed in the phrasing of definitions and the connotative nuances which may be heightened or suppressed. Similarly, the ideal of impartiality can soon fracture when faced with the historical positioning of ideologies of gender, race, and class.

Bradley's entry for *gent* is, for instance, written from a perspective which clearly reveals an intensely personal distaste for the word as well as his implied superiority to those who use it. Its use was *vulgar*, he noted, his choice of status label revealing a striking alliance with Johnson's socio-linguistic stigmatization of words such as *cajole* as indubitably 'low'. For Bradley, *gent* was a shibboleth in the true sense of the word – acting as a dividing mark between two social groupings, here those he constructed as socially acceptable or otherwise. It is, he continued, 'a mark of low breeding . . . except as applied derisively to men of the vulgar and pretentious class who are supposed to use the word, and in tradesmen's notices'. Its remoteness from Bradley's own standards of usage was obvious. *Flummox* ('to bring to confusion') revealed Bradley in a similar mode. Its use was colloquial and vulgar, he opined in the dictionary, a verdict which sits at odds with the accompanying 1892 citation from the *Pall Mall Gazette*: 'The Unionists appear to be completely flummoxed by the failure of Mr. Balfour's Land Act.'

Murray too, in spite of his iterated insistence on the validity of usage, could succumb to similar displays of class feeling, proscribing the use of *do* ('something done in a set or formal manner; a performance') as undeniably 'vulgar', and extending similar condemnation to words such as *party*. His entry for the latter makes it all too obvious that it could not be recommended in constructions such as 'The party was not known to me, though she lived at Hawkshead' – even though these particular words had been written by William Wordsworth.[55] Instead, as Murray asserted, 'the proper word' was *person*. *Party* was, he wrote, unquestionably 'shoppy', 'vulgar', or, at best, 'jocular'. For entries such as these, popular prescriptive texts such as Oliver Bunce's *Don't* again display a worrying parallelism. 'Don't say *gents* for *gentlemen*, nor *pants* for *pantaloons*. These are inexcusable vulgarisms', Bunce had declared,[56] endorsing prevalent language attitudes with all the authority of assumed correctness. 'Don't say *party* for *person*', he likewise affirmed, setting up a clear precedent for Murray's later entry in the *OED*. 'The word *party* for a man is especially offensive', Alford had likewise confirmed.[57] Images of class and associated class stereotypes did in fact pervade the dictionary. Transparent in Murray's conviction that *bloody* as an intensifier was not used outside the lower sections of society,[58] they are also evident in the choice of phrasing in definitions such as that given for *mobbish*. Here *lower class* comes to operate as a virtual synonym for the disorderly, the mob-like – and, again, the 'vulgar' ('characteristic of, or appealing to "the mob" or lower classes; vulgar, clap-trap'). Other definitions affirm this form of social equation. 'Of or pertaining to the lower orders of the community; hence, vulgar, common, popular', Murray noted for *proletical*. If such socially constructed edicts are in keeping with a self-styled manual on 'good' usage, then they can seem disconcertingly normative when they appear within the intentionally objective domain of the *OED* in which empiricism rather than language attitudes – particularly those based on convictions of one's place in the social order – had been given categorical pre-eminence.

Notions of editing the language – along with the dictionary – can, as here, take on a closer relationship than Murray's formal adherence to descriptive principle overtly allowed. Instead, if one examines the language practices that were in reality to come into play within and between entries, it is evident that images of an absolute and impartial neutrality often founder. Race, and its attendant agendas of empire and imperialism, raise a number of potentially disturbing issues as realized within the *OED*. Even the making of the dictionary as originally conceived by Murray had placed the lexicographer in the role of a pioneer in 'an untrodden forest, where no white man's axe has been before'.[59] Similar images appeared in Murray's published decision to restrict the number of entries in the section of the dictionary dealing with K. 'Our constant effort has been to keep down, rather than to exaggerate, this part of the "white man's burden"', he affirmed, referring to the deliberate exclusion of a number of 'exotic' words beginning with combinations such as *Kn*, *Kr*, or *Ku*.[60] Craigie's later entry for *white man* – 'A man of honourable character such as one associates with a European (as distinguished from a negro)' – evidently participated in the same ideas, though it is notable that, in *OED2*, rather different intersections of history and race have led to some conspicuous rephrasing (and the entire elimination of the section in parentheses within this entry).[61] The original entry for *negro* too has been modified by the dictionary's later editors under shifting conditions of acceptability and appropriateness. 'An individual (esp. a male) belonging to the African race of mankind, which is distinguished by black skin, black woolly hair, flat nose and thick protruding lips', the fascicle *N–Niche* had originally recorded in 1906 in a definition which now seems far from the impartiality which the dictionary formally professed.[62] History thus proves malleable, even as realized within different editions of the *OED*. Transplanted to a new era, Murray's unself-conscious use of terms such as *blacky* in the course of defining other entry-words now forces us to face less comfortable aspects of our own past. 'A negro, a blacky', the entry for *darky* in *OED1* states, with no apparent sense that anything other than the purely descriptive truth is being given.[63]

Such prejudiced discourse in which other nations and cultures are negatively figured as 'Other' was commonplace in the nineteenth century. 'Black folk are not remarkable for their powers of reasoning', states Dr Gibson in Gaskell's *Wives and Daughters*; 'certainly if [Roger Hamley] shares my taste, their peculiarity of complexion will only make him appreciate white skins the more', he continues.[64] Similarly untoward images pervade the work of Dinah Craik, another popular novelist in the nineteenth century. As Cora Caplan has noted of Craik's redemptive story 'The Half-Caste' (published in 1851), the beauty of its heroine Zillah Le Poer is almost invariably constructed in a negative mode, framed by the disadvantage of her birth ('Even though her skin was that of a half-caste, and her little hands were not white, but brown, there was no denying that she was a very beautiful woman').[65] The rhetoric of imperialism was dominant and images of difference and deviance were, it seemed, readily equated. The demonstrable fondness, in the first edition of the *OED*, for the use of 'civilized' or 'savage' in a whole range of dictionary entries hence stands as a further manifestation of this ideological bias, once again prompting a policy of discreetly significant rewording in later editions. As cultural antonyms, both 'savage' and 'civilization' are of course self-evidently laden with ideological baggage. It was 'a remarkable instance of what civilization can do' to find schoolchildren in Luxor studying the Old Testament, with their answers to questions being given 'in tolerable English or tolerable correctness', as George Curzon, Viceroy of India, categorically stated in the early 1880s.[66] His words betray a clear conviction that English and its assumed proprieties encapsulated the very definition of civilization, as well as revealing the role of such assumptions within the imperialist agenda of the late nineteenth century. As here, 'civilization' can act as a cultural marker in ways that likewise pervade the dictionary, further delineating attendant notions of inferiority and superiority, of inadequacy or its antonyms.

Murray's entry for *king* can in this respect be seen to maintain a striking cultural binarism. When used 'in European and other more or less civilized countries', *king*, we are told, 'came to be the title of the ruler of an independent organized state called a *kingdom*'. It is a role which is placed in self-evident contrast to its use in designating 'the native rulers of petty African states, towns, or tribes, Polynesian islands, and the like'. Perhaps predictably, *chief* would attract similar cultural hierarchies in its definition in the first edition of the dictionary. 'The head man . . . of a small uncivilized community', Murray's original entry affirmed in a form of words which has been conspicuously rephrased in *OED2* on the evident assumption that the connotations of *primitive* are less derogatory. 'The head man or ruler of a clan, tribe, or small primitive community', modern editions of the dictionary record. A parallel process has evidently been at work in *chieftain*, again silently rewritten in *OED2* to obliterate the cultural codings of the past by which *tribe* automatically seemed to attract a collocational pairing with *uncivilized*: '[the chief] of an uncivilized tribe or primitive peoples', as Murray had written. A shared set of ideological assumptions of this order can be seen throughout the first edition of the *OED*. 'An aboriginal of Australia who has not come under the influence of white civilization' stands, for instance, as the selected definition of *myall*. Even *day* as defined by Murray participates in socially normative visions of precisely the same kind. The entry for the latter once more enforces a useful corrective to the often assumed neutrality of the *OED*: 'in civilized countries generally . . . the period from midnight to midnight, similarly adjusted to its mean length'. Outside the civilized, as the *OED*'s entry for *uncivilized* makes clear, stands the 'barbarous', with its negative cultural associations. Captain Cook's *Voyage to the Pacific Ocean* of 1784 was selected as apposite illustration. 'They shew as much ingenuity, both in invention and execution, as any uncivilized nations under similar circumstances', Cook wrote in his description of the domestic habits of 'the inhabitants of Van Dieman's land'.[67]

A similar fondness for 'savage' as a defining term throughout the first edition enforces other departures from the ideological objectivity which is often taken to be the *OED*'s natural home, rendering even seemingly innocuous items such as blankets sites of cultural assumption and conflict. As *OED1* declared (in a definition which has once more been quietly changed in *OED2*), a *blanket* is 'a large oblong sheet of soft loose woollen cloth, used for the purposes of retaining heat, chiefly as one of the coverings of a bed; also . . . by savages or destitute persons, for clothing'. Entries for *cabin* ('A permanent human habitation of rude construction. Applied esp. to the mud or turf-built hovels of slaves or impoverished peasantry, as distinguished from the more comfortable "cottage" of working men, or from the "hut" of the savage') or indeed *hut* itself reveal further instances of such cultural bias. In *OED2* the entry for the latter has once again succumbed to the changed ideological preoccupations of another age. 'A dwelling of ruder and meaner construction . . . often of branches, turf, or mud, such as is inhabited by savages', wrote Murray for *hut* in 1899. 'A dwelling of ruder and meaner construction and (usually) smaller size than a house, often of branches, turf, or mud, such as is inhabited in primitive societies', states the sanitized entry of *OED2*, removing a phrase which now seems incontrovertibly prejudiced in its implications and association. The 'barbarous races' who once featured prominently in Bradley's definition of *fire-water* ('chiefly with reference to the pernicious effects of alcoholic liquors on barbarous races') have likewise fallen victim to revision, changing the images of history which once dominated the dictionary.

Entries such as *marriage* and *petticoat*, *pounce* (verb) and *medicine* present a similar history, their participation in cultural agendas of this kind having been edited out in the continuing process of revision within later versions of the dictionary. *Medicine* is here particularly worthy of note in the cultural translation which has in effect taken place between the first and second editions. 'As savages usually regard the operation of medicine as due to what we should call magic, it is probable that their words for magical agencies would often first be heard by civilized men as applied to medicine', Murray had written. *OED2* instead presents the image of a different world in which terms such as 'savage' and 'civilized' are no longer deemed acceptable ('As primitive peoples usually regard the operation of medicines as due to what we should call magic, it is probable that their words for magical agencies would often be first heard by outsiders as applied to medicine'). The continued embedding of this earlier negative metalanguage within the workings of the *OED* can, however, still at times be detected. As the dictionary continues to state in its definition of *reclaim*, for example, it is an action by which 'rude qualities' are 'removed . . . by means of instruction or culture' or by which 'savage people' are brought to 'a state of civilization'. The agendas of the past, as here, evidently linger on.

Gender too operates as a further fault line in language and culture as reflected – and endorsed – within the *OED*. In a dictionary which still defines *petticoat* as 'the characteristic or typical feminine garment; . . . the symbol of the female sex or character', the fact that the intended empiricism of the dictionary is filtered through distinctly male-as-norm ideologies is perhaps unsurprising. *Pensions* were (and are) delineated in dominantly male terms which rest on the apparent conviction that women cannot be famous artists or writers (paid 'as a matter of bounty, to aged artists, authors, etc., in recognition of eminent achievements, or to their widows or orphans when left in straitened circumstances').[68] *Learned* in a similar way gains a gloss as 'men of learning' while other designations (*artist*, *Bohemian*, *first-fruit*) formally exclude the female from their expected range. 'A gipsy of society; one who either cuts himself off, or is by his habits cut off, from society for which he is otherwise fitted; especially an artist, literary man, or actor, who leads a free, vagabond, or irregular life, not being particular as to the society he frequents, and despising conventionalities generally', Murray defined *bohemian*.[69] Bradley's entry for *first-fruit* maintained a similar point of view: 'the first products of a man's work or endeavour'. More interesting perhaps are terms such as *arson* and *cockney* which are likewise made to operate along clear gender lines. 'The act of wilfully and maliciously setting fire to another man's house, ship, forest, or similar property; or to one's own, when insured, with intent to defraud the insurers', Murray wrote, explicitly disallowing the possibility of arson with reference to a house which might belong to a woman. In *cockney* women are also effaced and Murray's terms of comparison assume an exclusively male form: 'One born in the city of London . . . Always more or less contemptuous or bantering, and particularly used to connote the characteristics in which the born Londoner is supposed to be inferior to other Englishmen'. *Meridian* too reveals a significant divide: 'The middle period of a man's life, when his powers are at the full'. Such examples are multiplied indefinitely in the first edition. Cultural bias underpins Murray's definition of *too* ('an emotional feminine colloquialism' when used as an intensifier to signify 'very, exceedingly') and Bradley's entry for *horrid*. Folk linguistics in both displaces the objectivity of that science of language which the dictionary formally espoused. Bradley noted, for instance, that *horrid* is 'especially frequent as a feminine term of strong aversion' – a judgement at variance with the accompanying evidence in which the majority of usages derive from writers who are undeniably male. As these and other instances suggest, pure descriptivism could indeed be a hard taskmaster as well as one which was, in the long run, almost impossible to satisfy. As Henri Béjoint has pertinently stressed, the level to which lexicographers are able to disentangle themselves 'from generally accepted prejudices' in providing a record of the language remains a real and fundamental problem.[70] The level of incomplete 'disentangling' in the *OED* is hence both predictable and, to a large extent, understandable. Almost invariably the human interface between dictionary-maker and dictionary creates a certain latitude in which, alongside the ideals of impartial objectivity, the all too fallible preoccupations and predilections of ordinary life can creep in.

Controlling the Language

That such preoccupations and prejudices could extend to language in use as recorded in the dictionary is simply another consequence of the fact that lexicographers necessarily remain ordinary speakers of the language alongside the professional roles which they also assume. Dictionary-makers too can succumb to prevailing language attitudes, and may even share popular assumptions about 'good' and 'bad' in matters of ordinary usage. Just as in the anxieties of Murray's many correspondents, language – even for the ostensibly impartial lexicographer – can sometimes seem to be amiss, displaying, in effect, that potential for 'misgrowth' of which Derwent Coleridge had warned.[71] The fact that so many letter-writers also saw fit to complain about the undue liberality of the dictionary in these matters nevertheless serves as a useful index of the level of descriptive impartiality which the dictionary did indeed achieve. However, if one examines individual entries in more detail it becomes clear that sympathies about 'incorrect' usage were sometimes shared by readers and editors, and that the resistance to change advocated by writers such as Alford and Oliphant could find its own counterpart within the ostensibly descriptive territory of the *OED*.

Murray's entry for *avocation* provides an early example of this problem as intentionally impartial evidence is filtered through the preoccupations of a dictionary-maker whose own impartiality occasionally disappears. A loan word from Latin, *avocation* had been used in English for several centuries, first appearing in the Renaissance, after which it gradually acclimatized itself to its new surroundings, taking on new senses as it did so. Polysemy is of course a normal linguistic process by which a pattern of coexisting meanings gradually evolves around a single word. As the *OED*'s entry for *line* confirms, for instance, if in its earliest uses *line* had signified simply cord or string, it has since acquired a complex of other senses which include the 'lines' of the spider's web, the 'lines' of telegraph or telephone wires (or other wires which carry electric current), as well as figurative uses in which it signifies the 'line of life'. *Avocation* was no different in the way it gradually gained a set of radiating and transferred senses. To its original meaning in English ('the calling away or withdrawal (of a person) from an employment') were added later senses: *avocation* could also signify 'the condition of being called away, or having one's attention diverted' as well as 'a minor and less important occupation'. The latter stands as the *OED*'s third sense, a meaning further elucidated by Murray's comment that an avocation in this context was something 'which has the effect of calling away or withdrawing one from [one's main] occupation'. So far, so good. The fourth sense, however, was clearly one with which Murray felt uncomfortable. 'Ordinary employment, usual occupation, vocation, calling', he noted. This was 'the new meaning' but rather than registering it in the expected impartialities of descriptive theory, Murray instead informs us that it is a sense which has been 'improperly foisted upon the word'. The emotively loaded *foist* further confirms his antipathy to the change. As Bradley later confirmed in the course of *Flexuosity–Foister*, *foist* in this sense was distinctly negative – 'to palm or put off; to fasten or fix stealthily or unwarrantably *on* or *upon*'. In terms of *avocation* therefore, while the other meanings were evidently deemed legitimate from Murray's point of view, that in which it was used to signify 'one's usual occupation' could not be accorded the same sanction. Prescriptivism again intervenes, its presence confirmed by Murray's deliberate polarization of instances where the word is 'rightly used' (as in the 1840 citation which he provides from Lord Macaulay: 'Found, even in the midst of his most pressing avocations, time for private prayer') against those instances where no such approval can be given – as in Henry Buckle's *History of Civilization in England* ('War and religion were the only two avocations worthy of being followed'). Here at least Murray regarded usage as both fallible and flawed, explicit issues of correctness (and its converse) influencing what he chose to admit as the acceptable consensus norms of English. True in part to his principles, he provided the evidence for the ongoing change, undeniably attested as it was in Henry Buckle's prose and, still earlier, in Thomas Moore's *Lalla Rookh* of 1817 ('Poetry was by no means his proper avocation'). Murray would, however, also deliberately and categorically withhold the final editorial sanction of approval from such semantic shifts. The meaning was 'improper', a verdict which *OED2* maintains.

Murray's feelings as a speaker of the language obviously played their part in this expressed resistance, in spite of his constant denial of subjectivity of this kind in his private letters to anxious correspondents. *Avocation* was, after all, a prominent issue in popular language attitudes and Murray was by no means alone in his attempted resistance. This new sense was a 'monster', Alford had declared; it was a journalistic corruption which threatened to destroy the 'real' meaning of the word. Vigilance was, he stressed, necessary lest its effects prove even more damaging.[72] Heald offered a similar caution: 'The word "avocation" is frequently wrongly employed to denote profession, calling, vocation, business, trade . . .'.[73] The *OED* here came to display an uneasy alliance with popular prescriptive discourses, based in a shared sense of linguistic conservatism and a joint conviction that contemporary usages of *avocation* were simply wrong. Similar too was Murray's later entry for *transpire* in which he again deliberately chose to endorse older against newer meanings. Figurative uses in which the word could mean 'to escape from secrecy to notice' or 'to leak out' were admitted without further comment. Nevertheless Murray evidently felt that sanction could not similarly be given to that transference by which *transpire* had also come to signify 'to occur, to happen, to take place'. Here, as the dictionary categorically stated, the word was 'misused'. And as Bradley's earlier entry in the *OED* had confirmed, *misuse* was unambiguously normative in its implications: 'To use or to employ wrongly or improperly; to apply to a wrong purpose'. Writers such as Dickens and Nathaniel Hawthorne, as well as the travel writer (and novelist) Lawrence Oliphant, all of whom had deployed this sense of *transpire*, were thereby convicted of error. 'His account of what transpired was so utterly unlike what I expected', Lawrence Oliphant had written in his novel *Altiora Peto* of 1883. 'Few changes – hardly any – have transpired among his ship's company', Dickens had stated thirty-five years earlier in *Dombey and Son*. Murray in his role as historian carefully traced such usage back to 1775. In his role as critic, however, he flatly refused to countenance this particular change in ways which bear striking affinities with the normative verdicts of texts such as *Don't*. 'Don't say *transpire* when you mean *occur*. *Transpire* means to become known, and hence is erroneously used in the sense of taking place', Oliver Bunce had dictated in 1884.[74] This change in progress was to be regarded as similarly suspect in the *OED*. Taking a stand against the assembled evidence of the slips, Murray resolutely adhered to the older forms and usages of his youth. Bradley, too, shared Murray's feelings on this matter (this modern sense of *transpire* was simply the consequence of 'ignorant misapprehension', he declared in 1904).[75]

While issues of linguistic controversy can be handled with impeccable objectivity in the *OED*, as in Murray's entry for *averse to*/ *from* (in which he refuses to endorse the evident susceptibilities of contemporary opinion, asserting instead that usage confirms the validity of both), his entry for *hideously* offers a further glimpse of somewhat different sensibilities in action. Murray obviously regarded its recent use as an intensifier with distaste and he overtly gives preference in the dictionary to older and more conservative senses in which it signified 'in a hideous manner'. The shift away from this more literal meaning was, he decreed, a 'misuse'. Supporting evidence within the entry is paradoxically used to justify a prescriptive rather than descriptive credo. 'There is a calmness about your life which makes me hideously envious', the effusive Mrs Fairfax-Torrington declares in the accompanying quotation from Mary Braddon's novel *Mount Royal* (1882). Though Murray's critical attitude in this matter would no doubt have pleased Gibbs – whose stringent opinions on 'hasty' women writers have already been discussed[76] – the tension between cited usage and stated incorrectness remains unresolved. The fact that Murray had evidently been unable to locate a single nineteenth-century example of this notionally 'correct' use of *hideously* makes the problems still more plain. In the entry as it stands, a conviction of mass error is clearly made to attend contemporary usage in an equation which remains distinctly problematic.

Murray's verdict on the relative proprieties of *rime* and *rhyme* was to present parallel problems. These forms notionally fell within Craigie's province as editor of R, a section of the dictionary which had already proved a more arduous business than Craigie might have preferred.[77] The spelling of *rhyme/ rime* was particularly contentious. *Rime* was the older form and its spelling revealed its etymological descent from Old French *rime*. *Rhyme* as a variant spelling had appeared in the Renaissance and over the years it had gradually come to dominate in English usage. Craigie diligently observed the workings of linguistic history in the citations he had before him, coming to the entirely justified conclusion that *rhyme* had to be given as the 'standard spelling' in the dictionary. As such, he concluded, it was *rhyme* rather than the outdated *rime* which ought to be the form which was used in the explanations, definitions, and associated entry-words. To Craigie's astonishment, however, Murray categorically disagreed. Craigie's descriptive reasoning was discounted and Murray instead sought to prescribe what was, in essence, a qualitative rather than objective norm. *Rime* was 'intrinsically the best', he had stated in the Preface which accompanied the dictionary's first part in 1884.[78] This was the spelling that Murray had subsequently imposed as a norm throughout the dictionary. As a result, he argued, it would damage the dictionary – 'introduce anarchy' – if Craigie were to use the spelling 'rhyme' in the definitions, as well as providing it with an entry on its own terms. Rather than being legitimized as a form in its own right, *rhyme* ought to appear as a mere variant under *rime*, Murray insisted. Tempers once more flared. Craigie maintained the significance of the descriptive norm of *rhyme* which, over and over again, he observed before him in the accumulated piles of slips. Murray meanwhile continued to assert that, whatever usage appeared to suggest in this instance, *rime* and *rime* alone was 'correct' and that it was this which must appear as a headword in the dictionary and in the surrounding text. 'Would you mind telling me the precise grounds on which the spelling *rime* was adopted in the Dictionary?' Craigie ventured to ask.[79] Murray refused to comply. 'I must insist upon it', he stressed, the authoritarian voice of the editor-in-chief once more in evidence; 'if any public animadversion is made upon it, you are always at liberty to say that was one of the points on which you were overruled . . . I am quite prepared to defend the action publicly, whereas I could offer no defence of the practice which occurs in the made-up sheet.'[80] Usage was inadequate to resolve the clash of principles involved. Craigie as a result found himself acknowledging *rhyme* as the usual form while paradoxically being compelled to use *rime* every time he wanted to discuss the word or any of its derivatives. *Rhymeless*, he wrote, his submission to Murray evident in the definition which follows: 'Without rime; unrimed'. In a similar way he was forced to define *rhymer* as 'one who makes rimes', *rhymery* as 'the making of rimes', *rhymeful* as 'abounding in rimes'. To his mind, the lack of logic in what he was made to do was even stronger when the accompanying citations were considered. All, without exception, used the spelling with *rhyme-* ('Compositions in verse . . . rhymeful and cutting', 'Rhymeful as a nursery ballad', 'Written in blank verse, or at least in rhymeless lines'). This evident dichotomy of principle and practice still acts as a telling image of the difficulties that writing the dictionary could bring.[81]

Henry Bradley and the Culture of Correctness

If descriptive precept lost out in instances such as these or, indeed, was to prove demonstrably lacking in Onions's later dealings with the proprieties of *who* and *whom*,[82] it is undeniable that neutrality does nevertheless serve to provide the overarching structure of the *OED*. But if even Murray found his professional impartiality fading as he faced the semantic slippage of words such as *transpire*, then for Henry Bradley the conflict of interests which such shifts represented was often still more pronounced. Bradley was, after all, a man famed not only for his philological precision and wide-ranging knowledge of languages, but also for his heightened awareness of linguistic nicety and all that this involved. As the poet and language reformer Robert Bridges recalled in his 1928 memoir of Bradley, the latter 'could only speak in correct grammar'.[83] Bradley's consciousness of correctness was such that he was unremitting in his observance of its norms, displaying a meticulous concern for what he deemed the proper linguistic standards in each and every act of communication, spoken or written. As a result, as Bridges continued, whereas other individuals might 'heedlessly . . . embark on a sentence in a manner that leads up to a grammatical impass', such unplanned infelicities were impossible for Bradley, given his command of language. Instead Bradley habitually began every sentence several times 'before he was satisfied that he had got hold of a construction that would carry him through'. Bradley's every word would betray a 'conscious way of talking', a heightened awareness of the putative rights and wrongs of language. Usage, as least as far as his own words were concerned, evidently had to be controlled. And if, in his utterances, he maintained a continued vigilance against the potential occurrence of some linguistic *faux pas*, then the attention he paid to the language habits of others was perhaps still more rigorous. Extending the habit of gathering citations for the *OED* into his own daily engagement with language in use, Bradley therefore amassed 'treasured samples' of 'unintentional malaprops, . . . accidental equivokes, solecisms and literary blunders' which he happily brought out in general conversation.[84] Bradley's favoured anecdotes were thus linguistic rather than personal, with lists of semantic shibboleths or grammatical 'howlers' being recounted for general amusement as well as incidental erudition. As Bridges ruefully concluded, 'when once embarked on one of these old stories, no protest or quizzing of mine could prevent him from completing it in full'. This was Bradley's private obsession, a detailing of the linguistic fallibilities which could and did attend the actualities of ordinary usage.

It was an odd preoccupation for a dictionary-maker engaged on a work such as the *OED*. Yet the influence of Bradley's unremitting attention to the problems of linguistic nicety and proper expression can, in a number of ways, be detected in the fascicles under his control, revealing the intervention of unexpected sympathies (or antipathies). What emerges, in consequence, is a markedly personal engagement with the facts of usage, presented in ways that stress resistance to current practice rather than a commitment to its empirical (and objective) observation. *Emergency*, for instance, was a word which was in the process of shifting its meanings in the nineteenth century. The drift had already begun when Johnson published his *Dictionary* in 1755: 'A sense not proper', he observed, categorically dismissing the tendency to use the word to mean 'urgency'. Addison's comment that 'In any case of emergency, he would employ the whole wealth of his empire, which he had thus amassed together in his subterraneous empire' was thus given in entirely negative illustration. 'Proper' use was located in meanings such as 'any sudden occasion' as well as 'the act or rising into view', senses which Johnson unequivocally commended. Almost a century and a half later, Bradley was to find himself in distinct agreement with his august predecessor. Indeed in the *OED* the construction 'It is a case of great emergency' is provided only to be immediately condemned by the addition of ¶ – the symbol used throughout the dictionary for what was termed catachrestic usage ('wrongly used, misapplied, wrested from its proper form', as the relevant entry in *Cast–Clivy* explained). This generalized sense of *emergency* was untenable, Bradley insisted, withholding lexicographical sanction. Far better were those uses in which *emergency* denoted something which had unexpectedly arisen and for which immediate action was necessary, as in Byron's 'On great emergencies/ The law must be remodell'd or amended', which Bradley cites from the poem 'Marino Faliero, Doge of Venice' of 1820. Byron's propriety in this instance contrasts with that evidently fallible usage which Johnson had recorded from Addison (and which Bradley repeats) in which the standards of the great prose stylist had ostensibly slipped. The shift was a 'distortion of meaning', Bradley later wrote, further confirming his normative predilections on this matter.[85] As for Johnson, change in language could be construed as degeneration or decline. Bradley's peculiarly overt judgement on the fallibilities which modern uses of *emergency* displayed both illustrates and confirms his constant thesis that language at times stood in need of active 'correction'. Like Johnson, he could be trapped within apparently irreconcilable beliefs about the rightful actions of the lexicographer. The dictionary-maker should 'register, and not form' the language, Johnson had written in his own Preface.[86] Yet he also stated – on the same page – that 'every language has likewise its improprieties and absurdities which it is the duty of the lexicographer to correct or proscribe'. For Bradley, the use of ¶ in the dictionary entry for *emergency* was at least one step in the direction of the latter. The fact that even Henry Alford had rejected Johnson's condemnation of *emergency* in this context serves, however, as a disturbing indication of the conservatism Bradley had deliberately chosen to display on this matter in the pages of the *OED*.[87] The disputed meaning, as Alford had argued in

1864, was 'now universal'. 'That Johnson, who gives this sense, should have characterised [it] as "A sense not proper," can only be classed among the many blemishes of his great work', he added, clearly distancing himself from a judgement which he regarded as flawed.

Bradley's work as a lexicographer on many occasions revealed sympathies which ran counter to the apparently errant ways of modern usage. His entry for *enthuse* shows a parallel disjunction between evidence and opinion as provided by the dictionary. The word is 'an ignorant back-formation from *enthusiasm*', Bradley wrote, his disapproval evident in his censorious selection of 'ignorant' as an appropriate label in this context. 'Destitute of knowledge, either in general or with respect to a particular fact or subject; unknowing, uninformed, unlearned', the entry for *ignorant* confirmed. Back-formation, a process evident in, say, the coining of *burgle* from *burglar*, is of course a pattern of long standing in the language.[88] Descriptively speaking, it is therefore no more deserving of censure than any other form of change. Citations such as 'I admit he began to enthuse a little' from James Grant's *Confessions of a Frivolous Girl* of 1880 and 'I don't get enthused at all, sir, over this Greek business', as H. P. Kimball admitted in the *Pall Mall Gazette* in 1887, were nevertheless determinedly stigmatized in the entry for *enthuse* as it appeared in the first edition of the *OED* (and indeed still in *OED2)*. Precisely as in Johnson's disfavoured uses,[89] the selection of 'ignorant' is made to stand like a prescriptive beacon, condemning and proscribing forms of which the lexicographer could not approve – in spite of the undoubted currency of such forms. Bradley's entry for *expect* betrays the same sympathies in operation so that the now dominant modern use ('to suppose, to surmise') is roundly condemned. This is a 'misuse', Bradley declared. Even if it was 'very common', such frequency was, Bradley insisted, limited to 'dialectal, vulgar, or carelessly colloquial speech', a trio of adjectives (the last heightened by adverbial condemnation) which blends seamlessly with the kind of prescriptive metalanguage happily deployed by earlier writers such as Thomas Sheridan as he urged his own readers to avoid the evident fallibilities of current speech in favour of the long-established proprieties of the past.

Behind the perceived 'errors' which Bradley sought to condemn, glimpses of linguistic reality nevertheless remain, contrasting sharply with his negative verdicts on certain shifting usages of the late nineteenth century. Was the Oxford-educated author William Mallock really being 'vulgar' or 'carelessly colloquial' in the use of *expect* in his *New Republic: or Culture, Faith and Philosophy in an English Country House* of 1877? The context of the quotation (as well as the setting) certainly seem at odds with such a view: 'Now I expect, Lady Ambrose, that, in its true sense, you know a good deal more history than you are aware of', the upper-class Otho Lawrence declares.[90] Similarly, could the same charge legitimately be levelled at Sir George Dasent in his comment, made in the impeccably scholarly Preface to his famous and highly regarded translation of the Icelandic *Story of Burnt Njals*, that 'It is an old saying, that a story never loses in telling, and so we may expect it must have been with this story'? Bradley's selected citations here seem to exist apart from his framing comments, enforcing a necessary reassessment of the censure he had chosen to accord this change of sense. While such examples can be multiplied in the first volume under Bradley's editorship (as in the ostensibly 'incorrect' use of *enormity* when intended to signify 'hugeness, vastness'),[91] they remain equally perceptible in other areas of the dictionary. Prescriptive edict and descriptive fact once more fail to coincide in terms of *feasible* when used with the sense 'likely, probable', for example. This was 'hardly a justifiable sense etymologically', as Bradley declared, attempting to lend further credence to his position by pointing out that this sense of *feasible* had hitherto failed to appear in any dictionary. In a work publicly committed to being a 'new garment throughout', this provided little justification. Against the alliances forged in terms of prescriptive inclination between Bradley and writers such as Alford and Heald, the assembled evidence again tells the true story. Charles Lyell's statement from his *Principles of Geology* of 1833 that 'The only feasible theory . . . that has yet been proposed' is that of adaptive variation, or David Livingstone's 'It seems feasible that a legitimate . . . trade might take the place of the present unlawful traffic' from his *Narrative of an Expedition to the Zambesi* of 1865, reveal the thrust of ongoing change and the 'vitality' which Murray had earlier praised, even if this dynamism was to remain largely unappreciated in the entry as it stood. *Literally*, as documented by Bradley in the *OED*, revealed other affinities with popular prescriptive assumptions about language use. The comments of Robert Heald in his guise of 'Anglophil' were to find a surprisingly precise echo in this entry in the dictionary. It is 'improperly used' to signify 'absolutely, actually, really', Heald had written in 1892;[92] it is 'improperly used' in spite of its frequency, Bradley affirmed eleven years later. Usage, as in *enthuse* and *emergency*, *enormity* and *expect*, meanwhile went on regardless.

Change, and attitudes to change, remained the central issue. The 'constituent elements' of language, as Murray had stressed in the 'General Explanations', are 'in a state of slow but incessant dissolution and renovation'. This recognition was fundamental to his vision of the *OED*. Bradley's attitudes, however, could be significantly different. Obviously each and every entry in the *OED* reflected a detailed engagement with the facts of change. Bradley likewise spent countless hours tracing derivation and descent, the mutabilities of form and meaning which the passage of time had brought. If such research occupied his professional hours – it is like 'groping in the dark', he lamented to Murray of his quest to elucidate the etymology and historical development of *beat* and *bait*[93] – his personal convictions on the flux of language remained at odds with such essentially descriptive cataloguing. 'Because people used to ignore the fact of language being a natural growth, and to propound futilities about "improving" it, there has arisen a tendency to run into the opposite extreme', Bradley wrote to Robert Bridges in a private letter. In his view, such passivity was not always wise. Instead, he added, 'I think that so far as [changes] are mischievous we ought to try and resist them'.[94] Forms such as *swashbuckling* were hence deemed reprehensible, and he expressed the earnest hope that this at least would 'not obtain general currency', even if its usage was increasingly common.[95] Bradley's long-time membership of the Society for Pure English – and his status as one of its founding members (along with Bridges, the critic Sir Walter Raleigh, and Logan Pearsall Smith, another conspicuous devotee of 'correct' English) – confirmed him in such views. As the original Prospectus for the Society declared in 1913, its aims were explicitly to include 'preserving all the richness in differentiation in our vocabulary, [and] its nice grammatical usages'. It stressed its equal commitment to opposing 'whatever is slip-slop and careless, and all blurring of hard-won distinctions'.[96] The engagement with language which the Society advocated was thus determinedly interventionist, in individual as well as general terms. Where it was thought necessary, its members were encouraged to 'introduce . . . certain slight modifications and advantageous changes' into current usage.[97] Bradley's opinion that change could be 'mischievous' here found additional expression and support.

'There are, however, some "spelling-pronunciations" that are positively mischievous', Bradley averred in one of the pieces he wrote for the Society, condemning the process by which *forehead*, once uniformly pronounced /fɒrɪd/, had, under the influence of its written form, gained a (now dominant) pronunciation as /fɔːhɛd/.[98] His own entry for *mischievous* in the *OED* once more sets the tone. 'Having harmful effects or results', as the fascicle *Misbode–Monopoly* explained. In the context of the natural processes by which words, spellings, pronunciations, and meanings all prove mutable over the course of time, this conviction once again placed change within a framework in which it could be constructed as profoundly and essentially negative. If in most cases 'we shall be beaten', the effort was still worth while.[99] It is, in turn, this which underlies Bradley's subsequent resistance to the consequences of such changes, whether this was to pronouncing *forehead* as /fɔ:hɛd/ or with reference to the shifting semantics of words such as *transpire* and *premises*.[100] Uses of the latter to signify 'a house with its appurtenances' were merely based on a popular misapprehension of legal discourse, Bradley stressed. Legal conventions by which 'in the body of a document it is usual to employ the expression "the premises"' did not therefore legitimize a new sense; this merely referred back to items which had been specified in full at the beginning of a written lease or similar text. As Bradley carefully pointed out, just as the premises of an argument are stated at the outset, so in a lease 'the premises' are 'the things specified at the beginning as the things to which the following stipulations have reference'. Here he sought to provide a logical refutation of the semantic departures in which *premises* seemed to be engaged. The meaning of 'buildings', 'houses', or 'lands' was cast outside 'good' English.[101] As Bradley argued, the term was not recognized in dictionaries. Ironically time itself would prove him wrong, even within the *OED*. Five years later Murray's entry for *premises* objectively verified the disfavoured form, tracing usage back into the early eighteenth century.

Bradley's personal predilections as a speaker and writer certainly heightened the recurrent conflicts of descriptive theory and prescriptive practice that attended the making of the *OED*. Even if his entry for a word such as *eventuate* displays an impeccable regard for the evidence at his disposal, neatly running counter to the prejudices expressed by Alford and Heald on this head (it was 'another horrible word . . . fast getting into our language through the provincial press', Alford had contended),[102] headwords such as *everybody*[103] return us once more to Bradley as an ordinary speaker of the language, still ineluctably enmeshed in the web of popular assumptions and attitudes towards correctness and its converse. Being a lexicographer was by no means easy. 'He . . . frequently had to translate his knowledge into uncongenial forms', as Bridges later recalled of Bradley's work on the dictionary.[104] Quelling one's natural sympathies (or distaste) for various instances of language could require heroic endeavours. And behind the heroic, the human is at times all too visible.

CHAPTER 6

Ended but not Complete

Editing the dictionary, as the previous chapters have shown, continued to present Murray and his co-editors with a whole range of problems to which solutions were not easily found. Words such as *hay-cratch* refused to yield up their meaning, driving Murray to exasperated conjecture: 'Is it the sparred place over a horse's head in a stall, through which he pulls out the hay? Is it the sparred arrangement on or near the ground in a cow-house . . .? Is it a portable thing I have seen in fields, through the spars of which . . . beasts pull out hay in winter?' 'Is it all or any of these, or something else?' He drew careful diagrams to illustrate what he meant (see p. 180). 'Pray enlighten me', he concluded.[1] Poetic creativity would likewise test Murray's patience to the limits, leading to the markedly unsatisfactory entry that he felt compelled to give for *harvestry*: 'The act or work of harvesting; also, that which is harvested. (Ogilvie, *Suppl.*, citing Swinburne)'. No citations appear to verify usage and Murray merely acknowledges his dependence on John Ogilvie's earlier lexicographical work. Even a direct appeal to Swinburne himself had given little illumination. 'I have no idea where I may have used the word "harvestry". I suppose I must have done if lexicographers say so: but when or how I cannot guess', the poet had replied.[2]

Nevertheless as work on the *OED* moved into the twentieth century a renewed sense of confidence and certainty attended both its making and publication. 'Already the joke of wishing a friend length of years in the form "May you live to see the Oxford Dictionary completed" has lost its point', as one review from this time confirmed.[3] 'Indeed', it added, 'there is . . . no reason why subscribers who are now all considerably on the wrong side of middle age should not regard hopefully the prospect of seeing the complete series of massive volumes of this great survey of English speech standing ready upon their shelves'. At the Press too the crises of the 1890s were placed firmly in the past. Under the new

At Kenwick's Park, between Cockshutt ~~& Oswestry~~: also at Stanwardine this is called a sheep-cratch. At Wem sheep-racks
? Sheep-cratch in Cheshire

winter? The shape I have seen was like this. Is it all or any of these, or something else? Kindly give me as explicit account as you can.

The word is immensely common in M.E., unfortunately without contextual description; as the name of the 'manger' at Bethlehem, it occurs everywhere in devotional books.

Miss Jackson has 2 modern quotations for 'sheep-cratches' from Shropshire Auctioneers' sale-catalogues. Mr [illegible] wonders if these are the flat-bottomed troughs out of which sheep are fed in winter.

You see Cratch is to Northerns and Southrons an unknown mysterious word as to the sense of which we can only form (perhaps) wild guesses;

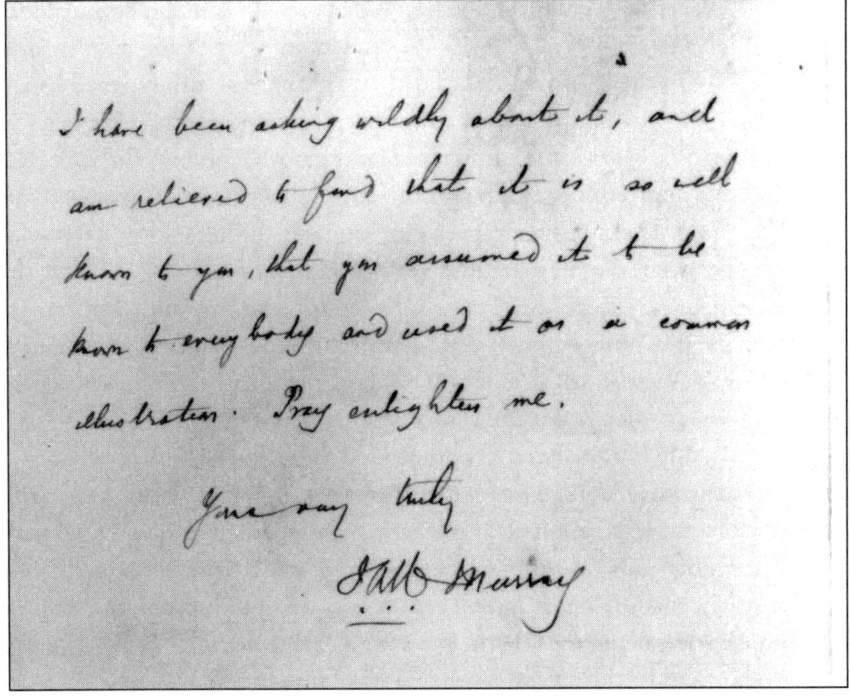

I have been asking wildly about it, and am relieved to find that it is so well known to you, that you assumed it to be known to everybody and used it as a common illustration. Pray enlighten me.

Yours very truly

J A H Murray

Figure 6 Annotated and illustrated letter from J. A. H. Murray to Mr Darlington, 26 November 1892 (MP/26/11/92).

Secretaryship of Charles Cannan,[4] even the Delegates seemed to have settled down into a more positive relationship with their most costly progeny. Cannan even enjoyed reading the proofs of the dictionary, a habit which Gell had certainly not shared. Moreover, instead of the two-year gap which had intervened between the appearance of *Ant–Batten* and *Batter–Boz*, the dictionary, much to the Delegates' relief, had adopted a steady rhythm of publication. In 1900, for instance, seven sections – each of sixty-four pages – had appeared. The following year saw publication of *Jew–Kairine*, *Kaiser–Kyx*, and *L–Lap*. With Craigie finally taking on the role of a formally independent editor in the same year, the three editorial teams began to work in close and productive synchronicity. In the Old Ashmolean Craigie busied himself with Q and Bradley concentrated on L. Murray toiled at M in his Scriptorium on Banbury Road. A further four sections of the dictionary appeared in 1902. Experience evidently brought its own rewards. By 1900, for example, Murray and Bradley had jointly amassed some thirty-five years of practical expertise on the dictionary. Assistants such as Arthur Maling and William Worrall had likewise been with the *OED* for sixteen and seventeen years respectively. The dictionary had a firmly established pattern for the writing of entries and their composite parts. Like cogs in a machine, the various dictionary teams moved surely through the lexicon, drafting, editing, and revising an endless flow of words. 'The great Oxford Dictionary pursues its course through the letters of the alphabet with the majestic and regular march of the sun through the signs of the zodiac', as the *Times* later commented in approbation. Its productivity did not go unnoticed. 'Punctually four times a year a new number of this great serial makes its appearance, and the interest, as we say in lesser matters, is magnificently maintained'.[5]

The very scale of the dictionary confirmed the advances which were being made. 'The words recorded [in] *Jew* to *Jywel* are almost twice as many as in any other dictionary', a notice in the *Periodical* recorded in July 1901; 'with regard to quotations the difference is still more remarkable', it added.[6] The immensity of the *OED* as it moved towards its mid-point prompted a range of enthusiastic calculations. If the type from each column of the dictionary were to be reset vertically end to end, it would extend almost four times as high as Snowdon, and be only 602 yards below the top of Mont Blanc (as well as fourteen times higher than the Eiffel Tower), one correspondent to the *Periodical* painstakingly reckoned in 1900.[7] Were the same hypothetical resetting to take place horizontally, the single line of type would moreover go a fair way towards encompassing the nation as well as the language, reaching from Charing Cross to Folkestone. Seen in these terms the dictionary was a bargain. A single penny bought '1 yard 1 foot and 8 odd inches of solid printed matter, 2½ inches wide, on unexceptionable paper, turned out in the best manner of the University Press'. Nine years later a correspondent from Yorkshire went one better in the attempt to establish the economic advantages of purchasing the *OED*. As he appreciatively confirmed, since publication of its first volume the net cost had been less than a halfpenny a day – excluding Sundays.[8] Contrary to the earlier financial pessimism of the Delegates, from this point of view the dictionary was clearly a success.

As the Delegates also came to realize, there was after all a certain grandeur in the ways in which the *OED* consistently exceeded its American predecessor. Webster's 1864 *Dictionary* remained of course the token benchmark, along with the requirement that the dictionary should – in principle – maintain a scale no greater than eight times the extent of Webster's work on any given section. In line with this the Delegates continued to monitor the scale – and the costs – of the dictionary, requiring regular reports on the progress of the different editors at their meetings. In January 1902, for instance, they were informed that Craigie had produced four pages against Murray's eight and a half while Bradley had reached a total of just over twelve. In June Craigie produced seventeen pages, Bradley just over sixteen, and Murray twenty-two. Against Webster's 'gold standard', such figures could still be deemed amiss – Craigie's sudden shift in November 1902 to a scale of nineteen pages of the *OED* where a single side of Webster had sufficed led the Delegates to resolve that 'an explanation of the high ratio be obtained'. Continued excesses later in the same year were formally noted at their meeting in December: 'The Secretary was instructed to write to the three Editors, urging the necessity of keeping the scale of the Dictionary down to eight times that of Webster, and pointing out that they had lately been gravely and constantly exceeding this scale.'[9] The diction of this new century is nevertheless significantly different. The Delegates urge rather than command and there are no stringent instructions for the formation of a further dictionary committee to intervene actively in determining the dictionary's scale. Though occasional remonstrations continued to be made on the grounds of cost, the Delegates tended to confine themselves to noting the steady progress of the dictionary at their meetings, and providing a token equivalence of the *OED* against Webster (however unsatisfactory the latter might at times prove to be). Resistance, as they gradually perceived, was futile; after all, it was clear that the three editors were striving to limit the scale of the dictionary as much as possible while still endeavouring to remain true to its founding ideals. For some sections of the dictionary, it was inevitable – and right – that Webster should be left behind.

Earlier expectations that the dictionary would bring immediate financial results had by this stage also been discarded. Instead the Delegates realized that the dictionary would prove its worth in terms of a wider symbolic capital which went far beyond the negative entries on a balance sheet.[10] This could not be denied. 'To 31st March 1904 which was the close of our last financial year the expenditure upon the Dictionary has been £101,254', Murray was informed. The same letter confirmed that receipts had so far totalled just £33,176, leaving a deficit of almost £70,000.[11] Given that each volume seemed to cost at least £11,000 net (and rising), such deficits should be expected to increase. But, just as Max Müller had stressed in his own role as Delegate in 1878, the *OED* was best seen in a much wider context – as 'an undertaking . . . in which one might almost say the national honour of England is engaged'.[12] Henry Hucks Gibbs concurred. For the Delegates, he wrote, 'their recompense will be great in the gratitude of the Nation for their liberality in taking so great a national burden on their own shoulders'. If it remained undeniable that 'the cost has been excessive', it was of greater significance that 'the money will have been most worthily expended'.[13]

This rhetoric of national honour surrounded the *OED* as an almost automatic response, particularly after the dedication of the third volume of the dictionary to Queen Victoria in 1897. It was of course also in evidence before. 'To make a dictionary worthy of the present state of philology and of the great English nation is certainly a project of national interest', a report in the *Times* had stated in January 1882. 'The Great Oxford Dictionary. A National Undertaking', the *Academy* agreed in March 1899. Murray's Romanes Lecture of 1900 and the lecture on 'Dictionaries' which he delivered to the Royal Institution in May 1903 were followed by lengthy reports in newspapers such as the *Times* and the *Morning Post*. 'Dr. Murray is a man of whom not merely Oxford . . . but the whole country may be justly proud', the *Daily News* proclaimed.[14] His appearance at Mill Hill School for the opening of the Murray Scriptorium later in 1903 generated still more extensive coverage. The *Times*, the *Westminster Gazette*, the *Standard*, and the *Daily News*, as well as the *Telegraph* and the *Pall Mall Gazette*, all devoted considerable column inches to the celebration of the new building which had been erected on the site of Murray's original Scriptorium – the place where the first pages of the dictionary had assumed their published form.

Popular culture too began to appropriate the dictionary in the early years of the twentieth century. The *Pall Mall Gazette* produced a poem to celebrate *Incircumscriptibleness*, the longest word which had so far been included. 'As we behold you, our awe is renewed in us/ Yes, with emotion our bosoms are stirred,/ Septisyllabic, immense, amplitudinous,/ Largest, leviathan, limitless word!' it declaimed.[15] The popular novelist Beatrice Harraden – a friend of Furnivall's – likewise drew literary inspiration from the slow crafting of the pages of the *OED*, publishing *The Scholar's Daughter* in 1906. This was 'an entertaining tale', James Bartlett told Murray. One of the sub-editors on the dictionary, Bartlett had read it with interest. As he explained, keen to know whether Murray had read it too, the novel dealt with the 'Editor of a monumental English Dictionary who wishes his daughter to engage in the work with all his enthusiasm, at which she rebels'. [16] Murray's earlier meeting with Harraden, who had visited the Oxford Scriptorium some years before,[17] was, however, to be subject to the transformative power of fiction. The Scriptorium had clearly been declared an unsuitable location for romance. As a writer in the *Christian Leader* had confirmed in 1887, the reality of what

Murray termed his 'lexicographical laboratory' was indeed less than congenial: 'There is one building in Oxford to which I have made a pilgrimage which neither has nor pretends to have any architecture. By the side of a villa, it looks like a toolhouse, a washhouse, or a stable'.[18] This was not the stuff of which fiction was made and Harraden duly turned Murray's corrugated iron workplace into 'a picturesque old manor house dating back to the Tudors'. Murray's own fictional counterpart was subject to further changes. A scholar 'engaged in the compilation of a dictionary which was to be the abiding pride of the Anglo-Saxon race',[19] Harraden's Professor Grant is significantly removed from the 'quiet, placid, genial man' with a 'rippling humour' who was described in contemporary interviews with Murray.[20] Instead Grant is 'an ice-berg of a human being' whose devotion to the world of words is deemed to preclude the world of human emotion. 'The impersonality of comparative philology has been a mighty resource and comfort to me', he declares. 'Where other people in their troubles and perplexities have turned to Nature . . . I have found absorbing pleasure in studying the history and the romance of words, their changes of meaning, yes, their vicissitudes of social condition and circumstance.'[21]

Nor did Murray's daughters bear much resemblance to Geraldine Grant, the 'scholar's daughter' of the title. If they shared her 'wonderful grasp of etymology' and the ability 'to do a fine piece of scholarship', they expressed none of her resistance to the work of the dictionary. 'I'm supposed to be a scholar . . . But I'm not one, thank goodness', Geraldine avers; 'I would much prefer to serve in a sausage-shop'. Her real ambition is to be an actress. Rosfrith and Elsie had in contrast submitted to work for the dictionary since their earliest days, along with the rest of their siblings.[22] By 1906 they were a respected part of their father's dictionary team (even if, in a further example of the gendered working of the dictionary, they received only half the salary of their male colleagues). Indeed, far from rebelling, Rosfrith would remain at her lexicographical labours until the very last word of the dictionary had been completed (Elsie left in 1920 upon her marriage). Art and life here firmly diverged.

Public appreciation of the real work of the dictionary came in a more formal way with the knighthood which was conferred upon Murray in 1908, even if this also raised a number of scruples about its rightful acceptance. Murray too saw the dictionary in national rather than individual terms; a knighthood was personal and as such disturbed his preferred convictions of his role. 'I am only an instrument', Murray had stressed in a letter to James Bryce in 1903; 'there is no credit due to me, except that of trying to do my duty'.[23] The task was a God-given one, undertaken for the greater glory of the language and the nation. He was tempted to decline. 'I do not believe in titles', he told his son Harold.[24] Yet the very offer of a knighthood stood, as Harold argued, as a symbol of the national honour which was increasingly accruing to the dictionary: it served to validate the collective endeavours of all who had worked on it. As in Murray's eventual letter of acceptance, it was this which ultimately triumphed. While despising such 'gewgaws' in themselves, 'public duty' and, as Harold prompted, 'the state recognition of philological work' (as well as 'a national recognition of a life spent in a national service')[25] were the motives that were therefore to predominate in Murray's reasoning. The knighthood 'expressed recognition of the Dictionary as a service to English literature', Murray carefully explained to the Prime Minister, Herbert Asquith.[26] As he had early stressed, 'one of my chief regrets is that the names of all workers at the Dictionary cannot figure before the public as much as my own'.[27] Murray accepted his knighthood as a collective honour, and with the collective future of the dictionary in mind.

Figure 7 James Murray and his assistants. From left to right: Elsie Murray, James Murray, Rosfrith Murray (*seated*); A. T. Maling, F. J. Sweatman, F. A. Yockney (*standing*).

Pounding through P

'To think that you will shortly be Pounding thro' P, Prancing and Pricking along like a Proud Prince, Persevering and Pioneering', Skeat had joyously exclaimed in 1902; 'it will be a high time'.[28] Skeat's optimism at times seemed as remote from the truth as Harraden's literary creativity. Murray's first new letter of the new century proved a daunting task. The single word *pass*, for example, took some 150 hours before Murray felt that he had managed to achieve even 'a semi-orderly state' for the material. Even so, he knew that this was merely a temporary resolution and that 'much of it will have to be pulled to pieces again'. *Pass* would eventually occupy sixteen columns in the dictionary. It was not surprising that Murray confessed himself 'brain-weary'. 'A run of such words would soon give me apoplexy', he informed Furnivall. 'Unfortunately I am faced by *passage*, with materials 9 inches deep, and unknown terrors'.[29] And after *passage* came still other feats of necessary endurance. He declared to Edward Arber that he could have written two books in less time than it had taken to come to a satisfactory way of ordering the information on *pelican* and *penguin*.[30] And as the Philological Society was informed at its Dictionary Evening in 1908, if time had permitted he could have written a further volume on the intricacies of *post* and *potato*.

Murray's work on P ultimately proved it to be one of the three gigantic letters of the modern English dictionary with 23,000 main words, each of which had to be carefully drafted and revised by Murray and his team of assistants and sub-editors. Many words necessitated individual searches for material as well as the painstaking verification of presumed facts. 'I want as early as possible an instance of the phrase "Old Age Pensions"', the sixty-eight-year-old Murray wrote to the Reverend Canon William Blackley in December 1904: 'The Dictionary ought to show the history of a phrase which has such a future'.[31] Further quests were initiated for words as diverse as *pot-hook* and *polar*, *poonah-painting* and *postural*. The replies illustrate the wide-ranging enterprise which the *OED* had become by the early years of the twentieth century. Sir Alexander Hiers, based at the University Museum in Oxford, wrote in detail on the meaning of *polar*. John Evans at the Imperial Institute in London tracked down the nuances and history of *plumbago*, a word with a peculiarly complex development since it designated both a form of lead ore and a plant. In the dictionary it would require a note of forty-four lines in further explanation. W. H. Wesley of the Royal Astronomical Society delved into the Society archives to find the earliest use of *polaris*. Sir William Osler, Regius Professor of Medicine at Oxford, tried to answer Murray's questions on the precise meaning of *posterior albuminuria*, an entry which, like a number of other scientific forms, was originally included in the proofs for the dictionary but later excised.[32] Any respite was rare. As he told Craigie in May 1901, he had not had a single day off, even at Christmas, since the previous August.[33] Even when ill, as he was throughout February of that year, he continued to work, producing over eighteen pages of the dictionary before 8 March (in comparison with the fourteen composed by Bradley over the same period). By April, Murray had produced a further twenty-one pages while Bradley had managed less than fifteen. The illness of his wife caused further problems. Ada Murray had not been outside since the previous December (and had been confined to bed for the whole of January). 'Over & above the domestic distress' which this had caused, the loss to the dictionary was also 'exceedingly serious', Murray explained to James Johnston, since she was usually able to give 'a great deal of help in dealing with non-dictionary business & correspondence'.[34]

There is an often perceptible sense of strain in Murray's letters of this period. The stress of work was undeniable. As well as working on his own sections of the dictionary, he was carefully monitoring Craigie's early editorial work, often actively reducing it by a tenth ('I think it desirable that everything possible be done to keep Q down', he advised, 'both by restricting quotations, & etymologies to a minimum, & by studying conciseness of definition'),[35] as well of course as continuing to keep a watchful eye on Bradley. Even with Bradley's undoubted experience, a second opinion could often prove beneficial, as in the revisions which Murray carefully supplied on the proofs of *loft*. Here he rewrote Bradley's third sense ('To strike (a ball) so as to lift it over an obstacle') to give instead 'To hit (a ball) into the air or strike it. Also, to hit the ball over an obstacle'. As each new section of the dictionary approached, queries had to be answered and new ones initiated, sub-editors' (and co-editors') work had to be checked, new entries and senses formulated and written. New material arrived on a daily basis at the Scriptorium and the Old Ashmolean, and was swiftly processed by the relevant editorial teams. Volunteer helpers such as W. Gribble sent in batches of sorted slips for entries which were about to be written (in this instance for *police*).[36] Meanwhile other scholars such as Ingram Bywater and Ernest Weekley read and corrected batches of proof entries which had already been set in type. 'The dictionary . . . must now be the largest single engine of research working anywhere in the world', Charles Cannan conjectured.[37] The industrial metaphor seemed apt. The dictionary was the 'factory' for Bradley, churning out its pages and pages of words.[38] Murray had recourse to similar images. 'It is like the work of a machine & not of human beings struggling with some of the most difficult problems in human history', he wrote to Arber.[39] Like the irreconcilable tensions between machines and men which dominated the industrial novels of the mid-nineteenth century, the human could get lost in the wider process. Murray at times despaired at the extent of the labours involved. 'At the age of 68, I begin to wonder if I shall myself ever see its completion, so much of the work remains to do', he wrote. Time which had throughout been the mainspring of the dictionary seemed to be turning against him.[40] He developed a form of tunnel vision, his horizons limited to the immediate part of the dictionary on which he was working. 'My opinion is of no value today beyond the word *Pitch*', he wrote to Wilberforce Jenkinson early in the following year. 'Next week I may be able to tell something of *Pith* and *Pity*; at present they lie in the unexplored territory'.[41]

Murray defined *productivity* in time for the fascicle *Premisal–Prophesier* which appeared in December 1908. 'The quality or fact of being productive; capacity to produce', he wrote, no doubt taking quiet pleasure in the citation with which he chose to end the sense: 'A publisher . . . doing all in his power to stimulate the productivity of an author'. Deriving from Leslie Stephen's *Studies of a Biographer* of 1898, it provided a wry commentary on the earlier fortunes of the *OED*. Yet as P approached its close (its last part was published in September 1909), it appeared possible to anticipate the end of the dictionary. Craigie was almost half-way through R and Bradley had begun the daunting task of editing S. Murray would begin work on T in 1910 which, in spite of containing words such as *take* ('the most terrible verb I have had to do', Murray declared),[42] was overall to prove a much more manageable task. The machinery of the dictionary moved into its accepted course. New quests for material on words such as *tene* or *throstling* were initiated while preliminary phases of drafting and correction began on other words for which the necessary information was complete. Assistants, editors, and critical readers worked in careful symbiosis and while Murray was often his own sharpest critic (his dissatisfaction with his draft of *temple* meant that a new definition had to be pasted on to the proof),[43] Craigie and Bradley also regularly read Murray's proofs, offering constructive suggestions and changes. Craigie emerged as a colleague whose linguistic credentials were respected and from whom he often – as in the midst of drafting *thane* – requested advice. The earlier autocratic dicta – and Murray's habitual stress on his role as editor-in-chief – increasingly faded into the background.

Though the work remained both demanding and time-consuming ('*T* promises to be a letter of bottomless difficulty', Murray announced in momentary despair to Furnivall),[44] a pattern of sustained and shared endeavour encompassed all three editorial teams. The Dictionary Evening at the Philological Society that year celebrated the fact that Murray had finished P (and with it the first half of Volume VII), Craigie had finished R, and in July Bradley had managed to complete Volume VI. While Bradley still had to finish S, work on the last volume had now officially begun. Sub-editing for the whole of the remaining portion was moreover substantially complete. Only two sub-editors remained at work, finalizing the last stretches of U and V. So Craigie's confidence in 1910 did not seem misplaced when he stated that 'seven more years should finish the Dictionary'.[45] Murray was still more confident. 'We shall finish in four years', he wrote in 1912 while half-way through T.[46] He wrote a detailed letter to Walter Skeat setting out the projected schedule for the completion of the *OED*. By 1914, he calculated, he would be working on V and Bradley would already have reached the end of words in Sh– while Craigie would also have completed his own sections of S. 'All will be done from A to Tz, and all three editors will be working at the last half vol. U to Z, of which W is the only considerable letter', he announced. And W surely should only take a further two years before that too would be completed. 'We may . . . reckon that the end of 1916 will see the Dictionary finished', Murray concluded. 'If I live to then, I shall be 80, and it will also be my Golden Wedding; let us hope that the Grand Conjunction of all these cycles will really take place.'[47]

The 'Grand Conjunction'

Murray's 'Grand Conjunction' was, however, framed by hypotheses. '*If* I live to then', he wrote to Skeat; '*If* I can get assistants enough, the work [could] be finished in 4½ or five years', he similarly conjectured in a letter to the German philologist, Friedrich Kluge.[48] In a further letter to Skeat in September 1912, the tone is the same, balanced between optimism and uncertainty: 'I hope I'm spared to finish Z at the end of 1916'. Murray's private letters of these years reveal his underlying anxieties. In 1912 he was already seventy-six, approaching the age when almost all other contributors to the dictionary had either slowed down or indeed stopped work altogether. The eighty-year-old Benjamin Dawson had, for example, sensibly decided in 1905 to limit his activities for the dictionary to two hours a day at most. Ill with heart disease in 1911, the German scholar Eduard Sievers likewise resolved that henceforth his reading of the proofs would have to be curtailed. While he remained 'pleased to contribute whatever little share I may have to offer . . . I am afraid that share will be even smaller than it has been of late'.[49] Murray, on the other hand, seemed to be working even longer hours. He had worked through Christmas of 1910 without a break, managing 'by unremitting effort to complete 16 more pages than the people at the Press thought possible'.[50] Two years later an address which Murray gave to the Philological Society at its annual Dictionary Evening revealed him to be working eighty or ninety hours a week in the attempt to complete the double section of *TH* which was due on 1 April.[51] And even after reaching this deadline, the pace did not slacken. He was working 'from 6 a.m. to 11 p.m.', he informed Skeat in September.[52]

'The past year has been one of great difficulty', Murray admitted three months later. He had been 'terribly pressed with the work of getting the next section into the printers' hands' and the stresses had been compounded by the fact that, since September 1911, he had in effect been trying to compensate for the loss of one of his assistants. Only in the past few months had he gained someone who might perhaps be a suitable replacement.[53] Yet replacements for other dictionary workers were not so easily found. The Prefaces to the individual parts and volumes of the dictionary often came to stand as an eloquent testimony to those who were no longer there. 'Five of our zealous helpers in this department have been removed by death during the preparation of this volume', Murray wrote in his Preface to Volume VII in 1909. Sykes had died in 1906 and Gibbs in 1907. Henry Chichester Hart (who had been an important contributor on Renaissance language) and Edward Brandreth, a regular sub-editor and reader of proofs, were memorialized alongside them. Murray recorded too the death of Janet Brown, 'one of the most devoted and enthusiastic of our volunteer helpers', who had been involved with the dictionary since its inception, sub-editing large sections of B, C, I, and P.[54]

Mutability had provided the overriding impetus for the dictionary as it documented the shifting forms of English. In one fascicle after another, Murray and his co-editors had repeatedly traced words through their birth and death, their obsolescence and decline. Yet the human side of mutability seemed to accelerate in the twentieth century with the demise of many of those who had been involved with the dictionary – and with Murray – since the earliest days. Fitzedward Hall's death in 1901 had been an inauspicious start to the new era. This had been 'a bad day for the Dictionary', Frederick

Furnivall wrote in sympathy to Murray.[55] Hall's death was an 'incalculable loss', the Preface to *H–K* later stated, lamenting the end of his meticulous work on the proofs and citations.[56] Murray seemed to be confronted by the remorseless fragility of circumstance. Even as he desperately strove to complete his life's work, those on whom he had relied for so long were falling away. Murray added the writing of obituaries and letters of condolence to his already pressed days. 'Alas! To many contemporaries his loss leaves Oxford the poorer', his eloquent tribute to William Morfill concluded.[57] Morfill, Professor of Russian and Slavonic Languages at Oxford and a regular helper with those philological cruces which so often plagued the dictionary, had died in 1909. One year later Murray found himself watching the seventy-six-year-old Robinson Ellis (one of his most regular correspondents) with concern. 'I fear that my friend Robinson Ellis, who has been kinder to me than [any] one else in Oxford, is also going rapidly down the hill. He is terribly thin & worn and has eyesight getting very feeble', he confided to Frederick Furnivall. While Ellis would in fact survive until 1913, Furnivall died before the year was out. 'Would it give you any satisfaction to see the gigantic TAKE in final? Before it is too late?' Murray asked, his attempts at consolation likewise being bound up with the dictionary.[58] Other colleagues and helpers likewise succumbed to the ravages of time. James Platt died in 1910. Two years later he would be followed by Walker Skeat.

This litany of loss touched on some of Murray's deepest fears. 'It was the fond hope of the editors that he might be spared to see the completion of the work in which he had by his indefatigable and scholarly labours contributed so much', Murray wrote in his moving obituary for Edward Brandreth. He ended with the impassioned 'May his name never be forgotten when its story is told.'[59] Murray's letter to James Platt's widow is similarly intense in its sense of barely repressed emotion. 'One does not at 73 (as I am this sad day) make new friends like the friends of one's youth or early manhood', he wrote; 'sometimes it seems as if all the friends I had when the Dictionary began will be gone before it is finished, and that I too may never see the end'.[60]

Given the collective import of these losses, and the impossibility in effect of finding anyone who could, for instance, replace Skeat's many years of involvement or James Platt's varied linguistic expertise, Murray's 'Grand Conjunction' began to seem one based on markedly insecure projections. Whereas once a letter to James Platt on a word in some unfamiliar language would have elicited a swift (and illuminating) reply, henceforth 'hours and days will have to be spent in finding out what a brief letter to *him* would have brought'. The loss was 'immeasurable', he stressed; the cost to the dictionary 'irreparable'.[61] Charles Balk's decision to retire in 1913 after twenty-eight years on the dictionary as one of Murray's editorial assistants was a further set-back to the progress Murray had hoped to see. As with Platt, there was no easy way of regaining such accumulated knowledge and expertise.

There were of course positive developments too. Charles Onions was appointed as a fully independent editor in 1914 in a move which promised to compensate at least partially for the losses sustained. He already had almost twenty years of lexicographical experience and his promotion to editor meant that henceforth the remaining tranches of the dictionary could be divided up amongst four separate editorial teams. But the outbreak of the First World War in August of that year was a conjunction of forces far outside Murray's control. Its impact on the Press was immediate. The declaration of war came on 4 August during the annual holiday of Oxford University Press, and more than sixty members of staff had left for the front by the end of the day. Almost a hundred more had joined them by Christmas. By the end of the war 356 men from OUP (over two-thirds of the total) would have enlisted. 'It is not too much to claim that wherever the British Army was represented the Press was represented too', Allpress Hinson recalled in the official *War Record of the University Press*.[62] Compositors, operators from the machine-room and from the printing divisions, men from the type foundry, the paper mill, and the binders all variously left Oxford. C. M. Barfoot, for instance, a skilled compositor, enlisted on 1 September 1914 and was killed three years later in Salonika; E. Edmonds, another compositor, enlisted in August 1914 though was fortunate to return to the Press after demobilization in 1919. Many of his colleagues, however, did not survive and D. Jones, R. Litchen, and P. Lines were all killed in action before 1918. A whole range of erstwhile machine-room operators became accustomed to the noise of battle rather than the clatter of the presses. A. Best left Oxford on 4 August and was not demobilized until 26 June 1919. F. Carter accompanied him, likewise returning in 1919. Others, such as W. Clack, were never to see Oxford again; after enlisting on 14 September 1915, Clack was killed on the Hindenburg Line in 1917. Even the Assistant Secretary to the Delegates, R. W. Chapman, decided that there were more important things than the commissioning and production schedules of books. He left to serve for three years as a heavy gunner in Salonika, where he found that his skills as a classical scholar were at times paradoxically almost as useful as his military training. May (the daughter of Charles Cannan, who remained as Secretary in Oxford) had later recalled that Chapman's comrades in Greece found their language difficulties solved by 'the silent Gunner Scholar who arranged everything, communicating with the local schoolmaster in the Greek of the Classical writers with which they were both gloriously familiar'.[63]

In Oxford the Press gradually emptied and Cannan, who remained as Secretary but with 'practically no staff left', followed the precedents established by Murray and by Bradley[64] and brought his daughters in to work. May, Joanna, and Dorothea became volunteers at the Press for the duration of much of the war, coping with the *Journal of Theological Studies*, the *Quarterly Journal of Medicine* or, in May's case, with the production of the Press Catalogue on which she was frequently to enlist Onions's help in dealing with the entries in Middle English. For those who remained, life was necessarily very different. The scholarly life of the university was disrupted, the Examination Schools on the High being turned into a military hospital while many of the colleges were taken over by officer cadets. The imperatives of producing the dictionary were suddenly relaxed, not least because the skills of those who were still at work at the Press were frequently appropriated by the war effort. War printing took precedence over other publications, occupying some 200 employees in 1917–18, with a new set of female workers 'contributing of their best, eager to do their share equally with the men and the boys'.[65] 'The printed page never played so important a part in war', Admiral Sir Reginald Hall later claimed as he unveiled the War Memorial which still stands in the quadrangle at Oxford University Press.[66] Even outside the secrecy of the Whitehall documents which the Press was commissioned to produce, resources had to be deployed on works which earlier had not even been contemplated. The printing of *War Songs* and the Oxford Pamphlet *Why We Are at War*, for instance, almost fully occupied the presses in November 1914, the latter having been translated into Swedish, Danish, Italian, Spanish, and French, as well as Dutch. The German translation had already been printed by October and widely distributed. 'The pressure of war books and the absence on service of many members of the staff both here and in Oxford . . . have delayed all our non-topical books terribly', Humphrey Milford, the London publisher of OUP, wrote to Robert Bridges in November 1914.[67]

In London and in Oxford, the costs of war were readily apparent, not merely in the depleted staff but also in the rising prices of the fabric used for binding and of paper itself. Within weeks of the outbreak of war, paper costs had risen substantially, whether that produced in the Press's own mill at Wolvercote in Oxfordshire, or that which the Press was forced to purchase externally. 'We are much handicapped just now because of advanced prices in almost every material that is used in our business', Milford lamented in October.[68] It was clear that work already commissioned would have to be postponed, while new works were often simply not accepted. The concerns of the *OED* and its own exigencies of production could seem somewhat remote. Nevertheless inside the Scriptorium and the dictionary offices at the Old Ashmolean, work on drafting the dictionary in some ways seemed to proceed much as usual. The age of many of those who worked on the *OED* was here an advantage: Walter Worrall, Henry Bayliss, and Wilfrid Lewis were, for instance, well into their forties when war broke out. While the twenty-six-year-old John Birt did enlist, depriving Onions of one of his editorial team, the majority of the staff stayed where they were, carefully crafting the final stages of the alphabet. Murray's letters record the accustomed habits of years in the quests which were initiated for a variety of words. He wrote a lengthy letter about *trim-tram*, trying to trace the details of its current usage. It proved to have a lineage going back to 1523 in a surprising variety of meanings even though it was, Murray decided, restricted to the regional in terms of modern English: 'A lich-gate; also a gate which opens in a V-shaped enclosure, a kissing-gate. *dial.*' He likewise searched after the origin of *travat* (it proved to be merely a variant form of *travado* and *trevat*, a word with the highly specific meaning 'An instrument with a sharp blade formerly used for cutting the loops which form the pile of velvet, Wilton carpets, etc., when hand-woven'). He received ample assistance from a carpet firm in Kidderminster which sent him a travat to examine. *Trichina* ('A genus of minute parasitic nematoid worms') posed further problems. Murray wrote to William Osler (appointed Regius Professor of Medicine at Oxford in 1905) to ask how it should be pronounced, duly recording his answer in the dictionary.[69]

Yet alongside such continued industry it was evident that Murray's health was noticeably fragile in the summer and autumn of 1914. 'You must mind and not overdo it', Ingram Bywater admonished in September; 'I feel sometimes that you overwork yourself in your anxiety to be up to time with your sections'.[70] Henry Bradley too was concerned. 'I fervently hope you will not risk a relapse by beginning hard work too soon', he wrote, trying to answer a detailed question on the etymology of *trust*.[71] The nature of his letter – and the etymological details that dominate – suggest, however, that Murray was still manifesting his habitual industry. 'The illness of any of the three editors might, as things are, result in failure to bring out even the *promised* instalment at the proper time', Bradley diplomatically wrote one month later to his senior colleague.[72] He urged that some sort of contingency plan might be devised – the building up of a reserve for the dictionary perhaps in case of accidents or other inadvertencies. Murray's reply does not survive though it is clear that he too was increasingly aware of the effects of time and the passing of years. 'I am awfully pressed with the preparation of this section, and my own inability to work as long hours as I formerly could', he confessed to Herbert Warren in April 1915 as he strove to complete the double section of *Trink–Turn-down*.[73] *Turn-down* seemed an inauspicious note on which to conclude.

'I had hoped by a slight enlargement of this issue to reach the end of T, but my long and serious illness, which lasted from May to November, robbed us of that satisfaction', Murray publicly stated in his 'Prefatory Note' when this section finally made its appearance in June 1915. He recognized that the 'Grand Conjunction' might have to be deferred, perhaps to 1917, as a private letter of January 1915 notes. Even this, however, was to prove impossible. By June, though he was still 'hard at work', Murray was also, as Bradley recorded, 'showing marked signs of physical weakness'. Whilst he rallied in part from the pleurisy which had assailed him ('one of the commonest diseases', as his own entry for the latter had confirmed), his decision to return to work in the Scriptorium proved a misguided one. 'He presumed too much on his recovered strength', Bradley noted with regretful hindsight.[74] Murray's death, on 26 July 1915, brought his own ambitions for the dictionary to an end.

'Death of Sir James Murray. Great Dictionary-Maker's Unfinished Volume', the *Daily Graphic* announced the following day. Other newspapers provided similar coverage, paying tribute to the man and the dictionary he had hoped to complete. 'In his race with time he has fallen with the goal in sight', the *Daily Telegraph* eloquently opined; '"a few small letters of the alphabet", as he bravely called them, remain to be finished by another hand'. Bradley memorialized Murray's lost hopes in the next part of the dictionary to be published. His 'great wish that he might live to finish the Dictionary on his eightieth birthday, in 1917, has not been fulfilled', he wrote.[75] Like Herbert Coleridge, Brandreth, and Platt before him, Murray had worked almost to the end. And as Bradley recorded in the ultimate scholarly commendation of his colleague, 'even in his last days the quality of his workmanship would have done him no discredit in his prime'.[76] The eighty-four completed columns of the final part of T, with much of the remainder already drafted, stood as further testimony to both his dedication – and his determination. Even in his weakened state, Murray's organizational skill and capacity for research had left the materials in such a condition that the remaining part could easily be finished by his well-trained staff, with Craigie's editorial revision where necessary. Rosfrith and Elsie, photographed flanking their father two weeks before his death, were able to aid in completing the last section at which he had worked. Though Murray would no longer 'write the last pages', Bradley continued to affirm the collective resolution of those who remained at work on the *OED*. The dictionary would continue, the individual sections 'will not be affected'. Collective endeavour once more triumphed. As Bradley concluded, 'the long and efficient working of the great engine of research by which the Dictionary has been produced' would continue, even without the figure whose name had been associated so closely with its detailed operation.

Nevertheless, to look at the dictionary in the years after Murray's death is to see an inevitable slowing of the famed 'engine'. The war continued to have an impact on the Press and on publication in general. Printing the *OED* required a minimum of twelve compositors, two readers, one electrotyper, and at least one and sometimes two machines in full operation. In all it meant a working staff of around twenty – a heavy burden at a time when much of the workforce remained absent and other learned works were being laid aside.[77] Paper too was scarce. Mr Skinner, the man in charge of the Press's paper stocks, governed a 'precious dwindling store'[78] which was reserved for essential publications. These, as Craigie informed the Philological Society, did not necessarily include the *OED*. 'Owing to a scarcity in the supply of materials for the covers of the sections, it has been decided not to issue any part of the Dictionary this quarter', he informed them in April 1917.[79] A single part of the dictionary appeared in 1918 and Onions temporarily relinquished his editorial role, transferring his skills to naval intelligence and becoming an honorary captain in the Royal Marines. As he noted in 1919 as the first part of Volume IX appeared, 'The progress of this portion of the Dictionary has been retarded by the withdrawal in succession of several members of the staff, and, in the second half of the year 1918, of the editor, for war service of different kinds'.[80] Even the proofs had been affected. As the *Periodical* announced in 1917, 'should the history of the *Oxford Dictionary* ever be written, it may be of interest that one of the staff opened up a packet of proofs in a dug-out that had once belonged to the Germans, but had been taken by our troops'. Proof-reading had never been so exciting – or so dangerous. As the *Periodical* continued, 'While the member of staff was perusing the proofs some German shells burst not far away, and fragments struck the sides of the dug-out.' Proofs were read by candle-light in the intervals between raids.[81]

Even after the war ended, the Press was slow to return to its previous levels of production. The shortages continued and demobilization proved a lengthy process. Many workers did not return until late in 1919. The dictionary was temporarily suspended with *Visor–Vywer* not appearing until 1920, followed by Bradley's own final part (*W–Wash*) in 1921. W, for which work had begun in 1881, would not be finished until 1928, five years after Bradley's own death, three years after Craigie had become a professor in Chicago, and eight years after Onions had become a university lecturer at Oxford – from 1927 he was Reader in English Philology in the university. This, and not *Z–Zygt*, marked the end of the dictionary, bringing to a conclusion, as the *Times Literary Supplement* recorded in April 1928, its vast tally of 15,488 pages, 178 miles of type, 50 million words, and almost two million quotations.[82] At the celebratory dinner given in June 1928 at Goldsmiths' Hall in London, and attended by the Prime Minister, the Delegates of the Press, literary scholars such as E. V. Gordon and H. C. Wyld, as well as the remaining editors and assistants on the dictionary (and Murray's sons Oswyn and Harold), Rosfrith Murray sat on the balcony. Excluded because of her sex from a seat in the hall, she watched the proceedings with equanimity. 'I always felt deeply that my Father would like one of his name to be "in on the finish" since this was denied to him himself', she later wrote to Chapman.[83] Along with Craigie and Onions, and some other stalwarts such as Edith Thompson (as well as Bradley's daughter, Eleanor, who also continued to work on the dictionary), she had indeed been there to have the last word.

Ended but not Complete

'No dictionary of a living tongue ever can be perfect', Samuel Johnson had written in 1755. The same was, of course, true of the *OED*, even if its scale was immeasurably larger than the two folio volumes – and 40,000 words – of Johnson's first edition. Even as the dictionary began, letters and reviews had picked out absences and omissions. Though, as Murray had noted, these had 'upon the whole . . . been surprisingly few', he recognized that they constituted 'a mere nothing . . . in comparison with what the experience of future times will suggest'.[84] As the dictionary moved through the alphabet, Murray's prescience was indeed fulfilled. 'I find *brought up* used in a sense which does not seem to be mentioned in the N.E.D.', noted L. P. H. Eijkhan after reading Florence Montgomery's novel *Misunderstood*. He provided a full reference in case Murray would care to insert it in a later revision.[85] Edward White picked out another absence in 1911. 'The word "Nitrary" I cannot find in the Oxford English Dictionary', he wrote. 'It should, it seems to me, appear therein under "N", page 162, second column, between "Nitransic" and "Nitrate"'.[86] Reviewers too cast a sharp eye over newly published fascicles in search of unrecorded words and senses, and Craigie was castigated in the *Athenaeum* for his failure to keep pace with the changing language. 'Dr. Craigie may have ignored the "siren" of motor-cars because the pest has not come under his notice in books or papers, for it seems unlikely that he has had so little experience of it as not to know the term', the reviewer commented.[87] Sirens in the dictionary were limited in this sense to steamships ('An instrument . . . used on steamships for giving fog-signals, warnings etc.', Craigie had written in 1911). Even as the letters of the alphabet settled into the stasis of the published page, language and usage repeatedly moved beyond them. Words such as *aeronaut* reflected a bygone age. 'One who makes balloon ascents', as Murray had defined the word in 1884. *Car* was similar. 'In some provincial towns (e.g. Birmingham) "car" means a four-wheeled hackney carriage, "cab" meaning a hansom', Murray had written in 1888, providing what was emphatically given as a '*Modern*' example of usage (and one invented by Murray himself). Yet within a decade *car* was beginning to shift markedly in its uses. Constructions in which it signified a motorized vehicle were common by 1900. Later iterations of the dictionary would record 'the first car built by the Daimler Company at Coventry' in 1902. *Car-owner* was recorded from 1905.

Readers moreover began to suspect the *OED* of an unwarranted conservatism in the attitudes to language it displayed. 'I suppose it will be twenty years before philologists recognise that the word *pram* is as good English as *cab* . . . it is now well established in colloquial literature', one correspondent had expostulated in 1899.[88] Eight years later his words proved entirely true. 'A shortened form of PERAMBULATOR', Murray noted, explicitly confining it to the *vulgar* and colloquial. Even if the seventy-year-old Murray might have considered it vulgar (and certainly not what his own children had lain in), language and usage had in this respect decisively moved on. The language of the First World War revealed further conspicuous tensions between current usage and the reference model which the *OED* was able to provide. 'The war has . . . introduced scores of new words with which Murray's successors will have to wrestle', the *Star* wrote in its obituary of Murray.[89] It gave *minenwerfer* as an example, the ravages of which were becoming all too common among the British troops in 1915. The fascicles dealing with M had, however, been completed in 1908; no further emendation could take place within the first edition of the dictionary. *Minenwerfer* – or *minnies*, as the German trench mortars came to be known – would remain outside the margins of the language as registered in the first edition.[90] Yet the problem transparently extended beyond the inclusion or otherwise of an isolated word. As newspapers in September 1914 reported on the bombing of Paris, their words reached far beyond the realities which Murray had documented in the early fascicles of the dictionary. Combinations such as *aerial fleet*, *aerial pirate*, or *air battalion* all figure in contemporary reports of the military action ten months before Murray's death; the *Daily Express* described the activities of *air scouts*, the *Evening News* discussed the quality of *airmanship* which was now required. Yet those who turned to the dictionary found little elucidation. A *battalion* was limited to troops on foot while *airmanship* in Murray's first fascicle refers to 'skill in managing a balloon'. Murray had been preoccupied by these absences. 'The whole terminology of aeroplanes and aeronautics is wanting', Murray had announced to the Philological Society in 1912. The ways in which journalists and writers sought to express the shifting nature of experience in the early days of war necessarily transcended the historical principles of the dictionary. While the published fascicles remained in the past, history itself advanced, its linguistic consequences emerging with a terrible and telling rapidity. *Projectiles* in the dictionary are limited to the shot fired from cannons; in the conflicts of September 1914 they were fired from *airships* (which in themselves bear little resemblance to Murray's definition of 1884 which refers to a boat 'propelled by an air-engine'). The *aerial raiders* described in the *Scotsman* on Tuesday, 13 October 1914 ('The German aerial raiders have not ceased paying their attention to Paris') have no counterparts in the *OED*. Similarly *air-raid* does not exist within its pages. War brought a fearful creativity to the language, whether in soldiers' slang (in which the front line becomes the *bumper* and a *bump* an opportunity of fighting, neither of which is in *OED*), or in the new collocations which express the unprecedented events that took place. Forms such as *petticoat troop* (soldiers using women and children as protection) and *living shield* still remain unregistered in the dictionary.

While there were some attempts to incorporate this vast new tranche of material in the fascicles which remained unpublished as war began, the task was far beyond the scope of the first edition. Craigie's inclusion of *strafe*, for example, deservedly brought praise from the *Periodical* in 1917. 'Used (originally by British soldiers in the war against Germany) in various senses suggested by its origin: To punish; to do damage to; to attack fiercely; to heap imprecations on', Craigie had written, providing evidence and etymology for a word which had come into sudden and prominent use in the early days of the war. 'From the Ger[man] phrase *Gott strafe England*, "God punish England", a common salutation in Germany in 1914 and the following years', he further explained. On the whole, however, precisely as Murray had indicated in 1911, the dictionary's prime allegiance at this stage had to remain largely to the past. While he could not have foreseen the linguistic and human consequences which, within a few years, war would start to bring, his general point remained valid for the principles that had to govern the completion of the *OED*. The material already at the dictionary's disposal was overwhelming. It was simply impossible to gather and collate the results of the ongoing creativity which erupted in 1914–18 (or, indeed, to do justice to all the new words and senses in other spheres which had emerged since 1884). Encompassing the language was inconceivable. If some newer usages were duly recorded, as in Onions's decision to give *a place in the sun* in the fascicle *Sullen–Supple* with the note 'its present currency in this country is due to its use by the Emperor of Germany in a speech made at Hamburg on 27th August 1911', coverage at this stage of the dictionary's making could not hope to be systematic. As Murray had always stressed, 'language is mobile and liable to change'.[91] Fixed norms and a finite span for words and their varying senses were alike impossible.

As war progressed, bringing new forms such as *Blighty* ('In the war of 1914–18 applied to a wound that secured return to England', *OED2* now records) and a wide-ranging vocabulary of attack and manoeuvre in which the German siege guns were variously figured as *Black Marias*, *coal boxes*, or *Jack Johnsons*, the gaps between language in the dictionary and language in use widened still further. No one could have envisaged the new salience of *entanglements* made of barbed wire or the semantic transformations which took place in *gas*. Bradley in 1899 had commented on 'colloquial' uses in which *gas* signified 'A jet . . . used to light a room, etc.; a gas-light'. He had also enumerated senses in which it referred to the nitrous oxide recently used by dentists as an anaesthetic and 'the hydrogen or coal-gas employed to fill a balloon', as well, of course, as its dominant meaning of an 'aeriform or completely elastic fluid; matter in the condition of an aeriform fluid', as illustrated by Thomas Henry Huxley's *Physiography* of 1878: 'The specific gravities of the three gases which composed the atmosphere'.

Bradley had not, however, been able to conceive the role of gas as a weapon in the First World War, forever immortalized in Wilfred Owen's 'Dulce et Decorum Est' ('Gas! Gas! Quick, boys! – An ecstasy of fumbling,/ Fitting the clumsy helmets just in time').[92] Even the *OED* could not document history before it had happened. The confidence expressed by the *Times* in 1914 in relation to the dictionary and the changing language hence seemed misplaced. 'In the Oxford Dictionary, where the appearance of each new word and idiom is accurately dated, we are now able to observe English as a living language, ever developing and changing as it keeps pace with new developments of life and thought', it had stressed, praising the *OED* in its role as a national record of both England and English.[93]

Outside such hyperbole, however, it was clear to many – including Murray and his co-editors – that completing the dictionary would in no way mean completing the record of the language for either past or present usage. The absence of *bondmaid* and *collide*, or words such as *radium* and *appendicitis* had already been a cause for comment. Yet the knowledge that the *OED* was merely one stage in a far larger attempt to document the language had almost always been there. Even in 1905 Murray had been aware of how much remained to be done beyond what the *OED* would itself achieve. He already had '*shelves* of material accumulated' for a future supplement. Organizing it and extending the reading programme to incorporate the necessary further research, however, lay outside his present means 'or I shall never see the end of the current Dictionary', he warned Furnivall.[94] His letter makes clear that alongside the making of what Murray here referred to as simply the 'current' dictionary was a still larger project which would strive to encompass still more of the language.

'We have never ceased to collect for the *Supplement* from the issue of the first part of A', he wrote. As each fascicle appeared, the dictionary staff had concurrently been noting corrections, additions, further words and senses which might appear in a future supplementary volume, or indeed, a revised version of the dictionary in entirety. Already in 1896 Bradley was certain that any such volume had to 'be much longer than 450 pages if it is to be at all complete'.[95] It is here, for instance, that Hamilton's material on *cunt* was to be filed alongside the correct etymology (and recommended deletion) of *delta-metal*[96] or the information on the recent use of *imagonary* which Murray had received in 1899, five months after completing the relevant section. 'I will relegate your memo to our pigeon-hole of Supplementary matter', he responded, though he was unable to provide any guarantee of future inclusion. 'Most scholars will, I dare say, be glad not to be horrified by a word so "barbarously" formed', Murray added, pointing out that, at least from an etymological point of view, 'the only legitimate derivation is imag*in*ary'.[97] Receiving a letter from Sykes five years later on the word *alexic*, Murray likewise filed it away for future use, neatly inscribing the abbreviation '*Supple*' along its outer margin.[98]

Murray's correspondents did, in fact, seem all too aware of the potential which continuing revision of the dictionary might offer. 'I venture to forward you a word *Anaerobic* which I do not find in your splendid dictionary. If it appears in any Supplementary volume I shall be highly gratified', Vernon Dowell volunteered in 1907.[99] 'I presume there will be an appendix to the Oxford Dictionary in which certain additions (entirely new words, or new uses of old ones) will appear and omissions be rectified', William Stathers wrote to Murray in 1912, proffering 'a use of the word "policeman" which has escaped you'.[100] *Actinology* ('The science of the chemical action of light') had presumably 'been missed through inadvertence', the American scholar Henry Metcalf similarly conjectured.[101] The absence of *doxographer* and *doxographical* similarly prompted Theodore Stanton to write to Murray in 1914.[102] In general such errors were carefully noted for the benefit of future readers, though they could on occasion provoke an intemperate reply. 'I am sorry that you condemn my small (would-be) addition to your information on the word "Cooper" as "irrelevant & superfluous"', a letter from H. Halliday Sparling opens in December 1891.[103] Not all efforts to swell the dictionary's files were equally appreciated and on a number of occasions Murray was unable to resist the urge to provide a stringently edifying reply. A drafted letter of 1911 with reference to a possible antedating of *protoplasm* provides an apt illustration of the kind of response which simply erroneous suggestions for the supplement could provoke. 'What you write about *protoplasm* is quite incomprehensible to me', Murray declared. The dictionary confirmed that the word had been coined by von Mohl in 1846. As a result, the suggestion that an example had been located in 'a 15th century book, is no more credible than if you had found a telephone there', Murray informed the unfortunate recipient.[104]

On the other hand, instances of what Murray regarded as legitimate criticism were indeed taken seriously and often received with conspicuous thanks. The specification in the published text of 'a genus of extinct crocodilian reptiles' as the appropriate definition of *tetrabeloden* was simply wrong, Harold Row wrote to Murray. His interest was in the accuracy of the record which the dictionary presented. 'May I point out that it belongs to the *Elephant* and not the above named group', he continued.[105] Edmund Simpson likewise criticized the decision to label *oisivity* ('idleness, indolence') as a nonce-word. He had found earlier examples which proved that this could not be the case. The 'collection and arrangement of the material for the Supplement . . . steadily flows on', Murray informed the annual gathering for the Dictionary Evening at the Philological Society in 1908. While he reported satisfactory progress on what he termed the 'Principal' dictionary, the supplement was making similar advances in its own right.

As a review in the *Manchester Guardian* would later state, 'Truly our dictionary-makers are toilers at a Sisyphean task – just as soon as they have got "Z" neatly caged an enlarged and adipose "A" has broken loose at the other end of the menagerie'.[106] Language, as the *Guardian*'s reviewer recognized, was never ultimately tamed. The lexicographer's control was illusory. Usage constantly moved beyond the entries which had so painstakingly been crafted in Murray's Scriptorium or in the dictionary offices in the Old Ashmolean. Heading his article 'Language in the Making', the reviewer focused on the paradox that the long-awaited completion of the *OED* merely heralded a new beginning. George Loane had already amply made the same point to the Philological Society. His 'Thousand and Two Notes on "A New English Dictionary"' recorded a catalogue of omissions and antedatings.[107] Even before the formal completion of the first edition, Onions and Craigie were already at work on the *Supplement*. 'Words too young to have been placed in the book itself' were being organized and edited in February 1928.[108] Echoing the precedents of the past, Onions eloquently discoursed to the Philological Society on the need for a new reading programme to create a new inventory of the language which will 'fill up the gaps unavoidable in a dictionary composed on historical principles'. Just like Murray so many years before, he stressed the importance of 'the colloquialism, the slang, the modern literary affectation, and the like' which 'constantly escape record'. Indeed, as Onions confirmed one year later, thirty pages of this new work had already been drafted, detailing words and meanings in the first letter of the alphabet which had simply not existed when the first edition had been written. A further four years saw the first *Supplement* complete, taking account of 'the growth and change of the vocabulary over nearly half a century'. Here were to be found words such as *cinema* and *cinematographer*, *photographess* (dated to 1926) and *photon* (from the same year), *surrealist* (from 1927) and *Wellsian*, the latter immortalizing H. G. Wells and the futuristic associations of his name. 'And we hear stories, like Wellsian prophecies, of a garage that will accommodate motor-cars like books on a bookshelf and which is to be erected in the heart of Soho', the *Observer* declared in 1928. Entries such as *azoimide* ('hydrazoic acid') and *chætotaxy* ('The arrangement or plan of distribution of the bristles on the bodies of insects') illustrate the continued commitment to the language of science. The omission of *actinology*, as earlier spotted by Metcalf, was here duly rectified, together with associated forms such as *actinologous*, *actinologue*.[109] Similarly Craigie rectifies his earlier decision to omit *radium* ('a rare metallic element, now regarded as the most important of the radio-active group . . .') and provides an entry for *pacifist*, another word whose absence had attracted comment. Entries span the language of new discoveries and the ordinariness of the everyday as, for instance, in the decision to include *bike* as a colloquial abbreviation for bicycle. Even if the *Times* in 1910 had noted that '"Bike" has a very low-bred sound at present', its diffusion over the next twenty years had made its continued absence from the dictionary a cause for regret. *Bike*, like countless other words, gained due restitution in the *Supplement* of 1933. Five citations deriving from 1890–1901 affirmed its undoubted currency. Other colloquialisms such as *billy-o*, verified since 1885, entered the dictionary at the same point, together with a more extensive set of Americanisms (*ginger-cake*, *corner-tree*, *moon-down*).

But this was not, of course, the end of the story. The *Supplement* was itself a compromise. Even in 1928 too much material had been gathered to fit into the single volume allowed (and which had moreover been promised free to all those who had previously purchased the *OED*). Against a possible supplement 'on a grand scale' which would indeed 'treat the new words and meanings that had come into being during the publication of the successive sections' (as well as inserting the corrections of which some of that material already stood in need)[110] was placed the exigency of issuing a single volume within a relatively short space of time. Like Murray and Bradley before them, Craigie and Onions had 'found themselves forced by facts to enlarge their plans', while simultaneously being compelled to prioritize, to select and to reject.[111] A thorough revision of the material, together with the verification of all the new material which the *OED* now possessed, 'would demand intensive researches by experienced workers extending over many years', they stressed. It was for this reason that a deliberately 'restricted' version was produced which focused on the previous fifty years while also rectifying obvious omissions and the gaps in American usage, as well as the gaps which modern usage had made all too perceptible in the earlier entries for, say, *navigation* or *park*. Craigie's original definition of the former had made no mention of aircraft, unlike the new sense which the 1933 *Supplement* carefully inserted ('The action or practice of travelling through the air by means of aircraft; flying'). *Park* in the first edition of the dictionary had likewise predictably failed to take note of uses involving cars.

Further *Supplements* would therefore be rendered necessary in the 1970s and 1980s. Robert Burchfield's four-volume *Supplement*, originally projected in the 1950s as a single volume to be completed in seven years, added thousands more usages to the material it incorporated from the 1933 *Supplement*. 'We have kept constantly before us the opposing concepts of permanence and ephemerality', Burchfield wrote in 1972, as he too deliberated on the inclusion (or exclusion) of words, determining to retain 'vocabulary that seemed likely to be of interest now and to future generations, and rejecting only those words, phrases, and senses that seemed transitory or too narrowly restricted in currency'.[112] Words which had seemed potentially ephemeral in 1933 (and so had been placed outside the line which the lexicographer must draw) are now given explicit entry into the dictionary – *usherette*, for instance, received lexicographical recognition almost sixty years after its date of first use in 1925. Similar were *wimpish* (also dated to 1925) and the euphemistic use of *upholstered*. 'Plump, stocky', Burchfield helpfully explained, deriving its first use from P. G. Wodehouse ('This sumptuously upholstered young woman').

New senses for words such as *cat's eye* ('One of the chain of light-reflecting studs used to demarcate traffic lanes on roads at night') further attest the changing habits of a new century. Here too, as the *New Statesman* recorded in 1940, Oxford seemed to have been in the forefront of development: 'Few motorists . . . in Oxfordshire will deny that the "cats-eyes", with which the County Council has studded its main roads, are an improvement for night driving on the old white line'. Words such as *Edwardian* ('the collective characteristics of the reign of Edward VII'), *movie* (and its catalogue of associated forms such as *movie actor*, *movie projector*, *movie star*), or *negritude* ('The quality or characteristic of being a Negro; affirmation of the value of Black or African culture, identity') attest other strands of culture and development. Words such as *iffy* and *Kilner jar*, *Kilroy* ('The name of a mythical person, popularized by American servicemen in the war of 1939–45, who left such inscriptions as "Kilroy was here" on walls, etc., all over the world') and *spacewoman* reveal further disparate coinages of a new era. Other entries receive conspicuous recoding. *Millionairess* is, for example, no longer declared to be *jocular* but is admitted as a legitimate term. *Toupees* gained the dubious distinction of no longer being declared *rare*. On a more serious note, *Hitlerite* and *Nazi* made their appearance in the dictionary, confirming the legacies of another discourse of war.

The domains of literary usage too reflected a new orientation, with James Joyce and Dylan Thomas occupying prominent places in the data files of the new dictionary, next to D. H. Lawrence and W. H. Auden, though alongside such canonical figures came a greater level of representativeness for the ordinary and colloquial, just as Onions had wished in 1928. Entries such as *video*, *psychedelic*, *vegan*, and *VAT* served at least in part to bring the dictionary up to date. *Head-on* and *hipster*, *tight-ass* and *tightwad* similarly traced the idiomatic expressions of modern life and thought. Continuities with the past are nevertheless transparent in complaints about the excessive liberality of this new version of the dictionary. Science, Americanisms, and the coinages of modern poets remained targets for attack. As Burchfield noted in the first of his T. S. Eliot Memorial Lectures of 1988, 'the scholars to whom the specimen was sent objected principally to the inclusion of technical and scientific words, American and Australian slang, and to quotations from modern poetry. My publishing overlords within OUP seemed to hold the same views.' Even if the words were different, Murray would no doubt have felt in familiar territory within such disputes.

Burchfield's *Supplements* nevertheless reveal a practical resistance of which Murray would have been proud. In a policy of marked insularity that seemed remote from linguistic reality in the second half of the twentieth century, Kenneth Sisam (Secretary to the Delegates, 1942–48) had directed that the English of the *Supplements* should be the 'English of educated people in England'.[113] However, in contrast they record the abundant forms of English outside England, a domain into which Burchfield reported that he had made 'bold forays' in order to retrieve terms such as *murumuru* (a Brazilian palm) and *nogako* ('the Japanese dramatic form called Noh'), *jilleroo* (an Australian term which denotes 'a female station-hand'), and *kotuku*, a word which, deriving from Maori, signifies the 'white heron' in the English of New Zealand. South Africa, Australia, India, New Zealand, and Pakistan, among others, became fertile sources of new domains of usage which were now 'accorded the treatment that lexicographers of a former generation might have reserved for the English of Britain alone'. Yet even this – including as it did a determined engagement with the new language of science (as well as the long-disputed areas of linguistic and cultural taboo) – would, as Burchfield recognized, necessarily fall short in any attempt to encompass the language in entirety. Intuition, the problems of editability, the inevitable gaps in evidence, the continuity of policies (even in a modified form) by which proper names and proprietary designations ought to be excluded,[114] all stand as factors – among a range of others – that fracture the image of total inclusivity. While *supplement* is defined (precisely as written by Onions in 1917) as 'A part added to complete a literary work or any written account or document', it was yet again clear that completeness could not be achieved, even by four further volumes or, in 1989, by the addition of a further 5,000 words in the production of *OED2*. As John Simpson, editor of *OED2* and, in a new millennium, chief editor of *OED Online*, has stressed, the dictionary is in essence a moving picture, its successive forms tracing the constant and inescapable mutability of language. Completeness remains a myth, even if one which still remains in the forefront of popular discussion of the dictionary.[115] 'It should be understood that fully comprehensive coverage of all elements of the language is a chimera', he states in his Preface to *OED Online* under the illuminating heading of 'Distractions'.[116] While 'the present revision gives the editors the opportunity to add many terms which have been overlooked in the past', the illusion of a word-book that contains each and every word in the language is cast aside as a distraction to the real business of lexicography.

CHAPTER 7

Into the Future

Delivering his Romanes Lecture in Oxford in June 1900, Murray strove to dispel any illusions his audience might possess about a static and unitary dictionary in English. Evolution inspired both his title and the substance of his address. Dictionaries, like language, constantly assumed new forms, responding to the changing currents of the time. The 'hard word' dictionaries of the Renaissance arose in response to the conspicuous influx of new words that might not be understood by, for example, the 'vnskilfull persons' to whom Robert Cawdrey had addressed his text.[1] A European zeal for ascertainment by which, as Murray noted, 'all succeeding ages . . . should find their ideal of speech and writing fixed for ever',[2] would later provide a central impetus for Johnson's work. Still later Charles Richardson had 'started on a new track altogether', amplifying the element of quotation used in Johnson's entries but excluding the definitions on the presumption that chronological citations were alone enough to illuminate meaning. The same operation of time and change was evident in the foundation of the *OED*. Its adoption of both historicism and empiricism as fundamental aspects of lexicography was entirely in keeping with the changing emphases of the nineteenth century in matters of linguistic enquiry. There are 'dictionaries *and* dictionaries', Murray stressed in 1903 as he spoke to the assembled members of the Royal Institution. It was the 'plurality and variety' of such works that should, above all, be borne in mind.

Seen in this light, the English dictionary was to emerge as a fluid rather than static construct, with the capacity to change and evolve as circumstances might demand. While it remains true that 'the lexicographer cannot anticipate the future', as a report on the dictionary's dedication to Queen Victoria had declared in 1897,[3] those who worked on the first edition were all too aware that the *OED* would inevitably partake in further processes of transformation. A '*living tongue*', Murray emphasized, served 'the changing needs and . . . the changing knowledge and views, of millions of men'.

Dictionaries in this sense – even those founded on historical principles – must prove equally responsive to the temporal frameworks in which they have their being. 'Think of tying down Huxley and Tyndall, Darwin and Spencer, the chemists, anthropologists, geologists, electricians, the sociologists, telepathists . . . and aeronauts to the vocabulary of Dr. Johnson', as Murray exclaimed in the course of another lecture, in 1910.[4] While the first edition of the *OED* undeniably transcended Johnson's 1755 *Dictionary* in this respect, it was in turn also deeply bound to its own place and time. Definitions (as well as the occasional strategic absence) often reveal the preoccupations and prejudices of the past. Entries for words such as *balloon* and *pyjamas* reveal the horizons of the nineteenth and early twentieth centuries rather than our own. 'An air-tight envelope of paper, silk, or similar material, usually globose or pear-shaped, which, when inflated with light gas, rises in the air, and will carry with it a considerable weight; to large balloons a *car* strong enough to carry human beings can be attached, and hence they are used for observing atmospheric phenomena, for military reconnoitring, and, though with little success at present, as a means of travelling through the air', as Murray had defined *balloon* in 1885 (in a form of words which still remains intact in *OED2*). *Pyjamas* has been silently re-edited for the modern text, so as to eliminate the cultural bias of the original. 'Loose drawers or trousers, usually of silk or cotton, tied round the waist, worn by both sexes by the Mohammedans, and adopted by Europeans, especially for night wear . . .', the first edition informed its readers.

Details of the dictionary's making likewise concisely illustrate the temporal bounds of progress. The writing of letters remained the central mode of communication with outside readers, scientific specialists, and indeed between the editors themselves. So great was the flow of information that a pillar-box was installed outside Murray's house in Oxford. As many archival missives confirm, merely writing the words 'Dr Murray, Oxford' on an envelope provided enough information for the efficient delivery of a letter or the return of a page of proofs. Pen and ink remained the preferred medium of Murray and his co-editors, as well as of the many volunteer helpers for the dictionary (see fig. 8). Typewriters were relatively new. 'Thus made, the type writer is the simplest, most perfectly adapted to its work', as C. L. Sholes announced, filing his patent at the US Patent Office (and duly being cited in the *OED* when it confirmed the introduction of the word in 1868). While a typewriter was occasionally employed by Henry Hucks Gibbs, it is by no means clear that this would have been his preferred choice had he not lost his right hand while out shooting in Mannhead, Devon in 1864. Gibbs learnt to write with his left hand, providing hundreds of precariously sloping annotations on the proofs (even if he tended to resort to typing for more lengthy communications). Telephones were still rare. While Gell had one installed at the offices of Oxford University Press in Walton Street in the early 1890s, its redundancy for communication on the dictionary was obvious. As Murray instructed Craigie in 1901, 'it would be better to send your copyist assistant straight up here . . . for the books or anything else wanted', rather than using the Press as an intermediary. As he added, a bicycle was quick; if matters seemed more urgent, the assistant 'could take a tram'.[5]

Such processes of course contributed to the immense archival resources for the dictionary which still exist, allowing us to reconstruct its making in unprecedented detail. As Murray noted in 1903, he was currently in possession of some six tons of material (a figure which did not include the assembled evidence of the letters or that of the proofs and their many iterations). The dominance of paper necessitated the building of Murray's Scriptorium in the form it assumed. Murray recounted the early history of the materials for the dictionary to his audience at the London Institute in 1910, noting that the original plan of leasing an adjoining cottage in Mill Hill had been abandoned, 'for the cottage was one of a row with much timber and thatch, which might one day catch fire, and be burned to ashes, dictionary and all'. Nevertheless, he added, '*fire* suggested *fire-proof* and fire-proof raised the thought of iron, and my wife exclaimed "Why not put up a detached iron room out in the garden" . . . And so the iron room rose, and we called it first in sport, and then in earnest, the Scriptorium.' The same concerns governed the treatment of the dictionary once in Oxford. Murray, as we have seen, built a second iron Scriptorium in his garden on Banbury Road. Material for completed sections of the dictionary was transferred to similarly protective environments at the Press. Six bundles of slips had been placed in the fireproof room, as a letter from J. Griffiths, the warehouseman at OUP, confirmed in 1882.[6]

The era of electronic communication was of course unknown. 'It is not easy to conceive what new feature can now be added to English lexicography', Murray stated in 1900.[7] *Digital*, as he had confirmed in the fascicle *Diffluent–Disburden* in 1896, meant 'Of or pertaining to a finger, or to the fingers or digits'. *Electronic* came into existence in 1902, too late for Bradley to include it in the first volume under his independent editorship. Even when added by Craigie and Onions in 1933, *electronic* was simply accorded the meaning 'Of or pertaining to an electron or electrons'. Burchfield in 1972 extended the range of senses to include 'Of or pertaining to electronics', and included citations which once more seemed to herald the onset of a new era. 'As we experience the new electronic and organic age with ever stronger indications of its main outlines, the preceding mechanical age becomes quite intelligible', Marshall McLuhan stated in 1962. Subsequent compounds in *OEDS* announce the introduction of electronic computers ('The servomechanism is part of the computer, and . . . computers of this type have become known as electronic computers', as a citation from the journal *Electronics* affirms), together with devices such as the *electronic calculator* and the *electronic flash camera*. Language and history are again densely intertwined. The technological revolutions of the later twentieth century were, however, to have profound implications not just for innovations in available lexis but also for the lexicographic retrieval, processing, and recording of such data. Even *OED2* would fail to keep pace with the speed of change. 'The marvellous maze of internetted motions', states the only entry for *internet* in 1989, recording the words of the astronomer Alexander Herschel in 1883 precisely as they had appeared in Murray's original entry (in *Input–Kairine*), published in 1901.

'The Internet is an integral part of modern lexicography', John Simpson claims, noting that modern editors of the *OED* 'benefit from being able to maintain a range of handpicked specialist advisors around the academic world who respond by e-mail to lexicographical enquiries both authoritatively and, in some cases, almost instantaneously'.[8] In *OED Online*, the (ongoing) third edition of the dictionary,[9] we enter an entirely different lexicographical world, equipped with a diction that would have baffled Murray. Here the desire to find a word requires not the presence of a physical text (and the hefty volumes that many correspondents to the dictionary bewailed)[10] but instead a computer equipped with keyboard, screen, and mouse, as well as the requisite site licence and software. After having located the dictionary's *home page* by means of a *webbrowser*, typing the desired word in the box in the top right-hand corner of the *browser-window* generates a *list of results* or, if a single *result* is proffered, the entry itself will appear and the user may *scroll* through it at will. *Wildcards* and *proximity searches* are available, as are *simple* and *complex searches*. One can search by source language, by etymology, by date, or by citations. One can subject data to a scrutiny which is only laboriously achievable (if at all) in the first edition. 'Everything from simple word look-ups to sophisticated Boolean searching, using any of the fields in the Dictionary, can be done with speed and ease', the website triumphantly proclaims.[11] It is a far cry from the manual turning of a page or the scanning by the human eye by which the first edition was used and read.

Figure 8 The antithesis of the paperless office: James Murray in his Scriptorium.

Murray had, of course, discoursed authoritatively on the professional jargons that make up one strand of the world of words. He too had made his own constructions in this way; *nonce-words* and *Anglicity* became elements of specialist lexicographic terminology for the first edition. In their work on the *OED*, editors and assistants crafted what were termed *articles*, basing their information on the assembled *slips* sent in by *readers* who not only read but also isolated (and documented) potentially useful elements of usage. Yet, as Murray repeatedly affirmed, 'No man's English is all English'. The intricacies of *data capture assistants* and *software engineers* or the demands on the *online publication manager* (all of whom form part of the staff listing for the modern *OED*)[12] remained outside his own lexicographical experience. Similarly, while editors and editorial assistants, as well as the vital contributors to the dictionary, retain a significant role in crafting this new edition of the dictionary, it is evident that they too have often experienced parallel transformative processes in the ways they carry out their work. E-mails as well as index cards record new documentary evidence of word usage. Text-files and bytes, rather than slips crammed into pigeonholes, offer an enduring record of assembled data. Extensive databases present the results of specialized reading programmes, enabling electronic searching of material rather than that laborious shuffling of slips like the pieces of a giant game of chess in which Murray and his co-editors so often found themselves engaged. 'What once was a paper slip has become an electronic text file . . . A staff of computer keyboarders work from the actual text sources, keying quotations directly into a computer', generating files which are 'loaded directly into the Reading Programme database, where [they] can be accessed immediately by Oxford lexicographers', a further statement on the *OED* website explains.[13]

Like the first edition, *OED Online* is, in effect, to be 'a new garment throughout'.[14] Each and every entry from previous iterations of the dictionary is subjected to a new and meticulous scrutiny while the varied discourses of modern English (and Englishes) are incorporated in order to bring the work as a whole up to date. A budget of £34 million dwarfs the £300,000 which ultimately covered the costs (and losses) of *OED1*. The 'amazing efficiencies of electronic technology' which are proudly proclaimed would, in this respect, clearly have impressed Murray, not least since such technology allows a liberality of entry which Murray so often felt himself denied. A page which is constructed electronically above all lacks the 'definite limits' which confronted its counterparts in the nineteenth and early twentieth centuries. Quotations from 1995, 1996, 1997, 1998, and 2001 accompany the entry for *-rage* ('the second element in compounds: denoting an outburst of esp. pent-up anger and aggression triggered by a specific incident'). 'Ignorance, bad attitude and pavement rage seems to be the in thing', the accompanying citation from the electronic edition of the *Leicester Mercury* states. *Lad* ('*Brit. colloq.* A young man characterized by his enjoyment of social drinking, sport, and other activities considered to be male-oriented, his engagement in casual sexual relationships, and often by attitudes or behaviour regarded as irresponsible, sexist, or boorish') is similar, possessing an array of four quotations which encompass a span of a mere thirteen years. Entries for *girlpower* ('a self-reliant attitude among girls and young women manifested in ambition, assertiveness, and individualism'), *alcopop* (three citations in four years), and *surf* (three citations in as many years for its intransitive use 'To move from site to site on the Internet, *esp.* to browse or skim through web pages') reveal a lexicographical generosity such as Murray often found himself forced to curtail. *Girlpower* has, for example, two citations from 1992 alone (and seven spanning 1986–2001), including prominent reference to the Spice Girls as a framework for definition which inevitably signals the temporality of this edition of the dictionary too ('the term has been particularly and repeatedly associated with popular music; most notably . . . in the late 1990s, with the British all-female group The Spice Girls').

Liberality is also conspicuous in the selected source texts for this new edition of the dictionary. Citations from the *Beano* and the electronic edition of the *Glasgow Herald* fracture the canonical inclinations which were so often imposed on the editing of the first edition ('They will tour Scottish schools, initiating partnerships with Scots children through internet links and video diaries', the latter states under a new entry for *video diary*). Journals such as *Internet World* and *Classic CD*, *World of Interiors* and *Discount Store News* offer authoritative evidence of usage. 'It's music for nail-biters anonymous, full of high-strung punk, screech and distortion', the *Vancouver Sun* stated in 1995, incidentally providing a dictionary citation for *nail-biter* as it did so. *Yahoo! Internet Life* in a similar way serves to document modern uses of *web* ('As legislators look to find some way to control the Web, they have latched on to everything from censorship to cybersquatting'). *Cybersquatting* itself is comprehensively referenced by means of the *New York Law Journal*, the *Independent* and the *Economist*. *Full monty* is verified against the film script of the same name ('*Horse*. No one said owt about going the full monty to me. . . *Gaz*: We've got to give 'em something your average ten-bob stripper don't') as well as by other accompanying citations from the *Sunday Mirror* and the *Evening Express*. *Blag* ('To talk persuasively, if disingenuously, in an attempt to obtain or achieve something; to bluff; to scrounge, esp. by clever or deceitful talk') receives its first intransitive citation from the *Face* in 1993; *sorted* ('streetwise, "cool"') is documented with reference to the *New Musical Express* of 1991, as well as the television script of *Hollyoaks*. 'Sorted music – none of that bogus jungle crap', the quotation from the latter demotically avers.

The reservations of the Delegates of the past about the level of linguistic legitimacy which might be offered by non-canonical texts are here intransigently put to rest. This new version of the *OED* is indeed an inventory which embraces that democracy of discourse which Furnivall had earlier extolled. 'Fling our doors wide! all, all, not one, but all must enter', he had proclaimed, stressing the agenda of inclusiveness which the dictionary should observe.[15] It is the diction of *new brooming* ('Behaviour that causes widespread or fundamental change, esp. as made by a newly appointed person'), of *negaholism* ('The condition of being habitually negative or pessimistic') and *negaholic*, which signals the dictionary entries of a new era. 'In today's complex, competitive society, negaholism may sometimes be an unfortunate result of self-imposed pressures to excel in work, friendships, love', as a citation from *Cosmopolitan* categorically states. Under *news sheet*, the *Sunday Correspondent* in 1989 informs us that 'The Natural Health Centre offers cranial osteopathy and a free news sheet listing astrology workshops, retreats, evenings of rebirthing and psychodrama'. If entries can smack of the popular and contemporaneous, it is nevertheless clear that words such as *docusoap* and *doh* ('"Look out, you dern fool! You're gonna cut off your . . ." "D'oh!!!"', as a citation from *Simpsons Comics Strike Back*! attests), *dotcom* and *dumbing down* have their own linguistic history which is here substantiated with the impeccable scholarship which characterizes the dictionary as a whole. *Generation X* and *lad culture*, *postcode lottery* and *retail therapy*, *student loan* and *screenager* ('A young person (typically in his or her teens or twenties) who is at ease with and adept at using new technology and media, esp. computers') locate the lexis of modern life in ways which continue to reveal the impartial operation of historical principles (and the claims of ongoing history).

Science and technology too reveal a liberality entirely in keeping with Murray's own instincts as a lexicographer, as well as confirming the increasing prominence of this domain in modern lexical creation. *Html* (hypertext mark-up language) and *web-centric*, *web design*, and *higgsino* ('A hypothetical particle which is the supersymmetric fermion counterpart of a Higgs boson'), *wired* ('*Computing slang*. Making use of computers and information technology to send or receive information; *esp.* connected to the Internet') and *necrotizing fasciitis*, among hundreds of other entries, reveal the thrust of modern creativity in this respect. *Neurotrophically* and *neutralino*, *neutron capture therapy* and *neutrinosphere* ('In theories of supernovae: a layer at the surface of a collapsing star in which the stellar material is transparent to neutrinos, and from which neutrinos can be emitted') document areas of discourse which can no longer be excluded from the inventory of English. New entries for *cyberphobia* ('Fear of or anxiety about computing or technology; reluctance to engage with computers') and other related words meanwhile map out conflicting areas of experience. *Cyber-* itself reveals a compelling creativity. 'Type in any disease on your computer and page after page of descriptions, symptoms . . . will cascade across your screen. Hypochondriacs are becoming cyberchondriacs', the *Daily Telegraph* announced in 2000. Not only are we potentially *cyberchondriacs*, however, but forms such as *cyberfriend*, *cyberhick*, *cybersnob* and *cyberfeminist* offer a range of competing identities for an entirely modern era.

Other cultural filters have also been removed. Murray's evident qualms about the possible increase in the 'white man's burden' by virtue of the admission of English words of diverse origin and form have predictably been rejected.[16] New entries for words such as *ngapi* ('In Burma (Myanmar): a condiment consisting of fish or prawns which have been left to rot and then salted and dried') and *ngaka* ('A traditional African healer. Occas. used of people supposed to possess malign powers') reveal radically reconfigured policies of entrance to those which operated in the first edition. 'Somehow, foreignness is not as foreign now as it was', as Edmund Weiner confirmed in 1990.[17] Burchfield's *Supplements* began a policy of lexicographic redress which is still in operation, reified further by the impeccably neutral presentation in *OED Online* of words such as *ngoma* (in an entry which carefully discriminates between southern and eastern African usage)[18] and *Ngqika* ('A member of one of the major branches of the Rharhabe division of the Xhosa people, centred mainly in the Eastern Cape province'). Entries such as that for *karoshi* ('In Japan: death brought on by overwork or job-related exhaustion') reveal other areas of lexical expansion and asssimilation.

Gender too provides an illuminating link to the past. 'Furnivall has a fancy that it is good to quote women, because the writings of women are a characteristic of the Age', Gibbs wrote to Murray (in apparent dissent) in 1883.[19] If the published version of the first edition failed to accord with this intent as much as Furnivall might have hoped, the newest edition of the dictionary has triumphantly returned to this expressed agenda. 'In addition to the "traditional" canon of literary works, today's Reading Programme covers women's writing and non-literary texts which have been published in recent times, such as wills, probate inventories, account books, diaries, and letters', as we are now informed.[20] The art of definition – or redefinition – pays more than lip service to these new political principles. 'A sense of self-esteem engendered by a person's (public) acknowledgement of his or her homosexuality', reads a new entry (from June 2003) for *gay pride*; 'a popular older or elderly person; *esp.* a veteran performer, etc., who retains his or her popularity or appeal', as the new entry for *golden oldie* proclaims. The dominance of an exclusively male frame of reference is lost. *Cookies* (as used in computing) 'identify the user or monitor *his or her* access to the server'; *mindstyle* is 'the cumulative attitudes and consistent habits of thinking that a person develops about *his or her* chosen lifestyle'. A *mucker-in*, as a draft entry from March 2003 affirms, is 'a person who "mucks in"; a person prepared to do any kind of work, to pull *his or her* weight, or to cooperate or share with others on equal terms' (emphases added).

'The greater the extension of the language, the more important does it become to throw around it the lustre of literary authority, and to preserve it as far as possible from the innovations which tend to vulgarise and degrade it', John Marsden had urged in 1859.[21] *OED Online* adopts a position which contrasts sharply with such inclinations, instead embracing a policy of unquestioned representativeness. It displays the wholehearted engagement with the complexity and essential dynamism of 'English' which so often emerged as a central theme in Murray's many lectures and addresses. If the static nature of Murray's finished text seemed at times to belie his chosen thesis, the capacity of electronic entries to respond to ongoing change would no doubt have been received by Murray as an entirely apposite image for the dictionary on which he spent the majority of his life. Murray and his co-editors were limited by existing technology. Even after the information at their disposal had changed, earlier entries could not be changed or emended. Skeat, for example, had pointed out on the proofs that Bradley's definition of *freeze* used the word *contamination* in a way which remained undefined in the relevant fascicle. 'As technically used here, this word is not in the D[ictionary]', he wrote.[22] Rectification of such problems remained impossible until a new revision of the dictionary took place. The editors of the first editions were forced to relegate vital corrections and additions to a *Supplement* which Murray knew would be beyond his own means to bring into being. If *OED Online* therefore manifests clear continuities with the past in its adoption of serial publication (beginning in this instance with M rather than A on the grounds of the 'editorial stability which the First Edition had achieved by this point'), it is nevertheless self-evident that the serial publication of the modern day has some significant advantages. The draft entries released in each new quarterly tranche of *OED Online* remain open to further revision, and can be 'refreshed' should circumstances demand. *Cat flap* was transmuted to include a new citation which enabled a date of first use in 1957 to be established (rather than the previous date of 1967); the recent adverbial use of *early doors* ('Early on; near the beginning'), dated to 1991 in the revised draft entry as originally issued, was also able to incorporate new evidence from twenty years earlier ('Early doors it was vital to me that they like me, too. But I became so attached to them as players that when I left Derby I found I liked them more than they liked me', Brian Clough stated in the *Observer* in 1979). While the enduring hazards of serial publication mean that, as yet, *refresh* itself has not been redefined to incorporate this flux of sense, its reality as a process is indeed being implemented in the dictionary as it evolves. The digital text of *OED Online* hence triumphantly obviates the temporal gaps that attended Murray's desire for corrections in entries such as that for *tetrahelodon*, which was forced, in *OED1*, to present an entirely erroneous definition to the world for some two decades.[23] This is, however, not to suggest that each and every linguistic change can be reflected with the immediacy which the flux of a living language might demand. Some 900 entirely new words come into existence each year, as a recent survey suggested;[24] thousands of new senses and new shades of meaning accumulate for other words which are already present in the language. If the new dictionary is to advance through the alphabet, not all of these can be included. Continuities are present here too. 'A liberty of selection must be allowed', as Derwent Coleridge had argued in 1860.[25] The same remains true for the dictionaries of a modern age.

Alongside the lexically new, the agendas of historicism and objectivity also remain intact. Entries for older and obsolete words continue to supplement the record of the language, to realize the 'inventory' which Trench had proclaimed. A new draft entry for *niggerality* ('niggardliness') appeared in September 2003, documenting a newly discovered a nonce-word of the past. *Niggerkin* ('A small black person or child'), first used by Thackeray in 1853 ('Another niggerkin yet smaller was deputed to do nothing but watch the process of dinner'), assumed its place in the inventory of English at the same time. Three months earlier *nebulochaotic* ('hazily confused') as deployed by George Macdonald in his *Mary Marston* of 1881 had made its own appearance. Historical principles hold firm. 'The definitive record of the English language', states the new rhetoric of the *OED*'s website. 'Having the character of finality as a product; determinate, definite, fixed and final. Of an edition of a literary work, a textbook, etc.: authoritative; the most complete and authoritative to date', the corresponding entry for *definitive* states. A justifiable degree of hyperbole, just as in the publicity material for the first edition, proclaims the image of transcendent advance. Yet it is important to realize that alongside this liberality and democracy a new and undeniable élitism has, in one important respect, simultaneously come into being. It was, after all, the 'wonderful cheapness' of the first edition which the *Scotsman* had singled out for praise in 1891.[26] The same cannot necessarily be said of *OED Online*. Rather than a format which enabled a net cost of sixpence a day,[27] we enter a world of site licences and subscribers, a domain which can be accessed only by possession of a password (and payment of the requisite fee), and which allows use of the dictionary only for the duration of the subscription itself. There is inevitably a world of difference between the two. Even if Walter Skeat complained about the physical burden of the volumes of the original *OED*,[28] it is clear that the modern dictionary can no longer be an open book to all who might wish to consult it. The images of the new *OED* are in this sense conflicting, divided. Alongside its agenda of transparent inclusivity come issues of potential exclusivity, necessitating (in 2003) almost £200 for a year's access by private subscription to its documentation of the language. Privilege coexists uneasily with the real and undeniable diversity of English as represented in the dictionary itself. So being able to access the dictionary in its most modern on-line version confronts us with other issues of access that perhaps inevitably remain unresolved.

In linguistic terms alone, however, it is indisputable that the revisions of this new incarnation of the *OED* make a number of significant advances towards breaking down the barriers of class and culture as conventionally represented in the English dictionary. The essential mutability of an on-line text moreover confirms its salience as an evocative image of the language itself. Neither language nor its representation, as Murray repeatedly stressed, can ever really be fixed. The proofs, as we have seen, consistently reflect the divergent possibilities of language for the first edition. The nuances of inclusion, definition, labelling, shift between different versions. In this respect the continuities with *OED Online* remain clear. Clicking on *martyr* also enables the antecedent entry in *OED2* to be revealed, charting the flux of definition and of sense. To click on *masculine* is to confront oneself with the diversity of readings that the word has previously received. 'Said of inanimate objects to which the male sex was attributed on the ground of some quality, e.g. relative superiority, strength, activity, etc. ***masculine hour*** (*Astrol.*): one ruled by a masculine planet. Obs.', as *OED2* declared in a precise echo of the first edition. 'Designating an object deemed to be of the male sex on the basis of some quality, such as strength or activity, esp. as contrasted with a corresponding object deemed female', states the new draft entry of December 2000, paying careful attention to the politics of representation and association of gender bias. Like a digital palimpsest, *OED Online* continually presents images of its own evolution, documenting its own history alongside that of the words and senses it consistently strives to encompass. The 'same' entry can demonstrably possess divergent readings and other forms, just as the earlier versions in the making of *OED1* offered alternative constructions of the ways in which entries might eventually emerge. Like language itself, there can be no single and definitive version in which words are immutably pinned down. The dictionary of the digital age endlessly offers images of its own potential for regeneration and for change. Murray would undoubtedly have approved.

Notes

Preface

[1] R. McLintock, 'The New English Dictionary and Some of Its Predecessors. Paper read before the Literary and Philosophical Society of Liverpool', 29 April 1889, 16.

[2] See further p. 7.

[3] R. Browning, *The Ring and the Book* (London: Smith, Elder, 1868–69), i, 127: 'Words as ready and as big/ As the part he played, the bold abashless one'.

[4] See pp. 38–9.

[5] On Hall's work for the *OED*, see further E. Knowles, 'Making the OED: Readers and Editors. A Critical Survey'. In L. C. Mugglestone, *Lexicography and the OED. Pioneers in the Untrodden Forest* (Oxford: Oxford University Press, 2002a), 22–39.

[6] J. A. H. Murray, 'Preface to Volume I', *A New English Dictionary on Historical Principles, Founded Mainly on the Materials Collected by the Philological Society*, Vol. I: *A and B* (Oxford: Clarendon Press, 1888), xiii.

[7] [Philological Society], *Proposal for the Publication of a New English Dictionary by the Philological Society* (London: Trübner, 1859), 8.

[8] OED/MISC/59/2/1. *National Observer*, 29 December 1894.

[9] E. B. Tribble, 'Like a Looking-Glass in the Frame. From the Marginal Note to the Footnote'. In D. C. Greetham (ed.), *The Margins of the Text* (Ann Arbor: University of Michigan Press, 1997), 229.

[10] T. Hilton, *John Ruskin. The Early Years* (New Haven and London: Yale University Press, 1985). So pervasive are the comments that a further reader was prompted to marginal annotations of a particularly trenchant kind, transforming the text into the kind of discourse that the proofs of the *OED* were often to become. Hence Hilton's discussion of Ruskin's *Modern Painters* ('It is philosophy and aesthetics, and much more than that. It is poetry') elicits the acerbic 'which is more than can be said for your writing' from the first reader, prompting in response 'since when has poetry been a criterion of biography, you pompous, too-clever-by-half idiot?' in the hand of a different – and far more sympathetic – reader. No text generates a single unified response, and this fact remains equally relevant for the reading(s) of the provisional versions of the *OED*.

[11] MP/[n.d.]/10/83. W. W. Skeat to J. A. H. Murray, October 1883.

[12] MP/27/10/83. W. W. Skeat to J. A. H. Murray, 27 October 1883.

[13] H. J. Jackson, *Marginalia. Readers Writing in Books* (New Haven and London: Yale University Press, 2001), 13.

14 J. Schäfer, *Documentation in the OED: Shakespeare and Nashe as Test Cases* (Oxford: Clarendon Press, 1980), 3.
15 R. W. McConchie, *Lexicography and Physicke. The Record of Sixteenth-Century Medical Terminology* (Oxford: Clarendon Press, 1997), 182.
16 D. R. Raymond, *Dispatches from the Front: The Prefaces to the Oxford English Dictionary* (Waterloo, Ontario: Centre for the New Oxford English Dictionary, University of Waterloo, 1987), Preface.
17 Murray (1888), ix.
18 MP/15/12/03. J. A. H. Murray to Dr J. Bryce, 15 December 1903.
19 A committee of ten Delegates (including the Vice-Chancellor of Oxford University) was the norm in the second half of the nineteenth century. As the minutes of their meetings record, they were responsible for approving and at times overseeing the publication of all books to be printed by the Press.
20 T. H. Huxley to J. Hooker, 5 September 1858. In L. Huxley, *Life and Letters of Thomas Henry Huxley* (London: Macmillan, 1900), i, 160.
21 See further pp. 152–4.
22 For a detailed account of the publishing history of the dictionary's fascicles, see J. McMorris, '*OED* Sections and Parts'. In Mugglestone (2002a), 228–31.
23 J. A. H. Murray, *The Evolution of English Lexicography* (Oxford: Clarendon Press, 1900), 6–7.
24 J. A. H. Murray, 'Shaksperian Illustrations and the Philological Society's Dictionary', *Academy*, 1 January 1881, 8.
25 J. Simpson and E. Weiner (eds), *Oxford English Dictionary Additions Series*, Vols I–II (Oxford: Clarendon Press, 1993); M. Proffitt (ed.), *Oxford English Dictionary Additions Series*, Vol. III (Oxford: Clarendon Press, 1997).

Chapter 1: The Ideal Dictionary

1 MP/15/12/03. J. A. H. Murray to Dr J. Bryce, 15 December 1903.
2 The history of the dictionary's change of title is by no means straightforward. While *A New English Dictionary* continued to appear on the title pages of the various parts and sections of the first edition 1884–1928, its designation as the *Oxford English Dictionary* was established from 1895 on the covers and the wrappers of the individual parts. It was not, however, until the 1933 edition by W. A. Craigie and C. T. Onions that *Oxford English Dictionary* also appeared on the title page.
3 See R. Bridges, 'Henry Bradley. A Memoir'. In R. Bridges (ed.), *The Collected Papers of Henry Bradley* (Oxford: Clarendon Press, 1928), 1–58.
4 The formal span of the dictionary in the first edition was from *c.*1150 onwards, though, as we shall see, the admission of what were deemed to be unduly 'modern' words was a subject of continued controversy.
5 MP/31/1/87. P. L. Gell to J. A. H. Murray, 31 January 1887. The Secretary's role was important; in effect, he acted as the executive head of the Press.
6 [R. Cawdrey], *A Table Alphabeticall, conteyning and teaching the true vvriting, and vunderstanding of hard vsuall English wordes* (London: I. R. for Edmund Weaver, 1604).
7 S. Johnson, *The Plan of a Dictionary of the English Language* (London: J. and P. Knapton, 1747), 32.

8 See S. Johnson, *A Dictionary of the English Language: In which the Words are Deduced from their Originals, and Illustrated in their different Significations by Examples from the Best Writers* (London: W. Strahan, 1755).

9 'The New English Dictionary', *Saturday Review*, 16 February (1884), 226.

10 The lectures, delivered on 5 and 19 November 1857, were reprinted in a revised and extended version from which all subsequent quotations are given. See R. C. Trench, *On Some Deficiencies in Our English Dictionaries* (London: John W. Parker & Sons, 1860).

11 W. Benzie, *Dr. F. J. Furnivall. A Victorian Scholar Adventurer* (Norman, Oklahoma: Pilgrim Books, 1983), contains a useful account of Furnivall's connections with the *OED*.

12 Johnson (1755), B2^{v}.

13 For a detailed survey of the changes in linguistic understanding and knowledge over this time, see A. Morpurgo Davies, *Nineteenth-Century Linguistics* (London: Longman, 1992).

14 Littré's *Dictionnaire de la langue française* was published between 1863 and 1873, and was the product of some thirty years' work. For a discussion of the work of Grimm and Littré in the context of the *OED* and nineteenth-century philological science, see N. Osselton, 'Murray and his European Counterparts', in Mugglestone (2002a), 59–76.

15 See T. Sheridan, *A General Dictionary of the English Language. One Main Object of Which, is, to Establish a Plain and Permanent Standard of Pronunciation* (London: J. Dodsley, C. Dilly & J. Wilkie, 1780); J. Walker, *A Critical Pronouncing Dictionary and Expositor of the English Language* (London: G. G. J. & J. Robinson, 1791). For a discussion of these developments in the English dictionary, see Chapter 1 of L. C. Mugglestone, *Talking Proper. The Rise of Accent as Social Symbol* 2nd edn (Oxford: Oxford University Press, 2003).

16 C. Richardson, *A New Dictionary of the English Language, Combining Explanation with Etymology* 2 vols (London: William Pickering, 1836–37).

17 Tooke in his *Diversions of Purley* (2nd edn, London: for the author, 1798–1805) believed that etymology contained the 'primordial meaning' of all lexical units, a conception which, in Murray's more scholarly view, resulted in merely a 'fabric of conjectures'.

18 Trench (1860), 10, 29.

19 Ibid., 4–5.

20 Johnson (1755), C1^{v}.

21 Trench (1860), 6.

22 See, for example, his evident distaste for the 'jargon' of science and technology (which are 'not, for the most part, except by an abuse of language, words at all'), and his preferences for canonical writers against the *ad hoc* creativity of modern journalism. The legacies of these assumptions for the *OED* are discussed further in Chapters 3 and 4.

23 Trench (1860), 1.

24 [Philological Society], *Proposal*, 3.

25 See further Chapter 4.

26 [Philological Society], *Proposal*, 5.

27 H. Coleridge, *A Letter to the Very Rev. The Dean of Westminster*. This appears as an Appendix to Trench's 1860 edition of *On Some Deficiencies in Our English Dictionaries* (pp. 71–78). An on-line version appears at: http://dictionary.oed.com/public/archive/Papers/Deficiencies/Deficiencies_71.htm.

[28] F. J. Furnivall, *An Alphabetical List of English Words occurring in the Literature of the Eighteenth and Nineteenth Centuries; and forming a Basis of Comparison for the Use of Contributors to the New Dictionary of the Philological Society*. Pt II (E–L) (London: The Philological Society, 1861).

[29] See F. J. Furnivall, *Circular to the Members of the Philological Society* (London: The Philological Society, 1865), 4.

[30] A. J. Ellis, 'Second Annual Address of the President to the Philological Society', *Transactions of the Philological Society* (1873–74), 245.

[31] F. J. Furnivall, *Circular to the Members of the Philological Society* (London: The Philological Society, 1862), 3.

[32] See p. 94.

[33] Cited in G. Wheelwright, *Appeal to the English-Speaking Public on behalf of a New English Dictionary* (London: The Philological Society, 1875), 3. One of the sub-editors for the dictionary under Furnivall, Wheelwright intended his pamphlet to spur fresh interest in the dictionary.

[34] A. J. Ellis, 'Third Annual Address of the President to the Philological Society', *Transactions of the Philological Society* (1873–74), 354.

[35] MP/20/4/77. H. Sweet to B. Price, 20 April 1877. This letter is reprinted in entirety in K. M. E. Murray, *Caught in the Web of Words. James A. H. Murray and the* Oxford English Dictionary (New Haven and London: Yale University Press, 1977), 342–6. Henceforth abbreviated as *CWW*.

[36] Sweet's estimates seem to be based on the confident assessments published two years earlier by George Wheelwright in his own *Appeal*. As Wheelwright noted (1875, 3): 'I have made the most careful survey I could as detailed in the Philological Society Circulars, and upon a rough calculation (which was all that circumstances admitted of) I believe I am right in affirming that nearly half . . . of the whole work has been completed by the various sub-editors. And remember that this included what is by far the most difficult stage in such an undertaking, viz. for getting it under weigh [*sic*]. . . Contributors of the present time have but to scan their books carefully and pick out the plums, the scarce words and phrases . . . whereas the earliest readers had a far more laborious and comprehensive task before them.'

[37] MP/19/6/82. J. A. H. Murray to B. Price, 19 June 1882. Other views on Furnivall could be more condemnatory. If Murray acknowledged to Price that 'Furnivall has an itch for annoying people', his words were certainly borne out by Edward Freeman who referred to Furnivall as 'the Society's madman', demanding 'why do not some of the saner members of the Society chain him up . . . or gag him?' MP/22/6/73. E. Freeman to J. A. H. Murray, 22 June 1873.

[38] See S. Smiles, *Self-help; With Illustrations of Character and Conduct* (London: John Murray, 1859).

[39] See in particular *CWW* for an illuminating biography of James Murray by his granddaughter. This supplies a detailed account of the early history of the dictionary under Murray's editorship. P. Sutcliffe, *The Oxford University Press. An Informal History* (Oxford: Clarendon Press, 1978), offers an account of the making of the *OED* from the point of view of the Press.

[40] H. Bradley, 'Sir James Murray, 1837–1915', *Proceedings of the British Academy*, 8 (1917), 546.

[41] On Müller's life and his contributions to nineteenth-century linguistic science, see N. C. Chaudhuri, *Scholar Extraordinary. The Life of Professor the Rt. Hon. Friedrich Max Müller P. C.* (London: Chatto & Windus, 1974).

42 Ibid., 186.

43 F. Max Müller, *Observations by Professor Max Müller on the Lists of Readers and Books Read for the Proposed English Dictionary* (Oxford: Clarendon Press, 1878). The original, now uncatalogued in the *OED* archives at OUP, was conspicuously headed 'Private. – For the Delegates of the Press Only'.

44 See e.g. his letter of 26 April 1878 on the details of the etymological treatment of words to be given in the dictionary (MP/26/4/78. F. Max Müller to J. A. H. Murray).

45 MP/25/11/78. J. A. H. Murray to B. Brice, 25 November 1878.

46 MP/6/4/76. W. W. Skeat to J. A. H. Murray, 6 April 1876.

47 MP/[n.d]/78. Undated draft of a letter from J. A. H. Murray to B. Price.

48 J. A. H. Murray, 'Eighth Annual Address of the President to the Philological Society', *Transactions of the Philological Society* (1879a), 569.

49 MP/10/5/79a. J. A. H. Murray to F. J. Furnivall, 10 May 1879. It was eventually traced to an erstwhile sub-editor living near Loughborough.

50 MP/10/5/79b. F. J. Furnivall to J. A. H. Murray, 10 May 1879.

51 It was eventually located in the stables which belonged to the house of this sub-editor.

52 See point 4 of Murray's letter to Price of 25 November 1878 (MP/25/11/78) which deals in detail with the financial arrangements for the dictionary. Murray was often to be seriously affected by the financial problems which resulted. 'I have seen myself becoming poorer and poorer every year since I came here, through inadequate income which I have had to make up from capital', he lamented to Furnivall in 1893, for example; 'I shall be insolvent some day soon, and then the crash will come' (MP/5/7/93. J. A. H. Murray to F. J. Furnivall, 5 July 1893).

53 OED/MISC/13/24. J. A. H. Murray to F. Hall, 11 April 1899.

54 As the *Athenaeum* recorded, 'the articles on [this] subject in the *Athenaeum* and other English journals were quoted in full by the New York press, and thence in the local papers and periodicals over the whole extent of the Union, from all parts of which eager offers of assistance continue to be received'. 'The New English Dictionary of the Philological Society', *The Athenaeum*, 13 September 1879, 338.

55 'The Philological Society's English Dictionary', *The Academy*, 10 May 1879, 413.

56 J. A. H. Murray, *An Appeal to the English-Speaking and English-Reading Public to Read Books and Make Extracts for the Philological Society's New Dictionary* (Oxford: Clarendon Press, 1879b), 3. See also http://dictionary.oed.com/public/archive/ where all three editions of this are available on-line.

57 MP/H. Harley, 'The Philological Society's New English Dictionary', *The Sweep Papers*, 43 (1879), 6–7.

58 'The New English Dictionary of the Philological Society', *The Athenaeum* (1879a), 337.

59 J. A. H. Murray, 'Ninth Annual Address of the President to the Philological Society', *Transactions of the Philological Society* (1880–81), 123.

60 Murray (1879b), 570.

61 MP/17/4/79. B. Wesley to J. A. H. Murray, 17 April 1879.

62 MP/18/4/79. W. White to J. A. H. Murray, 18 April 1879. Murray's 'old boys' – alongside his current students – could be diligent contributors to the dictionary. As the 1879 *Appeal* records, 'Dr. Murray's own pupils have supplied him with 5000 good quotations during the past month'.

63 MP/1/1/80. H. R. Helwych to J. A. H. Murray, 1 January 1880; MP/17/8/81. C. Y. Potts to J. A. H. Murray, 17 August 1881; MP/1/3/83. H. H. Gibbs to J. A. H. Murray, 1 March 1883.

64 MP/23/1/84. J. Randall to J. A. H. Murray, 23 January 1884.

65 This was an important departure from the instructions for reading as set out by the 1859 *Proposal* which had instead referred to the especial need to record 'remarkable words'. As Murray found, the consequences of this were all too apparent in the absence of many common words of the language as initially exhibited by the data files of the dictionary.

66 MP/12/2/82. J. A. H. Murray to H. H. Gibbs, 12 February 1882.

67 MP/24/6/86. J. A. H. Murray to P. L. Gell, 24 June 1886.

68 See e.g. Murray's further comment to Gibbs (MP/12/2/82) that 'the matter which troubles me most, is the doubt whether I am acting a straightforward part in not expressly pointing out to the Delegates what I now know to be the requisite time'.

69 See *CWW*, 207–8.

70 The first Dictionary Committee, consisting of William Markby, Benjamin Jowett, Henry Liddell, Friedrich Max Müller, and Ingram Bywater, was appointed in April 1882 'to consider the execution of the Dictionary'.

71 MP/9/6/82. Copy of a letter from J. A. H. Murray to B. Price, 9 June 1882. The letter is headed, in Murray's hand, 'In answer to request from the Delegates not to use newspaper quotations'.

72 In the later pressures to save space in the dictionary, such qualitative coding can nevertheless come into play. See further pp. 92–6.

73 OUP/ Delegates' Orders. Minutes of a Meeting of the Committee of the Delegates of the Press Appointed to Consider the English Dictionary, 10 March 1883.

74 MP/8/11/83. A. J. Ellis to J. A. H. Murray, 8 November 1883.

75 MP/18/4/83. *The New English Dictionary. Suggestions for Guidance in Preparing Copy for the Press* [Annotations by J. A. H. Murray].

76 J. H. Marsden, 'Dr. Trench', *Edinburgh Review*, 109 (1859), 376. Cited in L. Dowling, *Language and Decadence in the Victorian Fin de Siècle* (Princeton: Princeton University Press, 1996), 97.

77 See further pp. 74–5.

78 Johnson (1755), C2^{v}.

79 MP/1/7/84. W. Markby to B. Price, 1 July 1884.

80 'A New English Dictionary', *The Times*, 26 January 1884, 6.

81 Review of *A New English Dictionary on Historical Principles*. Edited by James A. H. Murray. Part I. *A–Ant*, *The Athenaeum*, 9 February 1884, 177.

82 J. A. H. Murray, 'Thirteenth Annual Address of the President to the Philological Society', *Transactions of the Philological Society* (1882–84), 524.

83 Review of *A New English Dictionary on Historical Principles*. Edited by James A. H. Murray. Part I. *A–Ant*, *The Athenaeum*, 9 February 1884, 177.

84 OUP/ Delegates' Orders. Minutes of a Meeting of the Delegates of Oxford University Press, 25 April 1884.

85 'Powell and the Press', *The Periodical*, 2 (1906), 78.

86 MP/22/7/84. H. H. Gibbs to B. Price, 22 July 1884. Gibbs was often required to act as an intermediary between dictionary and Delegates. He had, for example, formally been requested to explain to the Philological Society 'the wish of the Delegates to complete the Dictionary as speedily as possible' at the meeting of the Delegates of the Clarendon Press on 17 July 1884.

87 MP/25/2/82. J. A. H. Murray to H. H. Gibbs, 25 February 1882.

88 OED/MISC/13/6. J. A. H. Murray to F. Hall, 29 June 1894.

89 Murray (1884), 510.

[90] See e.g. MP/13/2/84. E. P. Thomson to J. A. H. Murray, 13 February 1884: 'I am sorry that you feel weary and embittered, but perhaps it is natural after such long labours'.

[91] MP/17/1/84. Copy of a letter from J. A. H. Murray to B. Price, 17 January 1884.

[92] MP/8/6/86. H. Frowde to P. L. Gell, 8 June 1886. The letter was subsequently sent on to Murray at the request of the Delegates.

[93] See e.g. MP/23/6/86. P. L. Gell to J. A. H. Murray, 23 June 1886.

[94] MP/23/3/87. P. L. Gell to J. A. H. Murray, 23 March 1887.

[95] See further p. 131. The slowness of Bradley's editing became a regular topic of many of the Delegates' meetings. In April 1893, for example, Bradley had produced 26 pages against Murray's 56. Six months later the respective tallies were 42 pages against 106.

[96] MP/17/4/86. H. Bradley to B. Price, 17 April 1886.

[97] MP/19/1/87. H. Bradley to B. Price, 19 January 1887.

[98] See p. 44.

[99] OUP/Delegates' Orders. Minutes of a Meeting of the Delegates of Oxford University Press, 7 February 1896.

[100] MP/31/1/87. P. L. Gell to J. A. H. Murray, 31 January 1887.

[101] MP/24/12/04. J. A. H. Murray to E. Arber, 24 December 1904.

[102] MP/Skeat Correspondence/Poems.

[103] MP/7/12/92. P. L. Gell to F. J. Furnivall, 7 December 1892.

[104] See further pp. 65, 99.

[105] See N. Webster, *Webster's Dictionary of the English Language*, rev. C. A. Goodrich and N. Porter (London: Bell & Daldy, 1864).

[106] See *CWW*, 207–9. This had in practice regularly been exceeded. From *A–Age*, for example, the average ratio for the *OED* to Webster was 10:1 and this was by no means atypical.

[107] I. Bywater to P. L. Gell, 21 February 1896. This letter appears in the Delegates' Order Book for 1896 in the archives of Oxford University Press.

[108] Uncatalogued draft of a letter in OED Archives at OUP from P. L. Gell to Murray and Bradley [April 1896].

[109] Ibid.

[110] Ibid.

[111] Uncatalogued letter in OED Archives at OUP from J. A. H. Murray to F. J. Furnivall. Enclosure. 11 December 1892.

[112] OED/MISC/59/1/13. *The Athenaeum* 1891. Review of H. Bradley (ed.), *A New English Dictionary on Historical Principles*, Vol. III. Part I, *E–Every*.

[113] MP/15/12/03. J. A. H. Murray to Dr J. Bryce, 15 December 1903.

[114] MP/5/3/96. J. A. H. Murray to P. L. Gell, 5 March 1896.

[115] Skeat's poem 'The Words in D.' which he sent to Murray early in 1897 likewise reflects a changed tenor in the making of the dictionary.

[116] OED/MISC/59/1/14/ii. *Manchester Guardian*, 1 January 1895.

[117] [C. A. M. Fennell], 'Review of *NED*, *Development–Dziggetai*; *Field–Foister*', *The Athenaeum*, 9 October 1897, 484.

[118] MP/26/6/94. C. E. Doble to J. A. H. Murray, 26 June 1894.

[119] MP/27/1/96. Draft of a letter from J. A. H. Murray to P. L. Gell, 27 January 1896.

[120] MP/5/11/97. First draft of a letter from J. A. H. Murray to J. R. Magrath, 5 November 1897.

[121] MP/24/4/96. *New English Dictionary. Correspondence and Minutes Printed by Order of the Board*. P. L. Gell to H. Bradley and J. A. H. Murray, 25 February 1896.

122 Ibid. H. Bradley to P. L. Gell, 2 March 1896.
123 MP/26/2/96. H. Bradley to J. A. H. Murray, 26 February 1896.
124 MP/24/4/96. *New English Dictionary. Correspondence and Minutes Printed by Order of the Board.* J. A. H. Murray to P. L. Gell, 5 March 1896.
125 Ibid. F. Hall to P. L. Gell, 16 March 1896.
126 MP/2/12/92. H. H. Gibbs to J. A. H. Murray, 2 December 1892.
127 MP/26/2/96. H. Bradley to J. A. H. Murray, 26 February 1896.
128 Murray (1900), 47.
129 See further Chapter 3.
130 Murray (1884), 523.
131 MP/24/4/96. *New English Dictionary. Correspondence and Minutes Printed by Order of the Board.* J. A. H. Murray to P. L. Gell, 5 March 1896.
132 'The English Dictionary and the Clarendon Press', *Saturday Review*, 18 April 1896, 393.
133 MP/24/4/96. *New English Dictionary. Correspondence and Minutes Printed by Order of the Board.* J. A. H. Murray to P. L. Gell, 5 March 1896.
134 MP/10/5/01. J. A. H. Murray to W. A. Craigie, 10 May 1901.
135 See S. Winchester, *The Meaning of Everything* (Oxford: Oxford University Press, 2003).
136 McConchie (1997), 219–20.
137 See further Chapter 6.
138 *Zyxt*, an obsolete present tense form of the verb *to see*, was published in July 1921. While this records the last word in the alphabetic sequence of the first edition, the last word in publishing terms was in fact *wyzen* (a Scandinavian or northern form of *weasand*, meaning 'gullet') edited by Craigie and published in 1928 as the final entry in the concluding fascicle.
139 MP/3/4/82. H. Sweet to J. A. H. Murray, 3 April 1882.
140 MP/[9]/83a. Proof of *Notice of Publication for A New English Dictionary on Historical Principles*. Part 1. A–APO.
141 Murray (1884), 521.

Chapter 2: Palimpsests

1 This citation was included by Robert Burchfield in *OEDS* as part of the later history of *palimpsest* and its figurative deployment.
2 Lloyd provides a detailed account of his work as a sub-editor on H in 'First Steps in Dictionary-Making', a paper which he delivered to the Literary and Philosophical Society of Liverpool on 29 April 1889.
3 See MP/15/6/97. J. A. H. Murray to P. L. Gell, 15 June 1897.
4 'The Oxford English Dictionary Completed 1884–1928', *The Periodical*, 13 (1928), 17.
5 Murray (1880), 129.
6 Further revision in the first revise was in this instance to lead to an entirely new definition ('One versed in the science of language') in the published fascicles.
7 The definition, presumably under renewed pressures of space, was shortened to 'a hand' in the final text.
8 That other mistakes were not is of course inevitable. 'Mr Henry Jones . . . points out

to me a misprint under *Cent*[2]', Gibbs, for example, wrote to Murray on the erroneous substitution of *glebe* for *gleke* in a 1577 citation from John Northbrooke's *Treatise wherein Dicing, Dauncing . . . are reproved* (OED/JH/26/6/1. H. H. Gibbs to J. A. H. Murray, n.d.). 'Glebe is nonsense', Gibbs adds, though as critical reader, he too admits his share in the responsibility ('I wonder that I should not have noticed it'). Marked '*Suppl[ement]*' by Murray in red, it was a correction clearly intended to be filed and incorporated when the time came for making necessary changes to the published text. In *OED2*, however, the problem persists, *glebe* still appearing where *gleke* should rightly have been restored ('To play – post, cente, glebe, or such other games'). Other errors detected only after the event likewise stand uncorrected in *OED2*. Murray, for instance, was particularly mortified by one under *great* in which a citation from Richard Eden's *A Treatyse of the Newe India* in 1553 ('That myghtie kyng . . . Alexander the great') in fact meant 'Alexander greteth thee', and hence was in the wrong entry altogether (OED/EP/MURRA/7. J. A. H. Murray to H. Bradley, 27 April 1904).

9 OED/MISC/13/13. J. A. H. Murray to F. Hall, 13 December 1893.

10 See H. Bradley, Review of *A New English Dictionary on Historical Principles*, Pt I: *A–Ant*, *The Academy*, 25 (1884), 105–6.

11 The earliest citation hitherto available was from Hall's *Chronicles* of 1548 ('The fore~frontes of euery gallery were hanged with . . . Sarcenet'). The addition made on the page proofs instead took usage back to 1470, as *OED* still records (Henry *Wallace* ix. 831: 'He gert thaim tak Syllys off ayk, and a stark barres mak, At a foyr frount, fast in the forest syd').

12 Prior to this, the dictionary had declared usage of *lexicography* in English to begin with Johnson himself: '1755 Johnson *Dict*. Pref. B ij: "Such is the fate of hapless lexicography, that not only darkness, but light, impedes and distresses it; things may be not only too little, but too much known, to be happily illustrated".'

13 See further p. 75.

14 The fact that in the published fascicle three further citations are included, all of which are earlier (ultimately taking the sense back to 1625 in a quotation from Bacon), further confirms the very real flux of information which continued to attend production of the dictionary at this stage.

15 OED/BL/323/15. First proof of *cheque*, 17 November 1888 [Annotations by H. H. Gibbs and J. A. H. Murray].

16 MP/14/3/83. H. H. Gibbs to J. A. H. Murray, 14 March 1883.

17 Murray (1884), 509–10.

18 Sutcliffe (1978), 61.

19 See further p. 26.

20 MP/17/1/84. Copy of a letter from J. A. H. Murray to B. Price, 17 January 1884.

21 See S. Landau, *Dictionaries. The Art and Craft of Lexicography*, 2nd edn (Cambridge: Cambridge University Press, 2001), 43.

22 Murray (1880), 128.

23 See further p. 31. It is important to realize that this ranking was accepted – and indeed endorsed – by Bradley from the beginning. As he had written to Gell on taking up his own editorship of the dictionary, 'The way in which I wish the matter to go before the public is that Dr Murray is still chief editor of the dictionary, but that it has been found necessary to depute certain portions of the editing to me'. See MP/30/11/87. P. L. Gell to J. A. H. Murray, 30 November 1887.

24 MP/17/1/84. Copy of a letter from J. A. H. Murray to B. Price, 17 January 1884.

25 MP/6/6/87. P. L. Gell to J. A. H. Murray, 6 June 1887.

26 In theory Murray ceased to work on Bradley's proof sheets after volume F of the dictionary, as an (undated) *Report* on the dictionary produced by the Press avers (*Rough Report as to Work done for Mr. Bradley at the Scriptorium, or by Dr. Murray personally, in Connexion with the N. E. D.*; uncatalogued document in OED Archives at OUP).

27 OED/MISC/13/6. J. A. H. Murray to F. Hall, 26 June 1894.

28 OED/MISC/13/36. J. A. H. Murray to R. Hall, 18 April 1901.

29 OED/MISC/13/6. J. A. H. Murray to F. Hall, 26 June 1894.

30 OED/MISC/58/8/29. Anonymous review of *Leisureness–Lief*.

31 See the entry in *OED*: 1591 Shakespeare. *1 Hen. VI*, i. iii. 53 *Winch*. 'Gloster, thou wilt answere this before the Pope'. *Glost*. 'Winchester Goose, I cry, a Rope, a Rope'.

32 Bradley here retained the transcriptions as originally given in the proofs, explicitly discounting the validity of Gibbs's evidence on coexisting variants (and incidentally revealing certain cracks within the descriptive adequacy of the dictionary). Bradley's own agendas of correctness would, as we will see, at times impede the impartiality which was formally professed. See further Chapter 5.

33 MP/30/7/82. H. H. Gibbs to J. A. H. Murray, 30 July 1882.

34 Bradley discounted Gibbs's annotations, providing /geɪlə/ as the only pronunciation in the dictionary entry as finally published and thereby excluding all information on the nineteenth-century variations which underpin the modern form.

35 Bradley's solution was instead to omit 'used': 'Now only in pa. pple. *laden*, loaded, fraught, heavily charged', as the published entry states, neatly obviating the prescriptive nicety detected by Skeat.

36 See further Chapter 5 on the role of prescriptive sensibilities in the making of the dictionary.

37 Murray (1884), 9.

38 W. W. Skeat, 'Report upon "Ghost-words", or Words Which Have No Real Existence', *Transactions of the Philological Society* (1886), ii, 350–1.

39 Ibid., 352.

40 See Murray's informative article on 'Abacot: The Story of a Spurious Word' in *The Athenaeum*, 4 February 1882, 157.

41 Ibid.

42 MP/Cuttings/37. 'Dr. Murray on Dictionaries', *The Standard*, 23 May 1903.

43 'One in whose hands money belonging to a debtor or defendant is attached at the suit of the creditor or plaintiff'.

44 MP/J. A. H. Murray, lecture on 'Dictionaries', delivered at the Royal Institution on Friday, 22 May 1903.

45 MP/24/8/83. J. A. H. Murray to B. Jowett, 24 August 1883.

46 'I should be obliged to say publicly that I myself considered the treatment inadequate. Indeed I do not feel that I could allow it to pass without an appeal to the Delegates, and a judgement on their part that they think it sufficient. I would infinitely rather not have to do this; and it might all be avoided by your wording the definition thus . . .'. OED/EP/MURRA/27. J. A. H. Murray to W. A. Craigie, 9 March 1909.

47 *Railway porter* provided another occasion for dispute, Murray going so far as to bring the offending entry to the attention of the Secretary of the Delegates, as well as to refuse to sanction the printing of the sheet. Both actions, he assured Craigie, were again motivated by 'the most friendly feeling' and a real sense of pain in thus having to interfere. OED/MISC/12/ 24/ ii/iii. J. A. H. Murray to W. A. Craigie, 3 December 1902.

48 'Please look at the enclosed . . . but don't send it to the Scriptorium' thus stands at the head of one sheet, written in Craigie's distinctive hand. Craigie and Murray continued to work in different locations throughout the history of the dictionary, Murray at this point being based on Banbury Road in Oxford, and Craigie in the Old Ashmolean, in the same city but – perhaps fortunately in this context – separated by a distance of almost a mile. See also *CWW*, 288.

49 See further pp. 138–40.

50 MP/19/4/98. J. A. H. Murray to Dr P. Fairbairn, 19 April 1898.

51 OED/BL/322/32. H. H. Gibbs to J. A. H. Murray, 16 October 1888.

52 OED/MISC/13/17. J. A. H. Murray to F. Hall, 6 April 1897.

53 See further p. 162.

54 L. D. Benson (ed.), *King Arthur's Death: The Middle English Stanzaic Morte Arthur and Alliterative Morte Arthur* (Exeter: Exeter University Press, 1988), comments on the 'hastily written and uncorrected copy' which constitutes the manuscript of the *Alliterative Morte Arthur*, adding that 'it contains many words and lines that make little or no sense'. It is presumably for this reason that Benson emends the relevant line, thereby eliminating all reference to *landon* in the poem.

55 MP/29/3/82. J. A. H. Murray to H. Sweet, 29 March 1882.

56 See, for example, the statement he made to Gell in June 1897: 'The real work is the Sematology, the power of seeing the sense of quotations, of formulating the scheme of the senses of words, of writing good definitions' (MP/15/6/97. Draft of a letter from J. A. H. Murray to P. L. Gell).

57 MP/18/4/83. *The New English Dictionary. Suggestions for Guidance in Preparing Copy for the Press.*

58 MP/24/4/96. *New English Dictionary. Correspondence and Minutes Printed by Order of the Board.* P. L. Gell to J. A. H. Murray and H. Bradley, 2 April 1896.

59 MP/17/1/84. Copy of a letter from J. A. H. Murray to B. Price, 17 January 1884.

60 MP/29/12/89. H. H. Gibbs to J. A. H. Murray, 29 December 1889.

61 See p. 231 n.37.

62 MP/29/10/83. B. Dawson to J. A. H. Murray, 29 October 1883.

63 OED/MISC/58/8/3. *The Scotsman*, 5 October [n.d]. Review of *A New English Dictionary on Historical Principles* ed. J. A. H. Murray. Vol. VI, *Lock–Lynn* by Henry Bradley.

64 MP/26/6/94. C. E. Doble to J. A. H. Murray, 26 June 1894.

65 OED/MISC/13/17. J. A. H. Murray to F. Hall, 6 April 1897.

66 1526 Tindale Mark iii. 20: 'They had nott leesar so moche as to eate breed'; 1553 T. Wilson *Rhet*. Ep. A ij: 'I traveyled so muche as my leasure myghte serve therunto'; 1599 Shakes. *Much Ado*, iii. ii. 84: 'If your leisure seru'd, I would speake with you'.

67 OED/MISC/12/21. J. A. H. Murray to W. A. Craigie, 19 July 190[1].

68 'I would have willingly believed the grossest figment the swaggering ass could have invented' from *The Fair Maid of Perth* (1828) was originally cited for *Gross*; 'His Lordship himself being the greatest grimalkin to whom they are to be given over to be devoured' (*Woodstock, or the Cavalier*, 1826) appeared under *grimalkin*. 'One loop of this substance is drawn under each foot', the entry for *loop* originally stated, again citing *The Fair Maid of Perth*. These represent merely a few of the instances which can be adduced in this context.

69 OUP/ Delegates' Orders. Report of the Dictionary Committee, 4 February 1893.

70 M. Laski, 'Revising OED', *Times Literary Supplement*, 13 October 1972, 1226.
71 MP/4/11/83. H. H. Gibbs to J. A. H. Murray, 4 November 1883.

Chapter 3: Lost Words

1 As Johnson explained to Thomas Tyer, 'I might have quoted *Hobbes* as an authority in language, as well as many others of his time: but I scorned, sir, to quote him at all; because I did not like his principles'. See A. Reddick, *The Making of Johnson's Dictionary 1746–1773*. rev. edn (Cambridge: Cambridge University Press, 1996), 34 ff.
2 W. A. Craigie and C. T. Onions, 'Historical Introduction', in *A New English Dictionary on Historical Principles*. Introduction, Supplement, and Bibliography. Vol. 1. A–B (Oxford: Clarendon Press, 1933), vii.
3 On Johnson's policies of selection in this respect, see further L. C. Mugglestone, 'Departures and Returns. Writing the English Dictionary in the Eighteenth and Nineteenth Centuries'. In F. O'Gorman and K. Turner (eds), *The Victorians and the Eighteenth Century* (London: Ashgate Press, 2004), pp. 144–62.
4 R. W. Burchfield, 'The Genealogy of Dictionaries'. In R. W. Burchfield, *Unlocking the English Language* (London: Faber & Faber, 1989), 149.
5 Trench (1860), 64, 69.
6 MP/[1883a]. Proof of first draft of 'Preface' to *A New English Dictionary on Historical Principles*. Part I. A–APO, 3.
7 MP/[1883b]. Proof of *Preface to Part I* for *A New English Dictionary on a Historical Basis*. Part 1. A–APO, 3 [Annotations by F. J. Furnivall].
8 MP/[1883c]. Proof of *Preface to Part I* for *A New English Dictionary on a Historical Basis*. Part 1. A–APO [Annotations by A. J. Ellis].
9 MP/17/9/83a. Proof 'for revise' of *Preface to Part I* for *A New English Dictionary on a Historical Basis*. Part 1. A–ANT [Annotations by J. A. H. Murray].
10 Trench (1860), 57. See further Chapter 5.
11 This did not, however, include a commitment to record every scientific coinage in existence. As a spirited debate with William Sykes carried out in the pages of *Notes and Queries* in the 1880s confirms, while Murray sought to include the discourse of science as part of the proper territory of the dictionary, this did not mean that an exhaustive documentation could be given. See e.g. W. Sykes, 'New English Dictionary', *Notes and Queries* 2, ser. 7 (1886a), 53; W. Sykes, 'Additions and Emendations to "New English Dictionary"', *Notes and Queries* 2, ser. 7 (1886b), 238, 282–3; J. A. H. Murray, 'The New English Dictionary', *Notes and Queries* 1, ser. 7 (1886), 370–1, 471.
12 Though even here there are problems, as Murray admits: 'to every man the domain of "common words" widens out in the direction of his own reading, research, business, provincial or foreign residence, and contracts in the direction with which he has no practical connexion: no one man's English is *all* English.' Murray (1888), xvii.
13 MP/[n.d.]/9/83a. First proof of 'General Explanations', September 1883.
14 MP/[n.d.]/9/83b. J. A. H. Murray's corrected and annotated copy of the first proof of the 'General Explanations'. The metaphor of the astronomer was added at this stage of the text, handwritten on a separate slip of paper and pasted to the side of the printed sheet.
15 *Anglicity*: 'English quality, as of speech or style; English idiom'.
16 Murray (1880), 131.

17 Murray (1888), xxviii.

18 A. F. Chamberlain in *Encyclopaedia Britannica*, Vol. XIV, 470/1 (1910): 'The wood art of the Indians of the North Pacific coast (masks, utensils, houses, totem-poles, furniture, &c.)'.

19 Murray (1884), 517.

20 R. Harris, 'The History Men', *Times Literary Supplement*, 3 September 1982, 935. See further p. 101.

21 Oral evidence is occasionally used, as in the entry for *cat* signifying 'a vessel formerly used in the coal and timber trade on the north-east coast of England'. Here Murray's research – and the information he chose to include – moves beyond the limitations of printed books. As the dictionary states: 'the name is unknown to the oldest of the Elder Brethren of Trinity House, Newcastle (aged 82), and to the oldest North Sea pilots there. One of the latter, however, remembers to have heard as a boy the joke "Do you know when the mouse caught the cat?" (the *Mouse* being a sand-bank in the Thames); and several remember the expression *cat-built* in the early part of the century.'

22 Review of *A New English Dictionary on Historical Principles*. Edited by James A. H. Murray. Part I. *A–Ant*, *The Athenaeum*, 9 February 1884, 177.

23 MP/14/7/82. H. H. Gibbs to J. A. H. Murray, 14 July 1882. Murray included the word, recording it with admirable neutrality in spite of Gibbs's protestations. *Absinthiate* met a markedly negative response from one reader, as Edith Thompson informed Murray: 'I confess I *did* show this [proof] sheet to [the historian] Mr. Freeman, and, as you foresaw, he objected that some of the words – particularly *Absinthiate* – were in his opinion not English at all, & should not be put into an English Dictionary' (MP/25/6/82. E. P. Thompson to J. A. H. Murray, 25 June 1882). Mr Freeman may, however, have had a point since *absinthiate* is provided with no accompanying citations or any other evidence of usage. Liberalities of this kind tended to disappear in the later fascicles as 'doubtful words' were subjected to ever more stringent review.

24 MP/22/2/84. J. A. H. Murray to unnamed correspondent, 22 February 1884.

25 MP/30/7/82. H. H. Gibbs to J. A. H. Murray, 30 July 1882.

26 Coined respectively by William Thackeray, Robert Browning, John Ruskin, and Charles Dickens. All are included in the *OED*. See further pp. 98–102 on the theory and practice of nonce-words in the *OED*.

27 *Landlord* (v. intr.) 'To play the landlord'. 1844. W. H. Maxwell, *Sports & Adv. Scotl.*, viii. (1855), 84: 'Landlording it over "the Admiral Benbow"'.

28 See pp. 152–4.

29 Murray (1888), xxxii.

30 MP/ Cuttings/ 82. 'How to Compile a Great Dictionary. A Chat with Dr. Murray in his Scriptorium at Oxford', *Westminster Gazette*, 23 June 1893.

31 MP/6/5/97. J. A. H. Murray to P. L. Gell, 6 May 1897.

32 MP/21/10/83. H. H. Gibbs to J. A. H. Murray, 21 October 1883.

33 MP/11/11/83a. B. Jowett to H. H. Gibbs, 11 November 1883.

34 See p. 20.

35 MP/18/10/83. J. A. H. Murray to B. Price, 18 October 1883.

36 MP/17/1/84. Copy of a letter from J. A. H. Murray to B. Price, 17 January 1884.

37 MP/13/8/01. J. A. H. Murray to unnamed correspondent, 13 August 1901.

38 MP/[22]/11/01. J. A. H. Murray to H. Bradley, [22] November 1901.

39 MP/24/1/02. Sir W. H. Preece to J. A. H. Murray, 24 January 1902.

40 Proprietary terms were usually regarded as not part of the proper territory of the dictionary though certain words – such as *nylon* and *Hoover* – clearly merited their inclusion in the later *Supplements*. See further pp. 82–3.

41 MP/11/2/14. J. A. H. Murray to unnamed correspondent, 11 February 1914. Murray concluded by promising to file the information among that already being generated for a future supplement to the dictionary 'so that the 2½ lines may be amended or cut out, in the next edition'. In *OED2*, however, the entry remains precisely identical in form to that in which it first appeared.

42 Dixon was a regular contributor to the *OED*, especially for medical terminology. See further pp. 84–5 and also P. Gilliver, 'OED Personalia'. In Mugglestone (2002a), 236.

43 MP/6/12/88. J. Dixon to J. A. H. Murray, 6 December 1888.

44 Even Dixon's evidence was, however, limited. 'I never saw it in print, so I spell the word phonetically', he noted. Dixon's reading evidently did not extend to *My Secret Life* (1888–94), from which Burchfield extracted one illustrative and explicit citation for *OEDS*. Burchfield was to trace usage back to 1706.

45 See p. 71.

46 MP/17/2/91. J. Dixon to J. A. H. Murray, 17 February 1891.

47 MP/[n.d]/3/90. R. Ellis to J. A. H. Murray, March 1890.

48 MP/4/9/99. J. A. H. Murray to J. Hamilton, 4 September 1899. See further L. C. Mugglestone, 'Pioneers in the Untrodden Forest – The *New* English Dictionary'. In Mugglestone (2002a), 11.

49 MP/1/9/99. J. Hamilton to J. A. H. Murray, 1 September 1899.

50 In spite of the opacity of the definition Murray provides, this was a word on which he had been forced to spend a considerable amount of energy – not least in resolving the problems associated with Robert Browning's use of the word in 1848 in his poem 'Pippa Passes'. 'Then owls and bats/Cowls and twats/Monks and nuns, in cloister's moods/Adjourn to the oak-stump pantry' (IV. ii. 96), Browning had written, under the evident apprehension that the word signified some part of a nun's attire. 'Browning constantly uses words without regard to their proper meaning. He has added greatly to the difficulties of the Dictionary', as Murray expostulated to his son Oswyn. See *CWW*, 235.

51 See G. L. Brook, *The Language of Dickens* (London: André Deutsch, 1970), 189 ff.

52 See e.g. M. Mason, *The Making of Victorian Sexuality* (Oxford: Oxford University Press, 1994).

53 See further pp. 162–8. L. C. Mugglestone, 'Balance and Bias: Cracking the Impartial Face of Dictionaries', *The English Review*, 9 (1999), 13–15 discusses other similar problems.

54 MP/27/3/05. J. A. H. Murray to E. Arber, 27 March 1905.

55 That editorial sensitivities were in existence with regard to the latter is evidenced by the careful rephrasing in proof of a number of entries referring to the condition of (il)legitimacy in which the word 'bastard' had originally appeared. *Legitimation*, for example, appeared in the published fascicle (and still in *OED2*) with the definition 'The action or process of rendering or authoritatively declaring (a person) legitimate'. 'A bastard or one whose birth is questionable' had, however, appeared in earlier versions, the change being made in the second revise of the appropriate sheet. While *bastard* here was clearly being used in its legal sense, the negative connotations of those other uses later to be tracked down by Burchfield for the nineteenth and twentieth centuries evidently made rephrasing desirable.

56 That such cultural sensitivities are not entirely a feature of the past is amply illustrated by Elisabeth Murray who, discussing her grandfather's decision to suppress *cunt* in the *OED* (*CWW*, 195), refers throughout to *pudendum* – another word entirely and one which Murray did in fact include. See further Mugglestone (2002a), 11.

57 See further p. 162.

58 Onions nevertheless decided to include *windfucker* ('*fig.* as a term of opprobrium') in 1923, basing his entry on a set of eminently literary citations from writers such as Ben Jonson, the dramatists Beaumont and Fletcher, and George Chapman's seventeenth-century translation of Homer (*Iliad*, Pref. A 4: 'There is a certaine enuious Windfucker, that houers vp and downe, laboriously ingrossing al the air with his luxurious ambition').

59 See further J. Butt and K. Tillotson, *Dickens at Work* (London: Methuen, 1957), 22 ff. R. L. Patten, *Charles Dickens and his Publishers* (Oxford: Clarendon Press, 1978), offers a similarly detailed analysis of the publishing process as it affected the writing of individual novels.

60 OED/EP/ALD/1/2.i. J. A. H. Murray to H. H. Gibbs, 7 December 1900.

61 See further pp. 64–9.

62 MP/15/11/76. W. W. Skeat to J. A. H. Murray, 15 November 1876.

63 See p. xv.

64 R. C. Trench, *On the Study of Words* (London: John W. Parker & Sons, 1851), 126.

65 Uncatalogued draft of a letter in OED Archives at OUP from P. L. Gell to Murray and Bradley [April 1896].

66 See *OED prune*, v.², 3. *fig.* a.

67 It is a consideration which is, however, always open to reassessment. *Frib*, for example, presented problems of precisely this kind, Bradley and his assistants having failed to find a satisfactory definition by the first revise of the relevant fascicle. At this point the entry (and its accompanying citation from the *Journal of Rural Agriculture* of 1893) was deleted. Some eighty years later, the word was reinserted in *OEDS* by Burchfield, who provided a full definition ('short wool pieces and second cuts'). Not having the benefit of the proof sheets of *OED1* he was, however, unable to provide a nineteenth-century example of its use. The word's origin is hence erroneously located in the twentieth century.

68 MP/14/6/82. H. H. Gibbs to J. A. H. Murray, 14 June 1882.

69 See p. 22.

70 See p. 68.

71 See e.g. the account given by Murray's youngest son of sorting slips for the dictionary in the 1890s: 'We enlivened the task by reading out tit-bits from Dr Furnivall's newspaper cuttings, & bundles of slips from Dr Furnivall were in demand in spite of bad handwriting' (cited in *CWW*, 180).

72 See pp. 131–3.

73 J. Simpson, 'The New Vocabulary of English'. In E. G. Stanley and T. F. Hoad (eds), *Words: For Robert Burchfield's Sixty-Fifth Birthday* (Cambridge: D. S. Brewer, 1988), 144.

74 Uncatalogued letter in OED Archives at OUP from J. A. H. Murray to F. J. Furnivall. Enclosure. 11 December 1892.

75 MP/14/7/82. H. H. Gibbs to J. A. H. Murray, 14 July 1882. On prescriptive considerations and the dictionary, see further Chapter 5.

76 Harris (1982), 936.

77 Defined as 'light, cheerful', and identified as *rare*, this use of *lightful* had originally

been granted a separate entry in the *OED*, distinct from *lightful* in the sense of 'bright'. Only the latter now remains.

78 J. A. H. Murray to F. J. Furnivall, 11 December 1892. Uncatalogued letter in OED Archives at OUP.

79 MP/24/4/96. *New English Dictionary. Correspondence and Minutes Printed by Order of the Board.* P. L. Gell to J. A. H. Murray and H. Bradley, 2 April 1896. See further Chapter 1.

80 Uncatalogued letter in OED Archives at OUP from J. A. H. Murray to F. J. Furnivall. Enclosure. 11 December 1892.

81 R. W. Burchfield, 'The Treatment of Controversial Vocabulary in the *Oxford English Dictionary*'. In Burchfield (1989), 89.

82 Schäfer (1980), 15.

83 As *DNB* records, Ward was of 'low extraction' and with little education.

84 Laski (1972), 1226.

85 As Kenneth Budd has noted, however, even this level of revision could leave something to be desired. As he affirms, 'A modern reader who persevered through even a quarter of the revised novel's sixty four chapters might wonder what the original version could have been like, if this was less prolix and Blackmore here less guilty of "involution of diction".' See K. Budd, *The Last Victorian. R. D. Blackmore and his Novels* (London: Centaur Press, 1960), 43.

86 Harris (1982), 935.

87 Trench (1860), 29: 'if their author and proposer was anything better than one of that rabble of scribblers who hang on the skirts of literature, doing their worst to profane and degrade it and language which is its vehicle, those words should not on this account the less find place among those archives of a language which it is the business of a Dictionary to preserve'.

88 Murray's criticisms prompted Bradley to edit the quotation (from the *Athenaeum*) so that whereas the entry now reads 'A mother-in-law so Gorgonesque even as the ex-*coryphée*', this was originally preceded by the words 'We are less ready to believe in his quailing before [a mother-in-law . . .].'

89 H. Bradley to P. L. Gell, 11 April 1896. Uncatalogued letter in *OED* Archives at OUP.

90 MP/2/12/92. H. H. Gibbs to J. A. H. Murray, 2 December 1892.

91 MP/8/11/87. H. H. Gibbs to J. A. H. Murray, 8 November 1887: 'I would unhesitatingly reject Ça . . . even if used by the very best authority . . . Take courage and slay all such vermin without mercy.'

92 That Murray's instincts were right in this particular case is of course amply confirmed by the revised entry of *OED2* in which four additional citations attest the established use of *garçon* in English.

93 *Lagniappe*, like a number of other words discussed in the course of this chapter, was later to receive citizenship once more via the 1933 *Supplement*. It is, however, conspicuously labelled *U.S.*

94 R. Morgan, *Cancelled Words. Rediscovering Thomas Hardy* (London: Routledge, 1994), 2.

95 MP/10/5/01. J. A. H. Murray to W. A. Craigie, 10 May 1901.

96 OED/MISC/13/15. J. A. H. Murray to F. Hall, 21 September 1896.

97 MP/10/11/78. J. A. H. Murray to B. Price, 10 November 1878.

98 As the *Canones* of 1860 had stated, separating regional from non-regional usages in the dictionary 'would deprive them of half their value for philological purposes; and as the claims of Philology, in such a work as this, must be looked upon as paramount

to all others, we have resolved to give them a place in the pages of the Main Dictionary'. [Trench *et al.*], *Canones Lexicographici; or, Rules to be Observed in Editing the New English Dictionary of the Philological Society* (London: The Philological Society, 1860), 11.

99 MP/10/5/01. J. A. H. Murray to W. A. Craigie, 10 May 1901. The excision of *fuffit* ('A local (East Lothian) name for the long tailed titmouse, *Acredula rosea*') in the first revise of *Frank-law–Glass-coach* can be seen as an earlier example of this process.

100 MP/Cuttings/23–4. 'The Historical English Dictionary', *Manchester Guardian*, 13 October 1897.

101 D. Berg, *A User's Guide to the Oxford English Dictionary* (Oxford: Oxford University Press, 1991), 4.

102 R. W. Burchfield, 'The *Oxford English Dictionary* and its Historical Principles'. In Burchfield (1989), 172.

Chapter 4: Science and the Principles of Selection

1 Murray (1900), 51.

2 Johnson (1755), *Preface*, C1^{v}.

3 MP/30/10/89. J. A. H. Murray to P. L. Gell, 30 October 1889.

4 MP/17/9/83b. Proof of *Preface to Part I* for *A New English Dictionary on a Historical Basis*. Part 1. A–ANT [Annotations by J. A. H. Murray]. This section was later omitted.

5 MP/20/12/06. J. A. H. Murray to Mr Jenkinson, 20 December 1906.

6 C. Dickens, *Hard Times, for these Times* (London: Bradbury & Evans, 1854), 236.

7 T. H. Huxley to C. Lyell, 27 November 1865. In L. Huxley (ed.), *Life and Letters of Thomas Henry Huxley* (London: Macmillan, 1900), i, 263.

8 G. Beer, *Darwin's Plots. Evolutionary Narrative in Darwin, George Eliot, and Nineteenth-Century Fiction* (London: Routledge & Kegan Paul, 1983), 5.

9 As Peter Gilliver has noted on such judgements of ephemerality, they are 'notoriously liable to be proved wrong in the course of time'. See P. Gilliver, 'Specialized Lexis in the *Oxford English Dictionary*', in L. Hoffman, H. Kälverkamper, and H. E. Wiegand (eds), *Fachsprachen/Languages for Special Purposes. Ein internationales Handbuch zur Fachsprachen-forschung und Terminologiewissenschaft*, ii (Berlin, 1999), 1681.

10 The term is dated to 1876 in the *OED*, its first citation deriving from Darwin's *The Effects of Cross and Self-Fertilization in the Vegetable Kingdom* ('Cross-fertilization is sometimes ensured by the sexes being separated').

11 G. Eliot, *Middlemarch, A Study of Provincial Life* (Edinburgh and London: William Blackwood & Sons, 1871–72), iii, 32.

12 E. C. Gaskell, *Wives and Daughters. An Every-Day Story* (London: Smith, Elder, 1866), ii, 285, 35.

13 C. Kingsley, *The Water-Babies: A Fairy-Tale for a Land-Baby* (London and Cambridge: Macmillan, 1863), 283.

14 T. Hardy, *A Pair of Blue Eyes* (London: Tinsley Brothers, 1873), ii, 183, 173.

15 G. Gissing, *Born in Exile* (London and Edinburgh: A. & C. Black, 1892), 269.

16 Ussher (1581–1656) was an Anglo-Irish prelate now remembered principally for his research on the chronology of the Old Testament and, in particular, for his dating of the creation to 4004 BC.

[17] R. W. Emerson, *Essays. Second Series*. Essay 1: 'The Poet' (London: Geoffrey Chapman, 1844), 14.

[18] 'As much mud in the streets, as if the waters had but lately retired from the face of the earth, and it would not be wonderful to meet a Megalosaurus, forty feet long or so, waddling like an elephantine lizard up Holborn Hill'. C. Dickens, *Bleak House* (London: Bradbury & Evans, 1853), 1.

[19] Cited in S. G. Alter, *Darwinism and the Linguistic Image. Language, Race, and Natural Theology in the Nineteenth Century* (Baltimore and London: Johns Hopkins University Press, 1999), 16–17.

[20] Hensleigh Wedgwood was appointed to the Etymological Committee for the proposed dictionary in 1860. His dictionary on the origins of word meaning – *A Dictionary of English Etymology* – appeared between 1855 and 1865. He published *On the Origin of Language* one year later, in 1866.

[21] C. Darwin, *Notebooks*. Cited in A. Desmond and J. Moore, *Darwin* (London: Michael Joseph, 1991), 216. Darwin here conspicuously echoes the astronomer John Herschel's famous letter to the geologist, John Lyell, in 1836: 'Words are to the anthropologist what rolled pebbles are to the geologist – battered relics of past ages often containing within them indelible records capable of intelligent interpretation'. See further Alter (1999), 12 ff.

[22] Review of 'On the Connexion of the Physical Sciences' by Mrs Somerville. *Quarterly Review*, 51 (1834), 59.

[23] MP/15/12/03. J. A. H. Murray to Dr Bryce, 15 December 1903.

[24] MP/Ms of Lecture to the Ashmolean Natural History Society [n.d.].

[25] T. H. Huxley to [?] Dyster 27 February 1855. In Huxley (1900), i, 138.

[26] Trench (1860), 57, 58.

[27] Ibid., 58.

[28] [Trench *et al.*] (1860), 3.

[29] Ibid., 8.

[30] [Philological Society] (1859), 3.

[31] W. Whewell, *History of the Inductive Sciences* (London: J. W. Parker, 1837), iii, 307.

[32] T. H. Huxley, *The Crayfish. An Introduction to the Study of Zoology* (London: C. Kegan Paul, 1880), 14.

[33] Cited in W. Irvine, *Apes, Angels & Victorians. A Joint Biography of Darwin & Huxley* (London: Weidenfeld & Nicolson, 1956), 13.

[34] Respectively 'Concave on both sides, double concave. Applied to vertebræ, as in the backbone of a fish' (coined by Huxley in the *Journal of Geology* in 1869); 'Of or pertaining to the *Amphipoda*' (coined in his *Manual of the Anatomy of Invertebrate Animals* of 1877); 'Having pillars or piers on both sides: applied to the skulls of certain sharks, having piers supporting both upper and lower mandibular arches', a neologism deployed in the *Proceedings of the Zoological Society* in 1876. *Pholidogaster* is unrecorded in the *OED* but is presumably a designation linked to the scales of a reptile.

[35] T. H. Huxley to J. Hooker, 5 September 1858. In Huxley (1900), i, 160.

[36] *Ceratodus*: 'A popular name for the Australian lungfish, *Neoceratodus forsteri*, belonging to the order Dipteriformes; also, a genus of fossil fish related to this lungfish'.

[37] Gissing (1892), i, 57.

[38] Trench (1851), 2.

[39] Ibid., 9.

40 The language of doctrine came readily to Darwin in this context: 'my species doctrine', he wrote, for instance, to W. D. Fox in October 1856; 'I cannot too strongly express my conviction of the truth of my doctrines', he assured Charles Lyell in September 1859, two months before the *Origin of Species* made its public appearance. That doctrines required converts was equally explicit in his letters: 'Further reflection and new facts have made [Joseph] Hooker a convert', he informed the American botanist Gray in August 1858. In F. Darwin (ed.), *The Life and Letters of Charles Darwin* rev. edn (London: John Murray, 1888), ii, 84, 167, 135.

41 T. H. Huxley to Henrietta Huxley, 22 March 1861. In Huxley (1900), i, 190.

42 See p. xviii.

43 See *CWW*, 33.

44 This accompanied the third edition of the *Appeal*.

45 OED/MISC/90/8. 'The Philological Society's New Dictionary', *The Journal of the Linnean Society*, 17 (1880).

46 Though see also p. 122 on the limits which influenced such inclusion.

47 MP/11/11/83b. Proof of 'The English Dictionary of the Philological Society'. 'Explanations'.

48 Murray (1888), xxviii.

49 Respectively, 'Not connected with germination', 'Pertaining to the study of the nature and functions of spines', and 'That which rubs or wears down a surface'.

50 See further McConchie (1997), 201: 'What is less clear to the student of the completed *OED* is that hard-and-fast rules governing the treatment of such words were ever devised or put into effect. Not that final consistency would ever have been more than a pipe-dream; but the practice, as it is now enshrined in the pages of the dictionary, is a cacophony of indecision.'

51 MP/23/8/83. H. Liddell to H. H. Gibbs, 23 August 1883.

52 See p. 20.

53 MP/18/4/83. *The New English Dictionary. Suggestions for Guidance in Preparing Copy for the Press* [Annotations by J. A. H. Murray].

54 Ibid.

55 MP/8/11/83. A. J. Ellis to J. A. H. Murray, 8 November 1883.

56 MP/29/10/83. B. Dawson to J. A. H. Murray, 29 October 1883.

57 MP/28/10/83. E. Brandreth to J. A. H. Murray, 28 October 1883.

58 See Preface.

59 Johnson (1755), B2[v].

60 After-dinner speech given by T. H. Huxley at an 1860 meeting in aid of the Literary Fund. Cited in Huxley (1900), i, 215.

61 S. Oliver, *A General Critical Grammar of the Inglish Language on a System Novel and Extensive* (London: Baldwin, Cradock & Joy, 1825), 227.

62 W. Nash, *Jargon. Its Uses and Abuses* (London: Blackwell, 1993), 3.

63 MP/8/12/91. J. Dixon to J. A. H. Murray, 8 December 1891.

64 MP/29/12/91. J. Dixon to J. A. H. Murray, 29 December 1891.

65 C. Darwin, *On the Origin of Species by Means of Natural Selection, or the Preservation of Favoured Races in the Struggle for Life* (London, 1859), ed. J. W. Burrow (London: John Murray, 1982), 116.

66 C. Darwin to A. Gray, 5 September 1857. In Darwin (1888), ii, 122.

67 In Huxley (1900), ii, 303.

68 See p. 71.

[69] Cited in H. M. Vernon and K. D. Vernon, *A History of the Oxford Museum* (Oxford: Clarendon Press, 1909), 51.

[70] See e.g. his *Lectures on the Science of Language* (Oxford: Clarendon Press, 1864), 309–10: 'It was the idea of *natural Selection* that was wanted, and being wanted it was found . . . if naturalists are proud to affix their names to a new species which they discover, Mr. Darwin may be prouder, for his name will remain affixed to a new idea, a new genus of thought'. On the other hand, Max Müller continued to resist the theory of transmutationism, affirming instead his belief in the static – and ordained – shape of organic forms. See further Alter (1999), 80 ff.

[71] MP/18/10/83. J. A. H. Murray to B. Price, 18 October 1883.

[72] E. Weiner, 'The Federation of English'. In *The State of the Language* ed. C. Ricks and L. Michaels (London: Faber & Faber, 1990), 494.

[73] OED/MISC/59/1/11. Review of *A New English Dictionary on Historical Principles*, Vol. III, Part I, *E–Every*, *The Manchester Guardian*, 14 July 1891.

[74] OED/MISC/59/1/13. Review of *A New English Dictionary on Historical Principles*, Vol. III, Part I, *E–Every*, *The Athenaeum* (1891).

[75] MP/1/1/99. Letter from unknown correspondent to J. A. H. Murray, 1 January 1899.

[76] Respectively '*Mod*. Its structure shows an approach to the Acephelan type' and '*Mod. Bot*. The alation of the stem is more conspicuous in other species of the pea'. The entries once more prove Murray in his role of polymath, able to provide appropriate usages for zoological discussion of jellyfish (*acephela*) or for winged structures (*alation*) in botanical classification.

[77] MP/15/6/86. H. Bradley to J. A. H. Murray, 15 June 1886.

[78] See Sutcliffe (1978), 85 ff.

[79] OUP/Delegates' Orders. Report of the Dictionary Subcommittee, 4 February 1893.

[80] See further p. 31.

[81] OUP/ Delegates' Orders. Minutes of a Meeting of the Delegates of Oxford University Press, 17 May 1895.

[82] The loss of *fragilis* was, however, to be permanent. See further p. 135.

[83] MP/26/6/94. C. E. Doble to J. A. H. Murray, 26 June 1894.

[84] MP/24/4/96. *New English Dictionary. Correspondence and Minutes Printed by Order of the Board*. P. L. Gell to J. A. H. Murray and H. Bradley, 2 April 1896.

[85] Darwin (1982), 117.

[86] This is not of course to suggest that Darwin was not used extensively within the *OED* but more to illustrate the principles of selection in action, and their necessary arbitrariness.

[87] Gilliver (1999), 1681.

[88] See further pp. 103–7. This designation within the first edition of the dictionary would of course have rendered the term additionally susceptible to excision.

[89] See p. 27.

[90] Trench had stressed that a dictionary 'must everywhere know how to preserve the line firm and distinct between itself and an encyclopaedia'. This was echoed by Murray in the Preface which accompanied the first volume of the *OED*: 'it has to be borne in mind, that a Dictionary of the English Language is not a Cyclopaedia: the Cyclopaedia *describes things*; the Dictionary *explains words*, and deals with the description of things only so far as is necessary to fix the exact signification and uses of words'. Murray (1888), vi.

[91] Scanning the database of *OED2* gives a total of 4,955 results for entries relating to genus types.

92 R. W. Burchfield, 'The Treatment of Controversial Vocabulary in the *Oxford English Dictionary*'. In Burchfield (1989), 104.

93 *Glycollide*, *glycosine*, *glyoxylic*, and *glyoxylate* moreover are all based on precisely parallel evidence from Henry Watts's *Dictionary of Chemistry*, a popular source for words within this area of research.

94 *Glyoxylic* supplies another example of this ongoing process of revision; Burchfield declared it to be 'an important metabolic intermediate and occurs in animal and plant tissues and fluids, esp. in unripe fruit' and duly inserted it in *OEDS*. Bradley had earlier defined it as 'an acid occurring in the leaves and unripe fruits of many plants' and had excised it.

95 C. Darwin to W. D. Fox, July 1837. In Darwin (1888), i, 280.

96 MP/29/6/11. J. A. H. Murray to Mr Dodgson, 29 June 1911.

97 See p. 39.

98 OED/MISC/210/326/1. W. Sykes to H. Bradley, 5 February 1888.

99 OED/MISC/210/362/2. W. Sykes to H. Bradley, 10 March 1902.

100 *Lime-wash* had originally been defined as 'a coating for walls . . . of a solution of lime and water'. However, as Sykes pointed out in the adjacent margin while checking the proofs, in fact 'in lime-wash only a very little lime is dissolved. The main quantity is undissolved and in diffusion or suspension'. The definition was subsequently rewritten ('a mixture of lime and water, used for coating walls').

101 OED/AA/105. W. Sykes to J. A. H. Murray, 6 December 1901.

102 MP/26/1/96. W. Sykes to J. A. H. Murray, 26 January 1896.

103 See further p. 203.

104 MP/29/12/1891. J. Dixon to J. A. H. Murray, 29 December 1891.

105 That Max Müller was one of the Delegates whose preferences for the exclusion of the technical and scientific had, as we have seen, been prominent in the making of the *OED* was an irony which was presumably not lost on Murray.

106 OED/MISC/147/7A. W. Sykes to J. A. H. Murray, 22 September 1904.

107 Darwin (1982), 133.

108 Weiner (1990), 492.

109 Respectively '*Computing*. A token or packet of data that is passed between computers or programs to allow access or to activate certain features; (in recent use *spec.*) a packet of data sent by an Internet server to a browser, which is returned by the browser each time it subsequently accesses the same server, thereby identifying the user or monitoring his or her access to the server'; '*Computing*, million floating-point operations per second'.

110 See further Chapter 7.

Chapter 5: 'I am not the editor of the English language'

1 MP/11/4/78. Dr A. Ball to J. A. H. Murray, 11 April 1878.

2 MP/24/10/88. J. W. Davidson to J. A. H. Murray, 24 October 1888.

3 MP/24/5/82. J. Graham to J. A. H. Murray, 24 May 1882; MP/7/10/13. A. Church to J. A. H. Murray, 7 October 1913; MP/21/10/11. J. A. H. Murray to unnamed correspondent, 21 October 1911.

4 MP/3/6/13. W. A. Read to J. A. H. Murray, 3 June 1913. *Cheyne* had not been included in *Cast–Clivy*, published in 1899, on the grounds that it was a proper name

and as such should not be considered for inclusion as an entry-word. See further pp. 82–3.

5 MP/8/12/06. G. K. Harrison to J. A. H. Murray, 8 December 1906.

6 MP/10/12/06. J. A. H. Murray to G. K. Harrison, 10 December 1906. Both spellings were duly given in the fascicle *Wh–Wise* which Onions completed in May 1923 though, as he added, 'In modern trade usage, Scotch *whisky* and Irish *whiskey* are thus distinguished in spelling'. *OED2* was to add a further clarification of usage for the late twentieth century, noting that '*whisky* is the usual spelling in Britain and *whiskey* that in the U.S.'

7 MP/21/10/11. J. A. H. Murray to unnamed correspondent, 21 October 1911.

8 OED/EP/MURRA/3. J. A. H. Murray to unnamed correspondent, 5 January 1895.

9 Ibid. As Murray's letter here makes plain, there were limits to descriptive tolerance, and his comment that usage must be 'well-grounded' is an important one.

10 H. Alford, *A Plea for the Queen's English. Stray Notes on Speaking and Spelling* (London: W. Strahan, 1864), 193. The seventh edition, under the revised title *The Queen's English. A Manual of Idiom and Usage*, appeared in 1888.

11 [O. Bunce], *Don't: A Manual of Mistakes & Improprieties More or Less Prevalent in Conduct and Speech By Censor* (London: Griffith & Farran, 1884), 58, 56, 59. This was still being reprinted in the early twentieth century.

12 T. L. Kington-Oliphant, *The New English* (London: Macmillan, 1886), ii, 220.

13 Johnson (1755), C2^{r}.

14 [R. Heald], *The Queen's English (?) Up to Date. An Exposition of the Prevailing Grammatical Errors of the Day, with Numerous Examples. By 'Anglophil'* (London: The Literary Revision and Translation Office, 1892), 7–8.

15 Ibid., 150.

16 MP/1/1/99. Letter from an unknown correspondent to J. A. H. Murray, 1 January 1899.

17 OED/MISC/58/8/28. Anonymous review of *Leisureness–Lief.*

18 MP/9/1/07. E. Parry to J. A. H. Murray, 9 January 1907.

19 Trench (1860), 5.

20 MP/4/1/85. J. A. H. Murray to H. Warren, 4 January 1885.

21 True to his descriptive principles, Murray included both spellings, though *disyllable* is listed first.

22 D. Coleridge, 'Observations on the Plan of the Society's Proposed New English Dictionary', *Transactions of the Philological Society* (1860–61), 155, 157.

23 Ibid., 162, 158.

24 MP/7/3/80. E. B. Nicholson to J. A. H. Murray, 7 March 1880. For a discussion of Sheridan's ambitions in this respect, see further Mugglestone (2003), Chapter 1.

25 Beazeley was a regular reader for the dictionary, and supplied over 30,000 quotations. See further P. Gilliver, '*OED* Personalia'. In Mugglestone (2002a), 233.

26 OED/BL/300/29. A. Beazeley to J. A. H. Murray, 8 January 1884.

27 F. Hall, 'English Rational and Irrational', *Nineteenth Century*, 8 (1880), 424.

28 See e.g. [Heald] (1892), 150.

29 MP/12/10/83a. Proof of *A New English Dictionary on a Historical Basis.* 'General Explanations' [Annotations by F. Hall].

30 MP/12/10/83b. Proof of *A New English Dictionary on a Historical Basis.* 'General Explanations' [Annotations by W. W. Skeat].

31 MP/[1883d]. Proof of *Preface to Part I* for *A New English Dictionary on a Historical Basis* [Henry Hucks Gibbs's copy, with annotations].

[32] See e.g. R. W. Burchfield, *The New Fowler's Modern English Usage* (Oxford: Clarendon Press, 1996), 22: 'Certain adjectives are normally incapable of modification by adverbs like *largely*, *more*, *quite*, *too*, or *very*: e.g. *absolute*, *complete*, *equal*, *excellent*, *impossible* . . .'. As he also adds, however, 'English is not a language of unbreakable rules, and contextual needs often bring theoretically unconventional uses into being'.

[33] As *OED2* records, this construction was 'Described as "erroneous" by W. A. Craigie in the *Dict. of Amer. Eng.*, and said by H. W. Fowler in *Mod. Eng. Usage* (1926) to be "often used by the illiterate as though it had passed, like *owing to*, into a mere compound preposition".' As it adds, however, it is 'now widely current though still firmly rejected by many grammarians'.

[34] MP/[9]/83b. Proof of *A New English Dictionary on a Historical Basis*. *Preface to Part I*. 'General Explanations' [Annotations by B. Jowett].

[35] MP/12/10/83b. Proof of *A New English Dictionary on a Historical Basis*. 'General Explanations' [Annotations by W. W. Skeat].

[36] MP/[n.d]/9/83c. Proof of *Preface to Part I* [Annotations by F. Hall].

[37] F. Hall, *Modern English* (London and New York: Scribner, Armstrong, 1873), xi.

[38] MP/18/4/88. Proof of 'Preface. Vol. I' [Annotations by F. Hall]. Hall headed the sheet 'Excuse all impertinence, hypercriticism, and other offences'.

[39] MP/28/4/88. Proof of 'Preface. Vol. I' [Annotations by F. Hall].

[40] MP/28/3/84. J. A. H. Murray to unnamed correspondent, 28 March 1884.

[41] MP/1883/Proof of 'Part I. A–ANT'. Title page [Annotations by B. Jowett].

[42] MP/17/9/83c. Proof of *Preface to Part I* for *A New English Dictionary on a Historical Basis*. Part 1. A–ANT. [Annotations by W. W. Skeat].

[43] MP/8/10/83. Proof of *A New English Dictionary on a Historical Basis*. Title page and 'General Explanations' [Annotations by F. Hall].

[44] MP/19/11/83. J. A. H. Murray to B. Price, 19 November 1883. This was the third and final draft of a letter which had evidently proved extremely difficult to write.

[45] MP/9/10/83. Proof of *Preface to Part I*. A–ANT [Annotations by W. W. Skeat].

[46] Trench (1860), 4.

[47] See pp. 42–6.

[48] MP/5/1/83. A. J. Ellis to J. A. H. Murray, 5 January 1883.

[49] Alford (1864), 253.

[50] See the *OED*'s entry for this word: 'That may be relied upon; in which reliance or confidence may be put; trustworthy, safe, sure. In current use only from about 1850, and at first perhaps more frequent in American works, but from 1855 freely employed by British writers, though often protested against as an innovation or an Americanism. The formation has been objected to (as by Worcester in 1860) on the ground of irregularity, but has analogies in *available*, *dependable*, *dispensable*, *laughable* (Webster 1864). The question has been fully discussed by F. Hall in his work *On English Adjectives in -able, with special reference to Reliable* (1877).'

[51] On the flux of appropriate labelling in the *OED* (and the associated problems of lexicographical assumptions about usage), see further L. C. Mugglestone, 'Labels Revisited: The Problems of Objectivity and the *OED*', *Dictionaries*, 21 (2000), 27–36.

[52] In W. Scott, *Tales of the Crusaders* (Edinburgh: Archibald Constable, 1825), ii, 137.

[53] MP/[n.d.]/97. J. A. H. Murray to H. Bradley, [n.d.] 1897.

[54] Johnson (1755), B2^{r}.

[55] Revd. A. B. Grosart (ed.), *The Prose Works of William Wordsworth. For the First Time Collected, with Additions from Unpublished Manuscripts* (London: Edward

Moxon, Son, & Co, 1876), iii, *Critical and Ethical*, 'Notes and Illustrations of the Poems', 206.

56 [Bunce] (1884), 53.

57 Alford (1864), 178.

58 See pp. xi, xv.

59 Murray (1884), 509.

60 J. A. H. Murray, 'Preface to Volume V', in *A New English Dictionary on Historical Principles*. Vol. V. *H to K* (Oxford: Clarendon Press, 1901), vi.

61 'A man of honourable character (such as was conventionally associated with one of European extraction)'.

62 The entry as recast in Burchfield's *Supplement* of 1976 (and incorporated in *OED2*) reads 'An individual (esp. a male) belonging to the African race of mankind, which is distinguished by a black skin, black tightly-curled hair, and a nose flatter and lips thicker and more protruding than is common amongst white Europeans. In the nineteenth and twentieth centuries also applied (now somewhat less frequently because of the increasing use of the word *Black*) to individuals of African ancestry born in or resident in the United States or in other English-speaking countries.'

63 This has likewise been emended in *OED2*. 'A Black, esp. a Southern U.S. Black (usu. considered patronizing or mildly offensive)', the entry now states, though one could still argue that the label 'mildly offensive' remains open to considerable debate.

64 Gaskell (1866), ii, 60–1.

65 D. Craik, *Olive* and *The Half-Caste* ed. C. Caplan (Oxford: Oxford University Press, 1999), 384.

66 G. Curzon, *Diary* 1882–83. Cited in D. Gilmour, *Curzon* (London: John Murray, 1994), 36.

67 J. Cook, *A Voyage to the Pacific Ocean. Undertaken, by the Command of his Majesty, for Making Discoveries in the Northern Hemisphere* (London: Printed for John Stockdale, Scatcherd and Whitaker, John Fielding, and John Hardy, 1784), i, 159. The reference as given in the *OED* is slightly inaccurate.

68 Entries for both *horrid* and *too* are emended in the second edition as part of the intent to eliminate bias of this kind.

69 Such terms have often been subject to inconsistent revision in *OED2* so that, whereas the entries for *artist* and *Bohemian* remain unchanged, that for *client*, for instance, has been made to abandon its earlier gender bias. Murray's sense 4 ('A person who employs the services of a professional or business man in any branch of business, or for whom the latter acts in his professional capacity; a customer') has hence been rephrased: 'A person who employs the services of a professional or business man or woman in any branch of business, or for whom the latter acts in a professional capacity; a customer'.

70 H. Béjoint, *Modern Lexicography. An Introduction* (Oxford: Clarendon Press, 2000), 136.

71 See p. 150.

72 Alford (1864), 250.

73 [Heald] (1892), 160.

74 [Bunce] (1884), 55.

75 H. Bradley, *The Making of English* (London and New York: Macmillan, 1904), 208. Bradley also proscribes *transpire* as a characteristic feature of 'bad modern newspaper English' as well as a 'blunder' which has given 'a perverted meaning' to current uses of the word.

76 See pp. 96–7.

77 See further p. 63.

78 This was repeated in the Preface to Volume I. As Murray elaborated, 'Where a decided reason of any kind exists for giving a preference to a particular spelling, this is briefly stated at the end of the etymology: especially this is done in the few cases where the spelling preferred (e.g. *ax*, *connexion*, *rime*) is not that at present favoured by the preponderance of usage, but is intrinsically the best, and therefore is recommended' (Murray, 1888, x).

79 MP/18/5/08. W. A. Craigie to J. A. H. Murray, 18 May 1908.

80 MP/22/5/08. J. A. H. Murray to W. A. Craigie, 22 May 1908.

81 Murray was not alone in such preconceptions about the relevant nuances of correctness in this matter. 'Henceforward . . . I shall continue to spell "Ryme" without our wrongly added *h*', Ruskin declared in his essay 'Fiction – Fair and Foul'. See J. Ruskin, *On the Old Road. A Collection of Miscellaneous Essays, Pamphlets, etc* (Orpington: G. Allen, 1885), ii, 57 n.

82 Onions's insistence on the politics of correctness with reference to *who/whom*, or *whoever/ whomsoever* – in spite of the evidence at his disposal – proves a further striking example of the rejection of the observational adequacy of usage. As the relevant entries attest, 'ungrammatical' uses of *who* for *whom* had, in effect, been current since the fifteenth century, leading Onions into a policy by which, like eighteenth-century grammarians such as Robert Lowth, he was forced to condemn linguistic reality in favour of a somewhat more abstruse ideal of 'good' usage, castigating a range of writers such as Shakespeare, Dickens, and Ruskin in the process.

83 Bridges (1928), 41.

84 Ibid., 45–6.

85 Bradley (1904), 208.

86 Johnson (1755), A2^{r}.

87 Alford (1864), 67.

88 See p. 246 n.95.

89 See e.g. the perceptible tensions which emerge in Johnson's statement that 'Modern writers have ignorantly written veil' in his entry for what, in the face of such usage, he resolutely includes as *vail* in the dictionary itself.

90 W. H. Mallock, *The New Republic: or, Culture, Faith and Philosophy in an English Country House* (London: Chatto & Windus, 1877), ii, 13.

91 See further L. C. Mugglestone, '"An Historian and not a Critic". The Standard of Usage in the *OED*', in Mugglestone (2002a), 201, and also E. Ward-Gilman, 'Dictionaries as a Source of Usage Controversy', *Dictionaries*, 12 (1990), 75–84.

92 [Heald] (1892), 162.

93 MP/8/10/85. H. Bradley to J. A. H. Murray, 8 October 1885.

94 H. Bradley to R. Bridges, 19 August 1904. In R. S. Bridges (ed.), *Correspondence of Robert Bridges and Henry Bradley, 1900–1923* (Oxford: Clarendon Press, 1940), 57–8.

95 Bradley (1904), 144. *Swashbuckling* was another back-formation, deriving from *swashbuckler* ('one who swashes or flourishes his buckler'). *Buckler*, as an earlier fascicle of the *OED* had painstakingly confirmed, signifies 'A small round shield; in England the buckler was usually carried by a handle at the back'. Entries for *swashbuckling* (and other derivative forms) appeared with conspicuous neutrality in the dictionary.

96 The Prospectus is reprinted in *Society for Pure English. Tract No.1: Preliminary Announcement* (Oxford: Clarendon Press, 1919), 5–12.

97 It was eventually to publish sixty-six *Tracts* between 1919 and 1946, the majority inspired by what Tom McArthur in the *Oxford Companion to the English Language* (Oxford: Oxford University Press, 1992) has described as its 'quasi-missionary approach' to language.

98 H. Bradley, 'Spelling Pronunciations', in L. Pearsall Smith, *A Few Practical Suggestions*, Society for Pure English. Tract No. III (Oxford: Clarendon Press, 1920), 19.

99 Letter to Bridges, 19 August 1904. Cited in Bridges (1928), 26.

100 See pp. 173–4.

101 Bradley (1904), 208–9.

102 Alford (1864), 250.

103 For a full discussion of the problems of *everybody* in the *OED*, see Mugglestone (2002c), 198–9.

104 Bridges (1928), 52.

Chapter 6: Ended but not Complete

1 MP/26/11/92. J. A. H. Murray to Mr Darlington, 26 November 1892. The results of his search were included in the detailed entry for *cratch* which appeared in the following year in the fascicle *Consignificant–Crouching* ('A rack or crib to hold fodder for horses and cattle in a stable or a cowshed; in early use sometimes, a manger').

2 MP/7/6/97. A. Swinburne to J. A. H. Murray, 7 June 1897. See further Mugglestone (2002a), 16.

3 OED/MISC/58/7/21. 'The Great Oxford Dictionary'. Anonymous review of *Lap–Leisurely*.

4 Cannan took over as Secretary in December 1897.

5 Cited in 'Obiter Scripta', *The Periodical*, 4 (1913), 162.

6 'Obiter Scripta', *The Periodical*, 1 (1901), 13.

7 'The Oxford English Dictionary', *The Periodical*, 1 (1900), 14.

8 'Obiter Scripta', *The Periodical*, 3 (1909), 30.

9 OUP/Delegates' Orders. Minutes of a Meeting of the Delegates of the Press, 5 December 1902.

10 'Far more than a convenient place to look up words and their origins, the *Oxford English Dictionary* is an irreplaceable part of English culture', as the *OED* website now proclaims. See http://dictionary.oed.com/about/history.html.

11 OED/PP/1905/2. Unsigned copy of a letter to J. A. H. Murray from C. Cannan, 23 January 1905.

12 Max Müller (1878). See further pp. 12–13.

13 OED/PP/1903/1/2. H. H. Gibbs to unknown correspondent, 19 February 1903.

14 MP/Cuttings/28. 'English Dictionaries', *Daily News*, 25 June 1900.

15 MP/Cuttings/75. 'To The Largest Word', *Pall Mall Gazette*, 9 April 1900.

16 MP/26/3/07. J. Bartlett to J. A. H. Murray, 26 March 1907.

17 An account of her visit appears in *Frederick James Furnivall. A Volume of Personal Record* ed. J. J. Munro (London and New York: H. Frowde, 1911), 71: 'On another

occasion I went to Oxford to the head-quarters of the great Dictionary; and there, as always, a postcard [from Furnivall] had been duly received, stating my needs and disclosing with unguarded truthfulness the plot of my story! Some of the complications and secrets of dictionary-making were unfolded to me with a willing generosity which I shall never forget; and off I went, armed with fresh knowledge and new friends.'

18 MP/Cuttings/73. 'Dr. Murray of Oxford', *Christian Leader*, 14 July 1887.

19 B. Harraden, *The Scholar's Daughter* (London: Methuen, 1906), 8.

20 MP/Cuttings/73. 'Dr. Murray of Oxford', *Christian Leader*, 14 July 1887.

21 Harraden (1906), 52.

22 See *CWW*, 178–80.

23 MP/15/12/03. J. A. H. Murray to Dr Bryce, 15 December 1903.

24 MP/11/6/08. J. A. H. Murray to Harold Murray, 11 June 1908.

25 MP/12/6/08. Harold Murray to J. A. H. Murray, 12 June 1908.

26 MP/18/6/08. J. A. H. Murray to H. Asquith, 18 June 1908.

27 MP/20/4/86. J. A. H. Murray to unnamed correspondent, 20 April 1886.

28 MP/7/4/02. W. W. Skeat to J. A. H. Murray, 7 April 1902.

29 MP/31/3/04. J. A. H. Murray to F. J. Furnivall, 31 March 1904.

30 MP/24/12/04. J. A. H. Murray to E. Arber, 24 December 1904.

31 MP/16/12/04. J. A. H. Murray to Canon W. Blackley. The phrase was included under *pension* with an explicit reference to the recipient of the letter: C. Booth, *Pauperism* (1892), ii. iv. 60: 'The father of the movement in favour of old-age pensions is Canon Blackley. With him must always remain the credit of whatever good may finally come out of any of these proposals'.

32 See further Chapter 4.

33 MP/10/5/01. J. A. H. Murray to W. A. Craigie, 10 May 1901.

34 MP/1/4/01. J. A. H. Murray to J. Johnston, 1 April 1901.

35 MP/10/5/01. J. A. H. Murray to W. A. Craigie, 10 May 1901.

36 MP/23/1/06. W. Gribble to J. A. H. Murray, 23 January 1906.

37 OED/PP/1905/2. Unsigned copy of a letter to J. A. H. Murray from C. Cannan.

38 Bradley Letters/H. Bradley to R. Bridges [n.d]/1915, fol. 171.

39 MP/14/1/00. J. A. H. Murray to E. Arber, 14 January 1900.

40 MP/3/6/05. J. A. H. Murray. Draft of a letter to [Thomas] Shaw, 3 June 1905.

41 MP/10/3/06. J. A. H. Murray to W. Jenkinson, 10 March 1906.

42 MP/2/3/10. J. A. H. Murray to H. J. Price, 2 March 1910.

43 'An edifice dedicated to the worship of a deity or deities' was changed in December 1910 to 'An edifice or place regarded primarily as the dwelling-place or "house" of a deity or deities; hence, an edifice devoted to divine worship'.

44 MP/17/4/10. J. A. H. Murray to F. J. Furnivall, 17 April 1910.

45 'Obiter Scripta', *The Periodical*, 3 (1910), 83.

46 MP/8/12/12. J. A. H. Murray to Revd W. Stathers, 8 December 1912.

47 MP/22/7/12. J. A. H. Murray to W. W. Skeat, 22 July 1912.

48 MP/22/6/12. Draft of a letter from J. A. H. Murray to F. Kluge, 22 June 1912.

49 MP/6/7/11. E. Sievers to J. A. H. Murray, 6 July 1911.

50 MP/[n.d.]/1/11. Draft of a letter from J. A. H. Murray to H. Warren, January 1911.

51 MP/Ms notes for address to be given at the Dictionary Evening at the Philological Society in 1912.

52 MP/28/9/12. J. A. H. Murray to W. W. Skeat, 28 September 1912.

53 MP/8/12/12. J. A. H. Murray to Revd W. Stathers, 8 December 1912.

54 J. A. H. Murray, 'Preface to Volume VII', in *A New English Dictionary on Historical Principles*. Vol. VII. *O, P* (Oxford: Clarendon Press, 1909a), [iii].
55 MP/5/2/01. F. J. Furnivall to J. A. H. Murray, 5 February 1901.
56 Murray (1901), vi.
57 J. A. H. Murray. Obituary notice of Professor William Morfill, *Oxford Magazine*, 18 November (1909b), 7.
58 MP/17/4/10. J. A. H. Murray to F. J. Furnivall, 17 April 1910.
59 MP/Murray/Obituaries and Notices/Brandreth. MS draft of obituary notice for E. Brandreth [n.d.].
60 W. Platt, *James Platt the Younger. A Study in the Personality of a Great Scholar* (London: Simpkin Marshall, 1910), 24–5.
61 J. A. H. Murray to Maria Platt. The letter is cited in full in Platt (1910), 24.
62 [A. Hinson], *War Record of the University Press, Oxford* (Oxford: Clarendon Press, 1923), 2.
63 M. Wedderburn Cannan, *Grey Ghosts and Voices* (Kineton: Roundwood Press, 1976), 97.
64 Bradley's daughter Eleanor began work in her father's editorial team in 1897. She continued to work at the dictionary until 1932.
65 [Hinson] (1923), 73.
66 Cited ibid., 7.
67 OUP/The Letter Books of Humphrey Milford. Book No. 60. H. Milford to R. Bridges, 27 November 1914.
68 Ibid. Book No. 59. H. Milford to Mr Murray, 10 October 1914.
69 MP/21/2/14. W. Osler to J. A. H. Murray, 21 February 1914.
70 MP/18/9/14. I. Bywater to J. A. H. Murray, 18 September 1914.
71 MP/[n.d]/9/14. H. Bradley to J. A. H. Murray, September 1914.
72 MP/ [n.d.]/10/14. H. Bradley to J. A. H. Murray, October 1914.
73 MP/26/4/15. J. A. H. Murray to H. Warren, 26 April 1915.
74 Bradley (1917), 552.
75 H. Bradley, Obituary Notice for James Murray, in *A New English Dictionary on Historical Principles*. Vol. IX. *Standard–Stead* (Oxford: Clarendon Press, 1915).
76 Bradley (1917), 552.
77 See Cannan (1976), 107.
78 Ibid., 112.
79 W. A. Craigie, 'Report on the Society's Dictionary, with Special Reference to the Letter V', *Transactions of the Philological Society*, 1917–20, 15.
80 C. T. Onions, 'Preface to SU–SZ', in *A New English Dictionary on Historical Principles* Vol. IX. Part II. *SU–TH* (Oxford: Clarendon Press, 1919), vi.
81 'Obiter Scripta', *The Periodical*, 6 (1917), 232.
82 'Our Dictionary', *Times Literary Supplement*, 19 April 1928, 277.
83 OED/FF/37. R. A. Murray to R. W. Chapman, 9 October 1928.
84 Murray (1884), 523.
85 MP/22/2/10. L. P. H. Eijkhan to J. A. H. Murray, 22 February 1910.
86 MP/3/12/11. E. White to J. A. H. Murray, 3 December 1911.
87 OED/JH/218/2. Review of *Simple–Sleep*, *The Athenaeum*, 4 November 1911.
88 MP/1/1/99. Letter from an unknown correspondent to J. A. H. Murray, 1 January 1899.
89 MP/Cuttings/43. 'Dr. Murray Dead', *The Star*, 27 July 1915.
90 Entries for both were included in *OEDS*.

91 OED/EP/MURRA/3. J. A. H. Murray to unnamed correspondent, 5 January 1895.

92 W. Owen, *Poems by Wilfred Owen* (London: Chatto & Windus, 1920), 15.

93 'Obiter Scripta', *The Periodical*, 5 (1914), 17–18.

94 MP/7/7/05. J. A. H. Murray to F. J. Furnivall, 7 July 1905.

95 MP/13/7/96. H. Bradley to P. L. Gell, 13 July 1896.

96 See pp. 82–3. As Murray had noted in his reply to his correspondent on *delta-metal* (MP/11/2/14), 'I will place your letter & the accompanying book among the Supplemental material'. Editors of the later supplements (and indeed of *OED2*) evidently did not have access to the same files. The word remains in current versions of the dictionary.

97 MP/16/9/99. J. A. H. Murray to unnamed correspondent, 16 September 1899.

98 OED/MISC/147/7A. W. Sykes to J. A. H. Murray, 22 September 1904. The word remains unrecorded.

99 MP/[n.d.]/1907. V. W. Dowell to J. A. H. Murray.

100 MP/1/12/12. Revd W. Stathers to J. A. H. Murray, 1 December 1912.

101 MP/22/9/99. H. Metcalf to J. A. H. Murray, 22 September 1899.

102 MP/2/4/14. T. Stanton to J. A. H. Murray, 2 April 1914.

103 MP/7/12/91. H. H. Sparling to J. A. H. Murray, 7 December 1891. As the letter concluded, 'Please believe that I am always actuated by a sincere desire to do what I can to add a little pebble to the cairn which you have so marvellously built, and not in the least to chuck that pebble at anybody in an "irrelevant and superfluous" way'.

104 MP/29/6/11. J. A. H. Murray to Mr Dodgson, 29 June 1911.

105 MP/28/7/11. R. W. H. Row to J. A. H. Murray, 28 July 1911. The entry was later revised. 'A genus of elephantine beasts', as *OED2* records.

106 OED/MISC/60/1/2. 'Language in the Making', *Manchester Guardian*, 29 December 1928.

107 G. Loane, 'A Thousand and Two Notes on "A New English Dictionary"', *Transactions of the Philological Society* (1925–30), 38–129.

108 C. T. Onions, 'Report on the Society's Dictionary', *Transactions of the Philological Society* (1928), 4–5.

109 Metcalf's other suggested omissions, concerning the absence of *acropodium*, *adamantology*, and *adelite* were, however, not to be rectified. All remain unrecorded in the dictionary.

110 See Craigie and Onions (1933), v.

111 See R. W. Chapman, 'A Supplement to the Oxford Dictionary', *Times Literary Supplement*, 21 September 1933, 631.

112 R. W. Burchfield (ed.), *A Supplement to the Oxford English Dictionary* (Oxford: Clarendon Press, 1972), i, *A–G*. Preface, v.

113 See R. W. Burchfield, 'The End of the Innings but not the End of the Game', *The Incorporated Linguist*, 23 (1984), 116.

114 Though see e.g. Burchfield's decision to include *nylon* in *OEDS* 'after much deliberation'. *Velcro* and *viyella* were similarly granted entry, with usage for the latter being traced to 1894; *velcro* was dated to 1960.

115 See Winchester (2003).

116 http://dictionary.oed.com/public/guide/preface_6.htm#distractions.

Chapter 7: Into the Future

1 See pp. 3–4.
2 Murray (1900), 37.
3 MP/Cuttings/20. Untitled newspaper report on the dedication of the dictionary to Queen Victoria, 14 October 1897.
4 MP/J. A. H. Murray/Ms of Lecture to London Institute, delivered on 9 November 1910.
5 OED/MISC/12/3. J. A. H. Murray to W. A. Craigie, 25 April 1901.
6 MP/19/4/82. J. Griffiths to J. A. H. Murray, 19 April 1882.
7 Murray (1900), 49.
8 J. Simpson, 'The Revolution in English Lexicography', *Dictionaries*, 23 (2002), 11.
9 See http://dictionary.oed.com/.
10 See further p. 251 n.28.
11 http://dictionary.oed.com/about/oed-online/.
12 See http://dictionary.oed.com/about/staff.html
13 http://dictionary.oed.com/public/inside/reading_2.htm.
14 See Trench (1860), 1.
15 Furnivall (1862), 3.
16 See p. 163.
17 Weiner (1990), 499.
18 1. In eastern and southern Africa: any of various kinds of drum; (*spec.* in *S. Afr.*) a large single-headed drum of a type traditionally used by the Venda in certain religious ceremonies; 2. *E. Afr.* A dance; a social gathering where dancing takes place; a night of dancing.
19 MP/3/5/83. H. H. Gibbs to J. A. H. Murray, 3 May 1883.
20 http://dictionary.oed.com/public/inside/reading_2.htm.
21 Cited in Dowling (1996), 97.
22 'Some scholars assume contamination with the Aryan root **qreus*, *qrus* to freeze, whence Gr. κρύσταλλος ice', as Bradley had written. He decided to retain the etymological information, irrespective of the discrepancies it generated with earlier sections of the dictionary.
23 See pp. 203–4.
24 R. Young, 'English Growing by 900 Words a Year', *The Times*, 9 October 2003, 17.
25 See p. 182.
26 MP/'The "New" Dictionary', *The Scotsman*, 2 October 1891. Each fascicle of the first edition cost 12 shillings and sixpence.
27 See p. 182.
28 'I am not equal to the task of handling A & B in one volume, not yet C', as Skeat informed Charles Doble. Instead he had C cut in half, and had all the other letters bound separately. 'The result satisfied *me*, because I only want to use the book *practically*', Skeat continued, acknowledging that others might find the results less than satisfactory given that some sheets had had to be cut in half. MP/28/2/99. W. W. Skeat to C. Doble, 28 February 1899.

References

Unpublished sources

Bradley Letters: Bodleian Library, Oxford.

H. Bradley to R. Bridges [n.d.]/1915, fol. 171.

Murray Papers: Bodleian Library, Oxford.

MP/Cuttings/20. Untitled newspaper report on the dedication of the dictionary to Queen Victoria, 14 October 1897.

MP/Cuttings/23–4. 'The Historical English Dictionary', *Manchester Guardian*, 13 October 1897.

MP/Cuttings/28. 'English Dictionaries', *Daily News*, 25 June 1900.

MP/Cuttings/37. 'Dr. Murray on Dictionaries', *The Standard*, 23 May 1903.

MP/Cuttings/43. 'Dr. Murray Dead', *The Star*, 27 July 1915.

MP/Cuttings/73. 'Dr. Murray of Oxford', *Christian Leader*, 14 July 1887.

MP/Cuttings/75. 'To The Largest Word', *Pall Mall Gazette*, 9 April 1900.

MP/Cuttings/82. 'How to Compile a Great Dictionary. A Chat with Dr. Murray in his Scriptorium at Oxford', *Westminster Gazette*, 23 June 1893.

MP/H. Harley, 'The Philological Society's New English Dictionary', *The Sweep Papers*, 43 (1879), 6–7.

MP/J. A. H. Murray, lecture on 'Dictionaries', delivered at the Royal Institution on Friday, 22 May 1903.

MP/J. A. H. Murray/Ms of Lecture to London Institute, delivered on 9 November 1910.

MP/Ms of lecture to the Ashmolean Natural History Society [n.d.].

MP/Ms notes for address to be given at the Dictionary Evening at the Philological Society in 1912.

MP/Murray/Obituaries and Notices/Brandreth. MS draft of obituary notice for E. Brandreth [n.d.].

MP/Skeat Correspondence/Poems.

MP/22/6/73. E. Freeman to J. A. H. Murray, 22 June 1873.
MP/6/4/76. W. W. Skeat to J. A. H. Murray, 6 April 1876.
MP/15/11/76. W. W. Skeat to J. A. H. Murray, 15 November 1876.
MP/20/4/77. H. Sweet to B. Price, 20 April 1877.
MP/ [n.d] /78. Undated draft of a letter from J. A. H. Murray to B. Price.
MP/11/4/78. Dr A. Ball to J. A. H. Murray, 11 April 1878.
MP/26/4/78. F. Max Müller to J. A. H. Murray, 26 April 1878.
MP/10/11/78. J. A. H. Murray to B. Price, 10 November 1878.
MP/25/11/78. J. A. H. Murray to B. Price, 25 November 1878.
MP/17/4/79. B. Wesley to J. A. H. Murray, 17 April 1879.
MP/18/4/79. W. White to J. A. H. Murray, 18 April 1879.
MP/10/5/79a. J. A. H. Murray to F. J. Furnivall, 10 May 1879.
MP/10/5/79b. F. J. Furnivall to J. A. H. Murray, 10 May 1879.
MP/1/1/80. H. R. Helwych to J. A. H. Murray, 1 January 1880.
MP/7/3/80. E. B. Nicholson to J. A. H. Murray, 7 March 1880.
MP/17/8/81. C. Y. Potts to J. A. H. Murray, 17 August 1881.
MP/12/2/82. J. A. H. Murray to H. H. Gibbs, 12 February 1882.
MP/25/2/82. J. A. H. Murray to H. H. Gibbs, 25 February 1882.
MP/29/3/82. J. A. H. Murray to H. Sweet, 29 March 1882.
MP/3/4/82. H. Sweet to J. A. H. Murray, 3 April 1882.
MP/19/4/82. J. Griffiths to J. A. H. Murray, 19 April 1882.
MP/24/5/82. J. Graham to J. A. H. Murray, 24 May 1882.
MP/9/6/82. Copy of a letter from J. A. H. Murray to B. Price, 9 June 1882.
MP/14/6/82. H. H. Gibbs to J. A. H. Murray, 14 June 1882.
MP/19/6/82. J. A. H. Murray to B. Price, 19 June 1882.
MP/25/6/82. E. P. Thompson to J. A. H. Murray, 25 June 1882.
MP/14/7/82. H. H. Gibbs to J. A. H. Murray, 14 July 1882.
MP/30/7/82. H. H. Gibbs to J. A. H. Murray, 30 July 1882.
MP/1883. Proof of Part I. A–ANT. Title Page. [Annotations by B. Jowett]
MP/[1883a]. Proof of first draft of 'Preface' to *A New English Dictionary on Historical Principles*. Part I. A–APO, 3.
MP/[1883b]. Proof of *Preface to Part I* for *A New English Dictionary on a Historical Basis*. Part 1. A–APO, 3. [Annotations by F. J. Furnivall]
MP/[1883c]. Proof of *Preface to Part I* for *A New English Dictionary on a Historical Basis*. Part 1. A–APO. [Annotations by A. J. Ellis]
MP/[1883d]. *Proof of Preface to Part I* for *A New English Dictionary on a Historical Basis*. [Henry Hucks Gibbs's copy, with annotations]
MP/5/1/83. A. J. Ellis to J. A. H. Murray, 5 January 1883.
MP/1/3/83. H. H. Gibbs to J. A. H. Murray, 1 March 1883.
MP/14/3/83. H. H. Gibbs to J. A. H. Murray, 14 March 1883.
MP/18/4/83. *The New English Dictionary. Suggestions for Guidance in Preparing Copy for the Press*. [Annotations by J. A. H. Murray]
MP/3/5/83. H. H. Gibbs to J. A. H. Murray, 3 May 1883.
MP/23/8/83. H. Liddell to H. H. Gibbs, 23 August 1883.
MP/24/8/83. J. A. H. Murray to B. Jowett, 24 August 1883.

MP/[9]/83a. Proof of *Notice of Publication for A New English Dictionary on Historical Principles* Part 1. A–APO.

MP/[9]/83b. Proof of *A New English Dictionary on a Historical Basis. Preface to Part I.* 'General Explanations'. [Annotations by B. Jowett]

MP/[n.d]/9/83a. First proof of 'General Explanations', September 1883 .

MP/[n.d]/9/83b. J. A. H. Murray's corrected and annotated copy of the first proof of the 'General Explanations'.

MP/[n.d]/9/83c. Proof of *Preface to Part I.* [Annotations by F. Hall]

MP/17/9/83a. Proof 'for revise' of *Preface to Part I* for *A New English Dictionary on a Historical Basis*. Part I. A–ANT. [Annotations by J. A. H. Murray]

MP/17/9/83b. Proof of *Preface to Part I* for *A New English Dictionary on a Historical Basis*. Part 1. A–ANT. [Annotations by J. A. H. Murray]

MP/17/9/83c. Proof of *Preface to Part I* for *A New English Dictionary on a Historical Basis*. Part 1. A–ANT. [Annotations by W. W. Skeat]

MP/[n.d.]/10/83. W. W. Skeat to J. A. H. Murray, October 1883.

MP/8/10/83. Proof of *A New English Dictionary on a Historical Basis*. Title page and 'General Explanations'. [Annotations by F. Hall]

MP/9/10/83. Proof of *Preface to Part I*. A–ANT. [Annotations by W. W. Skeat]

MP/12/10/83a. Proof of *A New English Dictionary on a Historical Basis*. 'General Explanations'. [Annotations by F. Hall]

MP/12/10/83b. Proof of *A New English Dictionary on a Historical Basis*. 'General Explanations'. [Annotations by W. W. Skeat]

MP/18/10/83. J. A. H. Murray to B. Price, 18 October 1883.

MP/21/10/83. H. H. Gibbs to J. A. H. Murray, 21 October 1883.

MP/27/10/83. W. W. Skeat to J. A. H. Murray, 27 October 1883.

MP/28/10/83. E. Brandreth to J. A. H. Murray, 28 October 1883.

MP/29/10/83. B. Dawson to J. A. H. Murray, 29 October 1883.

MP/4/11/83. H. H. Gibbs to J. A. H. Murray, 4 November 1883.

MP/8/11/83. A. J. Ellis to J. A. H. Murray, 8 November 1883.

MP/11/11/83a. B. Jowett to H. H. Gibbs, 11 November 1883.

MP/11/11/83b. Proof of 'The English Dictionary of the Philological Society'. 'Explanations'.

MP/19/11/83. J. A. H. Murray to B. Price, 19 November 1883.

MP/17/1/84. J. A. H. Murray to B. Price, 17 January 1884.

MP/23/1/84. J. Randall to J. A. H. Murray, 23 January 1884.

MP/13/2/84. E. P. Thompson to J. A. H. Murray, 13 February 1884.

MP/22/2/84. J. A. H. Murray to unnamed correspondent, 22 February 1884.

MP/28/3/84. J. A. H. Murray to unnamed correspondent, 28 February 1884.

MP/1/7/84. W. Markby to B. Price, 1 July 1884.

MP/22/7/84. H. H. Gibbs to B. Price, 22 July 1884.

MP/4/1/85. J. A. H. Murray to H. Warren, 4 January 1885.

MP/8/10/85. H. Bradley to J. A. H. Murray, 8 October 1885.

MP/17/4/86. H. Bradley to B. Price, 17 April 1886.

MP/20/4/86. J. A. H. Murray to unnamed correspondent, 20 April 1886.

MP/8/6/86. H. Frowde to P. L. Gell, 8 June 1886.

MP/15/6/86. H. Bradley to J. A. H. Murray, 15 June 1886.
MP/23/6/86. P. L. Gell to J. A. H. Murray, 23 June 1886.
MP/24/6/86. J. A. H. Murray to P. L. Gell, 24 June 1886.
MP/19/1/87. H. Bradley to B. Price, 19 January 1887.
MP/31/1/87. P. L. Gell to J. A. H. Murray, 31 January 1887.
MP/23/3/87. P. L. Gell to J. A. H. Murray, 23 March 1887.
MP/6/6/87. P. L. Gell to J. A. H. Murray, 6 June 1887.
MP/8/11/87. H. H. Gibbs to J. A. H. Murray, 8 November 1887.
MP/30/11/87. P. L. Gell to J. A. H. Murray, 30 November 1887.
MP/18/4/88. Proof of 'Preface. Vol. I'. [Annotations by F. Hall]
MP/28/4/88. Proof of 'Preface. Vol. I'. [Annotations by F. Hall]
MP/24/10/88. J. W. Davidson to J. A. H. Murray, 24 October 1888.
MP/6/12/88. J. Dixon to J. A. H. Murray, 6 December 1888.
MP/30/10/89. J. A. H. Murray to P. L. Gell, 30 October 1889.
MP/29/12/89. H. H. Gibbs to J. A. H. Murray, 29 December 1889.
MP/[n.d]/3/90. R. Ellis to J. A. H. Murray, March 1890.
MP/17/2/91. J. Dixon to J. A. H. Murray, 17 February 1891.
MP/(1891). 'The "New" Dictionary', *The Scotsman*, 2 October 1891.
MP/7/12/91. H. H. Sparling to J. A. H. Murray, 7 December 1891.
MP/8/12/91. J. Dixon to J. A. H. Murray, 8 December 1891.
MP/29/12/91. J. Dixon to J. A. H. Murray, 29 December 1891.
MP/26/11/92. J. A. H. Murray to Mr Darlington, 26 November 1892.
MP/2/12/92. H. H. Gibbs to J. A. H. Murray, 2 December 1892.
MP/7/12/92. P. L. Gell to F. J. Furnivall, 7 December 1892.
MP/5/7/93. J. A. H. Murray to F. J. Furnivall, 5 July 1893.
MP/26/6/94. C. E. Doble to J. A. H. Murray, 26 June 1894.
MP/26/1/96. W. Sykes to J. A. H. Murray, 26 January 1896.
MP/27/1/96. Draft of a letter from J. A. H. Murray to P. L. Gell, 27 January 1896.
MP/26/2/96. H. Bradley to J. A. H. Murray, 26 February 1896.
MP/5/3/96. J. A. H. Murray to P. L. Gell, 5 March 1896.
MP/24/4/96. *New English Dictionary. Correspondence and Minutes Printed by Order of the Board.*
MP/13/7/96. H. Bradley to P. L. Gell, 13 July 1896.
MP/[n.d.]/97. J. A. H. Murray to H. Bradley, [n.d.] 1897.
MP/6/5/97. J. A. H. Murray to P. L. Gell, 6 May 1897.
MP/7/6/97. A. Swinburne to J. A. H. Murray, 7 June 1897.
MP/15/6/97. J. A. H. Murray to P. L. Gell, 15 June 1897.
MP/5/11/97. First draft of a letter from J. A. H. Murray to J. R. Magrath, 5 November 1897.
MP/19/4/98. J. A. H. Murray to Dr P. Fairbairn, 19 April 1898.
MP/1/1/99. Letter from unknown correspondent to J. A. H. Murray, 1 January 1899.
MP/28/2/99. W. W. Skeat to C. Doble, 28 February 1899.
MP/1/9/99. J. Hamilton to J. A. H. Murray, 1 September 1899.
MP/4/9/99. J. A. H. Murray to J. Hamilton, 4 September 1899.
MP/16/9/99. J. A. H. Murray to unnamed correspondent, 16 September 1899.

MP/22/9/99. H. Metcalf to J. A. H. Murray, 22 September 1899.
MP/14/1/00. J. A. H. Murray to E. Arber, 14 January 1900.
MP/5/2/01. F. J. Furnivall to J. A. H. Murray, 5 February 1901.
MP/1/4/01. J. A. H. Murray to J. Johnston, 1 April 1901.
MP/10/5/01. J. A. H. Murray to W. A. Craigie, 10 May 1901.
MP/13/8/01. J. A. H. Murray to unnamed correspondent, 13 August 1901.
MP/[22]/11/01. J. A. H. Murray to H. Bradley, [22] November 1901.
MP/24/1/02. Sir W. H. Preece to J. A. H. Murray, 24 January 1902.
MP/7/4/02. W. W. Skeat to J. A. H. Murray, 7 April 1902.
MP/15/12/03. J. A. H. Murray to Dr J. Bryce, 15 December 1903.
MP/31/3/04. J. A. H. Murray to F. J. Furnivall, 31 March 1904.
MP/16/12/04. J. A. H. Murray to Canon W. Blackley, 16 December 1904.
MP/24/12/04. J. A. H. Murray to E. Arber, 24 December 1904.
MP/27/3/05. J. A. H. Murray to E. Arber, 27 March 1905.
MP/3/6/05. J. A. H. Murray. Draft of a letter to [Thomas] Shaw, 3 June 1905.
MP/7/7/05. J. A. H. Murray to F. J. Furnivall, 7 July 1905.
MP/23/1/06. W. Gribble to J. A. H. Murray, 23 January 1906.
MP/10/3/06. J. A. H. Murray to W. Jenkinson, 10 March 1906.
MP/28/10/06. J. A. H. Murray to Professor Yolland, 28 October 1906.
MP/8/12/06. G. K. Harrison to J. A. H. Murray, 8 December 1906.
MP/10/12/06. J. A. H. Murray to G. K. Harrison, 10 December 1906.
MP/20/12/06. J. A. H. Murray to Mr Jenkinson, 20 December 1906.
MP/[n.d.]/07. V. W. Dowell to J. A. H. Murray.
MP/9/1/07. E. Parry to J. A. H. Murray, 9 January 1907.
MP/26/3/07. J. Bartlett to J. A. H. Murray, 26 March 1907.
MP/18/5/08. W. A. Craigie to J. A. H. Murray, 18 May 1908.
MP/22/5/08. J. A. H. Murray to W. A. Craigie, 22 May 1908.
MP/11/6/08. J. A. H. Murray to Harold Murray, 11 June 1908.
MP/12/6/08. Harold Murray to J. A. H. Murray, 12 June 1908.
MP/18/6/08. J. A. H. Murray to H. Asquith, 18 June 1908.
MP/22/2/10. L. P. H. Eijkhan to J. A. H. Murray, 22 February 1910.
MP/2/3/10. J. A. H. Murray to H. J. Price, 2 March 1910.
MP/17/4/10. J. A. H. Murray to F. J. Furnivall, 17 April 1910.
MP/[n.d.]/1/11. Draft of a letter from J. A. H. Murray to H. Warren, January 1911.
MP/29/6/11. J. A. H. Murray to Mr Dodgson, 29 June 1911.
MP/6/7/11. E. Sievers to J. A. H. Murray, 6 July 1911.
MP/28/7/11. R. W. H. Row to J. A. H. Murray, 28 July 1911.
MP/21/10/11. J. A. H. Murray to unnamed correspondent, 21 October 1911.
MP/29/6/11. J. A. H. Murray to Mr Dodgson, 29 June 1911.
MP/3/12/11. E. White to J. A. H. Murray, 3 December 1911.
MP/22/6/12. Draft of a letter from J. A. H. Murray to F. Kluge, 22 June 1912.
MP/22/7/12. J. A. H. Murray to W. W. Skeat, 22 July 1912.
MP/28/9/12. J. A. H. Murray to W. W. Skeat, 28 September 1912.
MP/1/12/12. Revd W. Stathers to J. A. H. Murray, 1 December 1912.
MP/8/12/12. J. A. H. Murray to Revd W. Stathers, 8 December 1912.

MP/3/6/13. W. A. Read to J. A. H. Murray, 3 June 1913.
MP/7/10/13. A. Church to J. A. H. Murray, 7 October 1913.
MP/11/2/14. J. A. H. Murray to unnamed correspondent, 11 February 1914.
MP/21/2/14. W. Osler to J. A. H. Murray, 21 February 1914.
MP/2/4/14. T. Stanton to J. A. H. Murray, 2 April 1914.
MP/[n.d]/9/14. H. Bradley to J. A. H. Murray, September 1914.
MP/18/9/14. I. Bywater to J. A. H. Murray, 18 September 1914.
MP/[n.d.]/10/14. H. Bradley to J. A. H. Murray, October 1914.
MP/26/4/15. J. A. H. Murray to H. Warren, 26 April 1915.

OED Archives at Oxford University Press

OED/AA/105. W. Sykes to J. A. H. Murray, 6 December 1901.
OED/BL/300/29. A. Beazeley to J. A. H. Murray, 8 January 1884.
OED/BL/322/32. H. H. Gibbs to J. A. H. Murray, 16 October 1888.
OED/BL/323/15. First proof of *cheque*, 17 November 1888. [Annotations by H. H. Gibbs and J. A. H. Murray]
OED/EP/ALD/1/2.i. J. A. H. Murray to H. H. Gibbs, 7 December 1900.
OED/EP/MURRA/3. J. A. H. Murray to unnamed correspondent, 5 January 1895.
OED/EP/MURRA/7. J. A. H. Murray to F. Hall, 13 December 1893.
OED/EP/MURRA/27. J. A. H. Murray to W. A. Craigie, 9 March 1909.
OED/FF/37. R. A. Murray to R. W. Chapman, 9 October 1928.
OED/JH/26/6/1. H. H. Gibbs to J. A. H. Murray, n.d.
OED/JH/218/2. Review of *Simple–Sleep*, *The Athenaeum*, 4 November 1911.
OED/MISC/12/3. J. A. H. Murray to W. A. Craigie, 25 April 1901.
OED/MISC/12/21. J. A. H. Murray to W. A. Craigie, 19 July 190[1].
OED/MISC/12/ 24/ ii/iii. J. A. H. Murray to W. A. Craigie, 3 December 1902.
OED/MISC/13/6. J. A. H. Murray to F. Hall, 29 June 1894.
OED/MISC/13/13. J. A. H. Murray to F. Hall, 13 December 1893.
OED/MISC/13/15. J. A. H. Murray to F. Hall, 21 September 1896.
OED/MISC/13/17. J. A. H. Murray to F. Hall, 6 April 1897.
OED/MISC/13/24. J. A. H. Murray to F. Hall, 11 April 1899.
OED/MISC/13/36. J. A. H. Murray to R. Hall, 18 April 1901.
OED/MISC/58/7/21. 'The Great Oxford Dictionary'. Review of *Lap–Leisurely*.
OED/MISC/58/8/3. *The Scotsman*, 5 October [n.d]. Review of *A New English Dictionary on Historical Principles*, ed. J. A. H. Murray. Vol. VI. *Lock–Lynn* by Henry Bradley.
OED/MISC/58/8/28. Anonymous review of *Leisureness–Lief*.
OED/MISC/58/8/29. Anonymous review of *Leisureness–Lief*.
OED/MISC/59/1/11. Review of *A New English Dictionary on Historical Principles*, Vol. III, Part I, *E–Every*, in *Manchester Guardian*, 14 July 1891.
OED/MISC/59/1/13. Review of *A New English Dictionary on Historical Principles*, Vol. III, Part I, *E–Every*, in *The Athenaeum* (1891).
OED/MISC/59/1/14/ii. *Manchester Guardian*, 1 January 1895.
OED/MISC/59/2/1. *National Observer*, 29 December 1894.

OED/MISC/60/1/2. 'Language in the Making', *Manchester Guardian*, 29 December 1928.
OED/MISC/90/8. 'The Philological Society's New Dictionary', *The Journal of the Linnean Society*, 17 (1880).
OED/MISC/147/7A. W. Sykes to J. A. H. Murray, 22 September 1904.
OED/MISC/210/326/1. W. Sykes to H. Bradley, 5 February 1888.
OED/MISC/210/362/2. W. Sykes to H. Bradley, 10 March 1902.
OED/PP/1903/1/2. H. H. Gibbs to unknown correspondent, 19 February 1903.
OED/PP/1905/2. Unsigned copy of a letter to J. A. H. Murray from C. Cannan 23 January 1905.
OUP/Delegates' Order Books.
OUP/The Letter Books of Humphrey Milford.

Published works

Works published anonymously

(1834). Review of 'On the Connection of the Physical Sciences' by Mrs. Somerville, *Quarterly Review*, 51: 54–68.
(1879a). 'The New English Dictionary of the Philological Society', *The Athenaeum*, 13 September: 337–8.
(1879b). 'The Philological Society's English Dictionary', *The Academy*, 10 May: 413.
(1884a). 'A New English Dictionary', *The Times*, 26 January: 6.
(1884b). Review of *A New English Dictionary on Historical Principles*. Edited by James A. H. Murray. Part I. *A–Ant*, *The Athenaeum*, 9 February: 177–8.
(1884c). 'The New English Dictionary', *Saturday Review*, 16 February: 226.
(1896). 'The English Dictionary and the Clarendon Press', *Saturday Review*, 18 April: 393–4.
(1900). 'The Oxford English Dictionary', *The Periodical*, 1: 14.
(1901). 'Obiter Scripta', *The Periodical*, 1: 13.
(1906). 'Powell and the Press', *The Periodical*, 2: 78.
(1909). 'Obiter Scripta', *The Periodical*, 3: 30.
(1910). 'Obiter Scripta', *The Periodical*, 3: 83.
(1913). 'Obiter Scripta', *The Periodical*, 4: 162.
(1914). 'Obiter Scripta', *The Periodical*, 5: 17–18.
(1917). 'Obiter Scripta', *The Periodical*, 6: 232.
(1919). *Society for Pure English. Tract No. 1: Preliminary Announcement*. Oxford: Clarendon Press: 5–12.
(1928a). 'Our Dictionary', *Times Literary Supplement*, 19 April: 277.
(1928b). 'The Oxford English Dictionary Completed 1884–1928', *The Periodical*, 13: 1–32.
(1928c). *The Oxford English Dictionary 1884–1928*. Oxford: Clarendon Press.

Alford H. (1864). *A Plea for the Queen's English. Stray Notes on Speaking and Spelling*. London: W. Strahan.

—— (1888). *The Queen's English. A Manual of Idiom and Usage*. London: W. Strahan.

Alter, S. G. (1999). *Darwinism and the Linguistic Image. Language, Race, and Natural Theology in the Nineteenth Century*. Baltimore and London: Johns Hopkins University Press.

Ash, J. (1775). *The New and Complete Dictionary of the English Language*. London: Edward & Charles Dilly, and R. Baldwin.

Bailey, N. (1721). *An Universal Etymological English Dictionary*. London: E. Bell.

Barclay, J. (1774). *A Complete and Universal Dictionary on a New Plan*. London: Richardson & Urquhart.

Barlow, F. (1772). *The Complete English Dictionary: or, General Repository of the English Language*. London: the Author.

Beer, G. (1983). *Darwin's Plots. Evolutionary Narrative in Darwin, George Eliot, and Nineteenth-Century Fiction*. London: Routledge & Kegan Paul.

Béjoint, H. (2000). *Modern Lexicography. An Introduction*. Oxford: Clarendon Press.

Benson, L. D. (ed.) (1988). *King Arthur's Death: The Middle English Stanzaic Morte Arthur and Alliterative Morte Arthur*. Exeter: Exeter University Press.

Benzie, W. (1983). *Dr. F. J. Furnivall. A Victorian Scholar Adventurer*. Norman, Oklahoma: Pilgrim Books.

Berg, D. (1991). *A User's Guide to the Oxford English Dictionary*. Oxford: Oxford University Press.

Boag, J. (1848). *A Popular and Complete English Dictionary*. Glasgow: William Collins.

Bradley, H. (1884). Review of *A New English Dictionary on Historical Principles*, Pt I: *A–Ant*, *The Academy*, 25: 105–6.

—— (1904). *The Making of English*. London and New York: Macmillan.

—— (1915). Obituary Notice for Sir James A. H. Murray, in *A New English Dictionary on Historical Principles*. Vol. IX. *Standard–Stead*. Oxford: Clarendon Press.

—— (1917). 'Sir James Murray, 1837–1915', *Proceedings of the British Academy*, 8: 545–51.

—— (1920) 'Spelling Pronunciations', in L. Pearsall Smith, *A Few Practical Suggestions*, Society for Pure English. Tract No. III (Oxford: Clarendon Press), 19.

Bridges, R. S. (1928). 'Henry Bradley. A Memoir', in *The Collected Papers of Henry Bradley*. Oxford: Clarendon Press: 1–58.

—— (ed.) (1940). *Correspondence of Robert Bridges and Henry Bradley, 1900–1923*. Oxford: Clarendon Press.

Brook, G. L. (1970). *The Language of Dickens*. London: André Deutsch.

Browning, R. (1868–69). *The Ring and the Book*, 4 vols. London: Smith, Elder.

Budd, K. (1960). *The Last Victorian. R. D. Blackmore and his Novels*. London: Centaur Press.

[Bunce, O]. (1884). *Don't: A Manual of Mistakes & Improprieties More or Less Prevalent in Conduct & Speech. By Censor*. London: Griffith & Farran.

Burchfield, R. W. (1972–86). *A Supplement to the Oxford English Dictionary*, 4 vols. Oxford: Clarendon Press.

—— (1984). 'The End of the Innings but not the End of the Game', *The Incorporated Linguist*, 23: 114–19.

—— (1989). *Unlocking the English Language*. London: Faber & Faber.

—— (1996). *The New Fowler's Modern English Usage*. Oxford: Clarendon Press.

Butt, J. and Tillotson, K. (1957). *Dickens at Work*. London: Methuen.

Cannan, M. Wedderburn (1976). *Grey Ghosts and Voices*. Kineton: Roundwood Press.

[Cawdrey, R.] (1604). *A Table Alphabeticall, conteyning and teaching the true vvriting, and vunderstanding of hard vsuall English wordes*. London: I. R. for Edmund Weaver.

Chapman, R. W. (1933). 'A Supplement to the Oxford Dictionary', *Times Literary Supplement*, 21 September: 631.

Chaudhuri, N. C. (1974). *Scholar Extraordinary. The Life of Professor the Rt. Hon. Friedrich Max Müller P. C.* London: Chatto & Windus.

Coleridge, D. (1860). 'Observations on the Plan of the Society's Proposed New English Dictionary', *Transactions of the Philological Society*, 1860–61: 152–68.

Cook, J. (1784). *A Voyage to the Pacific Ocean. Undertaken, by the Command of his Majesty, for Making Discoveries in the Northern Hemisphere*, 3 vols [Vol. 3 by J. King]. London: Printed for John Stockdale, Scatcherd and Whitaker, John Fielding, and John Hardy.

Craigie, W. A. (1917–18). 'Report on the Society's Dictionary, with Special Reference to the Letter V', *Transactions of the Philological Society*, 1917–20: 15.

—— and Onions C. T. (eds) (1933). *A New English Dictionary on Historical Principles. Founded on the Materials Collected by the Philological Society. Edited by James A. H. Murray, Henry Bradley, William A. Craigie, C. T. Onions. Introduction, Supplement, and Bibliography*. Oxford: Clarendon Press.

Craik, D. (1999). *Olive* and *The Half-Caste*, ed. C. Caplan. Oxford: Oxford University Press.

Darwin, C. (1982). *On the Origin of Species by Means of Natural Selection, or the Preservation of Favoured Races in the Struggle for Life* (1859), ed. J. W. Burrow, London: John Murray.

Darwin, F. (ed.) (1888). *The Life and Letters of Charles Darwin*, rev. edn. 3 vols. London: John Murray.

Davies, A. Morpurgo (1992). *Nineteenth-Century Linguistics*. London: Longman.

Desmond, A. and Moore, J. (1991). *Darwin*. London: Michael Joseph.

Dickens, C. (1853). *Bleak House*. London: Bradbury & Evans.

—— (1854). *Hard Times, for these Times*. London: Bradbury & Evans.

Dowling, L. (1996). *Language and Decadence in the Victorian Fin de Siècle*. Princeton: Princeton University Press.

Eliot, G. (1871–72). *Middlemarch, A Study of Provincial Life*, 4 vols. Edinburgh and London: William Blackwood & Sons.

Ellis, A. J. (1873). 'Second Annual Address of the President to the Philological Society', *Transactions of the Philological Society*, 1873–74: 200–252.

—— (1874). 'Third Annual Address of the President to the Philological Society', *Transactions of the Philological Society*, 1873–74: 354–460.

Emerson, R. W. (1844). *Essays. Second Series*. London: Geoffrey Chapman.

[Fennell, C. A. M.] (1897). 'Review of *NED*, *Development–Dziggetai*; *Field–Foister*', *The Athenaeum*, 9 October: 484.

Florio, G. (1598). *A Worlde of Wordes, or Most Copious and Exact Dictionarie in Italian and English*. London: A. Hatfield for L. Blount.

Furnivall, F. J. (1861). *An Alphabetical List of English Words occurring in the Literature of the Eighteenth and Nineteenth Centuries; and forming a Basis of Comparison for the Use of Contributors to the New Dictionary of the Philological Society*. Pt II (E–L). London: The Philological Society.

—— (1862). *Circular to the Members of the Philological Society*. London: The Philological Society.

—— (1865). *Circular to the Members of the Philological Society*. London: The Philological Society.

Gaskell, E. C. (1866). *Wives and Daughters. An Every-Day Story*, 2 vols. London: Smith, Elder.

Gilliver, P. (1999). 'Specialized Lexis in the Oxford English Dictionary', in L. Hoffman, H. Kälverkamper, and H. E. Wiegand (eds), *Fachsprachen/ Languages for Special Purposes. Ein Internationales Handbuch zur Fachsprachen-forschung und Terminologiewissenschaft*, 2 vols. Berlin: 1676–84.

—— (2002). '*OED* Personalia', in Mugglestone (2002a): 232–51.

Gilmour, D. (1994). *Curzon*. London: John Murray.

Gissing, G. (1892). *Born in Exile*. London and Edinburgh: A. & C. Black.

Grosart, Revd A. B. (ed.) (1876). *The Prose Works of William Wordsworth. For the First Time Collected, with Additions from Unpublished Manuscripts*, 3 vols. London: Edward Moxon, Son, & Co.

Hall, F. (1873). *Modern English*. London and New York: Scribner, Armstrong.

—— (1880). 'English Rational and Irrational', *Nineteenth Century*, 8: 424–44.

Hardy, T. (1873). *A Pair of Blue Eyes*, 3 vols. London: Tinsley Brothers.

Harraden, B. (1906). *The Scholar's Daughter*. London: Methuen.

Harris, J. (1704–10). *Lexicon Technicum: or, an Universal English Dictionary of Arts and Sciences*, 2 vols. London: Dan Brown, Tim Goodwin.

Harris, R. (1982). 'The History Men', *Times Literary Supplement*, 3 September: 935–6.

[Heald, R.] (1892). *The Queen's English (?) Up to Date. An Exposition of the Prevailing Grammatical Errors of the Day, with Numerous Examples. By 'Anglophil'*. London: The Literary Revision and Translation Office.

Hilton, T. (1985). *John Ruskin. The Early Years*. New Haven and London: Yale University Press.

[Hinson, A.] (1923). *War Record of the University Press, Oxford*. Oxford: Clarendon Press.

Huxley, L. (1900). *Life and Letters of Thomas Henry Huxley*, 2 vols. London: Macmillan.

Huxley, T. H. (1880). *The Crayfish. An Introduction to the Study of Zoology*. London: C. Kegan Paul.

Irvine, W. (1956). *Apes, Angels & Victorians. A Joint Biography of Darwin & Huxley*. London: Weidenfeld & Nicolson.

Jackson, H. J. (2001). *Marginalia: Readers Writing in Books*. New Haven and London: Yale University Press.

Johnson, S. (1747). *The Plan of a Dictionary of the English Language*. London: J. and P. Knapton.

—— (1755). *A Dictionary of the English Language: In which the Words are Deduced from their Originals, and Illustrated in their different Significations by Examples from the Best Writers*, 2 vols. London: W. Strahan; 4 edn London: W. Strahan, 1773.

Kingsley, C. (1863). *The Water-Babies: A Fairy-Tale for a Land-Baby*. London and Cambridge: Macmillan.

Kington-Oliphant, T. L. (1886). *The New English*, 2 vols. London: Macmillan.

Knowles, E. (2002). 'Making the OED: Readers and Editors. A Critical Survey', in Mugglestone (2002a): 22–39.

Landau, S. I. (2001). *Dictionaries. The Art and Craft of Lexicography*, 2nd edn. Cambridge: Cambridge University Press.

Laski, M. (1972). 'Revising OED', *Times Literary Supplement*, 13 October: 1226.

Lloyd, R. (1889). 'First Steps in Dictionary-making: Illustrated Mainly by the Word "High" and its Compounds', *Proceedings of the Literary & Philosophical Society of Liverpool*, 43: 167–84.

Loane, G. (1925–30). 'A Thousand and Two Notes on "A New English Dictionary"', *Transactions of the Philological Society*, 1925–30: 38–129.

Lyell, C. (1851). *A Manual of Elementary Geology*, 3rd rev. edn. London: John Murray.

McArthur, T. (ed.) (1992). *The Oxford Companion to the English Language*. Oxford: Oxford University Press.

McConchie, R. W. (1997). *Lexicography and Physicke: The Record of Sixteenth Century English Medical Terminology*. Oxford: Clarendon Press.

McLintock, R. (1889). 'The New English Dictionary and Some of Its Predecessors. Paper read before the Literary and Philosophical Society of Liverpool', 29 April.

McMorris, J. (2002). '*OED* Sections and Parts', in Mugglestone (2002a): 228–31.

Mallock, W. H. (1877). *The New Republic: or, Culture, Faith and Philosophy in an English Country House*, 2 vols. London: Chatto & Windus.

Mason, M. (1994). *The Making of Victorian Sexuality*. Oxford: Oxford University Press.

Morgan, R. (1994). *Cancelled Words. Rediscovering Thomas Hardy*. London: Routledge.

Mugglestone, L. C. (1999). 'Balance and Bias: Cracking the Impartial Face of Dictionaries', *The English Review*, 9: 13–15.

—— (2000). 'Labels Revisited: The Problems of Objectivity and the *OED*', *Dictionaries*, 21: 27–36.

—— (ed.) (2002a). *Lexicography and the* OED*: Pioneers in the Untrodden Forest*. Oxford: Oxford University Press.

—— (2002b). 'Pioneers in the Untrodden Forest: *The* New *English Dictionary*', in Mugglestone (2002a): 1–21.

—— (2002c). '"An Historian and not a Critic": The Standard of Usage in the *OED*', in Mugglestone (2002a): 189–206.

—— (2003). *Talking Proper: The Rise of Accent as Social Symbol*, 2nd edn. Oxford: Oxford University Press.

—— (2004). 'Departures and Returns. Writing the English Dictionary in the Eighteenth and Nineteenth Centuries', in F. O'Gorman and K. Turner (eds), *The Victorians and the Eighteenth Century*. London: Ashgate Press.

Müller, F. M. (1864). *Lectures on the Science of Language*. Oxford: Clarendon Press.

—— (1878). *Observations by Professor Max Müller on the Lists of Readers and Books Read for the Proposed English Dictionary*. Oxford: Clarendon Press.

Munro, J. J. (ed.) (1911). *Frederick James Furnivall. A Volume of Personal Record*. London and New York: H. Frowde.

Murray, J. A. H. (1873). *The Dialect of the Southern Counties of Scotland: Its Pronunciation, Grammar, and Historical Relations*. London: Asher.

—— (1879a). 'Eighth Annual Address of the President to the Philological Society', *Transactions of the Philological Society*, 1877–79: 561–621.

—— (1879b). *An Appeal to the English-Speaking and English-Reading Public to Read Books and Make Extracts for the Philological Society's New Dictionary*. Oxford: Clarendon Press.

—— (1880). 'Ninth Annual Address of the President to the Philological Society'. *Transactions of the Philological Society*, 1880–81: 117–74.

—— (1881a). 'Report on the Dictionary of the Philological Society', *Transactions of the Philological Society*, 1880–81: 260–9.

—— (1881b). 'Shaksperian Illustrations and the Philological Society's Dictionary', *The Academy*, 1 January: 8.

—— (1882). 'Abacot: The Story of a Spurious Word', *The Athenaeum*, 4 February: 157.

—— (1884). 'Thirteenth Annual Address of the President to the Philological Society', *Transactions of the Philological Society*, 1882–84: 501–31.

—— (1886). 'The New English Dictionary', *Notes and Queries* 1, ser. 7: 370–1, 471.

—— (1888). 'Preface to Volume I', in *A New English Dictionary on Historical Principles, Founded Mainly on the Materials Collected by the Philological Society*. Vol. I. *A and B*. Oxford: Clarendon Press, pp. v-xiv.

—— (1900). *The Evolution of English Lexicography*. Oxford: Clarendon Press.

—— (1901). 'Preface to Volume V', in *A New English Dictionary on Historical Principles*. Vol. V. *H to K*. Oxford: Clarendon Press.

—— (1909a). 'Preface to Volume VII', in *A New English Dictionary on Historical Principles*. Vol. VII. *O, P*. Oxford: Clarendon Press.

—— (1909b). Obituary Notice of Professor William Morfill, *Oxford Magazine*, 18 November: 7.

—— (1915). 'Prefatory Note', in *A New English Dictionary on Historical Principles*. Vol. X. *Trink–Turn-down*. Oxford: Clarendon Press.

Murray, J. A. H., Bradley, H., Craigie, W. A., and Onions, C. T. (eds.) (1884–1928). *A New English Dictionary on Historical Principles*. Oxford: Clarendon Press.

Murray, K. M. E. (1977). *Caught in the Web of Words. James A. H. Murray and the* Oxford English Dictionary. London and New Haven: Yale University Press.

Nash, W. (1993). *Jargon. Its Uses and Abuses*. Oxford: Blackwell.

Oliver, S. (1825). *A General Critical Grammar of the Inglish Language on a System Novel and Extensive*. London: Baldwin, Cradock & Joy.

Onions, C. T. (1919). 'Preface to SU–SZ', in *A New English Dictionary on Historical Principles*. Vol. IX. Part II. *SU–TH*. Oxford: Clarendon Press.

—— (1928). 'Report on the Society's Dictionary', *Transactions of the Philological Society*, 1925–30: 4–5.

Osselton, N. (2002). 'Murray and his European Counterparts', in Mugglestone (2002a): 59–76.

Owen, W. (1920). *Poems by Wilfred Owen*. London: Chatto & Windus.

Patten, R. L. (1978). *Charles Dickens and his Publishers*. Oxford: Clarendon Press.

Phillips, E. (1706). *The New World of English Words*, 6th edn. Revised J[ohn]. K[ersey]. London: J. Phillips, H. Rhodes & J. Taylor.

[Philological Society]. (1859). *Proposal for the Publication of a New English Dictionary by the Philological Society*. London: Trübner.

Platt, W. (1910). *James Platt the Younger. A Study in the Personality of a Great Scholar*. London: Simpkin Marshall.

Proffitt, M. (ed.) (1997). *Oxford English Dictionary Additions Series*, Vol. III. Oxford: Clarendon Press.

Raymond, D. R. (1987). *Dispatches from the Front: The Prefaces to the Oxford English Dictionary*. Waterloo, Ontario: Centre for the New Oxford English Dictionary, University of Waterloo.

Reddick, A. (1996). *The Making of Johnson's Dictionary, 1746–1773*, rev. edn. Cambridge: Cambridge University Press.

Richardson, C. (1836–37). *A New Dictionary of the English Language, Combining Explanation with Etymology*, 2 vols. London: William Pickering.

Ruskin, J. (1885). *On the Old Road. A Collection of Miscellaneous Essays, Pamphlets, etc.*, 3 vols. Orpington: G. Allen.

Schäfer, J. (1980). *Documentation in the O.E.D.: Shakespeare and Nashe as Test Cases*. Oxford: Clarendon Press.

Scott, Sir W. (1825). *Tales of the Crusaders*, 4 vols. Edinburgh: Archibald Constable.

Sheridan, T. (1780). *A General Dictionary of the English Language. One Main Object of Which, is, to Establish a Plain and Permanent Standard of Pronunciation*. London: J. Dodsley, C. Dilly & J. Wilkie.

Simpson, J. (1988). 'The New Vocabulary of English', in E. G. Stanley and T. F. Hoad (eds), *Words: For Robert Burchfield's Sixty-Fifth Birthday*. Cambridge: D. S. Brewer: 143–52.

—— (ed.) (2000–). *Oxford English Dictionary*, 3rd edn. *OED Online*. Oxford: Clarendon Press. <http://dictionary.oed.com>

—— (2002). 'The Revolution in English Lexicography', *Dictionaries*, 23: 1–15.

—— and Weiner, E. (eds) (1993). *Oxford English Dictionary Additions Series*, Vols I–II. Oxford: Clarendon Press.

Skeat, W. W. (1886). 'Report upon "Ghost-words", or Words Which Have No Real Existence', *Transactions of the Philological Society*, 1885–87, ii: 350–74.

Smiles, S. (1859). *Self-help; With Illustrations of Character and Conduct*. London: John Murray.

Sutcliffe, P. (1978). *The Oxford University Press. An Informal History*. Oxford: Clarendon Press.

Sykes, W. (1886a). 'New English Dictionary', *Notes and Queries* 2, ser. 7: 53.

—— (1886b). 'Additions and Emendations to "New English Dictionary"', *Notes and Queries* 2, ser. 7: 238, 282–3.

Tooke, J. Horne (1798–1805). *Epea Pteroenta [Greek]. Or, The Diversions of Purley*, 2nd edn. 2 vols. London: for the Author.

Trench, R. C. (1851). *On the Study of Words*. London: John W. Parker & Sons.

—— (1860). *On Some Deficiencies in Our English Dictionaries*, 2nd rev. edn. London: John W. Parker & Sons.

[Trench *et al.*] (1860). *Canones Lexicographici; or Rules to be Observed in Editing the New English Dictionary of the Philological Society*. London: The Philological Society.

Tribble, E. B. (1997). 'Like a Looking-Glass in the Frame. From the Marginal Note to the Footnote', in D. C. Greetham (ed.), *The Margins of the Text*. Ann Arbor: University of Michigan Press: 229–44.

Vernon, H. M. and Vernon, K. D. (1909). *A History of the Oxford Museum*. Oxford: Clarendon Press.

Walker, J. (1791). *A Critical Pronouncing Dictionary and Expositor of the English Language*. London: G. G. J. & J. Robinson.

Ward-Gilman, E. (1990). 'Dictionaries as a Source of Usage Controversy', *Dictionaries*, 12: 75–84.

Webster, N. (1864). *Webster's Dictionary of the English Language*, rev. C. A. Goodrich and N. Porter. London: Bell & Daldy.

Weiner, E. (1990). 'The Federation of English', in C. Ricks and L. Michaels (eds), *The State of the Language*. London: Faber & Faber: 492–502.

Wheelwright, G. (1875). *Appeal to the English-Speaking Public on behalf of a New English Dictionary*. London: The Philological Society.

Whewell, W. (1837). *History of the Inductive Sciences*, 3 vols. London: J. W. Parker.

Winchester, S. (2003). *The Meaning of Everything*. Oxford: Oxford University Press.

Young, R. (2003). 'English Growing by 900 Words a Year', *The Times*, 9 October: 17.

On-line references

http://dictionary.oed.com/
http://dictionary.oed.com/about/history.html
http://dictionary.oed.com/about/oed-online/
http://dictionary.oed.com/about/staff.html
http://dictionary.oed.com/public/archive/
http://dictionary.oed.com/public/archive/Papers/Deficiencies/Deficiencies_71.htm
http://dictionary.oed.com/public/guide/preface_6.htm#distractions
http://dictionary.oed.com/public/inside/reading_2.htm

Index

abacot 52
abashless xi–xii, xv, xvi
accommodated 76–7
advertisemental 76–7
aged 75
Alford, H. 145–6, 152, 155, 158, 162–3, 168, 170, 178
all 42
alms 42
Americanisms 20, 27, 28, 103, 135, 205, 207, 237*n*.93, 244*n*.50
Appeal to the English-Speaking and English-Reading Public 15–18, 21, 121, 226*n*.54; *see also Oxford English Dictionary*, reading programme for
appendicitis 140
approve 18–19
Arber, E. 26, 36, 87, 187
arcade 151
archaisms 6, 158–60
art 43
Asquith, H. 186
Austin, T. 17
Australian English 207
averse to/from 170
avocation 168–70

back-formation 175, 246*n*.95
Bailey, N. 37, 45, 52, 85
Baldwin, S. 109
Balk, C. 193
balloon 210
Barclay, J. 45
Barlow, F. 70
Bartlett, J. 184
Bayliss, H. 195
Birt, J. 195
black 19, 26
Blackmore, R. D. 100–01
blanket 165
bloody 87
bondmaid 82
Bopp, F. 5
Braddon, M. 171
Bradley, E. 198, 249*n*.64
Bradley, H. 2, 12, 54, 63, 103, 147, 169, 170, 181–2, 189, 190, 194, 201–2
  attitudes to linguistic change 170, 174, 175, 177–8
  concerns for Murray's health 195–6
  edits dictionary v, 24–5, 30–32, 40–41, 43–5, 46, 48–9, 53–4, 58–9, 60–61, 131–2, 158–9, 230*n*.23
  and gender 167
  on Murray 196–7
  as philologist 172–3
  and prescriptive sensibilities 162, 172–8, 245*n*.75, 246*n*.95
  productivity as editor 25, 30–31, 131, 183, 188, 228*n*.95
  need to curb scale of dictionary 64, 78–9, 88–9, 90–91, 108, 131–3, 134–5
Brandreth, E. 125, 191, 192, 196
Bridges, R. 173, 177, 178
Broughton, R. 96–7
Brown, J. 191
Browning, R. xiii, 93, 235*n*.50
Bunce, O. 146–7, 162, 170
Burchfield, R. 71, 92, 95, 104, 109, 134, 135, 136, 142, 206–7, 235*n*.55, 236*n*.236, 244*n*.32, 250*n*.114
  on excision of words 134–5
  see also Supplement (1972–86)
Bywater, I. 27–8, 188, 227*n*.70

candle 26
Cannan, C. 181, 188, 194
Cannan, M. 193–4
car 199
Cawdrey, R. 3–4, 209
Chapman, R. W. 193–4, 198
chasuble 58
cheque 41–2
citations xix, 38–41, 78, 213, 214
  collection of xiv, 1, 8–9, 11–12, 14–15, 16–18, 41, 212–13, 230*n*.11, 230*n*.14; *see also Oxford English Dictionary*, reading programme for
  evidence of 58, 79, 170, 174–5, 209
  invention of 41, 75, 199, 241*n*.76
  in *OED Online* 214–15
  problems in xv, 14–16, 36, 41, 53–5, 61–2, 75, 91, 130, 227*n*.65
  protection of 211
  qualitative discrimination in 20, 22, 64, 66–9, 92–7, 100–01
  need to reduce number of xix, xx, 30, 35, 64–8, 90, 188
  searches for xiv, 75, 138, 187, 189, 195
  sources of xiv, 10, 19–20, 22, 28, 64–6, 76, 78, 89, 92–4, 171, 195, 215–18
class, and representation of xxi, 87, 162, 220
Coleridge, D. 150, 168, 219
Coleridge, H. 8–9, 10, 11, 14, 81, 120, 121, 150, 196
Coleridge, S. T. 8, 95, 97, 101
comparative philology 5, 13, 114–15, 185; *see also* philology
compositors 53, 193, 197
condom 84, 85, 86, 87
Craigie, W. 2, 31, 35, 63, 65, 105, 107–8, 113, 188, 189, 190, 211
  as editor 35, 56–7, 58, 171–2, 181, 183, 199, 200–01, 231*n*.46–47, 232*n*.48
  becomes professor in Chicago 198
  edits 1933 *Supplement* 70, 136, 141, 198, 205–8
Craik, D. 164
critical readers xiv, xv, xvii–xviii, 38–9, 40, 41, 48–53, 61, 138, 152, 210
cultoist 79–80
cunt 84–5, 202, 236*n*.56
Curzan, G. 164

Darwin, C. xx, 111, 112–14, 117–18, 120, 121, 127–8, 129–30, 133, 141–2, 210
  on language 114, 137–8, 239*n*.21
Dawson, B. 64, 125, 190–91
definition 3, 35, 39, 41–2, 62, 63, 162, 209
  and gender 166–7
  problems of xviii, 39, 42–6, 47, 49–50, 57–9, 60–62, 85, 91–2, 179–81, 195, 199, 210, 248*n*.96
  and race 163–4, 165–6
  subjectivity in 59–60, 85, 87, 163
Delegates of Oxford University Press 2, 3, 11, 12, 13, 19, 154, 183, 198, 215
  anxieties about cost of dictionary 21–22, 24, 26–7, 80, 130–31, 183
  anxieties about scale of dictionary 2, 26, 27–8, 30–32, 34, 46–7, 62, 64–8, 80, 89, 91, 131–2, 183
  anxieties about speed of publication 21, 22–5, 26, 30, 46–7
  pressures on Murray 23, 24, 25
  recommendations for the dictionary xx, 19–21, 27–8, 62, 64, 65, 67–8, 80–90, 98, 99, 124–5, 128–30
  role of 223*n*.19
derivative words xi, xiv, xvii, 20, 93–4
descriptivism xx, 20, 21, 76–7, 145–6, 148–9, 152, 154
  problems of 147, 148–9, 154, 160, 162–3, 167–9
dialect 107–8, 151, 159, 160, 237*n*.98, 238*n*.99
Dickens, C. 86, 88, 93, 97, 99, 111–12, 114, 246*n*.81
dictionaries, history of 3–4, 6, 85, 110–11, 209
different to/from 145–6
digital 211
Dixon, J. 84–5, 127, 140, 235*n*.42, 235*n*.44
do 43
Doble, C. 30, 132
due to 153, 154

electronic 211–12
Eliot, G. 113
Ellis, A. J. 10, 11, 20, 71, 125, 153, 157–8
Ellis, R. 84, 192
emergency 173–4
enthuse 175
entries, cutting of xi, xix, 32–3, 35, 62, 77–81, 88–9, 90–93, 94–6, 97–8, 104–6, 108, 133–6, 137, 188
etymology 25, 34, 39, 42, 48, 83, 110–11, 176, 177, 188, 195, 202, 203, 212
euphemism 86–8
eventuate 150
expect 175–6
exquisite 46, 56

facts
  as basis of dictionary 51, 55, 83–4
  interpretation of 56–7, 58–9
Faraday, M. 112–13, 114, 121
feasible 176
figurative language, treatment of 98–9
first-fruit 167
First World War 193–5, 197–8
  language of xix, 199–202
  impact of on dictionary *see under Oxford English Dictionary*
Florio, G. 85
folk-linguistics 167
Fowler, J. 57
fray 160–61
freelance xv
frotteur 105–6
froudacious 96
Frowde, H. 24
Furnivall, F. J. 4, 9–11, 12, 15, 28, 65–6, 71, 79, 94, 191–2, 225*n*.37, 226*n*.52, 248*n*.17
furry 61

gas 201–2
Gaskell, E. 113, 164
Gell, P. L. 3, 24–5, 28, 30, 44, 47, 91, 211, 230*n*.23
gender, representation of xxi, 162, 163, 166–7, 217–18, 245*n*.69
gent 162
ghost-words 51–3
Gibbs, H. H. xiv, 11, 32–3, 57, 77, 89, 124, 137, 183–4, 191, 210–11
  as critical reader 39, 41–2, 49–50, 58, 59–61, 158–9, 231*n*.32, 234*n*.23
  role as intermediary 18–19, 23, 32–3, 227*n*.86
  prescriptive sympathies of 76, 154
  recommends cutting of entries 32–3, 76, 96, 105–6
  on women writers 171, 217
girlpower 215
Gissing, G. 114, 119
Gordon, E. V. 198
Gray, A. 127, 240*n*.40
greasy-pole 60
Grimm, J. and W. xiv, 5, 8, 224*n*.14
grin 58–9
grotto 45–6, 55–6
ground-floor 60

Hall, F. 15, 23, 32, 34, 38, 47, 58, 64–5, 107, 191–2
  as critical reader xiv, xv, 40, 152
  on descriptivism 152, 154
  prescriptive sensibilities of 151–3, 154, 155
Hamilton, J. 85
handsome 58
Hardy, T. 107, 113–14
Harraden, B. 184–5, 187, 247–8*n*.17
Harris, J. 126
Harris, R. 75–6, 101, 102
Hart, H. C. 191
Heald, R. 147, 150, 170, 176, 178
Herrtage, S. 14
hideously 171
high 38–9
High-Churchman 57–8
historicism 2, 10, 38, 55, 114–15, 161, 163, 166, 209
Humphreys, J. 17
Huxley, T. H. xx, 112, 114, 118–19, 120, 123, 125, 126, 128, 129, 201, 210

ideology 87, 105, 162, 210; *see also* class; gender; race
imperialism 164

inclusivity xviii, 7–8, 10, 18, 28, 29, 32–3, 42, 70, 71, 73, 77, 82, 117–18, 208, 215–16
  and compromise in 35, 53–4, 62, 71–4, 77–8, 83–6, 87, 88–9, 90, 105–6, 107–8, 117, 128–9, 198–9
  see also Oxford English Dictionary, as inventory; scientific vocabulary
inmew xv
internet 212

jargon 126–7, 224*n*.22; *see also* scientific vocabulary
Johnson, S. 19, 26, 29, 37, 38, 45, 52, 59, 70–71, 77, 85–6, 110–11, 115, 116, 126, 128, 161, 174, 198, 209, 210
  attitudes to linguistic change 74, 75, 147
  and philology 5, 6
  and prescriptivism 4, 7–8, 157, 173–4
Johnston, J. xiv, 188
Jones, W. 5
Jowett, B. 22–3, 24, 56, 81, 125, 146, 150–51, 227*n*.70
  corrects Murray's prose 153
  objections to title of dictionary 154–6
Jumbo 59–60

Kemble, J. 5
Kersey, J. 37
Kingsley, C. 113
Kington-Oliphant, T. L. 146–7, 168, 174–6

labels and labelling xviii, xix, 41, 42, 87, 105, 122, 158–62, 162, 199, 174–6
landon 62
landscaping 94, 95, 96
langa 91–2
Laski, M. 68
leary 61–2
Lewis, W. 195
lexicographer 5, 6, 8, 168
  duties of 28, 33, 89
  as historian 7, 70, 79, 115, 117, 157, 161–2
  necessary impartiality of 7–8, 28, 76, 102–3, 117, 161–2
  as judge 77, 79–80, 103–4, 144, 148, 149
  as pioneer 163
library 43–4
Liddell, H. 6, 124, 227*n*.70
limeade 94–5
literary language 179, 204, 207, 235*n*.50
Littré, É. 5, 224*n*.14
Lloyd, R. 38
loanwords 3, [illegible], 103–7, 168, 171, 237*n*.92
lunching 94–5, 96

Maling, A. 182, 186
marginalia xvi–xviii, 222*n*.10; *see also* proofs, annotations on
Markby, W. 21, 22, 227*n*.70
Marsden, J. 21
meaning *see* definition
Morfill, W. 92
Morris, R. 4
Müller, F. M. 12–13, 125, 129, 140, 183, 227*n*.70, 241*n*.70, 242*n*.103
Murray, A. 75, 187
Murray, E. 185, 186, 197
Murray, H. 186, 198
Murray, J. A. H. xiv, xv, xvii, xix, 1, 10, 12, 40, 42, 46, 52–3, 79, 179, 181–2, 184, 186, 192, 194, 198, 214
  agrees to edit dictionary xv, 1, 13, 179
  attitudes to usage 143–6, 149, 154, 157–8, 168–72
  on change in language xxi, 59, 74, 75, 115, 176, 200, 201, 209–10, 220
  his children and the dictionary 94
  on completion of dictionary 190, 192, 196
  correspondence of xv, 14, 28–9, 57, 144, 187–8, 190, 192, 195, 196, 203, 210
  death 196
  declining health of 195–6
  on definition 39, 232*n*.56
  on Delegates 19
  disputes with Craigie 56–8, 231*n*.46–47
  on editing dictionary xix, 1, 3, 13–15, 18–19, 26, 28–9, 39, 42–4, 46–7, 168–72, 179, 189

as editor-in-chief xvi, 31, 46, 56–7, 60, 63, 82, 189, 230*n*.23
financial problems of 15, 226*n*.52
and gender 167
invention of citations by 75, 130, 199, 241*n*.76; *see also* citations
on Johnson 110–11, 209, 210
on literary language 179, 235*n*.50
on need to curb dictionary's scale 28–9, 62, 63, 65, 71, 79, 81, 89, 90, 95, 99, 102–3, 107, 108, 124–5, 188, 201
and prescriptivism 102, 149, 162, 168–72
productivity of 23–4, 183, 188
and race 163–5
receives knighthood 185–6
revision of co-editors' entries xvi, xx, 45–7, 56–7, 60, 63, 188, 231*n*.26, 231*n*.46
delivers Romanes lecture xxi, 184, 209
as schoolmaster 12, 14, 24, 27, 184, 211
on scientific vocabulary 71, 81, 110, 112–13, 121–2, 123, 126, 126–7, 129
as scientist 116, 121–2, 123
on *Supplement* for dictionary 202–4
Victorianism of 87
work, pressures of 18–19, 23–4, 43, 47–8, 191, 196, 228*n*.90
Murray, O. 198, 235*n*.50
Murray, R. 185, 186, 197, 198

Nazi 207
negro 163–4
New English Dictionary see Oxford English Dictionary
Nicholson, E. 150–51
nonce-words 78, 89–90, 96, 97, 98–102, 204, 213, 219

obscenities 71, 84–6, 235*n*.50, 235*n*.55
obsolete words, treatment of 6, 28, 32–3, 61–2, 152, 158–9, 160–61
Ogilvie, J. 179
Old Ashmolean 188, 195, 204
Onions, C. T. 2, 36, 172, 194, 201
appointment as editor 193
attitudes to usage 246*n*.81
edits (1933) *Supplement* 70, 136, 141, 198, 204, 205–8
and First World War 197
later career of 198
Osler, W. 188, 195
over-matter 88
Owen, W. 202
Oxford English Dictionary (first edition) xix, 1, 3–4, 73
assistants on 110, 182, 187, 190, 191, 192, 195, 213
as collective enterprise xiv, 8, 186, 197
completion of 1–2, 35–6, 109, 142, 179, 189–90, 198, 202, 204, 229*n*.138
Canones Lexicographici for 118, 120, 237–8*n*.98
errors in 39–40, 50–51, 82, 198–9, 203–4, 218, 219, 229–30*n*.8, 232*n*.68
expense of xx, 24, 26, 27, 32, 35, 36, 43, 46, 80, 87, 182, 183, 184
'General Explanations' for xx, 33, 73–4, 77, 121–2, 123, 152–4, 233*n*.14
historical principles of 1, 3, 5, 7, 28, 40, 74, 76–7, 84, 108, 191, 200
impact of First World War on 194, 195, 197–8, 200–07
independence of 36, 45, 50, 62, 176
as inventory xi, xxi, 7, 20, 23, 28, 34, 79, 82, 117, 162, 215; *see also* inclusivity
and national honour xxi, 13, 16, 17, 22, 183–4, 185–6
and prescriptivism xx–xxi, 7, 142–3, 149, 168–70, 172–6
Proposal for xiv, 8, 71, 95, 118, 227*n*.65
reading programmes for 1, 8–11, 17–18, 27, 38, 41, 51, 53–4, 55, 90, 121, 204, 213–14
reviews of 1, 4, 22, 29, 30, 34, 64, 76, 129, 130, 147, 179, 181, 184, 198, 199, 202

Oxford English Dictionary (first edition) (*Continued*)
scale of (and attendant problems) xx, 1–2, 10, 18–19, 30, 31, 33, 63, 64–5, 68, 70, 79–80, 92, 182, 183, 187, 198, 201, 211, 220, 225*n*.36, 251*n*.28
serial publication of xx, xxi, 2, 11, 13–14, 18–19, 23, 25–6, 54, 74, 88, 112, 123, 181, 200, 218–19
title of 1, 154–7, 223*n*.2
use of oral evidence in 234*n*.21
working methods xiv, xviii, xix, 38–9, 42–3, 213–14, 228*n*.90
Oxford English Dictionary (Second edition) xxi, 46, 62, 66, 95, 98, 169, 175, 201, 210, 212, 220, 230*n*.8, 235*n*.41, 237*n*.92, 243*n*.6
changing of definitions in 163–7
Oxford English Dictionary Online xxi, 142, 208, 212–21
Oxford University Press xx, 1, 3, 11, 13, 15, 16, 24, 34, 35, 80, 128, 143, 179, 182, 211
impact of First World War on 193–5, 197–8
installation of telephone 211
see also Delegates of Oxford University Press

palimpsest 37–8
party 162–3
pass 187
Passow, F. 5, 6
Philological Society xiv, xx, 4–5, 8, 10, 12, 15–16, 21, 114, 117, 125, 147, 187, 190, 191, 197, 200, 204
philology 4–5, 8, 10, 12, 13, 26, 28, 110, 114, 148, 192, 237–8*n*.98; *see also Oxford English Dictionary*, historical principles of
Platt, J. 192–3, 196
Pollock, Sir F. xv, 53, 54
Preece, Sir W. 83
premises 178
prescriptivism xxi, 22, 50, 76–7, 143–9, 152, 154–7, 162
and Philological Society 150
and writing the dictionary xx–xxi, 21, 143, 151–4
see also entries for individual OED editors
Price, B. 13, 14, 20, 21, 22, 23–4, 43, 46, 62, 80–81, 129, 130, 154
pronunciation xviii, xix, 143, 144, 231*n*.32, 231*n*.34
change in 151
variation of 18, 19, 143, 231*n*.32, 231*n*.34
proofs xi, xiv–xviii, xx, 26, 33–4, 38–40, 42–4, 46–50, 54, 56–61, 63, 66, 88–90, 125, 138–9, 155–7, 181, 189, 191, 210, 211, 232*n*.48
and addition of new material 40–41, 136
reading of xx, 19, 40–42, 197–8
proprietary names, treatment of in dictionary 82–3, 202, 235*n*.40–41, 250*n*.96, 250*n*.114
pyjamas 210

race
and nineteenth century 164
representation of xxii, 162, 163–6, 210, 217, 245*n*.62
radium 113, 142, 205
railway porter 63, 231*n*.37
Rask, R. 5
reliable 158, 244*n*.50
rhyme 171–2, 246*n*.81
Richardson, C. 6, 209
Rime see rhyme
Roman Catholic 56–8
Ruskin, J. xvii, 97, 246*n*.81
Ruthven, H. 14

Sanskrit 5
Schäfer, J. xviii, 100
science 115–16
science 118–20, 126, 128–9; *see also* Darwin, C.; Faraday, M.; Huxley, T. H.
scientific vocabulary xvii, xx, 8, 20–21, 57, 73, 76, 77, 81, 82–3, 111–14, 121–3, 126–8, 129, 134–5, 141–2, 187–8, 207, 210, 233*n*.11
collection of evidence on 138–41

excision of 125–6, 129, 131–2, 133–6, 137, 188, 242*n*.94
problems of 82–3, 195
scientist 116
Scott, R. 6
Scott, Sir W. xv, 65, 160, 232*n*.68
Scriptorium 14, 17, 18, 24, 38, 48, 58, 181, 184–5, 188, 195, 196, 204, 211
semantic change 115, 151, 168–71, 172, 173–4, 175–8, 199, 201–2, 210
sense-division xviii, 20, 38–9, 42, 43–4, 57, 62–3, 81
Sheridan, T. 6, 151
Sievers, E. 110, 191
Simpson, J. 208, 212
Sisam, K. 207
Skeat, W. W. xiv, 14, 26–7, 38, 90, 159, 187, 190, 191, 192, 220, 251*n*.28
as critical reader xiii, xvii, 39, 48–9, 50–51, 55, 61, 62, 65, 103
and prescriptive sympathies 153, 154, 155
recommendations for excision of words xi, xix, 103, 125
slang 20, 27, 71, 84, 103, 204
Society for Pure English 177, 247*n*.97
spelling, variation of 144, 149–50, 171–2, 243*n*.6, 246*n*.78
sub-editors for the dictionary xiv, 11, 15, 38–9, 125, 157, 184, 187, 190, 191
Supplement (1933) xxi, 46, 95, 113, 140, 141, 142, 205–7, 218–19, 223*n*.2; *see also* Craigie, W.; Onions, C. T.
collection of material for 202–4, 230*n*.8, 235*n*.41
Supplement (1972–86) xxi, 95, 98, 104, 134–5, 142, 206–8, 211–12, 235*n*.44, 236*n*.67; *see also* Burchfield, R.
swashbuckling 246*n*.95
Sweet, H. 11–12, 13, 14, 22, 36, 62, 78, 80, 103, 225*n*.36
Swinburne, A. 179
Sykes, W. xiv, 39, 57, 138–9, 191, 203, 233*n*.11, 242*n*.100
as critical reader 138–41

telegram 150
telephones 211
Tennyson, A. Lord 93
Thompson, E. xiv, 198, 228*n*.90, 234*n*.23
Thompson, P. xiv
Thorpe, B. 5
Tooke, H. 6
transpire 168, 172, 245*n*.75
Trench, R. C. 4, 5–7, 20, 21, 23, 28, 86, 102, 124, 129, 145, 157, 149, 150
on language of science 73, 76, 117–21, 129, 224*n*.22
Lectures to Philological Society 4, 6–8, 70, 116–17, 149
typewriters 210–11
typography xi, 40, 42

usage 157–8

Victoria, Queen 13, 108, 184, 209
vocabulary, extent of 33, 72–4, 77–8, 102, 133, 213, 233*n*.12
regional 108; *see also* dialect

Walker, J. 6
Warren, H. 28, 149, 196
Webster, N. 26, 27–8, 29, 30–32, 34–5, 52, 70, 182–3, 228*n*.106
Wedgwood, H. 4, 114, 239*n*.20
Weekley, E. 188
Weiner, E. 142, 217
Wheelwright, G. 225*n*.33, 225*n*.36
whisky 144
Worrall, W. 182, 195
Wyld, H. C. 198

Yonge, C. xv
York Powell, F. 23

Zupitza, J. 78, 110

4.00

KT-419-702

BEND'OR

DUKE OF WESTMINSTER

BEND'OR
DUKE OF WESTMINSTER

A Personal Memoir

by

George Ridley with Frank Welsh

With a Foreword by
Anne, Duchess of Westminster

ROBIN CLARK LTD

First published in 1985 by
Robin Clark Ltd
A member of the Namara Group
27/29 Goodge Street
London W1P 1FD

Copyright © George Ridley 1985

All rights reserved

British Library Cataloguing in Publication Data

Ridley, George
Bend'Or, Duke of Westminster.
1. Westminster, Hugh Richard Arthur Grosvenor,
Duke of 2. Great Britain——Nobility——Biography
I. Title
941.081'092'4 DA566.9W44

ISBN 0-86072-096-9

Printed and bound in Great Britain by
Mackays of Chatham, Kent

For Mary

Contents

Acknowledgements ix
List of Illustrations xi
Foreword by Anne, Duchess of Westminster xiii
Introduction 1
1 The Grosvenor Family 6
2 South Africa 29
3 The Young Duke 54
4 The First World War 76
5 Life on the Eaton Estate 110
6 His Occupation Gone 130
7 Sunlit Uplands 151
8 The Grosvenor Heritage 199
Index 203

Acknowledgements

I should like to thank the following people for the help they have given me in the preparation of this book:

Anne, Duchess of Westminster, for her constant encouragement and the use of photographs and personal papers; Lady Mary Grosvenor for the most valuable use of albums and other photographic material and for her encouragement; Gerald, sixth Duke of Westminster, for his help in making available papers in the strong room at the Eaton Estate office and in the Grosvenor Office, London and for his permission to photograph pictures at Eaton and his general support; Mr J.N.C. James (trustee of the Grosvenor Estate) for all his assistance in the provision of documents and his desire to see the book completed; Mrs Ivor Griffiths (George Powell's daughter) for the loan of invaluable photographs of the 1914–18 war and for some very special anecdotes; Mr Frank Welsh who has co-operated in the writing of the book, relieving me of the burden of some of the research at both estate offices; Mrs Beryl Hayter, my secretary for forty years, who has patiently borne with me while I have worked spasmodically on this book, which she has typed and retyped without complaint. She has also resurrected information out of files which I had long forgotten and has endeavoured at all times to keep me to the task.

Acknowledgement is also made to the following publishers for the consultation of *The Cousins*, Max Egremont (Collins, London); *Clementine Churchill*, Mary Soames (Cassell, London); *The War Hitler Won*, Nicholas Bethell (Futura Publications, London); *The Boer War*, Thomas Pakenham (Weidenfeld and Nicolson, London); *Oscar Wilde*,

Frank Harris (Constable & Co., London); *Within the Fringe. An Autobiography*, Viscount Stuart of Findhorn (Bodley Head, London); *A Dictionary of Artists of the English School*, Samuel Redgrave (London, 1878); *Victorian Duke: The Life of Hugh Lupus Grosvenor 1st Duke of Westminster*, Gervas Huxley (Oxford University Press, London); *Grace and Favour*, Loelia, Duchess of Westminster (Weidenfeld and Nicolson, London) and *The Autobiography of Margot Asquith* (Methuen, London).

List of Illustrations

1. Eaton Hall
2. Bend'Or as a boy at Saighton
3. Bend'Or in South Africa 1901; uniform of the Blues
4. Bend'Or in stable yard archway, Eaton 1901
5. Bend'Or's house in the Orange Free State
6. King Edward VII at Eaton, December 1909
7. Sir John Lavery's painting of the famous armoured car squadron
8. *Daily Sketch* of 1 September 1914, showing that Bend'Or was in the fighting from the beginning
9. Bend'Or in his armoured Rolls-Royce . . .
10. . . . and the man who drove it through the war, Bend'Or's chauffeur George Powell
11. The Armoured Car Squadron 1915. Bend'Or in centre front row. George Powell in chauffeur's uniform on left
12. The Duke of Westminster being presented with a silver souvenir of his armoured car exploit
13. Bend'Or and Shelagh with the King of Spain at Eaton
14. One night's catch. The river Alten, 7 July 1926. Thirty-three salmon weighing 800 lbs, the average weight being 24 lbs
15. Gamekeepers at Eaton in the late thirties: Sandy Myles, head keeper, with (in green livery) Fred Grass, George Grass Snr, Fred Milton and Tom Lamont

16. Bend'Or with his old friend Basil Kerr, World's End, 1930s

17. Sandy Myles with beaters at the Lower lanes, Aldford, 1930s

18. Bend'Or with Lord Derby, Winston Churchill and Basil Kerr. Aintree, mid-1930s

19. The *Cutty Sark*

20. Drawing of Bend'Or by Drian

21. Photograph of Anne, Duchess of Westminster, in the robes of a peeress at the time of the Coronation

22. George Ridley and the fourth and fifth Dukes of Westminster at the opening of the Annacis Island Industrial Estate in 1955

23. Annacis Island Industrial Estate, Canada

24. The attractive landscaped grounds of one of the factories on Annacis Island

Foreword

I know of no person better qualified than George Ridley to write an accurate and comprehensive book on the life of my husband.

George was Bend'Or's guide, philosopher and very dear friend for many years. He served him with complete loyalty and devotion and offered far-seeing and inspired advice on all financial matters; together they gave endless thought to the future and well-being of the family and the security of the Grosvenor Estates. I think my husband would be proud of and well satisfied with the result of their long-term planning.

So much has been written about Bend'Or, chiefly on the subject of how many yachts and how many marriages, and so little on all his achievements, his immense patriotism and service to his country and the utter loyalty and devotion shown to him by his many tenants, employees and friends.

The author of this book appreciated to the full these qualities and his great kindness and generosity.

I hope and think it will help succeeding generations to appreciate the unique and splendid qualities of the second Duke of Westminster.

Anne Westminster, 1985

Introduction

On a morning in December, 1926, I left my lodgings in Eccleston to arrive by bicycle at the keeper's cottage on the Belgrave drive at Eaton by eight o'clock. It was a cold, damp day – an extension of November weather before the advent of the frosts that would sharpen and clear the air.

Although it was not yet light, there were already assembled on and around the drive, just below the obelisk and within a stone's throw of the head keeper's house, a conclave of men and dogs upon whose efforts, together with the co-operation – however unwilling – of the birds, would depend the success of the day's shoot. I had only been at Eaton a few weeks and this was my initiation into the world of grand-scale pheasant shoots of which I was, unwittingly, to be a witness for some years to come.

As the light strengthened, I gained a somewhat awesome knowledge of the scene around me: the head keeper, Stark, and his keepers, each of whom controlled his own 'beat' on the estate, were dressed in rich green velvet jackets and waistcoats, light fawn Bedford cord breeches and fawn gaiters, and the whole was topped by billycock hats with gold lace bands. Bearded, Dorset-bred Stark was to me – a green seventeen-year-old from the town – a fearsome figure in his everyday tweeds, but in his livery he commanded a respect bordering on terror, which no headmaster had ever achieved.

The under keepers were dressed in hard tweed suits and breeches of almost clerical grey, topped with trilby hats to match. They were the younger men assisting each keeper with his pheasant rearing and his beat, and aspiring ultimately to full keepership with which went the coveted accolade of the green jacket and waistcoat. Each keeper had his labrador and, to augment the dog team for the day's retrieving, keepers from neighbouring estates in Cheshire and North Wales had brought their ladbradors or spaniels. While operating under the vigilant eye and stentorian word of command of Stark they moved, I noticed, with a sense of freedom that no Eaton keeper would be permitted by this sternest of commanders, who I was later to learn was one of the greatest masters of his craft. I was also to learn that he was himself serving a master whose knowledge of what was required was unsurpassed and whose standards never fell below the highest.

Aside from the keepers were congregated the beaters, presenting a sight which added to my bewilderment. They were estate workers chosen from the various departments – forestry, gardens and home farm – some seventy in number and selected for their experience in the art of 'beating' a wood slowly under the guidance of the keepers. Each dressed in a white smock pulled in by a stout leather belt, brown leather leggings and a scarlet hat of the shape worn by the Anzacs in the 1914–18 war, they added a splash of colour which would have done credit to a Covent Garden opera setting but which was, in fact, a safety measure to make them easily visible to the guns as they progressed through a wood. They worked in two teams – as one drove wood A, team number two assembled on the edge of wood B ready to move forward as the guns were taking up position. As this wood was driven so number one party moved to wood C.

In the course of time I learned that delay was not tolerated and, without any appearance of fuss, shooting days functioned with military precision, achieving success which was the pride of all who participated.

Last in the line of responsibility in status were the 'stops'. Many of them were younger employees or newcomers, inexperienced, who could not boast of any form of livery and wore the most waterproof and warm attire their wardrobes could supply. Their task, a tedious yet onerous one, was to take up posts within close proximity of each wood to be shot that day and by gentle tapping of stick upon fence or tree to make their presence known to the pheasants in the wood, so as to contain them and prevent them from straying. As their particular wood was shot, their day was made more interesting by joining with the teams of beaters, being on the move and seeing something of the sport. Those stops surrounding the last wood to be shot would have their patience strained by the fact that their immobility extended from eight in the morning to possibly three in the afternoon. Meanwhile they were kept aware of the activity around them by the sound of shooting drawing nearer, thus heightening the tension and willing the success of the drive for which one felt in one's innocent mind such grave responsibility. As a pupil forester, I was one of the stops and due to my junior status and as a newcomer, was posted to guard a hedge one hundred yards or so from the last wood of the day.

From eight o'clock until the first sound of the guns at about half-past ten seemed an eternity and my early diligence, more reminiscent of a wartime sentry guarding his prisoners than the guardian of a thousand or more pheasants, gave way to sufficient self-confidence to permit me to walk to meet my neighbour, a certain Walter Huxley, a first-class countryman later to gain almost national renown as a gold medallist hedge layer (appearing on television) and superb gardener, winner of prizes at the leading shows.

We chose our lunch-time at midday and while keeping a watch upon our charges, Walter found within the hedgerows enough sticks to give us a cheerful fire which was screened from any critical keeper by a nearby loose-box.

From then on time moved more quickly. The guns who had returned to Eaton Hall for lunch had been brought from there by the Duke's private train to the afternoon shoot. The first drive after lunch had taken place only half a mile away and now through the fields to the south came the first sign of movement. Two keepers, on whose beat we stood, with their small army of beaters were moving to encircle the wood – 'The Brickyard' – followed shortly by the balance of keepers, the loaders who (with the exception of the Duke's loader, Fred Milton, who was a keeper and had loaded for him for many years) were tenant farmers often accompanied by their sons or friends as cartridge carriers and, finally, the guns. They, for the most part, were men well known in political, military and social circles, many of them handsome, of good carriage and supported and enhanced by the presence of their ladies. They moved in two or three groups, engaged in animated conversation inspired by a day's good sport and with the pleasant anticipation of the day's final stand, which experience had taught them would not be disappointing.

Some little distance behind the others came the Duke of Westminster, accompanied by a lady and followed by the smart and dignified figure of his loader, who walked with military bearing. This was the moment I had waited for and even if I had not been acquainted in my few weeks at Eaton with glowing and inspiring descriptions of his appearance and his character, I would have felt that same instinct which told me that I was in 'the Presence'. Well over six feet tall, appropriately broad, wearing his fawn tweeds with a casualness that belied their quality, with a turned-down felt hat of uncertain age, he walked with body slightly bent forward, but with an air of alertness and vitality that was arresting. My feelings, as a youth of seventeen, were inevitably telescoped through inexperience and the brevity of the occasion, but uppermost in my mind was the thought that I was looking upon a great man. I was taken aback by his handsome and vigorous appearance and, while I had expected a man of his great wealth to bear all the characteristics of his possessions with a lively air of arrogance, his demeanour portrayed to me a sense of modest acknowledgement of his position. This was heightened in my juvenile mind when, to my great surprise, he extended a friendly greeting as he passed.

The territorial operations of the last drive meant that keepers, loaders, beaters and stops met up at the same point at the end of the shoot and past this the guns walked on their way to rejoin the Duke's train on the narrow gauge railway for the short journey to Eaton. As we lined the wood side the guests bade us an appropriate 'good night' after a great day's sport and finally the Duke himself slowly walked by with a special word of thanks to his head keeper and members of his staff whom he knew so well, but also surprisingly he thanked the likes of me in a charming manner as though I had done him a great kindness.

My admiration, evoked by stories from his old retainers, had been stimulated by this, our first brief meeting, and was now to rise to dizzy heights which could have been attributed to the youthful enthusiasm which produces hero worship and might well have been the subject of later disillusionment. In the ensuing years I was to learn that the judgement I had so readily made, with starry eyes, was not founded upon false premises and that the character of Bend'Or, Duke, as he was affectionately known, contained qualities unrecognized by many: not least the ability to acknowledge his own weaknesses and the greatest the sense of forgiveness for the weaknesses of others.

He was forty-seven when I first saw him and of much that happened in his life from then until his death in 1953, at the age of seventy-four, I was either a spectator on the sidelines or an active participant in the game. Of those years I can write with reasonable knowledge and accuracy. It is unfortunate, however, that of his early years too little recorded evidence is to be found to enable anyone to paint as full a picture of an exciting life lived fearlessly, as it deserves; but sufficient is available to show that a man endowed with great gifts fought, like many others, for his country at a tender age, showing qualities which would, without rank and great wealth, have taken him far, but that his career was cut short on the threshold by his inheritance of the dukedom and estates and the almost automatic restriction of his ability to work in the way he wished most.

I

The Grosvenor Family

Ever since the first chapter of the Gospel according to St Matthew it has been customary to begin biographies with a genealogy. Too often this is now skipped as tedious, but in order to understand the life and character of the Most Noble Hugh Richard Arthur Grosvenor, Duke of Westminster, Marquess of Westminster, Earl Grosvenor and Viscount Belgrave, Baron Grosvenor, Knight Grand Cross of the Royal Victorian Order, Member of the Distinguished Service Order, it is necessary to follow the history of that ancient Cheshire family, the Grosvenors, and their progress in the national life.

Although the Westminsters may be the last of the British dukes, the family of Grosvenor has been established as a patrician group, exercising great influence in its own territories, for many centuries. At a time when Cecils, Russells and Cavendishes were small farmers or lawyers the Grosvenors were leaders in feudal society. They have remained, settled on their own estates, for the better part of a millennium, in what may be seen as an ideal pattern of the solid continuity of English life.

It is true that the suggestion that the family is descended from the hereditary chief huntsman of the Dukes of Normandy (*le gros veneur*) is something of a romance; had such a 'high and powerful office' existed we might have expected something of a record to have been kept. Since nicknames were popular – Ralph the Ganger, William the Bastard, Curthose, Rufus, Lackland – the name was probably given originally to a hunter of generous habit of body. It is, though, highly likely that the family can trace its descent from one Gilbert Grosvenor, a nephew of Hugh Lupus, first Norman Earl of Chester.

A good deal is known about the Grosvenor descent as a result of a fourteenth-century dispute into which the family were precipitated; the affair was documented with meticulous care and included a trial in the Court of Chivalry which lasted for four years, with evidence being given by the Dukes of York and Lancaster, the Earls of Derby, Arundel and Northumberland, and many other lords, abbots, knights and gentlemen. Not its least effect was, somewhat indirectly, to provide the nickname by which the second Duke of Westminster was universally to be known, Bend'Or.

The cause of it all was described by one of the witnesses, Geoffrey Chaucer, in French that was, like the Wife of Bath's, very much of Stratford atte Bow. He is recorded as saying 'il estoit une foitz en Friday Strete en Loundres, com il alast en la rewer il vist pendant hors une novell signe faitz dez diz armez'. He asked if the arms were those of Scrope, a Yorkshire family, and was told that, no, they were the arms of 'une chivaler del counte de Chestre . . . mons. Robert Grosvenor'.

Sir Richard Scrope, Chancellor of England, first Baron Scrope of Bolton, had made his mark on fourteenth-century England. He had been knighted on the field of Nevile's Cross, when the Scots were beaten back from the outskirts of Durham, and had fought in almost all the campaigns of the time against the French and Scots. Sir Richard was furious, at reports that another was bearing arms he saw as his, with the ire of a man not too sure of himself. The Grosvenors had usurped, as he saw it, his own armorial bearings – a golden diagonal stripe on a blue background, or in the precise terminology of arms, azure, a bend'Or – a simple device, and for that reason highly prized, since the simplest coats were the oldest. It was not the first time that this matter had caused trouble. At the time of the battle of Poitiers a Cornish squire 'appelle Carminow' had appeared with the arms, and received a Grosvenor complaint; he had earlier, at Crécy, had an objection from the Scropes.

This time, it was generally felt, the matter had to be settled once and for all. A trial was therefore held before the Duke of Gloucester, Constable of England, and evidence gathered from all over the country. In so important a matter money was no object, and the veracity of much of the testimony is more than usually uncertain. The crucial point was the relative antiquity of the families; since he who had first borne the arms had the right to them. The Grosvenors had a strong case, for there was no doubt that the Grosvenors had been established in Cheshire for many generations. A forbear of Sir Robert, Robert Grosvenor of Holme, had been Sheriff of Chester between 1284–88. The Grosvenors of Budworth were hereditary foresters of Delamere Forest in the twelfth century, and quite possibly both were descendants of the original Gilbert, Hugh Lupus's nephew.

There was a good deal too much evidence, capable, were it true, of proving either side's case up to the pommel, and giving us an instructive view of medieval society. A damaging attack on the Grosvenors' case had been made by a neighbour, Lord Grey of Ruthven, who claimed that he knew nothing of the Grosvenors except that he had once bought a black mare from one Emma Grosvenor. It is not unknown now, and was probably not unknown in the fourteenth century, for purchasers of horses subsequently to regret their bargain, and it may be that Lady Emma was an astute saleswoman.

With hindsight, it seems that the stronger case was indeed that of the Grosvenors. They criticized, with justification, the gentle status of the Scropes. Sir Richard's father had certainly been a lawyer, never a profession held in the very highest esteem, even though he was Chief Justice of the King's Bench, and his grandfather a mere bailiff from an obscure Yorkshire family. Johnny-come-latelys the Scropes may have been, but they were men of weight in the country. Scrope, who had been Lord Treasurer and Steward of the King's Household as well as Chancellor, was able to call upon John of Gaunt, his son the Earl of Derby, later Henry IV, Harry Hotspur and many others, including Sir John Sully who was 105 and swore to having seen the arms borne by Scrope at Halidon Hill (1333) and Najara (1367); all doubtless true, but beside the point, which was who bore the arms in the thirteenth century and before?

It was hardly surprising, in view of the Scropes' influence, that after hearing 300 witnesses the Constable found in favour of Scrope, but added that 'la partie du dit Robert avons trouves grandes evidences et presumptions semblables en sa defense', and should be allowed to bear the bend'Or with a silver border (une plaine bordure d'Argent). Robert refused this concession 'and took unto him the coat of Azure, une garbe d'or: which coate his heyres and successoures hae ever borne to this present, scorning to bear the other coate with a difference'.

The judgement rankled somewhat, and was recalled in the nineteenth century when the first Duke named one of his most successful racehorses 'Bend'Or'; when his grandson, Hugh was born, his baby auburn curls reminded everyone of the chestnut horse and he was given the nickname 'Bend'Or'.

This exposure to the fierce light of history was the last for some centuries. The family continued to prosper quietly, adding to their estates many others, including some in Wales which contained lead mines and 'una minera Carbonn' voc' a Coole Myne', and properties in Leicestershire and Chester. The ancestral properties in Cheshire were strategic, and now included substantial parts of the town. Chester had been for many centuries the chief port of the North West and was to continue so for much longer – the first performance of *Messiah* is said to have taken place there as Handel waited for the Dublin packet. As agricultural land Cheshire was as rich as any in England; when in 1857 Hugh Lupus, later the first Duke, was arguing for compensation to be paid to farmers in order to help them over the effects of the rinderpest epidemic, he pointed out that the losses in the county of Cheshire alone were thirty per cent of the English total, an indication of the relative numbers of livestock.

The Grosvenor holdings stretched from Chester to the Halkyn and Berwyn Mountains. In the hills the lead and coal mines became increasingly important as the economy grew. This regional wealth did not produce national importance. Some members of the family gained individual renown: Robert Grosvenor, a certain forbear, fought with Richard the Lionheart in the Holy Land, Sicily and Cyprus; Sir Thomas Grosvenor, who died in 1549, was immortalized by Wyatt in an epitaph that would as well have served for many other Grosvenors:

> Under this stone there lyethe at rest
> A friendly mane a worthy knight
> Whose heart and mynde were ever prest
> To favor truthe to farther right.

But in general the Grosvenors avoided the great mischance of civil war and disturbance that brought so many distinguished families of the Middle Ages to ruin. Among these their old contestants, the Scrope family, may be numbered. Sir Richard Scrope's eldest son, William, became that Earl of Wiltshire who, with Bussy and Green, had his head removed by Henry IV; his godson, Richard of Masham, Archbishop of York, lost his in the same way, as recorded in *Henry IV*

Part II; while the Archbishop's nephew, Henry, was that 'kind Lord of Masham' ('What shall I say to thee, Lord Scroop, thou cruel, Ingrateful, savage and inhuman creature!' *Henry V* Act II Scene 2) who was sentenced to death in the Red Lion at Southampton, where one may still drink to either family's health.

Happy the family not mentioned in the history plays! Sir Robert Grosvenor's son, Thomas, certainly was to be found on the losing side at the battle of Shrewsbury but, wisely pleading that it was 'by the evil enticement fine words and promises of Monsieur Henry Percy' that he joined, procured a pardon. Had he been as prominent as the Scropes, this would have been less likely, which may have been some consolation for relative obscurity. Thomas's son, Ralph, made a considerable advance in the family fortunes by marrying, about 1435, Joan de Eton, heir to the manor of Eaton, which was to become the family seat, but did not thrust himself forward in public affairs.

During the Reformation, when the last of the great nobility of the Middle Ages came to an end and the new men of the Tudors made their way to the top, the Grosvenors continued to avoid the centre stage, and contented themselves with improving their estates and holding local offices. The first hereditary honour did not come until 1622 when Richard Grosvenor became the first baronet, a title invented by James I more in order to raise revenue than anything else. Sir Richard was Member of Parliament for Chester and successively Sheriff of Cheshire, Denbighshire and Flintshire; it is worth recalling that even then it was four and a half centuries since his direct ancestor had held the same office.

His career exemplified an energetic and somewhat combative Grosvenor streak. Charles Gatty describes him as a 'tough worthy, who loved his kin, but loathed the Pope, the poacher and the publican'. He was a Parliament man, though loyal to the Stuarts. 'A Parliament is the most honorable and highest Court of the Kingdom having an absolute jurisdiction and an unlimited power to dispose of the lives, limbs, states, goods, honours and liberties of the subjects, and of their religion too' (speech in 1623).

His parliamentary career came to an end in 1629 when he was thrown into the Fleet prison for debt. In 1638 he had thirty-four processes of outlawry for debt advanced against him and was again in prison. He managed, in spite of being 'greatlie dampnified in his estate', to arrange matters, and was Sheriff of Chester again in 1642, when he was able to condemn public houses as 'the very bane of the country, a receptacle for knaves and harlots, and the beggar's nursery, the drunkard's academy, the thieve's sanctuary'.

His son, also Richard, who succeeded in 1645, also found himself in the Fleet in 1646 for a cause he thought unjust. He had paid a large fine (£2,550) in 1646 in recompense for having supported the royal and losing side and claimed that since 1645 he had been active in sending men to fight for Parliament. His plea was successful and in 1651 he was back at Eaton. The family support for the royal cause fell to his son, Roger, who took part in the abortive 'New Royalist' rising of 1659. This was meant to be a general rebellion with the purpose of restoring Charles II, but was nipped in the bud by Thurloe's intelligence system and surfaced only in Cheshire, where it was speedily squashed by General Lambert at Nantwich. The leader of the plot, Sir George Booth, escaped disguised as a woman, but was arrested when he bought a razor. The conspirators, who included Edward Herbert of Cherbury 'a very big fat man', the Earl of Derby and Sir Thomas Middleton as well as Roger Grosvenor, escaped unscathed since the Restoration was by then generally felt to be inevitable.

Roger did not survive it long, since he was killed in a foolish fight with his brother-in-law, Hugh Roberts, at Heron Bridge on the road between Eaton and Chester. Roberts was forced to run him through in defending himself from Roger's fierce attack. When Sir Richard died, in 1664, he was succeeded by Roger's son, Thomas, then a boy of eight. In spite of the financial difficulties of his grandfather and great-grandfather, Thomas succeeded to a rich and powerful inheritance.

The importance of the family may be judged from the arrangement of the old baronet's funeral where, after his standard, his horse in the black trappings, his lance trailed, came Sir William Stanley, Roger Mostyn and Thomas Cholmondely, representing the great families of the North West, and carrying Sir Richard's banner, helmet and coat of arms.

His wealth can be judged by the fines levied on his forbears for recusancy. The 1646 fine was probably one year's income; if this had been accurately estimated it represented a capital value of perhaps £50,000. In addition there was a fine in 1648 of one twentieth part of his estate. Young Thomas's guardians determined that this fortune should be increased and looked around for a suitable heiress; they found Mary Davies. Mary was perhaps hardly ready for marriage – she was twelve when it took place – but she was not without other attractions, having inherited the manor of Ebury from her father Alexander Davies, who had been the partner of Hugh Awdely.

One of the great characters of the seventeenth century Hugh Awdely or Audley, whose name is commemorated in Audley Street, was, like other merchant bankers since, a lawyer by training, who amassed a large fortune by dealings always hard and occasionally sharp, and by a life of frugality. In 1605 he was worth £200; on his death in 1662 he left £400,000, an enormous sum for that time. He was always ready to advance money to needy young gallants – on the security, of course, of their lands and expectations, security which he was ruthless in exercising. He was regular in his attendance at church, and always appeared, when clients were expected, to be reading a devotional book. *The Dictionary of National Biography* records, 'The expensive habits of the clergy caused him some anxiety, and he would often sigh for the simplicity of living that prevailed in the days of his youth . . . he was, indeed, a most heartless bloodsucker.'

On his death, which was commemorated by the publication of a book, *The Way to be Rich According to the Practice of the Great Audley*, his immense fortune was divided, the portion which Alexander Davies received being but a fraction of the whole. Alexander died in 1665, the year in which Mary was born. His grave is the only one remaining in St Margaret's Churchyard, Westminster – saved, I understand, by Bend'Or at the time when the churchyard was being cleared of gravestones as I understood to make St Margaret's more attractive for its fashionable weddings. The wording on the gravestone is:

> Here lyeth interred the Body of Alexander Davis of Ebury in the County of Middlesex Esquire who dyed July 2nd Anno Domini 1665 – aged 30.

It has often been, quite incorrectly, assumed that the wealth of the Grosvenors stems from this marriage to an heiress. In fact at the time not only were the Grosvenors one of the most solidly established of the families of landed gentry, but in terms of personal wealth they were equal to a number of the most elevated aristocracy. Mary had previously been engaged – the transaction was entirely commercial – to the young Charles Berkley, son and heir of Lord Berkley of

Stratton. The contract was that Lord Berkley would advance £5,000 in cash and settle £3,000 in land. He did this in part but was unable to complete the transaction satisfactorily. Thomas Grosvenor, or his advisers, stepped into the breach, and not only met all the conditions but paid to Lord Berkley the interest accumulated on his down payment, so securing the bride.

The major part of Mary Davies's assets was the estate of Ebury on the fringes of what was then the built-up area of London. It adjoined the Millbank home of the Grosvenors and extended between Tyburn (Marble Arch) and the Thames. Awdely had bought the estate in 1626 for £9,400. The land certainly was a substantial asset, and the sum advanced by the bridegroom was calculated in relation to it, but its true importance became clear only as London expanded. This took place quickly, but even Bend'Or's grandfather, the first Duke, could remember shooting snipe in what is now Belgrave Square.

The marriage of Thomas and Mary Davies did more than augment the Grosvenors' already not inconsiderable fortunes: it brought them firmly into London society. Whereas for six centuries they had been a county family, serving only from time to time in a wider sphere, they were now drawn by their possession of an increasingly valuable estate in the capital into the main stream of national life. They accepted this with some reluctance.

Thomas was MP for Chester during the reigns of Charles II, James II and William and Mary. He was offered a peerage by James II in return for his support in repealing the penal laws against Catholics, which bribe he refused. His son Richard was Grand Cupbearer at the coronation of George II, and his grandson, another Richard, fulfilled the same office for George III, so initiating a tradition of family participation in coronations for which Bend'Or was to show a lively appreciation.

This Richard, the seventh Baronet, was raised to the peerage as Baron Grosvenor of Eaton in 1761 and Earl Grosvenor in 1784. His life in London society was not happy; his wife Henrietta was a flibbertigibbet 'whom a good person, moderate beauty, no understanding and excessive vanity had rendered too accessible'. The Duke of Cumberland found her easily accessible, and Grosvenor successfully sued him for £10,000 in recompense. Richard was happiest in Cheshire, where he led a civil and generous existence, doing quite a deal of good. The first Earl's generosity and open-handedness was not without its effects. By 1779 his debts amounted to over £150,000 and were speedily increasing to the extent that his London agent pressed him to sell off all his London property apart from the Mayfair Hundred Acres. Fortunately this short-sighted advice was not taken, but his affairs were placed in the hands of trustees, including two of the Drummond banking family, who promptly set about putting things right. All the estates were mortgaged to them, and Lord Grosvenor was allowed £4,000 a year to live on; he also agreed to give up his racing system by selling and disposing of his horses as soon as the next meeting should be over, which engagement he did not in fact fulfil. As a result, on his death in 1802 the debt was still over £108,000.

The new Earl, Robert, later to become the first Marquis, was a very different man, who determined to salvage the family fortunes, which he did vigorously and speedily. In six years he had discharged the debt, spent £30,000 on extending the Cheshire estates, started rebuilding Eaton Hall, and bought the remarkable Agar Ellis collection of pictures for 30,000 guineas – which included the splendid *Adoration of the Magi* by Rubens, now in King's College Chapel, Cambridge. He also rebuilt Gloucester House in Upper Grosvenor Street, as Grosvenor House, leaving the original Grosvenor home on Millbank. By the time Robert died his income from the Mayfair estate rents alone was over £60,000; there were in addition the premiums paid on renewals of leases and the rents from the Belgravia, Pimlico and Cheshire estates.

Earl Robert was a considerable figure in politics. He had from 1788 been a supporter of Pitt's in the House of Commons but changed his allegiance to the Whig cause on Pitt's death, and was on the Liberal side in all the controversies of the day – Catholic Emancipation, the Reform Bill and the Repeal of the Corn Laws – for which services he was raised in the peerage as a marquess by Lord Grey in 1831.

His son Richard, second Marquess, at first continued his father's political activities, but spent most of his time on looking after his estates, which were, under his father's will, entailed. The restrictions were not onerous. By 1869, when he died, the Mayfair rents alone were £80,000 a year and he had been able to buy, out of his income alone, some £200,000 worth of further land. Richard was also quite surprisingly mean. The richest man in England wrote to his son and heir, Hugh Lupus: 'Your habits are expensive and you live in expensive society. I believe that every-day-clean-shirt system at Eton did your temperament much harm and to have unfitted you for assistance when there is a question of expense.' If this is an indication of the Marquess's personal standards of hygiene he must have been just as unpleasant as some of his contemporaries portrayed him: 'He lived for the pleasure of getting money which he had not the heart to enjoy.'

Hugh Lupus was in fact anything but a spendthrift, although his first wife made up for this. He was perhaps more than any other man an archetype of the Victorian virtues. He was sympathetic, generous with a rigorous sense of responsibility and duty to his country, his family, tenants and servants, and his party; and probably in that admirable order. He was personally attractive, handsome, active, with a lively sense of humour. In all these things his grandson, Bend'Or, closely resembled him, but, quite unlike Bend'Or, Hugh was a serious politician.

He adhered to the family tradition of Liberalism and not only to the aristocratic tradition of the Whigs, but to the newer more radical Liberalism of Gladstone, who was loathed by so many of the Victorian aristocracy and magnates. It was Gladstone who promoted Hugh Lupus to the highest rank of the peerage as Duke of Westminster in 1874. Although he was very rich, mere wealth would never have obtained this elevation, especially from the hands of Gladstone, and it seems that Hugh Lupus's promotion was for the good reason that he had the same reputation for probity, energy and wisdom in civil affairs as the only other similar nineteenth-century duke, Wellington, had in military life.

Since Bend'Or lost his father as an infant it was his grandfather who represented authority and an older generation; if children may be expected to react against their parents it was Hugh Lupus who would fill the role of parent. He was a difficult man to react against.

Hugh Lupus had succceeded his father in 1869. He was then, thanks to his forbears' prudence and good fortune and in particular to his father's strictness, the richest landowner, and probably the richest man, in England. There were landowners with more acres, but none with a greater income from land. It is probable that this never fell below £60,000, and often exceeded £100,000 in any year.

It is difficult to estimate wealth in the nineteenth century in contemporary terms. Many things were much cheaper. A 'skilled artisan' might earn £2 a week when today he would earn £200, but merely applying a multiplier is deceptive. However the assessment may be made, wealth of such magnitude carried formidable responsibility. Hugh Lupus fulfilled this with dedication. In public life he did not hesitate, although a convinced Liberal, to dissent from his party when he believed them to be wrong. When Gladstone brought in his fudged and untidy Reform Bill in 1866, Hugh stuck his heels in, not against the principle of reform, but in defence of the principle of agreed bi-partisan reform, insisting that expansion of the franchise must go hand in hand with the progressive elimination of the remaining rotten boroughs. His opposition was the main cause, according to Gladstone, of the defeat of the bill and the fall of the Liberal government, but when the succeeding Disraeli government brought in their own Reform Bill, which was considerably more liberal than Gladstone's, Grosvenor gave it his full support.

In contemporary terms it seems unbelievable that having toppled Gladstone's government, the Duke and Gladstone should remain friends, which they clearly did. Hugh continued to support the party until he disagreed, as did many others, with Gladstone's Irish Policy. In spite of this quarrel Hugh Lupus continued on the best of personal terms with Gladstone, who in 1892 was godfather to Hugh's eldest son by his second marriage. Their last joint campaign was one of support of Russia against the Turks, who had just perpetrated one of their periodic massacres of the Armenians. Gladstone's last publication was in the form of a letter to Hugh on this question, to which the Duke replied 'who is there in their heart of hearts in England who cannot but agree with you in the sentiments expressed?'

As well as a national political figure, the first Duke was also a major philanthropist, not only giving a great deal of money, but a good deal of his time and talent. He was president of five London hospitals, treasurer of another, chairman of the Queen's Jubilee Nurses Fund, which initiated the provision of district nursing, and was a pioneer in the protection of shop workers. An unexpected enthusiasm for so great a landlord was his support as chairman of the Hampstead Heath Protection Society, an offshoot of the Commons Protection Society founded by Thomas Hughes, the Christian Socialist MP and friend of the Duke's, who was also a neighbour at Uffington House in Chester.

The broadness of the first Duke's sympathies is also shown by his successful pressure, in the face of Lord's Day Observance fanatics, to have museums and art galleries opened on Sundays. His own action, in opening Eaton Park freely, and in keeping it open in spite of occasional abuses, was prompted by the same feeling of obligation to ensure that national and personal treasures should be available to working people on the only day that they could take advantage of them. As a landlord the Duke was a model. He personally supervised the planning and rebuilding of the farms, cottages and estate buildings at Eaton – forty-eight farmhouses, three hundred and sixty cottages, eleven lodges, eight schools and seven village halls, all in an attractive rural-romantic style, were built or rebuilt in his time. This was no less than any Grosvenor would have thought necessary, but was not invariably the practice of even the richest landlords: the Rowntree Trust investigating rural conditions in the 1890s found that a high proportion of labourers on the Duke of Bedford's estates were living in dismal and insanitary slums. The Duke also encouraged scientific farming, giving grants for fertilizers, pioneering the use of silage and reducing rents when times were bad.

Bend'Or was clear in his own mind that Hugh was a model duke, and a model man, and that his own ambition must be to emulate him. His admiration for his grandfather was informed by a warm affection. The first Duke has sometimes been represented as a dry and unsympathetic character but Bend'Or did not find him so. His letters to 'Dearest Dads' are full of trust and affection. Hugh was certainly a disciplined man: never idle or superficial; a keen racing man, winning the Derby four times, without ever betting himself. Bend'Or never achieved the same self-discipline, but increasingly came to share the same qualities of obligation and compassion that his admired grandfather had. He also added some personal virtues of dash and humour that were very much his own.

In one aspect Hugh was a typical Victorian patriarch. He had fifteen children, eleven by his first wife. Bend'Or's father, Victor, was the third child, and eldest son, born in 1853. His birth, as heir to a marquisate and great fortune, was suitably marked by a christening in Buckingham Palace, with the Queen as godmother. He was 'a very fine child, and screamed dreadfully', but developed in early manhood a fatal illness. The Queen wrote to the Duke in June 1881, two years after Bend'Or's birth on 19 March 1879, 'Much and truly grieved is the Queen at the terribly distressing account which the Duke gives of poor Grosvenor.' Before Bend'Or was five his father was dead: a short time for a child to receive impressions of his father and, given his grave ill health, Victor must have been an almost entire stranger to the boy. To his mother, who lived until 1929, Bend'Or was always very close and when she married again in 1887 Bend'Or, at eight, was given another father figure, of a different generation and nature to Hugh, but who also exercised an important influence on him.

Bend'Or's mother was born Lady Sibell Lumley, youngest daughter of the Earl of Scarborough, and married Victor when she was only nineteen and the bridegroom just twenty-one. She became a great favourite of her father-in-law as she did of everyone she came close to. It was hardly to be expected that she would remain a widow for long.

Lady Sibell Grosvenor, as she became on her first marriage, fascinated her generation. Lord Hartington said: 'Of her beauty of person and character, of her grace and sweetness it would be impertinent to speak here.' 'Lady Grosvenor was by far the most dangerous siren in London and . . . he would not answer for any man keeping his head or his heart when with her.' Her brother, Osric Lumley, once calculated that, after Grosvenor's early death, there were over eighty people in love with her, including the curates, for she was of a religious disposition. One of the eighty was George Curzon, then a young Fellow of All Souls: 'I can't see you Sibell, though my whole soul is straining after you. What am I to do, Sibell? . . . Angel, love me in a letter do . . . God bless you my own darling.' This is an aspect of that George Nathaniel Curzon, that 'most superior person', which reveals a sympathetic human weakness: anyone who could make that grand figure call them 'Duck', as he did in another letter, must have had quite extraordinary qualities.

Her fascination was by no means limited to the opposite sex. Mary Gladstone said of her: 'She is a sweet little soul and the keynote is unselfishness.' 'We have seen many ladies,' said a cottager on the Island of Achill, 'but you are the first that has been kind to us.'

It was not Curzon with whom she fell in love after her husband's death, but George Wyndham. Wyndham was eight years her junior: he was twenty-four when they married, she thirty-two. Wyndham was therefore only sixteen years older than Bend'Or, and the relationship became, largely because of Wyndham's sensitivity, that of a younger and elder brother, in contrast to the more formal connection between Bend'Or and his grandfather. Wyndham's influence on Bend'Or may be assessed in the letters Bend'Or wrote to him, and in Bend'Or's constant reading, in later life, of Wyndham's collected works, a volume which he often pressed on his guests as bedside reading. But it also seems likely that Bend'Or had an important influence on Wyndham, which will be discussed later in this book.

The Wyndhams were a family as old as the Grosvenors and at one time nearly as rich. George's great-grandfather had been third Earl of Egremont and owned great agricultural estates in Sussex and the West Country as well as rich coal mines in Cumberland. On his death a division was made between his illegitimate son, who received Petworth in Sussex, and became Lord Leconfield, and a nephew. George's father, Percy, was a younger son of Lord Leconfield, and therefore, although affluent enough, of modest means by Grosvenor standards.

Young George followed his father into the Guards and saw service in the 1885 punitive expedition to the Sudan. He was a good regimental officer, but found the untaxing and superficial life of a Guards officer in peacetime boring. He gambled and fell into debt, a usual form of alleviating tedium, but more unusually, at least for a guardsman, took to reading romantic verse and fell in love with Lady Sibell. George Wyndham was often described as the handsomest man of his time, and had in addition a chivalrous and romantic streak that matched that of Sibell.

They married, and settled down in Saighton Grange, a lovely house of medieval origin near Eaton called the Dower House, and the children were brought up there. George became stepfather to Bend'Or and his two elder sisters, Lettice and Constance, always known as 'Cuckoo'. They were rapidly joined by a half-brother, Percy or 'Perf', and formed a household that was cultivated and affectionate, where dogs and horses were part of a life that also included George's translations of Ronsard and Scawen Blunt's highly unconventional opinions. A flavour of their family life may be conveyed by George's description of his birthday in 1887.

> We had a most festive day. It began before 7 in the morning when we were woken by the most hideous figure I ever saw, Bend'Or strapped into a perambulator in white petticoats with his face blacked with coal (it had taken from 5.30 to complete that difficult process). In the morning we had athletic sports, high jump, long jump, then swinging till luncheon. In the afternoon

> cricket. Lettice and I against Bend'Or, Cuckoo, Maudie Grosvenor and two of the coachman's children . . . after dinner we let off all the fireworks in Chester . . . After the fireworks all the children went to swing again till half-past ten o'clock.

If Sibell Grosvenor possessed charm in superabundance it was at least equalled by that of George Wyndham. He was extraordinarily good-looking in a romantic Byronic fashion. Like Byron he was a poet and a soldier, although much less distinguished as the one and considerably more effective as the other.

Wyndham was more complex than the essentially simple and candid Sibell. Although a lifelong Tory he was a great admirer of William Morris, the founding father of the peculiarly English socialism that goes with walking tours and real ale, rural crafts and madrigals. Towards the end of his life his closest friend was Hilaire Belloc, then a radical MP at a time when George was an ardent imperialist, who nevertheless shared to the full George's romantic and active enthusiasms.

A greater, since enduring from his birth, influence was that of his cousin Wilfred Scawen Blunt, a most unsuitable relative for a conventional Conservative politician, but much loved and admired. Blunt was a strong anti-imperialist, famous for his defence of Arabi Pasha, the Egyptian nationalist imprisoned by the British Government. Blunt was even imprisoned himself in 1887 when he organized an illegal meeting in Ireland in support of Home Rule. Since George was at that time private secretary to Arthur Balfour, Chief Secretary for Ireland, this was extremely embarrassing.

Cousinly oddities did not prevent George from being on the closest terms with Blunt and attending his famous all-male house parties with George Curzon, Lord Alfred Douglas and Oscar Wilde. 'There is a great deal of the schoolboy in all Englishmen, that is what makes them so lovable. When they came out [of the lake] they . . . began playing lawn tennis, just as they were, stark naked, the future rulers of England. I shall never forget the scene' (Wilde quoted in Frank Harris's *Oscar Wilde*). The tone of the parties was, however, decidedly literary, duels of wit were the order of the day: in the artificial society of *fin-de-siècle* England, Blunt and his friends were a healthy and stimulating influence.

Sir Shane Leslie saw Wyndham from a sympathetic Irish viewpoint: 'like an eighteenth-century statesman at his best. Romantic scholar, fearless rider with the blood of Lord Edward Fitzgerald in his veins . . . the last romantic figure in the House of Commons, I cherish every glimpse of memory of him.' He recalled life at Saighton: 'the highest ritual of the High Church brightened the chapel. George Wyndham kneeling in his riding clothes while the visiting priest prayed and Lady Grosvenor swung the censer was like a scene out of the *Idylls of the King*.'

To modern ears this sounds a little exaggerated, and some of Sibell's friends may have thought her silly. She was certainly unworldly, if that should be still accounted folly, but in her relations with Bend'Or she proved herself an eminently practical and sympathetic mother. She also kept all his letters, which allow the opportunity of seeing Bend'Or grow up, month by month, from infancy to his marriage. They show him consistently frank, open, affectionate, anxious to please, anxious to do his duty – a model schoolboy save in the matter of academic advancement.

They also indicate the natural and commonplace fashion in which some late Victorians treated their children. The Wyndhams were perhaps an advanced family, convinced of the benefits of open air and exercise, Dr Jaeger's underwear and easy communication. There was nothing of the stiffness often associated with Victorian families. Bend'Or called his mother 'Darling', his stepfather 'George', and even the magnificent first Duke, his grandfather, was addressed to the end of his life as 'Daddy' or 'Dads'. There is nowhere any suggestion that Bend'Or, as Viscount Belgrave, had been since he was five heir to the greatest fortune in the country and a dukedom. His privileges – a modest allowance, ponies, space to develop – were those of any reasonably prosperous family. One of his earliest letters does show something of the difference in background: children's drawings of houses generally show a smoking chimney, a door and four windows. Bend'Or's effort is on a more ducal scale, influenced by the splendours of Eaton.

At first his correspondence stood in need of stimulation. When he went to school Sibell wrote enclosing a list of questions he had to answer: Are you quite well? – Yes. Does your new suit fit? – Very well. Do you want any money? – I would like about 10/- more. Are you higher in your class than last term? – Yes, yes. Nails!! – Better much. Which lesson goes best? – I don't know. Is happy? – Yes, very.

This last answer was something of an inaccuracy. Bend'Or was packed off to prep school in 1889, aged ten; this custom, although quite common among the English, still tends to surprise foreigners. At that time Bend'Or was already heir not only to the dukedom, and the seat in the House of Lords, but also to Eaton, Cliveden, Grosvenor House, the London estate and tens of thousands of English acres. In Germany or France he would have had private tutors and led a sheltered life in an exclusively aristocratic society; in England he lived cheek by jowl with clergymen's sons, squires' sons, respectable grocers' sons and so on.

The school chosen, St David's at Reigate, was well regarded. Sixty boys were governed, very strictly, by a clergyman, the Reverend W.H. Churchill. One of Bend'Or's contemporaries there was Edward Halifax, later Lord Halifax, whose biographer, Lord Birkenhead, describes the atmosphere: 'Work, play and discipline were the order of the day . . .' St David's had the sinister reputation of turning out 'good specimens in brain and brawn with a high sense of duty . . .' The headmaster was a firm believer in the moral and educational value of flogging . . . 'for such faults as having a boot lace undone, or not eating a piece of dry bread provided before early school'.

Naturally enough, Bend'Or was extremely unhappy. The contrast with the easy and affectionate home life of Saighton could hardly have been starker. His unhappiness continued through the three years he spent there. In his last year, 1892 (31 January), he wrote:

> Darling Mother,
>
> I am going to tell you all my little sorrows which I have felt for a long time. I always feel so dull and miserable here and miss you so awfully, and for example if my watch stopped it would make me miserable and wretched for the whole day. The boys all seem to be so full of fun. I long to be but I can't I always feel so miserable. I am not going to eat Casie's sweets because I am afraid of losing one they are so precious as they come from her . . .
>
> P.S. This has not only been this term but all the terms.

It was not that he was an unpopular boy. Churchill wrote to Lady Sibell on 6 December 1891: 'He is very well and growing big and strong and does not suffer from lack of character. The servants often call him Master Belgrave – which is delightful! He is working hard but you know that he is far from clever, yet we shall manage Eton.'

He certainly had a less than brilliant academic career. In 1890 he was the oldest boy in his form, the 3rd, while younger boys were already in the 5th. Yet it is difficult not to feel that a sensitive affectionate and friendly boy capable of great enthusiasm would have done much better in a less restrictive and more stimulating environment, and it is interesting to remark the close parallel with young Winston Churchill, who suffered quite as much at his school in Brighton without a loving and concerned family to support him. The not-so-distant prospect of Eton encouraged him, and 1892 found him feeling livelier. 'Can he have some foreign stamps from Daddy's waste paper basket . . . Tennyson the poet has written something for St David's and his grandson is coming here soon. Can he have an air gun of his own, most of the other boys do, and go to a play?'

Eton, where he went in the autumn in 1892, was much better. Lord Birkenhead describes it as living in the past, the world outside having come to an uneasy pause.

> Little change too had taken place in the school by 1894. There were still the old rabbit warrens of the boarding houses, the black walls of their twisting passages carved with the names of generations of Eton boys . . . the boys were given as much beer as they wanted, with the choice of a glass of port or sherry on Sunday, solemnly handed round to all boys, large or small, by the fat old butler.

After the narrow confines of prep school the tolerant and lively society of Eton must have seemed a brave new world. Bend'Or gave some lively accounts of school life: 'I was looking at a match today and saw Nigel Lindsey streched [*sic*] out on the ground covered with coats and he was there all the afternoon . . . I don't know whether he was badly hurt or not.'

His tutor described his 'ingenuous frankness', a characteristic he never lost. He was dutiful in satisfying maternal worries. 'I have had my waiscoat lined with flannel so I shall keep quite warm, I have not begun thick jagers yet. Please do not give Mr Spot too many biscuits at dinner.' Spot's affairs and health were the subject of an entire letter – 'bring him to see a good vet in London, or if you are staying in Cheshire let him see Mr Henry Dobie, who understands animals'. An older dog, Jib, died, and Bend'Or wrote:

> Darling,
> It is really too sad to think that I won't ever see dear old Jib again, he was such a dear. I will miss him awfully. Please have him

buried somewhere nice. And please mind that Spot is taken the greatest care of, as he will be doubly precious. I did love the dear old dog so very much. Will you thank George for taking such care of him. And it was so dear of you all to look after him as you did . . .

Bless you darling,

Your ever loving Tommy [Bend'Or was calling himself this at the time],

Best love to Lettice and Cuckoo.

P.S. I am up to a man called Benson. Please write and tell me all about the dear old dog's death.

He was also worried about his tutor's health. At Eton, where boys live in a domestic setting, on close everyday terms with their tutors, this is perhaps less unusual than may be thought. Bend'Or himself was often ill, and missed a good deal of school, with recurrent chest infections, which may have brought the reality of illness home to him.

Apart from this and the desire to reassure his mother, his concerns were those of any schoolboy. 'Has Perf got his bicycle yet? Can he switch from Greek to German? What terrible news about the loss of the Victoria'; he is getting his House Colours, rowing in a four, doing well at fencing. He had some modest requests – a fixed allowance please, 'I should be very glad if a pheasant or two found their way down here' (they did), could they get him tickets for *The Geisha* – and responded in a brotherly fashion to demands made on him: 'Please tell Cuckoo I am nearly sure her button hook was not packed up and sent here as I have had my room searched . . . will you ask John to look inside my riding boots as it may have fallen into one of them, as I used it to help pull them on . . .' but he did discover a nail cleaner.

As he went up the school his interests became more serious. Perhaps inspired by a visit from Scawen Blunt he decided to take part in a debate on the wickedness of the Turkish Sultan. Before the debate he was worried that Abdul the Damned might be assassinated and all his work wasted, but the Sultan survived and Bend'Or was able to say that 'the Sultan ought to be deposed . . . with the aid of the other powers and to turn Turkey into a republic. However the majority had it that he ought not to be deposed, so we had to let him stay on.'

He did well in German, but was less happy with the classics. One letter has him anxiously asking for the fourth volume of *Tom Jones*, since he must find out what happens, a predicament that would win him sympathy from addicts of the novel but hardly argues a single-minded application to the syllabus.

While at Eton Bend'Or enjoyed playing football, and in the holidays played for Saighton Village until his grandfather discovered that he had been involved in a fight while playing against Aldford, the next estate village. The Duke felt that such occurrences would hardly benefit landlord–tenant relationships. Bend'Or was happy enough to desist, since he yearned for tougher opponents, and petitioned for a transfer to Waverton, who played against such good sides as Tattenhall and Malpas.

He also showed some sign of commercial acumen by persuading the very attractive keeper of the school tuckshop to extend him credit, since the Duke kept him on a tight financial rein; this lady subsequently married the regimental sergeant major of the Blues, regarded at that time as the smartest soldier in the army. RSM Potter later transferred to the Cheshire Yeomanry, so Bend'Or's benefactor, whom he installed comfortably in Aldford Lodge, reaped the rewards of her generosity to the hungry young Viscount as Bend'Or had engineered the transfer of RSM Potter from the Blues to the Yeomanry.

His school copybook was blotted by one serious crime – he cut off to Ascot and had another boy answer his name at roll call. For this offence Bend'Or was flogged: a less physically distressing punishment than it sounds, but it had a dramatic effect on the open and ingenuous boy. He wrote immediately to his mother:

> Darling dearest Mother,
>
> I am too miserable about this . . . I never dreamt I should have to tell so many untruths . . . Darling I don't want to and I don't mean to grow into a man like [obliterated] please don't think I will, I feel sure I won't. I am so sorry to have distressed you so darling and I hope this letter will comfort you a little.
>
> Your ever loving son, Bend'Or who loves you so much.

The grown-ups took the matter seriously, although they did not reproach Bend'Or but rallied round him in his unhappiness. He wrote to his grandfather a letter which is a good illustration of his character, and of the affectionate family relationships:

> Darling Dads,
>
> I am too distressed about this affair . . . I knew I would not have done such a foolish act if I had thought twice about it, but however it is done now and cannot be undone . . . It was kind of

you to write such a dear letter to me full of kindness . . . I could not I am sure have had a greater lesson, or greater proof of the love of all my friends which they bear to me. It makes me quite miserable to think of it. God grant that I may grow up half as noble, honourable and unselfish as you, and then I should be quite happy.

Goodbye Darling Dads,
Your ever loving grandson, Bend'Or

The old Duke, having seen Bend'Or's letter, wrote to Sibell: 'This is a very nice letter and I believe from what I hear that he *is* very unhappy about the affair. Yours affectionately, Westminster.'

In spite of this setback he did well enough to be entered for Cambridge, an idea he welcomed. 'Cambridge is a splendid place and will be all right if Daddy will agree to it.' Some polishing was however thought necessary and in September 1897 he was sent to a tutor at Hensingham House near Woodstock. He enjoyed the greater liberty afforded:

> This seems a jolly place . . . you would laugh at the people here – when I first arrived I met a cat as big as an ordinary Bengal tiger and then with a series of trips over woollen mats, etc. I arrived in the dimly lit drawing room where I met two elderly women I think they must be sisters by the way they fight and contradict one another . . . There are two other fellows here, one an old Etonian called Cox an awful good fellow . . . and a solemn looking youth who has not yet talked, who goes about in a long black coat and a top hat as black as his hands and face.

He found the work 'very easy', and had time to follow the local drag hunt, and for such diversions as a tennis party 'to which all the pimply-faced parson's daughters of the locality were asked. I have not proposed to any of them yet.'

During his stay at Woodstock it seems that he changed from the Cambridge examinations to the army examination, which took, in those unregenerate times, rather more work. He was successful and, either as a reward or as a further stage in his education, was sent to learn French. George chose a most beautiful setting for this, the Château of Azay le Rideau on the Loire. On 5 July 1898 he wrote to Sibell, 'This is indeed a glorious place . . . it is really like the sort of place you dream of, and occasionally read about, but never expect to see.'

The establishment was a sort of superior guest house, kept by one

Count de Mauny, with French and English visitors. Bend'Or took to France and the French, made the acquaintance of the local general and officers in the camp 'so I have great fun there. I hack over in the evenings when the band plays and have tea there.' 'Went to Mass on Sunday as it is less monotonous than the prayers in the house.' He approved of the countryside and the people: 'I get on very well with the people I have met down here, and they interest me very much, I think the French who are really what one calls good sorts differ very little from the English, and the sooner one gets the idea out of one's head that they only eat frogs, snails and garlic &c the better.'

Some of the English guests took his fancy rather less. 'I have come to the conclusion that Scott is an ass and quite in the wrong box here, he would be all right if placed on an empty cask and addressing the tow-rows in Hyde Park on socialism, but his views are too absurd about everything in life, that he bores me.' But Bend'Or was rarely ungenerous even about those he didn't take to: 'I am sorry for him at the same time, because I don't think he has had the best of times before this and it makes him a bit cynicle (I can't spell it)!' He did not much take to some more aristocratic guests: 'Lady Francis Cecil is staying here for a day or two, her two boys are with her and seem to be terrified of her.' He had amusing gossipy snippets about many other guests.

> The old grandmama here is still alive, and in a horrible fear of being assassinated as an unfortunate curé and his wife were battered into a jelly near here by burglars, so she is in a terrible state and sleeps with the electric light full on . . . there is a Miss Ethel Cadogan staying here who does nothing but talk and jump about although she is well over 50 . . .

What was clearly an idyllic summer, with fine weather, pleasant rides and progress in the language, came to a dramatic end. There had been some signs of apprehension: 'Lord Normanby comes out for a bit soon, I feel I shall not take to him, but perhaps that won't matter,' followed in the next letter by 'What I wrote in my last letter and all that about Ld Normanby was ridiculous, so don't think of it darling, it was only because your son at that time was a bit worried about something.' The something was probably the situation that came to a head in October.

Bend'Or wrote a serious letter to George on the fifteenth in which he said that he had been told on good authority that de Mauny was a homosexual, which at the time was a matter of grave concern. Any scandal could have the most serious effects on the family and mark Bend'Or for life. He was deeply worried and perplexed.

> By personal observation I have had a suspicion of it for a month or two back, and now there is no more doubt whatever especially when he has such old busters as Ward Cook whom you probably know, staying here, it isn't good enough if a man like that goes back to town, and says he has met so and so there &c . . . it rather gives you away . . . I am probably going to have the whole thing out with de Mauney [*sic*] tonight – I haven't written to Dads about anything yet, as I thought it best to let you know first of all.

This was decisive action from a boy of nineteen: he made it clear that it was George's career that was the prime concern. In the same letter he refers to George's possible appointment as Under Secretary at the Foreign Office, and also says '. . . with such a man, Good God if any row happened to take place where should we all be here?' The interview was unsatisfactory, and two days later Bend'Or wrote again from the Hotel de l'Univers at Tours:

> I have had this interview with de Mauney, with the result that, of all we suspected him is true, he has owned up that it is so . . . In consequence of this three of us have left at once. Hudson [his secretary in Scott's place], Peto, and myself. I am here now, and shall be here until I get a wire from you, either to recall me home, or in fact anything you should deem right to wire me . . .
>
> P.S. I am sorry about the FO but at the same time I feel that there is really something in the end that will be much better or at least lead to a bigger thing – must be in fact.

The episode left Bend'Or with an abiding dislike of homosexuals. He had previously had a high opinion of de Mauny, 'De M. is a capital sort and is the only person who has really ever understood me at all, and we get on well' (15 July 1889), and felt betrayed that such an attachment could have had ulterior motives.

To some extent he made up for the strain of the last days at Azay by spending a short holiday in Silesia at the magnificent Castle Pless, the home of Prince Hans and Princess Daisy of Pless, who had previously been the handsome Miss Cornwallis West, a country neighbour of the Grosvenors, with whose even more beautiful younger sister, Shelagh, Bend'Or was very much in love.

2

South Africa

It is not clear when Bend'Or's immediate future was settled, but it was not to be Cambridge. To understand the reason it is necessary to see what had been happening to George Wyndham since his marriage.

George had been rescued from a military career which had become unsympathetic by Arthur Balfour, who interrupted the honeymoon by an invitation to George to become Balfour's private secretary. Balfour was at that time Chief Secretary for Ireland: the British minister responsible for Irish affairs. This proved an excellent introduction to political life, marred only by the exasperating incident when cousin Wilfred contrived to get himself sent to prison. A by-election gave him the chance to enter Parliament as Conservative member for Dover in 1889, but his political career was slow to develop. He did not immediately gain office, and after the election of 1892 found himself as a member of the opposition to Gladstone's last government and spent much of his time on writing, specializing in the French poets of the fifteenth and sixteenth centuries, between Charles d'Orleans and the Pleiade.

He had much in common with both the soldier-poet Charles and the flamboyant Villon, and his romantic nature was stimulated by the Jameson Raid of 1896. This led him to visit South Africa to see for himself and he was captivated by the beauty of the country, as is every visitor. More importantly for the future, he was taken with the imperial aspirations of Cecil Rhodes, as were many others.

When the Conservative government was again returned in 1895 Wyndham hoped for a post but it seemed that some of his colleagues distrusted him as a poet and intellectual. His talents, however, were too clear to be overlooked and in 1898 he was appointed Under

Secretary of State for War, which, since the Secretary of State, Lord Lansdowne, was in the House of Lords, made Wyndham the government spokesman in the Commons, at a time when great things were stirring.

It was clear by then that South Africa would be a focus of intense interest. The diamond and gold finds offered prospects of tremendous wealth. Many wars had been fought with the Boers, Zulus and Matabeles, and more trouble was brewing. The UK High Commissioner there was Sir Alfred Milner, widely admired, the 'great pro-consul', who was gathering about him his 'nursery' of brilliant young men who included John Buchan and Leo Amery and all of whom were to be a significant influence on future politics. George saw this as a brilliant opportunity for Bend'Or. He was to pass his army examinations, take a commission and join Milner as ADC.

There was no time for anything but a crash course on the elements of military skills, and Bend'Or was sent in November 1898 to the King's Hussars at Shorncliffe for a brief period of instruction, which would have covered primarily such topics as musketry and map reading. He was made to work hard: 'I am quite a soldier by now, and enjoy the life thoroughly – up at six this morning and feel as fit as a fiddle. Such a good lot of fellows here.' He took to army life so well that by the end of November the Colonel, a 'delightful man', had said that he had learnt all that was needful. Nevertheless he found time to ride in a point to point and to visit the 'palace' – presumably a bioscope – in company with Lord Suffolk and Gerry Ward, since he saw 'George receiving the Sirdar at Dover'.

After the course and with Christmas celebrated, he sailed in January 1899 for South Africa. His more academic tuition had been equally successful since he passed the examinations and was duly commissioned. Not yet twenty, and full of enthusiasm, Bend'Or disembarked in February, a short time after the return of his new chief, Milner, from an interlude of conversations on policy with London. The policy that had been agreed during this visit was to turn the screw on Kruger to bring matters to a head – and to a head matters were brought.

Trouble had been brewing since Cecil Rhodes, four years previously, had launched the 'idiotic' and unscrupulous Jameson Raid on Johannesburg, an episode discreditable enough in itself but even more discreditable in the shuffling and lying that was resorted to in order to extricate the Salisbury government from its aftermath. This time

Rhodes was banished temporarily from South Africa, Milner was in charge, and there was to be no mistake. Rhodes sought some consolation with the Westminster family and in his thank-you letter to the Duchess wrote, 'I hope matters will be settled one way or the other when I reach Africa as they are sure otherwise to credit me with instigating some evil design. It is unfortunate when you are credited with being the cause of all evil.'

The prize was high – £700 million or so in gold and more in the great areas of the Transvaal and Orange Free State. Disliking everything about the British Empire, and obstinate in their own traditions of bigotry and independence, many Boers had migrated to the North from the Cape out of the sphere of British influence, and, expelling the natives with Afrikaner ruthlessness, had founded their own states – the South African Republic, the Transvaal and the Orange Free State. These had already had to defend their independence once in the first Boer war which had culminated in a British defeat at Majuba and the patched up Conventions of London and Pretoria, agreements neither side was anxious to keep.

The Boers had reservations about the British claim to hegemony in South Africa; the British were concerned about the Boers' high-handed disregard of the rights of non-Boers, white, brown, yellow or black. Most importantly some of the British had their eyes firmly on the loot. The discovery of immensely productive gold reserves in the 1880s had made the Transvaal the richest state in Africa and an object of considerable interest. In the words of Thomas Pakenham, the writer of the definitive history of the times, 'two multi-millionaires, Cecil Rhodes and Alfred Beit, conspired to take over the Transvaal for themselves and the Empire'. The grounds for their conspiracy lay in the grievances of the 'Uitlanders', those non-Afrikaners who had come to the South African Republic after the discovery of gold. Many, although perhaps not a majority, were British and the others included American, Irish, German and French. The Uitlanders were treated in the usual high-handed Afrikaner fashion. They were intruders, they were not of the 'Volk' or the Church, and they were denied a vote. Had they been given the vote they would have been in a majority, and would have radically changed the character of the Republic, a change which would probably have brought it nearer to the British, and certainly nearer to the nineteenth century. Neither of these appealed to Kruger and the Volk.

The first act of this 'conspiracy' had been the Jameson Raid when six hundred of Rhodes's mercenaries attempted to invade the Transvaal and were forced to surrender, under the white flag of a black servant's apron. The Boers of the Transvaal, who had earlier showed some willingness to accede to British demands, now had their suspicions reinforced and their intransigence redoubled. Their leader, President Kruger, Oom (Uncle) Paul, bigoted, stubborn and cunning, was not likely to attempt to mollify them. The Colonial Secretary, Joseph Chamberlain, knew all about the raid, and had to spend a great deal of effort in tidying up the aftermath. He visited Jameson secretly in prison and persuaded him to keep his mouth shut; Rhodes and Beit agreed to suppress the telegrams that proved Chamberlain's complicity, in return for their own immunities. Chamberlain's efforts 'passed into folklore as the Lying-in-State at Westminster'. After this dangerous and humiliating experience Chamberlain was most reluctant to tamper further with South Africa; the purpose of Milner's visit had been to persuade him otherwise.

Sir Alfred Milner had been sent to South Africa in 1897 as High Commissioner to tidy things up after the Jameson fiasco. Milner was a man of quite extraordinary ability and charm; these combined with a clarity of vision in a most persuasive alchemy. The vision was that of a British Empire, Liberal, and democratic, united economically and loyal to the Crown. It was an ideal that to modern ears sounds trite and old-fashioned, but has proved neither. Milner can claim to be a progenitor of the British Commonwealth, which continues, amid many alarums and excursions, to be a positive force for decency and goodwill: it is a sad irony that South Africa has withdrawn from it.

When Bend'Or joined the High Commissioner as ADC he was nineteen years old and almost fresh from school; his sympathies had been formed by George Wyndham, who shared most of Milner's views. In later life Bend'Or was to remain constant to the ideal of a civilizing and prosperous Empire. He supported this politically and, more importantly, by the imaginative deployment of some of his great wealth. He proved just as susceptible as everyone else to Milner's charm, as shown in his first letters home:

> I am slipping into the ways of the place well now, and know my way about. Sir Alfred is charming and we are all like a family together. We have got a gymkhana meeting this afternoon on the race course. I am riding one of the Chief's ponies perhaps two –

> H. Williams, Chester Martens and self are thinking of starting a racing establishment for ourselves and are getting three ponies from Basutoland.

His first duties were confined to that social round which has been the task of ADCs since time immemorial. 'We are so busy about a Garden party which has just taken place. It went off very well . . .' 'I want Lettice to send me if she will any old waltzes for the band to play, the *Runaway Girl* lancers and ditto of *The Belle of New York*.' When things occasionally went wrong Bend'Or did not take them too seriously. 'I asked an old Lady, by invitation, to dine the other day, she has been dead 9 years. I sent the husband's letter to S [Shelagh] it was rather amusing . . .'

Social duties became supplemented by more important activities as Bend'Or was drawn into Milner's confidence. The High Commissioner's plan to 'screw Kruger' advanced rapidly. By 7 April his ADC was writing to George Wyndham 'as the staff is small here one gets a lot of information, several interesting things are passing in, and concerning the Transvaal, which one is not able to talk about'. It did not take long either for Bend'Or to start exercising his critical faculties; his experiences in South Africa led him to distrust and dislike generals of all sorts, with the exception always of 'Bobs', Lord Roberts. Although he had only the most basic of military training Bend'Or was able to put his finger on what was to become the crucial point of the war that had not even started in a letter to George Wyndham on 19 April 1899.

> Dear George,
>
> This is a subject which may interest you. Through several chats I have had with both subalterns of my own age &c and Colonials, it appears that the transport system out here is very poor and insufficient. This experiment of South American horses in this country seems a farce entirely . . . if matters come to an extremity out here none of these S. American horses would be the slightest use. Could write a good deal more but I daresay you know all about it. But if not it would be a good plan to institute enquiries.

As things hotted up the new ADC became increasingly involved in the to-ing and fro-ing between Milner and Chamberlain. He wrote to the old Duke on 17 May a strikingly prescient letter:

Dear Dads,

By the time you get this letter I hope you will have won the Derby with Flying Fox. Matters are getting really most interesting here, and now it will I am sure be shortly settled one way or the other with the Transvaal. Personally I think it will end in an interview between Sir Alfred and Paul Kruger at some neutral place; even if this does come off, people out here say that Kruger will still play the same game that he has played so often before in uttering these promises which are never kept and of which everyone out here, besides the Uitlanders themselves, are tired.

Milner's plan to 'screw Kruger' had been threatened by Kruger himself. In spite of his antipathy to the British he was not anxious to press matters to breaking point. He therefore put forward proposals to enfranchise the Uitlanders as full citizens of the Transvaal after a waiting period of fourteen years, an unacceptably long time, but one that was clearly capable of negotiation. Milner was determined to scupper this, and did his best to stimulate opinion in South Africa and Britain, as in his famous despatch to Chamberlain when he referred to 'thousands of British subjects kept permanently in the position of helots . . . calling vainly to Her Majesty's Government for redress'. He was confident that this would ensure that 'never again would people reproach him with discretion'. In these efforts Milner was supported by Wyndham who, as well as acting as Parliamentary Under Secretary at the War Office, controlled the South African lobby; he wrote to Milner just before Bloemfontein: 'The Press are ready and under complete control. I can switch on an agitation at your direction.'

The peacemongers however kept at him, and Milner reluctantly agreed to a conference with Kruger on quasi-neutral territory at Bloemfontein, the capital of the Orange Free State. The talks started on 30 May 1899 and Milner was accompanied by his new ADC, an indication that Bend'Or had already proved himself to be something more than an engaging young man. The main item on the agenda was ostensibly to secure satisfactory representation and rights for the Uitlanders in the Dutch republics, but it became clear that no compromise would be acceptable to Sir Alfred. Bend'Or wrote to his grandfather from the conference.

Dear Dads,

I must just drop you a line from here as it may interest you to

> hear from the seat of operations whither these late troubles throughout S. Africa and chiefly concerning the SAR have been brought to a head – I have been fortunate enough in being admitted into the conference itself; it is most interesting, I am in fact writing you this from the conference itself – an interpreter sits at the head of the table and on his left Pres. Kruger and on his right, HE &c. &c. I am not in a position to tell you how it is all progressing, but this much I can tell, viz: that S. Alfred is without doubt the very man to see it through in the most satisfactory manner to both parties. It is a difficult position for him, as you will yourself see, on the one side an honest straightforward English Gentleman, and on the other an ignorant, cunning, unscrupulous scoundrel, but I think Oom Paul has really met his match and will have to give in whether to force, or go out quietly and alter the franchise law, and dynamite monopolies &c. it would amuse you to see the way in which he tried to wriggle out of the most important matters . . .

And to his mother:

> Dearest,
>
> This is a line written in haste from the conference itself. Old Kruger is sitting almost opposite, and it is most exciting, this is the 2nd day and I think Paul is getting pretty well tired. He looks very old, blind in one eye and wears green spectacles . . .
>
> Just begun conference again till 4. Really exciting this afternoon. Kruger thumping the table and HE laughing at him, he is delightful over it – I never dreamt I should be able to get to the conference itself, but have got in and mean to stay till I am kicked out – Kruger just going to make a long harangue on franchise, I wish I were able to write you all the details, but I should be jugged if I were to . . .
>
> Kruger is grunting away now, he is wriggling and trying his best to keep from facing the music – slight sketch – of the old man.

An interesting incident of the Bloemfontein Conference was that Bend'Or received a telegram announcing 'Derby victory of Flying Fox', and was congratulated on the 'joyful intelligence by President Kruger'. Allowing for youthful enthusiasm and his attachment to Milner, the perspicacity of Bend'Or's twenty-year-old judgement is striking. George Wyndham certainly took his letters seriously, and read them to his friends and colleagues, who spoke in their praise.

What happened at Bloemfontein was that once again Milner was nearly outmanoeuvred by Kruger who, on the third day of the conference, produced a draft bill for the reform of the Transvaal constitution which would give a good deal of what had been demanded and was certainly a sound base for negotiation – if Kruger could be trusted. There was a strong feeling among the British that he could not, and Milner was not willing to give him the benefit of the doubt. In this intransigence he was consciously moving ahead of Chamberlain, who cabled him at Bloemfontein, 'I hope you do not break off hastily . . . you should be very patient.' Milner was anything but patient and brought the conference to an untimely end, and with it the last serious hopes of avoiding war.

Back in Cape Town, Bend'Or wrote to the Duke urging support for Milner:

> We out here all trust that everyone in England will back up to the letter and thoroughly endorse what our chief out here has proposed to the President of the South African Republic . . . If you don't it is obvious that his position out here would become at once impossible and he would resign. But I can't help thinking that you will back us up and everyone else – I see the Press is practically unanimous about the matter, barring such scurrilous scrawls as the *Daily Chronicle*.

In the same letter he points again to the likely problems of transport: 'Horse sickness . . . is also very prevalent now amongst the mounted infantry horses, this is rather serious as it affects transport and other matters which as you see will form an important factor if war is declared.'

On the same day he wrote to George Wyndham a letter which, coming from a subaltern to the Under Secretary of State for War, was remarkable.

> Dear George,
>
> Just a line unofficially &c &c about one little matter out here, of rather an important nature. It is very hard on HE that the GOC should almost I may say refuse to help or back him up in any way or work jointly with him at all – but of course you will hear about all this officially. Of course one doesn't like writing this, as I think he is a very nice man socially –
>
> I know that you must really all be backing up HE's proposals, and won't let it slide this time. Afraid they wont fight but after a little delay will come down some way or other – most people think there are only two alternatives:

1. to climb down
2. to fight.

They in my humble opinion will do neither. They will blooming well *fall down* – directly there is any military demonstration out here to back up an ultimatum.

In haste,
Yours,
Ben

The GOC referred to was General Sir William Butler, who had been doing his best to undermine Milner's warlike policy. An Irishman, educated by the Jesuits, a friend of Parnell's and an admirer of O'Connell, he had much sympathy with the Boers. It is difficult not to believe that he was right in his conviction that war could be avoided, and that if it did come it would be disastrous. He recorded his opinion at the time: 'In the event of crisis arising the situation will be more of a civil war than regular military operations . . . War between white races coming as a sequel to the Jameson Raid . . . would be greatest calamity that ever occurred.'

Butler's concern was such that he, quite improperly if understandably, produced no plan for a strategy should war occur, and resigned on 4 July. Bend'Or shared no such inhibitions and in a letter to his mother on 5 July wrote, 'things are buzzing along here now better than a week or so back and I think we shall get what we all pray for here, namely war'.

Although Bend'Or disagreed with Butler he did not let that interfere with his friendly concern, and wrote to his mother to ask her to look after the eldest Miss Butler, 'an awful good sort and we were great pals out here, so you might make a little bit of fuss over her as I shouldn't think she has the cheeriest time of it'. His attachment was hardly very serious since he had earlier written, 'I have quite fallen in love with Miss Butler and have written to tell S [Shelagh].'

It is probable that Milner wanted a war, as the only way of clearing the air, but even if he did not, a threat, if it was to work, must be seen to be credible. Bend'Or was typical of those who felt that a short sharp conflict would solve the problem. 'The only thing for the Transvaal is 2 regiments of cavalry, 6 batteries of artillery – and squash they would go . . .' and, on 6 September 1899, 'Tell George we have only to kill 200 Boers in the first round and the others will go home quietly.'

Bend'Or was of course to be proved wrong: the war cost 60,000 lives, hundreds of millions of pounds, and by damaging British military prestige encouraged Germany in the aggressive foreign policy that led to the First World War. Bend'Or was to discover this the hard way, in the field; he learned much from his experience and took the lessons of the war to heart to such good effect that in August 1914 he was able to put his finger precisely on the key military problem – mobility – and its solution – armour.

The war that broke out in October 1899 was characterized by grave errors on both sides, but there is no doubt that the British came out of it worse than the Boers; lessons were learned, but not well enough, and the First World War found British generals repeating many of the blunders they had committed earlier against the Boers. The Boers were aggressive, well-armed, and immediately took the initiative. It proved, as General White had forecast, impossible to defend the frontiers of Natal and Cape Province. The correct response would have been to withdraw to defensible positions, but instead, grimly hanging on, the British found themselves cut off in the little towns of Ladysmith, Kimberley and Mafeking.

For Bend'Or the lessons began gently. He wrote to his mother on 18 October 1899, a week after the beginning of hostilities:

> Dearest,
>
> Many thanks for long letter of this last mail – Thank goodness they have now begun and we all feel very anxious about Mafeking of course all telegraph communication is cut off from it – Ed Cecil and Charlie Bentinck are there, and their two little ladies are staying at Groot [*sic*] Schuur and are wonderfully plucky. Rhodes is shut up in Kimberly [*sic*] and is in consequence in a very tight place, and doesn't like it a bit – Mrs Maguire of course followed him there, and I imagine they are both down a mine by now, too ridiculous her going . . .
>
> Boers fired 13 shells at the armoured train near Kimberly and missed altogether. So we don't believe all we hear about their unfailing marksmanship! You will see all news in the papers –
>
> Ever yr Son

Edward Cecil's little lady was Violet, for whom Milner developed a great admiration and married, after Lord Edward's death. There is a photograph of Milner and his staff taken at Groote Schuur at about this time which shows young Bend'Or, the very pattern of a High Commissioner's aide, towering over Violet. It forms a contrast to one taken a year later, when Bend'Or was a tired, lean and battle-wise ADC to the energetic Lord Roberts.

Bend'Or was naturally anxious to be in at the fighting before all was over: the single initial British success at Elandslaagte on 21 October, when the invading Johannesburg commando was wiped out, seemed to counterbalance the other failures. 'Guy [George Wyndham's brother] has now seen two good fights, Elandslaagte and Ladysmith. It was rather disappointing to me as Col. Ian Hamilton had offered me a billet there . . . But we have all we can to do here for the present' (26 December 1899). A week later (1 November) he was beginning to fret:

> General Buller arrived yesterday very much to everyone's joy, he received a tremendous ovation from all hands, at the same time we didn't get very reassuring news from Ladysmith. Have got no plans made about myself as yet . . . People aren't very excited here, but we are awfully relieved that it has come to war, the Boers appear to be fighting with great determination and pluck, more than we thought.

General Sir Redvers Buller had come to take charge of the Natal front; his endeavours to force the Boers back from strongly defended positions on the Tugela river, although ultimately successful, were to be costly.

Even at twenty Bend'Or was a difficult man to resist, and he managed to persuade General French to offer him a post as ADC. This was a most exciting prospect, since John French was the cavalry commander who had ordered the famous charge at Elandslaagte when the lancers had ridden through the retreating Boers, 'most excellent pig-sticking . . . for about 10 minutes, the bag being about 60', and his ADC would inevitably have seen as much action as anyone might have wished.

The prospect was promptly squashed by orders from home. A future Duke of Westminster was much too important a figure to be risked in battle. Bend'Or was furious: he wrote incoherently to his mother: 'My Dearest, I am indeed deeply disappointed and annoyed at extraordinary action taken by those at home . . . I can't write more it is absolutely disheartening. Your son.' He also wrote a longer and careful letter to his grandfather explaining his views.

12th December 1899

My dear Dads,

George's 2 cables of yesterday the 11th and of today the 12th surprised me a good deal and annoyed me as I do not understand my position.

It is difficult to imagine a better billet being given to one of my age at such a time as this, as that which General French offered me the other day as galloper to him, on a Divisional staff mind you not a Brigade staff. Leave not having been sanctioned by you surprised me . . .

Let me quote now a similar case which I think ought to disgust you. When Christian Victor was out here the other day everyone was saying – where shall we put this fellow so as to keep him out of harm's way where there will be no danger of his getting hit. Well I feel the same thing is happening about your grandson out here, for no other reason than that he is your grandson.

And after all to have to refuse to take a post like that is nothing short of a disgrace. It is a false position to be in and the mere idea of a Grosvenor not being allowed to go up – what is the use of wearing a sword, it surely isn't only meant for ornament like a footman's livery.

I dare say it does not seem to you an awful thing, but I can assure you to sit down at Cape Town and play the footman whilst great things are going on, is entirely against the grain; it may not be with some people anyhow it is with me and the sooner a glass case is bought measured for me and I put into it and carefully consigned to the Chester Museum – the better. You see it isn't as if I were any more use down here to HE. If I thought so I would not write like this.

The old Duke never received Bend'Or's letter: he died on 22 December and his grandson succeeded to the title and estate. This necessitated his return to England; it would have been natural and perhaps desirable that he should have stayed there to assume the very considerable responsibilities that were brought by his inheritance, but Bend'Or much preferred the front line to the life of the richest man in England, and was back in South Africa as soon as possible.

On his return at the beginning of March 1900 he was appointed ADC to Lord Roberts, a much more responsible position than that of galloper to French, for the Field Marshal was the most distinguished of British soldiers, sent out to deal firmly with the Boers as he had previously with the Afghans. Earl Roberts of Kandahar was then sixty-seven, an age when most generals would have retired, and indeed after a lifetime of soldiering in India he had been put out to grass as C in C in Ireland. While in India he had, like Wellington before him, perfected the art of moving large armies over considerable distances, and remains the only general ever to have brought the Afghans to submission. 'Bobs' was loved by his men, but not necessarily by his colleagues; the loss of his only son in the early days of the war had severely affected him, and he welcomed Bend'Or with great warmth and affection. The Field Marshal's greatest gift was his organizing ability: refusing to be distracted by the urgent calls for help from Ladysmith and Kimberley he constructed a transport system capable of moving the army effectively and rapidly in a very short time.

It was the largest force ever seen in Africa: a whole army corps, fifty thousand men, a hundred field guns, and a division of cavalry under French, with Lord Kitchener as chief of staff. The advance had started on 11 February. Kimberley was relieved and Rhodes liberated. Kitchener took command from the quite competent Kelly-Kenny and fought a foolishly bloody battle at Paardeburg, opening the way for the final advance on Bloemfontein. When Bend'Or arrived he made his way straight to the fighting line, and recorded his first impressions of war in enthusiastic, but not insensitive letters:

Bloemfontein
13th March 1900

Hurrah,

I head all my letters like this, as my Chief has done a really wonderful march from Kimberley and Modder . . . What with the transport for all these hungry men, it has been worked admirably. In the last fight at Driefontein I was lucky enough to get up into the fighting line, and enjoyed it in a casual, excited sort of way while it lasted.

I saw a Kopje gallantly taken and stormed by the Welsh Regiment, and the Buffs supporting them – it was splendid. But what one really feels about a battle is the morning after, when one goes out and finds the wounded who have been left out all night. Some of us went out with water for them early in the morning, when it was light. One case was very pathetic, as a young subaltern in the Essex regiment died just as Eddy Stanley and I were giving him some water – poor fellow, desperately wounded by shrapnel, quite young, and he evidently lay out all night in great agony.

Bloemfontein
14th March

We are here in this rather nice tin roofed little town. It is delightful to be a bit quiet after the bustle, dash and heat of that march from Kimberley. It was a splendid thing. The fight at Poplar Grove was merely a stampede on part of the Boers. I was with the Mounted Infantry for about two and a half hours taking messages, and was under fire when with Colonel Le Gallois' Mounted Infantry; they shelled us with shrapnel from One Tree Hill, which name you will recognize from the papers. Our Cavalry could not catch them. We saw them in front of us, not very far, and dropped some shells into them, the pick up was small however. The most interesting feature of it was that Kruger was present at the battle urging the Burghers on, but, alas! for him, they did not pay much heed.

The fight on the 11th at Driefontein, was a very different affair, as the Boers took up a very strong position of a figure 3, with the body of it facing you . . . The Boers consisted of the Johannesburg police, headed by De la Rey. They, as I have mentioned here, offered a most stubborn resistance; the Kopjes on the right were those that the Welsh Regiment, supported by the Buffs, took so gallantly . . . It was there that the Boers held up their arms, also the inevitable white flag, promptly putting three vollies [*sic*] into our men as they advanced, killing twenty-three men and two officers. I think this is right about the numbers. Lord Roberts witnessed this himself, and wired to our Government accordingly. I was sent on messages from the Commander in Chief to General Kelly-Kenny and General French, and in consequence saw a lot of it. The morning part of it I witnessed from an adjacent Kopje, but in the afternoon had plenty of it close up. You cannot imagine the pluck of the wounded. I always imagined a man would be delighted to get a bullet through the fleshy part of his leg, and retire to the comparative safety of the ambulance, I must mention something about this later, but not a bit of it, they are mad to go on, although badly hit. I saw many instances of this.

About the Ambulance Division, I had to pass through it on my way, and all the bearers were sitting behind rocks, as the bullets came there comparatively freely, and also two shells fell just short of it, they say they were only spent, but I doubt it about the shells.

Our Artillery horses were very beat. It was a beautiful sight to see a Battery come into action, and the men working like machines under a heavy fire, it is a sight worth seeing, and one I shall never forget. The coolness and bravery of our Infantry in storming some of these Kopjes is beyond all human praise. The Boers meant business, as the men I saw dead were not killed running away in the usual style, but were shot where they stood. One man was sitting with his back against a rock with his rifle to his shoulder, one eye closed, as dead as the rock he was leaning against.

This is the part of the war that one objects to, and also one's friends going down. Poor little Billy Bunbury died at Kimberley. At the Poplar Grove fight David Keswick of the 12th, an old Eton and Reigate boy with me, was killed. I may run down to Cape Town for my 21st birthday, which you know is on the 19th darling, as I have various papers to sign, and we may be here for a month or so yet. I have got a good bit of loot. It is very strange to be back in Bloemfontein under these circumstances, there are lots of old friends here – Dutch – including the dear English nurse at the Hospital – she is not pretty. Kerry and I went to tea with her, where we met 6 officers captured, wounded at Stormberg, and 40 men and several Boers.

The Scots Guards fife and drum, aided by their bagpipes have squeezed out 'God Save the Queen' and the last post has just sounded and this post is off, so Blessings to all and Goodnight.

Later: I am going with the dispatches to Cape Town. Lord Roberts is a *Saint* George.

Bend'Or

The young Duke had seen the hardest fighting of the war; Roberts had planned carefully and, deploying a much superior force, made sweeping initial victories, rolling up the Boer armies and advancing on their capitals. He was opposed by General Koos De la Rey, one of the best Boer commanders, who continued the war to the bitter end, always contriving to outwit the British generals; had he not been hampered by the incompetent Cronje, the British would have suffered even more at the battles of Modder River and Magersfontein. The Johannesburg police, the ZARPS, were also the élite fighting force of the Boer army who later made a great stand at the battle of Belfast, at which Bend'Or was also present; according to Thomas Pakenham they 'came to be regarded by the British as heroes cast in their own mould'.

After this fighting Bend'Or entered Bloemfontein on 13 March riding behind Roberts with the other three ADCs in a scene described by one of them, Lord Kerry: 'First Chief riding alone, then 4 ADCs, then rest of HQ staff in fours, military attachés kept in order by Lord Down, escort of a cavalry regiment, men decorated with red, white and blue rosettes walked alongside singing "Soldiers of the Queen", "Tommy Atkins" and other popular airs (some had drink taken).'

The advance had been rapid, and crushing: Bend'Or, in the thick of it, had seen how effective generalship could meet the challenge of great distances by mobility and careful planning.

On the nineteenth Bend'Or came of age, and in unfettered control of 120,000 acres, several hundred servants and employees, and perhaps fifteen million pounds. He had to go to Cape Town to sign papers, and while staying at the Mount Nelson Hotel wrote to his mother.

Mount Nelson Hotel
Cape Town
4th April 1900

Dearest,

I forgot whether I wrote and told you that I was rather seedy with fever and tummy troubles at Bloemf: but am all right now having spent a week in Cape Town. I go up Friday next –

I am afraid the Boers having captured another battery will buck up like anything and give us a lot of trouble –

Three aunts rolled up yesterday and the Cape Town streets are blocked with their luggage. No more must be encouraged to come out as they are really in the way as regards room, etc. etc. Fortunately I see the Queen is paying due attention to this matter.

Ever your Son

The fever he mentions was to prove a constant threat to his health, and was later to be the cause of his having to give up his squadron in the First World War. In spite of this he wasted no time in Cape Town and was promptly in action again. He wrote from Bloemfontein of a fight he had in company with another Duke, Marlborough, who was also an aide of Roberts.

Bloemfontein
2nd April 1900

I had one of the best days of my life yesterday, and had my first shot at Brother Boer at about 500 yards, and was too excited to be frightened. The day before yesterday Seymour Fortescue, self, and a Mr Gwynne [Reuter's War Correspondents] went out about 8 miles SE of here towards Paardekop, and sat on a Kopje overlooking what we took to be a small Boer laager (we thought small) but I had my doubts as we could only see 7 tents and there appeared to be a good many Boers going about and rounding in cattle, etc. These 7 tents were just on our side of a long ridge on to the top of which we could not go, as we should have shown going over the skyline. So we went home. I ruminated over this, and made certain in my own mind that there must have been a big laager over the side of that ridge (above mentioned). So on Sunday morning, I said to Marlborough, who had not yet seen a fight, and in consequence was very keen, 'Get leave and come out with me, and I think we shall see something.' We started at 12, heard firing at 2 p.m. rode straight to it as hard as we could stretch, we then sat behind a battery of Field Artillery, and I took the enclosed magnificent sketch! This battery, the 83rd, was endeavouring by pumping shrapnel and lyddite at a pom-pom, to make it cease from pouring. This it eventually did, but not until having been at it an hour. It was firing at General Stevenson's Brigade, who were attacking a Kopje. Straight to their front, the Welsh, Warwick and Essex Regiments, I think. Another big Boer gun was sending shells into them and into us, as we rode down to them and occupied a dried up dam near a farmhouse, where we sat pretty cunning within 600 yards of the enemy's position. I got off two shots at a couple of Boers. I did not down them, but picked my man each time with a carbine which I borrowed. While we were plugging at the Boers from this dam, the Warwicks were ordered out to take a Kopje on our right, but I am sorry to say had to fall back with heavy loss. Meanwhile we were having a very hot time and were being shelled from our left – we had given all our drink away to the wounded. On our extreme right, the Guards appeared to be most hotly engaged – and I hear did not do much good – and certainly the fellows our side had not done much. True, we took one Kopje with a heavy cross fire, which was unpleasant. I am quite contented now I have seen as much of a fight as anyone and had a lot of squeaks. There was a correspondent following us about and, having taken a very heavy toss in a ploughed field near this farm which was being shelled, I was very annoyed with him because he would not catch my horse, but I got him eventually. We had a very difficult ride home last night – I am afraid I cannot tell you the whole truth about this fight nor even its name (which I think will even be Paardekop or Leaw Berg), as it only happened yesterday afternoon (Sunday), and this is 6 a.m. Monday. Mr Gwynne and I go out scouting sometimes, and see a lot. We are having the most glorious weather, cold nights and bright sunshine during the day, to warm us up. I am very fit. I rode an old black horse of mine yesterday, that is to say when I was not lying face down. I always used to shove him into a sluit out of sight if there was one handy, and once I found him lying on his back, and nibbling at the grass unconcernedly, so I left him there, as I knew he could

> not get away. I believe Lord Roberts thinks that I can take care of myself, and as there is going to be 'Bloody War' again today, he is going to send me out to report back by Heliograph. He has done that twice before to me and I love nothing better than to take a couple of good ponies and hammer about from place to place, and see everything with a free pass anywhere. I take nothing but a big 'shelalagh' and I always borrow a shooting iron if I feel I want a shot. The pluck of the wounded indeed was wonderful. It was interesting to see how the Welsh Regiment left the shelter of the trench we were behind, and went out into the open to our right and also into a very hot fire, which we tried to keep down by our fire. We got one Maxim up with us, and blazed away – it made a great noise, and seemed to frighten some of the Boers from behind the rocks. Marlborough is one of the pluckiest I have met, and a bit too so, I thought once or twice.

Bend'Or's new commitments were taken as seriously as could be expected of an active junior staff officer. He wrote to his mother about a living that was in his gift: 'I have had little time for business, but as to increasing Pulford salary (as I have not the figures before me) I leave it to you to make it quite a possible living as it is ridiculous in a place like that to have a miserably paid parson.' It cannot often have fallen to the lot of a subaltern on active service to have to concern himself with a clergyman's stipend.

Roberts stayed at Bloemfontein for six weeks; both his transport and hospital arrangements had been stretched, and even in spite of his enormous numerical superiority he had suffered a humiliating defeat when a tiny raiding force, under de Wet, defeated a division under General Broadwood at Sannah's Post, took five hundred prisoners and escaped south to capture an entire regiment of Royal Irish Rifles, who surrendered after quite modest casualties. Bend'Or's distrust of generals, even the extremely popular and likeable 'Bobs', must have been exacerbated by the spectacle of 40,000 British troops being held up for so long by a handful – no Boer group had more than 6,000 – of citizen militia.

There was not much large-scale fighting in the march to Johannesburg that started at the beginning of May when the great army moved forward once more, since the Boers had decided to concentrate on the guerilla tactics that proved so successful in the later stages of the war, but what action there was Bend'Or contrived to take part in. He fought at the Zand river crossing on 9 May, a brief account of which he wrote at the time having 'only just jumped off my horse'. In this he saw the outcome of the fears he had expressed from his first arrival in South Africa. The army had been held up already for many weeks for want of horse transport and in this, the first battle of the advance on Johannesburg, the defeated Boers were able to make good their escape due to the lack of fit cavalry horses. Bend'Or wrote:

> Ventersberg
> 9th May 1900
>
> Just had a running fight from Zand River. I have just come in from Gordon's Brigade Cavalry and M.J. I hear some of the Dragoon guards have lost heavily. We saw three badly shelled and pom-pommed. We were lucky, as we had very few casualties. On the whole we are rather disappointed as we expected to bottle the lot, but am afraid French had missed there from what I saw, as he was abreast of them as they treked North, instead of ahead of the game, but I only speak from what I saw – things may turn out differently, since I have only just jumped off my horse to scribble in haste this note, after giving in messages, and taking orders. We are having the most glorious weather now, hot in the day, and awfully cold at night. Mail Off . . .

One action he missed was the fight at the Rand, when the City Imperial volunteers, one of George Wyndham's yeomanry units, distinguished itself, fighting well and intelligently on foot. Its achievement is commemorated in the name of a sailing barge, the *City Imperial Volunteer*, still to be seen around English coasts.

At Kroonstadt, the half-way mark, the still fire-eating Bend'Or wrote on 21 May:

> I fear there will not be much more fighting. I think it is a pity from the point of view of our not being able to kill and really terrorize more Boers than we do, and bring the horrors of war a bit more forcibly, burn more farms &c. and keep them stricter prisoners than we do, so that no disturbance of our line of march would occur again – this would shorten the war by months.

In spite of its apparently bloodthirsty tone this was a perceptive analysis! If Roberts had attacked the commandos much more aggressively at this stage De la Rey and De Wet might well have been dissuaded from their guerilla campaigns and the war actually brought to an end when Pretoria was taken and Kruger captured, rather than dragging on for another painful two years. The same letter described a communication he had received from 'one Temple or pimple I can't quite read it except one bit in which he says "I am ready to do anything, except that my people do not much wish me to fight"!!! . . . I imagine this poor creature is son and heir to the Archbishop Cantuarius!'

The Roberts steamroller crushed what opposition there was, and on 7 June Bend'Or was able to write home from the South African Republic's capital Pretoria, 'Here we all are, dearest, very pleased at having got to the promised land.' He attempted to consummate an ambition he had nursed since the Bloemfontein conference – laying felonious hands on President Kruger's hat:

> Yesterday Jim Clowes and myself thought we would visit Mrs Kruger, but it seemed a hopeless job as she flatly refused to see any Englishmen when I called in the morning but I went again with Jim in the evening and hit upon the excellent plan of saying that I knew Kruger personally having met him at Bloemfontein during the conference. This worked like magic and we were ushered in to a room with 5 old ladies in it who looked rather glum but spotted Mrs Kruger who I told by means of the interpreter that I had had the pleasure of meeting Mr K &c. it all went off well except that the real object of the visit was to bone Uncle Paul's top hat, which we didn't succeed in doing!

Bend'Or was in fact the first British officer to fly the Union Jack over Pretoria. This earned him a cigar, which had been left with the message: 'To the officer who hoists the Union Jack at Pretoria: Heartiest congratulations and thanks. Have a cigar. W.H. Knowles, Great Harwood, England. 24.1.1900.' By all the rules of nineteenth-century warfare the occupation of the enemy's capital ought to have ended the war; but the Boers refused to accept defeat and, prolonging the war for another two years, fought a classic guerilla campaign.

Bend'Or was kept busy on the routine business of confidential messages, travelling between the army in the Transvaal and Cape Town. His early boyish enthusiasm for a scrap had been much modified by his experience of the real thing. He wrote to his mother on 11 July from the RMS *Saxon*, en route for Durban with despatches, 'Everyone is longing for the war to end, which event I feel sure will take place if Christian De Wet is given a knock; we expected this to come off at Bethlehem, but on reading the papers I see it has not.' Again on 24 July: 'It looks now as if this war would never cease dragging on and on . . . lots of people want Lansdowne's blood out here no less than the Boers'. China has now I suppose cut this place out, one feels one is never going to have peace again.'

Lord Lansdowne, George Wyndham's chief, was not the most successful or popular of ministers, and was indeed soon replaced by St John Broderick; the China affair Bend'Or alluded to was the Boxer Rebellion, which led to the famous siege of Peking.

In the course of these journeys Bend'Or made one lifelong friend, Winston Churchill, who became famous throughout South Africa for his capture by the Boers from an armoured train and his subsequent daring escape. Churchill described this as follows:

> I had one more adventure in South Africa. After taking part a fortnight later in the action of Diamond Hill, fought to drive the Boers farther away from Pretoria, I decided to return home. Our operations were at an end. The war had become a guerilla and promised to be shapeless and indefinite. A general election could not long be delayed. With the consent of the authorities I resumed my full civilian status and took the train for Cape Town.
>
> All went well till we reached the neighbourhood beyond Kopjes Station, about 100 miles south of Johannesburg. In the first light of morning I was breakfasting with West-Roberts, when suddenly the train stopped with a jerk. We got out on to the line, and at the same moment there arrived almost at our feet a shell from a small Boer gun. It burst with a startling bang, throwing up clods from the embankment. A hundred yards ahead of us a temporary wooden bridge was in flames. The train was enormously long, and crowded with soldiers from a score of regiments, who for one reason or another were being sent south or home. No one was in command. The soldiers began to get out of the carriages in confusion. I saw no officers. Kopjes Station, where there was a fortified camp surmounted by two 5-inch guns, was three miles back. My memories of the armoured train made me extremely sensitive about our line of retreat. I had no wish to repeat the experiences of 15 November; I therefore ran along the railway line to the engine, climbed into the cab, and ordered the engine-driver to blow his whistle to make the men re-train, and steam back instantly to Kopjes Station. He obeyed. While I was standing on the foot-plate to make sure the soldiers had got back into the train, I saw, less than a hundred yards away in the dry watercourse under the burning bridge, a cluster of dark figures. These were the last Boers I was to see as enemies. I fitted the wooden stock to the Mauser pistol and fired six or seven times at them. They scattered without firing back. Then the engine started, and we were soon all safely within the entrench-

> ment at Kopjes Station. Here we learned that a fierce action was proceeding at Honing Spruit, a station farther down the line. The train before ours had been held up, and was at that moment being attacked by a considerable Boer force with artillery. The line had been broken in front of our train, no doubt to prevent reinforcements coming to their aid. However, with a loss of sixty or seventy men our friends at Honing Spruit managed to hold out till the next day when help arrived from the south and the Boers retreated. As it would take several days to repair the line, we borrowed horses and marched all night from Kopjes Station with a troop of Australian Lancers, coming through without misadventure. I thought for many years that the 2-inch Creusot shell which had burst so near us on the embankment was the last projectile I should ever see fired in anger. This expectation, however, proved unfounded.

Bend'Or was, typically, more laconic: 'I got stuck up in a train the other day when carrying despatches down to Cape Town but managed to ride through in time which I am rather elated at . . . Have now been shot at enough, so son is all right now, and darling need *not* worry any more.'

In fact he did manage to be present at the last set piece battle of the war, that of Belfast or Bergendal where Buller, watched by Roberts, crushed Botha's last field army. The ZARPS, whom Bend'Or had seen in action before at Driefontein, made their last stand and were annihilated. He wrote home:

> The last 2 days have been quite exciting for me. On Sunday I went up to Monument Hill by way of meeting the Chief (who for reasons given below never got there), anyhow, from the moment I arrived there, till the moment I left, I was in a trench lying flat, with dear old General 'Bawb' and 'The Viscount', whilst brother Boer poured in every kind of missile at 800 yards for two hours, from Long Tom shells to Mauser bullets; as long as we lay in the trench we were all right, and in consequence out of about 30 men, we had only 1 killed and 3 wounded, but the Scots Guards had 43 casualties in about 1 hour. Dear Canon Knox Little did wonderful work amongst the bullets, and goes about smiling and likes it, am afraid he is if anything rather imprudent. Yesterday, again I was sent on message out to General Buller whom, as luck would have it, I found in rather a hot engagement, where we straightened a good many burghers on Bergendal Kopje. Poor Captain Lysley was shot here (killed), it was very sad in this way, he had just been promoted to another Battalion in England and was really on

his way home, and secondly it was his birthday.

We hope the Boers will put up a big fight for us soon. We ought to be in Machadodorp tomorrow. It has been terribly cold lately, sleeping out of doors, so in consequence have got bad cold in my face, one side of which is puffed out like a balloon, so tonight have got a room in General Bawb's house, and am just going to have poultice put on it. Gen. Bawb, the Viscount, Eddy and I are still sitting round a table writing home. Must stop now, as have to get up at sunrise.

Good night darling,
from your Son

Love to sisters and Percy, afraid shall not be back in time to see him to Eton.

After Belfast the Boers fled to Mozambique, and Roberts prepared to hand over to Kitchener and proclaimed the war 'practically over'. There were still 30,000 Boers under arms, led by De Wet, Botha and De la Rey, to be dealt with before peace was finally signed in June 1902 but 'Bobs' was now out of the fighting.

With him too, went Bend'Or, who had now received a regular commission in the Blues. After riding successfully at a Belfast Natal race meeting and relaxing somewhat after his war he returned home to take on the responsibilities of a great landed proprietor.

Reviewing Bend'Or's performance during the South African war it is clear that he had the makings of a first-class officer. Roberts was admittedly prone to appoint his ADCs from the higher ranks of the nobility, and was subjected to some derisive criticism when he was seen to have no fewer than three dukes on his staff – Marlborough, Norfolk and Westminster. When he reacted to this it was Bend'Or he chose to keep rather than either of the more experienced aides. It is also probable that he valued Bend'Or as a means of communication with Wyndham, for Lord Landsdowne's son, Lord Kerry, was also on the Field Marshal's staff, doubtless for the same reason.

Like many young men Bend'Or loved the outdoor life, the excitement, and accepted the dangers, discomforts and responsibilities happily enough. His sense of fun appealed to everyone with whom he came into contact; a contemporary recalled him cutting a fellow-ADC's hair with a pair of horse-clippers, having previously submitted himself to the same operation. In time he would have made, and in the First World War did make, a first-class regimental officer.

But there was more to Bend'Or than that: he was a man of

considerable imagination, although progressively disguised as he grew older under a protective façade. At an early stage of the war he saw what would prove to be the central problem – mobility – and was the first to advance the idea of bringing the yeomanry out to the front.

This was a suggestion much more revolutionary than it sounds today. The nineteenth century had seen the evolution of a thoroughly professional army. Earlier lessons had been forgotten – Cromwell and Blake, perhaps the most successful English general and admiral, had after all been rank amateurs; most of Napoleon's marshals, who thrashed the highly trained armies of Austria and Prussia, had no professional training; George Washington was a surveyor, Andrew Jackson, who crushed a much superior British army at New Orleans, a farmer.

The British army, in spite of these examples, had evolved into an entirely professional body, with a structure of examinations and an organization along Prussian lines. It was a compact force, designed for rapid deployment in any part of the world. It followed the rules, and originality was not encouraged. Generals like Napier, who won the Punjab carrying a green umbrella and wearing shoulder-length hair, had been replaced within a generation by officers usually competent but by no means inspired. This professional army was intended for service abroad: defence of the homeland was left to the militia, who had been reformed in the 1850s, under the threat of resurgent Bonapartism, into a volunteer corps of half-a-million – more than twice the size of the regular army.

The yeomanry cavalry were the oldest part of this volunteer force, having originated during the Napoleonic wars when as a response to 'the threat of invasion', counties were authorized to raise regiments of 'provisional cavalry'. In the nature of things recruits, who served on a part-time basis, were drawn from the countryside, farmers, tenants and gentry. When invasion fears subsided, the yeomanry were retained as an emergency police force, and, being used by the repressive government of Lord Liverpool, gained a generally unjustified reputation for brutality in the Peterloo Massacre of 1819.

With the establishment of a regular police force their original role was no longer necessary and the yeomanry, although it continued in being, did so without any very clear task, and of course took no part in any actions. Life in a yeomanry regiment was certainly great fun. Training was superficial: a month's attachment to a regular regiment some time during his first two years' service was all that was required of officers; annual training was only seven days, and only then between 8.30 and 1 p.m., the rest of the time being spent in those convivial pastimes well known to all soldiers. In spite of these deficiencies the yeomanry had real virtues – enthusiasm, initiative and vigour, and experience in horse management. The troopers were independent farmers, used to making their own decisions, if not as skilled in working together as were the regular cavalry. They possessed many of the virtues of the Boers they were fighting except that, as Bend'Or recorded, they could not shoot as straight.

The South African war was something the War Office had not prepared for; the enemy was armed with the latest weapons, quick-firing guns and magazine rifles, at least as good if not better than those of the British. They were brave and resourceful, and capable of moving rapidly over immense distances. Roberts's advance from Cape Town to Pretoria covered the same distance as between London and Rome, Madrid and Munich, Paris and Warsaw. In this vast space the Boer commandos could disappear with the greatest of ease, while the advance of the vast British army was invincible only where it happened to be.

Fighting of this sort demanded a different type of soldier, and for the last two years of the war was largely a mounted infantry fight. Although in hindsight the idea that the yeomanry should go abroad seems obvious, at the time the suggestion that the yeomanry could serve as far afield as South Africa and in a full-scale war was unprecedented and highly original. It first came from Bend'Or in a letter to Wyndham, and while too much importance should not be attached to the letters of a subaltern at the front, George took these communications seriously. He read them at dinner parties and circulated them among his government colleagues, having some printed for the purpose. The decision to send the yeomanry out was entirely Wyndham's, and was executed with great alacrity. The suggestion was the first example of those imaginative military proposals that Bend'Or was to bring to fruition in the First World War.

3

The Young Duke

Bend'Or came back to England from the South African war to take up his responsibilities as the second Duke and to get married. Unlike that of his ancestor Thomas, who married Mary Davies in a dynastic alliance, this was a love match. Bend'Or had been in love with his bride Shelagh Cornwallis-West since boyhood.

If the first Duke represented tolerant Liberalism and George Wyndham romantic Toryism, the West family represented the cosmopolitan smart set. Their roots were similar – the Wests were a family of gentry with aristocratic links of comparable antiquity, and Shelagh's father possessed an ancestral mansion at Ruthin Castle in Flintshire with 12,000 acres, but their whole tenor of life was quite different.

Colonel William Cornwallis-West (he was a colonel only of the Kentucky variety, by virtue of being Lord Lieutenant of his county and honorary colonel of the yeomanry, but never smelt powder other than that discharged at game) never undertook any public duty that was other than honorific, or at least modestly undemanding. He spent all his early life in Italy, and returned to England only on the death of his father, leaving behind him three illegitimate daughters in Italy. These were but the first of charges on the West (the Cornwallis was not added until 1895) estate that the Colonel's son was finally left to cope with.

Colonel West married on his return a 'beautiful Irish savage', Mary Fitz Patrick. She was not only beautiful but endearingly gay, full of fun and agreeably irresponsible: all gifts attractive in the young but becoming progressively irritating with advancing years. Mrs West produced two daughters, even more beautiful than herself, and a son, who was another Adonis. All were charming as well as beautiful, but none had the invaluable quality that Dr Johnson described as 'bottom', and that the first Duke and Bend'Or had in abundance.

Being neighbours, in the country, Bend'Or was thrown into close contact with them, and became captivated by the younger daughter, Constance, always known as Shelagh. Her sister, Daisy, remembered that they had all when in the nursery played at weddings, with Shelagh marrying Bend'Or. He had written to her from his earliest days at Reigate and spent some holidays with her family, including a visit to Castle Pless in Silesia, since Daisy had increased the family consequence considerably by marrying in 1891 the heir to the Principality of Pless. George, the brother, did very much the opposite by marrying Jenny, Lady Randolph Churchill, in 1901; he was only a few months younger than Jenny's own son, Winston.

In spite of any reservations Countess Grosvenor and George Wyndham may have had about Bend'Or's choice (Countess Grosvenor had retained her title after her marriage to George Wyndham), there was no withstanding Bend'Or's devotion to Shelagh, and Lady Sibell did not attempt any opposition. Bend'Or confided everything to her. While he was at Woodstock he wrote a breathless letter to Sibell asking for reassurance: he was asked to stay at a country house where Shelagh was also to be a guest.

> They want me to dine there and if possible stay the night; well as S [Shelagh] is going to be there I suppose dining would be sufficient, and also in this case it would practically be a natural sort of coincidence, because I suppose we must meet sometimes even accidentally and really I don't think it would matter as being so near it would only be natural to go over. But Minnie wrote and told me to ask you, so darling write and let me know, will you?

The answer must have been satisfactory, for a little later he wrote, 'I spent a delightful Sat. to Monday at Newlands [the Wests' home]. Shelagh is really a great dear. I think you will love her, she said you had written her such a dear little letter.'

While Bend'Or was in South Africa Lady Sibell was helping him with Shelagh. He wrote to her on 28 April 1900,

> I agree *entirely* in what you have said to S [Shelagh] and so does she – have never heard a word from parents, and you know that your boy is up to anything of that kind . . . you have been a more

> than dear mother to me about S and we all feel comfy about it as it is and can feel also that whatever does happen now is God's will, and it is in his hands.

In 1900, back from South Africa, there were no difficulties. Bend'Or was twenty-two, one of the richest men in England, tall (six foot two) and handsome, fit and well (although the fever he had experienced in South Africa was to recur), amusing and intelligent with an unforced and natural charm and ease. He had a close and affectionate family, had matured in a hard war, and the world was at his feet.

When fortune lavishes so many gifts upon a single man there are likely to be many envious detractors, and self-seeking hangers on. It has been suggested that Bend'Or was pushed into marriage by King Edward VII, who was a close friend of the Wests and ready to do them a good turn. This is nonsense; Bend'Or was head over heels in love with Shelagh, and made it clear to everyone around him. His letter to his mother, quoted in Chapter 2, when he jokingly refers to having fallen for Miss Butler, and told Shelagh, is a sample of his happy confident love.

The wedding was held as quickly as possible, on 18 February 1901, Bend'Or being twenty-two and Shelagh two years older. Since the old Queen had died recently it was a quieter affair than it would otherwise have been, but the press recorded 'the many friends of the contracting parties showed great anxiety to obtain seats for the ceremony, consequently application forms for tickets of admission were most numerous'. The immediate royal family, being in mourning, could not attend, but sent presents, including a gold-topped cane for the bridegroom and star sapphire and diamond pendant for the bride from the King and Queen. The best of respectable society was there however, the Dukes of Teck and Marlborough, Marquesses of Ormonde and Headfort, the Maharajah of Kuch Behar. The pages were dressed as the *Blue Boy*, the famous Gainsborough portrait that hung in Grosvenor House, the cake was seven feet high, and weighed over 200 pounds, with the castles and country houses of the young couple depicted on the lower, and their armorial bearings on the upper, tier. All in all Shelagh can hardly have been disappointed. Bend'Or's wedding gift for his bride included a diamond and ruby tiara, turquoise and diamond aigrettes, collars, necklaces, bracelets and rings.

The honeymoon was spent at Eaton Hall, the most palatial of country houses. They left the train at Waverton Station and were driven to Eaton Hall: at the park gates they were met by the estate staff, the horses were unharnessed and the carriage drawn to the house – a not inconsiderable distance – by the cheering men. It was not the first time that Bend'Or entered Eaton Hall as its owner, but Shelagh, at the height of her beauty and charm, must have seemed like a fairytale princess.

Thus Shelagh became hostess of Grosvenor House, the finest private house in London, and of Eaton Hall, one of the largest houses and best sporting estates in the country. It was a considerable task for a young woman without much common-sense backing from parents, but she responded to the challenge.

Her first ball gives an indication. Held on 2 July 1902, it was attended by Princess Louise Margaret, Princess Alice, the Duchess of Albany, the Crown Prince of Sweden and Norway (this was before Norway became completely independent), Prince George of Greece, Prince Leopold of Bavaria, the Grand Duke of Hesse and the Aga Khan, who, asking whether he should appear in court dress, evening dress or oriental costume, was told the latter, which must have contributed to the splendour of the occasion. The ball was a great success in spite of the fact that the immediate royal family, still being in mourning for Queen Victoria, could not attend. Grosvenor House was an unrivalled setting for such an event. It had been rebuilt for the first Marquess in 1808, when much of the Gillow furniture was made, and was described by *The Times*: 'Never do we recollect to have seen a more judicious and pleasing application of classical enrichments to domiciliary character and accommodation.' The first Duke had added to its many modern refinements, including a steel roof capable of being raised for later expansion.

Lady Helen Seymour, daughter of Hugh Lupus by his second marriage, described Grosvenor House at the turn of the century.

> The large and magnificent drawing rooms were all on the ground floor . . . the picture gallery . . . was a perfect room for entertaining. Large double doors opened into the once famous Rubens room where hung three immense paintings by Rubens, completely covering the wall on each side of the door, and filling the huge wall space facing with windows . . . From the French windows (of the saloon) steps led directly down to the garden,

> which was spacious for London, with grassy lawns and huge shady plane trees. From the saloon you passed into the huge dining room containing the most wonderful pictures of all.

There was however only one bathroom, which even at that time was thought a little too little of a good thing.

It was a town house, with only the family living there, and little provision was made for guests. The entertainments, when they were given, were of such a scale as to need supplementary staff to be supplied by the caterers. Permanent servants were relatively few, being only a hall porter, an usher, carpenter, housekeeper, still-room maid and five housemaids. Personal servants – footmen, ladies' maids, valets and butlers would be brought from Eaton with the family. Large dinner parties were held in a splendour that could hardly be matched at the Palace. Guests sat under the Rubens in the dining room or the Gainsboroughs in the drawing room and dined off a gold service which included a hugh candelabra and the Doncaster Gold Cup, filled with carnations.

One such special event was a supper party given after a ball on 26 June 1911. The guest list was as follows:

HIH Crown Prince of Germany	The Duchess of Westminster
The Duke of Westminster	HIH Crown Princess of Germany
HIH Hereditary Prince Yousseuf of Turkey	HIH Princess Higashi Fushimi of Japan
HIH Archduke Karl Franz of Austria	HRH Crown Princess of Greece
HIH Grand Duke Boris of Russia	HRH Crown Princess of Romania
HRH Infante Don Fernando of Spain	HRH Crown Princess of Sweden
HIH Prince Higashi Fushimi of Japan	HRH Princess Militze of Montenegro
HRH Crown Prince of Greece	HRH Grand Duchesse of Hesse
HRH Crown Prince of Romania	HRH Grand Duchess of Mecklenburg Schwerin
HRH Prince Alexander of Serbia	HRH Princess Patricia of Connaught
HRH Crown Prince of Denmark	HRH Duchess of Coburg
HRH Crown Prince of Sweden	HRH Princess Henry of

HRH Crown Prince of Bulgaria
HRH Prince Danilo of Montenegro
HRH Prince Chatrabhongs of Pitsmulck
HRH Grand Duke of Hesse
HRH Grand Duke of Mecklenburg Schwerin
Mr John Hayes Hammond
Vice Admiral Fangues de Jonquières
HRH Duke of Connaught
HE the Russian Ambassador
HE the Austrian Ambassador

HE the United States Ambassador
HE the Spanish Ambassador
HE the Japanese Ambassador

HRGH Prince Henry of Prussia
HRH Duke Albrecht of Wurtenburg
HRH Prince Rupert of Bavaria
HRH Prince John George of Saxony
HRH Prince Henry of the Netherlands
HRH The Duke of Coburg

HRH Prince George of Greece
HIH Hereditary Grand Duke of Mecklenburg Streltiz
HRH Duke George William of Brunswick Luneburg
HRH Prince Philip of Saxe Coburg
HRH Prince Arthur of Battenberg
Mrs Hayes Hammond
HRH Duchess of Connaught

Duchess of Rutland

HRH Princess Alexandra of Teck
Countess Beckendorff

Mrs Whitelaw Reid
Madame de Villa Urrutia

Madame Kato
Countess Torby
HRH Princess Frederick Charles of Hesse
HRH Princess John George of Saxony
HRH Princess George of Greece
HRH Princess Maximilian of Baden
Marchioness of Winchester
Marchioness of Graham

The Duchess of Teck
The Duchess of Santona

HH The Nawab Sultan Begam of Bhopal
Katherine, Dowager Duchess of Westminster
HH Maharani of Kuch Behar
Duchess of Devonshire

Marchioness of Lansdowne

Duchess of Montrose

Countess Gleichan

Connaught
HH Prince Maximilian of Baden
HH Duke Ernst Gunther of Schleswig-Holstein
HH Prince Frederick Charles of Hesse
HH Prince Alexander of Battenberg
HH Prince Leopold of Battenberg
HH Prince Maurice of Battenberg
HH The Duke of Teck
Desgamatch Kassa of Ethiopia
HSH The Prince of Monaco
HSH Prince Alexander of Teck
HSH The Prince George of Battenberg
HSH Prince Pless
HH Maharajah Gaekwar of Baroda
HH Maharajah Seimdia of Gwalior
HH Maharajah Dhiraja Hoker of Indore
HH Maharajah of Patial
The Prince de Ligne
HH Maharajah of Kuch Behar
HH Maharana Shri of Rajpipla
HH Rajah of Pudukota
HH Rajah Aga Khan
Count Wrangel
HE Monsieur Johannes Irgens
The Prime Minister
Rt Hon Sir Wilfrid Laurier
Rt Hon Sir Joseph Ward
Gen Rt Hon Louis Botha
The Hon Sir Edward P. Morris
Admiral Count Herhachiro Togo
Duke of Norfolk
Duke of Somerset

Duchess of Leeds
Duchess of Somerset
Duchess of Portland
Duchess of Manchester
Duchess of Beaufort
Duchess of Wellington
Lady Londonderry
Countess of Dundonald
Marchioness of Salisbury
Marchioness of Waterford
Marchioness of Exeter
Marchioness of Camden
Marchioness of Ripon
Marchioness of Ormonde
Marchioness of Zetland
Marchioness of Tullibardine
Countess of Chesterfield
Countess of Granard
Countess of Essex
Countess of Pembroke
Countess of Mar & Kellie
Countess of Denbigh
Countess of Shaftesbury
Countess of Minto
Georgiana, Countess of Dudley
Countess of Darnely
Countess of Beauchamp
Countess of Derby
Countess Grosvenor
Lady Ward
Mrs Botha

Duke of Beaufort	Lady Morris

It would be difficult today to have a private supper party for 144, where the junior guests, in strict order of precedence, were the Dukes of Norfolk, Somerset and Beaufort. Preparations for an event such as this were on the scale of a military operation. The extra staff included twenty policemen, forty-five electricians and gardeners, twenty-two bandsmen, eight men to wash up, three men to lay up early and two to help, eight waiters for the servants and two to lay up for band, to help in stewards' room and to serve. In addition there were eighteen waiters for the tables, five for the soup stations, three on 'hot supply', two in the cellars, two scouts on glass and two on china, four buffet and two wine men, four in the cloakroom and one on 'cold supply'.

This was probably when the Crown Prince of Germany, 'Little Willie', blotted his copybook. The story as told by J. Wentworth Day is that after the ball the Prince went missing. 'His equerry was in a ferment, the Duchess was distraught. Bend'Or was puzzled – but, knowing his guest, had his suspicions. "Search the house," he ordered . . . In a bedroom they discovered Little Willie with a beautiful but rather forward lady. He was never asked to Grosvenor House again' (*Liverpool Echo*, 12 December 1960). Within a few years most of those colourful guests, including Bend'Or and Little Willie, were to be at each other's throats in the First World War with Count Wrangel fighting the Bolsheviks, and Bend'Or's old enemy, Louis Botha, fighting even more efficiently on the British side in East Africa.

By comparison with the splendours of Grosvenor House entertainments Eaton was a homely place – parties were smaller, since everybody had to be put up either in the house or in one of the neighbouring Grosvenor properties. Homely would, otherwise than by comparison with Grosvenor House, be a decidedly misleading description of Eaton Hall.

Eaton had been the Grosvenor seat since 1420, but the first fully described building was that erected by William Samwell for Sir Thomas Grosvenor in 1680. It was a large and elegant house, with a frontage of 157 feet, bays and a high-pitched roof with tall chimneys and a central lantern. Its setting in the lee of a ridge, looking down to the Dee on the east and sheltered by the Welsh Hills, allows still a magnificent prospect. Approaching by the carriage drive from the Chester to Wrexham road, which runs dead straight for more than a mile, the magnificent range of wrought iron railings and gates, twenty feet high, come gradually into view. They were made by the Brothers Davies of Bersham near Wrexham, who had served their apprenticeship with the famous metalworkers of Liège.

Unfortunately, Samwell's house is no longer disclosed behind them. A white flat-roofed building, on the merits of which opinions differ, appears instead, being the latest in a series of rebuildings. The first, in the Strawberry Hill Gothic style, was by William Porden between 1804 and 1812. A contemporary description gives some flavour of the result. 'Porden has not scrupled to avail himself of the low Tudor arch and the forms of any other age, that suited his purpose, which was to adapt the rich variety of our ancient ecclesiastical architecture to modern domestic convenience.' Porden was given the task in his capacity as surveyor of the London Estates, but it does not seem that his work at Eaton met with his employer's approbation. According to Redgrave's *Dictionary of Artists* Porden's death was hastened by his dismissal from Lord Grosvenor's service.

An attempt was made to refurbish Porden's work by William Burn in 1845–54, which fell between the two stools of Porden's imaginative but frivolous work and the later more ponderous and serious taste of Waterhouse, and satisfied nobody. Taste in matters of architecture is variable: a generation ago few would have admired the enormous complex designed by Alfred Waterhouse to replace the Porden building, but now many mourn his largely lost house as one of the glories of Victorian architecture. Many, also, do not!

Waterhouse was certainly one of the most prolific of architects, and there is no denying the magnificence of his work – the Prudential building in Holborn, the Natural History Museum in South Kensington, the National Liberal Club in Whitehall, the Manchester Town Hall and the Hotel Metropole in Brighton. His work at Eaton was on a similar scale. Francis Grenfell indeed described it as 'the most enormous place I was ever in – just like the Natural History Museum with two wings'. His plan utilized the foundations and some of the features of the Porden house, fragments of which survive, as in the chapel corridor. Eaton should not be thought of as a house; there was a house contained in the complex – the private wing – but the whole is understandable only as a combination of house, headquarters of a business – the Eaton Estate, private hotel and museum.

The family normally spent their time in the private wing, a

relatively modest house of some eleven thousand square feet, which today would be regarded as a substantial, but not impossible country house; the modern house built for the 5th Duke in 1971 is about the same size. The private dining room was, for example, a comfortable twenty by thirty feet, allowing respectable elbow room, but hardly a size for ducal splendour. The main wing, however, had ducal splendour in abundance. It was 250 feet long: the dining room was fifty-five feet long, and extended into an ante-dining room and recess with a combined length of 105 feet. The library was ninety feet long and of similar size to that at Blenheim.

The interior furnishings were splendid beyond comparison. Stacy Marks had painted an enormous mural of the Canterbury Pilgrims for the saloon, which was a continuation of the entrance hall, and bird murals for the ante-drawing room. Gertrude Jekyll designed a delectable series of panels for the drawing room, some of which fortunately survive. The library was painted in off-white, gilded with panels and bookcases of walnut inlaid with boxwood, and mother-of-pearl. Even the shutter panels were painted with birds and flowers together in their appropriate seasons. The chimney pieces throughout were decorated with carvings of Shakespearean characters and historical figures. One, in the hall, illustrated the Scrope and Grosvenor trial, with the Grosvenor witnesses standing on one side of King Richard and the Scrope witnesses, including Chaucer, on the other.

Some idea of the effect can be had from the only surviving piece of Waterhouse's work, the chapel. This has all its fittings intact, and must be one of the finest examples of Victorian ecclesiastical architecture. As in the hall, the furnishings are superb. The windows and pier mosaics, designed by Frederick Sheild, represent a *Te Deum*, with the Noble Army of Martyrs including the English Protestants and John Huss, and the Incarnation and Atonement. These reflect something of the liberal conscience of the first Duke: one of the windows shows Love, teaching a white child to kiss a liberated black child. A rather more frivolous note is struck, literally, by the twenty-eight-bell carillon, made in Louvain, which has a repertoire of thirty-one tunes, including 'Home Sweet Home' played when the first Duke returned to Eaton, and is now allowed to play on high days and holidays. The internal magnificence was continued outside. The terrace, overlooking the River Dee, is 350 feet long; the house gardens, quite apart from the park, stud farm, polo ground, cricket ground and kitchen gardens covered 100 acres – of which twelve consisted of glasshouses both utilitarian and decorative.

The staff required to run this vast enterprise were in keeping. In 1906 there were more than sixty:

steward,
groom of chambers (2),
valet,
under butler,
footmen (3),
nursery footman,
stewards' room footman,
usher of the hall,
oddmen (2),
clerks (2),
clerk of works (4),
upholsterer,
painter,
carpenter,
chef,
sculleryman,
laundry engineer,
stud groom,
coachman,
grooms (3),
housekeeper,
duchess's maids (2),
nurse,
nursery maids (2 – one French),
linen-room maid,
still-room maids (3),
housemaids (10),
kitchenmaids (3),
vegetable maid,
laundry matron,
laundry maids (8),
charwomen (daily) (3).

That was, of course, only inside, for every day. There were some fifty gardening staff, also a locomotive driver, brakesman and two linesmen for the private railway connecting the house with the main line, a golf groundsman and his assistant, and two ball boys. When the ball boys were not engaged in their proper avocation they gave a hand elsewhere, among the thirty-seven in the works department responsible for repairs and maintenance, the seventy-five looking after the forestry or the seventeen gamekeepers.

The object of all this was not merely to provide a comfortable country home; this could have been done with much less effort and expense, and indeed the Grosvenors always preferred to live in smaller houses, such as Saighton or Lochmore. Eaton was, as it appeared to be, an institution, and was seen at its best when used for its ceremonial social purposes. These revolved round sporting events – the Chester Races, polo meetings, the cricket and tennis weeks, and the shooting. The polo was Bend'Or's idea: he arranged a polo field and organized a team and an annual tournament. King Alfonso of Spain, who had visited Eaton in 1907 for the shooting, was a regular visitor. He and Bend'Or became close friends – he signed himself 'Your devoted friend Alfonso' when writing to Bend'Or – a friendship that was to be used to both countries' advantage in the war.

Even Eaton could not afford shelter to so extended a house party as that which took place at such a time, and Saighton was also pressed into service. Although large, these occasions were most un-royally informal and jolly. During one afternoon of less serious horse sports George Wyndham, Bend'Or – with a black moustache – and six others, properly accoutred as picadors, bandilleros and matadors, staged a bullfight. The bull turned out to be Lord Herbert and Mr Stanley; the King and Queen were amused.

Other royal parties included King Edward, with his raffish entourage, and, by way of complete contrast, the Prince and Princess of Wales, later George V and Queen Mary, who wrote a charming and quite typical thank-you letter from Marlborough House:

10th May 1903

My dear Westminster,

I wish to send you one line to tell you how much the Princess and I enjoyed our visit to Eaton. I do hope the Duchess will soon get well, but you must insist on her taking care of herself . . . I trust that several of your horses will win at Ascot.

Believe me very sincerely yours,

George

Other guests, besides the considerable number of family, included Churchill, of course, and other South African friends such as Milner, Roberts and Joe Laycock. The tone was generally conventional, and apart from such friends as Belloc no great names from the world outside 'Society' appear.

The arrangements at Eaton reflected both Bend'Or's and Shelagh's love for horses. George Wyndham wrote,

> the whole place has been turned into a glorified embodiment of a boy's holidays . . . he has constructed a steeple-chase course with a mile-and-a-half of high tarred rails . . . the old Deer house is now the home of badgers whose lives have been spared . . . the stables are crammed with hunters, chase-horses, polo ponies, Basutos, carriage horses, American trotters and two motor cars. But it is all very boyish and delightful: no luxury. I was quite glad to sleep in a room like a servant's room, with hard bed . . .

Although a very good rider, Bend'Or was, at six foot two and twelve stone, rather big even for steeple chasing and, after trying the Grand National and having a bad fall, gradually turned away from competitive riding.

For her part, Shelagh fulfilled her responsibilities as Duchess to the letter. She was beautiful, entertaining, original and kind-hearted. She produced a beautiful daughter, Ursula, who inherited her father's blond good looks, and a son and heir to the Dukedom, Edward. She brought with her, however, some unwelcome responsibilities in the shape of her family.

Bend'Or accepted that as head of the House of Grosvenor he had obligations to help indigent members. One statement of affairs (see overleaf) drawn up for his attention on behalf of an uncle, Lord Stalbridge, shows a sad condition.

While the young Duke had to do something about the Stalbridges he also had to do something for the Wests. Even before they were married Colonel West was seeking financial support, in the shape of a guarantee of £2,500 for six months in favour of the Wiltshire and Dorset Bank. This was repaid but on 10 October 1901 the Colonel was asking for another guarantee; there is no record of this having been discharged. Three years later the Colonel wrote on 17 October 1904 a letter addressed to 'My dear Ben', asking for a further guarantee of £5,000 and a loan of £500, and saying that he would have to go abroad unless this could be done. The Colonel pleaded, 'We live

Income	£	*Expenditure*	£
From Estate	7,500	Interest and premiums to Alliance	9,421
Railway chairmanship	4,000	Bank overdraft 4% on £35,000	1,400
Directorships	200	Premium on Lord Sudley's policy	443
Dividends	300	Lady Stalbridge's pin money	700
		Balance	36
	12,000		12,000

very quietly here and I have reduced my establishment to eight servants and three horses.' He also admitted that 'I have hesitated to tell my wife'. This may well have been so, for next month Mrs West wrote, on Grosvenor House paper to 'Benny dearest' – an appellation Bend'Or hated – asking for a guarantee of £500, 'It will mean nothing but in name.'

The parents' demands were equalled and surpassed by those of their son. George Cornwallis-West (the family liked their newly hyphenated name but many of their friends stuck to the simpler version) was a handsome, pleasant and entirely superficial man, who lived entirely on his expectations, which his parents were rapidly reducing. He added much to his burdens by marrying Jenny Churchill, and naturally applied to Bend'Or. 'I am in great trouble and crave your assistance . . . three years ago when I married I took over Jennie's liabilities and raised in all £15,000 on my reversionary interest . . . Unfortunately the full amount of these debts was not disclosed and furthermore she incurred a loss of nearly £4,000 on a literary venture called the *Anglo Saxon Review* . . . I have made arrangements to borrow £30,000 in order to start us both with a clean slate' (a somewhat unfortunate metaphor given the West propensity for running into debts). Once again 'my parents know nothing'. 'You know my affection for Jenny . . . money confidence often estranges friends and even relations.' The *Anglo Saxon Review* was as fine a money-losing prospect as could well be imagined. It appeared twice yearly as a magnificently bound, beautifully printed bound volume, all triumphs of the book producer's art. The first volume, for example, printed in June 1899, had a facsimile of a binding made in 1604 for King James I. The contents were however patchy, and the publication did not flourish, although Jenny, in her introduction, said firmly 'the first object of every publication is commercial'.

Bend'Or was intensely irritated with these constant applications, and indeed nearly was estranged; Winston however helped to soothe him, and a joint rescue was staged with the Duke of Marlborough and Sir Ernest Cassels. The extent to which George's expectations were eroded was made clear: his expected income on his father's death was £12,222 and £500 of this was already mortgaged and he was going to charge another £2,185; in the meantime he had only £500 a year to live on. George never changed his ways. He fell in love with Mrs Patrick Campbell, who was if anything more irresponsible than Jenny, married her, left her, and finally married a third time, ending up in circumstances far removed from those he had been brought up in.

The Wests were a problem Bend'Or could cope with. There were others he could not. In November of 1904 a son and heir was born, christened Edward George Hugh, with the King, George Wyndham and Katherine, the first Duke's widow, standing as sponsors. The birth of an heir was a great occasion, celebrated with church bells and rejoicing in Eaton and Chester; the future seemed secure. Young Edward grew a lively boy and a great favourite. Shelagh did not allow her responsibilities to overwhelm her and confided his care to his nurse and two nursemaids, and was not unduly perturbed when in February 1909 the young Earl developed a high temperature. The local general practitioner believed it at first to be only a bilious attack, but changed his diagnosis to appendicitis on the sixth. For some reason the operation was not carried out until the twelfth. It was done at Eaton, as was the custom of the time, since the better off had their doctors come to them rather than going to hospital, and what would now be regarded as impossibly unhygienic conditions must have contributed largely to the septicaemia that set in. The little boy died a week after the operation.

This was for Bend'Or a shattering blow. Wealth, dignity and power were suddenly dust and ashes. He was a man with a great capacity for loving, and the little boy had been a focus for this in a singular fashion. His love for his half-brother and his two sisters had shown early in life this same deep affection.

The funeral was most simple, no hearse, no mourning coaches, but the little body in a white coffin carried by the chief mourners – all members of the estate staff, including N.F. Barnes, the head gardener. The most conspicuous absentee was Shelagh herself, who had not felt able to face the occasion. Without any doubt Shelagh must have been deeply affected by her child's death. She had another girl the next year, Mary, dark-eyed and beautiful, like herself, but no son. There have been other reasons advanced for the gradual estrangement between Shelagh and Bend'Or but the loss of the child must have been a decisive blow, and one that increased Bend'Or's distaste for the artificial life of the time, which was typified by his in-laws.

Proof of his distancing himself from Shelagh is given in the arrangements which he made for a gravestone for the boy. Under normal conditions he would have discussed the matter with Shelagh, but he turned to his mother, whose love and staunch support had always been with him and was to remain so until her death in 1929. He wrote to her on 5 September 1909, sending her drawings of the suggested memorial and again on 7 September, seeking her approval of his final choice, which is shown in the charming memorial in Eccleston Churchyard today.

Bend'Or did the things that were expected of him: he gave generously to good causes, kept his estates in order and his tenants satisfied. He was reluctant to take an active part in politics, which he saw as a world of hypocrisy and double dealing, a perception that it is not easy to quarrel with. Earlier his mother had felt that he ought to do more, and remonstrated with him when he refused to make the speech in the House of Lords welcoming the loyal address at the opening of the 1903 Parliament. He replied on 24 January.

> Dearest,
>
> Your letter recd this morn. I was sorry in many ways to get it.
>
> Of course your ideas may be right, but you are actually thinking that I am lazy and will never begin, because you will never make believe that you would be proud of your son stuffed in a tight uniform repeating a few words parrot like, that he had been told to say. On the contrary if I had a boy I should be proud to see him get on his legs and say what he thought, without the pompous flourish and the ordinary routine of moving the address. Mind you I am in a position of knowing that in politics, one is not wanted personally but it is one's influence and money that is mostly needed, so before I hurriedly decide I am going to look round.

> Shall very likely make an independent speech if there is a S[outh] A[frica] debate – you will understand me I think.

The letter exemplifies many aspects of Bend'Or's thoughts at the time – his distaste for ceremony, and for the politics of party, his acknowledgement that he was pursued not for any personal merit but for his position and wealth, and his need to find a great cause, where he could speak with some authority. Although no public speaker, he made some effective speeches. His first, made in May 1905, gave his very sensible views on the importance of a generous settlement in South Africa: 'The British people, however, were developed politically to such an extent that they generally disagreed, no matter how organized, upon political procedure . . . like all British people they wanted their own way . . . this country was only the trustee for future generations of colonists in the Transvaal.'

His presidency of the Imperial South African Association was the most important political responsibility assumed by Bend'Or. The Association had been formed, largely at the instigation of George Wyndham, who became its first chairman, 'To maintain British supremacy and to promote good government in the various colonies in South Africa with a view to the establishment of a Dominion of South Africa under the British flag.' Although very much a favourite of the Tory imperialists the Association had enjoyed the support of Liberal governments and had done much to encourage the healing of old wounds by a policy of advocating economic development.

The success of the conciliatory policy in South Africa was striking. Within five years of the end of the war, which had been bitter and virulent, the former Boer republics became fully self-governing colonies. Almost immediately secret talks began on unity, which led to the preparation, by the colonies, of a draft constitution that was accepted by Britain and became law in 1909. Recent troubles have obscured the undeniable fact that at the time this was a most successful piece of reconstruction that reflected great credit on all concerned; its major weakness was that the question of black and coloured rights, on which very different views, then as now, prevailed, was left over for future settlement.

The Association was a victim of its own success, and dissolved itself after the new constitution was accepted. Bend'Or had been president for seven years, or during the whole reconstruction period and, on the winding up of the Association, Milner described him as having taken 'an unobtrusive but most important part in repairing the ravages of the war, who had supplemented by his private liberality immense public efforts made for its recuperation'. Bend'Or himself, in a typical phrase, said that they had been helped by being able to 'run their own show. They went on their own way: no one, no matter how powerful, ever tapped them on the shoulder and said "Do this or do that." '

In domestic politics he accepted the presidency of the Cheshire Liberal Unionist Association, describing himself as 'a strong imperialist and convinced Unionist', and joined the Tariff Reform League. Although it might seem that the political traditions of the Grosvenors had been reversed, it was rather following the split in the Liberal Party on the Irish question that Bend'Or, as his grandfather had done, had taken the Unionist part which, under pressure from the radical policies of Lloyd George, had begun to side with the Conservative opposition. Like his grandfather, Bend'Or never allowed political dissension to come between friends, and Churchill, although an ally of Lloyd George, was always welcome at Eaton.

There were more practical ways of strengthening the ties of Empire than by making speeches or giving garden parties, and Bend'Or found one. He had formed a great affection for South Africa, and for many of the people he had met there, including his old enemy Louis Botha. At Milner's suggestion he acquired 30,000 acres of land on the high veldt near Bloemfontein, the scene of his meeting with Oom Paul, and had the distinguished architect Sir Herbert Baker, who built South Africa House in Trafalgar Square, the Parliament buildings in Pretoria and worked with Lutyens in New Delhi, design sixteen farms with all roads and services.

The property was named 'Westminster' and developed to a standard to fit the name. Millions of trees were planted, the land ploughed, pedigree shorthorns sent out from Eaton to form the nucleus of a herd. It was originally proposed that a mansion should be built for Bend'Or to live in on his visits, which were intended to be frequent, but he had a preference for simplicity, and on his first visit in 1903 decided that the house intended for the agent would suffice. The houses and especially the farm buildings show how well Baker executed his commission. Life in South Africa is an outdoor one, and thoroughbreds and fox hounds were also imported for racing and to serve in the jackal hunts which he had enjoyed during his service career. In 1914 Water Baby, bred by Bend'Or, won the Cape Derby.

The original tenants were to be selected from young Cheshire farmers who would be enabled to buy the land over thirty years on favourable terms, and encouraged to take out their sweethearts, 'while even colonists' sisters will not be objected to if they will marry in the district', as Colonel Lloyd, the Duke's secretary, put it. This experiment, the success of which is described later, encouraged similar projects under the auspices of the Imperial South African Association.

In October 1905 he wrote from 'Westminster, Orange River Colony':

> Darling,
>
> We found this place delightful and I only wish you and George were here to enjoy it too. Curiously enough the house on a small scale reminds me of Clouds (the Wyndham family home).
>
> Baker has finished it all off very well. As regards the rest of the property I am full of hope – the settlers are all of good farming type and they all mean having a good try to make the thing a success.

The following year he 'found everything in capital working order, and the various tenants have made great strides'. He was very busy in the improving of the estate, but found time to attend a service in the school given by one of the St Augustine Anglican Fathers, which would have pleased the High Church Lady Sibell, and to play 'in a football match, Westminster v Thabanchu, one goal all and many bumps and bruises'.

He found, as always, the simplicity and freedom from the protocol insisted upon by society welcome, but was not able to spend as much time in South Africa as he would have liked. In 1908 he succumbed to another attack of the fever he had experienced during the war; when this recurred in 1916 in Egypt it was clear that hot climates should be avoided, and he never visited South Africa again after that.

Although he did not seek involvement in domestic politics he could hardly avoid being dragged into it, especially when Lloyd George found dukes as a class so convenient a target. At this distance in time it is difficult to see what all the fuss was about: Lloyd George singled out the Grosvenor estates for their wickedness in requiring a premium for the renewal of a lease, and having the temerity to ask for increased rents. But politicians on the make have at all times been able to work up spurious indignation over something.

Bend'Or's energies diversified into all forms of modern sports. It is expected of country magnates that they should assist with the pursuit of the fox, and Bend'Or served a six-year term as Master of the Cheshire hounds, but, being Bend'Or, also went one better. Being told there was good boar-hunting to be had in the Landes, he went to see for himself and discovered the little town of Mimizan on the coast some forty miles south of Bordeaux. The local Landais tell the story that after pursuing boar all day without any luck they suddenly came upon one on the banks of the lagoon. After killing it Bend'Or looked up at the scenery and was so struck by the beauty of the place that he decided there and then to build a house on the spot, and hunt boar. Being Bend'Or, he had to do it immediately: he would spend Christmas there.

Detmar Blow, the architect, was telegraphed for and came ready with plans for a simple Dutch villa (delightful but quite out of place in the Landes), the building of which was instantly put in hand, showing a remarkable speed in the purchase of land from the local inhabitants. It was a charming house with a terrace and a large enclosed courtyard and later had added to it some accommodation for guests and a good deal more accommodation for horses. Never more than a modest hunting lodge, it became one of Bend'Or's favourite places, where he could live the relaxed uncomplicated life he liked best in the close company of real friends. He kept a large stable there and brought hounds from England. The citizens of Mimizan adored him, calling him 'Notre Duke'. The housekeeper Thérèse Deleste, who came to work originally as a nursery maid, was a particular favourite of Bend'Or's. When Queen Elizabeth II was crowned, Bend'Or made sure that she and Fournier – his chauffeur – had an invitation to view the Coronation procession from his private stand in Park Lane, which he provided for members of his staff from all his estates. During the war the members of the staff at Mimizan had a miserable time, some of them being interned by the Germans, but Thérèse Deleste did a splendid job in hiding silver from the château in the forest and it was recovered intact after the war.

Another, equally distant and well frequented home, was Lochmore, the estate in Sutherland that the first Duke had rented from his relations, the Leveson-Gowers. The fishing and stalking were of the best, and the fuss and bother inseparable from the contemporary demands of rank and protocol could be ignored. Not that Bend'Or, even when he first succeeded, was anything other than very relaxed about much of the pomp affected by Edwardian society. Sir Shane Leslie contrasted him with his fellow duke, Marlborough. 'Staying at Blenheim was not unlike living in a mausoleum. Bend'Or's parties for the Grand National and the Chester Cup were very different.'

Among less conventional sports Bend'Or was much attracted by speed-boat racing. His first boat, *Ursula*, won the Coupe des Nations at Monte Carlo in 1909 and 1910; his second, the *Pioneer*, was less successful, capsizing on her trials and nearly drowning him. *Brunhilde*, launched in 1911, was a superb craft, fifty feet long with 760 horse power and capable of making nearly fifty knots.

Motor cars were a permanent enthusiasm. Francis Grenfell helped him 'try out a new motor car [probably a Mercedes] which could go at ninety miles per hour'. He was an excellent driver, but had one brush with the law in 1912 when he was fined thirty shillings for driving in Richmond Park at nineteen mph. The alternative of seven days imprisonment 'was greeted with loud laughter, in which the justices joined'.

Wilfred Scawen Blunt also described something of the young Westminster's life in his diary:

> 20 August 1908. At Clouds. George [Wyndham] arrived this afternoon . . . with him Shelagh, Duchess of Westminster. They had been at the manoeuvres all the morning, had motored over here, some thirty miles, stopped for tea, and were to motor back, and go out to dinner. This is a good example of the life at high pressure of our ladies of fashion. She has with her in camp a lady's maid, a footman, a chauffeur and a cook. The Duke in the meanwhile is away motoring in Ireland with another chauffeur, another cook, and more servants, besides a motor boat, the one he races with. The life of both of them is a perpetual gallop. This sort of society cannot last. It will end in Bedlam.

Blunt was fond of Bend'Or. In 1912, when he was living apart from the Duchess, Blunt wrote: 'He is a kindly, good-humoured fellow, like a great Newfoundland puppy, much given to riotous amusements and sports, with horses, motors and ladies. The fast life clearly suits him, for he looks a model of health and strength.'

Between the two meetings with Blunt the fairytale lovers had separated. At thirty Bend'Or was disillusioned and unhappy; the ardent young lover had become a cynical young man. From 1910 onwards they lived increasingly apart. Various reasons for the estrangement have been advanced, and it seems the death of young Edward was certainly a turning point, although they continued to have a considerable regard for each other.

With the winding up of the South African Association, Bend'Or had no major political task. The early death of George Wyndham in 1913 had deprived him of his political mentor, and an element of stability in his close relations. The fact that Wyndham had largely been rejected by his party and lost his place in the forefront of affairs had left Bend'Or even less enthusiastic about public life, and although he continued to take an active interest in the estates the strenuous occupation that might have served to settle him was denied. This was abruptly changed in 1914.

4

The First World War

The outbreak of world war came both as an irresistible challenge to Bend'Or and as a relief from a society he found tedious and unsympathetic. From the time of his marriage he had been virtually forced to accept a social round which involved dinner parties and balls at Grosvenor House, shooting, racing and polo parties at Eaton – all requiring vast numbers of invitations, many to people he did not know, thus demanding the courtesy expected from a host which put a strain upon an essentially shy man. Just as in South Africa he could not wait to get into action – and indeed he did not even wait for the declaration of hostilities, taking himself off to the side of the French, who he felt would certainly fight while he was doubtful about Asquith's firmness.

He was installed at the Hotel de l'Univers in Arras, still the best hotel in that fine city, when he wrote to his mother on 5 August a letter with at least two remarkably inaccurate prophecies:

> This place is in a state of cheerful siege but everyone happy and confident. My darling, my thoughts are with you and Ursula. From what I see here, and this is a busy place as far as soldiers are concerned, I think that any big fighting is some way off – especially on the frontier here. I know nothing but imagine a big naval battle will take place first. Anyhow just heard from the General here that England has definitely declared war on Germany. This being the case I shall have to get back if not too late. The French are very confident almost too much I think. This is a perfectly lovely old town. I can't think why one has never seen it before. We must come out again someday if there is anything left of it after the war. They [the French] are all very enthusiastic at England coming along with them. But are rather

> anxious to know when the expeditionary force is coming over. I shall see you both after or perhaps before you get this letter if I can get over. My love to Ursula.
>
> Your son

The British moved remarkably quickly and the expeditionary force which was to be given immortality by the Kaiser's description of it as 'a contemptible little army' disembarked within a week. Bend'Or stayed ahead of the game and was in le Cateau on the sixteenth. 'Have been here 2 days and got up long before the Headquarters staff who got hung up – I think the only other English was Col. Fowler here, Madge's husband. We were presented with bouquets by the excited inhabitants.'

Very soon however the distrust of generals that he had formed after his experiences in South Africa was shown to be well grounded. He wrote on the nineteenth,

> We have as usual made some awful mistakes and are now rectifying them, but they have cost many lives – and many miles of marching. I cannot make out why the Germans have not done us more harm than they have – by our gross stupidity we ought to have been wiped out by now. This only for yourself and I may be wrong. We shall see. I wish we had a great brain here. Would to God dear George were here.

He had found time to visit George and Sibell's son, Perf, who he found 'bursting with health and happiness. All he wants are 150 pairs of thick woollen socks for his men.'

He was typically laconic about his own doings: 'I had only five hours sleep for three nights and days . . . many excitements . . . I picked Francis Grenfell up after he was wounded and motored him into a town (in our possession).' This exploit was seized on and exaggerated by the popular press which had Bend'Or charging with the cavalry and sweeping up Grenfell in his arms; everything that Bend'Or did was distorted in this way – he was news, in much the same fashion as are royalty today. For a shy and private man, such as Bend'Or essentially was, this was hard to bear, even when the news was complimentary.

The truth was, in its less dramatic way, much more revealing of Bend'Or's loyalty to his friends. The Grenfell twins, Francis and Rivy, had been close friends of Bend'Or's for many years. They had played solo and practical jokes together, of which the most famous was the Cholmondely burglary, shivered in Bend'Or's fast cars, and had been as younger brothers in much the same way as had his half-brother Perf. Bend'Or had found Francis badly wounded on the battlefield and motored him off to a hospital staffed by nuns at Bavai, and had supervised the dressing of his wounds, the surgeon having refused to remove the victim's breeches 'car il y a trop de jeunes filles'! Francis wrote home: 'It is wonderful what Bend'Or has done for Rivy and me', and in his will wrote: 'My special thanks are due to the Duke of Westminster for his great generosity and kindness to me on many occasions. No man had ever a better friend.' Nor was this a generosity of money, which would have had minor significance, but of time, patience, affection and shared danger.

Bend'Or was much less forthcoming about his part in the First World War than he had been when writing from South Africa, partly because he threw himself with such enthusiasm into the battle that his letters are distinctly scrappy. We know from other accounts what Bend'Or was doing at the time, which was to act once more as galloper for the staff, but using his own Rolls-Royce instead of his charger, and covering considerable distances and having many narrow escapes. Bend'Or merely said, 'My work here is most interesting. Hugh Dawnay and I work together – link up with the different armies from HQ. We also do a bit of reconnoitring and pick up positions &c.' He was feeling decidedly ungenerous towards his in-laws: 'The Germans are behaving like savages. This is a good sign – if I find Hans Pless I shall cut his throat and thus show one's indignation at their conduct.'

The German advance was rapid and devastating. Bend'Or wrote from Soissons on 14 September that Rivy Grenfell had been killed, a blow he found hard, and that he 'had a hard day myself and got out all right'. His main personal concern was with his half-brother Perf, Percy Lyulph Wyndham, who like his father had been commissioned into the Coldstream Guards, but was faced with a war infinitely more savage than anything George had ever known. Whenever an opportunity arose Bend'Or called on him, supplying him with socks and chocolate 'which are the two absolute necessities of life'. Percy was having a hard time, in some of the fiercest fighting of the war, which he described graphically himself.

> . . . they were only ten or twenty yards off, and with a yowl they

sprang forward, and yelled 'Deutschland'. After that words fail me. Hell was let loose. Our men lay down flat and poured volley after volley into them. I flattened myself against a wall and quaked. In about three minutes it subsided and awful groans filled the air . . . Then they brought up a gun, at 200 yards, and fired lyddite point blank at us! My word it was a caper. They kept coming on, and at about 12.30 made a final desperate effort. I thought we could never stick it, but we did. I just said my prayers as I lay, nose buried in the ground, and waited for my bit of shell or bullet . . . They shot like demons, and absolutely straight. I got out of all my heavy kit, pack, revolver, knapsack &c. and piled it in front of me, and got a rifle and bayonet from one of the dead un's. We just shot and shot in great paralysing bursts of fire. When we retired twenty yards, I had to leave my kit, so now I have nothing but what I stand up in. No coat, no woolly, no nothing.

On 14 September the news came that Percy Wyndham had been killed. Bend'Or was distraught. He wrote immediately to Lord Ribblesdale, Perf's father-in-law:

My thoughts are with dear little Diana, and with my Mother, whom I hardly dare write to. I should like to see the latter if possible, and tell her I have written to you. I cannot write her, as I don't know when Rawlinson will break the news. Can you explain all this to her? I am heartbroken myself. When this is over I must come and see you. I know Diana will be braver than the brave. Perf was, and his example will last throughout the ages.

and to his sister:

I was allowed to wire to Sir H. Rawlinson to break the news, so I daren't write to Mother or Diana for fear they have not heard already. Will you some time explain my position to them. He went in good company with several friends in a way most befitting to him, with a heap of Germans slain round him.

My darlings I grieve with you all and feel hopelessly heartbroken, it is tragic. I have not time to write and this is a cold-blooded letter. My heart bleeds for Mother and Diana. We must think, dear ones, of Percy and George together. I cannot write more, and this letter you must explain to Mother and Diana. I have written more fully to Lord Ribblesdale. You must all gather round Mamma and little Diana. When Mother knows explain my not writing, my thoughts are so with her.

David Bingham was killed with him, so they go into a glorious partnership.

When he did bring himself to write to Sibell his pain was manifest: 'My darling, Your and Diana's Perf is at rest – to the last moment happy I know. He lies in a little wood where he had done so well . . . I cannot write more . . . I feel heartbroken.'

In the face of these personal losses Bend'Or longed for a more active combatant role; now he had seen enough to convince him, quite rightly, that the war could never be won by those then in charge and had identified the only man with enough imagination and courage to do things differently – his old South African friend and relation by marriage Winston Churchill.

Since 1900 Churchill had moved far and fast. From a young Conservative member elected for Oldham in the 'khaki election' of 1900 he had become a Liberal and had prospered, first at the Colonial Office, then the Board of Trade and the Home Office before becoming, in 1912, a superbly effective First Lord of the Admiralty. His mother, Jenny, who was always something of a trial, had married Shelagh's brother George, who was the same age as Winston and as charming and feckless as all the Wests. They were in permanent money troubles, and extricating them from their embarrassments had also brought Bend'Or and Winston closer together. Their experiences in South Africa had rendered both Churchill and Bend'Or distrustful of generals, a distrust speedily fortified by Bend'Or's experience on the Western Front. They were both surely right in this lack of confidence.

The reputation of British generalship was hardly enhanced by the First World War, and in the early days the War Office was quite unbelievably shortsighted and stupid. In satisfying contrast the navy was active and constructive, although this was due in no small extent to Winston Churchill. The Dreadnought building programme had been started previously, but Winston, with the enthusiastic backing of Lord Fisher, had stepped it up even further. While the army was still suspicious of machine guns, the Royal Navy had the liveliest appreciation of all new technologies.

Bend'Or's enthusiasm for motors, by sea and land, had led him to speedy appreciation of their potential in war. The Boer War had proved how essential was mobility in avoiding stalemate; the answer must be to provide motor cars with weapons and armour to enable them to take part in the fighting and to supersede horsed cavalry. It was fortuitous, and fortunate, that his friendship with Churchill enabled him to find an outlet for his ideas.

The development of the armoured car, and thence the tank, owed everything to the navy and was in fact carried through in spite of initial army obstruction. As part of their development of new weapons the navy had seized on the potential of the aircraft, and in the first days of the war Churchill wrote a memorandum which started a new phase in warfare.

> In order to discharge effectively the responsibilities which we have assumed for the aerial defence of England, it is necessary that we should maintain an aerial control over the area approximately 100 miles from Dunkirk. To do this, we must support the aeroplanes which are stationed on the French coast with efficient armed motor cars and personnel to enable advanced subsidiary aeroplane bases to be established 30, 40 and 50 miles inland.
>
> According to all accounts received the Germans, in so far as they have penetrated this region, have done it simply by bluff. Small parties of Uhlans, taking advantage of the terror inspired by their atrocities in Belgium, have made their way freely about the country, and have imposed themselves upon the population. We require in the first instance 200 or 300 men with 50 or 60 motor cars, who can support and defend our advanced aerial bases. I should propose to draw these from suitable volunteers from the Marine Brigade . . . The advantage of aerial reconnaissance is that the approach of any serious body of troops can be discovered while it is still at least two days' march away . . . Propose me plans for immediate action on these lines in detail.

The idea of an armoured motor car was not new: in May 1901 a Mr A.G. Hales had suggested that cars could be protected and armed with a Maxim gun, and the following year Mr Simms showed an armoured car at the Crystal Palace. Predictably enough, the War Office at the time showed a complete lack of enthusiasm and nothing was done.

It is somewhat remarkable that the Royal Navy should have assumed responsibility for the aerial defence of England, and one more indication of the vision and adaptability of that service. By the eleventh the Director of the Air Department, Commander Murray Sueter, had drawn up a complete programme for designing and producing the armed motor cars and training staff. Churchill made his alterations – the number of cars to be doubled to 100 – and authorized it the same day; the first armoured cars were in action within a month. These experimental cars were simply given 4mm armour to the sides with a fixed cover for the driver and armed with one Maxim gun, as Hales had suggested. However, since both the gunner and any other occupants of the car except the driver were quite unprotected from above, it was rapidly evident that an improvement had to be sought. Bend'Or made his own cars available for experimental work and by November the definitive armoured car design was evolved, a design that served the country well for the next quarter of a century. The car was completely protected, with its most prominent feature being the revolving gun turret that is till found on tanks and armoured cars. The navy was, of course, experienced in making turrets and the device of putting an essentially naval feature on a land vehicle was one of brilliant simplicity.

The armoured car squadrons were fortunate in their first leaders. The earliest cars were under Commander C.R. Samson, 'a fiery Captain Kettle-like figure' – who refused to leave Dunkirk when even the Royal Marines were withdrawn in front of the rapid German advance. Samson and his brother Felix reconnoitred as far afield as Bruges and the cars did particularly good work in the early stages of the battle of Ypres.

No. 1 Squadron of turret cars was led by Commander Oliver Locker Lamson, who later carried on what was almost his own private war in the Balkans and Russia. The cars came under the overall charge of Commodore (later Admiral Sir) Murray Frazer Sueter, who, like Bend'Or, had displayed great interest in new technologies. Sueter had served with the original Holland submarines, been in charge of the naval airship programme, and gone on to develop the Royal Naval Air Service. He also initiated, with Lt Douglas Hyde-Thomson, the use of torpedo-carrying aircraft, which were to prove such an important weapon in the Second World War.

Again like Bend'Or the restless and outspoken Sueter did not hit it off with the more hidebound of his superiors and his talents have never had the appreciation they deserved. He was however, with Churchill and Bend'Or, the right man in the right place at the right time. Sueter got on well with Bend'Or and affectionately recalled seeing the Duke holding a pay parade in the rain at Wormwood Scrubs, painfully counting out each man's pay to the last farthing, in coins he had probably never even seen before.

Among the squadron was his own chauffeur, George Powell, who was then still in his livery. Powell drove the Duke in his open Rolls tourer, with a machine gun mounting, but quite unprotected. Like young tank commanders later, Bend'Or preferred to do his fighting in the open air.

The Naval Airmen's Armoured Car Force was started at Wormwood Scrubs, in the *Daily Mail* airship shed – the War Office maintaining that complete lack of interest that led to the well-known story:

> Enquirer in Whitehall: 'Which side is the War Office on?'
> Officer: 'Ours, I believe, but opinions differ'

They were even unable to produce any data on the penetrative power of British rifles (the navy found it poor, while that of the German pieces was excellent). Naval experience of diesel power and fighting in confined spaces, as in submarines and gun turrets, was helpful, and within four months the first revolving-turret armoured cars had been designed and delivered. These cars remained, with very few modifications, the standard British vehicle until World War II.

Churchill found no difficulty in agreeing with Bend'Or that the army should adopt armour on a large scale, and the two men made an attempt to persuade the military to do so. They had shared the same experience in South Africa and had both a lively appreciation of modern developments. They jointly came to the view that a major change in tactics was needed. By this time the Allied armies had been driven back by the constant German advance to within artillery range of Paris. The conventional military wisdom had been seen to be deficient and new solutions were urgently demanded. The most effective of the new weapons, the tank, had yet to be formulated, but the armoured car was already pointing the way.

On 26 September Churchill and Bend'Or went, by destroyer, to visit Field Marshal Sir John French, in an attempt to convince him that the war could be won only by a rapid development and deployment of armoured vehicles. French, who should have been a decently retired cavalry colonel, was, unhappily for the lives of thousands of his soldiers, in command of the British Expeditionary Force. Even the *Dictionary of National Biography*, normally charitable, finds it difficult to be so about French.

French was unconvinced of any need to change and Churchill and Bend'Or decided to go their own way together. Bend'Or transferred from the army to the Royal Navy and was gazetted Lieutenant

Commander RNR on 21 November 1914 with authority to form his own squadron (No.2 Squadron RNAS) of armoured cars. The fiction that the cars were meant to protect airfields shielded them from a possible army takeover, lent some legitimacy to the Royal Navy's fighting on land, and was preserved by their being officially part of the Royal Navy Air Services.

Bend'Or's enthusiasm and resources were lavished on the project, but before the new cars were deployed in action another step was taken. In February 1915 the Duke gave a dinner where Churchill met some of his fellow officers in the Armoured Car Squadron. One of these, Major Hetherington, convinced Churchill that a much larger armoured car could operate off the road and negotiate trenches and other obstacles. Moving with a speed common with him but most rare elsewhere Churchill commissioned a study on the 'land ship' to be made by the Admiralty designers in co-operation with Hetherington. In order to keep the matter secret the new weapons were to be known as 'water carriers for Russia', but since it was clear that this would be abbreviated to 'Russian WCs' it was agreed to call them 'tanks'.

Within one week a committee had been set up, discussed the whole question, prepared recommendations and placed the order for the first tank with Messrs Fosters of Lincoln. If everything had gone forward with the same speed tanks would have been available in quantity by the end of the year, hundreds of thousands of lives saved and the war measurably shortened. But by May Churchill had been ejected from the Admiralty and the entirely unwarlike Balfour, his successor, wanted to scrap the whole project. Churchill wrote on 20 September 1915, 'It is odious to me to remain here watching sloth and folly with full knowledge and no occupation.'

Even if the tanks were stalled, the armoured cars, pushed hard by the Duke, advanced, and by March 1915 Bend'Or was able to lead No.2 Squadron, representing half the armoured might of the Empire, into battle. They were immediately successful. In that month during a comparative lull between the battles of Neuve Chapelle and Second Ypres, the Duke led part of the squadron into action. These were the Seabrook lorries which at first formed part of the armoured squadron but were later dropped in favour of the much faster cars.

He had instant success supporting the cavalry. A press report on 27 March 1915 illustrates this:

The Duke of Westminster was once again in action this week near La Bassée. He came home slightly wounded before Christmas and since then has been busy training an armoured car squadron under naval regime. He has entirely financed his squadron, barring, of course, the running expenses and the men's pay which the Admiralty meet. The cost – cars, guns, equipment of all kinds for men and machines – is something like £20,000. But, from the viewpoint of adventure, it is not such bad value for money. The enterprise offers something like the fascination of fitting out and commanding a privateer in former days. With this difference, that the privateer was often a 'commercial proposition'.

But the future of the naval cars is probably as irregulars attached to the French army. General Joffre has shown a healthy interest in them.

It was thought at one time that the new naval armoured cars would never get out to France, but the Duke of Westminster paid several visits to the French field and by working hard enlisted interest and brought over many an official to see 'the goods'. Eventually there was a big surprise when it was known he had permission to take the squadron to the fighting line.

About the action – this was at a bend in the line from Neuve Chapelle to La Bassée and Armentiers. Two of his gun lorries advanced and demolished a house occupied by snipers in a few minutes. These also trundled within range of a party of the enemy who were getting a 15-inch gun in position and scattered them.

In a letter home he says that they would have stood a poor chance though if the German shells had been anything but rotten. They fell all around the cars. Had they exploded properly they would have made scrap of them, he admits. One fell in front of a gun lorry and blew up the road. The car crew coolly got out and under direction of an officer took spades and filled in the road under fire. Then they went ahead. This was their first time under fire. Perhaps this is the first good word in print for chauffeurs. They compose the whole of the crews, from gunners to cook.

During this time Bend'Or discharged all the duties of a serving frontline officer with care and dedication; his letters home show something of his frustration with the progress of the war. He wrote to his mother congratulating her on another grandchild:

What good news my darling about Cuckoo. It is far the most intelligent thing to do in these days to produce the 1935 class of soldier . . . A parcel of socks, woolly tomtoms, soap, etc. arrived from you this morn. for which all thanks. Things quieter now –

> but this long line of battle makes it all seem most dull and unreal. One longs for a Crécy or Agincourt – anything except this long stretched line.

Another letter, which illustrates the confused line of command – he was responsible to the Admiralty but under military command – as well as a side of his character not always recognized, is dated 27 June 1915; 'My darling, I find that a real useful present to us out here would be a portable "Communion Set" – our parson has been promised one by the Admiralty but nothing has come of it and this was some time ago . . . You might send it out to me – it would be dear of you.' He also realized that Lady Sibell, who had lost a son, could best comfort other mothers, and asked her to write to the mother of one of his officers,

> Lt Wilding of Ohawa, New Zealand, who had been killed instantly by a shell. A great loss to me and everyone. He was one of the best officers and had just done very good work with a 3 pounder. A shell burst practically on him. All my light maxim cars are with the cavalry – which is good but we shall have to bide our time – as I cannot see the cavalry being used yet . . . We are getting on all right and I believe the French have done very well. I am afraid the Germans are not great gentlemen in the way they are conducting this war.

In spite of the initial successes of the cars it became clear after a time that in the trench warfare of the Western Front tanks, rather than armoured cars, were to be the decisive innovation and the RNAS was not too unhappy in making over its cars on that front to the War Office in September 1915. There were by then seventy-two Rolls, twenty-four Lanchesters and twenty Seabrook armoured lorries, together with 'a very large quantity of transport, spares, materials and despatch cycles for these'. The RNAS kept its two original squadrons in being for service outside Flanders where they would be able to operate free from the restrictions imposed by settled lines.

British generalship was more successful outside the Western Front. There were, it is true, fiascos – as at Kut and Gallipoli, but these were fiascos largely because of Western Front ideas and prejudices. In the war of mobility that was carried out in Africa and the Near East reputations were made rather than lost, with that of Allenby as the prime example.

An example of original and imaginative tactics was the successful use of armoured cars. The two squadrons of the RNAS were deployed as far afield as Romania, Persia and Libya, always with considerable success. As Commander of No.2 Squadron Bend'Or had opportunities to put his own theories of warfare into practice when in 1916 he was sent out to join General Peyton in Egypt.

Bend'Or started to enjoy himself immediately in the more congenial surroundings. He wrote home on 1 February 1916:

> . . . we are by the sea right out in the desert. Blue sea. Roman remains, camels, etc. Cars all going well and get over the country splendidly but for all that wish the war would end.
>
> . . . glorious hot sun which has done us all good . . . lots of sea bathing. It is a paradise after Flanders. Rowe [one of the Eaton men] got blown up in a small explosion yesterday, but none the worse except slight cut in head. He does very well and looks after our mess room &c. We eat your mince pies for which many thanks.
>
> Blessings from your son Bend'Or.

A new front had been opened in the previous December when an army of Senussi had invaded Egypt, led by Nuri Bey, a half-brother of the Turkish leader Enver Pasha, assured by Gaafar, or J'aafar Pasha, who was later Iraq's Ambassador to London. This was an unexpected threat. The Senussi were a widespread religious fraternity, regarded as unorthodox by fellow Mahommedans. There were some similarities to the fanatic followers of the Mahdi who had devastated the Sudan a generation earlier, but the leader of the Senussi, the Grand Sheik Sidi Ahmed, had always shown himself to be friendly with the British. It seemed however that his followers were susceptible to the blandishments of their co-religionists in Turkey, who supplied them with weapons and leaders. Tripoli, where the Senussi were concentrated, was officially under Italian suzerainty, but the Italians were neither able nor willing to offer effective opposition to the rising, which rapidly spilled over into Egypt. The menace of another Mahdist revolt was distinctly worrying, for the Senussi were both courageous fighters and, unlike the Mahdists, well officered and equipped with modern weapons.

The first incursion was repelled, as was the second in January 1916, but the lack of mobility made it impossible to pursue the fast-moving invaders. The British were therefore reorganized and a mobile column formed under the command of General H.T. Lukin, later Sir Henry

Lukin. General Lukin was an unconventional, fighting soldier who had worked his way up from a subaltern in a South African native cavalry regiment. He had fought against Basutos, Boers and Germans in South West Africa and had settled in South Africa. This background would hardly commend itself to the War Office, but was exactly right for a brilliant desert campaign.

The column was composed of the South African Infantry Brigade, a squadron of the Dorset Yeomanry, a Royal Engineers company, a field ambulance, a company of the Australian Camel Corps and the Armoured Car Squadron. This truly representative army was supplied by a camel train which enabled it to advance, although with some difficulty and at foot pace, across the desert.

The column caught up with the Senussi army at Agagia, near Mersa Matruh. They were to fight over exactly the same ground as their successors fought a generation later, and with as much success: many of the names will sound very familiar. The Senussi outnumbered the imperial column, and were strongly entrenched, having chosen a position off the highway in loose sand specifically to impede the cars, a new weapon of which they were much afraid. This worked, and although the cars were able to support the South Africans in the early stages of the battle they eventually all got stuck in the sand. There were considerable losses but the Senussi were forced to retreat and their field commander Gaafar Pasha captured. Before this happened the cars had more than proved their worth. The colonel of the South Africans and his adjutant both used cars and were able to advance right up to the enemy front which was supported by three ten-pounder field pieces and four Maxims. The fire from the armoured cars was so severe that the Turks fled, abandoning their guns. Even after the cars were immobilized the machine guns could be dismounted and used on foot, as was done by Lieutenant Jack Leslie.

That Bend'Or regarded this campaign as a proving ground for armoured warfare is indicated in a letter written after the fight.

> We had a good fight on the 27th [of February] and captured the Turkish general and killed his second in command. Killed about 300 others, captured camp and one maxim . . . I could have done much more than I did had the going been better but it was very sandy, but with very hard work we got there all right – very satisfactory. I hope now that we may go back to France . . . Fired over 3,000 rounds from the maxim in my car – she got hit pretty

often but the armour plate acted all right.

Joe Laycock's battery did well. Our casualties were pretty heavy – but worth it – the South Africans were magnificent and I am glad to say we went up in the attack with them. Dorset Yeomanry did very well.

General Lukin's column was able to advance along the coast road to Sidi Barrani – another familiar name, where they were able to regroup. The problem of supplying water, which had to be all brought up by camel, made consistently rapid advance impossible. Supplies had therefore to be built up at Sidi Barrani in readiness for the next push.

This advance, which was aimed at Sollum, was to be along the coast, but in order to effect this safely the ridge of high ground that paralleled the shore had to be taken. It proved to be desperately difficult work, with very bad going over the stony plain and up the escarpment under a hot sun. The official report says 'the men were suffering fiercely from the heat, lack of water and the accumulated weariness of the previous day's marches' before they gained the heights. They were met by the unwelcome news that the wells where they had expected to find water were dry and that their limited water supplies could be made to last only for another forty-eight hours. The capture of Sollum was therefore imperative.

It did not prove too difficult. The armoured cars, which had been forced to take a different route from the infantry, moved forward to occupy the Halfaia Pass – later known as the Hellfire Pass to the 8th Army – which they did successfully. As soon as the Senussi realized that the heights had been taken, and that the armoured cars had successfully struggled up there, a feat which they had considered impossible, they abandoned Sollum. The remainder of the army, a cavalry brigade with infantry and artillery support, was able to occupy Sollum.

In any previous campaign they would have been forced to wait there for some time to allow the men and transport animals to recover their condition and regroup for an advance. But now, for the first time in warfare, the armoured cars came into their own. The infantry were in a terrible state, collapsing with heat and want of water, quite unable to effect a pursuit. The General gave orders to Bend'Or to advance and left it to his discretion as to how far to pursue the retreating army; no support could be offered and Bend'Or was on his own, which suited him admirably. The cars rushed after the Senussi and caught up with them about seventeen miles from Sollum at the Bir Asisa Wells. They were by no means a routed army, being several thousand strong, well entrenched once more among sand dunes, with three field guns and two machine guns. Since the armoured cars carried only machine guns it should have been possible for the Turkish gunners, with an effective range of two miles, to have caused grave damage. In fact they were so taken aback by the speed of the attack that they managed to fire only eight rounds before the cars were on top of them and the gunners killed or captured. The speed and mobility of the cars was an entirely new element in warfare, and the engagement at Bir Asisa was the first of a new era. It was appreciated as such at the time. GOC Egypt described it as a record in the history of war. Reuter's correspondent sent a long dispatch:

> ARMOURED CAR CHASE
>
> . . . But they were by no means to be allowed to get away scot free. The armoured car battery, under the command of Major the Duke of Westminster, was hot on their tracks. The battery consisted of nine armoured cars and, in addition, one open car, on which a machine gun had been mounted, the total personnel only amounting to thirty-two all ranks. Quickly reaching and passing through the enemy's camp at Bir Waer, where a straggler was captured, who was afterwards to prove a most valuable prize, the cars dashed at racing speed down the Tobruk Road, which runs westward through the Libyan Desert, and along which the enemy had retired. Signs of their retreat shortly became visible, an abandoned horse being passed, then a few bunches of stragglers, who sniped the cars as they dashed past. Twenty-three miles had been covered at a terrific pace, when whipping round a bend in the road, the leading car came suddenly on top of the enemy's camp, which lay at the Bir Asisa Wells, about 300 yards to the south of the road. They were caught just as they were preparing to leave the camp. Their camels were standing loaded, and, indeed, masses of the enemy were already on the move. One of their ten-pounders, however, was still in position, and two machine guns, and with these the Turks who were manning them immediately opened fire as the leading car swung round the bend into sight. A sharp order from the commanding officer and the battery swung into line and charged! Now the method of an armoured car attack is much the same as that of infantry – alternate rushes by a portion of the line, supported by the covering fire of the other portions. And in this manner the cars

advanced on the enemy over the 300 yards of rough ground which lay between the road and the enemy's gun positions and camp. Ten-pounder shells whizzed just over the top of the cars, bursting nearly two miles behind them, but fortunately not a single direct hit was registered. And our machine guns were doing deadly work, which quickly silenced the enemy's guns, the Turkish officers and gun crews who were serving them being shot down almost to a man and the guns captured.

Turning their attention now to the retreating enemy forces who were thoroughly demoralized and scattering in every direction, the cars dashed here and there, scouring the battlefield, shooting down any of the enemy who still attempted to offer resistance, and searching for Turkish officers, whose capture was, of course, of importance. Most of the enemy were now throwing away their rifles and clearing as rapidly as they could, helter-skelter and utterly regardless of direction, into such a state of panic had they been thrown by the suddenness and irresistible nature of the attack. To prevent the escape of their camel supply train, some fifty camels, which were already on the move with their loads, were shot, with extraordinary results in several cases, for the moment they were struck they blew up sky-high with terrific explosions. The unfortunate beasts had been laden with petrol and bombs.

ENEMY SMASHED UP

After effecting as much damage and destruction on the enemy as possible the battery returned to Sollum, leaving three cars on the field to guard the prisoners and booty captured, until such time as empty cars could be sent out to bring the prisoners in. The enemy had been completely smashed up at the cost to us of only one casualty, one officer being slightly wounded in the head. It was a magnificent and unique piece of work from start to finish.

Of the gallant fellows who manned them it is impossible to speak too highly, and Major the Duke of Westminster's name will by now be on everybody's lips for the intrepid manner in which he pushed the pursuit home and committed his command to the final attack. In the action the enemy suffered heavy casualties, which included about thirty Turkish officers either killed or wounded. Three ten-pounder guns, nine machine guns, a great quantity of shell, and 300,000 rounds of small-arms ammunition were amongst the principal items of the booty captured, which included quantities of military stores of all descriptions, food supplies, camels, mules &c. It was a knock-out blow for the enemy and a fine finish for the campaign.

The single casualty was Lt Leslie, who was only slightly wounded.

Bend'Or rode as always, not in an armoured car, but in his own Rolls tourer, open to the elements and mounting a machine gun.

After the guns were captured the now demoralized enemy was pursued. The Senussi were left much to their own devices, but the Turkish officers were sought out. About fifty of all ranks were killed or wounded and many more captured. The enemies' supplies were also destroyed, and the Senussi as a fighting force finished.

In essence it had much of the qualities of a brilliant old-style cavalry action, and Bend'Or certainly had the dash and vigour of the best type of cavalry officer, riding in his open car at the head of his squadron. The difference was that no horsed cavalry could have made so rapid a move across desert – a hundred miles that day – or stormed machine guns and artillery without taking punishing casualties. This was something hitherto unknown in warfare and all subsequent armoured actions are the heirs of it.

There are two contemporary accounts of the battle, the first by the Reuter correspondent quoted above, and the second by Jack Leslie himself, who described the whole of the short campaign. (The extracts from this are published by kind permission of his daughter the Marchionness of Cholmondely.)

> We left Matruh on the 10th and made Barrani, when we proceeded thirty miles due south with ten armoured cars, eighteen Fords, and six staff cars carrying our petrol and transport. The object was to climb the Tereff Mountains for the attack on Sollum, which lies in a harbour surrounded by mountains except on this side, which road, of course, was completely held from the heights. We made a track up the pass, and succeeded in getting every car up without mishap. When I tell you that the desert we traversed has the exact appearance of the Brancaster Marshes, only dry with large tufts of camel scrub and many sand dunes in places, you can imagine some of our difficulties. Of course it was a compass bearing march, with no track except of a car sent down two days before to reconnoitre. When we reached the top we had no idea how far the dongas, of which there were some twenty, reached back and, of course, we had to go round them. That afternoon the helio failed to find the main force on the coast and receiving no orders by 10 p.m. Westminster and I motored right back to Bag-Bag on the coast where General Lukin's forces were. This place is twenty-five miles west of Barrani and twenty-five east of Sollum. We found the place, which consists of one hut in the sand dunes, in two

hours, doing thirty miles by the stars with no car lights and no track. We went slap through a Bedouin camp en route. We arrived back at camp, with orders to move at 4 a.m. We did forty miles the next day and succeeded in joining up with General Lukin and his South African brigade – very fine men – on top of the Medean Pass, about thirty miles south of Sollum. The stones and rocks on the top were so bad that some cars punctured six or seven times.

On the 13th we did a ten mile march north-west and the 14th morning we set out to take Sollum and attack the enemy who were expected to be at Bir-Waer, their arsenal and headquarters since the beginning, six miles south-west of Sollum. We arrived without event at the top of Holfara Pass, where we were going to meet the Camel Corps and Hampdens Yeomanry Brigade. We heard there that the enemy had blown up a lot of stores and left the day before on hearing of our arrival up the mountain. Of course we had outflanked them with the cars. Now the series of events of the next three days you would not believe if you read it in a book and certainly the relief of the *Tara* prisoners [described below] was almost too exaggerated for a Drury Lane melodrama, but I will relate them as I saw them.

After hearing of the evacuation of Bir-Waer General Peyton gave 'Bend'Or' leave to pursue unsupported, on what he said was a risky and hazardous exploit.

We proceeded six miles at once to Bir-Waer due west where we found one man left who unwillingly told us that the enemy had retreated down the road. This man eventually turned out to be the only man who had ever seen Bir Hakim where the *Tara* prisoners were and he had fed his flocks there thirty years ago. We were in Tripoli at Bir Waer and hit off the road – a good desert track – made by the Sultan years ago. We knew they would have gone far, but would not expect us in Italian territory. Nine cars, one Ford and the Duke's Rolls set off down the road doing 35 and came across many stragglers which we did not wait for. Mangles, 20th Hussars, had the leading car – I was next. Suddenly about four to five hundred camels loaded, many men, and tents appeared to our left stretching from the road to two miles south-west. Mangles and I never stopped till we had gone two miles past the convoy, when we turned south to head them off. We then collected the other seven cars and Ford with machine gun and forming line went straight for them. In this position we half-mooned them. The first shot they fired hit the side of my turret and splintering hit me in three places. I was firing the gun and had taken the top off the car to lighten it. However, I did not feel it much and had a splendid time. To make accurate practice one has to stop the car to shoot, which gives the fellow broadside on a good head and shoulders target. My main objective was a ten-pound gun which was firing at the seven cars. I got 200 yards off and fired ten rounds which went too high, but the next burst hit the five gunners – all Turks – and no movement could be seen. A machine gun had meanwhile opened on the car from my right hand and had to be attended to. As in the previous fight we had killed all their gunners. There is not so much competition to man the mitrailleuse in the Senussi army as formerly. After a rambling fight which stretched over some seven square miles we collected forty dead'uns, twenty five prisoners and six or eight Turks. We could have done in many more, but had not the means of taking away prisoners. Two cars were left out collecting munitions and breaking rifles. Three field guns, nine machine guns, shells and 300,000 rounds of ammunition were amongst the spoil. Most of it was on camels, already packed for a trek, so it was extremely urgent we pushed on after them. I went back with Westminster to bring out twelve Fords at night to collect the prisoners and wounded. We had wires of congratulation from Maxwell, the Sultan of Egypt and Kitchener, so felt rather bucked with ourselves. Peyton said we deserved special recognition and asked for the names of all the officers out that day. We gave him the names of the men but did not recommend any officer in particular – quite rightly. We came back the next day to Sollum where the trophies were all paraded and tremendous palaver for the whole garrison.

There was a result of the action that was to be more pleasing than the capture of Turkish officers or guns: one of the prisoners was carrying a letter from a British naval officer appealing for better treatment on behalf of his men who were being held prisoners by the Senussi. The letter was written in French, and the halting naval officer's French shows the desperate state they were in.

Monsieur le General Nouri Pasha,

Tous ces hommes ont grand besoin de souliers a marcher, a present les pieds de tout sont nues . . . tout ont grand faim toujours. Nous n'avons pas j'amais assez a manger et tout sont tres maigre et faible . . . Il y a chaque jour malade commle dyssentry entre 15 et 25 hommes. 2 sont tres serieux . . . depuis que nous sommes dans cettle localite il y a morte 3 personnes . . . Ils sont mort parce qu'il n'y a pas des medecines, des nourritures et des necessaires pour les malades . . . Dans l'esperance de votre consideration favorable a mon lettre, et a notre besoins tres grandes, et avec beaucoup de salutations et des compliments.

R.S. Gwatkin Williams
Capitaine de Vaisseau de Navire Anglais

It was dated more than a month previously – 8 February, and unless something had been done to improve the prisoners' lot they would clearly be in even worse straits by now.

The men were survivors of the auxiliary cruiser HMS *Tara*, formerly the Dublin–Holyhead ferry *Hibernia*, manned by her civilian crew including her former master, Lieutenant Tanner RNR. *Tara* had been armed with a single 3.6-pounder gun and given the task of intercepting seaborne supplies for the Senussi. On 5 November they were torpedoed by a German submarine, the *U 35*, and sank within seven minutes. Twelve men were killed but most of the crew managed to get to the boats, which were taken in tow by the submarine and the men landed at Bardia. The German commander wanted to take Captain Gwatkin Williams as a prisoner to Austria where he would certainly have been much better looked after, but he pleaded successfully to be allowed to stay with his men.

The capture represented something of a coup for the Turks – both Nuri and Gaafar came to inspect the prisoners – but also something of an embarrassment for they had to be removed to a safe place deep in the desert, and many were in no condition to march. One of the survivors had to have a mangled foot amputated, without anaesthetic, by a pair of scissors: he died. Many of the civilian crew were in their fifties and sixties and in no shape to cope with the demands of a desert march which would have taxed much younger men. March they had to, for twelve days through the desert, before they reached a 'camp' with no facilities and little food.

The camp was at the wells of El Hakim (Bir el Hakim Abbayar), described by Captain Williams as

> two old Roman wells with the usual white mound and grave on top, a small stone blockhouse, and the barest, flattest desert of stones we had yet seen, and with a single dwarf date palm growing out of an old lime kiln . . . these wells are of the usual Roman pattern. Bottle shaped, some 25 feet in diameter at the bottom, 15ft deep and with a square entrance on top a yard across.

This was to be their home for more than three months, where they had to provide what shelter they could for themselves in the desert winter. For some time this was one of the wells which happened to be conveniently dry.

A diary of their life was kept by the Captain, and another by a private soldier 'Willie', who had served as a gunner on *Tara*. It is interesting to compare some incidents seen from the quarterdeck and the lower deck.

> November 29. Rice has been our only food for some time now, and we gradually get thinner. No gram of it is ever wasted, we wait eagerly until it is cooked, and half have it at a time. It is levelled into the iron wash-basin and carefully divided into sectors clockwise, so that all may share exactly equally. Hunger makes us extremely jealous and watchful of any infringement of this.

Captain Gwatkin Williams wrote: 'Small quantity of rice only for ration. Men started to feel the hunger.'

On Christmas Day they were given a handful of beans, 'an undreamed-of luxury'. They had saved some flour, rice and sugar to make a Christmas pudding 'all boiled for five hours in the Master's trousers'. On 30 December they had a treat when a sheep was killed by a wolf, but even then the remains had to be bought from the villainous Captain Achmed, an Egyptian deserter who commanded the guard. A little later a young camel drowned in one of the wells. Captain Williams succeeded in getting it out, at some danger to himself, for which feat he was rewarded with a highly appreciated ship's biscuit, and for two days the men were able to feast on drowned camel. Apart from such pieces of good fortune their only available protein was in the form of snails, which were much appreciated but the cause of much dissension.

Inevitably there were further deaths. Unless something could be done rapidly it was clear that all the prisoners would die, in the not-too-distant future, of disease or starvation. Captain Williams, after his letter had been dispatched, felt that the only opportunity to save his men would be for him to escape and try to reach British lines across the desert, a venture which would have been suicidal to anyone without navigational ability. In fact he managed to make over fifty miles on foot before being recaptured, a fact that probably saved his life. Although the Turkish soldiers who caught him were decent enough, and, by stealing lambs from the Arabs, gave him the first good meal he had eaten for months, when he was returned to camp he was spat at and beaten by the guards.

They had been held prisoner for nearly twenty weeks when Captain Williams's letter to Nuri Pasha was discovered, and it was clearly imperative that they be rescued without further delay, especially since they had been warned that they would have to move, an appalling prospect when they could not even muster enough strength to search for firewood. Other prisoners' letters were also captured, and one of these had the name of the place they were being held; fortunately a guide was found from among the captured Arabs who claimed to know the wells of El Hakim; they were, he said, about sixty miles away.

Bend'Or asked for permission to attempt a rescue with the cars: any other method would have been impossible, since in their weakened condition the prisoners would hardly have been got out on foot and horse transport was impossible since the water shortage was already so great that the cavalry were sent back from Sollum as soon as that town was taken. General Peyton recorded:

> I gave his offer careful consideration; our information was scanty and conflicting, the country to be traversed practically unknown and unmapped, the distance most uncertain, and the fact of our prisoners being at the spot by no means established, finally it was more than possible that re-inforcing enemy in strength might be met with, coming from the West. However, encouraged by the Duke of Westminster's quiet confidence and having still fresh in my mind his brilliant leadership on March 14th and greatly influenced by the misery to which our fellow countrymen were being exposed and to the still greater misery to which they would be indefinitely condemned, unless a rescue was effected, I decided to accept the Duke's offer.

Bend'Or wrote that night to his mother:

> I cannot give you the details of a fight I had on the 14th but just the rough outline. After 2 days hard march over almost impossible country I was ordered to pursue the enemy who had retreated to take up a fresh position. They had 17 hours start, but I managed to catch them in 2 hours, found where their guns were, formed line with my cars and charged them. Turks manned the guns and fired at us till we were within 200 yards of them, luckily they missed us – and the net result was that with 9 cars and only 36 men I captured 3 cannon and 9 Maxims. Killed fifty of the enemy, including 4 Turkish officers killed round the

> guns, captured 3 more Turkish officers, 36 prisoners, 50 camels, 12 horses, 10 mules, 250,000 rounds ammunition and lots of loot. Am off on my last expedition at 2.30 tomorrow morning and hope to bring off a big thing. N.B. None of this success due to me but to my officers and men. Was in centre car in the charge, we went full speed – glorious feeling. I go 700 miles tonight into their country with 40 cars, 100 camels and one squadron cavalry; a nice force – but a difficult job before me am very proud of the command entrusted to me. Only had one officer wounded slightly in head – Jack Leslie 12th Lancers, very slight . . .

Thus a convoy of forty-two vehicles – nine armoured cars, three Fords armed with Maxims, eleven other Fords, ten ambulances, a Wolseley and five staff cars including the Duke's own Rolls set out. This was the first long-range motor desert raid, over unmapped and unknown country with no logistic support or pre-planning. An account was written by one of the officers who took part:

> The consent of the General having been obtained we got a number of Ford and Studebaker ambulances up the pass at Sollum and started off at 3 a.m. 42 motor vehicles in all 9ACs leading and 3 Fords mounted maxims forming additional escort – the Duke led the way in his *touring car* and immediately found the track leading into Tripoli (in itself remarkable) and we all went off in line eventually striking quite a decent road which brought us to the scene of the battle two days before; the moon then went down and we waited until daybreak and had breakfast. About 6 a.m. we started off on our journey and kept along this road in a westerly direction for 85 miles before striking off into the desert. We saw a large number of camels on each side of the road but no Senussi excepting a small party of Turkish officers who we took prisoners – only one escaping. After we left the main road we struck one of the most desolate pieces of country I have ever seen and what the guides steered by I have no conception – as a matter of fact I was getting very pessimistic by this time as every time we came to a ridge the guides would say, 'The well is over this ridge' which did not prove to be the case; this happened about 5 times, each ridge being about 4 to 5 miles beyond the last. When the guides themselves began quarrelling we thought it was up with us when lo and behold! we pulled up and the guides said they could see the well. We had then been 130 miles across unmapped, unknown country. The excitement was then intense we knew that if the news of the battle had reached the guards they would have removed the prisoners. Also we had received reports that they were somewhere else, but off charged the cars with the

Duke at their head and we following about a couple of hundred yards behind. We could see a mount in the desert with a large number of figures silhouetted against the skyline. I shouted 'It must be them' as they made no attempt to run away but stood like statues. When they got over the first shock of seeing us they started to beckon us with their arms and wave their clothes. The cars were a wonderful sight all charging across the desert in fact it became a race as to who got there first. The scene when we did get there was one I shall never forget – numbers of the prisoners crying without any effort to hide their tears while a number of our men found a great difficulty in not following suit. I personally had a very big lump in my throat if nothing more. The majority were so weak from dysentery and starvation that they could only just stand and most were half-naked and ravenous. We brought large supplies of hospital suits and luxuries for them and they were soon eating for all they were worth. Whilst this was going on we heard the rattle of the maxims and soon the cars had overtaken the guards who had run away and all the latter about 30 in number were killed. They could never stop shaking our hands and I was surprised to find them nearly all Welshmen. Captain Gwatkin Williams needless to say was one: he was the fittest of the whole party being the only one who had not had dysentery. When captured he weighed 16st and he now weighs about 10.7. I should think something in favour of being fat. The next thing was to get the party home and this was a very difficult job as the prisoners were like children. As soon as I arranged them in a car with blankets food &c and went to another car the first lot were all out again talking to their pals and congratulating one another and eventually about 5.30 p.m. we started home, following our old track. 91 extra people taking some carrying, and we had to put some outside the ACs. We had a terrible lot of tyre trouble and I was the last to reach our temporary camp, 20 miles from Sollum touring in 2 Ford cars at 1.30 a.m. dog tired, and happy when one looked at the pitiable condition of the men and realized that in another week or ten days it would have been too late.

The Duke has got the DSO and been recommended for the VC what a sportsman. When the prisoners reached Sollum the next day they had to be brought down the hill on camels as they could not walk. They had a great reception but it was a sad sight . . . Please don't let any of this letter get in the papers the Duke hates advertisement.

Captain Williams described it from the other side:

I had just put our supper to cook when someone came running into the tent and said the soldiers were very excited, had all gone off for their rifles and run up the mound. I hoped it was the long expected caravan (returning travellers often being greeted in this way) and went on writing. Suddenly someone shouted there was a motor car coming, and we all ran out to see, not daring to believe our eyes and fearful of disappointment. But there it was right enough its khaki body coming rapidly round the bend of the incline to the ENE the way I had gone to Sollum. Salin had not lied after all, and the two months truce with the Senussi, to be followed by permanent peace on 14th March must have taken effect and this must be a British envoy allowed to come and see us and arrange our release at last. But there was no flag, so we did not yet feel certain. Suddenly more cars appeared, and more and more, all tearing towards us over the stones. On sighting us they seemed to check for a moment, and then fly forward again. We were certain now. We went mad. We yelled ourselves hoarse. We could see now that some were armoured cars and some others ambulances. The latter drew up at our tattered tents, and in a moment we were tearing bully beef, bread and tinned chicken, and drinking condensed milk out of tins. We tore our food like famished wolves with tears in our eyes and wonder in our hearts. An officer approached and asked if I was Captain Williams and a second or two later I was shaking hands with the Duke of Westminster, in command of the whole. He asked where our guards were, and with my mouth full I indicated the bushy plain to the westward. I had no idea there was still work and went on eating. But the armoured cars dashed off round the mound to reconnoitre. Almost immediately, while the Duke was questioning me as to the treatment, I heard the maxims splutter. I shouted 'save them, they have been kind to us' and dashed up the old well mound for the last time, the Duke with me. But we were too late, the garrison (I suppose nine soldiers) had been wiped out in a few seconds, and I could see only prostrate forms lying amongst the desert scrub. Unhappily with them perished many women and children who had run out with the soldiers and could not be distinguished from them in the heat of action. Our guards had died like the brave Arabs they were, with arms in their hands, and 'in death they were not divided'. If only they had told me the truth sometimes, if only they had not always lied to us, their lives would probably have been saved, because I would have realized that England was still at war with the Senussi, and could have interceded in time on their behalf. There we left them, and in a few minutes had packed our mementoes and belongings and were ourselves being towed away in ambulances and armoured cars, warmly clad in blue hospital suits, the sick being tenderly carried on stretchers to their conveyances. The graves of the four who would never return were photographed, with many other interesting groups, and in about half an hour from our first sighting the cars we were all bumping joyously, and still only half believing over the desert stones. One of the last remarks I heard uttered, I think by a cockney, seemed to sum up tersely the whole matter. 'An' to think I went in there saying there was no Gawd.'

Jack Leslie's account gives some feeling of what it was like to serve under Bend'Or:

> From correspondence collected at Bir Waer, some letters written by the prisoners dated February 3rd Bir Hakim were found. It was this evidence alone and that of two Turks we captured that induced us to set out on this unmapped, unexplored desert in search of these one hundred starving prisoners. In the night of the 16th we collected thirty three Ford Studebaker ambulances, Talbot and Sunbeam touring cars and set off at 3 a.m. 17th. We went down the same road we had gone to the battle on two days before, and for ninety miles down it before branching off. We met two Turkish officers and six loaded camels on the way: amongst the loot we took off them were a dog, sheep, tea, coffee, cashmir shawls and toilet soap from the Rue de la Paix in Paris, which I kept in reminiscence of happy days!
>
> When we had gone ninety miles the guide said if we prayed there in the morning we should reach Bir Hakim at night, so we made it out to be thirty miles further. The going proved pretty good as the surface of caked sand bore the weight of the cars. We had two guides now, both were much at a loss as we passed objects so quickly in the cars their brains could not keep pace. Eventually after many punctures, etc. we pulled up six miles from a small mill which they assured us was the well. Someone could be seen running up to it too. The armoured cars then set off expecting considerable opposition from the guard if the prisoners were there. It was only at 400 yards off one could see these half-starved wretches waving and cheering – the guard having cleared off. They rushed out to meet us, half-naked, some shouting 'We are free', others 'We are starving', 'For Christ's sake a cigarette'. However, we were off in half a minute to pursue the guard, all of whom we killed.
>
> I never saw fellows eat like it in my life. They were all provided with dressing-gowns to wear. Wynn Williams, the officer with them, had had the gold cap taken off his tooth and been beaten and thrown into the latrine for trying to escape. A quarter of a pint of goat's milk was their full daily ration and absolutely nothing else. To cut a long story short, we got back at midnight

> with every car and man, more wires from Maxwell and the Sultan of Egypt. Bend'Or was given the DSO and recommended by Peyton for the VC. Nothing but his amazing confidence and innate optimism could have ever started off a convoy prepared to do 300 miles to find them. He would class with any general as a great leader of men, having extraordinary personality. The odds were considered about six to one against our getting them. To start with they had not been located for six weeks, and then had probably been moved miles since. General Peyton was almost beside himself with excitement I believe. Of course he commands the whole force and Lukin the infantry under him.
>
> Well I do not know if this will interest you at all, but it will have to do for all at home as I cannot write this out again. Commander Williams came back on my car and never stopped eating, except when he talked – they were all far too happy to sleep that night – poor devils.

The raid had covered two hundred and thirty miles within twenty-four hours and experienced no losses, either of men or cars: a considerable tribute to the toughness of the vehicles and the standards of maintenance achieved, and a clear precedent for subsequent desert actions.

Enthusiasm at the rescue, coming on top of the successful action at Asisa, was unbounded and tributes flowed. After the stalemates and bloody battles of the Western Front it seemed that a new form of warfare had become possible, as indeed it had. To a greater extent than almost any other innovation it was one man's doing. Bend'Or's enthusiasm for motors, his perception of the need for mobility, his personal backing of the design and production, his dedicated formation and training of the squadron culminating in his resourcefulness and dash in battle, had made this a unique episode.

He was thanked by Sirdar, the King of Egypt: 'Mon Cher Duc de Westminster, C'est avec un véritable plaisir que je vous confère la Médaille d'Or de Mohammed Aly, qui vous sera remise par le Colonel Renucy Bey . . . Vous êtes le premier officier à qui je remes cette Médaille. Vous l'avez hautement merité . . . c'est un des faîtes d'Armes le plus glorieux.' It was widely recognized as such. Bend'Or was thanked by the Lords of the Admiralty and the War Council, as became one who held commissions in both services. Lord Kitchener, no great friend of his, said in measured terms: 'The final action of the armoured cars under the Duke of Westminster was well managed and

Eaton Hall

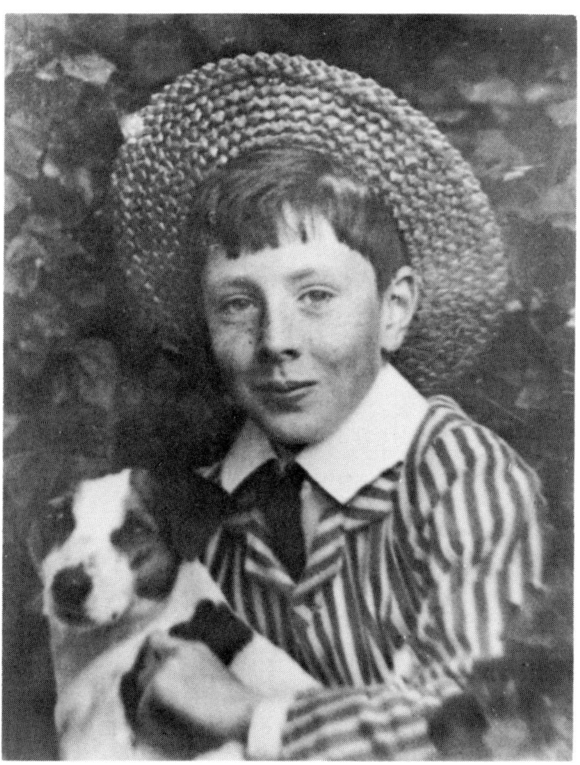

Bend'Or as a boy at Saighton

Bend'Or in South Africa 1901; uniform of the Blues

Bend'Or in stable yard archway, Eaton 1901

Bend'Or's house in the Orange Free State

King Edward VII at Eaton, December 1909

Sir John Lavery's painting of the famous armoured car division

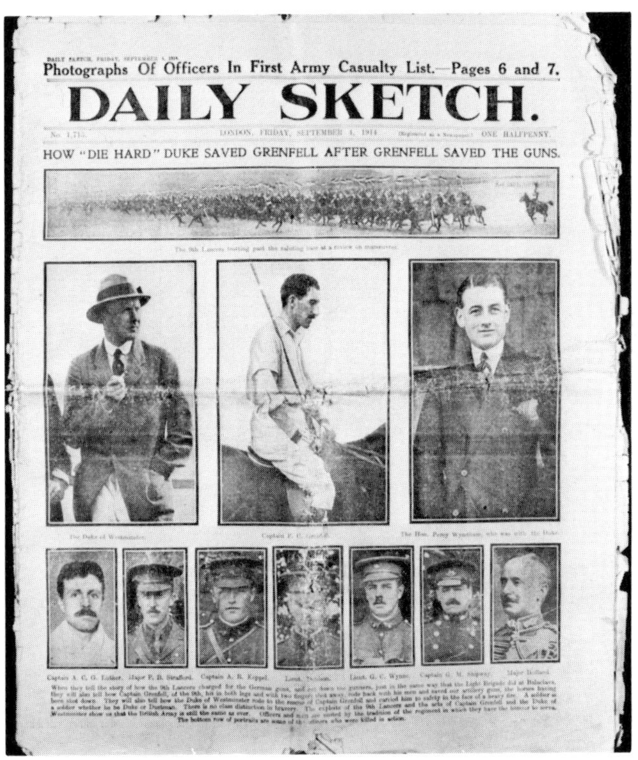

Photographs Of Officers In First Army Casualty List.—Pages 6 and 7.

DAILY SKETCH.

HOW "DIE HARD" DUKE SAVED GRENFELL AFTER GRENFELL SAVED THE GUNS.

Daily Sketch of 1 September 1914, showing that Bend'Or was in the fighting from the beginning

Bend'Or in his armoured Rolls-Royce . . .

. . . and the man who drove it through the war, Bend'Or's chauffeur George Powell

The Armoured Car Squadron 1915. Bend'Or in centre front row.
George Powell in chauffeur's uniform on left

REWARD FOR THE DUKE.—Capt. Gwatkin Williams (left) and Capt. Tanner (right), of the torpedoed Tara, visited Saighton Grange to present the Duke of Westminster with a silver souvenir of his armoured-car exploit. With the Duke is little Lady Mary Grosvenor.

The Duke of Westminster being presented with a silver souvenir
of his armoured car exploit

Bend'Or and Shelagh with the King of Spain at Eaton

One night's catch. The river Alton, 7 July 1926. 33 salmon weighing
800 lbs, the average weight being 24 lbs

Gamekeepers at Eaton in the late thirties: Sandy Myles, head keeper, with (in green livery) Fred Grass, George Grass Snr, Fred Milton and Tom Lamont

Sandy Myles with beaters at the Lower Lanes, Aldford, 1930s

Bend'Or with his old friend Basil Kerr, World's End, 1930s

Bend'Or with Lord Derby, Winston Churchill and Basil Kerr. Aintree, mid-1930s

The *Cutty Sark*

Drawing of Bend'Or by Drian

Photograph of Anne, Duchess of Westminster, in the robes of a peeress at the time of the Coronation

The opening of Annacis Island, the author is sixth from the left, with Colonel Robert Grosvenor, later 5th Duke of Westminster, immediately to the left, and Colonel Gerald Grosvenor the 4th Duke of Westminster behind him

Annacis Island Development, Canada

The attractive landscaped grounds of one of the factories on Annacis Island boldly led.' The GOC Sir John Maxwell wrote:

> My dear Westminster,
>
> I most heartily congratulate you on the truly magnificent performance of your motor cars.
>
> I congratulate you personally for I know well that these things depend entirely on the initiative, decision and courage of the Commander. I hope those in authority at home will realize what an extraordinary success this little campaign has been and how much is due to the actions of your cars. Had it not been for their dash our casualties would have been far greater and results far less decisive.
>
> People in England will be delighted to hear of the rescue of the poor ship-wrecked Britishers and I personally am very proud and happy that this should be the culminating episode of my command. I thank you.
>
> Yours very sincerely,
> J.G. Maxwell

He sent him the Grand Senussi's standard. More formally he reported to the Secretary of State for War:

> My Lord,
>
> The enclosed dispatches from Major General W.E. Peyton, CB, DSO, Commanding the Western Frontier Force, Egypt, were handed me as I was on the point of embarking for England on 22 March 1916.
>
> Before the receipt of these dispatches I had, in accordance with the powers conferred on me, bestowed the Distinguished Service Order on Major the Duke of Westminster for his gallantry and resource when in command of the light armoured car brigade on March 14th, 1916 at Bir Asisa, and subsequently on March 17th and 18th, 1916 at Bir Hakim. I desire to endorse Major General Peyton's high appreciation of the Duke of Westminster's services, a less determined and resourceful commander might well have shirked the responsibility of taking motor cars on the first occasion, 30 miles, and on the second, 115 miles, into an unknown desert with the uncertainty of the cars being able to negotiate the country or the amount of resistance that was likely to be encountered. I venture to think that these actions constitute a record in the History of War.
>
> The Duke of Westminster's modest account of his exploits I cannot improve on, therefore forward them for Your Lordship's perusal.
>
> Major General Peyton recommends that the name of Major the Duke of Westminster be submitted to His Majesty the King for a

> Victoria Cross in recognition of his gallantry in rescuing no less than 91 imprisoned British subjects. I feel I am in duty bound to forward this recommendation for it was entirely due to the Duke of Westminster that this magnificent enterprise was brought to a successful conclusion; had this opportunity been missed or had there been any hesitation in decision it is possible that these unfortunate people might never have been heard of again. Because so much depended on this decision I have no hesitation in forwarding Major General Peyton's recommendation for Your Lordship's consideration.

The recommendation for the Victoria Cross was, unusually, not sanctioned by London, much to General Peyton's fury. It was highly likely that Kitchener was responsible. Peyton wrote to Bend'Or from London on 1 May 1916: 'I know for certain one if not two of the committee who adjudicated these matters were in favour of it. Lord K told me you could not get it because you were in command!!!!! and the recommendation could not be accepted as I was not present!!! I know you don't care a damn but I do.' Winston Churchill was probably right when he said that it was only because he was a Duke that Bend'Or was denied the VC.

Bend'Or was never popular with the High Command, and his being proved so right cannot have improved his standing. But he was given a DSO, this being in Maxwell's gift, and, what must have been at least as much appreciated, received letters of thanks from both the South Africans and the Australians, who were not noted for excessive enthusiasm towards English dukes. Bend'Or was somewhat overwhelmed by all this attention, and in his letter home said only

> the last fight I had when I got the ninety-one prisoners back was at a well Bir Hakim built by the Romans – the water was good except for a moribund camel having been in it for sometime. Three of the prisoners knew me – stewards on the Holyhead boats – they nearly all come from Holyhead and district, so you might make some enquiries about them all – I was told their camp was only 60 miles away, but it turned out to be 120, so I had a long 240 mile drive through the enemy country, but took them by surprise and all went well – a good day but not as good as my fight on 14th. This prisoner episode happened on 17th.

There is one particularly nasty suggestion made, most recently by Mr Woodrow Wyatt, and passed on by Lesley Field in her life of Bend'Or, that he caused the guards of the *Tara* prisoners to be shot.

Captain Williams's diary shows quite conclusively that this was not so, that he was with Bend'Or when this took place, and that they both attempted to stop it. This was confirmed by an eyewitness account published in *The Times* of 15 March 1963:

> In the confusion, and through a misunderstanding, some of the armoured cars on the flanks of the advance had opened up with their machine guns and blood was shed. After hurried explanations and with the Duke at his side, Captain Gwatkin Williams dashed up the sloping ground and stayed the shooting, but not before many of the Arab garrison had been killed.

The canard is however typical of those that have been allowed to flourish.

In spite of the success of the Armoured Brigade Bend'Or was not allowed to participate in further fighting. He wrote in annoyance on 22 June from Alexandria:

> There is no prospect of anything here – the Italians won't let us over their Tripolitan frontier – if our weak knock-kneed non-fighting government would only be firm with them. I could do lots of good work – and plenty of fighting. But as it is we have to sit still and do nothing, and no prospects. I have written to Aquila G. to tell her what I think of her macaroni eating countrymen.

This inactivity was partly again due to Kitchener, who kept a large force pinned down in Egypt for no apparently good reason.

Shortly after this he went down with high fever, a legacy of his South African days, and was shipped back to France. The fever proved serious and recovery was delayed. As late as January 1917 he was waiting for the verdict of a medical board to pronounce him fit for service. This never came, but something happened that throws an unexpected light on his character and abilities. He had already proved himself to be a courageous and capable regimental officer, but he was now able to make himself valuable in a very different role, working with an old comrade.

Winston Churchill had experienced a serious reversal of fortunes after his initial success at the Admiralty. In May 1915, Lord Fisher, the First Sea Lord, then seventy-four and suffering from acute megalomania, petulantly resigned from his post. Although Churchill had the full backing of all the other Sea Lords, who had suffered from Fisher's tantrums themselves, the Conservative opposition were at that time virulently anti-Winston, and eager for any opportunity to damage him. They seized the chance of an apparent crisis at the Admiralty to demand a coalition government, from the centre of which Churchill must be excluded. Asquith, who had just been jilted by Venetia Stanley and was in no condition for a fight, agreed to these demands 'in an incredibly short time', as Lloyd George observed.

When her husband was forced out of the Admiralty Clementine Churchill said 'I thought he would die of grief'. He was given the placebo of being appointed the Chancellor of the Duchy of Lancaster, but his counsels, which showed that grasp of high strategy that he always displayed, were ignored. He stayed for only a short time: the first speech he was able to make in Parliament was his speech of resignation, in November 1915. It contained, in one phrase, advice that if it had been taken, would have changed the whole course of the war – 'Undertake no operation in the West that is more costly to us in life than to the enemy.' In a remarkable gesture he went off immediately to the front, where for six months he fought with panache and efficiency as a regimental commander. When his regiment was amalgamated with another he returned to London to try once more to influence the government to sanity: it was a useless task, and when he wrote to his brother Jack 'I am learning to hate', it was not only the Germans to whom he was referring.

In December 1916 Asquith, 'supine, sodden and supreme', was replaced by Lloyd George, Winston's old friend and colleague. Even so it was not until July 1917 that he was able to ease out Dr Addison, who had been a successful Minister of Munitions, and put Winston in his place. There was a tremendous row, for many Liberals as well as Conservatives detested Churchill. The Tories called him 'a national danger' and organized committees to protest against his appointment.

In these circumstances Churchill kept his head down – he made only one major speech during his tenure of office – and got on with the job, determined to retrieve some of his political power and reputation. One of his first acts was to ask Bend'Or to join him as his personal assistant. This action can hardly be construed as favouritism. Churchill was never one to give 'jobs to the boys' and at that exceedingly critical time in his career he would have been even less likely to indulge in whims. He had already described Bend'Or (28 September 1915) as 'very trustworthy' and quite clearly wanted him as an active member of his team.

The Duke accompanied him on his travels to the front. On 18 March 1918, just before Ludendorff's spring offensive, they visited Montreuil, where Winston promised the Tank HQ that he would deliver 4,000 tanks to the Western Front during 1919. They were still there when the offensive began on the twenty-first, and Winston was hurried off, protesting, out of harm's way, by Bend'Or. Leo Amery, another Boer War friend, agreed with this. 'Stray tourists are not popular with staffs in a crisis. I found Bend'Or shared this view very strongly and was going to ask me not to come [to the front]. He said Churchill couldn't realize that he wasn't popular on these occasions, just because people received him reasonably politely.'

The rapid German advance was so serious that Winston and Bend'Or both had to leave once more for Paris on 28 March. There was a row from the politicians about this, since Winston, a politician, was going to see the Supreme Commander, Foch, a soldier, and it was felt that he should rather see Clemenceau, the President. Winston was still too dangerous to be let too close to soldiers! When they arrived in Paris they spent some time with both chiefs. They stayed there until the fourteenth, co-ordinating Allied plans to meet the German threat. Lloyd George did not join them, at this most important meeting, until 4 April. In the interim there had been a whole series of meetings where Allied strategy was agreed, at all of which Bend'Or seems to have been present. It is possible, since his French was better than Winston's and since he was popular with the French, that Bend'Or was at least a useful emollient; it is quite clear that he was asked to be much more than a dashing cavalryman.

Two months later he was playing an even more important role as the Marques de Villavieja recorded in his memoirs *Life has been Good*:

> In 1918, just before the party [at the Magdalena Palace in Santander] was about to break up, I was taken by surprise by a team of four great Englishmen, headed by the Duke of Westminster. They had arrived from San Sebastian by car, were in a terrible hurry, and without even giving themselves time to change their dusty clothes, they went straight to the casino, hoping to find out where and when they could see King Alfonso. They wanted at all costs to speak to him as soon as possible . . . The great team had to wait until next morning . . . it was evident that they had come to bring some important news . . . and we were given to understand that before the end of the year there would be peace in Europe. One of the four Englishmen was Mr

Smith.

This embassy visit is still shrouded in some mystery. Mr Smith, presumably Lord Birkenhead, does not mention it, nor is it recorded in John Capbell's latest biography. Churchill's letter to Bend'Or on 22 April 1918 hardly seems to warrant such a high-powered team, but makes it clear that there had been a previous talk.

> My dear Benny,
>
> I am delighted you are going to Spain and it will be very kind of you to give my best respects and very sincere good wishes to the King . . . We have I think understood in England the difficulties of the Spanish position. I am sure I understand; and you have never underrated them. Still I believe in the end the force of events and the march of history will sweep away the difficulties, and offer a great and splendid opportunity to Spain and her wise Sovereign.
>
> I hope you will tell the King that I am absolutely confident of the final result. I do not think there will be any compromise . . . with every good wish for the success of your journey.
>
> Believe me, Your sincere Friend. W.

These events took place at a time of great crisis. The British Army had taken a terrible mauling on the Western Front. The German advance continued unremitting and furious to within forty miles of Calais. On 13 April the C in C, Douglas Haig, issued a desperate order of the day. 'There is no other course open to us but to fight it out. Every position must be held to the last man: there must be no retirement. With our backs to the wall, and believing in the justice of our cause, each of us must fight to the end.'

The mission that Bend'Or was given must have been to pave the way for bringing Spain into the war. Portugal was already fighting alongside the Allies, Bend'Or was closer to Alfonso than any other Englishman as he had entertained him at Eaton for polo and shooting, and Birkenhead was the most convincing advocate of his time. Churchill's strategy had always been one of diversifying the action from the Western Front, which had been the motive of the Dardenelles campaign. If Spain could be persuaded to enter the war against Germany it might be enough to stave off the immediate threat, distracting the enemy's attention for enough time to give the armies, which Churchill described as 'fighting for their lives', a brief respite.

Bend'Or spent some time in Spain, for on 7 June the British

Ambassador in Madrid, Sir Arthur Hardinge, sent a secret message to Balfour:

> I have told him [the Duke of Westminster] that W.C.'s visit would in my opinion be undesirable even if he could find time for it. His coming to Spain, in his position, would be deemed a grave political step on the part of His Majesty's Government, would be misinterpreted by Germans and might be construed by Spaniards as a bid for active Spanish assistance in the War.

Which is of course what it would have been construed as.

If it is typical of Churchill that, as Minister of Munitions, he should have been seeking to influence high strategy by the most direct of means, it is equally typical that he should have chosen Bend'Or to head, at the most important crisis of the war, such a mission. Churchill was, of course, looking ahead. He could not know that the Germans were exhausting their strength in a final assault and were about to crumble. He was already planning the 1919 strategy, and indeed in an extraordinary Cabinet memorandum he made the point forcibly: 'In this year the initiative can only be seized as the result of plans made nearly a year ahead . . . we must organize the offensive battle for 1919. It will be no use thinking about it this winter . . .'

There was an interesting sequel to this incident over twenty years later. In January 1940 Bend'Or was found extremely ill by his own doctor on the Channel ferry nearing Dover. He did not immediately recognize the doctor, who was in uniform, and for six months afterwards was seriously ill with pneumonia. The only information he ever gave was that he had just returned from a mission to Spain. It seems likely that once again Churchill had sent his old friend to use his influence to keep Spain neutral. Although Alfonso had abdicated, Bend'Or had still many influential friends, and in view of his influence with the Windsors would have been an obvious choice. Since he never spoke about the journey, even to his daughter, Mary, who was serving in the MTC and had her home at Churton, near Eaton, at the time, it seems clear that there was some matter of importance behind his mission.

5

Life on the Eaton Estate

At this time it may be appropriate to record a personal view of what life between the two World Wars was like on a major English estate.

Eaton Hall, one of the greatest of English houses, existed in its final form for only eighty years, and for more than half a century Bend'Or was master there. Life there was of a kind that is now gone for ever, and a personal reminiscence of what it was like may be interesting both for itself and the light it throws on Bend'Or. As a boy I suffered a good deal from asthma, and when the time came to leave school – Oldershaw Grammar School at Wallasey – my family felt that an outdoor life would be best for me. My father, who as North Wales area manager for the Atlas Assurance Company had a wide range of clients and friends, arranged for me to be accepted as a pupil forester.

The prescription must have been a good one, since I am now nearer eighty than seventy and have led a consistently demanding and energetic life, although one also full and rewarding, to a degree I could never have imagined when I arrived on 29 November 1926 at Chester station. I was met there by one of the estate lorries, an old Lacre which had been to the gasworks to collect coke for the agent's house. The coke and I arrived at my digs in Eccleston where the driver, George Johnson, carried my grip in and introduced me to my landlady, with the observation 'look after him, Missus, he looks pretty frail'. I was so shocked by the remark that I forgot to give him the half crown that should have been his tip.

I took a walk around Eccleston, the largest of the Eaton estate villages, built in its present form by John Douglas for the first Duke, and still a most beautiful village. It seemed then to reflect wealth applied in a diligent and responsible fashion to the creation and upkeep of a community. The church, inside and out, one of G.F. Bodley's finest works, seemed like a miniature cathedral, while I took the agent's house, The Paddocks, for Eaton Hall itself.

My landlady, Mrs Kate Debenham by name, had been married to one of the coachmen, who had died a year or two earlier. She was a neat lady of about fifty who had been in service herself, a fact reflected in the spotless manner in which her cottage was kept.

The next day I started work under the eye of my 'ganger', Bill Salisbury. It was still dark at 7.30 when he introduced me to my fellow workers to start my first day. Working hours were 7.30 a.m. to 4.30 p.m. during the winter time and 6.30 a.m. to 5 p.m. during the summer, except at harvest time when forestry workers joined in the harvesting and the hours were undefined!

The first task was to sweep the drive from Eccleston to Chester – a distance of roughly two miles, and only one of the five drives that led to the house. I was to lead the way, sweeping the middle of the road with a besom, the men following on both sides raking up the leaves into small heaps which were then loaded into a cart. It all seemed so easy, but by midday my back was breaking, my hands were sore and I realized that being in the presence of a stranger the men were loath to take a 'breather' as they obviously thought of me as a 'boss's' man.

After work I walked to Chester and bought a bicycle. My father was not going to spoil me and had told me I must buy it myself. It cost thirty shillings – and I agreed with Mr Crimes to pay two shillings and sixpence per week for twelve weeks. My wages were fifteen shillings and my father augmented this with seventeen shillings and sixpence a week so I had just enough to live on.

After sweeping the Overleigh drive the next job was to be hedge trimming on the Bretton drive, which seemed so far away that I thought I had ridden to Canada. The drive was hardly ever used and had been part of the extension of the Belgrave drive towards Hawarden at a time when the first Duke had been friendly with Mr Gladstone. The hedges were boundaries between the drive and farmland. I was not entrusted with a slashing hook, which was the privilege of the experienced, but was given a rake to rake up the cuttings and a pikel to load them into the inevitable horse-drawn cart which followed.

Raking thorns on a normal lawn or road is a simple task, but I learnt it was far from simple in anything like long grass and one had to be immaculate in the tidying up. Fortunately, we were not too many days on this job and the next task was one to which I looked forward with some excitement. The Crook O'Dee is a bend in the river Dee, about five miles upstream from Chester and, as the name indicates, is a very sharp bend. Some large trees in the saucer-shaped bank were slipping into the river and proving a danger to navigation. Our task was to fell these in such a way that they dropped up the bank, from where, after trimming out, they were hauled on to the roadside to be taken to the sawmill.

As a concession to my youth and size I was given a four-pound axe while the men with me wielded ones weighing five pounds. The axe was to be used primarily for putting a face into the tree so it fell the way you hoped it would go, and ultimately for the trimming out of the branches. The remainder of the work was done by cross-cutting, where one knelt on the ground on the other side of the tree to one's partner and pulled and shoved on the cross-cut saw, taking care not to get the saw trapped when the tree fell. I was given a tree smaller than the others were tackling, told what I had got to do, and started off with great enthusiasm, swinging the axe with rapidity and quietly critical of my companions with their slow methodical rhythm. It did not take long to learn that they were making much more headway than I and were much more accurate. I found it terribly hard to get the axe into the same place twice in succession. Before long, Sandy Myles, the head forester, drove up. He was a tall broad-shouldered Scot with a black moustache and rather fearsome looks. He stepped down the river bank, took one look at me swinging the axe and calmly said to Bill Salisbury – 'When that lad has his accident, Will, take him straight to the infirmary!'

After I had eventually got a face into my tree and had trimmed the base ready for the cross-cut, Bill Salisbury came to work the saw with me. Bill was in his fifties, knowledgeable, dour and of few words, but a strong character. We had not been working the cross-cut very long before my knees and thighs ached as well as my arms. I longed to ask for a 'breather' but pride would not allow it and very soon I was something of a passenger on the cross-cut, which drew appropriate comment from Bill! Eventually to my great relief we dropped the tree and I was given guidance on how to trim it out. This is certainly one of the most dangerous jobs with an axe as you are swinging it so often at shoulder level that any mistake could have serious consequences.

After lunch, timber waggoners with their teams of horses arrived to extract the timber on to the pole waggons and to make for the Belgrave sawmill three or four miles away. It would be about 3 p.m. in the afternoon when they departed and by this time I was swinging my axe at another tree.

The timber-waggon horses were splendid creatures and I still have vivid memories of them hauling these massive trees up the river bank to the roadside, the teamwork of the horses and men, the straining of harness and the rattle of chains. The waggoners were tough and I recall one of them, Dick Richardson, with flowing moustaches watching me, by then very tired, swing away somewhat pathetically. His voice boomed from the top bank, 'come on lad pick it up – God Almighty will send it down'.

Each waggoner took great pride in his horse and the smartness of his turn-out. Apart from timber hauling there was a variety of work to be carried on throughout the year and each man had to prove his versatility. The horses were stabled at Belgrave and the waggoners took it in turns to do the weekend work of feeding and watering.

This job introduced me to the use of the axe, and I was able to vary the work by rowing out to collect the branches that had fallen in the river. This task was then followed by felling the inferior trees and pruning those which were to remain at Sourbutts Wood, at Churton. While this was more enjoyable it served to prove that I had something to learn about the safe use of the axe, justifying Sandy Myles's edict that when I had my accident I was to be taken to the infirmary. I was felling a tree one day when in the line of fall, standing on a ride with his back to me, was Bill Salisbury. The tree was not very big, and did not justify a cross-cut saw so the work was all by axe. I gauged that it would fall short of Salisbury but – to my horror – when I dropped it the last six feet or so caught him and knocked him flat. It could well have been me that went to hospital after all since Bill thought I had done it deliberately. It rather flattered my ego that he should think I knew what I was doing!

A rather amusing incident in this wood happened when I got the top of a tree trapped in another one and asked for help in levering the butt which was on a bank leading to a slimy brook. Bert Smart helped me with the lever pole, but it slipped sending both of us rolling down the bank and into the brook, with me underneath. I came out covered in black slime. I took off my clothes and hung them round the log fire to dry, running about meantime to keep warm. However, as soon as Bill Salisbury saw me, he ordered me to put on my slimy clothes and cycle back to Eccleston for a change. Poor Mrs Debenham was horrified to see me. There was no bathroom, so she ran a tub in the wash-house for me to bath in and then washed my clothes in the copper.

Work was never free from more serious dangers. One which might have had an unfortunate sequel concerned Arthur O'Brien, a tall gangling Irishman, rather wild and careless, happier handling horses than axes. I was holding the bottom of a ladder while, against all the rules, he trimmed the branches of a tree with an axe. This he suddenly let slip from some height, just missing my head and burying itself at my feet. What I had to say was water off a duck's back to him as his sole comment was – 'Well, it did miss you.'

My first days were an introduction not only to some of the skills of forestry but to the diversity of characters with whom I was working. We used to eat our lunch in a little enclave made by heaping faggots into a square around the wood fire. John Williams, a handsome well-built fellow, had been Light Heavyweight Champion of Wales and at lunch time we used to do some boxing. He was very kind to me until one day he accidentally caught me with a 'good one' and I was completely knocked out. When I came round he insisted that we boxed on so as to restore my confidence.

Another member of the gang, Tommy Williams, came from Holt. He was a tough creature and had been a fairground bruiser in his time. Once when work had been stopped by heavy rain he and I boxed in the summerhouse at Eccleston overlooking the river. By mistake I split his mouth very badly, but he thought I had done it deliberately and came after me. Fortunately the other men held him off, for if he had set about me he would have been quite capable of putting me out for good! He was one of the strongest men I ever knew, and I was an eight-stone, five-foot-odd lad.

On another wet day in a building at the bottom of the village known as 'The Belgians' (because it had been occupied by Belgian refugees in the 1914–18 war) he lay on the ground, put a plank on his chest and said he would lift nine of us by deep breathing. I was the one in the middle. He certainly lifted the nine of us, he exhaled and I jumped on the plank with almost disastrous consequences!

Sammy Rathbone was a gypsy fellow of very few words, who

constantly chewed tobacco and spat with great proficiency. I used to hate it when he borrowed my bill hook!

Although Eaton Hall had a primitive form of central heating, fires were in great demand. At least 2,000 faggots a year had to be cut for the house and one man, Charlie Weaver, with a boy to help, spent his whole time in the stick house chopping the faggots into kindling wood. I found that while cutting was one thing, tying faggots together with osiers was extremely difficult and needed the patient instructions of Walter Huxley, who helped me so much and was expert in all manner of jobs. Walter once came second in the long jump for the Northern Counties and one day jumped a pile of faggots with the greatest of ease. I tried to follow suit, but succeeded only in taking the seat out of my trousers, forcing me to walk home to lunch with my jacket round my middle. He also won sixpence from me when I wagered that he couldn't jump Balderton Brook. When he sailed over easily I realized what a fine athlete he must have been.

Forestry was not only a matter of handling trees: a good deal of digging is needed, as I found out when we made a forestry nursery in Eccleston village. The instructions were to take the top sod off, dig two spades deep, bury the sod, plus manure, replace the soil and break it up and clean it for weed. The gang lined up and the men were each given eight yards while I was given six. After a few days Bill Salisbury said that as I had got so much time to talk I could take eight too.

Fencing was another forestry task, and provided me with an early taste of responsibility. We were to refence the Crook O'Dee meadow, the summer paddock for mares at Eaton Stud. A small gang was selected to do the job on piece-work and to my surprise I was put in charge. My enthusiasm to make money was not altogether shared by my colleagues and at four o'clock on the first afternoon O'Brien, the big Irishman who had nearly decapitated me in the Sourbutts Wood, exclaimed, 'When are we going to be allowed to straighten our backs?' This piece-work job no doubt sowed the seeds in my mind of the merits of payment by result and I have since taken every opportunity to use it. Providing the job is well done, it is most satisfying from the employer's and the employee's point of view.

We gradually moved on to the time to harvest the hay, which covered substantial areas in the park, back fields, the drives and other odd tracts which did not come within the orbit of the Home Farm. As we started work at 6.30 a.m. in the summer it was too early to go into the hayfields and odd jobs had to be done until the dew was off the ground. One of these was the repair of platts and bridges in the Duck Wood and it was here that I experienced my first very unpleasant accident. I was working with Billy Rowlands from Churton and he committed the almost unforgiveable sin of standing on the tree which he was clearing and swinging an axe. He slipped and the axe went right through his boot and was buried in his foot. We were alone and I had to get him up to the Pulford drive and run for help. It seemed an age before we got him to Chester Infirmary.

These were long days leaving home at 6 a.m. and often not returning until after 10 p.m. One took breakfast, lunch and tea and by teatime the bread and cake were pretty dry! One evening when we had been working in the hay in the park, Sandy Myles, who had been playing golf, came along and said – 'Ach! lad you look tired' and I said – 'Yes, sir, I am.' He replied – 'Ach! The day has only just started.'

However, with my eye on the money I loved the overtime of ninepence an hour and was delighted when I was told that I could not go home for the August Bank Holiday weekend. As this brought double pay for the Bank Holiday, I began to wish they came more often.

After the harvest came the hedge-cutting which again was a piece-work job. There were thirty-two miles of hedges, each one priced according to height, width and species. Measurement was by the chain – twenty-two yards. The highest price of five shillings per chain was for the yew hedges at Eccleston church and the agent's house, The Paddocks. These were all about nine feet in height and four feet in width. The ordinary thorn field hedges, approximately four foot six inches to five foot in height, were one shilling and sixpence a chain. The Stud paddock hedges, with double timber fencing to protect them, were over six feet in height and, as with the yew hedges, the tops had to be cut from trestles – a tedious part of the business being moving the trestles.

All the hedges had to be thoroughly 'badged' before cutting, which meant all grass and weeds were cut with a sickle and raked up to allow proper cutting at the bottom of the hedge to give the young growth a chance. For hedges which were a protection against stock, it was essential to have the bottom of the hedge clear to give the sun a chance to promote the growth of the young shoots. The quality of a hedge was judged by its bottom growth. It is sad today to see such hedges cut by machines which slice off the tops and upper sides and neglect the growth in the bottom. This, with the failure to carry out badging, is leading to the decay of stock-proof hedges – a sad indictment of our present-day methods and the loss of a fine rural art.

Later on I was privileged to be with Walter Huxley on his hedge-laying. He won the Gold Medal for Cheshire and was probably the first man to be televised in a hedge-laying competition. He taught me that the art of laying was by cutting the stow with as long a cut as possible, the cut finishing down to the ground. The stow could then be gently laid so as to be almost touching the ground. With a good thick hedge to work on an artist like Huxley could 'build' a hedge that was virtually rabbit-proof. In competitions there were great tricks among the old hands, such as cutting a stow and putting it into the ground as though it was growing in an attempt to deceive the judges that they had a 'close' hedge. I loved to see good hedge-laying with ditches cleaned and banked up under the hedge, creating a stock-proof hedge, which with good annual trimming would last more than a lifetime and was more than appreciated in hunting country, where every farmer on the Eaton estate received a letter in early October, advising him that all wire – plain and barbed – had to be down on his farm by 1 November. Stakes and rails to make good any gaps were provided at half cost.

Walter Huxley was not only a master of the art of hedge-laying, he was also a great countryman in his knowledge of rural crafts and was one of the finest vegetable gardeners in the North, once winning thirteen prizes at the famous Southport Show. He also created the Churton Silver Prize Band and was a prime mover in the Churton Sports, which had a great reputation in the community. Perhaps because of his successes in such diverse fields of activity and his passionate will to win he was never very popular among his colleagues, nor in the community. I am afraid he was so dedicated that he lost his sense of humour.

There were no tractors in the forestry department and, as I have said before, all the timber hauling was done by horses. There was a great art in pulling trees out of a wood and one of the first essentials was to map one's route, taking the lead horse through on the understanding that the horses following would be treading the same path and the tree or trees would follow.

I had a frightening experience of this in the Glebe Wood at

Eccleston one day when I was allowed to take the lead horse of three while pulling a big tree to the drive-side. With the horses at full stretch I stupidly looked round to see if all was well and tripped over a briar. With a wonderful presence of mind, Harry Barlow, following me with the second horse, jumped on my chest and diverted the lead horse. It was impossible to stop and the horses and tree went past me with a margin to spare, which was – to say the least – uncomfortable. I was white as a sheet and never ceased to thank Harry Barlow when we reminisced about this incident years afterwards.

Work in the department was not all forestry, as the park, golf course, cricket ground, the light railway and the maintenance of the drives all came within the purview of the head forester.

I enjoyed it immensely and physically it did me the world of good, but the time came when Myles thought I should learn something of office work. There was a one-roomed forestry office at Belgrave with stores attached; Rushton, the clerk, was a frail-looking character who came from Chester each day. His task was to write up the pay sheets once a fortnight from the time sheets collected from eighty-odd men. These pay sheets were taken by Myles every other Friday to the estate office, were they were checked. Myles would then go to the bank in Chester with his brown Gladstone bag and receive the appropriate money in notes and silver. After a drink in the front bar of the Grosvenor he would return by twelve o'clock and turn over the cash. The next job was the allocation of the money into the individual pay packets already prepared, and putting up the money for the pensioners. Rushton was completely lacking in method and it was often mid-afternoon before the foreman left the office with the pay packets in another Gladstone bag strapped to the back of his bicycle for distribution among the men working in all four corners of the estate. It was not unusual for men to have to wait until after knocking-off time before receiving their fortnight's wages.

To my horror I found that the ledgers were hopelessly out of date. Myles, being a tough outdoor man, had little regard for office work and the estate office was obviously not interested in the domestic accounting of the forestry department. The inevitable happened: the inefficient clerk was off sick and I took over. The writing up of the pay book and pay sheets from the time sheets took me only half a day and the ultimate filling of the pay packets and balancing twenty-five minutes. The clerk was not surprised when he was dismissed and I took over the task, with the added responsibility of understudying Myles in the outside work. Although I had received no training in accounting, I enjoyed improving the bookkeeping system, a task in which I was helped by my knowledge of the estate and what went on.

The next reorganization was that of the stores, with the introduction of a new system of checking and also an accounting system for the sawmill. Hitherto this had been non-existent, especially the measurement of timber in the round as it was brought in from the woods each day and the allocation of the sawn timber despatched.

After these reforms I was sent by Myles to the estate office to explain what I had done. Like Myles, but in a bigger way, the agent, Major Basil Kerr, had no time for figures; he delegated the tasks to his chief clerk, Edward Wells, and two others – Rhodes and White. Wells, in keeping with all departmental heads, was a most well-dressed man about seventy, who had been in the estate office for fifty-six years. He eventually retired after sixty-four years in the same office.

At this time I was nineteen, and the advent of a young 'pup' from the forestry department, regarded virtually as a colony, come to tell the finance office of the central government that they had been writing their books up all wrong for years, was hardly likely to endear me to them, especially when my enthusiasm knew no bounds. I was dismissed with a flea in my ear. Nevertheless my wages rose with new responsibilities until from fifteen shillings a week I was getting two pounds, which meant I could afford to be independent and, no doubt somewhat prematurely, I told my father I needed no more subsidy.

We were not without emergencies such as that which occurred on 29 October 1927, when a severe gale brought down over 2,000 mature trees throughout the estate. I was called out that night to join a squad of men to cut up trees across the road at Potts' Wood on the Eaton road near Chester. As we cut up one tree with cross-cuts and axes, another would fall across the road until Myles reckoned it was too dangerous to go on. We got back to Eccleston where a dance was taking place in the village school and learnt that Colonel Charles Hunter, the Duke's secretary, had been trapped in his car at Eccleston Hill, his home at the top of the village. We found his car in the drive which was in a cutting in the rock. A tree had fallen in front of the car, then one at the rear; the engine was running and the lights on, but no sign of the Colonel. We found him safely in the house, having very wisely made a dash for it with no time to switch off the engine or the lights.

It was a frightening night and most of the people at the dance were compelled to sleep in the school or be put up by villagers. The next day showed the devastation: every main road was blocked and most of the drives and farm roads. These were the days before power-saws and gangs of us worked to clear the fallen trees. Floods added to the chaos of fallen timber, broken power and telephone lines. It was a Saturday and instead of going to Wrexham for an international soccer match, I spent the afternoon helping to clear a line of poplars from the flooded road to Fearnie Williamson's farm to enable the milk lorry to get through. Fearnie Williamson was the farm tenant who, in 1949, was to win the Grand National with his home-bred Russian Hero.

The majority of the windblown trees were massive, but shallow-rooted, elms. Myles then gave me the job of selling the trees to timber merchants – two primarily – Musgraves, the old-established firm in Chester, and Leather. The measuring of the trees was always the subject of much argument as to where the quarter girth should be taken, and at times we had to take it in three places along the bole of the tree, with the added question of the length to be deducted for decay or 'splits'. I felt a novice among experienced buyers, but soon learnt that one's foot in the tape when measuring the girth compensated for loss of argument on length! It was a great experience.

My education advanced further when Myles promised the Bishop of Chester that the estate would drain the King's School playing fields in Lache Lane, a particularly flat and difficult area. I had to draw the plans, provide estimates for pipes and labour and supervise the job when Myles went down with appendicitis. I was taught a very good lesson by Bill and Hezekiah Jones – the estate drainers and ditchers. They needed no instruments to decide the fall of the land in any direction and despite my protestations about the water running uphill did a magnificent job. They really were artists.

Half a mile down the Wrexham road from Belgrave was 'The Cuckoo's Nest' the residence of the clerk of works, responsible for the buildings on the estate as distinct from the mansion and its appurtenances. Over forty men were engaged – bricklayers, carpenters, plumbers, painters and labourers. The clerk of works was James Morgan, promoted from head carpenter, and it was felt that he never exercised the appropriate authority over the men with whom he worked.

The light railway, which came under Myles's control, was a feature of the Eaton estate. It had been built by Sir Arthur Heywood for the first Duke: the engines were housed at Belgrave, the carriages at Eaton. The two steam engines were seldom used but when they were they made the petrol engine a dull affair. Harry Wilde, the engine driver, who Sir Arthur Heywood had produced when the railway was built, was a kindly character, well-known throughout England as a foremost campanologist. He was captain of the bellringers at Eccleston Church for many years and toured the country with teams of bellringers.

Several times he allowed me to drive the steam train while he stood on the plate and guided me. There was a straight run of approximately two miles from Eaton to the main Chester–Wrexham road, where one was required to halt to allow the guard with his red flag to stop the traffic while the train crossed the road on the way to Balderton. One day I put my back to the engine and talked to Wilde while we careered down the straight run alongside the Belgrave woods. I manoeuvred the lever behind my back and got up full steam before Wilde realized what had happened. When it came to the point where one applied the brakes I did so, but we failed to pull up before coming to the main road. We sailed across with our line of trucks with Harry Morgan, the guard, vainly waving his red flag and – by the grace of God and aided by the braking of vehicles in both directions – we crossed the road without being hit. In the excitement and with the rocking of the train, Wilde's false teeth fell out! It was a long time before I was allowed to drive the train again. Fortune smiled on me on many occasions during my life in the forestry department: there were many incidents for which I could justifiably have been sacked!

Gradually I was learning more about the operation of the estate, although I was baffled by the isolation of the individual departments. It was rather like the 'Iron Curtain' of post-war years, and probably stemmed from the attitudes of the heads of departments, who seldom mixed. We, as the forestry department, were apart from the estate works and its clerk of works, the home farm and its manager and the gamekeepers, who came under the control of the agent, and even further apart from the house staff at the Hall and the gardens, with their head gardener, who came under the control of the secretary's department in London.

The gamekeepers were a law unto themselves, although closer to us as they came within the purview of the agent, and we had to work with them in the wiring of the woods for pheasant rearing and as beaters and stops during shooting days. Years later I was to learn that keepers, stalkers and gillies by virtue of the fact that they had closer personal contact with the owner and gave happy and more often than not successful days to him, or her, and their guests, felt themselves privileged persons and expected to be treated with the greatest respect by all and sundry.

The head keeper at Eaton in my early years was Richard Stark, a fearsome Dorset man with grey beard and the energy of twenty. His knowledge of wild life and field sports was unsurpassable. One day he would be organizing a shoot with twelve guns and upwards of 2,000 birds shot; the next, in his knickerbocker suit, he would be riding to hounds and giving advice to the huntsman as to where a fox would be found; and on another occasion at the appropriate time he would accompany the Duke or a guest to the River Dee as gillie. At the time when the Duke had the famous World's End shoot at Llangollen, rented from Sir Watkin Williams Wynn, Stark had sixteen keepers under him, all of whom he ruled with a rod of iron.

One of my first encounters with him was on a morning when I had to go to Belgrave for some tools and reported there at 6.30 a.m. Cycling back up the mile-and-three-quarters-long Belgrave drive, I met Stark and very respectfully touched my cap and said, 'Good morning, Mr Stark.' 'I don' say marning to anybody after seven o'clock,' came the reply.

The pheasant rearing at Eaton doubled to 20,000 birds a year when the Duke took on World's End, so named because it was a dead-end valley of Eglwyseg. It was a marvellous setting for a wonderful shoot, with high birds flying across and down the valley. At the far end of the valley, 'World's End' was a splendid half-timbered farmhouse which we were allowed to use for shoot lunches. Over the door was the coat-of-arms of Elizabeth I, and it was said that it was here she had given birth to an illegitimate child. Sadly, during the last war the house was occupied by the army and much damage was done to the historic property.

Half the number of pheasants reared at Eaton were transported at six weeks old to World's End. With 10,000 pheasants put into the woods at Eaton and the same number at World's End, there could be two days' shooting at Eaton, followed by two days' at World's End.

Each estate had eight keepers who reared the birds, on a contract basis, to be bought by the Duke at six weeks old. I was given the job of purchaser for the Duke and throughout mid-summer there were days when I was up at 5 a.m. and in the pheasant field by 5.30 a.m. to see the keeper in charge of his particular beat. The trap of each coop which housed the broody hen and her chicks was lifted and I counted the chicks as they ran out and argued with the keeper as to how many I would discard as weaklings, unlikely to live for long in the woods. Tom Lamont, a rough-spoken Scotsman who had been with the Duke at Rosehall in Sutherland, was in charge of the World's End shoot, under Stark and Myles. The farmers, who remained tenants of Sir Watkin, naturally used their Welsh ingenuity to get the best deal they could with the Duke, a favourite gambit being to claim damage to crops they had never sown or planted. Lamont was hardly the tactful representative of a wealthy duke expected to dispense largesse in return for the pleasure of shooting over the farmer's land and there were critical conflicts which one wanted to avoid for the sake of both parties. Matters came to a head one day when Myles asked me to go up to World's End with him urgently. When we got there we found an irate Lamont who said that at one of the farms occupied by two spinster sisters they had alleged damage to a crop which he swore never existed.

Myles and I went to see the quiet Chapel-going ladies who were distraught and still suffering from their encounter with Lamont. They said, 'We can accept argument from Mr Lamont about the value of our claim, but we were horrified when he used language which indicated that we would be nicer people if our mother and father had married!' That was the finish! Lamont was brought back to Eaton, where he was an excellent man with his spaniels, especially for the Duke's snipe shooting, and a quiet-spoken diplomatic under keeper from Eaton, George Grass, was put in in his stead. Grass's father was a senior keeper at Eaton and two of his uncles were keepers there also: all quiet dedicated men.

It was Myles who hit upon the solution to the problems of farmers' claims for damage which plagued us each year, by appointing Lloyd-Jones, the auctioneer at Llangollen, as agent to settle all claims. It was a brilliant plan of psychology since Lloyd-Jones sold the tenants' cattle and sheep in the Llangollen market so they were anxious to be on the right side of him!

Winston Churchill shot often at Eaton and World's End, and on one occasion at World's End I was given the task of assisting his loader by carrying his cartridges. The great man asked if I would count the birds he shot at each stand as it was difficult for the gun to see what had happened on the hillsides when so many birds fell below in the valley. After one particularly successful drive when birds were coming over without break for some twenty minutes, he asked me how many he had got. I told him forty-seven, I received a charming smile and the words 'you are too generous'. At another shoot when following a barrage the barrels of his guns were getting hot and he had no mittens, he took out of his pocket a pair of suede 'London' gloves and asked me if I had a penknife, which I then produced and was astonished to see him cut the fingers off the gloves and turn them into mittens! I could not help but think of what they cost.

There was a splendid and well known bookmaker, a great character, called Harrison, who had a fine house near World's End and the Duke gave him permission to come to the shoots. He knew a number of the guests and would take it in turn to stand behind them at a drive and give them odds on a bird coming over!

World's End must have been one of the most difficult shoots in Britain and there was nothing the Duke liked more than to test the skill of friends, who were named among the best shots in the country, at the high-flying, swooping pheasants as they came off the hilltops, especially with the wind under their tails. There was only one stand at Eaton – the Lower Lanes at Aldford – comparable to the World's End stands. Sadly the war brought it to an end, but one of the last shoots brought together the following guests and this result: the Duke of Roxburghe, Lord Delamere, Sir Richard Molyneux, Mr Winston Churchill, Sir George Thursby, Sir Joseph Laycock, General Paynter, Colonel Leslie, Captain Cobbold, Captain Laycock – and 2,486 pheasants over the two days.

The staff at Eaton were well looked after from the sporting point of view. The cricket club, entirely financed by the Duke, was unusual in so far as it played all its matches at home. It was a good team with farmers and estate workers, strengthened by such players as General Charles Lyon, a former Derby county cricketer and footballer, Colonel Priestman of Western Command and, when home on leave, Mark, the soldier son of Basil Kerr. Jack I'Anson, the professional, was one of the old school who had played for Lancashire for some years and for Leyland in the Lancashire League. One of his proud possessions was the silver-mounted ball presented to him by Lancashire when he took eight for thirty-two against the Australians in 1899. He was a fine all-rounder who, opening with General Lyon, would expect, when each was aged sixty, to put on as many runs as their joint ages for the opening partnership.

Like a good north-countryman (I'Anson was born in Yorkshire although he played for Lancashire) he had an earthy approach to all matters and a typically dry and forthright manner of comment. When the Duke's sister, Countess Beauchamp, was living at Saighton, her younger son, Richard Lygon, who was at Westminster, played for Eaton in the summer holidays. The Countess brought Richard over to the ground on a practice evening when Richard had just returned from school. 'I'Anson,' she said, 'I want you to see Richard's new bowling style: he's taken a lot of wickets at school this term.' I'Anson threw a ball to Richard and asked him to bowl at the player in the nets. Richard, aged about eighteen, but even then some six foot three in height, took a run which started at the boundary fence; with legs and arms whirling, he hurled himself down and released the ball at great speed, but no accuracy. 'Now, I'Anson, what do you think?' was the Countess's query. 'He's only got to black his face and he's got the part,' was the reply! As well as cricket there was also tennis, badminton and soccer, not to mention the swimming pool that came slightly later.

In those days Eaton was a world of its own. The size of the Hall itself, like a palace, included the private wing, the adjoining chapel with its clock tower reminiscent of Big Ben, the contrasting stable yard built of red brick with stone facings and the upper structure in black and white half-timber, stabling for seventy carriage horses, an indoor riding school and an adjoining block in stone for hunters. The gardens covered 100 acres, including twelve acres of glass. There were forty-five gardeners under the firm discipline of Nicholas Friend Barnes, one of the finest gardeners of his day and the holder of one of the highest honours – the VMH (Victorian Medal for Horticulture). He was a most impressive figure, immaculately dressed, his white hair and Edwardian moustache adding to his dignified appearance. His authority was such that even the Duke was loath to pick flowers or fruit before first advising Barnes! On at least one occasion Barnes admonished his employer for daring to pick orchids himself, and damaging the plants. The kitchen gardens were some two miles away at Aldford. It would have been unthinkable to have grown vegetables and common fruit within the glory of Eaton gardens, with the exception of the hot-house fruits. Barnes was very forthright in his views, a true-blue Tory who considered it heresy to listen to any other political views. He also had strong ideas about the young and their need to play games. The first tee at the Eaton Golf Club adjoined the cricket pavilion, and one Saturday afternoon Barnes and I teed off together. After we had played our drives he noticed a young man watching us from alongside the pavilion. Barnes turned on him – told him he should be ashamed of himself – a fit young man like him walking about and idling away a Saturday afternoon when he should be playing games. Before Barnes walked away in high dudgeon, the embarrassed young man barely had time to say that he had come from Merseyside and was to play for a Liverpool cricket club against the Eaton XI.

The mutual respect and affection that existed between the Duke and his servants is made clear in his correspondence with Barnes, who had joined the Eaton staff in 1892. Bend'Or was never a good correspondent and his letter, written in longhand on Barnes's fiftieth anniversary at Eaton, is probably the longest he ever wrote.

15th May 1942

Dear Mr Barnes,

I am given to understand that on Monday next, 18th May, you will have completed a half-century at Eaton. Ten years with my Grandfather, and forty years with me.

Fifty not out, and still batting (as long as others in the team don't all get bowled out), I imagine and trust that you will go on for your century. A marvellous innings!

I have to thank you for your great loyalty, to me, and I blame myself for not having taken a deeper interest, as it seems to me, in your magnificent achievement in having made the Eaton gardens what they are, and what they stand for.

Believe me, however bad the present times are, and the future may be, you will always have the knowledge and satisfaction in knowing that your work is not only appreciated by me, but also by many thousands of people who have visited, and I hope enjoyed the gardens during the number of years that you have been responsible for them. I think you and I have seen England at its best – the future we cannot see under present circumstances.

I must give a secret away. I have never known where you grew the mushrooms, or from where those blue flowers came from that you used to put in my room – the ones I liked so much. They are simple things but stick in one's mind more than the highly bred orchids with their almost royal pedigrees. Also before the war the strawberries that suddenly appeared (earlier than any others I have ever heard of) a real delight, and gastronomically acceptable to a high degree.

Mrs Barnes must take this letter as addressed to her as well as you. She comes into the picture as having looked after you so well during these years of rough and tumble – whether it has been a hard task for her I don't know? But anyway she has succeeded, and I send her my best wishes.

How Mr C. Gatty would have enjoyed 'Honest Tom's' story when he got rather muddled up with Primulas and Prime Ministers. When Mr Gatty died you lost a great friend and enthusiastic admirer. I wish you and I could go back and meet our departed friends as they were. I hope to see you again winning my golf cup in years to come.

My sincere thanks go out to you for all you have done for me, and are doing, I hope that our long association together has been as pleasant for you, as it has for me.

I will drink yours, and Mrs Barnes health on Monday with deepest gratitude, and long life and health to you both.

Westminster

P.S. On my return to Eaton I have a small memento to present to you.

Barnes's reply is an indication of both the quality of the man and his relationship with his employer. The two men were joined by a devotion to a concept of life and a set of values. The fact that these values may no longer be fashionable is perhaps the worse for us.

20th May to His Grace, the Duke of Westminster GCVO DSO
Your Grace's kind telegram and your appreciative letter of my work since I have had the honour, and great pleasure of serving you in your gardens, has touched my wife, and myself very deeply and we thank you most sincerely for it.

Contrast this with what our industrialists have done. Profiting by the prosperity of the country, the only thing they have to show is miles of slum cottages and mountains of debris disfiguring the countryside.

I am leaving my wife to convey her gratitude to you in her own way. She unfortunately has become almost stone deaf, and though debarred from taking part in things she used to be able to do, her interest in Eaton is as keen as ever.

For nearly fifty years now she has made my morning porridge, and I am still not sure as to how much credit is due to her for what I am? I think honours must be divided between her, a healthy frame, inherited – and your Grace's golf course in keeping me fit.

Since you have mentioned 'Honest Tom' I am permitted to say that, among your closest friends, there is not one, that holds you in greater admiration and loyalty.

We have had very acceptable rain lately, and the surround of Eaton excepting the Huts is looking its best. Rhododendrons, lilacs, chestnuts are now full out.

There is nothing in this world that I value now, and shall continue to do so in the years that may come, than your kind appreciation of what I have tried to do these past years.

The one aim I have had, has been to serve a kind, and considerate master and that your gardens should compare favourably with other fine establishments in the country – which have stood for so much and done so much that has not been fully recognized. 'To beautify, not disfigure, to build up rather than pull down' has been the main incentive in this.

And I acknowledge with sincere gratitude, the freedom you have given me to act on these lines, and the great kindness I have always received from yourself, and members of your family. The grievous thing to me now is that the heavy burden of taxation may make it impossible for Eaton to be the same again after this wicked war ends. Can we hope that those who now speak so glibly about a better world after the war, will give thought to what our old establishments have done in the past? And the example set in housing, sanitation and other amenities of life, and in the planting of beautiful woodlands, that are such a fine feature of the country? And all this done at their own initiative, and expense, and without selfishness – and this at a time when there were few parks and gardens and picture gardens, of a public nature, open to the public.

I will close as I began, and again say with what sincere pleasure, and gratitude, I received your kind letter, and also that whatever changes and chances an uncertain future may have in store I shall enduringly value the honour and opportunity of having been your servant, and so long as you wish, and I am able, my only desire is to serve you to the end.

I beg to remain your Grace's respectful and obedient servant, to the end.

N.F. Barnes

While such eminent employees as Barnes were treated with the respect they deserved and to which they were entitled, the real affection Bend'Or had for them was extended to all his staff. One anecdote can stand for many others. Not long before he died the Duke was signing documents at Bourdon House when he suddenly stopped and said, 'How is Jobie Edge?' Jobie was a retired waggoner on the estate who had played left-back for Saighton at the same time that Bend'Or played for the team, sixty years before. I answered that Jobie was very well, but Bend'Or insisted on being given chapter and verse, which I was able to do, since I had walked down the church path with Jobie only the previous Sunday. Nevertheless Bend'Or insisted that on my return I must visit Jobie, tell him that the Duke had been asking after him, and find out if there was anything he needed.

The Duke's loyalty and affection for his staff was a byword and the name Barnes brings to my mind only one of many actions defining the character of a man whose staff held him in awe, coupled with implicit faith that in him they had a guardian who would care for them in times of trouble. Barnes's elder son was killed in the 1914–18 war. His second son, Wilfred, was an auctioneer with Manleys of Crewe. About 1950, some time after Barnes's retirement, Wilfred underwent a very serious operation in the Chester Infirmary. His father and mother were too old to do much, if anything, for him. As a matter of course I went to see him and found him desperately ill, but most of all terribly depressed and lonely. I went back to Eaton and reported this to the Duke. He instantly ordered a case of champagne to be delivered to the Infirmary and all Wilfred's meals to be cooked at Eaton and taken in to him. The result was dramatic. Wilfred regained his courage and confidence and next time I saw him he said with tears in his eyes, 'I should have known Eaton would not forget me.' Later when Wilfred Barnes's health had suffered as a result of his severe illness, I took him on to the estate staff to supervise the farm improvement schemes which we were carrying out at that time. When this was completed he took on the task of custodian of the chattels at Eaton.

The Hall itself was for some time sacred territory to me. Eventually I was asked by E.K. Willett, librarian and clerk of works, if I would like to see the dining room when it was laid for a dinner at the time of a big house party. It was an occasion when the gold plate was in use and I was overcome by the magnificence of the table display, the masses of flowers on the table and the banks of flowers elsewhere. To my young mind it resembled an Aladdin's cave.

6

His Occupation Gone

The First World War did not bring so uniformly a dramatic change to the life of the nation as is sometimes thought. There were profound social forces at work, but the movement was slow, and for many life went on much as before. The aristocracy in particular were able to resume much of the pre-war splendour.

Certainly there were changes, not least in that all families had suffered tragic losses, of which the Grosvenors had their share. Eaton Hall however continued in much the same fashion as before. The staff was not reduced: as late as 1931 there were ten housemaids and thirty-eight gardeners with other departments in proportion. Some simplifications had been introduced – carriages and horses need no longer be sent from Eaton to Lochmore by rail, since the journey could conveniently be done by motor – but the nineteenth-century mechanism of a great house with its reservoir of human energy continued. Housemaids still lit fires every morning in every room that was to be used. The stick-chopper in his hard hat still had a full-time occupation. Men from the golf club were used for runners to run the dishes from the kitchen to the state dining room using a baker's cart.

One most striking difference in Bend'Or's life was brought about by his divorce from Shelagh and second marriage, in November 1920, to Violet Rowley. She too had been divorced and already had a son, born in 1915. Violet was twenty-nine and Bend'Or forty-one; there seemed no reason why a son and heir might not in due course be expected.

Like all Bend'Or's wives, Violet was a remarkable woman, of great energy and originality. She was one of the finest horsewomen in the country. The marriage, which began with such high hopes, did not fulfil them. The heir did not appear, and Violet's decided character made life difficult. It was a marriage that needed at least one emollient partner. At this time in his life it did seem that Bend'Or was happiest single. Clemmie Churchill, who stayed with Winston at Mimizan, said when she met Bend'Or for the first time without Shelagh, 'The difference is great. Far more intelligent than he ever appeared in her company – the best of hosts.'

Within four years it was painfully clear that things were wrong. In June 1924 Bend'Or's elder daughter, Ursula, was married. The reception, in Grosvenor House, was one of the last touches of magnificence. Two hundred policemen were needed to control the traffic! The guests, who included all the Eaton staff, the Duchess's Airedale terrier, and an old crossing sweeper who had known her all her life, were received by Bend'Or, Shelagh, and Katharine the Dowager Duchess. Violet was a notable absentee, and by August she was applying for an injunction to restrain her husband from ejecting her from Bourdon House. With the ensuing divorce the continuity with pre-war life was broken.

Grosvenor House was sold to Lord Leverhulme, Bend'Or publicly explaining that this was a step forced on him by taxation and maintenance payments. It is likely that he was also by now thoroughly disillusioned with London society and found the vast entertainments which provided Grosvenor House's sole *raison d'être* both anachronistic and boring. His other London house, Bourdon House in Davies Street, now occupied by Malets, the antique and art dealers, was a much smaller affair, more suitable for the restricted entertaining of close friends which was all that he now wished to do. Leverhulme had intended Grosvenor House to become an art gallery, which purpose it would have admirably fulfilled, but his early death allowed his executors to sell the site for the construction of the present Grosvenor House Hotel.

Money was also raised by the sale of a number of the Grosvenor House pictures, an action much criticized at the time, especially as some, including the famous *Blue Boy* by Gainsborough, were sold abroad. In the conditions of the time it was difficult to see what else could be done. Some of the prices were extraordinary, the *Blue Boy* going for £200,000. The pictures had been bought by the first Marquis for Grosvenor House, which had been extended to accommodate them. But there was no room at Bourdon House, and it was pointless adding to the stock at Eaton, where they would be accessible only to a favoured few. Much better, it would seem, that they should be dispersed, especially since many found their way into public collections.

Bend'Or's life at Eaton changed less obviously. On the surface things went on much as before, but there were differences. Before the war extensive entertainments were given for royalty and the higher ranks of the aristocracy, European and English. After the war, Bend'Or was to mix only with those whom he regarded as friends, and the visitors' book at Eaton gives some indication of the variety of Bend'Or's friends. There were the old comrades from South Africa and the World War, Joe Laycock and Winston Churchill, Jack Leslie and Lord Birkenhead, his sisters and their families, the Grosvenor relations, but also a strikingly wide range of notable personalities – Hilaire Belloc, Shane Leslie, Gladys Cooper, Gerald du Maurier, Roger Keyes, Michael Arlen, and most of the Sitwell family.

Perhaps the oddest of these was Professor Lindemann, afterwards Lord Cherwell and always known as 'the Prof' who was a constant friend from 1922 until Bend'Or's death. At first sight the contrast between Lindemann the ascetic high-powered academic and Bend'Or the sporting peer seems hard to explain. The Prof would eat only vegetables, the whites of eggs and one cheese, Port Salut, which he considered safe perhaps by virtue of its name, and was a teetotaller. Bend'Or's last wife, Nancy, remembers Lindemann apparently lost in thought at luncheon; when she asked what great issues were passing through his mind he admitted that he was calculating how many pieces of asparagus were left for him. The men had two things however in common: both were good tennis players and both were fascinated by technology. Lindemann suggested that Bend'Or should establish a Duke of Westminster studentship at his college, Christ Church, which he did, and the two men worked together later on the development of new weapons.

Bend'Or's much publicized marital affairs were only part of the influences that led him to the dissatisfied restlessness that he displayed in his middle years. His mother died in 1929, and Hugh Lupus's second wife Katharine in 1942. They had represented the last links with their husbands, the men on whom Bend'Or had modelled himself in his early years, and whose standards he always accepted as right. Applying these standards he cannot have felt satisfied. Both

Hugh Lupus and George Wyndham had won great admiration: the first Duke had become a symbol of Victorian virtues, and Wyndham, as well as his great work in Ireland, had taken the lead in forming Tory imperialist policy. Neither had been without personal difficulties. Hugh Lupus's first wife had been notoriously unfaithful, George had been in love with Lady Plymouth for many years while married to Sibell, Bend'Or's mother. But both had conformed to the mores of their time, and kept a face of domesticity unbroken to the world.

Bend'Or was of a different generation, and was without the personal flexibility that might have enabled him to keep up appearances with Shelagh. He found compromise difficult, a serious disability in either husbands or politicians. Dishonesty in private and hypocrisy in public relations were alike anathema to him. The qualities of decision and courage and leadership he had shown in two wars were not appreciated in peace, especially since they were not accompanied by any feeling for party politics. His other gift, that of transcending temporary concerns and seeing into the future, was vitiated by his inability to explain himself with any fluency. Thirty generations of Cheshire Grosvenors had pointed him towards the long perspective, which with his natural ingenuity, was exemplified in his development of armoured warfare. Eton and the army had hardly encouraged any facility in self-expression he may have had, but the major factor in his reluctance to expose his feelings must have been his early assumption of rank and responsibility.

From the age of twenty he had been the richest man in England, with an income larger than that of the monarch, added to one of the highest positions in society. He was always highly conscious of the duties and obligations that these brought with them, and of the possible consequences of indiscretion or ill-judgement.

Only occasionally did something move him to put his views forward, and when he did so they were invariably germane and trenchantly expressed, often concerned with problems that are still relevant. An example that could bear repetition is the letter he had published in *The Times* in December 1923.

> At the recent election all parties alike, while differing widely on means and methods, were one in honestly recognizing the overpowering necessity of helping the 'bottom dog' – of tackling the problems of unemployment. Now that party interests, party policies, party tactics, are more to the fore, is there not a danger

> lest this supreme issue be made to take a subordinate place in our minds? No sensible man expects miracles from any political party. Improvement in trade can only be gradual. Meanwhile, surely nothing should be done to reduce to unemployment any now employed, or to discourage enterprise on the part of employers, or to prevent trading facilities within the Empire.

There is irony in the fact that these words could have been written with equal emphasis in 1985!

One aspect of his extensive land holdings in which he took a lively interest was the Reay Forest Estate, which had been leased by the Grosvenors from their relations, the Sutherlands, for a century and a half. A gazetteer of 1859 describes Reay Forest, 'Lord Reay's Country', as a 'wild tract of 800 square miles'. Lying just south of Cape Wrath the estate comprises the whole of the famous salmon river, the River Laxford, including Lock Stack and some of the best deer-stalking country in Scotland. The Laxford was so named 'salmon river' by the Vikings a millennium ago, and has been producing the finest salmon ever since, in a striking example of the fish's fidelity to its native waters. Although the Grosvenors had spent a good deal of money over the years improving the estates Bend'Or wanted to do more and in 1920 bought the freehold from the Duke of Sutherland. From that time on Lochmore became the place where Bend'Or was most himself, where he could spend his time in those outdoor pursuits that he most enjoyed, free from the demands of that society which became increasingly distasteful to him.

His other favourite spot was Mimizan, in the Landes. Both Lochmore and Mimizan are extremely difficult of access by land – Lochmore being almost at the extremity of the British Isles, and Mimizan accessible only by forest roads. Bend'Or solved this problem by speeding between the two in his yachts. He had acquired two of the largest private yachts in Europe. *Flying Cloud* was used for pleasure and kept for only five years, but for rapid transport Bend'Or depended upon a faster ship, much as today a private aeroplane might be used. *Cutty Sark*, not to be confused with the tea clipper, had been built as a destroyer at the Yarrow Yard in 1920 and converted to a yacht by Major Henry Keswick. With a 263-foot hull and 25-foot beam, her four steam turbines made her both fast and uncomfortable in anything like a sea. *Cutty Sark* was kept until the outbreak of the Second World War when Bend'Or gave her to the government to be used as the destroyer for which she had been designed. In that role she served all through the war, with some narrow escapes.

His restlessness was increased as the second marriage broke up, and was succeeded by a relationship with another tempestuous character, Coco Chanel. The divorce from Violet was a long-drawn-out affair, and Chanel became very close. She attended Lady Mary's coming-out ball and attracted such unlikely friends of Bend'Or as Clementine Churchill, who normally disapproved strongly of any irregular relationships, but was prepared to make an exception for Coco and Bend'Or, somewhat surprisingly in view of her own husband's enthusiasm for Coco. Winston was a great fan. He met Coco first at Mimizan in 1927.

> The famous Coco turned up and I took a great fancy to her – a most capable and agreeable woman – much the strongest personality Benny has yet been up against. She hunted vigorously all day, motored to Paris after dinner, and today is engaged in passing and improving dresses on endless streams of mannequins . . . she does it all with her own fingers, pinning, cutting, looping, &c.

They met later that year at Stack Lodge in the Reay Forest. 'Coco is here in place of Violet. She fishes from morn till night, and in two months has killed fifty salmon. She is very agreeable – really a great and strong being fit to rule a man or an Empire. Benny very well and think extremely happy to be mated with an equal – her ability balancing his power.'

Chanel herself said of Bend'Or, 'My real life began with Westminster . . . I'd finally found a shoulder to lean on . . . The simplest person in the world . . . he didn't know the meaning of the word "snobby". He was simplicity itself.' Both people were used to having their own way, however, and Chanel had her own great business to run. The affair came to an end at Mimizan, in a tremendous row when Coco insisted on leaving for the opening of her Paris show at a time when Bend'Or particularly wanted her to stay.

Although Bend'Or spent much time at Lochmore, Mimizan, St Saens and the South of France, Eaton was his base. Here his family and friends came for such annual feasts as Christmas, the Grand National and the Chester Races. It had lost nothing of its old glory, and it is here that Bend'Or is best remembered. If one man could prove the exception to Mme Cornuel's remark that no man was a hero to his valet, it was the second Duke of Westminster. He was uniformly loved and admired by all those who worked for him.

The house staff at that time were headed by Percy Smith the house steward who was, like all the Duke's senior staff, the most impressive of figures. He looked more like a church dignitary than a private servant. It is related that many guests unacquainted with the Duke arriving at Eaton for the first time, mistook him for the Duke when he greeted them in the hall. Percy had his own valet and changed his suits four times a day: short black jacket and striped trousers in early morning, to be followed by tail-coat; in the afternoon he played golf whenever he had the opportunity, and in the evening on formal occasions made his final appearance in white tie and tails. He was a member of Sandy Lodge Golf Club and the proud possessor of a set of clubs given him by Cyril Tolley – a frequent visitor at Eaton. He was also a prominent Freemason in London and enjoyed relating stories of his greeting visitors in his role as house steward, who had virtually bowed the knee to him at a Masonic function earlier in the week. As with all the Duke's senior staff he was the strictest of disciplinarians.

Next in command were the two grooms of the chambers, Ernest Jenkins and Richard Chapman, who with their black tail-coats wore orange and black horizontal-striped waistcoats. The tall, fair-haired, ex-guardsman Jenkins, was married to the sister of the Duke's chauffeur at Lochmore, Hughie Morrison. They lived in one of the most charming small houses on the estate just inside the park, overlooking the River Dee and the golf course. It was a half-timbered brick and stone building, very pleasing architecturally, and originally built as the deer keeper's lodge in the first Duke's time, when a herd of deer roamed the park. Richard Chapman was dark and swarthy, displaying an inscrutable face to the world, and nicknamed by the Duke, 'the Chinaman'. He was a man of great ability and character.

Albert Hopkins, the Duke's valet and factotum, had to be prepared at any time to move to any one of the likely places where the next action would take place. Boar-hunting at Mimizan or St Saens, tennis at Monte Carlo, brief social visit to the Lotti, lunches and dinners usually with leading politicians as guests at Bourdon House, shooting or tennis and golf at Eaton, stalking and fishing at Lochmore. In between these strenuous activities the Duke would be holding meetings with advisers concerning the administration of his estates. Secretarial staff were there to acquire the necessary travel tickets and reservations, but when the actual travel took place it was Hopkins upon whom the responsibility lay for smooth transport between car, train and boat and the care of documents and tickets. A task which would have driven normal men to distraction, more especially when plans were so often changed, to Hopkins appeared a normal way of life.

Down the line came the footmen, all very smart and military in their bearing, chosen for their decorative as well as other qualities, a number of whom played golf at Eaton in their spare time and who were always welcome in the competitions. It was always a great joy to the community life at Eaton when one of the Duke's house parties coincided with a village dance at Eccleston. In 1927 the Duke had built a new village hall with a dance-floor installed by the firm who did similar work for the Cunard line. At times there were over four hundred people attending the dances and the local maidens' hearts fluttered when just before midnight a fleet of cars would arrive from Eaton with the handsome young footmen and visiting chauffeurs and valets.

The female servants were under the rule of Mrs Beauchamp, the housekeeper, who had below her the head housemaid, and a small army of other maids, augmented by the cleaners who generally came from the village of Aldford. She was succeeded by Mrs Crockett, a Scot who transferred her services from Floors Castle. Some years after this the Duke of Roxburghe, who married the fifth Duke's younger daughter Jane, felt it was a slight on the name of Floors! Mrs Crockett was made in the same mould as the other heads of departments. Tall, handsome in an 'eagle' sort of way, she was complete mistress of her craft and a disciplinarian, which no doubt she had to be when so many of her staff of twenty-five housemaids were young girls. They started work at 4.30 a.m. for all living rooms, dining room and hall had to be cleaned and fires laid before breakfast.

The head housemaid married Fred Milton, an under keeper and loader for the Duke, who after the 1939–45 war became head keeper. Her successor, Elizabeth Harrison, could not live at peace with Mrs Crockett and after the war came to work for the Ridleys – to their great joy.

There were three chauffeurs, each a 'character'. The two senior, Jack Cable and George Powell, had both graduated from coachmen. George Gude, always regarded as a virtual newcomer, was the only one with appropriate training and had to bear the brunt of the long-distance driving. One of his most notable exploits was when he was doing duty at Lochmore. The Duke had a number of guests at a time when the weather was hot, the river low and fishing consequently poor. At dinner one evening the conversation turned to Italy and the Duke asked a guest if she had been to Naples, which she admitted she had not. Quictly the Duke ordered Captain Mack, the skipper of the *Cutty Sark* which was lying in Laxford Bay, to get up steam and prepare to sail immediately. Several of the guests, including the lady who had not seen Naples or Vesuvius, were taken on board not knowing for certain where they were going. Gude was ordered to drive to Naples and meet the yacht at ten o'clock on the following Wednesday morning. This meant he had to drive 500 miles to Eaton, pick up his passport and appropriate money – on to Dover and after crossing the Channel drive through France and Italy to Naples. He met the yacht as planned – the Duke disembarked with two or three guests. They drove to Vesuvius for lunch – and then returned to the *Cutty Sark* where the Duke said, 'Thank you, Gude, you can go back now.' The idea of hiring a car at Naples had never crossed his mind!

George Powell was a great personality who enjoyed a special relationship with the Duke, one reason for which was that they had served together in the Great War. When the Duke was awarded the DSO, after the rescue of the *Tara*'s crew, George received the DCM, and whenever thereafter describing the incident George's opening remarks were always, 'When me and the Duke received the DSO . . .' One of George's stories was that when in the desert one day George produced a tin of bully beef for lunch, the Duke took a piece of string out of his pocket, measured the tin of beef, folded the string double and then cut the tin. George asked him why he did so – the answer was, 'I'm not having you saying I had more than you!'

George's conversation was renowned. His forthright manner of expressing his views, intermingled with an inevitable cough and clearing of the throat (he was a chronic asthmatic and bronchitic), embraced the national and international political scene as well as any major current topic of interest. There were no grey areas in his opinions. His driving reflected his character – clear-cut and aggressive. One day driving the Duke and Basil Kerr back from Roehampton he faced a situation in Clapham requiring very delicate judgement – the decision whether to overtake a tram in time to pass it before meeting an oncoming one. He decided to go for it. Both the passengers closed their eyes and waited for the crash. It never came – they got through by a whisker. 'Never do that again, George,' said the Duke. 'What's the matter, I got you through didn't I?' came the reply.

Driving from Eaton to Aintree on Grand National day with the Duke and Anne, the Duchess, the Duke having set out, as usual, with no time to spare, they were snarled up in traffic, despite George having made wonderful progress by driving for some distance on the wrong side of the road. 'Get on, George, get on,' said the Duke. 'I'd get on much better if you'd keep quiet,' answered George. No one else in the world would have dared to give such an answer. Another time at Lochmore when there were several visiting chauffeurs gathered together on the gravel outside the side-door, George grumbled to the others – 'It's a nice state of affairs when His Grace comes out in the morning, greets all you lot and asks you how you are and never says a word to me.' The Duke heard this from his bathroom window and presently came out, walking past the other chauffeurs to George, whom he shook by the hand and felicitously asked how he was.

A few years before the Duke's death, as agent I was making my usual morning visit to Eaton when George stopped me in the stable yard and said he would like to see His Grace. 'But George, you know you can see him at any time.' 'Yes,' he replied, 'but this is special.' When the Duke was informed he said, as expected, 'Of course he can see me – he knows that – what's the matter with the old fool?' (always a term of endearment). George came up into the sitting room. 'What's the matter, George?' 'I want to retire.' 'What do you want to retire for?' 'Well I am getting old, and anyway I came here fifty years ago as a lad in the stables on a fortnight's trial and you haven't told me yet whether I've suited!'

With great reluctance George was retired. A few months later I was instructed by Bend'Or to see George and ask him to come back. He was not to do any work, not even to move a dustsheet off a car, but just to accompany the Duke and Duchess on their journeys. 'We do so miss his conversation.' George declined, feeling that his chest was so bad that he couldn't manage even a passenger's job. His clear understanding of the Duke and their close relationship left him completely unmoved by a request which would have flattered most men.

George, in a very special way, typified the intense loyalty which Bend'Or generated among his staff without a word of praise from either side. He was also the subject of treatment unostentatiously given to so many. The Duke was a firm believer that only the best was good enough for his staff. After one attack George was sent to Ruthin Castle to recuperate, and after another to Reid's Hotel in Madeira. When guests enquiring after George expressed surprise at the exclusive nature of that place, the answer was 'Why, isn't it very good?'

Much of the success of the social life at Eaton depended on the kitchens, which were controlled with great distinction by the chef, Maurice Le Gras, a cheerful, massive Frenchman, who had his home in Paris and a small house at Eccleston, between the head gardener's and the organist's, in a small attractive terrace designated in the *Estate Field Book* as 'Upper Servants' Cottages'.

Le Gras was an expert who refused to accept employment on a normal salaried basis, but controlled the catering at Eaton, Bourdon House, Lochmore, in France and on the yachts on a hotel-style basis, charging for meals pro rata for 'upstairs' and in the servants' hall. The kitchen in the main house at Eaton was like a miniature cathedral and Le Gras had his office adjoining at first-floor level. He was thus able to open a door on to a small balcony (more like a pulpit) and survey the operations of his chefs and kitchen maids. The work of the kitchen maids began each day with covering the floors with sawdust and marking them by means of their long brooms with an appropriate W. When Le Gras descended to the floor of the kitchen to pass comment it was customary for him to smack the behinds of the kitchen maids. He was an ebullient, extrovert character who would honour the village by attending bridge drives in the small Men's Reading Room at Eccleston. Playing against him one night I brought off two outrageous finesses. He slapped me on the knee with a force that nearly broke my leg and exclaimed, 'You are a lucky boy.'

Le Gras met a sad end – which could have been even more sad. He was driving Percy Smith between Lochmore and Kylestrome when he had a heart-attack, and the car went off the road and down a hillside. Le Gras was dead but by a miracle Percy Smith escaped unhurt.

It was fortunate for Bend'Or and later for Nancy, that, working in the kitchen under Le Gras was Florence Pickett, who ultimately took charge of the kitchen at Eaton, Bourdon House and Lochmore. It can truthfully be said that with Florence's splendid training the standard of cooking did not deteriorate. She was devoted to her task and to the family and was a great favourite, not only with Bend'Or and Nancy, but all members of the Grosvenor family who stayed at Eaton or Lochmore and who rightly regarded her as an old friend.

These were only the head servants who looked after the family and guests. The supporting cast, as it were, who attended to the needs of the upper servants, and to the maintenance of the house and gardens, were much more numerous. Between the steward's room, where the upper staff, the steward, grooms of the chamber, Duchess's maid and housekeeper ate, and the servants' hall which catered for the junior staff, a considerable gulf was fixed.

The young gardeners lived together in the Bothy, a communal hostel in the grounds, and by the standards of the time were well provided for. George Miller, who was head gardener between 1946, when N.F. Barnes retired, and 1976, lived there at a time when his wage as foreman gardener was fifty-two shillings and sixpence a week and his only expense nine shillings a fortnight for food, a sum which enabled him to eat extremely well.

Everyone enjoyed the distinction of working in one of the greatest of great houses, where everything was of the best and the standards were the highest. The long hours were repaid by the highest conditions of service and the excitement of the great occasions. Five young men, under the personal direction of the head gardener, did the table decorations, which always included a barrier down the middle of the table to discourage conversation across the table, a habit of which Bend'Or strongly disapproved. Anne, Duchess, recalls how a groom of the chamber once consulted her as to whether to use the large candelabra or a number of smaller candlesticks. When she replied that she didn't much care which, he replied, with great respect, that this was an answer that she should not have given, since he, and all the staff, cared very much indeed that things should always be of the best, since that was the object of all their work. Both the answer, and the story itself being told by the Duchess, give a piquant illustration of the way in which a great house was run.

Times have changed and much of the traditions of service have changed, and become commercialized. While they were still maintained they were, at their best, a dignified and rewarding framework of human relations.

In 1930 Bend'Or made a third marriage with Loelia Ponsonby, now Lady Lindsay, who has given her own very lively accounts of their life together in such detail as to make it difficult to add anything.

Throughout the ups and downs Bend'Or continued to see much of his oldest friend Winston Churchill, especially on the holidays they had together. In 1923 Winston went to Mimizan on *Flying Cloud* which he described as 'a most attractive yacht. Imagine a large four-masted cargo boat, fitted up in carved oak like a little country house, with front doors, staircases and lovely pictures.' Bend'Or and he paid a visit to the casino at Bayonne where 'Benny with persistent luck and without playing very high has won over half a million francs. I pursuing a most small and conservative game am nearly 30,000 to the good.' In February next year he was there again where 'he enjoyed himself so much'.

Bend'Or rented the Château of St Saens in the Forest of Eawy near Dieppe for boar-hunting to supplement that offered at Mimizan. Churchill gave an account of one hunt there:

> Yesterday we hunted the penwiper [he thought boars looked like dirty penwipers]. A dramatic moment occurred when he appeared from a lake where he had refreshed himself and galloped into our midst. The wire netting round a culvert prevented his escape. He turned to bay. Colonel Hunter fired repeatedly and missed. Benny advanced pistol in hand – but luckily on horseback – to fire the final shot. The pistol in bad order would not cock. The penwiper charged – grazed the horse, scattered the company and eventually makes good his retreat . . . the country people of all classes are enchanted at the hunt and follow it on foot or in motors or on any kind of quadruped. They are as eager to kill them as if they were Germans. It is all quite novel to them so far.

A holiday that did not come off was a projected cruise to North Africa. When this was mooted Bend'Or asked Winston to suggest other companions. He replied, 'The only other suggestion I can make is the Prof who is always most instructive and amusing and loves playing about with us. Somehow or other I feel that yachting with Hilaire Belloc would be rather a formidable undertaking.'

An indication of their continuing close relations is given in a letter Winston wrote from Rosehall, near Lochmore, where he had been staying with Bend'Or and Coco. Bend'Or had to absent himself to London for a ball, and Winston wrote to Clementine, 'Please do this [attend ball] because I am very fond of Benny and I know he would so like to see you and D there.'

Churchill was also the moving figure in Bend'Or's public life. Bend'Or's only major political involvement before the outbreak of World War Two was a direct result of his friendship with Churchill. During the early 1930s the National Government under Ramsay McDonald backed by an overwhelming majority of the Conservative Party, had decided on a policy of dominion status for India and the grant of progressively more self-government to the subcontinent.

Churchill was aware of the very considerable dangers, chiefly of communal strife, inherent in these proposals, and mounted the stiffest of resistances, which earned him very considerable opprobrium in his own party. The opprobrium came to a head in January 1935, when Randolph, then twenty-three, decided, off his own bat, to stand against the Conservative candidate in a by-election for the Wavertree division of Liverpool. Winston was not entirely happy with this, but threw himself into the fight on Randolph's side. One of his first steps was to appeal to Bend'Or for help, which was given unstintingly, in the form of funds, motor cars, canvassers and a message of support. It was a striking example of how far Bend'Or put personal feelings of loyalty far above the claims of party. The result was hardly satisfactory, for Randolph was beaten into third place, the seat going to the Labour candidate. Bend'Or sent a telegram of consolation to Winston: 'What a glorious fight Randolph put up. Never mind. The time will come. It has given the enemy a nasty shock.'

Bend'Or had already helped the previous year in providing funds to save the India Defence League, which was Churchill's instrument for fighting the official Conservative policy, and indeed he was consistently the largest subscriber to the league, and prominent in it from its initiation. Although Bend'Or certainly agreed with the aims of the league it cannot be doubted that, then as later, he was always willing to follow Churchill's lead in politics; it would have been hard to find a better leader. He was moved to write a rare letter on 17 April 1924 following a speech Churchill had made attacking the Conservative leaders:

> My dear Winston,
>
> My congratulations on your having shown up and having fairly cornered Sam H [Sir Samuel Hoare] and Eddy D [Lord Derby] . . . I don't see how these rascals can get out of it . . . I

must say Rothermere has put in some useful work for us . . . Am sure we are gaining ground and friends every day.

Bend'Or

My love to Clemmie.

Winston repaid the political debts he owed to Bend'Or by rescuing him, by his advice, from trouble he would otherwise have steered himself towards. Far too much fuss, often of the most hysterical variety, has been made about Bend'Or's views at the opening of the Second World War. Like many of his generation, especially those who had played an active part in the First World War, and had seen their relatives and friends killed by their sides, he was horrified at the thought of another, which it was thought at the time would be even more devastating than it turned out to be. He had no sympathy at all for Fascism, Communism or any other totalitarian doctrine, unlike, it should be said, many famous figures of the 1930s: Bend'Or remained at all times a resolute democrat in the dogged 'agin-the-government' fashion of the countryman that at heart he was, but as war threatened he became convinced that Britain was in no shape for such a conflict, and that an increase in military strength, and a concomitant avoidance of military action until this was achieved, was the only course. In time, he believed, Germany must strike against Russia, the country that presented the greater threat to the West.

Travelling back from France after a visit he found himself with Anthony Eden, and gave the Foreign Secretary his views on France. Having lived there on and off for thirty years Bend'Or doubted very much whether the French had the stomach for a fight. Eden was indignant, asserting that Bend'Or had been vamped by the Boche, to which Bend'Or replied that Eden must have been vamped by the French, and that he inevitably would be disillusioned; as, of course, he very soon was.

Holding these views the Duke was misled into taking part in a movement launched by a former Conservative MP, Henry Drummond-Wolff. When Winston heard of this he was very alarmed and wrote a long letter:

13 September 1939

My dear Benny,

Several of the cabinet were speaking to me this morning about the statement you read out at your private meeting yesterday. It seems to me on reading it that there are some very serious and

> bad things in it, the full bearing of which I feel you could not possibly have apprehended. It gave me great distress to read it, being one of your oldest friends. I am sure that pursuance of this line will lead you into measureless odium and vexation. When a country is fighting a war of this kind, very hard experiences lie before those who preach defeatism and set themselves up against the main will of the nation. Ramsay McDonald went through it all in the last war, and rose again when it was over, but I wonder whether you have really counted the cost, or whether you are being drawn into courses the true character of which you do not realize . . . I beg you not to spurn the counsels of a life-long friend, and I trust that before you take any further steps you will come to have a talk with me.

The letter had immediate effect; Bend'Or disassociated himself from the peace-mongers and did what he could for the war effort.

Yet it is permissible to wonder whether, in September 1939, such an attitude was all that reprehensible. It was after all shared by such unquestionably admirable persons as Queen Wilhelmina of the Netherlands. Perhaps the answer is given by Nicholas Bethell, whose book *The War Hitler Won* contains one of the most vicious attacks on Bend'Or, when he records Hitler as saying, at exactly that time, 'My only fear is that some bastard will propose a peace conference.' Be that as it may there is no question but that the good relations that subsisted between Bend'Or and Winston Churchill were in no way ruptured by this incident, but continued to flourish for the rest of their lives.

With his views set right by his old friend Bend'Or settled down to do what he could to beat the Germans and, as always, put his whole heart into it. His most dramatic intervention was the mysterious visit to Spain in 1940, the details and purpose of which still remain unclear. It is probable that this had something to do with the affairs of the Duke of Windsor, which much exercised Churchill at the time. The two dukes had been friends for some time: on the abdication Bend'Or had offered St Saens to the Duke. Churchill wrote on his behalf on 17 December 1936:

> Bend'Or would be delighted if you could use St Saens. His horses and hounds are there and every facility for the chase. I do not know whether your RH has ever hunted the boar. It is pretty good sport and I like it because although there is a great deal of rough and tricky riding through woodland and up and down hill, there are no fences to jump. This I fear you would regard as a disadvantage.

Eaton was immediately put at the disposal of the war effort, as Grosvenor House had been in 1914. It was quickly converted into a military convalescent hospital, housing French troops evacuated after Dunkirk. Enthusiasm for the Allied cause was by no means unanimous among them and when given a choice between returning to Vichy France or joining the Free French forces many opted for the former. It was not the French, however, who were responsible for betraying Eaton to the enemy: that was a different story.

When in the August of 1940 the German air raids on Liverpool began, warning was given that signals were being given, during the raids, by means of a light from one of the windows at Eaton Hall. Squads of the Home Guard were detailed to patrol the gardens and open fire on any window from which signals were being made, but never succeeded in finding the culprit. The true story of what was happening was revealed a few months later. Among the army staff at Eaton was a very handsome blond Norwegian sergeant PT instructor. He had apparently owned a private gymnasium in London before the war and, as he claimed to be a member of an aristocratic Norwegian family, was handsomely entertained by the local 'gentry', included in Western Command parties and soon built up a reputation as a very attractive and charming personality, especially among the girls. Before long he went missing and to many people's embarrassment was heard broadcasting on Lord Haw Haw's programme from Berlin. He had made his way to the east coast, found himself a boat and by prior arrangement was picked up by a German submarine. Having dined with the GOC Western Command and knowing the senior officers he was able to make play of his knowledge of military affairs at Chester. He was a Quisling who had been planted by the Germans in London before the war, and there could be little doubt that it was he who signalled to the German planes.

Not only the navy but the RAF and eventually the army partook of Eaton hospitality. An airfield was built in the park, close to the Hall, which necessitated felling some magnificent oaks, a cause of sadness to everyone. We all, including Bend'Or, took a hand in the defences of Eaton. I held the exalted rank of corporal in the Home Guard, where Basil Kerr commanded. At some times our work was very demanding: one night in six had to be spent on patrol around the estate. Three of us generally patrolled with only one break for coffee and sandwiches about two o'clock. So far as I was concerned it was a real

'Dad's Army', and for some time I was the only one armed as I had a .22 rifle! My companions (there was no change in the rota) were Charles Elen from the Eaton Stud (nephew of Gus Elen the cockney comedian) and Jack Davies – a gardener in the village, both ex-servicemen. Jack Davies had a cleft palate with the impediment forcing his words through his nose, while Charles Elen had a stutter. One night in six we would walk from the cricket pavilion, through the village, down the Rake Lane, along the Wrexham Road and up the Belgrave drive. Had anyone heard the conversation on the radio or gramophone they would never have believed it!

However, we did have real drama one night. As the only one with a car I was the one to be alerted in the event of trouble and it was my task to gather my own small squad together and to alert others. In the middle of one night the telephone rang and, expecting to have to take a long message, I threw on a dressing gown and hastened down. Alas the dressing gown cord caught under the bedroom door and I pitched headlong down the stairs. In a daze I picked up the phone and received a curt message to the effect that German parachutists had landed in woods on the Pulford drive. I was to gather up my squad and proceed forthwith. My fourth member was to be Lieutenant Heber Fearnall, a local farmer and a sniper with the Cheshire Yeomanry and the Camel Corps in the 1914–18 war, a really toughened veteran of unflappable character. He had always been Winston Churchill's loader in the days of the Eaton and World's End shoots.

We proceeded to the area of the Pulford drive where the parachutes had been spotted and sure enough even in the dark we could see half a dozen or more parachutes in the trees, but no sign of the enemy. We sat tight and waited for dawn. When it came we could see in a nearby field on Fair's farm the debris of a German bomber and when we advanced found a huge crater. The bomber had exploded when it hit the ground and this had forced the parachutes out. The bodies of the crew had been blown to smithereens and as we cautiously walked through the debris Heber Fearnall quietly bent down and picked up a hand. 'That's just the sort of ring I've been looking for,' he said, and promptly took the ring off the hand, put it on his own finger and threw the hand away without any emotion!

Heber was a tough customer. He had an excellent loft of racing pigeons, one of which won him the big race from Nantes and altogether over £2,000 in prize money. When, through age, it ceased to win races he wrung its neck. One of his friends was horrified and asked him why in view of the bird's achievements he had not kept it as a pet. 'What,' said Heber, 'feed the so-and-so when it's not earning any money!'

After the bombing of Dartmouth in 1942, the Duke was asked if he would agree to the Royal Naval College moving to Eaton and this he was delighted to do and during their occupation of Eaton he took a keen interest in their activities and entertained members of the staff, as well as some of the cadets from time to time. The negotiations with the Admiralty were conducted initially with Mr Palmer, the chief surveyor, Lands Branch, who then delegated the task to Derek Brice of the Lands Branch, Bath, who had been moved to Western Approaches, Liverpool. Brice and I worked closely for the period of Dartmouth's occupation of Eaton and I had a high opinion of his ability.

In 1961, I invited Brice to join us and he did so, taking over the management of the Bridgewater Estate at Ellesmere, Shropshire, and the Chester Urban Estates. In 1967 he went to Grosvenor International in Australia as property manager, retired at the end of December 1978, and returned to England to live in the Old Rectory at Colemere, Ellesmere.

With due respect to the army, the navy were so much easier to deal with. They regarded the RNC HMS *Britannia* as a ship with the result that the supplies captain could settle all accounts himself without reference to the Admiralty. With the War Office there was so much 'red tape' with accounts having to be approved by officers on the spot, submitted to Western Command and then the War Office for approval.

It was a joy to see the young cadets at Eaton. The cricket ground, golf course, tennis courts and other recreation grounds and squash court were in full use and they did their best to practise sailing under difficult conditions on the Dee. Their officers were hand-picked, while their civilian schoolmasters, who were billeted in the villages, brought a boost to the social life. They also swelled the numbers of the Home Guard and made life much easier.

A number of them joined my signal squad. They were not exactly immaculate on the parade ground, but I felt a fraud carrying two stripes when they could lose me in knowledge of signals. One of their number, Geoffrey Ghey, who was a scientist, was awarded the CBE at the end of the war. He was a charming, retiring man who, with his wife and small child, lived in a flat at Eccleston Hill, the residence of the captain of the college. He and I were engaged in an amusing incident towards the end of the war.

Having suffered from the complete lack of signals equipment for the Home Guard and relying upon the primitive method of 'runners' to augment or replace the telephone, we were as excited as schoolboys to receive two radio transmitters. Ghey and I arranged one Saturday afternoon that he would sit on the lawn at Eccleston Hill and I on the lawn of my house in the village and exchange communications. We played the fool by saying that German troops had landed and made up a story of what was happening. The next thing was that troops in armoured cars, etc. entered the village – Western Command Headquarters, only a couple of miles away, having picked up our signals. Our possession of the transmitters was short-lived. They were confiscated!

Bend'Or made only one essay into his old love of military technology, jointly with Professor Lindemann. They had both become interested in the work of a Greek scientist, Mitzakis, in the use of very high-powered searchlights for aerial use, and were anxious to see the potential for this weapon exploited, a project which Bend'Or was very willing to pay for. He wrote to Churchill:

> My dear W,
>
> Listening in to last night's wireless, I heard it mentioned that one of our pilots had encountered an enemy 'plane with very bright lights on it. It occurs to me that we ought to waste no time in getting our lamps trimmed like the wise virgins – you – better than anyone – know what happened about the tanks in the last war. The fatal delays, etc. – we must not repeat that error. It looks as if we are going to be done in again on this De Thoron plan and I pray that you will intervene with all your power. Professor has received a letter from A. Chief Marshal Dowding which he will tell you about.
>
> The great thing is to get a move on – there is no expense and you might get a stupendous result out of it – I would suggest that the expert Mitzakis, the professor and A.M. Dowding should meet soonest possible and have a talk. Can you possibly arrange this. I hate writing and bothering you just at this moment. You hold the greatest position in the world and are far better fitted for it than anyone else, that must be my excuse for this letter. In June 37 you very kindly wrote to the WO on behalf of the De Thoron

> Co. I do implore you to let me act as I suggested in my last letter and let us give the project a try out. To my mind at this moment speed is essential in this matter.
>
> The Prof will himself explain that the beam is in itself a protection to the pilot. It has been proved in the WO tests that you cannot shoot at the lights – so I do so hope it will not be necessary to go through long drawn out experiments again. We shall be beaten for time if we are beaten at all.

In a letter which looks much like a reply to a telephone call, Churchill had said to Bend'Or on the thirteenth, 'I am always in the closest touch with Dowding and so is the Prof. The Prof thinks well of aerial searchlights, and I have given directions for the subject to be presented as coming from me – Yours always WC.' Although tests were carried out nothing more came of this particular enthusiasm, and Bend'Or spent the war quietly; he was for a time very ill and when in better health devoted himself to the mundane but vital task of encouraging agricultural production, a subject in which he soon became absorbed and in which, when conditions permitted after the war, he again showed himself both enthusiastic and expert.

7

Sunlit Uplands

The end of the 1945 war, the election of a Labour government and the prolonged period of austerity made a much greater difference to English life than had the previous war. This time there was no question of Eaton being retained as a private house: those days were, for better or worse, gone and Bend'Or did not repine.

For some time Basil Kerr had groomed me to succeed him on his retirement, which he had planned for the end of the war. With great wisdom he had quietly arranged that I should see Bend'Or on estate matters instead of him, thus giving the 'Owner' ample time to decide whether I was the person he would like as his agent and, of equal if not more importance, as his confidant and adviser on personal matters. It was in this field that Basil Kerr had excelled and it was to him that Bend'Or would turn when difficult problems required to be resolved. Basil would never have claimed expertise in estate management – especially financial affairs – but for worldly common sense and judgement he was invaluable. His special piece of advice and guidance to me were the words 'common sense, courtesy and tact'. Quietly and unobtrusively he retired in November 1945, and I was appointed in his place.

He had enjoyed a remarkable life. A son of Charles Wyndham Rudolph Kerr, a grandson of the Marquess of Lothian, a great Border family, he received the minimum education at Hawtreys and then at the age of seventeen sailed for Australia to work as a jackaroo on a sheep station. He was dispatched with £100 and a saddle. On the voyage he lost the £100 and the saddle at cards, but learnt enough to be a master of card tricks worthy of a stage act from then on. In addition his arms were tattoed from wrist to elbow – a factor which prevented him from rolling up his sleeves when in years to come he returned to English society and the pursuits of polo, cricket and golf.

When he arrived at Sydney he was forced to work in a butcher's shop for six months to obtain his train fare to the sheep station. He roughed it and enjoyed it – especially one piece of incredible luck. In a saloon one night two miners from a neighbouring gold mine announced in their cups the find of an excellent seam. The next day Basil made off to Sydney and used all his savings to buy shares in the mining company. He got in before the news broke and made a killing. The money he made was soon needed for shortly afterwards the sheep station suffered a severe drought. Thousands of sheep died so he took himself off to the Argentine and was successful in obtaining a job as assistant manager on an Estancia.

For enjoyment this was the highlight of his life. Horses and cattle were his first love and the days in the saddle were to him idyllic. His ability as a horseman saw him involved in polo and eventually he was appointed as player-manager of the Argentine team to visit England. It was while playing at Roehampton and Hurlingham that he first met Bend'Or who was captaining his own team as well as playing for club sides. Bend'Or's relationship with his agent at Eaton, his uncle – the Hon Cecil Parker – was strained and he was looking for a new man. He offered the job to Basil, who refused it on the score that he was loath to abandon the freedoms of life on an Estancia and in the polo world of the Argentine for the comparative restrictions of an agent's life in England.

A year or two later, however, he suffered a bad fever and was advised to return home. He obtained a job as assistant to Mr Lightfoot who had a good land agency practice in Market Drayton, including five estates of value, among them Cheswardine, Adderley and Shavington. The owner at Adderley was Reggie Corbet who had succeeded Bend'Or as Master of the Cheshire Hounds. He gave Basil the added job of rough-rider and by coincidence he met Bend'Or in the hunting field, who repeated his offer of the job at Eaton, which this time was accepted. Cecil Parker, who had a great name in the land agency world, retired and Basil Kerr came to Eaton in 1910.

He was immediately popular with the staff and tenants, but the outbreak of war saw him joining Bend'Or's armoured car squadron with which he won the DSC in 1915, a naval decoration, emphasizing the formation of the squadron within the navy, although his rank was that of major.

Throughout his thirty-four years at Eaton, Basil Kerr earned and retained the respect and loyalty of tenants and employees and displayed a dignity appropriate to the representative of a noble landlord. He had an especially close relationship with the farming community and with the racing world, where he made contact through his management of the Eaton Stud.

At this time my own responsibilities were modest. The imposing head keeper, Stark, died after a long and painful illness; I remember the Duke, at the funeral in Eccleston Church, putting a comforting arm round the widow. Myles then combined the post of head forester and head keeper; I spent a couple of years as assistant forester, but with a variety of outside work in addition. It came as a surprise to me when, in January 1931, Myles walked across from his house to my little office to say that Major Kerr wished to see me at once at the estate office. I cannot remember that he ever warned me what it might be about. I cycled the three miles to Eccleston and was ushered into Major Kerr's office. I had met him occasionally at my work and in church affairs, but up till then had had no real conversation with him. He asked me, 'Do you know anything about property?' 'No, sir.' 'You don't know anything about shops, offices and residential property?' 'No, sir.' 'Do you know anything about rates and taxes?' 'No, sir.' 'Do you know anything about building construction?' 'No, sir.' 'You'll do, I want you to start next Monday and take over the Chester estate.' The sub-agent who managed the property had died a few weeks earlier, and I realized that I owed my good fortune to Myles, who had obviously recommended me.

One of the conditions Major Kerr laid down on my new appointment was that I should leave the Cheshire Yeomanry, where I had been for three years, joining at the time the Eaton troop was re-formed. There had been an Eaton troop consisting of men from the estate almost from the time of the formation of the regiment in 1797 up to the end of the 1914–18 war. The first Duke was colonel of the regiment and his second son, Lord Arthur Grosvenor, served with it for many years. The second Duke had joined on leaving Eton and had gone out on his second tour of duty to the South African War with the regiment before transferring to the Blues.

My new responsibility, the Chester estate, comprised shops and offices and about 200 cottages and flats. There was also a substantial area of farmland to the south of Chester, west of the Dee, all of which had development potential which had been promoted by the building of Westminster Park, a high-class residential area on long leaseholds, which in fifty years had produced no more than fifty leaseholds. My job was to collect the weekly rents on a Monday – many of the cottages were let at two or three shillings a week, including rates and repairs – receive notice of repairs, meet the builders and give them instructions. On Friday afternoon I visited the building work to see progress.

My work on the Chester estate soon expanded my knowledge of human nature, particularly as it was related to the management of the cottage properties – all terraced houses where neighbours' lives were intertwined and the agent was regarded as a resident magistrate, whose tasks did not end with the collection of rents and the efficient repair of the properties, but included the settlement of disputes, which were sometimes violent in character.

At the time of King George V's jubilee celebrations in 1935, Chester streets vied with one another in the decorations comprising Union Jacks and red, white and blue bunting and various motifs. The bunting across Greenway Street and around the houses was yellow and black – the Duke's racing colours. When I asked the reason for this I was told 'The Duke is our King!' They meant no disrespect for the royal family, but their loyalty to the Grosvenor family knew no bounds.

Many years later, about 1968, when I was chairman of the trustees, we held a trustees' and agents' meeting at Eaton which lasted several days. We went on a tour of the Chester properties, including Greenway Street. Sadly, to my mind, the corporation had condemned all the properties and arrangements were being made to rehouse the tenants prior to demolition and a rebuilding scheme. The fourth Duke, Gerald, and his brother, Lord Robert Grosvenor, their cousin and a fellow trustee, Colonel Michael Crichton, Tom Barty-King and I were standing together with various executives at the bottom of Greenway Street along the river bank where the drying posts stood for drying the salmon nets. Unexpectedly along came one of the old tenants whom I had not seen for years. 'It's Mr Ridley isn't it? How are you? Have you heard what they're going to do to our street – they're knocking it down 'cos they say we haven't got bathrooms. Who wants a bathroom, Mr Ridley? Missus and I have lived here for over fifty years an' if we want a bath we go in the blooming river!' Not knowing who was in our party he went on, 'It wouldn't have happened in our Duke's time would it Mr Ridley?' Then, turning to Gerald, the Duke, and Lord Robert, he said 'Our Duke was a gentleman, wasn't he Mr Ridley? He looked after us – always shoved half a ton of coal under our door every Christmas.' Up to the time of the last war every weekly tenant received ten hundredweight of coal at Christmas. Considering that their rents of two or three shillings a week included rates, water rate and all repairs this represented a half-year's rebate of rent.

I rather enjoyed that incident because no words of mine could have created a picture of the relationship between Bend'Or and his tenants as the colourful outburst of a typical, appreciative tenant. In times of trouble their rents were forgiven and, if necessary, they were given financial help – quietly, unobtrusively as the Duke would have been furious at any publicity; any such arrangements were personal between him and his tenants whom he regarded as his friends.

In 1940, Diana Kerr – Basil and Winifred Kerr's elder daughter – married Captain Henry Clowes of the Scots Guards. They had first met when Henry, as a contemporary of Mark Kerr at Eton, had visited Eccleston Paddocks. Mark Kerr, a Lieutenant-Colonel in the Rifle Brigade, sadly died in Italy in 1944. He receives very favourable mention in Lord Lovat's book and one of David Niven's. Henry survived the war in which he won a DSO and ultimately commanded the regiment. On his retirement from active service he was appointed a member of the Queen's Bodyguard, 'The Hon. Corps of Gentlemen-at-Arms', and rose through the various offices to be Lieutenant, a post he relinquished on reaching the age limit in 1971, when the Queen conferred on him a KCVO. Diana's and Henry's very close friendship with Nancy and with Bend'Or's daughter, Mary, conveys to me a most happy continuation of the Bend'Or–Basil Kerr almost life-long companionship.

With the end of the war it was understandable that the Admiralty would make plans for an early return of the Royal Naval College to Dartmouth. Their occupation of Eaton had given great pleasure to so many in the locality, but their leaving was immediately compensated for when General Sir Brian Horrocks, who was GOC Western Command, on learning of the Royal Naval College's departure asked if the Duke would be prepared to grant the War Office a long lease of

Eaton as an officer cadet school, or as he envisaged it – 'the Sandhurst of the North'. The Duke, with his military background and love of the army, was happy to agree to such a lease of the main house and gardens, the park, all the drive and adjoining woodlands, thus giving the cadet school about 2,000 acres of training area. It was an ideal site and with the proximity of the headquarters of Western Command and the city of Chester, the location could not have been bettered.

Henry Potts (whose family had been lawyers to the Grosvenor family for generations) and I spent many hours in the preparation of the all-important lease. The Duke was to retain the private wing and a small part of the gardens and the greenhouses for his life and twelve months thereafter. The rent of a peppercorn a year was obviously a nominal one, having regard to the accommodation provided, but the War Office were held responsible for all maintenance. Brian Horrocks was a most delightful person with whom to deal and was instrumental in cutting through a lot of the normal red tape. There was an interesting sequel of which he later told me. He was sent for to appear before the Army Council – Field Marshal Montgomery, then CIGS, was in the chair. Horrocks was severely reprimanded for having committed the War Office to the lease of Eaton in his capacity as GOC Western Command when he should have obtained prior approval from the War Office. His severest critic at the meeting was Monty, who appeared to be distinctly annoyed. Later he walked down the corridor with Horrocks and said, 'Well done, Jorrocks – it's just what I would have done!'

When the Officer Cadet School was installed, Monty decided to pay a visit of inspection. Brian Horrocks asked me would I help out and conduct Monty around the property and grounds. 'He'll ask the most detailed questions,' he said, of which he would not know the answers and Horrocks felt he had better delegate to someone who knew. His assessment was perfect and when the day came I led Monty around the property explaining the history of the building. When we came to the 'Golden Gates' in front of the Hall, I told him they had been made by the Brothers Davies of Bersham, who had served their apprenticeship in Liège, the home of the most famous gatemakers in the world. Monty's comment was typical of the others he made – a short, snappy 'How do you know?'

Brian Horrocks had moved into Eccleston Hill when it was leased by the Duke for a period coextensive with the lease of Eaton and was renamed Government House. Monty was very critical of it and said it was better than any house he had ever occupied and too good for a command general. To the Duke, to the estate and to the people of Eccleston the army's occupation was a happy period – particularly the use of Eccleston Hill as the GOC's home. Brian Horrocks was promoted to command the Army of the Rhine in 1948 and was succeeded by General Simpson and the succession continued through Cameron Nicholson, Charles Loewen, Otway Herbert, Edward Howard-Vyse, Charles Craddock, Tony Read, Napier Crookenden, on whose termination of office in 1975 Western Command was the subject, with other commands, of abolition. The Generals were splendid persons, the embodiment of all that is best in the British Army and, together with their wives, played their part in the community life.

The Officer Cadet School's first Commanding Officer was Douglas Darling – as far as we were concerned a happy choice as he had been at Eton and Sandhurst with Mark Kerr, Basil Kerr's son, and they joined the Rifle Brigade together. He was with Mark when he died in Italy in 1944. He went on to become a major-general but shortly before I wrote this there was the sad news of his death from a hunting accident while out with the Beaufort. He was succeeded by Dennis Gibbs of the Queen's Regiment and among the subsequent commanding officers was Basil Eugster, later to gain rapid promotion and to command the Army of the Rhine.

With the cut-back of the armed services in 1960 the War Office asked if they could surrender their fifty-year lease and this was agreed to with regret.

In 1942 the estate was approached by the Air Ministry and the Ministry of Agriculture for the building of an aerodrome at Eaton. The site chosen covered a substantial area of the park close to Eaton Hall and major portions of two tenant farms of Mullock and Denson and of two farms owned by the Liverpool Co-Op and W. Watson. The largest portion of the land being in the occupation or ownership of the Duke, the government were safe in relying upon his patriotism as against the choice of alternative sites. The felling of magnificent trees, oaks in particular, was a great sadness, but with commendable speed Wimpeys created Poulton Airfield for the RAF and there began another military occupation of the estate and I was much concerned with all the usual complicated negotiations as between the Air

Ministry, the estate and the tenants.

It was at this time, after a lifetime of success and disappointment, that Bend'Or at last settled into a happier state of mind and a more contented existence. This started with a journey to Ireland to visit an old friend, Ikey Bell, whom he had first met at an Eton–Harrow soccer match fifty years before. The match had been flooded off and the two boys set to wrestling in the gym. Ikey was a character straight out of Surtees, apart from the fact he was an American, who inherited a fortune from his uncle, Gordon Bennett, owner of the *New York Herald Tribune*. To make up for this, perhaps, he never actually visited the States. After Harrow, Ikey went to Cambridge and set a record, even for that university, of being up two terms without ever seeing Cambridge in daylight. This he achieved by hunting five days a week in the shires, leaving before dawn and returning each evening, climbing into his rooms from the roof of a hansom cab. On Fridays it was his habit to take the train to Holyhead, cross to Kingstown, and go by train to Galway to hunt with the Blazers on Saturday, returning to Cambridge on Sunday night. After two terms of this his tutor told him to make up his mind whether he wanted to be a Master of Arts or a Master of Foxhounds. Ikey unhesitatingly chose the latter, and became successively Master of the Galway Blazers, the Kilkenny and the South West Wilts, writing in his spare time books on foxhunting and hound breeding. His hunting career came to an unhappy end just before the war when his horse fell on him, crushing him against some iron railings and confining him thereafter to crutches.

During the visit Bend'Or and Ikey stayed with General Sullivan and Mrs Sullivan of Glanmire, County Cork, and met their delightful daughter, Anne (Nancy), who had just come home after six years' service with the FANY. Bend'Or immediately decided that Ireland was the place for him, and initiated one of the whirlwind operations which so entirely typified him. When he got back to Eaton he sent for me, and drew an arc on my RAC map of Eire, telling me to buy him a house with a farm, also a stud, which need not necessarily be with or near the residence and finally a dairy farm near Dublin. I was to go forthwith – it was the end of November – and meet Ikey Bell, who would accompany me, at the Shelbourne in Dublin. Reports of my progress had to be sent virtually daily.

By the greatest good fortune Ikey first introduced me to George McVeagh. George was a charming, yet dynamic personality, a quadruple 'Pink' at Trinity, Dublin, and a quadruple international, having played for Ireland at cricket, tennis, hockey and squash. He was just the type of lawyer we wanted, a man who would drop everything to concentrate on the job on hand and who would be prepared to use unorthodox methods to get results. These qualities were certainly needed in the next few months and George got a great kick out of being under maximum pressure to complete deals in a space of time unheard of in Ireland.

George gave me a list of possible properties from estate agents, as well as introductions to agents, and Ikey and I set off in a hired limousine. Ikey was also to take me to properties owned by people of his acquaintance who he thought would be prepared to sell. They proved to be mansions of charming Georgian architecture, but hopelessly neglected and unsuitable, many with roofs leaking like sieves. On his tour with Ikey the Duke had passed the drive gates of a property adjoining the Duke of Devonshire's Lismore Castle, then occupied by Lord Charles Cavendish's widow, Adele Astaire. I understood that this was a real possibility so I could not wait for our travels to take us there.

To my shame this came about on a Sunday morning. The property was Fortwilliam, an early Victorian house standing in about 160 acres – approached by a very pleasant mile-long drive lined with beeches, the farm building halfway down the drive and the fields beyond the house running down to the River Blackwater. The property, like so many in Ireland during the war, had been bought by a speculator, a Mr Dunne of Dungarvan, who owned a dairy business. Ikey and I arranged to meet him in the middle of the morning and after a quick look around the property I was satisfied that this was 'the thing'. The house was in first-class order and the only one I had seen that was as dry as a bone.

Naturally, I did not tell Mr Dunne whom I was representing and he, therefore, assumed that if I did a deal I would be buying the property for myself. I was very much at a loss as to what the value might be as I could not really compare Waterford prices with Cheshire. He suggested £12,000, but gradually, over a glass of sherry, I got him down to £8,000 and felt satisfied that before long I could make it £6,000, when to my surprise, Ikey intervened and said, 'If you do not buy it, George, I will', which committed me to the £8,000. Mr Dunne had some very nice furniture, carpets and curtains in the house;

also a small herd of pedigree Herefords on the farm. A deal was struck on a 'lock, stock and barrel' basis for £10,000, £2,000 being the price of all the furniture and effects, and the farm stock.

Ikey then had to return to Dublin and I went on the next day to see Bruree Stud Farm in County Limerick. This was a property of about 470 acres, with post and rail paddocks, boxes for seventy, two stallion boxes, a covered exercise yard and a good-sized house, but externally not very attractive, being of yellow brick and very Victorian, although the thirteen cottages included were good. The property had belonged to Mr Gubbins in the latter half of the nineteenth century, along with Knockaney Stud and it was here that were bred Galtee More and Ard Patrick, winners of the Derby in 1897 and 1902. In addition to being a good stud farm, Bruree had excellent fattening land for bullocks. Mr de Courcy, an estate agent in Limerick, was acting for the then owner, Mr Sheahan, and the three of us stood in one of the paddocks from mid-afternoon until it was dark arguing as to price. Eventually we agreed £14,000 but I was still not happy at this price and persuaded Mr Sheahan to pay half Mr de Courcy's fees of £700, as the purchaser was liable for fees in Eire, not the vendor as in England.

Having done a deal, I went back the next day when Mr de Courcy was not there and privately arranged with Mr Sheahan to buy all the live and dead stock for £5,000. Included was a thoroughbred mare with a foal at foot. This was Knocksouna, the dam of Knock Hard, the winner of the Cheltenham Gold Cup in 1953. Here again the purchase was in my name.

When I reported to the Duke, at Eaton, he was delighted, and told me to go over again as soon as possible to arrange for the staffing and complete equipment of Fortwilliam, so that he could take up residence early in the New Year. Unfortunately, I went down with flu after Christmas and the Duke sent his secretary from London over to make the necessary arrangements. On his return he reported that it was simply impossible to obtain staff, an incident which was to have a dramatic effect on my future as the Duke did not suffer failure gladly and made his views known. All personal staff wherever located were under the ultimate control of the secretary in London, but following this news the secretary came to see me while I was still on my sick bed and told me that from then on I would be in charge of all the Duke's personal staff. I protested and said I was a land agent and did not wish to have anything to do with the personnel side, but I was told I could tell this to the Duke and he, the secretary, had no say in the matter.

I received word that the Duke wished to come to Eccleston to see me, but I preferred to struggle out of bed and go up to see him. He was most apologetic for pressurizing me when I was not feeling well, but stressed that he wished to have Fortwilliam ready for his occupation by 23 January and confirmed that from that day onwards I would be responsible for all his personal staff, in addition to my tasks as agent for the Eaton estate.

My cousin, Bill Bryan, who at that time was in the navy, was on leave and staying with us, so I asked if I might take him to Ireland with me to help out as I felt some support was certainly needed in this Herculean task. We went over in the first week in January and took Richard Chapman, then butler, with us to see the house and to do the practical work of preparation.

The agent on the Duke of Devonshire's Lismore estate, which was only a part-time job, was Captain Gerald FitzGerald, a splendid Irishman who had spent quite some time in the oil business in California. I sought his help and persuaded him to release the head housemaid, the cook and the house boy from Lismore Castle, which was feasible since Lady Charles Cavendish had decided to return to America. He also helped in finding some more maids, but the Lismore staff and others who were in jobs had to give a month's notice, making it impossible for them to be at Fortwilliam until early February. I wired the Duke asking if I could have a fortnight's grace, which meant that he would take up residence at the end of the first week in February. I received a telegram in reply which read: 'Shall be at Fortwilliam 23 January. The House will be fully equipped and staffed. No excuses. Westminster.'

I was furious but accepted the challenge. Richard was splendid: he had dealt with 'panic stations' before. We drove up to Dublin, where the housekeeper at the Shelbourne Hotel – Miss Duffy – was most kind and helpful. Through her good offices we engaged the chef, a Swiss, from the Clarence Hotel, Dublin, for a month and as it was out of season for the Great Northern Hotel at Bundoran took the maids from there also for a month. The farm staff and gardeners had already been taken on so, together with a small garage owner at Lismore who was prepared to do part-time chauffeuring, we had a complete staff.

The next problem was the silver, glass, china, etc. which the Duke wished to send from Eaton. It was a great battle with the Irish authorities to obtain an import licence, but here George McVeagh was at his best. We had a dramatic moment when the authorities demanded a cheque for three times the value of the goods to be imported, the cheque to be deposited for six months as an insurance against the Duke selling all or any of the items. I wrote out the cheque for the appropriate amount and was horrified when George told me they would not accept it unless it was guaranteed by the bank. Another rushed visit to the bank manager for his endorsement and then after acceptance by the customs it was a question of getting the pantechnicon cleared in Dublin. I cannot say strongly enough how George McVeagh's personality and influence came to the fore.

Having cleared the goods through customs, we found that the pantechnicon could not be opened at Fortwilliam without the presence of another customs officer. The nearest man was situated at Fermoy and I arranged for one of George's partners to accompany the pantechnicon to Fortwilliam in his car overnight and then go on to Fermoy to collect the customs officer who would break the seals and grant the necessary certificate. This was done in splendid fashion, except the Fermoy customs officer was not too pleased about turning out in the early morning for such a task.

Richard Chapman, cool and calm as usual, superintended all the proceedings and when the Duke finally arrived – a day early on the twenty-second – the house was fully staffed and equipped, looking as though it had been lived in by the Duke for years. Only one thing could be called a complaint: when, a little while after the Duke had moved in, he asked me how much the chef was being paid and I told him the amount, which was larger than usual since it was intended as a temporary measure, he was horrified, saying that we could not possibly afford it and that the man must be got rid of! Needless to say this was not done and the chef remained until Mrs Lynch, the cook from Lismore Castle, arrived. The manner of the Duke's arrival and the establishment of his home within a few weeks was the talk of Ireland at the time: it was said in some quarters that, like an Arabian prince, he had come on a magic carpet.

While he loved the relaxed life in Ireland he nevertheless expected the continuance of those standards that he had been accustomed to all his life at Eaton, and asked me to keep my eyes open for ways in which things might be improved. The day after he asked me to do this

I was watching Paddy, the boy from the gardens, take a wheelbarrow from the house to the farm, a mile away down the drive, and some time later return with a sack of fertilizer. During the time he had taken to do this a farm tractor had made several trips from the farmsteadings to the meadows and back. I had a word with Lawlor, the farm manager, and pointed out how easy it would have been for the tractor to have dropped off a sack of fertilizer at the garden during its journey. He looked at me with amazement and said: 'Sure, Mr Ridley, you may be right, but what would I be doing with Paddy in the meantime?'

When I first set about the establishment of Fortwilliam the Duke had asked me to approach Miss Sullivan if I stood in need of any help, and in particular to ask her if she would do the flowers in the house before his first visit. It was not until some time later that I realized that the reason for the purchase of Fortwilliam had been to give the Duke a home close to Miss Sullivan! She often came over for the day from Glanmire and the Duke was often loath to return to Eaton from Fortwilliam. One occasion was typical of his determination to stay. He and I were due to leave Fortwilliam, drive to Dublin, and return to Eaton the next day, and planned to leave after luncheon. Miss Sullivan was there for lunch; I tried to persuade the Duke to leave while it was still daylight, but he decided to stay for tea. After tea my exhortations produced no further effect and we remained for dinner; it was only then that he allowed Miss Sullivan to take her leave.

All the way to Dublin he extolled her qualities, seeking my approval, which I did not find hard to give, for I liked her enormously. It was nearly midnight when we got to Maryborough, where I asked if we might stop for a drink, as was my habit on this journey. He replied that we could not possibly get a drink at that hour, but, knowing Ireland, and Kelly's Hotel, I felt that he might just be wrong! Accordingly I took him through the yard and in by the back door. The lounge was full of Irish soldiers, and it was significant of the respect he always commanded that everyone, not even knowing who he was, stood up as he entered. He joined me in a Guinness, which I do not think that he had ever drunk before, and from that time on whenever I stayed with him at Fortwilliam there was a bottle of Guinness on the sideboard. On our leaving, the company again stood and returned our goodnights in a warm and friendly fashion which was most impressive.

Before the end of the year he had persuaded Nancy to marry him as soon as he could obtain a divorce from Loelia, from whom he had been separated for more than ten years. This was done by January 1947 by which time the press had become aware of an impending marriage. It fell to my lot to arrange the wedding in such a way that there would be the minimum of publicity or, better still, none at all. I arranged, through Henry Potts, the Duke's lawyer in Chester, to meet the registrar, Alby Hull, a charming person who was also a musician and played the cello in a three-piece orchestra, which performed during tea at Bollands Restaurant.

Alby Hull, who came to lunch at Eaton with Potts, was splendid and readily fell in with the scheme of things. He had two books in which forthcoming weddings were inserted, one for Chester and another for West Cheshire. The Chester book was kept on the counter opposite the entrance to his office, while the West Cheshire book, in which very few people were interested, was kept on one side. The necessary three weeks' notice of impending marriage was given, and entered in the West Cheshire book, which was completely ignored by the reporters who came every day to inspect the Chester book.

The wedding was fixed for 7 February, just after the office opened at eight in the morning. The Duke arrived with Miss Sullivan and her brother, Major George Sullivan of the 14th/20th Hussars. I was there to greet them and to act as witness and I still recall the surprise on the face of Alby Hull's assistant, who was completely unaware of the names of the principals in the ceremony until he was introduced. It was all over in a very short space of time – very efficiently but in a dignified manner and it terminated in a very typical Bend'Or gesture. As we were walking out of the door of the office he put his hand in his pocket and took out a gold cigarette box which he handed very shyly to Alby Hull and thanked him for what he had done. He then turned to me and said, 'I suppose you had better have something as well', and gave me his gold-topped Malacca cane.

At eleven o'clock I called a press conference, made the announcement of the marriage and told them that the Duke and his new duchess had left for London. This information was a 'blind' to divert the press and it proved to be successful. That evening I accompanied them to the B and I boat at Liverpool where I had reserved accommodation in the names of Colonel and Mrs Bell. They thus made their way to Fortwilliam without any of the press being aware of their movements.

From that time on Bend'Or's life was, for the first time since his youth, happy and relaxed. It was a much less unequal match than any of his previous marriages: all Bend'Or's duchesses were ladies of beauty and character, but Nancy was not only young and high-spirited, but a wealthy lady in her own right. On the eve of his marriage to Nancy he asked me to call at Eaton, and handed me a document which had been brought to him 'by a gentleman from London in a black coat and striped trousers'. The document was a deed making over to Nancy part of the monies of a trust to which she became entitled on marriage. Bend'Or was astonished when he saw the size of the sums involved, and asked 'Did you know Nancy was rich? – Good heavens, you don't think, do you, that people will say I am marrying her for her money!'

On another occasion I was lunching at Bourdon House while Nancy's mother, Mrs Winifred Sullivan, was staying there. She had been to the jewellers in the morning to pick up a maple-leaf-shaped diamond brooch which she had ordered for Nancy, as Mrs Sullivan was herself Canadian and her father one of the early directors of the Bank of Nova Scotia. Having collected the brooch for Nancy, Mrs Sullivan thought it was unkind not to take a little present for Bend'Or, which she gave to him just before lunch. He was so obviously touched by the thought as he very seldom received presents. During lunch he put his hand on Mrs Sullivan's arm and said, 'Do you know – you are the nicest mother-in-law I have ever had.' This was a typical Bend'Or gesture – firstly of genuine gratitude and secondly an acknowledgement of the existence of other mothers-in-law.

Like that of Winston Churchill, Bend'Or's mind was at its most active late at night or in the early hours of the morning and it was customary after guests had retired to bed for him to open his letters and go through papers with me. At Fortwilliam, after midnight one night he opened his roll-top desk and, going through his letters, found one from George McVeagh, saying that George was captaining the Irish Davis Cup team against Sweden in Stockholm and as he did not know anyone in Sweden he would be grateful if the Duke could give him an introduction to anyone he knew. Bend'Or said to me, 'The only person I know in Sweden is the King. Do you think McVeagh would mind if I gave him an introduction to him?' I said I felt sure George would be delighted and it was decided to write an appropriate letter. Bend'Or then looked at McVeagh's letter again and said, 'Good heavens this was written a fortnight ago – the Irish team arrives in Stockholm today – we had better send a cable.' He than wrote a cable to the King of Sweden as follows:

> George McVeagh, Captain Irish Davis Cup team, personal friend. Would be grateful for any kindnesses you may wish to extend to him. Warmest regards and good wishes. Westminster.

Having despatched the cable Bend'Or then said, 'I suppose we had better let McVeagh know', and he promptly wrote another cable to McVeagh at his hotel in Stockholm – 'Have wired the King – Westminster.' George McVeagh was astonished to get the cable and delighted subsequently to get an invitation from the King to take his team to the palace as the King enjoyed tennis very much and was keen to have a game with them.

The story was picked up by Patrick Campbell (later of BBC fame), who was the *Irish Times* correspondent with the Davis Cup team and reported in the London papers. At dinner one night at Bourdon House a guest mentioned the fact that she had read the report and was fascinated by the fact that Bend'Or had wired the King. 'Tell me,' she said, 'how do you send a wire to a king?' Bend'Or said, 'It is quite easy, you just send a cable – The King of Sweden, Copenhagen.' 'But Benny,' she said, 'Copenhagen is the capital of Denmark.' 'Oh! that's all right,' he answered, 'those chaps all know one another!'

Another amusing episode occurred when an enquiry was received from a book dealer in New York to say that he had heard that Bend'Or possessed a copy of Audubon's *Birds of America* which he was anxious to buy, suggesting a price of £6,000. We looked up the record and found that Bend'Or had sold this book to his trustees in 1930 for £250. I suggested that he should buy the book back from them so we could then do a deal with the gentleman from New York. We found that pages from the book had been cut out – some were at Bruree, some at Lochmore and others generally scattered in houses around the country. These were rescued and I think Bend'Or himself stuck the pages back in the book. We were advised that the New York buyer was in London and was very anxious to conclude a deal. Since it was thought that the price of £6,000 was a very good one, I was asked to get in touch with him, invite him up to Eaton for lunch and endeavour to make a sale. As his wife was with him they were both asked. On arrival at Eaton the book dealer appeared a very quiet, sombre man, obviously a person of considerable intelligence, whereas his wife was a very lively person, good-looking with altogether a different outlook from her husband. A couple of dry martinis before lunch really warmed up the personality of the American lady, who was sitting on Bend'Or's right. She constantly put her hand on his arm and remarked, 'Duke I think you are wonderful. Duke, I think you are great.' Bend'Or took this in charming fashion and was not the least bit disturbed, but I could see that Nancy, at the other end of the table, was not at all pleased. This was the sort of situation in which Bend'Or quietly revelled.

After lunch I arranged for Bill Bryan to take the dealer and his wife into the part of the house where the books were stored and where the Audubon *Birds of America* had been laid out for him to see. This seemed to get rid of the lady for a while, but as Bend'Or and I were sitting in his sitting room, the lady, having escaped, burst into the room, flung her arms round Bend'Or's neck and once again said 'Duke I think you're wonderful' and, of course, it was just at this moment that Nancy entered the room. Bend'Or took it all with great aplomb and was perfectly charming to the lady. After the deal was done and the Americans were on their way back to London, Nancy said, 'I think that is the most ghastly woman I have ever seen.' Bend'Or's remark was, I thought, absolutely typical. He said 'Do you, darling? I think she showed great taste!'

Bend'Or lived through times of rapid social change: he was in charge of the greatest landed fortune in the country for fifty-four years, from the reign of Queen Victoria to that of Queen Elizabeth II, from an aristocratic to an egalitarian, if not socialist, society. Whatever his services to his country in war, his personal qualities and defects, he should be judged by his success or failure in discharging the responsibilities brought by his wealth.

On this test he comes out well. The Grosvenor estate in London, handed down from Mary Davies, has stayed intact with the exception of the Southern portion through nearly a century of death duties. It is an agreeable, well administered, well mixed area. The Cheshire estates, the Grosvenor heartland, continue to prosper. Grosvenor House has gone, but so has every other great private house in London; Eaton Hall has gone, but after Bend'Or's day.

Much more has come: the Grosvenors remain the richest landed family and developments started by Bend'Or are to be found in Canada and South Africa; a whole region of Scotland has been transformed; and all has been done to the highest standards of design and service.

Bend'Or succeeded in changing with the times, and even generally in being ahead of them. In London he had, to begin with, a 'hard act to follow'. The first Duke left his mark on the London estate for all to see. Under his leadership new workers' blocks had been built, whole new areas redeveloped, the best architects employed and his own ideals stamped on everything. Red-brick houses must have white railings and frames; plate glass must be used in windows; chocolate was a favourite colour for rendering. When Bend'Or succeeded the properties had taken up much of their present aspect and the need for large-scale redevelopment much restricted.

The day-to-day running was in the hands of the board of trustees: who were anxious to ensure that the Young Duke behaved prudently, and particularly sought to warn him against continuing the munificence of his grandfather in alienating large portions of the London estate for working-class housing. Twenty-three blocks had already been erected and this was quite enough. For the immediate future there could be little question of this but, in the long run, both instinct and his respect for the work of his grandfather always made Bend'Or a champion of the under-privileged. He also fought long and hard, often against the advice of the board of trustees, to secure the retention of some important buildings. Camelford House, on the corner of Oxford Street and Park Lane, could be preserved only by the sacrifice of £6,000 of annual income; this the Duke was willing to accept since 'something had to be sacrificed for sentiment and association'. It was not only an attractive house, but had played an important part in the history of London. A bench erected on its roof had served to view the executions at Tyburn. When the house eventually had to be demolished the Duke insisted that a man be employed to watch for any Roman remains that might be uncovered and to ensure their preservation – a precaution that might often with advantage have been taken by others.

According to the *Survey of London*, vol. XXXIX, the Duke was 'personally responsible for the preservation of several of the finest houses on his estate, despite the loss of income which sometimes resulted'. Among those saved were the remarkable pair of houses now 11–12 North Audley Street which have probably the finest Georgian interiors in London, 9–16 South Audley Street and 44 Grosvenor Square. This last one, most unfortunately, was demolished in 1966, after Bend'Or's death.

It was also no propitious time for new developments. Death duties, first levied by Sir William Harcourt in 1894, claimed the large sum of £600,000 from the first Duke's estate, which could be met only by the sale of properties. It was a bad time for property: until 1901 values had risen at about ten per cent per decade, but from that year they began to fall. In 1909 it was estimated that values had dropped by fifty per cent since the beginning of the decade. For six years, until 1906, assets had to be realized to meet these demands, at a time when this was by no means easy.

A new policy was adopted of selling longer – sixty-three-year – leases and insisting on substantial improvements being made to the properties. Unlike his grandfather Bend'Or was unsure of his own taste in architecture, and was therefore reluctant to impose it upon others. He relied much upon the advice of the state surveyor, Edward Wimperis, who nominated architects as one method of ensuring high standards of work.

One of these favoured architects was Detmar Blow, who became in 1916 Bend'Or's private secretary. Blow had benefited by an unusual training. He met Ruskin, who took him on a tour of France and Italy, which must have been an extraordinarily rewarding experience for a young man. After that he apprenticed himself to a working stone mason in order to gain an intimate knowledge of the fundamentals of his profession. He certainly developed a fine sense of detail, but, although he was a close friend of Lutyens, was always most successful on a small scale. His comparatively few large buildings cannot begin to compare with those of Lutyens; a good example is the elegant but unadventurous Queen Anne style house at 28 South Street. Blow's greatest contribution was probably to arrange the employment of Lutyens on estate work, of which the most striking examples are his design of the Grosvenor House Hotel and the Millbank flats that Bend'Or funded in Page Street and Victoria Street. One of Blow's best works outside London was the charming little Château Woolsack at Mimizan.

After becoming Bend'Or's secretary he seems to have dropped most of his architectural work: this was to prove remunerative. Bend'Or reposed near-absolute confidence in his agents and secretaries, a confidence that was entirely justified except in this single instance. The story has been told by Loelia, Duchess of Westminster, in her book, how 'Mr Waterloo' was caught out in what had been a systematic campaign of defalcation. 'Mr Waterloo' was Blow, who had over the years defrauded the Duke of a great sum. Bend'Or refused to take legal action to recover the money. Blow had been treated as a friend, and he would not pursue a friend. He wrote a dignified letter to Blow, telling him this and adding that of all the ways to make a living, stealing from a friend is not one he would have chosen. (Typically, when Bend'Or's confidence was betrayed he blamed himself for not paying enough attention to his affairs.) Blow should be given credit, however, for seconding Bend'Or's efforts in preserving the best of the estate against the depredations of others, of which the most vandalistic was the proposal to demolish St George's Hanover Square. This concern to protect the past led to Bend'Or buying back parts of the Mayfair estate that had previously been alienated, including the Connaught Hotel.

Certainly it cannot be truly said that Bend'Or, even although he never applied himself consistently to business and relied too much on Blow, neglected his London estates. Bend'Or was never inclined to let the board have things too much their own way; on 9 January 1902 they recorded, 'The Duke has heard that no systematic inspection of houses on the estate is carried out and asks if this is so. The board discussed the matter and think that a regular inspection should be made.' Not, one might think, before time.

In spite of the trustees, Bend'Or did what he could for deserving causes. One of the more interesting of these was advanced in July 1910 when Lord Lyttelton requested that he might find a site for the projected National Theatre. Bend'Or examined the maps and suggested that a suitable site could perhaps be found on the Horseferry Road estate, in which case he could make the terms easy. For some reason this was not pursued and the National Theatre took another sixty-five years to come about.

Both before and after the First World War the burden of taxation increased so much that some sales were inevitable: the most dramatic of these was that of Grosvenor House and its eventual replacement as an hotel. It is somewhat remarkable that at the same time Bend'Or was able to make, as had his grandfather, substantial contributions to the development of working-class housing on a charitable basis. There is a distinction to be made between the support given to good causes by self-made men and that of families with inherited wealth. Such men as Carnegie, Nuffield or Wolfson, who have by their own efforts and good fortune become extremely rich, are often most generous in disposing of money which is incontrovertibly their own and for which they owe little to their forbears.

A great landowner has a much more circumscribed freedom of movement. In the first place his wealth is for the most part usually in property which may produce a handsome income but which can be sold only with difficulty or even, if entailed, not at all. His command of spending money is often limited. Bend'Or was once told by his accountant that he had not enough cash to pay a rail fare to Inverness. But apart from this practical limitation there are even more powerful restraints. Inherited wealth places great obligations on its possessors, if they are willing to accept them. They are rich not by any merits of their own, but thanks to successive generations. The land they own has been created and transformed by their forbears, and they assume a duty to hand it down to their successors. They recognize themselves not as absolute owners but as trustees for the future generations.

There are other obligations – to the land and buildings themselves and above all to the people who work on them, and their own traditions. No landowner was more conscious than Bend'Or of these obligations. He took at all times the most active interest in the estate and insisted on the highest standards of management, design and building. In the same way the problems of his staff and tenants were his own; their rights and dignity were for him to protect.

For these reasons there are no Bedford, Devonshire or Westminster Foundations comparable to Ford or Nuffield. The only notable charitable bequest associated with one of the great landowning families is the Smithsonian Institute in Washington, founded by an illegitimate scion of the Percys, and therefore hardly typical.

In spite of the inhibitions he felt about alienating any of his forbears' estate there is one notable exception to this, which in its originality is very much a Bend'Or gesture. Severe flooding in January 1928 had destroyed many homes on Millbank and elsewhere, causing great distress among the many working-class occupiers. Acting together with the Mayor of Westminster, the Duke gave to the City five acres of land, which was then estimated to be worth £200,000 and today would be of enormous value. He also gave over £130,000 towards the cost of building and an annual grant to enable the rents of protected tenants to be maintained at the current level.

This was by no means the only example of Bend'Or's readiness to respond to appeals. He had already, in 1924, made over land in Pimlico sufficient to construct homes for 300 people for ninety-nine years at one pound per annum. This was done at a time when pictures were being sold, and this fact was noticed in the *Observer* of 31 May: 'His Grace (I use the title of courtesy because in this case, it really means something) has specified that preference must be given to tenants with families . . . It is a fine thing to preach social service: but the Duke's way of doing it is ever so much more useful.' In 1927 he gave a long lease of 128 Ebury Street to the National Playing Fields Association and, in 1929, in memory of his mother, a lease of two houses in St George's Street for a Toc H centre.

It was in the early 1930s that Bend'Or was confronted with a family problem which was extremely unpleasant and called for swift and positive action in order to save his sister, Lettice, and her family from what would have been disastrous consequences. Perhaps the most highly coloured and most serious charge advanced against Bend'Or was his 'persecution' of his brother-in-law, Earl Beauchamp. We must try to see things through the eyes of the time; it is arrogant to assume that the views of our own age, simply by virtue of being modern, are therefore necessarily right. Homosexuality was, until very recently, generally regarded as unmentionable, horrible, the greatest vice and quite unforgiveable. After his gaol sentence Oscar Wilde had to live abroad in order to avoid opprobrium. As late as 1958 people were still sent to prison for what would now be no offence. High rank – Lord Montagu of Beaulieu served six months in prison – was no protection. That things have changed so much should not obscure the detestation in which homosexuality was most generally held and the serious consequences that could attend exposure.

Earl Beauchamp was married to Bend'Or's sister, Lettice. The marriage seemed successful: they produced a number of attractive children and Beauchamp held many public offices. Bend'Or had maintained amicable, but not close, relations with his brother-in-law. They had few tastes in common, Beauchamp being no sportsman or warrior, but family relationships were maintained, especially since

Bend'Or had always been very fond of his sister. As he grew older Beauchamp's behaviour seems to have become more lurid, and became impossible to ignore in one who was to other appearances a pillar of the Church of England and the House of Lords. When the scandal threatened to break Bend'Or was furious at the thought of what it might do to his sister. Beauchamp would certainly have gone to prison and the thought of the Grosvenors being subjected, even by marriage, to such disgrace, was intolerable. Bend'Or had a strong sense of personal honour, which was exemplified in his letter to the old Duke from South Africa, and regarded homosexuality with abhorrence. He certainly used his influence to ensure that Beauchamp went abroad and stayed there, in order that Lettice might be spared the consequences of a public exposure.

This unhappy affair split the Lygon family: Lettice came to live at Saighton, bringing her younger son Richard with her. 'Cuckoo', Lady Shaftesbury, Lettice's sister, was every bit as insistent that scandal could be avoided only by her leaving Beauchamp. The girls sided with their father, and went so far as to attempt, in the *Oxford and Cambridge Magazine*, to blacken Bend'Or's name. This was unsuccessful and, faced with a libel suit, they were forced to apologize. Beauchamp's other children and friends did not see things in quite the same light either, but to Bend'Or his behaviour was a betrayal, and treachery was an unforgiveable crime.

Poor Lettice was somewhat baffled by the whole thing, having no idea of what exactly homosexuals did, but had little hesitation in accepting that her brother was anxious to protect her, and gratefully took up residence at the old house at Saighton, where they had both spent a happy childhood.

The most striking characteristic of Bend'Or was always his generosity. It may hardly be much accounted for virtue in so rich a man as he that this should be so, but it must be recognized that there is much more to generosity than the readiness of a rich man to disburse money. He did much of this, making gifts of land and money for good causes, and establishing the Duke of Westminster Studentships at Christ Church, Oxford. But to me, it was the quite unknown kindnesses to those whom he learnt were in distress which most marked the character of the man.

The Duke was now sending for me to Eaton, London, Lochmore or Fortwilliam regularly and although I was aware that he was seeking my advice on broader issues, it came as a great surprise to me when he sent for me to Eaton, with Basil Kerr present, and told me that he intended to write to his lawyers in London that he wished me to be appointed as trustee of his estates, chief agent of all his properties – including London and executor of his will. He told me that he felt that it was not appreciated that he had put the estates in trust as a young man of twenty-two in 1901, and there was an 'iron curtain' between him and his advisers and he intended to put me behind the 'iron curtain' in the expectation of obtaining more favourable results. He asked that his instructions be implemented forthwith and, on 2 May 1947, the documentation was completed.

When I first went up to London to take charge I was most embarrassed and occupied a very small room in the Grosvenor Office at 53 Davies Street as I did not wish to appear 'grand'. Eventually as I had to receive more and more staff and visitors I took over a nice panelled room off the reception hall – a room formerly occupied by Arthur Borrer, the senior partner of Boodle, Hatfield and Co. This I retained until my retirement twenty-five years later.

After my appointment I had discussions with the Duke's accountants and lawyers regarding the pattern of his investments and we agreed that there was too much emphasis on the London estate and that it would be wise to diversify. The Duke's love of the Eaton estate encouraged us to believe that an expansion of his agricultural interests would prove to be most acceptable to him and would meet with an enthusiastic response.

Spencer Beesly, the second senior partner in the Duke's firm of accountants – Champness, Corderoy and Company – became my principal adviser on this agricultural policy. Beesly was a quiet, diffident – but most able – man whom I shortly brought into the inner sanctum of Grosvenor estate advisers and who gave me loyal support as well as excellent advice over the years. I put the proposals to the Duke and, as I had hoped, received his enthusiastic blessing to proceed, not only with an agricultural policy but forestry as well. He thereupon gave me instructions to go out and buy agricultural estates.

I turned to John D. Woods and had meetings with their senior partners – Gordon Saunders and Algy Farrer – who from then on for the next twenty years gave invaluable advice: firstly over the purchase of properties, secondly on the Duke's death in 1953 on the agreement of valuations, not only on the agricultural estate but the urban properties including London, and lastly in the estate duty negotiations which followed. It was a happy association, involving other firms of agents as the need arose, but with Saunders and Farrer playing the leading role.

The first estate purchased was Whinfell, near Penrith, which was acquired from the Hothfield family. This was completed in 1947. In 1948 the Brancepeth estate was bought from the Boyne family and the Ketteringham estate from the Boileaus. In 1949 part of the Melton Constable estate, Norfolk, was purchased from Lord Hastings and the Manby portion of the Brocklesby estate from the Earl of Yarborough; also the Coddington estate in Cheshire from the Masseys. In 1950 we acquired the Bridgewater estate in Shropshire from Lord Brownlow, Gobernuisgach in Sutherland from the Gilmours and Pale from the Robertson family. In 1951 the Park Hatch estate in Surrey was bought from the Godmans. Upwards of 100,000 acres was bought at a cost of approximately £2½ million.

Having regard to the Duke's age it was essential that no time should be lost in carrying out repairs and improvements to the agricultural properties and the establishment of a forestry programme. I was at a loss to find a young man of energy to control the agents taken over with the agricultural estates and direct the improvement programme, but eventually appointed John Saunders – Gordon Saunders's son.

In regard to the woodlands, I had had a lot of dealings during the war with Langshaw Rowland of Hoseley, near Wrexham, who – although chairman of a family company owning a chain of chemist shops – had his first love for forestry and timber and had established a business in the Chester/Wrexham locality and had taken a lease of the estate sawmill at Belgrave. I felt it was imperative that, if we were to get the best out of the forestry and timber operations, we should own the company carrying out the work. So – on behalf of the Duke – I made Langshaw Rowland an offer to buy his business, to appoint him as director of woodlands to the Duke and managing director of the sawmilling and forestry company. We came to terms and from then on Langshaw directed the operations which involved the planting of 16,000 acres of woodlands on the various estates, coupled with a timber business controlling the sale of timber in the round and sawn. It was a signal honour to Langshaw, and indirectly to the Grosvenor estate, when Langshaw was later elected president of the Royal Forestry Society.

The London estate was a very different problem. Whereas with the agricultural properties one was starting with new acquisitions and creating new management, the Grosvenor estate in London had been in the hands of the family for nearly three hundred years and a pattern of management had grown up which had hardly been altered in that time. Much of the management was done by the lawyers – Boodle, Hatfield and Co. – whose senior partners over the years had virtually acted as agents. What account books were not kept by them were kept by the accountants and the estate office staff mainly comprised a rental department, one surveyor and one architect. Most of the lease negotiations were carried out by outside agents and there was no professional management team as such.

The estate surveyor – Geoffrey Singer – was first-class but his role was extremely limited. With his co-operation we set to work to establish a true estate office. The surveyors' department was expanded so that all lease negotiations could be conducted by the surveyors' staff. The architectural department was developed and an accounts department created by the engagement of a chartered accountant, with other accountants and appropriate staff working under him. We thus had a completely comprehensive estate management organization.

Boodle, Hatfield and Co. had enjoyed a monopoly of Grosvenor legal business from time immemorial and, while they had done some excellent work, the Duke felt the time had come for some competition. While leaving the work on the London estate in the hands of Boodles, the Duke decided to introduce William Charles Crocker as an additional legal adviser and to give work on the agricultural estates to Henry Potts, whose family – like Boodles – had done legal work on the Eaton and Chester estates, but only to a limited degree, for generations.

Crocker had made his reputation through his work in the insurance world, particularly when he was primarily responsible for breaking the fire-raising gang led by Leopold Harris. Crocker brought a clear and incisive mind to the problems of reorganization for the future. A most powerful figure – physically and mentally – later to become president of the Law Society, Crocker always claimed he did not know anything about the law, but he was a most able administrator and ran his office to a degree of efficiency which was unique in the legal world.

He delegated the Grosvenor work to Gerard Reyburn, who as a boy had escaped with his mother to England from Berlin, where his family had been hounded by the Nazis. Gerard Reyburn had a brilliant brain, one of the finest I have ever met in the legal profession. He took his degree in law at London University and ultimately became an examiner for the Law Society, in addition to his work at Crockers. He joined with Crocker in our inner sanctum of advisers. He later played a leading role in the rewriting of the Duke's will, a lengthy and intricate document, which succeeded in taking care of the needs of the family, employees and pensioners and has been regarded as a model document in the eyes of the legal world.

It is sometimes thought that the Grosvenor estates were entailed by the first Duke and the properties would pass automatically to the holder of the dukedom; this was not so and Bend'Or's will was unique in so far as he bequeathed the bulk of the estate ultimately to a year-old child – Gerald Cavendish Grosvenor – son of the then Lieutenant-Colonel Robert George Grosvenor (who became the fifth Duke); the principal heir to Bend'Or's fortune is now the sixth Duke.

Bend'Or's desire to protect the estates for the future was a wise and generous thought which saved in due course a treble penalty of death duties and provided his executors and advisers with the opportunity to rebuild the Grosvenor fortunes, the bulk of which the present Duke inherited on his eighteenth birthday.

I have vivid recollections of translating the Duke's wishes to paper when Reyburn, William Charles Crocker's brother, Walter, and I spent the whole of one Saturday in my office preparing the details in the course of which a 1/20th formula was prepared. This was a small table of fractions with alternative formulas related to the possibility of one or more sons being born to Colonel Gerald Grosvenor or his brother, Colonel Robert. The implementation of this formula took a step nearer to fulfilment when Bend'Or rang me on the night of 22 December 1951 and asked me if I had heard the news about Viola (wife of Robert Grosvenor). I said 'no' and he said 'she has had a son'. I answered 'that is splendid because that carries on the line' and he said 'come up tomorrow morning and we will check what we have put on the line'! The birth was of Gerald Cavendish, the present Duke.

At the same time as Henry Potts was given the whole of the legal work in the North, Warmsley, Henshall and Co., chartered accountants at Chester, were given the accountancy work for all the Northern agricultural estates. The division of legal and accountancy work created a delicate situation, when dealing with firms who had had a monopoly over such a long period of time, but it proved to be extremely beneficial as it provided not only 'on the spot' service, but also competition which sharpened the minds of those concerned.

Having established a new organization for the management of the Grosvenor estates, the next problem was to deal with the possible effects of estate duty in the event of the death of the Duke. With Crocker having been appointed trustee and an executor of the will, we agreed to set up a Death Duty Committee which would do nothing else but devise plans for valuation of the estate and assessment of estate duty liability and the payment thereof. As I was so heavily involved in property investment, in the Duke's personal affairs and in the management of properties, it was agreed between us that Crocker should be the chairman of this committee; Geoffrey Singer was, of course, one of the foremost members with Terence Coffey as the estate's accountant; Tom Barty-King was a member, Reyburn, as Crocker's working partner, Sir Bernard Blatch, having just retired as solicitor to the Inland Revenue, was invited on to the panel and we brought in from time to time on a consultancy basis Gordon Saunders and Algy Farrer, Spencer Beesly and Bill Champness, representing Champness, Corderoy and Co., Wilfred de Knoop of Rowe and Pitman, the stockbrokers, and Peter Wilson, chairman of Sothebys. This latter was a most valuable appointment because the Grosvenor chattels formed a very substantial part of the family's assets and Peter Wilson was ultimately to play an important part in the agreement of valuations with the Inland Revenue.

The first step to be taken was an up-to-date schedule of all properties wherever they might be situated with professional valuations; similarly valuations of Stock Exchange investments and lastly the chattels. This meant that when the time came that Bend'Or died we were able in a matter of weeks to present the Inland Revenue with completed schedules and valuations. This was particularly important because the Inland Revenue were not prepared for a sudden receipt of schedules and valuations of thousands of properties and it took them several years before they were able to prepare and finalize their own valuations, particularly of the London estate. The benefit accruing as a result of the formation of this committee will be shown later when I come to the protracted discussions with the Inland Revenue over valuations, negotiations which went on for sixteen-and-a-half years.

In the course of investigations I learnt from Boodles in 1949 that the Duke had in 1933 obtained an act through Parliament which enabled him to use trust money to provide £350,000 each to his two daughters by his first wife – Lady Ursula and Lady Mary Grosvenor. Unfortunately the approval of the scheme obtained from Parliament was never implemented. Crocker drew up the appropriate deeds for the Duke's signature and we flew to Bossekop in Norway, where the Duke was fishing the Alta River, to obtain this. Alas, as events turned out, the Duke did not live the necessary five years to avoid estate duty liability.

After I had become responsible for so much of the Duke's affairs I had to refer to him from time to time to obtain written authority to conclude contracts I was conducting. He soon became irritated by such requests and said he wished to sign a single authority which would give me power to carry out transactions on his behalf without reference back. The document which he signed was drawn up by the lawyers as follows:

> I, The Most Noble Hugh Richard Arthur Duke of Westminster, DSO hereby state that Mr George Kershaw Ridley of Eaton, Chester, is my duly appointed Agent in respect of my estates in England, Wales, Scotland and Ireland and France with authority from time to time to enter into agreements as he may in his absolute discretion deem proper and to perform and do all other acts whatsoever proper to be performed in connection with my estates and affairs generally.
>
> Westminster
> 14 December 1947

I was flattered that such an authority showed confidence in my ability to produce results and it proved invaluable in speeding up negotiations which were the essence of successful deals.

One of the problems on the Eaton estate in Cheshire which had prevailed for some years was that of housing the families occupying agricultural cottages in one or other of the estate villages when the cottages were required for agricultural or estate workers. It was resolved by building twenty-four houses and sixteen flats in Handbridge, which were named Westminster Green and Westminster Terrace, in 1947. This was the first private housing undertaken in Chester after the war and it created a controversy since at the time the supply of timber was under licence. Since we were unable to obtain licences, oak trees were felled on the Eaton estate and following kiln drying in the timber yard were used to enable us to complete the scheme on time. It was felt that this was somehow stealing a march, but the rehoused families were very grateful.

Having acquired the agricultural estates and embarked upon a large improvement programme the Duke was very alive to the need for Britain to expand its agricultural production – primarily to save the cost of imports from abroad. Unwittingly, not being aware of the quarters in which the Duke would use the information I gave him, I was very critical of the Socialist government's policy and the Tories' lack of appreciation of the part agriculture could play in the national economy. I was continually saying what the Tories should do about their propaganda for the next election. It was a great surprise to me one day when Bend'Or told me that he was arranging for me to see Mr Churchill so that I could explain my policies on agriculture to him.

Mr Churchill, being out of office and thus leader of the Opposition, granted me an interview at his home at Hyde Park Gate. Prior to my going to see him Bend'Or gave me some very firm advice. He told me, 'No matter what you say and how right you might be he will knock you down and it is what you say when you get up from the floor that will count. For goodness sake be firm without being rude, otherwise your visit will be completely wasted.' He emphasized that it was the Great Man's method of testing your knowledge to go on the completely reverse tack in his arguments. This proved to be very true. Mr Churchill greeted me very warmly, no doubt because of his very long friendship with Bend'Or, asked me if I would have a cigar and when I said, 'No thank you, sir, I don't smoke,' promptly said, 'You would be a better man if you did.' He then asked me if I would like a whisky and soda and when I said 'yes', he said, 'That's better.'

I outlined my views on what should be the agricultural policy of the party with the main plank being a system of quotas for all produce, emphasizing the success of the Milk Marketing Board and what it had achieved for the dairy farmer, the milk industry as a whole and the housewife in particular, stressing that the collection of milk from the farms, supervision of quality and distribution from central points, thus providing excellent service to the housewife, was the pattern which should be followed with other agricultural products. Mr Churchill looked very forbidding when he growled, 'So you believe in controls,' as though I believed in the Devil and all his works! He encouraged me to expand my theories, arguing all along the line, until his final shaft brought home to me the manner in which politics controlled governmental decisions. He asked me how many voters I represented and followed it up with 'and how many voters are there in Sheffield?' After further very strong discussion I did not think I had made any impact and moved to take my leave. I was, therefore, all the more surprised when, as he very kindly accompanied me to the door, he quietly said, 'And when can you come and see me again?'

This was the first of three visits when discussion widened from agricultural policy to the finances and management of the Tory Party. The last time I saw him I regarded it as a great compliment when he invited me to see him at ten o'clock in the morning; I was ushered up to his bedroom to find him in bed wearing his famous Chinese silk dressing gown and smoking the inevitable cigar. After our discussion he asked whether I was married and had any family. When I gave him the answer that we had two sons, and that the older was eleven, I was somewhat surprised when asked if he could read. On being assured that he could, the old statesman said, 'I will send him a book.' My son's proudest possession today is a copy of *My Early Life* inscribed on the fly-leaf, 'To Michael K. Ridley with all good wishes from Winston S. Churchill'.

Bend'Or by this time had become so interested in agricultural problems that I suggested he should meet the president of the National Farmers Union, Sir James Turner, later Lord Netherthorpe, and his deputy – Mr Harold Woolley, now Lord Woolley – who farmed as a neighbour of the Duke's at Hatton Heath near Chester. I knew them both and, having a high opinion of them felt confident they would make a very good impression on Bend'Or. He invited them to lunch at Bourdon House and I was delighted at the success of the luncheon, the Duke and Duchess creating the right atmosphere in which their guests could expound their views and forge an immediate understanding.

The sequel to this was that Bend'Or told Jim Turner he would arrange for him to meet Mr Churchill. I learned shortly afterwards that the president of the NFU was invited to lunch one Sunday at

Chartwell. I arranged a quick meeting with Jim Turner to give him the same warnings that Bend'Or had given me as to the treatment he might expect from Mr Churchill, and to advise that this should be accepted as something of a test. On the day after the lunch we met again and Jim Turner told me that during the meal Churchill had been so rude to him that immediately it was over he felt he should take his leave. To his surprise Winston linked his arm in his and took him into the garden. They sat down facing the goldfish pond without a word being uttered. Winston thereupon extracted a tin of maggots from under the seat and proceeded, in continued silence, to throw maggots into the pond. After what had seemed an age he said, 'Maggots to goldfish, subsidies to farmers!' This broke the ice and from then on they had a most useful talk.

Jim Turner proved not only to be one of the best presidents to serve the NFU but also one of the strongest characters in the higher echelons of the country's economy. He made a point in his discussions with the government of never asking for more than could be justified, thereby gaining the confidence of the Minister of Agriculture and the cabinet.

Under the existing legislation expenditure on agricultural and forestry estates was given favourable treatment in death duties, and since Bend'Or was then sixty-eight it was clear that no time should be lost in carrying out a programme of improvements. This was energetically done.

The Pale estate of 20,000 acres in the Vale of Edeyrnion was described in the *Liverpool Daily Post* of 28 July 1952:

> The crumbling roofs, rutted yards and stark poverty of its 100-odd farms were mute witnesses . . . the Duke, who is deliberately trying to show what class and political prejudice could never belittle – how the enlightened application of money, energy and initiative can be directed to the reconstruction of a big stretch of countryside . . . Perhaps no other agency short of another Tennessee Valley Authority could bring to bear such huge resources of money, materials, expert professional supervision and advice.

This scale of reconstruction was applied to all the other estates. The sum of £1,000 a week was spent in Reay Forest, which offered employment to all able-bodied men in the region. Using the same analogy this was described as 'a New Deal for Sutherland'.

Bend'Or had always been keenly interested in farming, and the home farm at Eaton was a show place, with everything spotless. The Eaton Dairy Shorthorns won prizes at many shows, including the Royal, and there were also Kerry Hill sheep, a poultry unit specializing in turkeys and geese, scores of which were given away each Christmas, and pigs. The policy of the home farm was that it should act as a model for tenant farmers and make first-class stock available to them at reasonable prices.

The Duke followed progress with real interest, and was a great believer in traditional methods, distrusting new ideas, especially when they involved a heavy dependence upon chemicals. In this, as in so many other ways, he was ahead of his times, quick to spot the dangers in fashionable ideas. It was therefore only to be expected that Bend'Or would be in the forefront of tuberculin-tested milk, and indeed he threw his weight into the campaign, writing to *The Times* to encourage others. Eaton was the first estate to be TT attested, largely because the terms made available to the farmers to enable the work to be carried out – £150,000 loaned at 2½% gross – were too attractive to be refused. The other estates rapidly followed and since time was of the essence contractors were put to work under the supervision of architects and quantity surveyors without preliminary tender. One of the contractors was John Laing & Son, who have been working for the estate ever since. In all 20,000 acres were eventually TT attested.

A very different problem existed on the Reay Forest estate. In an area of gross underemployment – although on the estate itself there was one hundred per cent employment – imaginative schemes were needed. The first of these was the afforestation of Reay Forest; it should be explained that the most noticeable aspect of a deer forest, such as Reay, is the complete absence of trees. No planting had been carried out there in historic times although roots of trees have been found in peat bogs. A total of 3,500 acres were laid down, and on the first day 106 men signed on, coming from many miles around.

At the same time the little haven of Kinlochberrie was developed to provide the facilities for a fishing port ice plant, auction room, offices, etc. A wholesale company in Aberdeen was bought in order to act as a depot. If the fishermen were not satisfied with the price available in Kinlochberrie market the fish were taken to Aberdeen and sold on their behalf. The Sutherland County Council, who were much impressed with what was being done, helped greatly by deepening the channel at Loch Bervie to allow access by larger vessels and providing housing for the fishermen who came from Banff, Buckie and Lossiemouth to settle on the west coast. As the county was so dependent upon road transport, the Sutherland Transport and Trading Company at Lairg was bought giving the Duke responsibility for running practically all the bus services in the county and the major lorry transport, as well as mail deliveries and ambulance services. This involved the construction of new garage and showrooms at Lairg, Kinlochberrie and Bonar Bridge.

Although realizing that most of the newly engaged men would wish to retain their croft houses because of the croft land and hill grazing which they enjoyed, the Duke offered to build houses on the Reay Forest estate which he made available, rent-free, to those wishing to move. Twelve houses were built and occupied by employees.

It was hoped that it would be possible to have the hill land carry cattle as well as sheep. For this purpose two large cattle shelters were built and potential grazing land fenced in; to support the scheme a farm was purchased at Morangie near Tain – sixty miles away – and some of the Duke's Welsh Blacks from the Pale estate in Wales and Dairy Shorthorns from Eaton were transported there. At Morangie a herd of pedigree Galloways was also established.

However, after a few years it was found that the extreme weather in the winter was too much for the cattle on the hill. Calves produced were small and eventually a compromise was made to retain a smaller number of cattle throughout the year on the Reay Forest supplemented by cattle for the hill from Morangie in summer. Hard frost and snow was no handicap to the cattle, but what did sap their physical resources was the almost constant rain throughout the winter months. The latest figures show only thirty-seven days in the year without rain, and an annual precipitation of 120″. In later years it was felt that even sheep were not suited to these conditions, and that it would be better to ranch deer as the indigenous stock.

Development on this scale – over 400 square miles of the Highlands, is normally the prerogative of government agencies. It gave Bend'Or especial pleasure to be able to marshal his own resources to such obviously socially valuable purpose.

As soon as possible after the end of the war work was started on restoring the London estates. The first private housing to be carried out in London after the war was started on a two-acre site at the junction of Ebury Street and Cundy Street. The area had been badly blitzed and plans to redevelop it with small terraced houses were abandoned so as to provide more accommodation on the site. Four seven-storey blocks of flats were designed by Sir Thomas Bennett, the intention being that they would be occupied by white-collar workers, a section of the community for whom such provision is not normally made. These blocks were named after features on the Reay Forest estate, i.e. Lochmore House, Laxford House, Stack House and Kylestrome House. They remain among the most practical and elegant post-war blocks in the capital and the 109 flats completed in 1952 represented a source of great personal satisfaction to Bend'Or who by then had made the same personal mark on the London estate as his great predecessor.

At the same time, two important decisions were taken regarding the London estate. First of all, a most unsatisfactory position existed over what was called the Southern portion, from Buckingham Palace Road to the Embankment, as many of the properties, all of which were on ninety-nine-year leases, had become dilapidated, after their occupation as billets in the 1914–18 war, which later led to many of them becoming brothels with constant prosecutions ensuing. Needless to say the press reports always announced that the landowner was the Duke of Westminster but although the 1939–45 war led to a further deterioration, both as regards structural conditions and use, the law protected the tenants and it was not possible to obtain possession. With such an unsatisfactory situation it was decided there should be a single sale to an institution and this was duly effected. Today, thirty years later, some of the properties have been restored, but all too many are in a dilapidated condition reflecting the unsatisfactory state of landlord and tenant legislation.

It was possible to be more constructive over the problems presented by Eaton Square, where 120 Regency terraced town houses had proved to be too large for single occupation. Leases were bought in and by amalgamating two or three adjoining properties, lateral conversion into flats was undertaken by a company which proved to be under-financed. After the estate had made substantial loans it was decided we should buy the company and carry out the balance of the conversions. All but a handful of the houses were included in the scheme which preserved the character of one of the most famous

London squares without outwardly showing the results of the conversion.

At about this time a major change took place in the heart of the London estate which attracted considerable comment. The American government had for some time occupied Grosvenor Square properties, the most considerable being the building on the east side now housing the Canadian High Commission, and wished to consolidate in a new embassy to occupy the whole of the west side of the square. In order to do this they asked the Grosvenor estate to acquire on their behalf the individual existing leases and then to grant the US government a long ground lease. This the estate was happy to do, and set about buying in the leases, somewhat hampered by the Americans' insistence that each purchase had to be approved by Washington, a practice that gave each owner the opportunity to extract the maximum price for the surrender of his lease and was as gall and wormwood to the hard-bitten negotiator, Geoffrey Singer.

It had been the estate's intention to rebuild the square entirely in the same style established by Fernand Billerey in the early years of the century, and reflected in the Canadian building, and the north and south sides of the square. The US government, however, commissioned Eero Saarinen to design the present building, and sent plans and elevations to the estate office for approval. This was not immediately forthcoming, and in spite of revisions the plans were rejected three times, causing some irritation in the White House and leading to pressure being put on the Foreign Secretary, then Anthony Eden, to persuade the estate to agree. A compromise was eventually arrived at whereby the estate accepted the design while insisting that harmony with the rest of the square should be to some extent maintained by having the sill lines continuous with those of the other three sides.

Following Anthony Eden's intervention I went to see the American Ambassador, Lewis Douglas, and in the course of conversation he asked why it was that the Grosvenor estate refused to sell the freehold to the American government. I think he said it was their only embassy in the world where the Americans did not own the freehold. I told him that it was not estate policy to sell freeholds as with a leasehold we retained control of the property for the period of the lease. Secondly, a condition in the lease was to the effect that if the American government became bankrupt the estate could take possession of the property! I added that the Duke, however, would be prepared to give the site to the American government if they in turn would return to the Duke the Grosvenor family property which was seized in the War of Independence. He asked me whereabouts and I told him it was now Miami! He was very amused and said, 'I do not think we will press this point any more.' Actually my statement that it was Miami was somewhat inaccurate as the Grosvenor property was, I believe, some 20,000 acres to the west of Miami on the St John's River, near Jacksonville. It appears too, from a document in the Grosvenor archives that it was agreed at the time that if General Grosvenor, who received the 20,000 acres in Florida, was not satisfied with it he could have an alternative choice at Cape Canaveral!

With the progress of the purchase of the agricultural estates, the commitment to a substantial forestry programme and the improvements on the London and Chester estates under way, Bend'Or decided that he now wished to fulfil a lifetime's ambition and expand his interests in the Commonwealth, which hitherto had been limited to the Westminster estate in the Orange Free State, South Africa. This decision was one of the most imaginative in a career marked by bold action.

Canada was to be the first objective in this new policy, but the situation *vis-à-vis* the acquisition of dollars made it virtually impossible to acquire what we needed from the Treasury. I was therefore sent, as a first step, in 1950, to America to see if I could persuade some of the major American companies like Gillette, who had substantial property holdings in the UK, to offer an arrangement for a switch of assets which was acceptable to the Treasury, but each of the companies I approached told me that they had substantial amounts of blocked sterling held in England since the war and they were not interested in acquiring any more.

In the following year my first visit to Montreal and Toronto proved abortive because, here again, the lack of Canadian dollars prevented any transactions being entered into. Later that year Bend'Or asked me to try again, when I was accompanied by Tom Barty-King and Langshaw Rowland, our director of woodlands, with the thought that we might make an investment in forestry and sawmilling if there was no opportunity of a property development. It was during this visit, which looked as if it was going to be abortive, that Harry Smith, who was trade commissioner in London for the Province of British

Columbia, and who had accompanied us to British Columbia, was standing at the window of the trade commissioner's office in New Westminster and pointed out Annacis Island lying in the Fraser River – just off New Westminster. It was a delta island of some 1,200 acres, half of which, we were told, could be acquired in England for sterling, following the death of Sir Edward Stracey whose family lived in Norfolk. If we could acquire half the island for sterling it was possible the Treasury might be persuaded to allow the acquisition of dollars to purchase the rest of the island and thus to create an industrial estate, as secondary industry was urgently required in the Province of British Columbia.

Back in England the 600 acres were successfully purchased for $200 an acre: at that time the equivalent of £70 an acre, which in due course proved to be an excellent purchase. We then approached the Treasury for permission to buy the necessary dollars to purchase the rest of the island, which was divided up into several ownerships, and we had a very sticky time. But eventually they agreed, I think under the misapprehension that as Annacis was close to New Westminster, New Westminster was Grosvenor property. There was a time when they thought I had misled them, but I can assure readers that this was not the case.

The British Columbian government was most enthusiastic at our proposals to create an industrial estate. The Duke would provide all the roads, sewerage and water systems, etc. and would build the factories from his own resources and lease them on the English leasehold system. The premier gave us every encouragement and so did the federal government at Ottawa. Between them they agreed to build a causeway and bridge to the island and to provide us with sandfill to raise the level of the island against the danger of floods. The island had never been flooded, even in the very worst floods just after the war, but with such a vast investment, risks of this sort should be obviated.

As Bend'Or's trust was subject to the laws of the Settled Land Act investment overseas required court approval. The trustees accordingly applied, on Bend'Or's behalf, to the courts for permission to invest in real estate abroad. Mr Justice Roxburgh heard the case and in giving his favourable judgement made the most complimentary remark about the Grosvenor estate. He said in effect that giving this favourable decision to the Grosvenor estate did not mean that the courts would readily accept applications from other landowners who were subject to the Settled Land Act. He said that he was giving the decision only because of the reputation of the Grosvenor estates of excellent management and he knew that wherever we intended to invest in the world we would first of all obtain the best professional advice before making a move. It was on this score that he gave Bend'Or the authority to invest £5 million.

The newspapers reported the decision prominently and a day or so later a guest sitting next to Bend'Or at dinner at Bourdon House said to him, 'Oh, Benny, I hear you are going to invest in property abroad.' On his agreeing she went on with some astonishment, 'They say you are going to invest £5 million!' With his charming ingenuousness he replied, 'Yes, my dear, it's that fool George Ridley – he never does think big enough!'

Approvals having been gained I went to British Columbia but when there I received a cable from England to say that the Treasury had reneged on their approval for us to acquire the necessary dollars. This was a terrible blow as we had received headline news in the Canadian papers of the scheme we were to carry out and the benefits which would accrue to British Columbia, and Canada as a whole, all stemming from a British investment.

I immediately saw Bryon Johnson, the premier of British Columbia, who proved a stalwart friend in drafting a telegram to Winston Churchill, telling him of the severe effects such a decision would have upon Anglo-Canadian relationships. After this was dispatched I hastened back to England for a meeting with the Treasury. Nigel Birch as financial secretary to the Treasury took the chair, and was supported by quite a number of Treasury officials, the senior of whom was Sir Leslie Rowan. I was accompanied by Tom Barty-King, Maurice Laing and Ernest Uren of Laings who prepared an excellent civil engineering report on Annacis. The meeting was rather terse and the Treasury stood firmly by their decision that they could not possibly help us, despite the fact that they were reneging on an earlier decision. However, when they were reminded of the favourable publicity which the Duke's proposals had received in the UK and that in Canada they had been welcomed throughout the Dominion, Bryon Johnson's warning of the harm which would be done by retraction influenced the Treasury who eventually agreed, while making a stringent proviso that nine Canadian or American dollars would have to be mounted for each dollar acquired in this country. In addition, the acquisition of dollars would require to be phased.

A few years later my wife and I were invited to a farewell party given by the agent-general for Ontario, Jim Armstrong, and his wife, and as we entered the hall of their house in Leinster Gardens to be greeted by them we were followed by Sir Leslie and Lady Rowan. Jim enquired of Leslie Rowan whether he knew me. Sir Leslie turned to my wife and said, 'Mrs Ridley, I was once told by Mr McNamara, the chairman of Fords in America, that for any business to be successful they must have the "son-of-a-bitch" at the top and this is what the Grosvenor estates have got!' This was said with considerable humour. Leslie Rowan, of course, subsequently left the Treasury and became chairman of Vickers. He had had a very distinguished career as one of Winston Churchill's principal private secretaries throughout the war and had gained the confidence of Churchill, which has been so appropriately expressed in numbers of books about the Great Man.

The question of the purchase of the balance of the property was now possible and was put in hand. Half of Annacis Island was divided into smallholdings occupied by Fraser River fishermen, a number of them of Norwegian extraction; when their land was bought by the Duke they were guaranteed their homes for life rent-free, and all went well. There was, however, one slice of land slap through the centre of the island owned by a Chinaman, Law Soong. He had bought the land many years before with considerable foresight, believing that one day there would be development. Gilbert Hardman, whom I had sent out from London as agent at the age of twenty-eight, tried and tried to get a price agreed commensurate with what we had paid for earlier purchases, but the old man was adamant as to what he wanted. Hardman even tried to exert influence through Law Soong's Tong – but all to no avail. Following successive visits to British Columbia I had reported to Bend'Or the old man's firm resolve to obtain his asking price and one day after such a visit and my report Bend'Or said, 'I don't blame him, I admire him. Ask him if he'll come into partnership with me. I've never had a Chinaman as a partner before!' On receipt of this news and with the thought of such a complication, Hardman promptly agreed Law Soong's price!

Having acquired Annacis and initiated the development it was indeed sad that Bend'Or did not live to see the fulfilment of the first stages of the scheme. But he had created an organization in Canada which sowed the seeds of ultimate success, not only at Annacis where there are now over 110 factories, but in the development of shopping centres, office blocks and other schemes – and provided the nucleus from which staff were assigned to new tasks in Hawaii and Western America.

The work at Annacis was extended by building up a 170-acre site on the south side of the Fraser River in the Municipality of Surrey, going towards the American border. This acquisition, all in small lots, was done by Gilbert Hardman, who had been so successful in buying Annacis. Since it was necessary to give a code name to this scheme in order to preserve the secrecy essential when buying land in small lots, we felt that 'Guildford' would be geographically suitable and indeed the completed development is now known as Guildford Town Centre.

A much larger site, 4,000 acres in one block, was bought nearby at Langley. Development on this scale required a partner, and these acquisitions were made jointly with Laings, with whom we formed a joint company – Grosvenor–Laing. When the assets of this company were divided between the partners in 1967–9, the original investment Bend'Or made – Annacis – remained with the family. It is now one of the most prosperous industrial centres in Canada, and a memorial to Bend'Or's ideals of Empire and Commonwealth to which he had been faithful for half a century. The photographs emphasize the parkland and garden setting of the factories – all of pleasing design. Annacis is written deep on my heart and it is to my great regret that Bend'Or did not live to see the achievement he inspired.

When not at Eaton, Bend'Or and Nancy spent most of the season at Lochmore with a trip to Norway to fish the Alta, accompanied by friends, in a chartered yacht.

London was visited occasionally – more often than not when Bend'Or wished to maintain his links with Winston and when journeying to and from Mimizan, which he still loved despite the fact that the château had been burnt to the ground in 1947; he made a home in the timber annexe. From Mimizan they would make occasional excursions to Monte Carlo, where the lure of the tables still prevailed. With the scarcity of foreign exchange in those days Bend'Or persuaded the Hotel de Paris to allow him to park a caravan in the grounds to save the cost of a suite!

In Paris he continued to use the Lotti as home – having financed the original purchase by Lotti – and Lotti's son was content for him to sign accounts and wait for the day when currency restrictions were eased and payment could be made.

While abroad he kept in constant touch by cable and expected those of us who had direct contact with him to do the same. His letters were few and far between – mostly consisting of hurried notes as some matter exercised his mind and demanded immediate action. Almost the last letter I had from him was written in Paris where he had read in the *Daily Telegraph* that Handel's *Zadok the Priest* would not be played at the Coronation. He stressed that it had been played at every Coronation since it was written and would I get in touch with the Dean of Westminster and ensure that it would be played. He concluded, 'You know how the moderns cut off all the beautiful things of the past and put in their sob stuff instead. I rather think this may happen in this case.' Fortunately, after making enquiries I was able to assure him that it would be played. His interest in *Zadok the Priest* was emphasized by the fact that in 1951 he had thus named one of his racehorses.

When at Eaton and Lochmore, Bend'Or was in constant touch with his daughter, Mary. In the 1930s he had bought Churton Lodge, a property on the boundary of the estate, for her and later gave her Kylestrome. Thus at both properties she was close to her father with whom she shared the love of horses, fishing and stalking. Mary made annual visits to Westminster in the Orange Free State, which Bend'Or had given her before the war and he loved to learn her news of the estate on her return.

Since Bend'Or's death, Mary and Nancy have maintained a close friendship, following the pattern at Eaton and the Reay Forest set by Bend'Or.

Bend'Or and Nancy's happy and contented life together came to an end in July 1953 at Lochmore. They had been on their annual fishing trip to the Alta River in Norway, for which he had chartered Lord Illiffe's yacht *Radiant*. Having had a strenuous time in Norway it would have been wise for him to rest when he returned to Lochmore, but with his usual determination to be active and his love of fishing, he was on the Laxford three times the day after returning from the Alta. On the night of 17 July, he suffered a massive heart attack. Dr William

Alford from Lairg attended him and realizing the seriousness, Nancy asked Bend'Or's old friend, Dr George Rossdale, to come up from London, which he did immediately.

It had been customary for me to go up to Lochmore and see Bend'Or after his return from Norway, and accordingly had been instructed by cable from *Radiant*: 'Letter received. Go Lochmore 18th. Keep in touch by wireless.' Together with my secretary, Beryl Taylor, I left Eaton on the afternoon of Friday the seventeenth, and stayed the night at Bridge of Allan. At 7.30 the next morning Albert Hopkins telephoned me giving me the news of Bend'Or's heart attack and asking me to hurry on to Lochmore, telephoning from Inverness to get the latest bulletin. I arrived at teatime and between five and six o'clock had two talks with Bend'Or. As a result of injections his heart pain had eased but he was under very strict instructions that he was on no account to move. He was anxious for me to confirm to him that if the worst happened everyone for whom he held a responsibility – the family and his staff – would be provided for, and I reassured him that he had no need for anxiety for their futures. A little while later he sent for me again as he wished further reassurance about the future of those for whom he was concerned. In particular he said, 'You promise me you will always take care of Nancy, Ursula and Mary.' This promise I gave him and took the opportunity to stress, what George Rossdale had told me, that he would need to pay heed to the doctors' instructions and be prepared for a long convalescence. His dry sense of humour came through and he promised me that he would be a very 'patient patient'. However, the thought of him ever being an invalid was beyond belief and it was perhaps all to the good when he died suddenly the following day.

Fortunately Basil and Winifred Kerr were among those at Lochmore and Mary Grosvenor was at Kylestrome, and they were a great comfort to a very distraught Nancy. We discussed plans for the funeral and memorial services. The funeral would, of course, be in the family church at Eccleston and the burial in the old churchyard among the Grosvenor graves. This would take place on Thursday, 23 July, and we would break with precedent and have the memorial service in Chester Cathedral on the following day and likewise in St Mark's North Audley Street.

The service at Eccleston church would be for the family and employees and tenants of the Eaton estate, while the service in St

Mark's North Audley Street would be for his many friends in London. At the same time as these services took place a service was held in the village hall at Achfary, which the estate employees of the Reay Forest and innumerable friends in the county of Sutherland attended.

Bend'Or in death was as controversial as he had been in life. The funeral service at Eccleston was taken by the Bishop of Chester: the *Church Times*, pursuing an old feud, implied that Bend'Or, though not formally excommunicated (on account of his divorce) certainly did not deserve the attendance of a Bishop at his funeral. The people were furious; the local paper wrote 'Church people in the Chester diocese will deeply regret, and with considerable indignation, the *Church Times*' comments.' And the Bishop of Chester, when asked to comment upon the *Church Times* criticism, defended his memory in the following words: 'There was no kinder man than the Duke. He did a vast amount for agriculture and he was good to his many workers and tenants. It was the personal touch – quite remarkable. He was so kind to them all.'

The real Bend'Or was rarely seen by the public – in spite of his panache and larger-than-life aspect he was essentially a private man. He preferred to do good by stealth: to some extent he was forced into this by his great wealth which made him a target for every good cause and every sponger. A normal social life was impossible: he could not belong to a club for he would be inevitably a target for all needy members.

His generosity was also that generosity of the spirit that is found among the best of all ranks of society. There are many examples of this known only to his friends. A certain person in the racing world, whom he had helped years before, had proceeded to blackguard Bend'Or. One day this man arrived in Chester from London and, lacking even the taxi fare, walked to Eaton. He was seen by Bend'Or who then sent for me and asked me to give the mendicant a substantial sum of money. I said I considered this unwise, and that having regard to the man's behaviour he did not deserve favourable treatment – in fact very much the reverse. Bend'Or replied, 'We are not here to judge this man. We do not know what he has gone through or what his mental anguish has been. I propose to help him and this I want you to do.'

Again, one day I was summoned from Eaton to Lochmore, some

500 miles, and found Bend'Or in a very unhappy state of mind. He had received a letter from a widow, one of his tenants in Pimlico, who had written three times to the Grosvenor Office about the back of her grate but nothing had been done. He was furious and said that the woman depended upon him to look after her: he was not concerned with the wealthy people of Grosvenor Square, Belgrave Square or Eaton Square – they could look after themselves but this widow could not and he felt he had let her down. I was told to go forthwith and apologize to her and see that the repairs to her grate were done immediately.

After his death Shane Leslie, his old friend, tried to put his feeling in verse.

> How generously you let your millions slip
> The public only saw your pleasure ship:
> A prince of sportsmen you were known to most,
> And to a hundred friends as splendid host.
> Few knew how sometimes you would stand beside
> A broken man or swerve a suicide.
> Scarce seemed your public life to seek a goal –
> But secretly I've watched you save a soul.

Sacheverell Sitwell, in the obituary published in the *Sunday Times*, emphasized some of the lesser-known aspects of his friend's character, in a way that, especially coming from such a source, refutes the concept of Bend'Or as a philistine playboy.

> . . . he was indeed unique in this modern world, and I think no one who fell under the spell of his friendship will ever forget his noble and manly character, compound of the finer qualities of the youthful Henry VIII, with a touch of Falstaff, more than a touch of Richard Coeur de Lion, and the paladin in him always lightened into comedy by his personal and delightful humour.
>
> He was noble in appearance at all ages of his life, of Tudor colouring, as in miniatures by Hilliard of the gallants of Queen Elizabeth, much resembling, indeed, when a young man, the portrait of the poet Earl of Surrey in scarlet doublet and hose at Hampton Court . . . What tales one could tell of him! Sir Winston Churchill always said that he was not good at speaking or explaining things: but he had that instinct that always led him to do what was chivalrous and daring . . . The second marriage of his mother, Countess Grosvenor, with George Wyndham, and the intelligent circle of their friends, left influences upon him that grew stronger in later life. Without detailed knowledge, but with

> unfailing instinct, he was never happier than when seeing some ancient abbey or cathedral. Albi, Santiago de Compostela, Alcobaca and Batalha occur to mind, and I well remember his delight at Poblet, one of the marvels of Spain, near Tarragona. This aspect of his character is stressed because it would be easy to romanticize over the lonely boar hunts of the descendant of the *gros-veneur* in the Norman forests or pine-haunted Landes.
>
> How rare and delightful to get a letter from him! He read his favourite books over and over again, Surtees and Mark Twain; and, if I may be allowed a personal note of reminiscence, I was always touched by the way he would try to conceal from me out of affection that he preferred my brother's books, many of whose short stories he knew almost by heart, to my own. Tact and consideration of that sort, again, were typical of him.
>
> Latterly, his thoughts turned more and more to the old world which in almost all ways had been so good to him; and his good fortune in material things, I know and am sure, he tried to his utmost to share with others. From long experience he developed strong judgement in affairs. His estates were conducted along model lines: indeed their conduct is perhaps the strongest argument for private fortunes.
>
> In his later years, with Eaton Hall taken over, he spent more time at Fortwilliam, in Ireland, and at a little house in North Wales. But it is difficult to speak of the old age of someone youthful in heart and humour, who in those respects was always young.

The last word must go to his closest friend, Winston Churchill.

> Bend'Or was my friend since the Boer War more than fifty years ago. We had a somewhat adventurous journey down from Pretoria to Cape Town in June 1900; and our relationship, which started then, was never ruffled even by the bitter forms of party strife which preceded the First World War. Between the wars he worked with me and my Conservative friends, who were opposing the Baldwin-Macdonald policy on India, and on, for him, a unique occasion, he took the chair at a great meeting in Liverpool.
>
> As a companion in danger or sport he was fearless, gay and delightful. He was deeply versed in all forms of animal sport and saw into the heart of them. In this and other fields he was happiest of all when he was giving pleasure to others. The arranging of a shoot for his friends interested him much more than his actual part in it. I remember going out deer-stalking at Lochmore several times with him when he would not shoot himself or take a stalker but showed all his art of venery in bringing me to the right

place to fire.

In the war of 1914–18 he moved among those from the ferment of whose minds emerged the armoured car and then the tank. His most gleaming personal exploit was to lead the armoured regiment he had formed in a daring and far-flung excursion against the Senussi. For this he received the Distinguished Service Order. Between the wars he helped forward research and experiments in a special field of tank warfare.

On his vast and varied estates, farming, reafforestation and other agricultural enterprises were brought, under his inspiration, to a high pitch. All the people on his estates were devoted to him and he did all he could to promote their welfare.

Although no good at explaining things or making speeches, he thought deeply on many subjects and had unusual qualities of wisdom and judgement. I always valued his opinion. His numerous friends, young and old, will mourn and miss him and I look back affectionately and thankfully over half a century of unbroken friendship.

A less formal version of Churchill's appreciation of Bend'Or is given in James Stuart's autobiography. Stuart was chief whip from 1941–51:

I always admired the fact that Winston appeared to me to be thinking at least thirty years ahead. Strangely enough, he greatly admired this quality in others – and in one (to me) very surprising case in particular. He had a great friend in the late Duke of Westminster (known as Bend'Or) with whom he used to dine quite often, even in the war when he seldom went out to a meal at all. I couldn't help asking him once why he usually accepted the Duke's invitations but seldom any others. 'Bend'Or,' he said, 'is one of my oldest friends. If he had not been a Duke, he would have got the VC in the First War. He is incapable of expressing himself, but he is always thinking a hundred years ahead.'

The two men, Bend'Or and Winston, had far more in common than has been generally realized: they both acknowledged that each was the only other person who could implicitly be trusted. This similarity is shown most interestingly in Beatrice Webb's first judgement of Churchill:

First impression: restless, almost intolerably so, without capacity for sustained and unexcited labour, egotistical, bumptious, shallow-minded, and reactionary, but with a certain personal magnetism, great pluck and some originality, not of intellect but of character.

It is of course a superficial and inaccurate judgement, but it reflects very precisely what an uninformed observer might well have made of Bend'Or. They would have been equally wrong.

In my possession at the Old Rectory, Eccleston, is an ivory and glass sand-timer which stood on Bend'Or's desk all his life and was given to me by Mary Grosvenor. On the base is the inscription 'Belgrave 1864' (his father) and on the top the words –

Seize the moments while they stay
Seize and use them
Lest you lose them
And lament the wasted day

So appropriate to Bend'Or's life.

8

The Grosvenor Heritage

Bend'Or's wisdom in seeking to provide for any eventualities in order to preserve the estates for the future has reaped its reward for the Grosvenor family, as I think it is true to say the Grosvenor Estate's assets are stronger than they have ever been.

With the greatest of all landed proprietors however, much care was needed to ensure that the inevitably enormous sums that would be due on Bend'Or's death could be provided without damaging the estate as a whole. During his lifetime we had as I have written set up a Death Duty Committee, with the brief of preparing valuations, assessing estate duty liability and making arrangements for eventual payment.

It was inevitable that negotiations with the Inland Revenue would be difficult. Their task was to obtain the appropriate amount of duty levied according to their valuations. Their professional valuers were competent men known to the valuers appointed by the executors. But, as with most valuations of land or chattels, it was a question of one man's opinion against another's. And, at times, the interpretation of the law. On this score we had had some experience in 1952 before Bend'Or's death. The Inland Revenue had contended that payments to pensioners by Deeds of Covenant were not eligible for tax relief and a hearing of our case was arranged before the commissioners. Mr John Pennycuick QC represented the Duke. A busload of pensioners was brought down to London for the hearing, and accommodated in an hotel for the period of the hearing and while they were waiting to be called as witnesses. I was the first witness, and therefore was able to sit in the court and hear everyone else. It was most illuminating: in particular with regard to George Powell, the chauffeur, whose character has earlier been described. Treasury Counsel asked him, 'I understand you travelled frequently with the Duke. Did he ever mention to you about your pension when you retired?' George gave a very curt 'No.' 'Did you mention ever yourself to the Duke about your pension?' – 'No.' 'Well how did you know you would get your pension?' and George replied very tartly, 'Of course I knew I would get it – everyone else got them and I knew I would.'

Despite the fact that we produced ledgers going back hundreds of years showing that all employees on retirement had received pensions, the Treasury held that such action on the part of the Grosvenor family was 'grace and favour'. There was no commitment to give a pension and any one of the Dukes or Marquesses or Earls going back over the years could have refused to have given a pension and the employee would have had no claim. Fortunately we had found among the documents in the estate office a paper which had been pinned up in the forestry bothy and in the home farm bothy in 1914, as the result of an employee making a direct approach to the Duke regarding his wages. The document stated that the employee had drawn a comparison with the estate's wages and those of neighbouring estates which he claimed were higher, but went on to say that in the case of the Grosvenor Estate employees they were entitled to a pension on their retirement and this was taken into account in assessing their wages. This evidence was invaluable and eventually won us the case. It seems anomalous that although it could be shown that for hundreds of years the Grosvenor Estate employees had always received pensions this was no proof of a commitment by the family!

The Duke was delighted at the result and sent me a telegram from Scotland, asking me to thank all the employees and pensioners for the part they had played on his behalf. I felt very proud of them all – for the way in which they bore themselves in the witness box and their general decorum. It even drew favourable comment from the Treasury Counsel and ultimately from the Commissioner.

Following the success of the tax case, Crockers advised that Bend'Or should enter into formal agreement with each and every one of his employees. Contracts were printed and signed by all members of the staff and by me on Bend'Or's behalf. These contracts provided a pension of 1½% of wage for each year of service on retirement, plus a free house for life, with other perquisites if these had been provided. In addition there was 60% of a man's pension for his widow if he should pre-decease his wife. This formed the basis of the Grosvenor

Estate Pension Scheme as it is today. I know of a number of pensioners who are as well of now as when they worked – not having made a penny contribution to the scheme. All the more credit to Bend'Or's successors for having maintained and cherished the scheme. This is a good time for me to recall that I once said to Bend'Or (to his surprise) – 'You are the first Socialist in the land!'.

As a result of all the work done by our Death Duty Committee it was possible on Bend'Or's death to present current valuations of property investments and works of art to the Inland Revenue. They however were but ill prepared and it finally took over sixteen and a half years to sort everything out. The valuations of the agricultural estates were agreed without too much difficulty, but the valuations of the London estate and chattels presented many bones of contention. Peter Wilson, chairman of Sotheby's, had advised the Death Duty Committee on the valuation of chattels. He was in a strong position here since he had previously negotiated a deal between the Inland Revenue and the Leconfield estate, who were handing over chattels in part payment of duty, and whose many fine pictures were comparable to those in the Grosvenor collection. The Inland Revenue had not made any detrimental comment on the values put forward by Peter Wilson until after the sale of the *Adoration of the Magi* by Rubens in 1959. The sale of this picture at Sotheby's realized £275,000 – then the highest price ever obtained for a painting. What the Inland Revenue had failed to realize, however, was that the sale was six years after Bend'Or's death and during that time there had been a dramatic increase in values.

They reopened the valuations, and we had a fascinating meeting at Somerset House. The Inland Revenue put their case for reopening the valuation and increasing the estate duty considerably. Peter Wilson, who had come with virtually a barrow-load of ledgers and documents, was absolutely splendid in his reply, first of all reminding the Inland Revenue that it was the valuation at the date of death which counted and that any subsequent sales had to be ignored. He then went back through his ledgers and sales just prior to Bend'Or's death and thus confirmed the valuations he had put on the major pictures. To my mind there really was no answer, but as an act of good faith we did agree to increase the valuation of the *Adoration of the Magi* and other pictures in dispute.

The valuation of the London estate was a constant bone of

contention which was resolved after our valuers' basis of valuation was confirmed by a tripartite Counsel's Opinion written by Mr John Pennycuick, the Hon Charles Russell and Mr S. Michael Young. Shortly after our presentation of this opinion to the Inland Revenue, both Mr Pennycuick and Mr Russell were appointed judges, which I sensed further strengthened our contention, following which we came to agreement with the Inland Revenue's valuers.

The settlement of the estate duty valuations and the ultimate payment of duty amounting in all to £19,100,000, paved the way for the implementation of plans for the future of the Grosvenor Estates. No praise could be sufficient for those who fought – not for financial reward – but for a cause. Geoffrey Singer, for instance, whose love of the London estate in particular was that of a husband for his bride – whose vast knowledge was backed by a fine negotiating ability. He was ably supported by others, in the forefront of whom were Tom Barty-King and Gerard Reyburn.

As I write this in May of 1985 I realize the many years it has taken me to put my thoughts on paper – the task always competing with my other responsibilities.

The reader may feel that I have portrayed Bend'Or in a more than favourable light, but he was to me a giant among men, a personality transcending all others whom I have ever met.

He could be impatient and intolerant, but it was for the best of reasons, the other side of a personality who judged, not on promises, but on results: a man who was not content to rest on his laurels, but who after success was achieved, immediately formulated a new plan to be embarked on, with progress to be reported forthwith; hard to live with, but stimulating, and creating a vitality which permeated his whole staff. I was the medium through whom the energy was passed, but the dynamism was felt even in the lowest echelons. To most of them he was but a name, but the name was magic. The magnetism which he conveyed in the 1914–18 war was still strong in the latter years of his life to his joy and the benefit of his successors. I have ever been grateful for the opportunity he gave me to interpret his wishes and after his death to see so much of the 'grand strategy' brought to fulfilment.

Taken all in all Bend'Or must be judged to have done his duty, and more than his duty, by his family, his employees, his tenants and the communities where he owned land. He would not have wished for more.

Index

Achmed, Captain, 96
Achfary, 194
Adderley, 152
Addison, Dr, 106
Aga Khan, 57, 60
Albrecht, Duke of Wurtenburg, 59
Aldford, 25, 126
Alexander, Prince of Battenberg, 60
Alexander, Prince of Teck, 60
Alexander, Prince of Serbia, 58
Alexandra, Princess of Teck, 59
Alfonso, King of Spain, 65, 107, 108
Alford, William, 192
Alice, Princess, 57
Amery, Leo, 30, 107
Annacis Island, 188–91
Arabi Pasha, 20
Ard Patrick, 160
Arlen, Michael, 132
Armstrong, Jim, 190
Arras, 76
Arthur, Prince of Connaught, 59
Ascot, 25
Asquith, H.H., 76, 106
Astaire, Adele, 159
Awdely, Hugh, 12, 13
Azay le Rideau, 26–7
Baker, Sir Herbert, 71, 72
Balfour, Arthur, 20, 29, 84
Barlow, Harry, 118
Barnes, Nicholas Friend, 69, 125–8, 129, 141
Barnes, Wilfred, 129
Barty-King, Tom, 154, 178, 187, 189, 202
Bayonne, 142
Beauchamp, Earl, 172–3
Beauchamp, Mrs, 137
Beesly, Spencer, 174, 178
Beit, Alfred, 31, 32
Bell, Ikey, 158–60
Belloc, Hilaire, 20, 66, 132, 142
Bennett, Gordon, 158
Bennett, Sir Thomas, 185
Bentinck, Charles, 38
Berkley, Charles, 12–13
Berkley, Lord, 13
Bethell, Nicholas, 145
Billerey, Fernard, 186
Bingham, David, 79
Birch, Nigel, 189
Birkenhead, Lord, 22, 23, 108, 132
Blatch, Sir Bernard, 178
Blenheim, 74
Bloemfontein Conference, 34–6
Blow, Detmar, 73, 169–70

Blunt, Wilfred Scawen, 19, 20, 24, 29, 74
Bodley, G. F., 111
Boer War, 37–52
Boileau family, 175
Bonar Bridge, 184
Boodle, Hatfield and Co., 174, 176, 179
Booth, Sir George, 11
Boris, Grand Duke, 58
Borrer, Arthur, 174
Botha, Louis, 50, 60, 61, 71
Botha, Mrs, 60
Bourdon House, 131, 140
Boyne family, 175
Brancepeth, 175
Brice, Derek, 148
Bridgewater Estate, 148, 175
British Columbia, 187–91
Broadwood, General, 46
Brocklesby, 175
Broderick, St John, 49
Brownlow, Lord, 175
Brunhilde, 74
Bruree Stud Farm, 160
Bryan, Bill, 161, 167
Buchan, John, 30
Budworth, 8
Buller, Sir Redvers, 39, 50
Bunbury, Billy, 43
Burn, William, 62
Bussy, 9
Butler, Miss, 37
Butler, Sir William, 37

Cable, Jack, 137
Cadogan, Ethel, 27
Cambridge University, 26, 29
Camelford House, 168
Campbell, John, 108
Campbell, Patrick, 166
Campbell, Mrs Patrick, 68
Canada, 187
Carminow, 7
Carnegie, Andrew, 171
Cassels, Sir Ernest, 68
Castle Pless, 28
Cavendish, Lady Charles, 159, 161
Cecil, Lord Edward, 38
Cecil, Lady Francis, 27
Chamberlain, Joseph, 32, 33, 36
Champness, Bill, 178
Champness, Corderoy and Company, 174, 178
Chanel, Coco, 135, 142
Chapman, Richard, 136, 161, 162
Charles II, King of England, 11
Chatrabhongs, Prince of Pitsmulk, 59
Chaucer, Geoffrey, 7
Cheshire Liberal Unionist Association, 71
Chester, 9, 194
Chester Estate, 153–4
Chester Urban Estates, 148
Cheswardine, 152
Cholmondely, Thomas, 11
Christ Church, Oxford, 132, 173
Church Times, 194
Churchill, Lady Clementine, 106, 131, 135
Churchill, Lady Jenny, *see* Cornwallis-West, Jenny
Churchill, Randolph, 143
Churchill, Sir Winston, 23, 49–50, 66, 68, 71, 80, 104, 105–9, 124, 132, 135, 142–5, 149–50,

180–2, 189–91, 196–7
Churchill, W.H, 22
Churton Lodge, 192
Churton Silver Prize Band, 117
Chemenceau, Georges, 107
Cliveden, 22
Clouds, 74
Clowes, Henry, 155
Clowes, Jim, 48
Cobbold, Captain, 124
Coddington, 175
Coffey, Terence, 178
Connaught Hotel, 170
Cook, Ward, 28
Cooper, Gladys, 132
Corbet, Reggie, 152
Cornwallis-West, George, 55, 67, 68
Cornwallis-West, Jenny, 55, 67–8, 80
Cornwallis-West, Mary, 54
Cornwallis-West, Shelagh, 28, 33, 37, 54–6; *see also* Grosvenor, Lady Shelagh
Cornwallis-West, William, 54, 66
Cox, 26
Craddock, Charles, 157
Crichton, Michael, 154
Crocker, Walter, 177
Crocker, William Charles, 176–7, 178, 179, 200
Crockett, Mrs, 137
Cronje, Piet, 43
Crookenden, Napier, 157
Curzon, George Nathaniel, 18, 20
Cutty Sark, 134, 138

Daisy, Princess of Pless, 28, 55
Danilo, Prince of Montenegro, 59
Darling, Douglas, 157
Davies, Alexander, 12
Davies, Jack, 147
Davies, Mary, 12–13, 167
Dawnay, Hugh, 78
Day, J. Wentworth, 61
De Courcy, Mr, 160
de Knoop, Wilfred, 178
De La Rey, Koos, 42, 43, 47, 51
De Villa Urrutia, Madame, 59
De Wet, Christian, 47, 48, 51
Death Duty Committee, 178, 199, 201
Debenham, Kate, 110, 114
Delamere, Lord, 124
Delamere Forest, 8
Deleste, Thérèse, 73
Denson, 157
Derby, Lord, 143
Desgamatch Kassa, 60
Disraeli, Benjamin, 16
Dobie, Henry, 23
Douglas, Lord Alfred, 20
Douglas, John, 110
Douglas, Lewis, 186
Dowding, Air Chief Marshal, 149–50
Down, Lord, 43
Drummond family, 14
Drummond-Wolff, Henry, 144
Dudley, Georgina, Countess of, 60
Du Maurier, Gerald, 132
Duffy, Miss, 161
Dunne, Mr, 159

Eaton Golf Club, 126
Eaton Hall, 1, 10, 17, 22, 57,

61–6, 110–29, 130, 132, 135–41, 146, 183
Eaton Square, 185–6
Eaton Stud, 152
Ebury, 13
Eccleston, 110–11, 193–4
Eccleston Hall, 15[illegible]
Eden, Anthony, 144, 186
Edge, Jobie, 129
Edward VII, King of England, 56, 65
Egremont, Earl of, 19
Egypt, 87–105
Elen, Charles, 147
Elen, Gus, 147
Ellesmere, 148
Ellis, Agar, 14
Enver Pasha, 87
Ernst Gunther, Duke of Schleswig-Holstein, 60
Eton, 22, 23–5
Eton, Joan de, 10
Eugster, Basil, 157

Farrer, Algy, 174–5, 178
Fearnall, Heber, 147–8
Fernando, Infante Don, 58
Field, Leslie, 104
Fisher, Lord, 80, 105
FitzGerald, Gerald, 161
Fitzgerald, Lord Edward, 21
Flying Cloud, 134, 142
Foch, Ferdinand, 107
Fortescue, Seymour, 44
Fortwilliam, 159, 160–3, 165
Fournier, 73
Fowler, Colonel, 77
Frederick, Princess of Hesse, 59
Frederick Charles, Prince of Hesse, 60
French, Sir John, 39, 40, 42, 83

Gaafar Pasha, 87, 95
Gainsborough, Thomas, 131
Galtee More, 160
Gatty, Charles, 10. 127
George, Prince of Battenberg, 60
George, Prince of Greece, 57, 59
George, Princess of Greece, 59
George II, King of England, 13
George III, King of England, 13
George V, King of England, 65
George William, Duke of Brunswick Luneberg, 59
Ghey, Geoffrey, 148–9
Gibbs, Dennis, 157
Gilmour family, 175
Gladstone, Mary, 18
Gladstone, William Ewart, 15, 16, 29, 111
Gleichan, Countess, 59
Gobernuisgach, 175
Godman family, 175
Grass, George, 123
Green, 9
Grenfell, Francis, 62, 74, 77–8
Grenfell, Rivy, 77–8
Grey, Lord, 8, 14
Grosvenor, Anne, Duchess of Westminster, *see*, Grosvenor, Nancy
Grosvenor, Lord Arthur, 153
Grosvenor, Contance 'Cuckoo', 19, 20; *see also*, Shaftesbury, Lady
Grosvenor, Edward, 66, 68, 75
Grosvenor, Lady Emma, 8
Grosvenor, Gerald, 4th Duke of

Westminster, 154, 155
Grosvenor, Gerald Cavendish, 6th Duke of Westminster, 177
Grosvenor, Gilbert, 6, 8
Grosvenor, Henrietta, 13
Grosvenor, Hugh Lupus, 1st Duke of Westminster, 14–16, 25, 26, 40, 132–3, 168
Grosvenor, Jane, 137
Grosvenor, Katherine, Duchess of Westminster, 59, 131, 132
Grosvenor, Lettice, 19, 20; *see also* Lygon, Lettice, Countess Beauchamp
Grosvenor, Loelia, Duchess of Westminster, 142, 164, 170
Grosvenor, Lady Mary, 69, 109, 155, 179, 192, 193
Grosvenor, Nancy (Anne), Duchess of Westminster, 132, 139, 140–1, 155, 158, 163–4, 167, 191, 192, 193
Grosvenor, Ralph, 10
Grosvenor, Richard, 11, 13
Grosvenor, Richard, Earl, 13–14
Grosvenor, Richard, 2nd Marquis, 14–15
Grosvenor, Sir Richard, 10–11
Grosvenor, Robert, 7, 9
Grosvenor, Robert, 1st Marquis, 14
Grosvenor, Sir Robert, 8, 10
Grosvenor, Robert, of Holme, 8
Grosvenor, Robert George, 5th Duke of Westminster, 154, 155, 177
Grosvenor, Roger, 11
Grosvenor, Shelagh, Duchess of Westminster, 56–7, 66, 69, 74–5, 130, 131, 133
Grosvenor, Lady Sibell, 18–22, 26, 55, 69, 86, 132
Grosvenor, Thomas, 10, 11–13, 54
Grosvenor, Sir Thomas, 9, 61
Grosvenor, Lady Ursula, 66, 131, 179
Grosvenor, Victor, 17–18
Grosvenor, Viola, Duchess of Westminster, 177
Grosvenor, Violet, Duchess of Westminster, 130–1, 135
Grosvenor Estate Pension Scheme, 200
Grosvenor family, 6–28, 168
Grosvenor House, 22, 57–61, 131, 170
Grosvenor-Laing, 191
Grosvenor Square, 186–7
Gubbins, Mr, 160
Gude, George, 137–8
Guildford Town Centre, 191
Gustav VI, King of Sweden, 165–6
Gwynne, Mr, 43, 45

Haig, Douglas, 108
El Hakim, 95–105
Hales, A.G., 81, 82
Halidon Hill, 8
Halifax, Edward, Lord, 22
Hamilton, Ian, 39
Hampstead Heath Protection Society, 16
Handel, George Frederick, 9
Handsbridge, 179–80
Hans, Prince of Pless, 28, 78
Harcourt, Sir William, 169

Hardinge, Sir Arthur, 109
Hardman, Gilbert, 190, 191
Harris, Leopold, 176
Harrison, 124
Harrison, Elizabeth, 137
Hartington, Lord, 18
Hastings, Lord, 175
Hawaii, 191
Hawtreys, 151
Hayes Hammond, John, 59
Hayes Hammond, Mrs, 59
Henry, Prince of Prussia, 59
Henry, Prince of the Netherlands, 59
Henry IV, King of England, 8, 9
Hensingham House, 26
Herbert, Edward, 11
Herbert, Lord, 65
Herbert, Otway, 157
Herhachiro Togo, Count, 60
Hesse, Grand Duke of, 57
Hetherington, Major, 84
Heywood, Sir Arthur, 121
Higashi Fushimi, Prince, 58
Higashi Fushimi, Princess, 58
Hitler, Adolf, 145
Hoare, Sir Samuel, 143
Hopkins, Albert, 136–7, 193
Horrocks, Sir Brian, 155–7
Hothfield family, 175
Howard-Vyse, Edward, 157
Hudson, 28
Hugh Lupus, Earl of Chester, 6, 9
Hughes, Thomas, 16
Hull, Alby, 164
Hunter, Charles, 119, 142
Huxley, Walter, 3, 115, 117
Hyde-Thomson, Douglas, 82

I'Anson, Jack, 124–5
Illiffe, Lord, 192
Imperial South African Association, 70–71, 72
India Defence League, 143
Inland Revenue, 178–9, 199–201
Ilgens, Johannes, 60

James I, King of England, 10
James II, King of England, 13
Jameson, Sir Leander Starr, 32
Jekyll, Gertrude, 63
Jenkins, Ernest, 136
Jib, 23–4
Joffre, General, 85
John of Gaunt, 8
John George, Prince of Saxony, 59
John George, Princess of Saxony, 59
Johnson, Bryon, 189
Jones, Bill, 120
Jones, Hezekiah, 120
Jonquières, Fangues de, 59

Karl Franz, Archduke, 58
Kato, Madame, 59
Kelly-Kenny, General, 42
Kerr, Basil, 118, 124, 138, 146, 151–3, 155, 174, 193
Kerr, Charles Wyndham Rudolph, 151
Kerr, Diana, 155
Kerr, Mark, 155, 157
Kerr, Winifred, 155, 193
Kerry, Lord, 43, 51
Keswick, David, 43
Keswick, Henry, 134
Ketteringham, 175

Keyes, Roger, 132
Kinlochberrie, 183–4
Kitchener, Lord, 41, 51, 94, 102, 104, 105
Knock Hard, 160
Knockaney Stud, 160
Knocksouna, 160
Knowles, W.H., 48
Knox Little, Canon, 50
Kruger, Mrs, 48
Kruger, Paul, 30, 31, 32, 33–6, 42, 47, 48
Kylestrome, 192

Lacock, Sir George, 124
Laing, John and Son, 183, 189, 191
Laing, Maurice, 189
Lairg, 184
Lamont, Tom, 123
Landes, 73, 134
Langley, 191
Lansdowne, Lord, 30, 48–9
Laurier, Sir Wilfred, 60
Lawlor, 163
Laxford, 134, 193
Laycock, Captain, 124
Laycock, Joe, 66, 89, 132
Le Gallois, Colonel, 42
Le Gras, Maurice, 140
Leather, 120
Leconfield, Lord, 19
Leopold, Prince of Battenberg, 60
Leopold, Prince of Bavaria, 57
Leslie, Jack, 88, 91–4, 98, 101–2, 124, 132
Leslie, Sir Shane, 20, 74, 132, 195
Levenson-Gower family, 73
Leverhulme, Lord, 131
Lighfoot, 152
Lindemann, Professor (Lord Cherwell), 132, 142, 149–50
Lindsay, Nigel, 23
Lismore Castle, 159, 161
Lloyd, Colonel, 72
Lloyd George, David, 71, 72, 106, 107
Lloyd-Jones, 123
Lochmore, 73–4, 134, 140, 191, 192–3
Locker Lamson, Oliver, 82
Loewen, Charles, 157
Louise Margaret, Princess, 57
Lovat, Lord, 155
Lukin, Sir Henry, 87–8, 89, 93
Lumley, Osric, 18
Lutyens, Edwin, 169
Lygon, Lettice, Countess Beauchamp, 125, 172–3
Lygon, Richard, 125, 172
Lynch, Mrs, 162
Lyon, Charles, 124, 125
Lysley, Captain, 50–1
Lyttleton, Lord, 170

MacDonald, Ramsay, 143, 145
Mack, Captain, 138
McVeagh, George, 158–9, 162, 165–6
Maguire, Mrs, 38
Mahdists, 87
Manby, 175
Mangles, 93
Marks, Stacey, 63
Marlborough, Duke of, 45, 51, 68, 74
Martens, Chester, 33
Mary, Queen Consort of George

V, 65
Massey family, 175
Mauny, Count de, 27–8
Maurice, Prince of Battenberg, 60
Maximilian, Prince of Baden, 60
Maximilian, Princess of Baden, 59
Maxwell, Sir John, 94, 103
Melton Constable, 175
Miami, 187
Middleton, Sir Thomas, 11
Militze, Princess of Montenegro, 58
Milk Marketing Board, 180
Miller, George, 141
Milner, Sir Alfred, 30, 31, 32–6, 66, 71
Milner, Lady Violet, 38
Milton, Fred, 3, 137
Mimizan, 73, 131, 134, 135, 142, 169, 191
Mitzakis, 149
Molyneux, Sir Richard, 124
Montagu, Lord, 172
Monte Carlo, 74, 192
Montgomery, Field Marshal, 156–7
Morangie, 184
Morgan, James, 120
Morris, Sir Edward P., 60
Morris, Lady, 61
Morris, William, 20
Morrison, Hughie, 136
Mostyn, Roger, 11
Mullock, 157
Musgraves, 120
Myles, Sandy, 112, 116, 118–19, 120, 121, 123, 153
Najara, 8
Napier, General, 52
Naples, 138
National Playing Fields Association, 172
National Theatre, 170
Nevile's Cross, 7
New Westminster, 188
Nicholson, Cameron, 157
Niven, David, 155
Norfolk, Duke of, 51
Normanby, Lord, 27
Nuffield, Lord, 171
Nuri Bey, 87, 95, 97

O'Brien, Arthur, 114, 115
Officer Cadet School, 156–7
Oldershaw Grammar School, 110

Pakenham, Thomas, 31, 43
Pale, 175, 182, 184
Palmer, Mr., 148
Park Hatch, 175
Parker, Cecil, 152
Paynter, General, 124
Pennycuick, John, 199, 201
Percy, Henry 'Hotspur', 8, 10
Percy family, 171
Peto, 28
Petworth, 19
Peyton, General, 87, 93, 97, 102, 103–4
Philip, Prince of Saxe Coburg, 59
Pickett, Florence, 140–1
Pimlico, 172, 195
Pioneer, 74
Pitt, William, 14
Plymouth, Lady, 133
Porden, William, 62

Potter, RSM, 25
Potts, Henry, 156, 164, 176, 177
Poulton Airfield, 157
Powell, George, 82–3, 137, 138–40, 199
Priestman, Colonel, 124

Queen's Jubilee Nurses' Fund, 16

Radiant, 192
Rathbone, Sammy, 114–15
Rawlinson, Sir H., 79
Read, Tony, 157
Reay Forest Estate, 134, 182, 183–4, 194
Reid, Mrs Whitelaw, 59
Reyburn, Gerard, 177, 178, 202
Rhodes, Cecil, 29, 30–1, 32, 38, 41
Rhodes (clerk), 119
Ribblesdale, Lord, 79
Richard the Lionheart, 9
Richard of Masham, 9
Richardson, Dick, 113
Ridley, Michael K., 181
Ridley family, 137
Roberts, Hugh, 11
Roberts, Lord, 33, 39, 40, 43, 44, 45, 48, 50–1, 66
Robertson family, 175
Ronsard, 19
Rosehall, 123, 142
Rossdale, George, 192
Rothermere, Lord, 144
Rowan, Lady, 190
Rowan, Sir Leslie, 189, 190
Rowe, 87
Rowe and Pitman, 178
Rowland, Langshaw, 175–6, 187
Rowlands, Billy, 116
Rowntree Trust, 17
Roxburgh, Mr Justice, 188–9
Roxburghe, Duke of, 124, 137
Royal Naval College, Dartmouth, 148, 155
Rubens, Sir Peter Paul, 14, 57, 201
Rupert, Prince of Bavaria, 59
Rushton, 118
Ruskin, John, 169
Russell, Charles, 201
Russian Hero, 120
Ruthin Castle, 54

Saarinen, Eero, 186
Saighton Grange, 19, 21, 65, 173
Saighton Village, 25
St David's School, Reigate, 22
St George's, Hanover Square, 170
St Saens, 135, 142, 145
Salisbury, Bill, 111, 112, 113, 114, 115
Samson, C.R., 82
Samson, Felix, 82
Samwell, William, 61
Saunders, Gordon, 174–5, 178
Saunders, John, 175
Scarborough, Earl of, 18
Scroop, Henry, 10
Scrope, Sir Richard, 7, 8
Scrope, William, Earl of Wiltshire, 9
Scrope family, 8
Senussi, 87–104
Seuter, Sir Murray Frazer, 81
Seymour, Lady Helen, 57
Shaftesbury, Lady, 173
Shavington, 152

Sheahan, Mr, 160
Sheild, Frederick, 63
Shorncliffe, 30
Shrewsbury, 10
Sidi Ahmed, Grand Sheik, 87
Simms, 81
Simpson, General, 157
Singer, Geoffrey, 176, 178, 186, 201–2
Sitwell, Sacheverell, 195
Sitwell family, 132
Smart, Bert, 113
Smith, Harry, 187–91
Smith, Percy, 136, 140
Smithsonian Institute, 171
Sollum, 89–94
Soong, Law, 190
Sotherby's, 178
South Africa, 29–53, 70, 71–2
Spain, 107–9, 145
Spot, 23, 24
Stack Lodge, 135
Stalbridge, Lord, 66
Stanley, 65
Stanley, Edward, 41
Stanley, Venetia, 106
Stanley, Sir William, 11
Stark, 1–2, 153
Stark, Richard, 122
Stracey, Sir Edward, 188
Stuart, James, 197
Suffolk, Lord, 30
Sullivan, General, 158
Sullivan, George, 164
Sullivan, Winifred, 158, 165
Sully, John, 8
Sutherland family, 134
Sutherland Transport and Trading Co., 184

Tanner, Lieutenant, 95
Tara, 95
Tariff Reform League, 71
Taylor, Beryl, 193
Tennyson, Alfred, Lord, 23
Thurloe, 11
Thursby, Sir George, 124
Toc H, 172
Tolley, Cyril, 136
Turks, 87–105
Turner, Sir James, Lord Netherthorpe, 181–2

United States Embassy, 186–7
Uren, Ernest, 189
Ursala, 74

Victoria, Queen, 17
Villavieja, Marques de, 107

Ward, Gerry, 30
Ward, Sir Joseph, 60
Ward, Lady, 60
Warmsley, Henshall and Co., 177–8
Water Baby, 72
Waterhouse, Alfred, 62, 63
Watson, W., 157
Waverton, 25
Weaver, Charlie, 115
Webb, Beatrice, 197–8
Wellington, Duke of, 15, 41
Wells, Edward, 119
West family, 54–5, 66–8; *see also* Cornwallis-West
Western Command, 155–7
Westminster, Orange Free State, 71–2, 187, 192
Westminster Park, 154

Whinfell, 175
White, General, 38
White (clerk), 119
Wilde, Harry, 121
Wilde, Oscar, 20, 172
Wilding, Lieutenant, 86
Wilhelmina, Queen of the Netherlands, 145
Willett, E.K., 129
William, Crown Prince of Germany, 61
Williams, Gwatkin, 95–7, 99–101, 102, 105
Williams, H, 33
Williams, John, 114
Williams, Tommy, 114
Williams Wynn, Sir Watkin, 122–3
Williamson, Fearnie, 120
Wilson, Peter, 178, 201
Wimperis, Edward, 169
Windsor, Duke of, 145
Wolfson, 171
Wollsack, Château, 169
Woods, John D., 174
Woodstock, 26
Woolley, Harold, Lord, 181
World War I, 76–109
World War II, 144–50
World's End, 122–4
Wrangel, Count, 60, 61
Wyatt, 9
Wyatt, Woodrow, 104
Wyndham, George, 18–22, 27–8, 29–30, 32, 34, 35, 51, 53, 65, 70, 75, 133
Wyndham, Guy, 39
Wyndham, Percy, 19
Wyndham, Percy 'Perf', 19, 77, 78–9
Wyndham family, 19, 21

Yarborough, Earl of, 175
Young, S. Michael, 201
Yousseuf, Prince, 58